Modern Arabic Sociolinguistics

Modern Arabic Sociolinguistics overviews and evaluates the major approaches and methods used in Arabic sociolinguistic research with respect to diglossia, codeswitching, language variation, language attitudes and social identity.

This book:

- outlines the main research findings in these core areas and relates them to a wide range of constructs, including social context, speech communities, prestige, power, language planning, gender and religion
- examines two emerging areas in Arabic sociolinguistic research, internet-mediated communication and heritage speakers, in relation to globalization, language dominance and interference and language loss and maintenance
- analyses the interplay among the various sociolinguistic aspects and examines the complex nature of the Arabic multidialectal, multinational, and multi-ethnic sociolinguistic situation.

Enriched by the author's recent fieldwork in four Arab countries, this book is an essential resource for researchers and students of sociolinguistics, Arabic linguistics, and Arabic studies.

Abdulkafi Albirini is an Associate Professor of Linguistics and Arabic at Utah State University.

Modern Arabic Sociolinguistics

Diglossia, variation, codeswitching, attitudes and identity

Abdulkafi Albirini

Routledge
Taylor & Francis Group

LONDON AND NEW YORK

First published 2016
by Routledge
2 Park Square, Milton Park, Abingdon, Oxon OX14 4RN

and by Routledge
711 Third Avenue, New York, NY 10017

Routledge is an imprint of the Taylor & Francis Group, an informa business

British Library Cataloguing-in-Publication Data
A catalogue record for this book is available from the British Library

Library of Congress Cataloging-in-Publication Data
A catalog record for this book has been requested

ISBN: 978-0-415-70746-6 (hbk)
ISBN: 978-0-415-70747-3 (pbk)
ISBN: 978-1-315-68373-7 (ebk)

Typeset in Berthold Akzidenz Grotesk
by Apex CoVantage, LLC

Contents

Map of the Arabic-speaking world

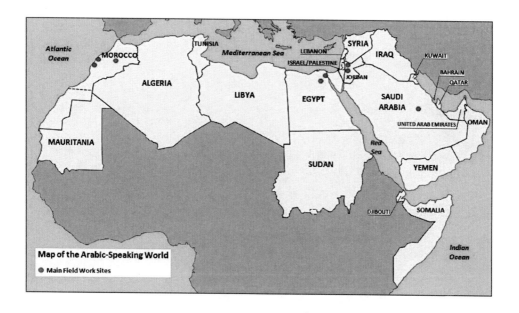

Figures and tables

FIGURE

TABLES

Acknowledgements

Several people have contributed to this work. I am grateful to Elabbas Benmamoun for directing me to Routledge and for his kind help with my fieldwork in Morocco. Elabbas Benmamoun has been of great help in addressing several logistical issues that arose during my writing of the book. I am also very grateful for his invaluable feedback and insightful suggestions on the book manuscript. I am thankful to Bradford Hall at Utah State University for his support of my fieldwork and other research activities.

I would like to express my indebtedness to all of the informants for giving me so much for their time and for sharing their ideas, opinions, and stories. The data was collected through the help of several people in the United States and in Egypt, Jordan, Morocco, and Saudi Arabia. I am grateful in particular to the following individuals for their direct involvement in the data-collection process: Muhammad Hussein, Enas Abbas Khedr, Noha Elsakka, Suleiman Elsakka, Ula Dabbagh, Nihaal Umaira, Samir Diouny, Naeem Sheikh, Abdellah Chekayri, Abdelrahim Slouihakim, Abdel Motaleb Mhaouer, and Abdelhady Aljuufan. Many thanks for Ali Salha for his help with the graphics. I would like to thank all of the students who helped with the transcription of the data.

I would like to express my gratitude to Andrea Hartill, Isabelle Cheng, and Egle Zigaite from Routledge for their kind support throughout the book-writing process. It has been a great pleasure to work with them. My gratitude also goes to Deepti Agarwal and Geraldine Martin for copy-editing the manuscript and printing the book.

Abbreviations and transcription conventions

*ABBREVIATIONS

Abbreviations used in the text		Abbreviations used in the glosses	
CA	Classical Arabic	1	First person
CS	Codeswitching	2	Second person
MSA	Modern Standard Arabic	3	Third person
QA	Colloquial Arabic	F	Feminine
SA	Standard Arabic	M	Masculine
		D	Dual
		P	Plural
		S	Singular
		INT	Interrogative
		NEG	Negation
		ASP	Aspect

TRANSCRIPTION CONVENTIONS

Consonants

أ	ʔ	ط	ṭ
ب	b	ظ	ẓ
ت	t	ع	ʕ
ث	θ	غ	ɣ
ج	j	ف	f
ح	ħ	ق	q
خ	x	ك	k
د	d	ل	l
ذ	ð	م	m
ر	r	ن	n
ز	z	ه	h
س	s	و	w

Consonants			
ش	š	ي	y
ص	ṣ	ج	g
ض	ḍ	ڤ	v

Vowels			
´	a	ـيـ	ii
ٔ	u	ـَو	aw
ٖ	i	ـَي	ay
ا	aa	Shortened vowels	ə
ـو	uu		

* The abbreviations and transcription used in examples cited from other works are adapted to the style of the book.

CHAPTER 1

Introduction

1.1 BACKGROUND

In 2009 during a summer trip to Syria, I was invited to give a seminar presentation at a Syrian university. Because I wanted to relate to my audience and simultaneously present about a topic on which I was working at the time, the topic of my presentation was the acquisition of agreement morphology in Syrian Arabic and American English. The lecture was in the English Department and so English was the medium of delivery. Most of the attendees were faculty and graduate students from the same Department and the College of Humanities.

At the end of my presentation, the audience had a thirty-minute period to ask questions about the presentation. The first question that I received was about the rationale for choosing to study the Syrian dialect instead of Al-Fusħa (Standard Arabic). After I had explained that the Syrian dialect is acquired naturally by Syrian children, new voices joined the discussion, which spanned the whole thirty-minute period and revolved mainly around the topic of whether the dialects were a topic worthy of study. The topic was continued at the end of the session when I had an informal conversation with an old colleague and friend who was in attendance. Our discussion started with general remarks about the presentation, the nature of the questions asked, and research in this area. However, it shortly turned into a deeper discussion about different issues related to the standard and colloquial varieties of Arabic. During our conversation, I noticed that my friend started shifting from his colloquial dialect to a high form of Standard Arabic. The move was surprising to me, given the nature of our conversation, our relationship as previous colleagues and friends, and the informal setting in which the conversation took place. However, after the shifting recurred more than once, I noticed that my interlocutor's switching to Standard Arabic coincided with earnest efforts on his part to explain, and possibly convince me of, the main point in his argument, namely, the "risks" involved in studying the dialects and "abandoning" the Standard variety.

As I reflect on this encounter now, I realize that my friend did not merely express his attitudinal stance on the topic verbally, but also *performed* it through his codeswitching behavior. This incident initially sparked my interest in the mechanisms that govern codeswitching. However, as I considered the motivations, emotions, and implications involved in this sociolinguistic phenomenon, that interest later developed into a broader consideration of language use and behavior and their relationship to a host of socioaffective and sociocontextual factors.

My research in the past five years or so has focused on interdialectal codeswitching between different Arabic varieties, particularly its sociolinguistic and pragmatic functions, and on heritage speakers of Arabic in the United States. Codeswitching, like any other sociolinguistic phenomenon, may not be fully understood in isolation. In the Arab context, codeswitching is intricately related to such issues as diglossia, identity, language attitudes, language variation and other aspects of the broader Arab sociolinguistic situation (speakers, communities, varieties, etc.). These sociolinguistic phenomena are always changing due to various historical, social, and political factors surrounding language use and language ideologies in the Arab region. The emergence of new technologies is one of the main influences on language use in many parts of the world, and the Arabic region is no exception. Heritage speakers are removed from the Arabic diglossic context and they diverge with respect to their facility with the Arabic language. However, they are still subject to the same influences as their monolingual counterparts in the Arab region. Heritage speakers display dissimilar attitudes toward the Arabic language and its importance in their daily lives. Their language usage is affected by the Standard–Colloquial dichotomy. Some may have strong attachment to Arabic for cultural and religious reasons, whereas others are only remotely related to their ancestral language and home. This variability may be explained by social, political, and historical factors that are not very different from those undergirding language attitudes, identity dynamics, and language use in the Arab region.

Modern Arabic Sociolinguistics: Diglossia, Variation, Codeswitching, Attitudes and Identity developed out of my interest in exploring the complex relationship between these important aspects of the Arabic sociolinguistic landscape and their individual and combined impact on the language behavior of Arabic speakers. As the title suggests, this book aims to provide an up-to-date account of these areas based on current theoretical and empirical work in the field. In this endeavor, I also aim to establish the historical background against which these important aspects have developed and taken their current shape. I believe that this approach will give the reader both diachronic and synchronic perspectives on the development and current statuses of the areas under discussion. As Heller (1988, 1992) remarks, language behavior may not be fully understood without considering the social and historical dimensions of the setting in which it occurs.

The book draws on the existing theoretical frameworks, empirical findings, and extensive discussions on the Arabic language, particularly the literature on Arabic sociolinguistics. At the same time, it brings a wealth of new and unpublished data related to the five main areas under investigation. Most of the new empirical data used in this book comes from four field trips that I have recently made to Egypt, Jordan, Morocco, and Saudi Arabia. The purpose of these trips was to collect firsthand and topical data necessary to answer empirical questions pertaining to the areas under study. Six main types of data were collected during these trips: elicited speech recordings, surveys, interviews, language–behavior observation, pictorial and textual information, and short casual question-and-answer discussions. The data was collected from university students and faculty, taxi drivers, passengers, passersby, shoppers and shopkeepers, hotel receptionists, and acquaintances. In addition, I use a variety of other data sources, such as online data and naturalistic data recordings collected during a 2009 summer business trip to Syria. Part of the data collected from Syria has already been published, but another part is published for the first time in this book.

1.2 THE SITUATION OF THE ARABIC LANGUAGE

Arabic is a Semitic language that is spoken natively by more than 200 million speakers in the Arab region, and it is spoken as a heritage language by several other millions in North America, Europe, Australia, and other parts of the world. It is the official language or one of the official languages of more than twenty countries of the Arab League, and it is one of the six official languages of the United Nations. As the language of Islamic scholarship and liturgy, Arabic is used by millions of non-Arab Muslims who can often read it but do not have oral fluency in it. It has an uninterrupted literary tradition that is more than fourteen hundred years old. While the systematic study of the Arabic language is as old as the codification of the language itself, the systematic research on the social aspects of the Arabic language has taken form only in the past century. Modern Arabic sociolinguistic research has been inspired by the pioneering work of the American sociolinguist Charles A. Ferguson (1959a), who was the first contemporary scholar to provide a formal framework describing the Arabic sociolinguistic landscape and its main historical, social, and linguistic variables.

The Arabic sociolinguistic situation is characterized by the coexistence of two varieties: Standard Arabic (SA) and Colloquial Arabic (QA). In this work, the term Standard Arabic (SA) is used to refer to the variety of Arabic that is taught at schools and has formal and official status throughout the Arab World.[1] SA therefore covers both Classical Arabic (CA) and Modern Standard Arabic (MSA). QA, on the other hand, refers to a number of Arabic dialects that are spoken routinely by speakers of these dialects and do not have an official status or standardized orthography. While SA is to some extent uniform across the Arab region, QA varies across and within countries with mutual intelligibility decreasing as the geographical distance increases. In his seminal 1959 study, Ferguson described the situation of SA and QA as a prototypical example of *diglossia* due to their complementary distribution in terms of contexts of use. SA represents the "High" and "superposed" variety, which is normally reserved for formal, semi-formal and literary contexts: governance, education, mass media, religious discourse, arts, formal spoken discourse, and high culture. QA represents the "Low" and "local" variety used in conversations and other informal communicative exchanges: sports, music, film, and some TV show broadcasts. Although Ferguson's early delineation of diglossia has been refined in a number of subsequent works (e.g., Albirini, 2011; Fishman, 1971; Gumperz, 1962; Hawkins, 1983; Hudson, 2002), this framework has remained a viable base for studying various areas in the Arabic sociolinguistic scene.

Ferguson's pioneering work laid the foundation for subsequent studies about the notion of diglossia as well as the use, distribution, functions, and statuses of SA and QA. Some of the main questions that motivated these studies were the following: (1) are SA and QA so rigidly compartmentalized across the lines of formality–informality that they never coexist in the same context or overlap in terms of use, distribution, and functions, (2) what motivates speakers' alternation between these varieties in certain domains, and (3) how is the depiction and use of SA and QA as High/superimposed and Low/local varieties, respectively, linked to speakers' language attitudes and social identities. These and similar questions have generated much research and discussion about the issues of diglossia, dialect use and variation, codeswitching, language attitudes and ideologies, and identity dynamics, which became crucial for understanding the Arabic diglossic situation and, eventually, the language behavior of Arabic speakers.

1.3 GOALS OF THE BOOK

This book revisits and expands the discussion on Arabic diglossia in conjunction with four interrelated areas, namely, language attitudes, social identity, variation and codeswitching. A central premise of this book is that an assessment of the current Arabic diglossic situation requires considering the role of socioaffective factors – i.e., language attitudes and identity sentiments – in determining the *values*, *roles*, and *distribution* of the High and Low codes. Moreover, diglossia as an active social phenomenon should be reflected in speakers' language behavior, which is why the study of variation and codeswitching is critical in understanding the Arabic diglossic situation. The book brings these five topics together into focus as a resource that serves three main goals. First, the book overviews and evaluates the major assumptions, approaches, theories, and methodologies used in research on diglossia, variation, codeswitching, language attitudes, and social identity as well as the major empirical findings emerging from this research. Second, the book offers an up-to-date account of these areas in the light of empirical data from recent research, including research projects carried out by the author during recent trips to the Arab region. The empirical approach to some of the fundamental questions under the areas of interest is well-suited to reflect the current trends in the Arabic sociolinguistic situation as perceived and enacted by speakers of Arabic. Lastly, the book provides a new perspective on the interplay of these sociolinguistic aspects in the language behavior of Arabic speakers as well as their role in defining a number of related sociolinguistic issues.

The need for providing an up-to-date account of these key areas stems from two interrelated factors. First, languages, their statuses, and their use are subject to change over time and space in tandem with changes in social life in general. Such a change necessitates a periodic reanalysis of language use as well as a reassessment of its social, socioaffective, and sociocontextual foundations. Second, Arabic sociolinguistics is still a developing field that is sensitive to developments in linguistic research. Within this field of study, claims are often introduced, revised, and countered by other researchers. The present work contributes to the ongoing discussion on a number of major topics in Arabic sociolinguistics. In particular, the book reexamines some of the main assumptions about the distribution of SA and QA, their functions, and the attitudes and identity-related motives underlying their deployment in the discursive practices of Arabic speakers. In addition, this book discusses the relationship of these areas to some of the recent political, sociocultural, and ideological developments and tensions in the Arab region. By interconnecting the areas under study to recent political, sociocultural, and ideological developments in the Arab region, the book seeks to shed new lights on the study of Arabic varieties and their statuses and functions in society. Moreover, since the examined sociolinguistic areas do not operate in isolation, the book examines their relationships to other key issues in Arabic sociolinguistics, such as language prestige, globalization, standardization, language planning, language maintenance, and so on. The study of these relationships extends the scope, depth, and focus of the book and simultaneously highlights the complex nature of the Arabic multidialectal, multinational, and multiethnic sociolinguistic situation.

The book covers two areas that have so far received little scholarly attention in the field of Arabic sociolinguistics. The first area is the virtual contact situations created by digital media. The goal is to examine the impact of digital media on the statuses of the Low and High varieties and speakers' use of these varieties in online and offline communications. The study of language use on digital media is critical to trace any potential changes in the patterns of communication and the distribution or functions of SA and QA in the virtual sphere. Moreover, the study of speakers' online language use may provide insights into speakers' identity sentiments and their attitudes toward the language varieties to which they are exposed in the virtual space. The second area concerns heritage speakers as a group of Arabic-speaking individuals who are detached from the diglossic situation of the Arab region, but are influenced by its identity dynamics and language attitudes due to their link to their parents' heritage language and culture. This area is also significant for understanding the impact of the Arabic diglossic context on speakers' language behavior and the role of language attitudes and identity sentiments in language use and maintenance.

1.4 OUTLINE OF THE BOOK

In addition to this introductory chapter, the book consists of nine chapters. The second chapter provides a historical overview of the main language varieties at play in the Arabic sociolinguistic arena, including SA, QA, Berber, English, French, and Kurdish. The chapter also surveys the major analytical representations of

Arabic diglossia and outlines the major debates concerning the distribution, functions, and uses of SA and QA in different social contexts. This chapter also revisits some of the controversies surrounding the labeling and grouping of different language varieties based on linguistic, political and geographic considerations. The notion of the third/middle language (e.g., Mahmoud, 1986; Mitchell, 1982; Ryding, 1991) receives special attention because of its implications for approaching diglossia and the other areas under investigation. The "classical" view of diglossia as context-based (Ferguson, 1959a, 1996) is reconsidered in the light of recent developments and research findings in Arabic sociolinguistics.

The third chapter examines the broad goals, paradigmatic assumptions, methodologies, and techniques used in sociolinguistic research. The methodologies used in researching the topics of diglossia, language attitudes, social identity, language variation, and codeswitching receive particular attention due to their germaneness to the themes of the book. The merits and limitations of using certain data-collection techniques in studying these subjects are evaluated. The chapter highlights the importance of using contextually relevant analytic frameworks and methods as well as the need for original approaches and techniques that are informed by empirical questions or problems emanating from the Arab context (Suleiman, 2011). The literature concerning the impact of the researcher and his/her relationship to the participants on the outcome of sociolinguistic research will be reviewed. This chapter concludes by explaining the research methodology used in the book and its suitability for researching the sociolinguistic constructs under study.

The fourth chapter explores the relevance of language attitudes to understanding the unequal statuses and functions of the language varieties at play in the Arabic sociolinguistic landscape. In addition, the chapter examines the impact of language attitudes on Arabic speakers' language behavior. A distinction is made between attitudes based on the "prestige" of particular language varieties, the status of their speakers, and their use in certain domains. This distinction is needed for understanding the relevant literature and explaining the discrepancy in the findings of recent research on Arabic speakers' attitudes toward different language varieties, such as those related to Standard Arabic versus a particular regional variety. Empirical data collected from 639 participants in four different Arab countries (Egypt, Jordan, Morocco, and Saudi Arabia) is used to explain the complexity of language attitudes, their link to a number of sociodemographic factors, and their role in orienting speakers' language behavior. Based on the findings, it will be argued that language attitudes are shaped by both affective and practical factors – though pragmatic considerations seem to be progressively overshadowing the affective ones. Last, the relationship of language attitudes to other sociolinguistic areas, such Arabicization, will be examined.

The fifth chapter overviews the concept of social identity as it relates to the Arab context. The national, ethnic, and religious dimensions of social identity are explored. The relationship between identity, language attitudes, and language use is examined within the framework of existing research and is furthered based on insights from fieldwork observations. It will be shown that identity is constructed through forged historical narratives and negotiated discursively by speakers to attain specific sociopragmatic goals (e.g., to maximize their benefit from social interactions). Empirical data is used to problematize the notions of the *local* versus *superposed* varieties as conceptualized by the classical view of diglossia and adopted widely in Arabic sociolinguistic research. In particular, the analysis of the existing accounts of SA draws links between speakers' identity management techniques, their language attitudes, and their view of "classical/standard/formal" Arabic as a *superposed/local* variety (in the sense of Ferguson, 1959a). Apart from the role of historical narratives, the chapter also highlights the need for examining identity statements and identity acts in the study of the identity sentiments prevailing in the Arab context.

The sixth chapter focuses on variation and change in the Arabic language. A distinction is made between region-based variation and socially motivated variation, which fall within the study of regional dialectology and social dialectology, respectively. These two areas are theoretically distinct, but intertwined in the real world. The chapter summarizes key developments in Arabic variationist research and explores their historical, social, ideological, and political roots. An attempt to disambiguate the outcome of language variation and change will always necessitate investigating a host of affective, social, historical, political, and power-related factors. Language variation and change often signify practices of linguistic convergence and divergence that reflect conflicting or harmonious attitudes, social identities, or sociopragmatic ends. Therefore, language variation is one manifestation of deeper dynamics underlying the relationships among language varieties and among their speakers. These relationships are not merely communicative, but also historical, social, and political.

The seventh chapter examines the phenomenon of codeswitching (CS) in the Arabic sociolinguistic situation (both bilingual and bidialectal), its historical background, and its relation to diglossia, language attitudes, and identity dynamics. The different sociolinguistic approaches to CS are reviewed within their global and Arab settings. Recent studies and approaches will be used to provide new insights into the pragmatic and social functions of CS between SA and QA and between different Arabic dialects. The findings from these studies, along with those from the relatively older literature, will explain the complexity of this social phenomenon, its relationship to several social factors, and the multiple motives for language choice and switching. A distinction will be made between monitored and unmonitored speech situations. This distinction is needed to account for the dissimilar functions of CS in these different forms of speech. The chapter also reports on a case study about educated Arabic speakers' ability to sustain conversations in SA and the implications of their speaking skills in SA for understanding their ability to use SA strategically in their discourse.

The eighth chapter reviews the literature on language use on digital media, particularly social media, as a new mode of communication. A comparison is made between language use and choice in face-to-face interactions and online

Facebook-based communication. To this end, the chapter includes a case study focusing on Facebook users' language practices and their utilization of SA, QA, and English in their online activities. It will be shown that the functional distribution of SA and QA in the physical and virtual worlds is relatively similar, which suggests that speakers somewhat replicate their face-to-face patterns of language use when they are online. New patterns of language use and language change, such as the increasing presence of English and Arabizi (Arabic and English mixed), emerge, and these are explicated in the light of language attitudes, identity dynamics, and the Arabic diglossic context in general. The chapter explores the prospect of the spread of multilingualism as a substitute to diglossia in the light of the increasing presence and use of English in online and offline communication.

The ninth chapter centers mainly around the question: what language usage, attitudinal, and identity construction patterns do we expect from speakers of Arabic who are removed from the diglossic context? To this end, the chapter focuses on heritage Arabic speakers in the United States, i.e., those who are born and raised to Arab parents in a context where Arabic diglossia is theoretically non-existent. This group is sociolinguistically interesting because they lack full exposure to SA and QA, are removed from the diglossic context, and live in speech communities that diverge from those inhabited by their monolingual Arab counterparts. Giving the circumstances surrounding their acquisition and use of Arabic, this group provides an illuminating example of the role of *diglossic context* and *speech community* in the socially appropriate use of SA and QA. Heritage speakers also demonstrate the importance of attitudinal and identity factors in language maintenance.

The tenth, and final, chapter summarizes the main themes, trends, and findings of the book and provides directions for future research. The chapter outlines some of the patterns of stasis and change in the Arabic sociolinguistic situation, and it outlines its possible trajectories based on the existing patterns.

NOTE

1   In this book, the "Arab World/Arab region" refers to the Arabic-speaking countries that are members of the Arab League and whose main official and everyday language is Arabic, including Algeria, Bahrain, Egypt, Iraq, Jordan, Kuwait, Lebanon, Libya, Mauritania, Morocco, Oman, State of Palestine, Qatar, Saudi Arabia, Sudan, Syria, Tunisia, United Arab Emirates, and Yemen.

CHAPTER 2

Arabic varieties and diglossia

As far back as our knowledge of Arabic extends, the sociolinguistic situation of Arabic has always been marked by the existence of multiple varieties that converge or diverge based on geographical and genealogical factors. Scholars working on Arabic have compiled various pieces of evidence indicating not only the existence of several varieties of Arabic, but also their historical, philological, and linguistic relatedness under the umbrella term "Arabic." These pieces of evidence come from a wide array of sources, such as the inscriptions found in different parts of the Arabic-speaking world (e.g., An-Namaara, Nabataea, Palmyra, Al-Ḥurayba, etc.), accounts of pre-Islamic linguistic, literary, and cultural traditions, the literature on the Qur'an (e.g., its collection, interpretations, and recitations), and Prophetic traditions (see Versteegh, 2001 for a review). Moreover, according to various accounts, both recent and old, these same pieces of evidence seem to indicate that SA may have enjoyed a widespread currency and esteem as a medium of oral and written communication even before the advent of Islam (Blau, 1981; Eid, 1990; Ferguson, 1996; Versteegh, 1996, 2001; Zaidan, 1988).

The current Arabic sociolinguistic landscape is not very different from how it was more than fourteen hundred years ago. The Arabic sociolinguistic scene is characterized by the existence of a number of language varieties that often vary from one country to another and sometimes from one region to another. Even within a geographically small region, urban, rural, and Bedouin populations may have their own distinct local dialects. Although mutual intelligibility may not always be guaranteed between speakers of the regional varieties (e.g., Yemeni and Moroccan), these varieties are often believed to share a collective history and a wide range of phonological, syntactic, morphological, and lexical features that justify their subsumability within the family of Arabic varieties. Standard Arabic is the vehicle of reading and writing that is commonly used for formal, literary, and educational purposes across the countries comprising the Arab League. However, the picture is not as simple as it may first appear. A number of world languages (e.g., English and French) and local languages (e.g., Berber and Kurdish) are claiming space in the Arabic sociolinguistic arena. Moreover, modern communication media are allowing for the rapid spread of new linguistic forms, concepts, and styles in the Arab sociocultural scene, while simultaneously providing a wide Arab audience with new veins of exposure to SA, the regional dialects, and a number of global and local languages. These developments have the potential to redraw the sociolinguistic map of the Arab region and dictate new patterns of language use in the Arab context.

The coexistence of multiple varieties of Arabic in the same context has naturally raised a number of sociolinguistically motivated questions that are still the subject of much scholarly discussion. One of these questions concerns the nature of the relationship between these varieties from structural, acquisitional, historical, and social perspectives. A second question involves the factors that determine the social functions and distribution of these varieties in the Arabic sociolinguistic scene. A third question has to do with their relative statuses and prestige as perceived and enacted by speakers of Arabic. Moreover, the presence of a number of languages in areas that had been reserved for the Arabic language necessitates examining the current and future roles that these languages may play in defining or redefining the Arabic sociolinguistic scene and Arabic speakers' language behavior. This chapter addresses these basic interrelated questions as they are integral for understanding the present sociolinguistic situation in the Arab region, particularly with regard to the notions of diglossia, language variation, codeswitching, identity, and attitudes. Before delving into these questions, it is necessary to establish the sociohistorical background of the two main varieties of Arabic, namely Standard Arabic (SA) and Colloquial Arabic (QA).[1]

2.1 STANDARD ARABIC

As noted in the introductory chapter, Standard Arabic (SA) is the term used in this book to refer to the variety that is officially recognized across the Arab region and is often associated with education and literary. It covers both Classical Arabic (CA) and its *modern* descendant, namely Modern Standard Arabic (MSA). SA is the official language of Arab governments, education, and print publications. It is more or less the same throughout the Arab World with minor variations mainly in lexical choice and phonological features due to the influence of the local dialects (Holes, 2004; Mitchell & El-Hassan, 1994; Parkinson, 1991, 1993; Schulz, 1981). In the Maghreb/North Africa, for example, one may find certain lexical items or expressions borrowed mainly from French, whereas most of the borrowed expressions come from English in the case of the Mashreq/Middle East.

Classical Arabic (CA) is often identified in the literature as the pre-renaissance formal and literary language, which is most closely related to the Qur'an and the medieval and pre-Islamic literary tradition. We still do not have adequate historical data to answer with any degree of certainty questions about the exact condition of CA before Islam. What is clear to us, however, is that the emergence of Islam in the seventh century CE enhanced the status of CA and ensured its durability for many ages to come. On one hand, the selection of CA to be the language of the Qur'an may be seen as an indication of both its wide presence in the Arab social life at the time and its prestige among other Arabic dialects. On the other hand,

the Qur'anic emphasis on the articulate and clarifying linguistic style and composition of CA (Chapter 12: 2) secured it not only high status relative to the other
varieties of Arabic but also wider distribution both inside and outside the Arabian
Peninsula. Apart from its link to the Qur'an, CA derives its importance from the
fact that the *Hadith*, which includes the reported words and acts of the Prophet of
Islam Muhammad, was recorded in CA.[2] In this sense, CA becomes essential for
understanding the Hadith, which is considered the second most important source
in Islamic traditions and law.

Three other developments have led to the predominance of CA in the Arab
sociolinguistic scene. The first concerns the evolution of scholarship in Qur'anic
sciences, Hadith, and Islamic jurisprudence. This has helped in the establishment of a definite and lasting link between CA and Islamic theology and law,
whose influences are still felt today. The link between CA and Islamic theology
and law has prompted many prominent Muslim scholars and intellectuals to consider learning CA as part of understanding Islam. For example, Ibn Taymia (AD
1263–1328), a well-known Muslim scholar, said "The Arabic language is in itself
part of the religion, and knowing it is an obligation, because understanding the
Qur'an and the Sunnah is an obligation that cannot be attained without the Arabic language . . ." (Abduljabbar, 1996, p. 469). The need for CA in the religious
practices of Muslim Arabs became an important factor in determining its role and
value in their daily social lives. The second development concerns the codification and standardization of CA following the spread of Islam outside the Arabian
Peninsula. The Arab tribes' exposure to linguistically diverse populations seems
to have led to concerns about the preservation of the language of the Qur'an
and the emergence of a relatively large body of literature on the structure and
form of CA (Blau, 1981; Owens, 1998; Versteegh, 2001). A main goal of this
literature was to impede any modifications that may affect the *purity*, *eloquence*,
and *beauty* of CA. Arab grammarians like Abu Al-Aswad Ad-Du'ali (AD 603–688),
Al-Khalil Bn Ahmad Al-Faraheedi (AD 719–786), Sibawayh (AD 757–796), and
their students described and prescribed the rules and the standards of CA based
on the Qur'an, pre-Islamic poetry, judgment of Bedouins, and directly observed
language use (Chejne, 1969; Owens, 2001). This suggests that, at least up to
that stage (around tenth century), CA was probably used in everyday interactions
by certain sectors, groups, or communities in the Arab societies. As a result of the
codification process, CA earned an official status, stability, and fixed orthography
and grammar. In addition to its religious importance, CA has therefore become
the language of high culture. The third development is the Arabization of administration under the Umayyad caliphate and interest in science and philosophy,
which will be discussed in detail in Chapter 5.

From the nineteenth century on, the Arab World has been in an unbalanced
contact situation with Europe in the sense that it has been on the receiving end
of a process of unidirectional transmission of language, literature, culture, and
science. This process started with Napoleon's 1798 campaign in Egypt, and it
is still in effect. This situation has brought forth important sociocultural, literary,

and educational transformations in the Arab societies, which became the precursor of palpable linguistic changes in CA (Abdulaziz, 1986; Van Mol, 2003; Versteegh, 2001). The linguistic changes started with a huge translation movement from European languages, especially French, to Arabic. However, because many sociocultural, political, economic, and scientific concepts in the source languages had no equivalents in the target language, new words, expressions, and stylistic features started to infiltrate Arabic. With the spread of many foreign terms and expressions, the Arabic language used by many educated speakers of Arabic diverged gradually from CA, particularly with respect to the lexicon. This led to the emergence of the term "Modern Standard Arabic," which was coined to reflect the changes that CA was undergoing while coping with concurrent changes in the Arabic sociocultural and historical scene.

Abdulaziz (1986, p. 12) argues that European influence was bolstered by "deliberate action on the part of the various agencies involved in the development of modern standard Arabic." He lists three main factors that have been actively involved in the development of MSA. The first factor is the modernization, secularization, and Westernization processes that were induced into many urban centers in the Arab region, such as Beirut, Cairo, and Baghdad. These processes were initiated by the upper and middle classes whose members received their education either in Europe or in European-model institutions in the Arab region. The upper and middle classes first adopted then introduced the Western lifestyle into the Arab social life, which was then emulated by other sectors of the Arab societies. More importantly, most members of this socioeconomic class were "multilingual." Thus, they used QA, MSA, and French/English in their daily interactions – a model that many members of the society followed. The adoption of a Western lifestyle along with the ability to use multiple languages paved the way for the entry of many new concepts and expressions into CA. The second factor is mass media and literary and intellectual movements that were captained by the same group of Western-educated intellectuals who initiated the modernization process, including Muslim reformists such as Jamal Al-Diin Al-Afghani and Mohammad Abdu. These intellectuals used different media outlets (newspapers, journals, radio, etc.) to discuss a wide range of topics that were a staple of the European social and intellectual life, but were then new to the Arab milieu (e.g., forms of government, nationalism, etc.). This necessitated the induction of many new concepts and terms into Arabic, both in its written and oral forms. The third factor is Arab academies, particularly those in Damascus, Cairo, and Baghdad, which were dedicated to establishing a single "Standard variety" that could be accessible to all Arabic-speaking people and simultaneously distinct from the regional colloquial varieties. As Abdulaziz notes, the efforts of these academies to "modernize" Arabic was more successful at the lexical and stylistic levels and less so at the grammatical level. Proposals to reform CA grammar were met with intense opposition from many intellectuals, nationalists, and literary figures. This may explain the relative uniformity of MSA across the Arab region and the relative structural homogeneity of MSA and CA, which is why this book uses SA as a cover term for both.

The diffusion of new digital technologies and media into the Arab societies along with the one-way flow of Western terms, expressions, and stylistic features into the Arabic language has brought with it a new set of challenges to SA. Many new terms related to computer, internet, and mobile technologies have become an integral part of everyday interactions and public discussions. They are also widely used in the media and education. These challenges may be viewed from two different perspectives. If one posits a genuine difference between CA and MSA, the physical encounter of CA with the Western linguistic, cultural, and scientific tradition has given birth to MSA, and therefore the virtual encounter that MSA is now experiencing with a new wave of technology-mediated Western linguistic, cultural, and scientific patterns may yield a newer form of CA – a post-MSA form of CA. When CA and MSA are viewed as basically identical, CA survived the first linguistic and cultural encounter with the West, and it may likely survive the electronic, social, and satellite encounter. Irrespective of the perspective adopted, one is obliged to admit the dramatic changes that SA is undergoing in tandem with the ongoing sociocultural changes that are occurring in several spheres of the Arab societies (see Chapter 8).

2.2 COLLOQUIAL ARABIC

Colloquial Arabic (QA) refers to several regional dialects that are spoken regularly by Arabic speakers in everyday conversations and other informal communicative exchanges: sports, music, film, and some TV show broadcasts. These varieties diverge in a number of ways, particularly in terms of their lexicons and phonology. However, they share a wide range of lexical, syntactic, phonological, and morphological features. As Mitchell and El-Hassan (1994, p. 2) note, "Regional differences are lexical (and phonological) before they are grammatical." The structural homogeneity of the Arabic dialects is confirmed by a number of studies on the structural comparability of the different Arabic dialects (e.g., Aoun, Benmamoun, & Choueiri, 2010; Benmamoun, 2000; Benmamoun et al., 2014; Soltan, 2007). Ferguson (1959b) identifies fourteen features that are shared by all modern dialects and argues for a common ancestor for all modern dialects, "a koine."[3] For example, all modern dialects have no feminine comparative (e.g., *kubra* "big.f."). Likewise, all use the suffix -*i* instead of the -*iyy* for marking *nisbah* nouns and adjectives. In addition, all have lost the dual category, dropped the gender-agreement feature in number+noun constructions, and come to have reduced verbal inflections.

Most of the early existing accounts of the old Arabic dialects present dialectal forms as eccentric accents (*laħn*) or linguistic corruption (*fasaad al-lugha*) that characterize the speech of the illiterate or the common people (*al-'aama*) (Ibn Khaldun's *Al-Muqaddima*, 1995, p. 480). As previously noted, the codification of the grammar of CA may partly have been stimulated by the need to preserve SA from the intervention of QA forms that started to creep into it after the Islamic conquests (Blau, 1981; Owens, 1998; Versteegh, 2001). Nowadays the Arab academies replicate the role of the early Arab grammarians, as they indirectly seek to maintain the gap between MSA and the colloquial varieties (Abdulaziz, 1986). However, it is doubtful that their directives will have a strong impact on QA development and use because of the somewhat uncontrollable virtual language contact situations that the new information technologies, social media, and television are creating in the Arab homes, schools, communities, and other social spheres. Blau (1981) provides an insightful proposition about the link between the medieval QA dialects and their modern counterparts. He suggests that the medieval dialects were themselves developments of pre-Islamic Arabic dialects that were very close to CA, but started to deviate notably from it due to language contact in the urban centers. The notion of minimal differences between CA and the dialects of the time is underlined by the common term *Lisaan Al-'Arab*, which was commonly used in reference to the pre-diaspora forms of Arabic. According to Blau, the codification of CA has ensured its structural stability, durability, and immunity to change, whereas the QA dialects have continued to change over time. The present dialects represent the outcome of this developmental process. Blau argues that "The gap between the standard literary language and the spoken vernaculars would have been bridged if the history of Arabic had taken its 'normal' course and the spoken vernaculars had influenced the literary language" (pp. 6–7).[4] Blau's argument raises important questions about the future of SA and QA in the light of the increasing interaction between the two varieties and the Arab populaces' access to the two varieties through different channels (TV, radio, movies, internet, social media, etc.), sometimes on daily basis.

Regardless of their origin, the Arabic colloquial dialects share a number of common features. First, Arabic dialects are acquired from parents and family by all speakers of Arabic. They are generally the medium of everyday interactions. Arabic dialects are not typically written, although a certain amount of literature exists in some of them. Unlike SA, QA does not have an official status in any of the Arabic-speaking countries. A few attempts have been made to bring recognition to QA, particularly when various parts of the Arab World were colonized, and to give it an official status alongside SA. These attempts found no appeal in many Arab social circles and were resolutely resisted by several intellectuals because of their weakening effects on counter-occupation, pan-Arab, and Islamic movements (Mejdell, 2006). Interest in QA has been recently revived by many scholars and researchers, mainly from the USA and Western Europe or Western-educated Arab scholars, who have engaged in important studies on the different dialects. These studies have fueled some of the current debates in the Arab region concerning the roles of QA in education, media, business, and public life. The debate may have political, economic, social, and ideological roots but language is always put at the forefront of the debate. This topic will be revisited in Chapter 4, where I discuss language attitudes.

Last, while both SA and QA have been influenced by the explosion of new concepts and expressions related to electronic, social, and satellite media, the changes undertaking QA seem to be more dramatic than those affecting SA. In my fieldwork in Jordan, Egypt, Morocco, and Saudi Arabia and my study-abroad experiences in 2012 and 2014, I noted such expressions as[5]:

(1)   jayyii-k bas **šayyik email**-e

        "I am coming to you after I check my email." (Jordanian)

(2)   laazem tiʕmil **restart** lal-**program** ...

        "You have to restart the program." (Jordanian)

(3)   ħaʕmal **search** marra tanya

        "I will do a search one more time." (Egyptian)

(4)   ħakuun **online** inšaaʔa Allah

        "I will be online, God willing." (Egyptian)

(5)   ma ʕindiiš **internet**

        "I do not have internet." (Moroccan)

(6)   l-**coverage** mahi zeina hina

        "the coverge is not good here." (Saudi)

In general, QA is constantly changing at a pace faster than SA due to three inter-related reasons. First, QA is not codified, and therefore new concepts, expressions, and styles can be easily introduced and befitted into it. Second, Arabic speakers sometimes disagree on what is acceptable and not acceptable in QA. This is evident in studies that use grammaticality judgment in one of the colloquial varieties (e.g., Albirini & Benmamoun, 2015; Khamis-Dakwar, Froud, & Gordon, 2012). This may have to do with the many factors that may influence the judgment of QA sentences (e.g., region, language contact situation, etc.). Third, some speakers of QA, especially from the younger generations, deliberately try to deviate from the "rules" or "standards" of their dialects by introducing new concepts, especially borrowed or modern ones, to indicate their sophistication, intelligence, modernity, and/or their socioeconomic class (see Chapter 8).

2.3 CONCEPTUALIZING THE RELATIONSHIP BETWEEN SA AND QA

A number of accounts have attempted to describe the relative statuses of SA and QA, their distribution in a number of social domains, and their social functions and roles in the Arabic-speaking communities. It is possible to classify these different accounts into two broad frameworks, one that maintains a basic structural and distributional distinction between SA and QA and another that posits intermediate varieties or a continuum of varieties between the SA and QA poles. We may refer to the first framework as "diglossia" and to the second as "polyglossia and contiglossia." In what follows, I outline the arguments and assumptions upon which these two frameworks are based.

2.3.1 Diglossia

The term diglossia was first used by the German linguist Karl Krumbacher (1902) and then by the French orientalist William Marçais (1930). However, the earliest, most comprehensive, and most widely discussed model for approaching the relationship between SA and QA is presented by Ferguson in his now-classic 1959 *Word* article. Ferguson's delineation of diglossia aimed to define a specific sociolinguistic phenomenon, describe its main variables, project its potential future trajectory, and provide a theoretical framework within which language varieties with specific sociohistorical and structural relationship can be defined. As Ferguson (1991, p. 215) later remarks, "My goals, in ascending order were: clear case, taxonomy, principles, theory . . ." Ferguson exemplified his model of diglossia through four prototypical situations, including Standard /Colloquial Arabic, Katharevousa/ Dhimotiki in Greece, Standard/Swiss German, and Standard /Creole French in Haiti. According to Ferguson,

> Diglossia is a relatively stable situation in which, in addition to the local dialect(s) of the language (which may include a standard or regional standards), there is a very divergent, a highly codified (often grammatically more complex) superimposed variety, the vehicle of a large and respected body of written literature, either of an earlier period or in another speech community, which is learned largely by formal education and is used for most written and formal spoken purposes but is not used by any sector of the community for ordinary conversation (1959a, p. 336).

Ferguson's definition of diglossia characterizes the two varieties by (1) their structural and somehow historical linkage; (2) their disproportionate prestige with one serving as the High (H) or prestigious variety and the other as the Low (L) and less prestigious variety; (3) their complementary distribution in terms of context of use; (4) their dichotomization in terms of acquisition and difficulty (H is learned in a formal setting and is difficult, whereas L is acquired natively by children and is easy); and (5) their unequal contribution to the literary and written tradition of the speech community (with H being the main contributor to this literary legacy).

The situation of SA and QA was introduced as a prototypical example of diglossia. Ferguson argued that the two varieties are diglossic due to their complementary distribution in terms of contexts of use. SA represents the "High" variety whose use is normally reserved for formal, semi-formal, and literary contexts, whereas QA represents the "Low" variety that is used in conversations and other informal communicative exchanges. To be more specific, Ferguson listed twelve contexts exemplifying the domains of use for H and L. H is used in

- sermons in church or mosque,
- personal letters,
- political speeches,
- university lectures,
- news broadcasts,
- newspaper editorials, news stories, and captions on pictures, and
- poetry.

On the other hand, L is employed in

- instructions to servants, waiters, workmen, and clerks,
- conversations with family, friends, and colleagues,
- radio soap opera,
- captions on political cartoons, and
- folk literature.

Ferguson (1991, p. 60) pinpoints the context-based nature of his model of diglossia as follows: "in the early twentieth century an Arab playwright (Mikhail Nu'aimeh) . . . had the educated people speak H and the less educated people speak L, although in real life everyone spoke L in the situations presented in his dramas." Later commentaries on Ferguson's model also noted its context-based configuration. For example, Hudson (2002, p. 6) asserts, ". . . the bulk, if not all, of the variance in the use of H and L appears to be explained by situational context." Likewise, Kaye (1994, p. 60) observes "Even Classical Arabic literature and grammar professors go home and speak their colloquial dialects with their children, families, and friends." According to Ferguson (1959a, p. 328), a person who uses the High variety in an informal setting or the Low variety in a formal setting becomes "an object of ridicule" due to his/her violation of the sociolinguistic rules associated with these two varieties. This rigid compartmentalization across the lines of formality–informality therefore negates the possibility of overlap in the context in which the two varieties are used.

Although his model disregarded the characteristics of the speaker (e.g., education, social class, etc.) and the social function of language use (Hudson, 2002), Ferguson acknowledges that only "some speakers possess the requisite linguistic versatility to be able to use H under one set of conditions and L under another" (1959a, p. 325). In particular, Ferguson was referring to educated speakers of Arabic who have the linguistic facility to utilize the two varieties based on situational factors. Moreover, although he described diglossia as a "stable" situation, Ferguson conjectured the social and historical conditions that may lead to the reconfiguration of diglossia in its original 1959 delineation. In one scenario, adult speakers may decide to deploy H in daily conversations, particularly with their children – a very unlikely situation that may lead eventually to the spread of H in both formal and informal domains. In another scenario, L may gradually prevail when literacy becomes widespread, when communication between the regions or speech communities in a given country become common, and when the populace seeks a "national" language that reflects their "autonomy" and "sovereignty" (Ferguson, 1959a p. 338). Later researchers have drawn upon Ferguson's predictions to propose a number of changes in his initial configuration of diglossia. For example, Walters (2003) argues that the three conditions of literacy, communication, and desire for a national variety are available in the Tunisian context. Walters points to the "changing nature of diglossia in Tunisia" (p. 77) and the emergence of a "postdiglossic" (p. 102) situation that is marked by "the growing conventionalization of new varieties like the Tunisian Arabic as spoken by younger Tunisians . . ." (p. 102). Tunisian Arabic, according to Walters, is increasingly occupying domains that were reserved for SA.

Ferguson's delineation of diglossia was reviewed and reformulated across five main lines of argument. The first line of argument concerns the restrictedness of the model to language varieties that are genealogically related, such as SA and QA. Fishman (1967, 1971) extended the notion of diglossia to include two separate languages, where the H language is usually used in official or formal settings and the L one is used in private or less formal settings. These settings are presented as *domains* that range from very intimate and private (e.g., home) to very official and formal (office). For Fishman, the most distinctive mark of diglossic communities concerns the availability of "compartmentalized roles [to their speakers] as well as access to these roles" (1971, p. 78). These roles are clearly differentiated "in terms of when, where, and with whom they are felt to be appropriate" (p. 79). The refined criteria correspond to what Fishman describes as *occasion*, *event*, and *interlocutor*. Fishman's contribution here lies not only in expanding the scope of the term *diglossia*, but also in specifying the principal contextual factors that determine language choice. However, the extension of the notion of diglossia was criticized in the relevant literature because it overlooked the basic principles based on which the notion of diglossia was founded, particularly the historical and structural relatedness of the two varieties and the fact that H is rarely used in daily interactions (e.g., Hudson, 2002).

The second line of reasoning concerns the distribution of the two varieties in the community. Gumperz (1962, p. 464) argues that diglossia can manifest itself as a "communication matrix" that represents the different functional roles adopted by different groups of speakers in the community. Since each role has its code or subcode that "serves as the norm for role behavior," there exists a "code matrix as the set of codes and subcodes functionally related to the communication matrix" (p. 464). Gumperz suggests that the codes and subcodes can be dialects, styles, or typologically distinct languages. In each case, a code or a subcode can be functionally appropriate for a certain group in the community in a particular context. For example, Sanskrit is part of the communication matrix of certain Hindu communities in India because it has a religious role in their lives, but it is not relevant for certain Muslim groups in the same communities. Therefore, for Gumperz, diglossia is a marker of functionally differentiated usage of languages, dialects, or registers by large or small groups of speakers in the same or different communities. Community is therefore the single most critical player in language use, function, and distribution. While it may be valid in a number of speech communities, Gumperz's contentions lack empirical support in the Arab context because several studies do show that, even when the construct of community is variable, the characteristics of the codes themselves, namely SA and QA, do play a role in their function and distribution (Albirini, 2011; Owens, 2001; Saeed, 1997).

A third reanalysis of Ferguson's model is related to the distinction between "linguistic communities" and "speech communities" (Caton, 1991). According to Caton, Ferguson's model is an abstract paradigm of rules of speech in specific *linguistic* communities rather than a practical model of actual speaking behavior in real *speech* communities. In other words, it is based more on ideology of appropriate usage than on pragmatics of actual use. Caton describes a linguistic situation in North Yemen, where an urban community and a rural community follow different approaches to CA and their local dialects. Because of the large number of educated people in the urban community, the written language is the lenses through which the city people view CA and the local dialects. In this speech community, CA has an elevated status in comparison to the urban and rural dialects, which are considered as distorted forms of CA. The rural community, however, relies more on oral tradition as a way to establish social relationships. Within this speech community, the local dialect is seen as a "pure" spoken Arabic that is different from, but not necessarily inferior to, CA. Caton refers to a poetic dialogue that was held in a Yemini village. The dialogue involved a highly educated urban poet and an illiterate rural poet. According to Caton, the urban poet disapproved the rural poet's imperfect use of CA without taking into account the pragmatics of the rural speech and the role of education. Caton acknowledges that it is the urban centers that dictate the rules of proper use and distribution of CA and the local dialects because of the socioeconomic power of the cities. However, he contends that Ferguson's model should not be based on the dominant ideology of proper language use but on how speech communities implement language varieties in everyday speech.

A fourth modification is related to the "static" and rigid nature of the model (Badawi, 1973; Hawkins, 1983; Hudson, 2002; Myers-Scotton, 1993b; Pauwels, 1986). Hawkins (1983), for example, critiques the compartmentalization of H and L in any given context and suggests that the two languages or dialects may overlap and mix in their forms and structures. Thus, an utterance may fall anywhere on a continuum of linguistic variation between H and L. The specific position of an utterance on the continuum depends not merely on the context of the speech, but also on speakers' variables, such as language proficiency, education, and socioeconomic status. Similarly, Kaye (1972) suggests that diglossia is an unstable situation where H and L interact constantly. Along similar lines, Hudson (2002) indicates that Ferguson's model negates the possibility of new varieties "to accommodate new (or imported) social functions" that may not be served by either H or L. This line of criticism has figured predominantly in the relevant literature and spawned a rich body of literature on Arabic diglossia and varieties. It has also resulted in terminological profusion of intermediary varieties, such as Educated Spoken Arabic, Formal Spoken Arabic, Oral Literacy Arabic, Colloquial of the Educated, Colloquial of the Literate, and Colloquial of the Illiterate (Badawi, 1973) and confusion about the exact features of each (particularly with the lack of empirical studies about the new varieties).

A fifth reconfiguration of Ferguson's model is presented by Albirini (2011), who proposes a functional representation of SA and QA in discourse. Albirini studied the distribution of SA and QA in three "monitored-speech" situations, namely religious speeches, political debates, and soccer commentaries (see Chapter 7). The data came from thirty-five audio and video recordings for educated speakers of the Egyptian, Levantine, and Gulf dialects. Albirini describes the data examined in all three contexts as a mixture of two codes that is characterized by frequent switching from one variety to another. Despite the apparent mixing of SA and QA in the same context, however, these two varieties are allocated to specific functions with little functional overlap.[6] For example, speakers switch to QA to simplify a preceding idea, exemplify, mark a shift in tone from serious to comic, discuss taboo or derogatory issues, introduce daily-life sayings, and scold, insult, or personally attack. However, speakers switch to SA to, for example, introduce formulaic expressions, signal a shift in tone from comic to serious, produce rhyming stretches of discourse, and take a pedantic stand. Albirini argues that speakers use SA and QA to encode and index sociolinguistic functions of varying levels of importance, complexity, and seriousness. These functions are preserved within this mixture, irrespective of the context in which they occur. This means that even in religious discourse, which is possibly the most formal form of discourse, QA may occur if such functions as joking, simplifying, exemplifying, and scolding are invoked. By the same token, joking is typically associated with QA whether it occurs in religious speeches, political debates, or soccer commentaries. While Ferguson (1959a p. 328) argues that "in one set of situations only H is appropriate and in another only L, with the two sets overlapping only very slightly," Albirini suggests that the use of one of the varieties or the other depends largely on the function to be performed and its relation to the High or Low code. Hence, he suggests, the construct of diglossia has to be reformulated – not abandoned – based on the functional, rather than the contextual, compartmentalization of SA and QA (Figure 2.1).

Although Ferguson's early delineation of diglossia has been refined in several other accounts, the distinction between the High and the Low codes persists in all subsequent accounts. Moreover, even when the two varieties are presented on a linguistic continuum, many scholars still acknowledge the disparate domains in which the two varieties appear or the unique functions to which they are put.

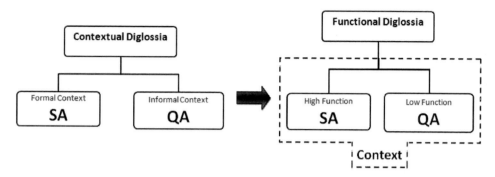

Figure 2.1 Contextual versus functional diglossia

2.3.2 Polyglossia and contiglossia

Although Ferguson's model was criticized at all levels (Eisele, 2002; Hudson, 2002), the most widely articulated criticism concerns the rigid intercontextual compartmentalization of SA and QA. This line of criticism generated much research and discussion on two related points: (1) the existence of a range of intermediate varieties or levels between SA/H and QA/L and (2) the possibility of the coexistence of SA and QA in the same context or domain. The latter point will be explicated in Chapter 7. In this section, however, the focus is on the models that presented the Arabic sociolinguistic situation as polyglossic or contiglossic, i.e., a continuum of varieties or levels. This line of research became one of the most visible trends in Arabic sociolinguistic studies in the 1970s through the early 1990s. A survey of the topics of the dissertations produced during this period clearly captures this trend (Abou-Seida, 1971; Belazi, 1991; Bouamrane, 1986; Hannaoui, 1987; Hussein, 1980; Jabeur, 1987; Rabie, 1991; Schmidt, 1974; Schulz, 1981, among many others).

Studies that posit intermediate varieties between SA and QA have followed two paths to critique the contextual polarization of SA and QA. A first approach identifies discrete varieties between SA and QA, often as instantiations of the mixing of SA and QA (e.g., Blanc, 1960; Cadora, 1992; El-Hassan, 1977; Harrell, 1964; Hawkins, 1983; Mahmoud, 1986; Meiseles, 1980; Mitchell, 1982, 1986; Ryding, 1991; Schulz, 1981; Youssi, 1995). For example, Blanc (1960) identifies five main varieties: classical, modified classical, elevated colloquial, koineised colloquial, and plain colloquial. Cadora (1992), on the other hand, identifies three spoken varieties: modern standard Arabic, intercommon spoken Arabic, and dialectal Arabic. For Meiseles (1980), four varieties are at play: literary or standard Arabic, oral literary Arabic, educated spoken Arabic, and plain vernacular. El-Hassan (1977) focuses mainly on one intermediate variety, which is Educated Spoken Arabic, and so does Mahmoud (1986), Mitchell (1982), Schulz (1981), and Ryding (1991), who sometimes call it the *Middle* or *Third* language or *Formal Spoken Arabic*. Educated Spoken Arabic (ESA) has been a standard term that figured predominantly in recent sociolinguistic work (e.g., Elverskog, 1999; Mazraani, 1997; Ryding, 2009; Suleiman, 2011; Van Mol, 2003; Wilmsen, 2006). Mitchell (1982, p. 125) defines ESA as "the virtually unregistered 'mixed' Arabics that provide the basis for the 'koineised' Arabic of intercommunication between Arabs of different countries. It is this 'inter-Arabic' *koine* or 'standard spoken Arabic' …" Ryding (1991, p. 212) defines ESA as "a supra-regional prestige form of spoken Arabic practical as a means of communication throughout the Arabic-speaking world." The definitions highlight three important aspects of ESA: (1) its nature as "mixed" variety, (2) its use in intercommunications between Arabs from different countries, and (3) its "standard/formal" status.

Although Mitchell (1986) and Ryding (1991) acknowledge the fluidity of the notion of ESA, they provide a number of specific features of this variety in terms of phonology, morphology, and syntax (see Ryding, 1991 for details). Obviously, the prescription of specific "rules" and yet simultaneously suggesting the fluidity of ESA makes the conceptualization of the nature of ESA elusive. That is why a wide disagreement exists in the literature about the exact definition and delineation of ESA (Boussofara-Omar, 1999; Mazraani, 1997; Nielsen, 1996; Wilmsen, 2006). Nielsen (1996) argues that ESA remains underspecified in terms of the type of mixing between SA and QA and the role of "personal and regional factors" in the outcome of this mixing. In fact, even if a number of rules of language mixing were to be specified, they would not be in themselves sufficient to posit the existence of a new language variety. Bassiouney (2009b, p. 17) underlines the difficulty of prescribing rules of "intercommunal communication" based on "the relationship between MSA and the different vernaculars" because this underestimates the differences between the various Arabic dialects. Moreover, studies on CS between SA and QA point to unpredictable patterns of SA–QA mixing where both SA and QA may provide lexical items, morphemes, and whole constituents in a single sentence (Albirini, 2010). Furthermore, lengthy stretches of SA or QA may be found in the discourse of a single interlocutor. Such cases pose a problem for ESA because they show that it may materialize selectively in some cases and not others. More problematic still are cases where whole sentences or episodes are rendered in one variety and not the other. For instance, in (7) below, two separate sentences are produced by a single speaker, each in a different variety. This example shows that the two varieties are not mixed either at the word level or the sentence level and therefore their grammars are kept intact. Stretches of discourse that do not mix SA and QA pose a challenge to the notion of ESA. This conclusion is supported by a recent study by Khamis-Dakwar and Froud (2007), who experimentally provide neurolinguistic evidence for separating the two varieties, particularly Modern Standard Arabic (MSA) and Palestinian Colloquial Arabic (PCA).

(7)   hal ʔad-dawla l-ubnaaniyya qaadira ʕala d-difaaʕ ʕan əl-januub? *Wein hiyyi l-ʔasliħa?*

INT the-state the-Lebanese capable on defending about the-South?
   Where it the-arms?
"Is the Lebanese state capable of defending the South (of Lebanon)?
   Where are the arms?" (Albirini, 2010)

The second approach to the mixing of SA and QA suggests a continuum of levels with varying degrees of overlap and borrowing from SA and QA. This approach is resembled by Badawi's *Mustawayat Al-lugha Al-'arabiyya Al-mu'asira fi Misr* "Levels of Contemporary Arabic in Egypt," which represents the most comprehensive work on intermediary levels of Arabic. Badawi identifies and describes in detail five *levels* of Arabic: *fuṣħa t-turaath* "inherited Classical Arabic," *fuṣħa l-ʕaṣr* "modern Classical Arabic," *ʕaamiyyat l-muthaqqafiin* "colloquial of the educated," *ʕaamiyyat l-mutanawwiriin* "colloquial of the literate/enlightened," *ʕaamiyyat l-ʔumiyyiin* "colloquial of the illiterate." Badawi builds his taxonomy on the analysis of Egyptian social media. Unlike Ferguson whose description of SA and QA focuses mainly on the situational factors governing their use, Badawi describes the events, context, format, and the speakers of each of his levels. For example, *fuṣħa t-turaath* is most closely associated with the Qur'an and classical Arabic literature, and it is well-defined in terms of rules, structures, and uses. *Fuṣħa t-turaath* is basically written; it is spoken only by religious leaders in religious contexts. *Fuṣħa l-ʕaṣr* is a simplified version of *fuṣħa t-turaath*. It is used in its spoken form mostly by reporters in news broadcasts. Otherwise, it is mostly the language of reading and writing. The remaining three varieties are not written with the main difference between them being the identity of the speaker and/or the event of the speech. For example, *ʕaamiyyat l-muthaqqafiin* is spoken by educated speakers in "serious" or "intellectual" discussions. This form of colloquial is used, for example, in political speeches, university lectures, and TV panel discussions and interviews involving educated people. *ʕaamiyyat l-mutanawwiriin* is spoken by literate people and sometimes by the educated speakers in "non-serious" or "non-intellectual" discussions. *ʕaamiyyat l-ʔumiyyiin* is the colloquial that is sometimes associated with slang that is basically confined to specific people in specific situations. Badawi argues that these levels have no clear boundaries and therefore can readily merge into one another. Moreover, most educated speakers are able to use and shift between these different levels depending on situational factors.

Badawi's model is based on the Egyptian situation, and it should be discussed within the Egyptian setting. The levels proposed by Badawi are not recognized by Arabic speakers in Jordan, Morocco, and Saudi Arabia. Only a few of the Egyptians with whom I interacted endorsed three varieties: *Al-fuṣħa, ʕaamiyyat l-muthaqqafiin*, and *ʕaamiyyat l-ʕaamma*. Badawi's classification of these varieties may be critiqued on three different grounds. The first concerns the exact characteristics and boundaries of each of these levels (Versteegh, 2001). There is little doubt that the purpose of Badawi's taxonomy was, at least partly, to show that an utterance may fall anywhere on the *fuṣħa-ʕaamiyya* continuum rather than at the extreme ends of this continuum. However, the fact that he identifies the location of utterances with specific levels requires distinguishing these labels from one another in a systematic way. In fact, the testability of any theoretical paradigm, like that of Badawi, rests on its ability to demarcate the lines between its main parameters. Second, if individual speakers may shift between the "levels" based on situational factors, the question is then how these levels are different from registers or styles (Bassiouney, 2009b). Badawi introduces the demographic variable of education into the taxonomic equation, which makes the classification even more complicated because education is a demographic variable (a characteristic of the speaker) rather than a linguistic variable (a characteristic of the language variety). In other words, speaker variables may not justify the distinction between the two varieties (although they may differentiate styles). Moreover, the notion of "educated person" is not easily defined with respect to language use unless we posit a correspondence between education and language use.

Ferguson was careful to describe two main varieties without positing any in-between dialects. The reason is simple: a dialect is, by definition, a language variety that differs from other mutually intelligible varieties in systematic ways. The factor of systematicity is crucial in delineating the exact properties of a given dialect. In addition, Ferguson was careful not to include speakers' variables in his model because this would lead to the fluidity of the linguistic constructs and model that he was describing. Badawi's observation concerning the gradient nature of Arabic speech with respect to how close or distant it is to SA and QA is valid. However, framing this variation within specific levels and associating these levels with particular groups of speakers is difficult. Ferguson retained only two varieties in his model allowing room for speaker variables to determine where between the SA and QA poles a certain word, sentence, or piece of discourse may fall.

2.4 REVISITING THE TAXONOMIES OF ARABIC VARIETIES

The plethora of terms and taxonomies describing the varieties and subvarieties of Arabic is a sign of healthy intellectual activity and development in the field of Arabic sociolinguistics and its affiliate disciplines (e.g., anthropology). However, it has sometimes become a source of controversy among speakers and scholars of Arabic and a cause of confusion for those who are less familiar with the Arabic sociolinguistic situation and those interested in the study of the Arabic language. This necessitates working toward a typological parsimony through revisiting some of the criteria based on which these taxonomies are based and thus reconstructing some of the terminological superfluity in the field. In this section, I will try to problematize or justify some of the classifications within the SA varieties (i.e., CA and MSA), within the QA varieties, and between SA and QA.

2.4.1 Standard varieties

The division between CA and MSA raises the unavoidable question of how distant or distinguishable are the two varieties from each other. Speaking of language varieties, one may find the distinction clear or unclear depending on the
criteria that one applies. I believe that the most important criterion for the distinction between CA and MSA is whether speakers of Arabic recognize this distinction. In my fieldwork in Egypt, Jordan, Morocco, and Saudi Arabia, I asked
two related questions to taxi drivers, passengers, pedestrians, shoppers and
shop keepers, hotel receptionists, college students and professors (during visits
to university campuses), and acquaintances: (1) Do they speak Arabic, and (2)
what *form* of Arabic do they speak? The majority of the respondents indicated
that they spoke the *Al-'Aamiyya/Ad-Darija* "the colloquial variety" of their country
(and some included their local dialects) and *Al-Fuṣħa*. Others stated that they
spoke *Al'aamiyya* and some or little *Fuṣħa*. Only a few mentioned that they used
Al-Fuṣħa most of the time and *Al'aamiyya* in particular contexts. None differentiated between CA and MSA (see also Parkinson, 1993, 2003). Several Arabic
sociolinguists have questioned the division between CA and MSA. For example,
Zughoul (1980, p. 207) remarks, "The concept of MSA is unheard of in the Arab
region and it is assumed in fact to be FA [Al-fuṣħa]. Other than the specialists
who have received their training in the West, particularly America, few people
recognize its existence. However, MSA has been hailed by some scholars as a
step toward the modernization and simplification of Arabic." Likewise, Bassiouney
(2009b, p. 11) observes, ". . . this distinction is a western invention that does not
correspond to any Arabic term . . ."

Historically speaking, the relationship between CA and MSA may be viewed
from two perspectives. First, MSA may be conceived as a *development* of CA,
which reflects historical developments that languages typically undergo. The new
words and forms found in MSA are part of this evolutionary process, just as many
of the new words found in present-day English were not existent in the English
language a few decades ago. Second, as Blau (1981) argues, the emergence of
MSA may be seen as a form of CA revival after years of decline in use (roughly
between the thirteenth and eighteenth century AD). This linguistic rebirth coincides with the Arab renaissance that overtook other aspects of the Arab social
and intellectual life. This linguistic revival helped restore CA into use, while still
retaining its ability to adsorb new ideas and forms of expression. A main characteristic of the restoration of CA is the maintenance of its basic structure and form.
This assumption, however, presumes that CA may have been in little use in the
"decay" period, which some historians and literary critics question on the basis of
the number and quality of literary and intellectual productions in this period.

From a structural viewpoint, many of those familiar with Arabic would agree
that the structural disparities between CA and MSA are not as striking as those
characterizing some of the medieval languages (e.g., Latin) and their contemporary counterparts (e.g., Portuguese) or between older versions of some languages

(e.g., Old English) and their modern counterparts (e.g., Modern English). As many scholars of Arabic have indicated (Abdulaziz, 1986; Bateson, 1967; Blau, 1981; Holes, 2004; Parkinson, 1991; Ryding, 2005; Versteegh, 2001), the variances between CA and MSA are mainly lexical and stylistic rather than morphosyntactic or phonological. The phonology of certain aspects of MSA may sometimes vary slightly from one Arab country to another due to the effects of QA, but the same may apply to CA as well. Based on his comparative study of a number of structures in CA and MSA, Lucas (2007, p. 402) suggests:

> MSA is syntactically largely identical to Classical Arabic, which is the language of the Qur'an (early seventh century) and of pre-modern literature. Such differences as exist between MSA and Classical Arabic are chiefly lexical and stylistic, which is to say that standard Arabic has throughout its history been highly conservative in terms of its syntax and phonology, having barely changed in the last fourteen centuries.

MSA has sometimes been claimed to have a more flexible word order. However, as Owens (2001, 1998, p. 55) observes, Sibawaih in his famous Al-Kitaab treatise records "a great deal of internal variation" in CA, which may reflect its flexible structure. Moreover, recent studies on the classic texts of CA, including the Qur'an, shows that they display notable structural flexibility, including its well-known verb-subject-object, subject-verb-object, and verb-object-subject word orders (Abdul-Raof, 2004; El-Yasin, 1985; Saidat, 2006). Structural simplification is another property often associated with MSA, but this property has not been verified empirically and is often not measured against the variables of the speakers/writers.

Overall, while one may justify the coinage of the term MSA considering the new words, expressions, and stylistic features that CA has assimilated, the division between CA and MSA is not without problems. The problematicity of this division becomes clear when one considers the historical and structural relationship between the two varieties and how they are perceived in the speech community where they are used. However, only studies using large corpora of old and modern texts can determine the need for positing two varieties within the SA category.

2.4.2 Standard versus colloquial varieties

While the split between CA and MSA is controversial on structural, historical, and social (community) bases, the SA–QA dichotomy is widely accepted by many speakers and scholars of Arabic and those familiar with the Arabic language. Even those with limited exposure to the Arabic language, such as learners of Arabic as a foreign language, can distinguish between SA and QA upon hearing them. SA and QA differ clearly from each other is systematic ways. Notwithstanding the notable differences between the two varieties, SA and QA share a large number of properties at the syntactic, phonological, lexical, and morphological levels (Aoun et al., 2010; Benmamoun, 2000; Benmamoun et al., 2014; Holes, 2004; Mitchell & El-Hassan, 1994; Soltan, 2007; Versteegh, 2001). To illustrate both the similarities and the differences between SA and the four colloquial varieties under study, let us consider the following two examples:

(8) a. aṭ-ṭaalibu kataba kitaabaan wa-ħaḍara muħaaḍaratan ṭawiilatan fii l-madiinah (SA)
     b. ṭ-ṭaalib katab kitaab w-ħaḍar muħaaḍra ṭwiila fi l-maddiina (Egyptian)
     c. ṭ-ṭaalib katab ktaab w-ħaḍar muħaaḍara ṭwiile fi l-madiine (Jordanian)
     d. ṭ-ṭaalib ktəb ktaab w-ħḍər muħaaḍara ṭwiila fi l-mdiina (Moroccan)
     e. ṭ-ṭaalib kətab kətaab w-ħəẓər muħaaẓara ṭwiila fi l-maddiina (Saudi)
         the-student wrote book and-attended lecture long in the-city

     "The student wrote a book and attended a long lecture in the city."

(9) a. yuridna ʔan yastaʔjirna aš-šaqqata llati raʔayna-ha ʔamsi fii haða l-ħayy(i) (SA)
     b. ʕaayziin yiʔaggaru eš-šaʔʔa lli šaafuu-ha mbaariħ fi-l-mintiʔa di (Egyptian)
     c. biddhən yistaʔjrən eš-šagga lli šaafən-ha mbaariħ bi-haað l-ħayy (Jordanian)
     d. baɣɣiin yi-kriw l-partma lli šaafuu-ha l-baariħ f-haad l-ħuuma (Moroccan)[7]
     e. yibɣuun yistaʔjruun eš-šəgga lli šaafoo-ha l-baarħa fi-ði l-mantiga (Saudi)
         Want.3FP rent the-apartment that saw-it yesterday in-this the-neighborhood

     "They (feminine) want to rent the apartment that they saw yesterday in this neighborhood."

The sentences in (8) are almost identical with the exception of some minor phonological and morphological differences, such as the presence of case markers in the SA sentence and their absence in the QA sentences. However, the sentences in (9) vary considerably between SA and the QA dialects in terms of word selection, case markings, morphological markers, and word order. For example, the demonstrative *di* occurs post-nominally in the Egyptian sentence, unlike the demonstratives in the other sentences which occur before the noun. Similarly, the five language varieties have different lexical items for *want* and *neighborhood*. Moreover, the SA sound [q] is realized as /ʔ/, /g/ or /q/ in the four colloquial dialects. In what follows, I will highlight some of the main differences between SA and QA to readers who are not familiar with the structure and form of these varieties.

SA is characterized by an elaborate morphological system. In terms of agreement, this system involves inflections for such features as number, gender, person, case, and definiteness. The combination of these morphological features often generates complex paradigms both in the verbal and the nominal domains. For example, in a phrase like *bintun kabiiratun* "a big girl," the post-nominal adjective *kabiiratun* "big" agrees with the noun *bintun* "a girl" in terms of number (singular). The adjective also agrees with the noun in gender (feminine), case (nominative), and indefiniteness, which are realized respectively by-*at,-u*, and-*n*. Compared to SA, QA has a more simplified morphological system that often lacks the representation of the dual and plural-feminine categories, except in some Gulf and Bedouin dialects that still retain feminine plural morphology (Brustad, 2000; Holes, 1987). Likewise, QA nouns and adjectives usually lack any overt case and idefiniteness endings. In the verbal domain, SA verbs do not carry any aspectual markers (Aoun et al., 2010; Benmamoun, 2000). Whereas, with the exception of some Gulf and Bedouin dialects, all of the colloquial Arabic dialects use different aspectual markers, such as *b-* (Egyptian), *b-/ʕam-* (Levantine), and *ta-/ka-* (Maghreb dialects), which encode the progressive aspect of the action (example (10)).

(10) a.   huwa ya-ʔkul (SA)
     b.   huwwa **bi**-ya-akul (Egyptian)
     c.   huwwa **b**-uu-kəl (Jordanian)
     d.   huwwa **ka**-ya-akul (Moroccan)
     e.   hu ya-akəl (Saudi)

     he **ASP**-3-eat
     "He is eating."

(11) a.   **ma**-saafar[8] (SA)
     b.   **ma**-saafir-**š** (Egyptian)
     c.   **ma**- saafər-(**š**) (Jordanain)
     d.   **ma**-saafər-**š** (Moroccan)
     e.   **ma**-saafar (Saudi)

     NEG-travel.3SM-**NEG**
     "He did not go."

(12) **hal** saafar? (SA)
     saafar/saafər? (Jordanian/Saudi)
     INT traveled.3SM?
     "Did he travel?"

(13) ʔayna l-kitaab? (SA)
     fein l-kitaab? (or) al-kitaaf fein? (Egyptian)
     where the-book the-book where
     "Where is the book?"

Sentential negation in SA is realized by five main negative particles: *laa, maa, lam, lan,* and *laysa.* Some of these negative particles are tensed (*lan/lam* "will not/did not"), while others are not (*laa/maa/laysa* "not"). Sentential negation in QA is typically realized by two negative particles, one often reserved for verbal sentences and the other for verbless sentences (Aoun et al., 2010; Benmamoun, 2000; Brustad, 2000; Soltan, 2007). These particles are *ma-š* and *miš/muš/maši* (Egyptian, Maghrebi, and some Levantine dialects), *maa* and *muu* (most Levantine dialects), and *maa* and *mahu/mahi* (most Gulf dialects) (Benmamoun, 2000; Brustad, 2000; Holes, 1987). One of the distinctive aspects of negation in some colloquial dialects is the deployment of a discontinuous form of negation, which allows for a proclitic and enclitic at the left and right edges of the verb (example (11)). In SA, yes/no questions are formed through the simple addition of the particle *hal* or *ʔa* at the beginning of the sentence, and wh-questions are typically formed by fronting the question word (Aoun et al., 2010). In most Arabic colloquial dialects, however, yes/no questions can have the same structure as declarative sentences with the change residing only in the intonation (example (12)). Moreover, some colloquial varieties allow for both the movement and in-situ options in wh-questions (e.g., Lebanese), and others display a strong preference for the in-situ option (Egyptian), which is rarely used in SA (example (13)).

There are a number of structures that are expressed uniquely in SA and QA. For example, affirmative existential constructions in SA are introduced by locative pro-form *hunaaka* "there" or the verb *yuujad* "exists." However, QA existential sentences are introduced by the preposition *fi* "in" (or its variants *bi/bu*) or the participial *kaayin* (Moroccan). In terms of phonology, some sounds found in SA words, such as /q/, /ð/, /θ/, and /j/, transpire differently in colloquial words. Thus, most Arabic dialects change the SA /q/ to /ʔ/, /g/, /y/, /k/, or /dʒ/; the interdentals /ð/ and /θ/ to the alveolar /d/ or /z/ and /s/ or /t/; and /j/ to /g/ or /y/. Thus, as example (9) above shows, an SA word like *šaqqa* "apartment" appears as *šagga* in Jordanian Arabic and *šaʔʔa* in Egyptian Arabic, and it may also appear as *šagga* in some Arabic dialects.

SA has a richer vocabulary and fewer foreign words in comparison to QA. For example, SA has various demonstratives that are used to refer to nouns that vary in number, gender, and case, including *haaða/ðaalika* (this/that.SM), *haaðihi/tilka* (this/that.SF), *haaðaani/haaðeini/ ðaanika* (these/those.DM), *haataani/ haateini/ taanika* (these/those.DF), and *haaʔulaaʔi/ ʔulaaʔika* (these/those.P). Likewise, SA deploys different relative complementizers (meaning "that"), including *allaði* (SM), *allati* (SF), *allaðaani/allatheini* (DM), *allataani/allateini* (DF), *allaðiina* (PM), and *allaati/allaaʔi/allawaati* (PF). QA generally is not as lexically rich as SA. For example, QA has fewer demonstratives than SA because the dual is not represented (Benmamoun, 2000; Brustad, 2000; Magidow, 2013). Thus, the Egyptian variety uses the demonstratives *da/daak* "this/that.M," *di/diik* "this/that.F," and *dool/ dukhum* "these/those" (or their variants). Likewise, most colloquial Arabic dialects use a single relative complementizer, namely *illi* "that" (or its variants *lli/yalli/halli*) and some use an additional relativizer, such as *aš* "that" (some Maghrebi dialects).

Last, many of the foreign words that are common in QA, such as *kindara* "shoes," *tarabeiza/tabla* "table," *booliis* "police," are not found in SA. All of the colloquial Arabic dialects contain a substantial number of borrowed words, many of which are shared by more than one Arabic dialect, such as *duɣri* "straight," *aṣanṣeir* "lift," *etikeit* "etiquette," *boliis* "police," *vella* "villa," *spirto* "alcohol," and *mitr* "meter." Some of these loanwords are unique to one dialect, such as *Pusṭa* "driver" and *ṭarabeiza* "table" in Egyptian Arabic and *kuuzina* "kitchen" and *karmuus* "fig" in Maghrebi Arabic. The bulk of these loanwords come from English, French, Greek, Italian, Spanish, Turkish, and Berber (in the case of Maghrebi Arabic). SA has fewer foreign words than QA partly because such words have more conventional counterparts in SA, and also because many foreign words are Arabicized by the Arab academies or through media outlets.

2.4.3 Colloquial varieties

A relatively large number of colloquial varieties coexist in the Arabic sociolinguistic arena. These varieties vary in terms of geographic distribution, linguistic features, and sometimes socioeconomic prestige. However, they often overlap geographically due to mobility and migration waves throughout ages and more recently from the countryside to the cities. Thus, it is not uncommon to find a Bedouin dialect spoken chiefly in a large city. Casablanca is an example of a metropolitan city where the Bedouin dialect is spoken predominantly (Hachimi, 2012). The varieties overlap linguistically due to genealogical and language-contact factors. For example, the dialect spoken in the eastern Syrian city of Deir Az-Zour is linguistically closer to the dialects found in Iraq than to those used in other Syrian cities (Albirini, 2014a). This is because many of the inhabitants of the eastern parts of Syria and the western parts of Iraq descend from a single northern Arabian tribe, namely Zubaid.[9] The geographic and linguistic overlap among the various colloquial dialects presents a challenge to drawing any clear-cut boundaries among them. However, because of the need to put some order within which these dialects can be analyzed and studied, researchers have developed diverse taxonomies to approach these dialects. These typologies are often based on extra-linguistic criteria (e.g., historical, social, ethnic, geographical, and demographic), although most are backed by studies involving different linguistic features (e.g., lexical, phonological, or prosodic similarities). Such studies have become more feasible thanks to recent developments in human language technologies (e.g., Abu Nasser & Benmamoun, in press; Akbacak et al., 2011; Embarki et al., 2007; Ghazali, Hamdi, & Barkat, 2002; Shaalan, 2014).

According to one common classification system, Arabic dialects may be divided into Eastern dialects and the Western dialects, corresponding respectively to the dialects spoken in the Mashreq/Middle East (including Egypt) and the Maghreb/North Africa (e.g., Barkat, Ohala, & Pellegrino, 1999; Bateson, 1967; Embarki et al., 2007; Ghazali et al., 2002; Newman, 2002; Palva, 2006). The division may appear to have been made on purely geographic grounds, but it has also been ascertained by linguistic analyses. Bateson (1967), for example, justifies this division by citing the divergent verbal affixation strategies used in these two big dialect groupings. In the Eastern dialects, the affixation patterns replicate those found in SA with the exclusion of only the dual and feminine plural, whereas in the Western dialects the /u/ suffix is generalized to all plural persons and the /n-/ prefix to all first persons. Likewise, the /ʔ/ sound is more retained in the Eastern dialects than in their Western counterparts. Palva (2006) distinguishes the Western dialects from its Eastern counterparts by a number of criteria, such as the dropping of the short vowels in the medial position, the aspiration of /t/, and the deployment of double-consonantal onsets (*ktəb*). Embarki et al. (2007) compared MSA, a representative Western dialect (Moroccan) and three representative Eastern dialects (Jordanian, Kuwaiti, and Yemini) in terms of the degree of coarticulation in CV syllables. Embarki and his associates used locus equations (i.e., linear regression techniques) to compare the degree of coarticulation between a consonant and an adjacent vowel in CV syllables. The findings point to two consonantal groups (pharyngealized *vs* non-pharyngealized), which yield a clear distinction between MSA and the colloquial varieties and also between the Western (Moroccan) and Eastern (Jordanian, Kuwaiti, and Yemini) dialects.

Another popular classification of Arabic dialects stipulates five regional zones: Egyptian, Gulf (including Yemen), Levantine (spoken in Syria, Jordan, Lebanon, and Palestine), Maghrebi (spoken in North Africa), and Mesopotamian/Iraqi (e.g., Abu Nasser, Benmamoun, & Hasegawa-Johnson, 2013; Akbacak et al., 2011; Holes, 2004; Shaalan, 2014; Versteegh, 2001). Again, this taxonomy is not merely based on geography but also reflects a large number of shared linguistic features in the dialects of the majority of speakers in these zones (Abu Nasser & Benmamoun, in press; Abu Nasser, Benmamoun, & Hasegawa-Johnson, 2013; Versteegh, 2001). For example, Abu Nasser, Benmamoun, and Hasegawa-Johnson (2013) used a pronunciation variation metric, which is based on word similarity (defined by whether the words are cognates and whether their sequence of phones share articulatory gestures and phonetic features) to examine the distance between the Egyptian, Gulf, Levantine, and Moroccan dialects. The findings indicate that the four varieties are distinct from one another. However, the Moroccan variety is relatively distant from the other varieties, whereas the Levantine is close to both Egyptian and Gulf. The distance between Egyptian and Gulf fell in the middle. It should be noted here that computational linguistic techniques have recently joined sociolinguistic and variationist research in the process of defining and classifying the different Arabic dialects.

Despite the popularity of the above taxonomies, much of the empirical research in the field of sociolinguistics is grounded in country-specific dialects, such as Moroccan, Bahraini, and Yemini. The vast majority of publications in sociolinguistics explicitly or implicitly adopt this division. The focus on the country-based dialects is often motivated by sheer practical reasons, such as feasibility of access to a larger population. Moreover, studies conducted in a single country – particularly those focusing on CS, dialect accommodation, and dialect-feature changes – sometimes adopt a demographically based typology of Arabic dialects that often recognizes three main varieties: urban, rural, and Bedouin. However, even linguistically, these "local" dialects may vary to a degree no less than that found between the regional or interstate varieties. Moreover, the properties of each of these local varieties may vary from one region to another. For example, the urban dialect used in Cairo is different from that used in Damascus or Rabat. The same applies to the rural and Bedouin dialects. However, most urban dialects are characterized by the substitution of the interdentals /θ/ /ð/ and /ẓ/ with the alveolars /s/, /t/, /d/, /z/, and /ḍ/, the lack of feminine plural affixes on verbs and adjectives, the loss of the indefinite markers, and the frequency of the genitive particles (e.g., tabaʕ, bitaaʕ, etc. "belonging to") (Palva, 2006). The Bedouin dialects often retain the interdentals /θ/, /ð/, and /ẓ/, realize feminine plural affixes on verbs and adjectives, deploy the indefinite markers, and use the analytic genitive sparingly (Palva, 2006). The rural dialects are often closer to the urban dialects, but they sometimes share features with the Bedouin dialects. Some of the rural dialects in the northern parts of Jordan and southern parts of Syria, for example, behave like the Bedouin dialects with respect to the retention of the interdental fricatives and the use of feminine plural morphology.

Mutual intelligibility may not always be guaranteed between speakers of regional varieties (e.g., Yemeni and Moroccan) across the Arab region. On the other hand, speakers in the same region or country do often understand one another, even when their local dialects are different, and some may master different dialects due to contact with other speakers. Since the 1960s, the Egyptian dialect has been the most widely understood variety of Arabic across the Arab region because of the popularity of Egyptian movies, plays, and other entertainment media. In situations where mutual intelligibility is not guaranteed, Arabs may resort to the Egyptian dialect or to SA to be able to communicate effectively. However, as it will be explained in the coming chapters, this may not always be related to illegibility per se, but to attitudinal and ideological factors (Hachimi, 2013; Shiri, 2002). During my fieldwork in Morocco, I shared a bench with two middle-aged ladies as I waited for my train from Casablanca to Fes. One of the ladies asked me about the location of the train going to Fes. She spoke to me in Moroccan Arabic. When I replied to her in Syrian Arabic, she shifted spontaneously to the Egyptian dialect. After a short conversation about the purpose of my visit to Morocco, I asked her about her use of the Egyptian dialect. She indicated that she shifted to the Egyptian dialect to help me understand her. Most of the male Moroccan informants, however, either conversed with me in the Moroccan dialect, SA, or a mixed Moroccan Arabic-SA speech.[10] In general, the dynamics of interdialectal communication are changing slowly, especially with the increasing presence of the Syrian, Lebanese, and Gulf dialects on satellite television. Television is also responsible for enhancing the familiarity of the Maghreb dialects in the eastern part of the Arab World.

Before concluding this section, it is important to point out that, although the Arabic dialects have been classified using different taxonomies, scholars and researchers often select the typology that is pertinent to their research focus, population, and overall approach to the topic of study. There is an awareness among the research community (as well as many speakers of Arabic) that any possible classification would not always map accurately on the linguistic features of a given dialect or the geographic areas or demographic characteristics of the speech community that it represents.

2.5 MOTHER TONGUE, NATIVE LANGUAGE, OR SECOND LANGUAGE?

One of the distinctions that Ferguson (1959a) made between the Low variety and the High variety is that the former is learned at home and the latter is learned at school. Ferguson made no attempt to identify either of the two varieties as *mother tongue* of the Arabic-speaking people. However, later scholarship has engaged in interesting discussions about whether SA is a mother tongue, native language, or second language (Cowan, 1968; Haeri, 2000; Hudson, 2002; Kaye, 1972, 1994; Mahmoud, 2000; Mitchell, 1982; Sabir & Safi, 2008; Schiffman, 1997; Schulz, 1981; Suleiman, 2011; Walters, 2003). As a representative of the viewpoint of SA being a second language, Schulz (1981, p. 10) maintains, "CA *has no native speakers*. Everybody who knows classical Arabic learned it in school. This means that, in reality, no matter how much MSA may resemble CEA [Colloquial Egyptian Arabic], it is a second language for all Egyptians (and other Arabs as well)." Suleiman (2011) argues that the "insider" and "nativist" view of diglossia dictates a dichotomy between "a native variety," namely SA, and "a mother-tongue" variety, namely QA. The various labels assigned to SA beg the question of what exactly a *mother-tongue* language means. In this book, for reasons explained below, I adopt the view that, together with QA, SA is the mother tongue of the Arabic-speaking people.

   Language acquisition studies often associate mother tongue with the language or variety acquired first by the speaker. From a purely acquisitional point of view, therefore, the Low variety may be viewed as the mother tongue and the High variety as a second language since mother tongue is typically associated with the first acquired language (e.g., Sabir & Safi, 2008). However, this distinction is problematic, when applied to SA, for two main reasons. First, even from an acquistional point of view, one may consider SA (the High variety) as a mother tongue because most Arab children are exposed to the two varieties from birth. Children acquire QA from parents, family, and community at large, but they are also exposed informally to SA from television (e.g., cartoons and news), radio, religious speeches and sermons, children's books, siblings' reading, adults' prayers, and Qur'anic recitations. Some children read the Qur'an and attend religious schools early in their lives (Aram, Korat, & Hassunah-Arafat, 2013; Haeri, 2000; Saiegh-Haddad et al., 2011). Their exposure to SA, though may not be as rich as their exposure to QA, allows them to develop at least receptive skills in SA. Thus, it is true that many Arab children may not be able to speak SA fluently, but most of them do understand it. This is similar to passive bilingualism, where children speak one language and can understand another but not speak it. It is also similar to the situation of many heritage speakers who do not necessarily speak their first language but do understand it.

Sabir and Safi (2008) remark that, even before they start attending school, Hijazi children in the city of Jeddah (Saudi Arabia) exhibit "diglossic awareness" in that they infuse their QA-based speech with items from SA early in their lives. The authors examined the oral output of a male child aged 5:6 over a period of nine months. The child has no formal schooling in SA. The interactions of the child with his parents, siblings, and friends were recorded manually immediately after their production. Most of these interactions occurred at home. Religious sayings, which could be mere memorized rehearsals in SA, were excluded from the data. The authors found a significant presence of SA elements in the daily conversations of the subject, which suggests that the acquisition of SA is not the result of formal education. The findings of this case study may not be generalizable to all children in the Arab societies. However, they present an important perspective on SA acquisition by Arab children. Leikin, Ibrahim, and Eghbaria (2013) investigated the effects of diglossia on the narrative ability of Palestinian pre-school children aged between 5:3 and 5:8 years. Thirty children took part in the study. The researchers narrated two unrelated stories (accompanied by illustrations from two books) in spoken Arabic (i.e., colloquial Palestinian dialect) and in literary Arabic (i.e., SA). The children were asked to retell the two stories in their dialect and in SA, respectively. The findings show that children are generally more successful in retelling the QA story than the SA story. At the same time, however, the researchers found that, ". . . children at this developmental stage already succeed in using linguistic structures from the literary language and to understand narrative texts. Therefore, children are capable of acquiring LA [Literary Arabic] parallel to SA [Spoken Arabic]" (p. 13).

During my fieldwork in Jordan, I conducted a pilot study that explored Arab children's comprehension of five video clips in SA. The study involved eight children (aged between 5 and 5:6), who had no developmental or linguistic problems.[11] The children were identified through (1) acquaintances in the cities of Amman, Irbid, and Al-Ramtha, (2) colleagues from two universities in Amman and Irbid, and (3) staff at a private school in Amman with whom I worked on a different project (see Albirini, 2015). At the time of the study, none of the participants had had formal education in SA. The clips were extracted from five cartoon shows: *Sinbad, Sasuki, Ḥikayaat 'Aalamiyya, Sinaan,* and *Abṭaal Al-Malaa'eb.* The topics covered in these topics were, respectively, adventures, fighting, child narrative stories, animals, and soccer. From a developmental perspective, cartoons are generally assumed to be thematically, structurally, lexically, and stylistically appropriate for children at this age.[12] The length of each clip was about sixty seconds with word counts ranging between ninety-one and 123 (see Appendices for video transcripts). Because language is always used and understood in context, the children, individually, heard and saw the video clips on my laptop. I made sure that no real action was displayed in the clips so that the children could not interpret the videos merely based on the course of events. After watching each video clip, each child was asked three comprehension questions: one about the general theme of the video clips and two questions about particular details. Two independent raters judged whether the children's responses were full answers (two points), partial answers (one point), or wrong answers (zero points). When a child gave a partial or wrong answer, I posed the question "what else?" until he/she came to a stop. The full, partial, and wrong answers were pre-defined in a simple rubric that I developed in consultation with a number of Jordanian colleagues (see Appendices). This procedure was necessary to make sure that their wrong or partial answers were due to lack of comprehension and not other reasons, such as shyness. The children were asked the questions in SA, but they were not given specific instructions about the use of SA and QA (because this is a comprehension task). The findings indicate that all of the eight children could recognize the general themes of the clips either completely or partially (92.5% comprehension accuracy). In addition, they could identify specific details that require meticulous understanding of SA in 83.1% of the cases. This shows that Arab children have at least receptive skills in SA. Based on everyday observation, one may find that even illiterate Arabs who had no formal education is SA can understand news reports, religious speeches, and other forms of SA-based discourse (Sabir & Safi, 2008).

Even if we accept that Arab children do not acquire SA in early childhood, the notion of mother tongue is *sociolinguistically* imprecise when based merely on the sequence of acquisition. In other words, language should not be viewed merely as a medium of communication, but should also be considered from ideological, political, and social perspectives (Makoni & Pennycook, 2007; Suleiman, 2011). The ideological, political, social, and communicative dimensions of language are central to the conception of sociolinguistics as an interdisciplinary field. Makoni and Pennycook (2007) suggest that language is a social, political, and historical construct, and therefore any definition of language should draw on its meaning to the local people who speak it or use it in their daily lives. A sociolinguistically based definition would better reflect the general understanding of the term *mother tongue* by Arabic speakers. An obvious starting point, then, is to look at how participants use their multilingual resources and how they themselves understand language use. One of the questions that I asked my interviewees (N = 76) in Egypt, Jordan, Morocco, and Saudi Arabia is: which do you consider as your mother tongue: *Al-fuṣħā* or *Al-ʕamiyya/Ad-Darija*? The responses fell under three different patterns. A first group of respondents, which include the majority of the interviewees (40.8%), identified SA as their mother tongue. When I asked for justification, the participants indicated that SA is attached to their Muslim faith (particularly the Qur'an), history, heritage, Arab identity, and social, economic, and political membership in the Arab community. A number of them indicated that SA is the "language" through which they could read, write, and get educated. It should be noted that more Moroccans were in this category than Egyptians, Jordanians, or Saudis. As will be explained in Chapter 7, my fieldwork in Morocco coincided with a heated debate in the media over the use of QA as the medium of instruction in the early years of children's education. Thus, the identification of SA as a mother tongue could partly be a reaction to this call. The second group identified QA as their mother tongue (25.0%). The interviewees in this group explained their choice by indicating that QA is the variety that they learn first, command better, use on daily basis with family and friends, and associate with their nation-state. The third and last group (34.2%) suggested that both SA and QA are mother tongues with the rationale that both are part of the social reality in which they live, are needed for different purposes, and are part of who they are as members of specific Arab states and the larger Arab community. A number of informants in this group distinguished between the variety that they learned from parents and family and the variety that represents them, and they identified QA as their mother tongue by acquisition and SA as their mother tongue in terms of representation.[13]

In conclusion, SA may be seen as mother tongue of Arabic speakers if we consider two important facts about their acquisition and their views of this variety. First, Arabic children are exposed to SA in the early stages of their language development, and therefore it may not be considered as a second language. Second, SA is linked to some form of their identities as users of this variety.[14] Undoubtedly, QA is the mother tongue of Arabic speakers not only because it is acquired at home or used in everyday communications, but also because it corresponds to another level of their identities, as I will explain in Chapter 5.

2.6 LANGUAGE PRESTIGE

Language prestige is a complex sociolinguistic construct because it has historical, socioeconomic, behavioral, and attitudinal dimensions. In this section, I will focus briefly on the sociohistorical, socioeconomic, and behavioral perspectives and leave the attitudinal/ideological dimension to Chapter 4 because it is, I believe, the most important determiner of language prestige in the Arab context.

Historically, SA has enjoyed a higher prestige than the spoken colloquial dialects for three main interrelated reasons. First, SA is a written language with well-defined rules, conventions, and orthography. As Haugen (1966) observes, written languages generally accrue more prestige and stability than their spoken counterparts. The standardization of any given language variety involves in many cases instating or reviving a written form of the language that has specific structure and standards (Haugen, 1966; Kahane, 1986).[15] Second, SA has been the medium of encoding the rich Arabic literary tradition, including the medieval and pre-Islamic poetry. The classic masterpieces of Arabic poetry have been viewed as exemplars of the *beauty* and *eloquence* of SA and, by extension, its *superiority* over QA. Third, SA is related to Islamic texts (particularly the Qur'an), liturgy, and scholarship. Due to its link to the Qur'an, SA came to be perceived as a superior and sacred language.[16] Ferguson (1968, p. 378) presents the following argument for the superiority of CA, as perceived by its speakers: "God is all-knowing, all powerful; He knows and can utilize all languages; He chose Arabic as the vehicle of his ultimate revelations to the world; consequently, the Arabic language must be, in important respects, better than other languages." These three factors have played an important role in sustaining the prestige of SA and in its enduring role as the High variety in the Arab speech communities.

From a socioeconomic perspective, SA is the language of education, administration, government, and print media, and therefore its acquisition may give speakers advantages in specific domains (e.g., media outlets; political speeches). As Kahane (1986) observes, prestige languages are typically associated with education, which often translates into a symbolic class value. Salam (1980) found that, regardless of their countries, educated Arabs, particularly politicians, always use the SA [q] variant, in their intercommunication. In my fieldwork in Egypt and Saudi Arabia, I had the chance to interact with two college students who reported using SA predominantly in public. One of the students was studying journalism and the other was a student of religion. When I inquired about their use of SA, they indicated that their command and use of SA would help them in their future careers as a reporter/journalist and a religious leader.[17] However, the historically endowed status of SA is not always convertible to prestige in everyday interactions. Ibrahim (1986, p. 115) suggests that the prestige of SA is based on common attitudes of "correct" or "good" language rather than actual use, thus calling for "the need to maintain a clear distinction between standard and prestige language in Arabic." Ibrahim argues that prestige languages are usually associated with social class and mobility, but these socioeconomic indices are not marked by SA. At the same time, however, he maintains, "Since H is inseparable from education, it would be wrong to attribute to H the power of affecting an individual's social class and mobility; these are the results of the individual's education and not his or her knowledge of H." Ibrahim, however, makes the correct observation that ". . . the L varieties of Arabic must have their own hierarchical order of prestige independently of H and any of the latter's features" (p. 118). In other words, the prestige of SA, which is often based on its historical, religious, educational, and literary value, is different from the prestige of the dialects (see also Abdel-Jawad, 1987).

A large number of studies have suggested that some, if not all, of the urban dialects are the prestige varieties in everyday interactions between urban and non-urban speakers of Arabic (Abdel-Jawad, 1986; Al-Wer, 2002, 2007; Amara, 2005; Behnstedt, 1997; Habib, 2010; Hussein, 1980; Wahba, 1996). The urban dialects derive their prestige from the socioeconomic status and power of the city where educational institutions (e.g., universities), businesses, services, and resources are concentrated. Moreover, the inhabitants of most Arab cities are generally more affluent than the rural and Bedouin populations and they have access to better education, infrastructure, and communications. The dialects of the capitals in each Arab country are often more prestigious than the other urban dialects (when multiple urban dialects are present) because of their sociopolitical position. For example, the Cairene and Damascene dialects are often considered the prestige dialects in Egypt and Syria, respectively (Ibrahim, 1986; Versteegh 2001). A number of studies have found that non-urban speakers may adopt certain urban linguistic features in their interactions with speakers of these dialects, which has often been attributed to the "prestige," "beauty," "sophistication," and "femininity" of the urban dialects (e.g., Abdel-Jawad, 1981, 1986; Al-Wer, 2002, 2007; Amara, 2005; Habib, 2010; Sawaie, 1994). For example, Jabeur (1987) points to a correlation between the use of the urban variant of /q/ in Rades, Tunisia, and the degree of social integration and education among rural migrants. Habib (2010) notes that younger rural migrants to the city of Hims, Syria, tend to adopt the [ʔ] form, which according to Habib is "the prestige marker" of the urban Himsi dialect, at the expense of the standardized [q] form, which is part of their rural dialect.

The Bedouin dialect is generally not considered as prestigious as the urban dialects mainly due to the socioeconomic and educational gap between the urban populace and the Bedouins in most Arab countries. However, the Bedouin varieties have sometimes been recognized for what Miller (2004) describes as *Aṣaalah* "pure origin" (see also Hussein & El-Ali, 1989; Nader, 1962). This type of prestige is based on the presumed historical and linguistic relationship between SA and the Bedouin dialects (e.g., proximity of the Bedouin dialects to SA), rather than socioeconomically based, as is the case of the urban dialects. For example, Ferguson (1968, p. 379) reports that his non-Bedouin subjects indicated that the Bedouin dialect is "better" than the rural and urban dialects in the Levant. Nader (1962, p. 25) suggested that "stating that Bedouin dialect was best was not being disloyal; it was expressing loyalty to widespread cultural ideal – that the Bedouin speaks the purest of Arabic." Al-Wer (2007) found that urban men in Jordan sometimes adopt features of the Jordanian Bedouin dialects as a way of relating to the Bedouin heritage. Hachimi (2012) reports of a language shift in the speech of two women who migrated from the city of Fes to Casablanca in Morocco. Whereas their "native" Fessi dialect is urban, the Casablancan dialect is historically Bedouin. For example, the two Fessi women in Hachimi's study deploy the Casablancan [gaal] and drop the Fessi [qaal].

Albirini (2014a) suggests that language *use* in naturalistic settings is shaped more by sociopragmatic factors than by language-prestige issues – though the latter is an important part of the language *ideologies* of many Arabic speakers. He further suggests that language prestige in the Arabic sociolinguistic context is complex and controversial because it is often intricately related to various factors (context, speaker variables, etc.), particularly with respect to the dialects. For example, Daher (1998) reports that the speech of the Damascene men is marked by the dominant use of the standardized variant [q], whereas the urbanized variant [ʔ] features predominantly in the speech of Damascene women, especially the young and educated. Similar results are reported by Al-Ali and Arafa (2010), who found that men and high schoolers in Irbid (Jordan) are more likely to utilize the local /θ/, /dʒ/, and /ð/ sounds, whereas women and university graduates tend to use the prestigious non-local variants of these sounds. Likewise, in their study the Arabic dialect spoken in Bethlehem, Amara (2005) and Amara, Spolsky, and Tushyeh (1999) discovered that, whereas Muslims and males tend to use [q] and [θ] sounds, Christians and women are more prone to the [ʔ] and [t] variants found in the *prestigious* urban dialect of Jerusalem. Mejdell (2006) reports of the use of various features of SA in the formal speech of educated women (see also Walters, 2003). Overall, language prestige is governed by complex interactions of historical, socioeconomic, pragmatic, and demographic factors. However, as noted above, the most critical determiner of language prestige in the Arab context is speakers' attitudes to these varieties or their speakers, which will be discussed in Chapter 4.

2.7 LOCAL AND GLOBAL LANGUAGES: BERBER, KURDISH, ENGLISH, AND FRENCH

A discussion of the Arabic sociolinguistic situation is incomplete without considering the role of global and local languages in the Arabic sociolinguistic scene. These languages are critical for understanding speakers' language attitudes, language identities, language choice, and other language-related issues. Throughout its history, the Arabic language has influenced and has been influenced by a number of languages due to processes of language contact (e.g., Berber), migration (e.g., Persian), translation (e.g., Greek), and colonialism (e.g., Spanish). However, the competitive presence of a number of local and global languages in the Arabic sociolinguistic situation unsettles the somewhat comfortable position that the Arabic language has enjoyed in the Arab region for the major part of its history.[18]

One of the local languages that is claiming a space and legitimacy in the Arabic sociolinguistic sphere is Berber. Berber is not a single language, but numerous languages that are spoken in the various countries of North Africa, including Algeria, Morocco, Tunisia, Mauritania, Libya, and Egypt (Sadiqi, 1997).[19] Berber communities are spread across North Africa with higher concentrations in Morocco and Algeria and lower concentrations in Libya, Tunisia, Egypt, and Mauritania (Keita, 2010). The most populous Berber communities exist in Morocco (Masmuda, Kutama, and Zenata) and in Algeria (Kabyle and Aures) (Benrabah, 2013). Mutual intelligibility may not always be guaranteed among speakers of the various Berber languages or varieties even within a single country (Keita, 2010). The existence of these languages in North Africa predates the presence of Arabic (Chakrani, 2010; Errihani, 2006; Keita, 2010; Miller, 2003). For a long time, Berber has been a spoken language whose use has traditionally been limited to certain rural areas and to the home domain in the urban centers (Hoffman, 2006; Sadiqi, 1997). However, there have recently been concerted efforts by various constituencies to codify and standardize Berber, using Latin and Tifinagh alphabets (Chakrani, 2010). Moreover, Berber became a national language of

Algeria in 2001, and ten years later it became a constitutionally official language in Morocco. These developments have extended the use of Berber to the public domain (e.g., some schools, media outlets, and magazines). Nonetheless, when a Moroccan Arab and a Moroccan Berber meet, the customarily medium of communication would be Moroccan Arabic possibly because Berber speakers also command Moroccan Arabic and not the opposite.

Kurdish is another language that competes for space in the Arabic sociolinguistic scene. Kurdish is not a single language, but several languages that are spoken by diverse speech communities spread over areas in southeastern Turkey, western Iran, northern Iraq, northeastern Syria, and smaller parts of Georgia and Armenia.[20] The existence of the Kurdish people in the north parts of the Arab Middle East predates the existence of Arabs in this region (McDowall, 2004; Vali, 2003).[21] Kurdish languages are not mutually intelligible, although they often share a wide range of linguistic properties (Hassanpour, 2012; McDowall, 2004; Meho & Maglaughlin, 2001; Vali, 2003). Within the Arab context, Kurdish is spoken mainly in northern Iraq and in small parts in northern Syria. Like Berber, Kurdish had conventionally been a spoken language (McDowall, 2004; Vali, 2003). Since 2003, however, Kurdish has become an official language in Iraq, and henceforward, it came to be used in administration, schools and universities, media, and print. With the current conflict in Syria, the Kurds may replicate the Iraq experience in terms of making Kurdish an official language within a prospective autonomous state. Outside the Kurd-dominated areas, however, Kurdish has often had meager presence and influence compared to the Syrian and Iraqi dialects (O'Shea, 2004; Sheyholislami, 2008). However, the situation is changing, particularly in the Iraqi context.

While the presence of Berber and Kurdish is confined to certain parts of the Arab World, English and, to a lesser extent, French are two global languages whose influence is felt in various parts of the Arabic sociolinguistic arena. French found its way into the Arab region by means of Catholic missionary education and humanitarian aid and through the gate of Lebanon (Burrows, 1986; Walker, 2000). According to Burrows (1986), the French introduced themselves as a protector of the Christians in Lebanon and thus paved the way for their linguistic, cultural, and military intervention in Greater Syria, which came into effect in 1920 after hostilities broke out between Shi'i and Christian factions in South Lebanon. The Lebanon experience aside, French was introduced into the Arab region as part of a colonial package, which included, in addition to military occupation of territory, an imposition of the French language and culture on the Arab societies.[22] The presence of French in the Arab region started in 1798 in Egypt and spread afterwards to Algeria, Morocco, Tunisia, Mauritania, Lebanon, and Syria. However, French was not spread merely by military force, so to speak; it was adopted, and sometimes propagated, by the local socioeconomic elites who in many cases are still seen as responsible for securing its place in the Arabic sociolinguistic space (Chakrani, 2010; Ennaji, 2007; Holt, 1994). This is particularly true in the Maghreb/North Africa and Lebanon, and less so in Syria and Egypt where

French plays a minor role. The influence of French is evident in the many French loanwords that are used routinely in several Arabic varieties (e.g., *ʔitikeit* = *étiquette* "etiquette"; *ʔokazion* = *occasion* "sale"; *ʔaṣanṣeir* = *ascenseur* "elevator"). French is also an everyday language of communication, writing, education, and print, electronic, and satellite media in the Maghreb. It is part of the multilingual reality of the Maghreb, and it is taken into account in language planning and policy and sometimes in socioeconomic and political decisions. However, the presence of French is gradually shrinking because of its waning international role – compared to English – and the entry of English as a strong rival in business and education. Other attitudinal and identity-related factors are involved, but these will be discussed later in the book.

Compared to French, English is not as strongly associated with the British colonial experience in the Arab region (Egypt, Sudan, Palestine, Jordan, Iraq, and the Gulf region) because the British were not as aggressive in promoting the English language and culture as their French counterparts (Suleiman, 2003). English started to recede gradually after the Arab countries gained their independence and initiated the Arabicization policies within some societal domains. However, the global status of English, the spread of modern technologies and communications, and the economic and political influence of the English-speaking countries, particularly the United States, have necessitated the reinception of English into the Arab sociolinguistic scene for the purposes of global communication, economic competitiveness, use of new technologies, and national development in general. As McArthur (2002, p. 450) suggests, English serves as "the primary vehicle of the world's commerce, science, technology, computer activity, electronics, media, popular culture and entertainment." In several Arab countries today, English is a required subject in elementary schools. It is used as the language of instruction in several Arab universities and schools. In most Arab countries, some subjects (e.g., medicine) are taught exclusively in English (or, less so, in French). Many newspapers, magazines, radio and television channels use English as the exclusive language. In 2012, I led a summer study-abroad program in Jordan. The program included visits to museums, art galleries, historical sites, media institutes, and financial institutions. The visits were arranged by the host university, and therefore we always had a guide in the target sites. Although they varied in education, experience, and training, almost all of the guides displayed remarkable proficiency in English. The instrumental use of English, however, may not by itself explain its fast spread. English is also a prestige language across the Arab region and it is rapidly occupying domains that were reserved for SA and French (in North African countries) (Al-Khatib, 2008; Battenburg, 2006).

The somehow competitive existence of these languages has generated lively debates among linguists, nationalists, social activists, educators, politicians, planners, and even ordinary citizens concerning their potential to challenge the role of Arabic in different social spheres or to enrich the Arabic communities with more linguistic diversity, more economic opportunities, and more windows open to the world. These debates have reverberated strongly through the sociolinguistic literature, because they involve social, political, economic, affective, and behavioral aspects, which will be discussed in the coming chapters.

2.8 SUMMARY AND CONCLUSION

This chapter discussed the two varieties recognized by the Arabic speakers, namely SA (the High code) and QA (the Low code). SA is the variety that is typically used in education, literature, print media, news reports, and religious discourses, whereas QA is the variety used in everyday interactions, entertainment media, and informal discussions. SA is often perceived by Arabic speakers as the "Arabic" language, whereas QA is identified as a later development or a derivative of SA. The relationship between these two varieties has been framed within two different perspectives. A first perspective maintains a structural distinction as well as a contextual or functional disparity between the two varieties. A second account, however, conceptualizes SA and QA as two extreme poles on a continuum or introduces in-between varieties whose boundaries are defined by contextual (e.g., setting) and demographic (e.g., speakers' educational level) factors.

The chapter presented an argument against the division between CA and MSA based on historical, structural, and social factors and also against the notion SA as a "second language." It was shown that, from an acquisitional point of view, Arabic children get exposed to SA at an early age and that, from a sociolinguistic perspective, adult speakers consider SA as an important facet of their linguistic self-representation and social identities. The different intricacies of the concept of prestige were explained in relation to SA and QA. SA derives its prestige from historical, literary, and religious factors as well as from its status as the official language of most Arab countries. On the other hand, the prestige of the urban dialects is built on the socioeconomic power of their speakers and the socioeconomic privileges of the urban centers in general. The Bedouin dialects are sometimes considered prestigious when viewed through romanticized, historical lenses as somewhat "pure" dialects. However, the notion of prestige is not always as straightforward as it may seem to be because it is typically related to a complex set of social, economic, contextual, demographic, and affective factors.

Last, the chapter pointed to a number of local languages (Berber and Kurdish) and global languages (English and French), which are gaining greater visibility across the Arab region. These languages have the potential to redistribute the main parameters of the Arabic diglossic landscape and to influence the language behavior of the Arabic speakers, particularly considering their presence in social domains and functions that were exclusive to SA and QA. Having set the general background of the Arabic sociolinguistic situation, I will move to tackle some of the main methodological considerations in the study of the five areas covered in the book.

NOTES

1 The abbreviation QA is used in reference to Colloquial Arabic to distinguish it from CA, which is reserved to Classical Arabic.

2 Most Muslim scholars and historians believe that Prophet Muhammad and many of his companions and contemporaries used CA in their oral and written communications (Versteegh, 2004; Wild, 2006). For example, the widely circulated story about the writing of the Qur'an at the time of the third caliph suggests that CA was the everyday language of Quraysh and the Prophet. Likewise, Muhammad is reported to have used CA in his correspondence with the leaders of the neighboring nations, including the emperors of Byzantium and Persia and the kings of Oman, Bahrain, Yamaama, Abyssinia, and other Arab leaders.

3 See Chapter 6.

4 See Al-Jallad (2009) for a similar account.

5 Throughout the book, glosses are provided only when needed for understanding specific details in the examples. Otherwise, only the English translation is presented.

6 All of the participants in this study were educated speakers, and therefore it is not likely that they switch to QA for lack of fluency in SA or to sustain their speech in SA.

7 Alternative lexical items and morphological endings may be used in each of the four varieties for the words used in these examples.

8 Alternative negative sentences are available in SA, such as *lam yusaafir* "He did not travel."

9 The name is still widely used in reference to a number of tribes, particularly in eastern and northern Iraq.

10 Some also used mixed forms that involved both Moroccan and SA (e.g., retention of /ʔ/ word medially "yisʔal" or the dropping of the aspectual marker ka "yruuh") and Moroccan-Syrian forms (e.g., /ʔ/ instead of /q/ and the use of aspectual prefix b-). See Chapter 8 on mixed forms.

11 I plan to extent this study to children from different Arab countries and to add production tasks to it. This study will be published in a separate work.

12 There are no empirical studies investigating the correspondence between the structures, vocabulary, style, and topics of these cartoons and the particular age group under study. However, I assume that cartoons in general are appropriate, age-wise, for this and older group ages.

13 Most of the respondents in this group asked for clarification of the meaning of "mother tongue" based on their awareness of its double meaning. My reaction was to confirm the dual meaning of "mother tongue" and to request that they describe SA and QA in terms of these two meanings.

14 See Chapter 5 for a discussion on the different forms of identity in the Arab context.

15 See Van Mol (2003) for a discussion on standardization as it relates to the Arabic language.

16 The notion of the superiority of SA has been reiterated in the writings of many scholars of religion, literature, and language (see Chejne, 1969 for a review).

17 Both indicated the importance of SA to them as individuals and community members. These atypical cases were not included in the interviewee sample.

18 The late periods of the Ottoman presence in the Arab World and the colonial period may be considered an exception.

19 Berber is spoken in a number of other African countries, but these are out of the scope of this book.
20 The assumption that the Kurdish people come from a single ethnic origin has been questioned in recent literature (see O'Shea, 2004).
21 There is disagreement in the literature about the origins of the Kurds (see Vali, 2003).
22 The French language made its first appearance into the Arab region through religious schools mainly in Mount Lebanon. However, its impact was limited in this role.

CHAPTER 3

Methodological considerations

Research methodology is one of the most basic requisites for any field dealing with human interaction. In researching sociolinguistic phenomena, researchers are always faced with challenges concerning the proper approach, contexts, populations, sampling procedures, data-collection methods, data-analysis techniques, and reporting formats. These issues are critical in sociolinguistic research because of the interdisciplinary nature of this field and its openness to various theories, methodologies, and techniques. Research and writing on even the most intriguing topic may descend into mere speculation if not backed up by supporting data. Similarly, very good data may be wasted when an inappropriate approach to the topic is adopted. This chapter has three main goals. First, the chapter discusses a number of methodological considerations in researching the Arabic sociolinguistic situation. Second, the chapter provides a critical review of the main methods used in researching the areas under study – namely, diglossia, language attitudes, social identities, language variation, and CS. Last, the chapter explains the methodology used in the research reported in this book.

As an interdisciplinary field, sociolinguistics has benefited from a number of disciplines, including linguistics, sociology, anthropology, philosophy, social psychology, communication, education, and cultural studies. It is not surprising therefore that theories and methodologies originating in diverse disciplines have made their way into sociolinguistic research and have added richness to the field. Bilingual CS, for example, has been analyzed through ethnographic methods, conversation-analysis techniques, interpretive and interactional frameworks, sociopragmatic principles, accommodation theories, rational choice processes, and optimality theory, among others (Auer, 1998; Bhatt & Bolonyai, 2011; Giles & Powesland, 1997; Gumperz, 1982; Heller, 1992; Myers-Scotton, 1993b; Myers-Scotton & Bolonyai, 2001). Sociolinguists have adopted these approaches as useful frameworks for analyzing data in different bilingual contexts. By contrast, the majority of studies on bidialectal CS between SA and QA have drawn largely on Ferguson's seminal work on diglossia (1959a). The use of Ferguson's model is often instigated by its contextual relevance to the Arabic sociolinguistic situation, but this does not mean that theories and methods initiated in bilingual situations may not be exploited in bidialectal CS. In fact, several studies on bidialectal CS have fruitfully used some of these frameworks and added much depth and richness to their analyses thereby. What is critical here is the illustration that a wide range of methodologies and analyses can be used to address a single research topic.

Research should not be confined to available theoretical frameworks and methodologies. The field of Arabic sociolinguistics is in dire need of new theoretical models and methodologies that spring from the Arab context and fit within its unique sociohistorical circumstances (Suleiman, 2011). In what follows, I discuss a number of methodological considerations relevant to researching the constructs under study, and to Arabic sociolinguistic research in general. As the title of the chapter suggests, the goal is not to cover the "research methods" used in studying these areas – which obviously need more than a single chapter and are beyond the scope of this book – but to consider and reflect on some of the important issues connected with sociolinguistic research in these areas, offer suggestions that may enhance research outcomes, and contextualize the research methods used in developing this book.

3.1 GOALS AND ELEMENTS OF SOCIOLINGUISTIC RESEARCH

Sociolinguistic research, like research in the social sciences in general, is led by three principal questions: (1) what epistemological assumptions guide the research process? (2) What methodologies are used to approach the topic? And (3) what techniques are implemented in conducting research? (Creswell, 2003; Crotty, 1998; Jones, Torres, & Arminio, 2014; Lincoln & Guba, 2000; Mertens, 2010; Tashakkori & Teddlie, 2010). These questions highlight the three main components of sociolinguistic research, which include *epistemology, methodology*, and *techniques*. Epistemology is concerned with questions of what we are learning from inquiry, how this knowledge is accessed and acquired, and what limitations may restrict our understanding of social reality. Methodology is the plan of action or design that informs the selection of particular methods. Techniques refer to specific methods used to collect and analyze data in exploring research questions. These three components are interdependent in the sense that a change in one component often entails changes in the other categories as well. The three components appear under disparate categories and formulations in several works (e.g., Creswell, 2003; Jones et al., 2014; Lincoln & Guba, 2000; Mertens, 2010; Tashakkori & Teddlie, 2010).

Much of the existing sociolinguistic research has been epistemologically guided by the *constructivist/interpretive* and *transformative* paradigms.[1] For researchers who adopt an *interpretive* epistemology, meaning is constructed socially by humans as they interact in a given context (Debrix, 2003; Gralewski, 2011; Halliday, 1978). Therefore, meaning requires a process of interpretation based on understanding the interlocutors themselves and the context in which meaning is situated. In other words, social meaning may not be imposed from outside. Johnstone (2000, p. 36) argues that "Sociolinguistic research is always 'interpretive,' whether the interpretation involves numbers or results of some other kind." Within the *transformative* paradigm, research focuses on exposing the various factors underlying language usage and manipulation, including power relationships, socioeconomic inequalities, ideologies, and political interests (Fairclough, 1989; Heller, 1992; May, 1997; Wodak & Meyer, 2009). This paradigm proposes dismantling the broader historical, political, and ideological processes involved in language use while at the same time scrutinizing immediate contextual and textual details. In some cases, researchers may adopt an "openly ideological research" (Lather, 2003, p. 186) in which the researcher's role is to advocate a certain position, perspective, or social group, or to engage in an action to *transform*, not merely describe, certain social inequalities through research.

These epistemological frameworks inform the broad goals of sociolinguistic research. Generally speaking, sociolinguistic research sets out to achieve three main goals: (1) to improve understanding of the relationship between language and social actors and communities, (2) to propose solutions to problems surrounding language perceptions, productions, behavior, and policies, and (3) to engage in solving inequalities stemming from language attitudes and praxes. For example, a study motivated by a question like "What are the social functions of CS between Moroccan Arabic and French in everyday speech?" may provide us with a better understanding of this linguistic behavior, which may offer insights into Moroccan speech communities. However, a study pursuing a different question like "Why do some Jordanian college students use English exclusively in Facebook mediated interactions?" provides venues for explaining this intriguing behavior, which, if seen as a "problem," may prompt the researcher to propose possible solutions for this behavior. More far-reaching still is the pursuit of the third goal, which would turn a research project into an action to influence or change a certain social reality. Labov's work on language-based stereotyping and discrimination in the case of African Americans is an example of a scholar–activist's use of research to solve a real-life problem (Labov, 1972). These broad goals translate into specific research questions in individual studies, which are arguably the pivotal element in any research enterprise around which other research components are structured. The goals are not mutually exclusive; researchers may, and often do, engage in more than one goal in a single research project. Sociolinguistic activism, for example, often entails improving our understanding of a social issue or providing practical solutions to problems in our social life.

The second component of research is *methodology*, which includes *quantitative research*, *qualitative research*, and *mixed methods* (Creswell, 2003). While epistemology reveals a researcher's assumptions about "how they will learn and what they will learn during their inquiry," methodology "provide[s] specific direction for procedures in a research design" (Creswell, p. 6 & p. 13). Quantitative research relies heavily on experimental, quasi-experimental, and correlational designs in which relationships among a specific set of variables are studied, sometimes with hypotheses specified (Gay & Airasian, 2000; Lincoln & Guba, 2000). Qualitative research involves more open-ended research questions and a more inductive, exploratory approach to investigating social phenomena (Creswell, 2003; Glesne, 2010; Mertens, 2010). Linguistic and critical ethnographies, case studies, narrative research, and discourse analyses are examples of qualitative research strategies. It is common for researchers, however, to use a mixed-method approach, which reflects a particular paradigmatic view that some social realities are more socially complex, historically rooted, and context-dependent than others. It is often assumed that the goal of qualitative data is to *maximize information*, whereas quantitative data seeks after *obtaining generalizations*. In my view, this argument does not pertain to sociolinguistic research. Given the relativeness of what "maximum" means, every study should aim to provide enough information to explain and interpret the results while simultaneously trying not to restrict its findings to the limited number participants in the study. Failure to do so may turn the focus of the study to individual people rather than sociolinguistic *patterns*. A focus on the social rather than the individual is part of the very definition of *socio*linguistics as a discipline.

The third and last basic component of research is *technique*, which refers to the specific methods or tools used to collect, analyze, and present data. Quantitative research relies heavily on controlled tests, elicitation measures, and questionnaires. These methods often entail measurement, statistical tests, and numerical results. By contrast, qualitative research relies more on participant observation, individual interviews, focus-group interviews, auto-reflections, media analysis, and textual analysis. These methods often involve the use of rich descriptions and participant discourse. Some techniques, such as observation, may be used in both quantitative and qualitative research methodologies. What is critical is the relatedness of the techniques chosen to the specific goals and methodologies of research. Understanding the goals and components of sociolinguistic research is critical for planning further details in the research process.

3.2 THEORY, METHODOLOGY, AND PRACTICE

Theory and practice are interlocked in a dialectic relationship in which the former derives its reference from the latter and the latter feeds the former with themes and serves as a testing ground. Methodology acts as a bridge between the two through which theory can be used in practice and practice can be turned into theory. Methodology also furnishes means for linking linguistic variables (e.g., phonology) to social factors (e.g., socioeconomic status) (Labov, 1972). Theory in this context refers to generalized frameworks or templates for interpreting language behavior, whereas practice denotes aspects of language behavior, such as language use, choice, and maintenance. Like any other field dealing with human subjects, sociolinguistics has employed several "subtheories" that address different aspects of the relationship between language, speakers, and society (Coupland, 2003; Hudson, 1996; Romaine, 1994). Accommodation theory (Giles et al.,

1991), politeness theory (Brown & Levinson, 1987), and social capital theory (Bourdieu, 1977) are examples of theoretical frameworks that have been used extensively in sociolinguistic research. Although sociolinguistic research is generally driven more by "problem solving" than by theory construction (Ferguson, 1996), sociolinguistic "subtheories" continue to evolve, providing conceptual maps that guide empirical work and help in data analysis and interpretation. Theories differ in their frames of reference, context, explanatory power, and applicability to new situations. Despite their importance, theories may become a source of confusion when they are not derived from – or grounded in – empirical data, or applied uncritically to contexts that are governed by different linguistic, social, political, and historical realities.

Definitions are an important consideration in dealing with theories and theoretical constructs. Theoretical frameworks delimit the scope of their transferability through conceptual and operational definitions, which are typically quite focused, concrete, and specific. Pitfalls may arise when these theoretical models are utilized without considering their circumscribing definitions. Take for example Ferguson's model of diglossia, which was carefully delineated in terms of defining SA and QA, their historical and structural relatedness, their respective statuses, their contexts of use, their relationship in the speech community, their complementary distribution in speakers' language behavior, and their potential evolutionary interplay. Some of the main theoretical controversies surrounding Ferguson's model stem from overlooking the very basic definitions delimiting the parameters of this model (see Hudson, 2002). The concept of identity has been couched in theoretical frameworks that define identity differently (e.g., Antaki & Widdicombe, 1998; Blommaert, 2010; Bucholtz, 2003; Bucholtz, Liang, & Sutton 1999; Fairclough, 1989; Hall, 1996; Kroskrity, 2000; Silverstein, 2003). Therefore, studying a complex sociolinguistic construct like identity depends first upon adopting the definition that works within one's approach. The same applies to an equally complex sociolinguistic construct like language attitudes, which have been defined and approached distinctly by different researchers. Although these social and socioaffective constructs are part of the social reality of every speech community, they are conceptualized differently in various theoretical frameworks, and this variability only further highlights the importance of proper definitions.

The question of definitions is a broader problem in sociolinguistic research because definitions are often ideologically laden. This is particularly true in historical narratives, which continue to play a major role in shaping and reshaping the Arabic sociolinguistic scene. Historical narratives refer to stories that are constructed at one point in the past, but are somehow linked to the realities or politics of the present. The construction of *pan-Arabism* – when charted on the current political map of the Arab World – is an example of a description that is based on ideologically mediated historical narratives. This means that understanding or untangling the ideological presumptions and implications of definitions becomes an integral part of conducting sociolinguistic research. Bourdieu's social capital theory provides an interesting case in point. Bourdieu (1977, 1999) argues that social actors' linguistic behavior is inextricably linked to such factors as their socio-economic situation, the structures of the social fields in which they operate, the nature of their relationships within a given social structure, and their socialization into what is valued and not valued in different *social fields* or *linguistic markets*. Although the theory focuses mainly on forms of social capital, for Bourdieu, language is not merely a medium of communication, but also an instrument and an index of power and power relationships. Understanding this part of Bourdieu's definition of language is critical for using this theoretical model and applying it to contexts where the researcher may think that power relationships are at work in language use.

The link between theory, methodology, and practice becomes critical in the process of theory construction and verification. Sociolinguistic theory construction typically relies on identifying general patterns of language use or social interaction in a given context(s), which in turn depends on suitable description or analysis of actual data from specific social context(s). In other words, it is methodologically grounded and is testable through empirical observation (Appadurai, 1986; Coupland, 2003). Ferguson's model of diglossia, for example, is derived from *systematic observation* of sociolinguistic norms and language behavior in a number of contexts, such as home, mosque/church, and university. Systematic observation may also characterize several other important contributions to the ongoing discussion of diglossia in the Arab region (e.g., Hudson, 2002; Kaye, 1994; Schiffman, 1997). The process of verifying theories or specific theoretical claims is subject to the same criteria; some level of descriptive or analytic account of language behavior in context is needed for evaluating any theoretical generalizations. However, this depends on whether these claims were, in the first place, derived empirically from linguistic practices in context and, equally importantly, whether they continue to be applicable to these contextually bound practices. The fact that some theoretical claims are more empirically verifiable in language behavior may help explain why some theories are more enduring than others. Because of its enduring relevance to language practices in language-contact situations, accommodation theory, for example, has figured predominantly in sociolinguistic research, including research on Arabic (Abu-Melhim, 1992; Albirini, in progress; Shiri, 2002).

Most linguistic theories have tried to establish universal rules that apply to all languages based on similarities in human cognitive abilities (Chomsky, 1965). A sociolinguistic theory, on the other hand, can make no such claim simply because sociolinguistic patterns are influenced by the idiosyncrasies of distinct cultural contexts (Heller, 1992). This does not mean that sociolinguistic theories cannot be used outside the contexts in which they evolved; rather they apply selectively to contexts undergirded by similar linguistic, sociocultural, and political conditions. In some cases, ready-made models that have been used effectively in one context may become unworkable in another context (Suleiman, 2011) because the theoretical issues or social problems that may have motivated the creation of a specific model do not map neatly on the questions and issues in the adopting context. The credit that Ferguson's model of diglossia has received stems partly from its originality with respect to the Arabic sociolinguistic situation. This leads to our next important question, namely, the importance of context in sociolinguistic research.

3.3 THE STUDY OF LANGUAGE IN CONTEXT

In sociolinguistic research, context is simply indispensable for understanding language as a social system, as a means of communication, and as a form of social behavior. Language use evolves and acquires meaning within a given context that informs its social significance. Gumperz (1992, p. 230) argues that the "situated interpretation of any utterance is always a matter of inferences made within the context of an interaction exchange . . ." According to Gumperz (1992), language use is a social activity that can be understood only through interpretation derived from the contextual cues surrounding the utterance as well as from the utterance itself. In other words, language, like other objects of social study, should be understood according to the relevant social, political, and economic context. Similarly, Labov (1972) maintains that language is a "social entity" that interacts with other social, historical, and economic factors in its community. To understand language, one has to know its relationship to this complex set of social factors.

Context operates at five different levels, namely those of language, speaker, interaction, occasion or event, and community or society (Akman, 2000; Auer, 1998; Bakhtin, 1986; Fairclough & Wodak, 1997; Gumperz, 1982, 1993; Harris, 1988; Hymes, 1972; Silverstein, 1992). Some or all of these levels may contribute to interpreting language use. At the language level, context implies understanding the complexities of language and its unique structures and meanings (Akman, 2000; Harris, 1988). At the speaker level, context involves the demographic, socioeconomic, and ideo-political background of the speakers (Gumperz, 1982). An utterance as simple as "life is worthless" may be interpreted differently based on whether the speaker is, for example, educated or uneducated, socioeconomically advantaged or disadvantaged, religious or non-religious. Even lacking other contextual information, we are more likely to interpret this utterance as a philosophical statement if made by an educated, affluent, and religious figure, whereas this very statement may be seen as a complaint if made by an uneducated, socioeconomically disadvantaged, or non-religious individual. At the interaction level, language use is influenced by the sequential position of an utterance within language negotiation or conversation (Auer, 1998). Thus, every utterance should be interpreted with reference to the preceding and following utterances and the organization of the interaction. Utterances are also bound by their "contextualization cues" (e.g., prosody, Gumperz, 1993) and "indexes" (e.g., specific references and associations in social reality, Silverstein, 1992). For example, an utterance like "I hate spaghetti" could be a mere statement of preference in a response to a preceding question like "what types of food do you hate most?"

but it could also be interpreted as an offensive response to a preceding question such as "would you like to have some of my spaghetti?" Interaction also involves the type of relationship that binds the interlocutors (Bakhtin, 1986; Gumperz, 1993). For example, a professor may not address a colleague in the same way he or she addresses his or her students. Recognizing the relationship between utterances and interlocutors is part of understanding their contextually specific social meaning.

At the occasion or event level, an utterance like "I am dying" may be taken more seriously if said by a man on his sickbed than by the same man watching a soccer game on his couch. At the community or society level, an utterance like "I am sorry to hear that" may be considered a form of condolence in the American society, but it is not so in Arab societies (Taha, 2006). Similarly, language choice has been found to carry different meanings or different weights based on established society-based conventions and historical details. For example, the use of French in the Morocco context correlates with the social functions of social mobility and modernity (Bentahila, 1983a; Chakrani, 2010), whereas the use of French in Canada is a form of resistance and national mobilization (Heller, 1992). In general, language use may not always evoke the same social meanings in different contexts. Utterances acquire their meanings contextually and should therefore be interpreted within the context in which they occur. Certain contextual cues acquire more prominence and visibility in some contexts than others. For example, historical data may be more relevant for studying language attitudes in the Arab World than in the United States, although it is needed in both contexts. The reason history is more important in the Arab context is that Arabic speakers' attitudes toward SA and QA derive much of their reference from historical events and figures, whereas language attitudes in the United States are not so deeply rooted in history.

Wolfson (1986) argues that contextual factors are responsible for much of the variation in language use. In Arab contexts, for instance, speakers change their speech according to the event, type or frame of interaction, dynamics of the interaction, ideological views about the interlocutors' spoken varieties, the relationship binding the interlocutors, interlocutors' religion, ethnicity, or nationality, and the interlocutors' demographics, such as socioeconomic status, gender, and education (Abdel-Jawad 1981, 1986; Abu-Haidar, 1989; Abu-Melhim, 1992; Al-Wer, 2002; Amara, 2005; Hachimi, 2012; Holes, 1987, 1995, 2006; Mejdell, 2006; Parkinson, 1996; Sawaie, 1994; Shiri, 2002; Suleiman, 1993; Walters, 2003). This suggests that some patterns of language use may simply be explained by contextual factors.

The question of context raises a number of challenges for the field of sociolinguistics. A first challenge relates to the nature and meaning of context: context is not fixed but may change in accordance to shifts in social, political, economic, and cultural circumstances (Gumperz, 1982; Hymes, 1972). The mutable nature of context carries with it fluctuations in the social meanings context lends to language use. This aspect of context is particularly important to Arabic because the Arab region is changing rapidly at the cultural, social, political, and economic levels (Nydell, 2012). These changes are redefining the meaning of relationships, communities, social norms, nations, belonging, among many other concepts. The Saudi Arabia of today is different from that of a few decades ago. Therefore, a discussion on tents, cattle, and nomadism in pre-oil-discovery Saudi Arabia does not carry the same meanings as in the current Saudi context. Sociolinguistic patterns and trends may change and evolve continually, and therefore a periodic assessment of emerging patterns is always needed. The meaning of context becomes particularly fluid in the absence of contextual cues such as space, time, speaker background, and community. In digitally mediated communications on the internet, for example, little may be known about the interactants' backgrounds, and the community of online users may not be easily defined (Ramirez et al., 2002). This contextual plasticity reflects directly on language use and communication patterns. For example, expressing emotions may not be done by tone of speech, facial expressions, or other contextual cues. Hence, online users have to create social and interactional meaning through their discursive practices, such as choice of vocabulary. In other words, language itself becomes a context-creating agent (van Dijk, 2008; Zimmerman, 1992). In fact, van Dijk (2008) argues that context is *always* redefinable by speakers based on their language use, implying that an understanding of language use necessitates a grasp of the ever-changing meaning of context in discourse.

A second challenge concerns the selection of proper setting for studying a given sociolinguistic phenomenon. To give an extreme example, language accommodation in the Gulf region takes an interesting form: Arabic speakers in the Gulf, who constitute the dominant group, linguistically accommodate Asian immigrants by addressing them with a pidginized form of Arabic (Bakir, 2010; Næss, 2008; Smart, 1990). The pidginized form is supposed to be structurally and lexically simpler and therefore more accessible to the Asian speakers than the local Gulf dialects. Studying this form of language accommodation among Gulf and Asian students in the United States, for instance, would yield completely different results because of contextual dissimilarities. In the United States, for example, there is an alternative code (i.e., English) that can be utilized by both groups, and therefore language accommodation may not transpire at all, or it may take a completely different social meaning. As another illustration, a researcher who opts to focus on the current sectarian-divided Iraq to study the link between SA and pan-Arabism in the Arab region may obtain results that do not reflect the overall trends in other Arab countries. Context selection should be considered at an early stage of research because research questions ideally stem from the need to understand well-defined contexts or to solve problems within them (Ferguson, 1996).

A last concern with respect to context is the implementation of theories and methodologies that originate in American and European contexts with little consideration paid to differences in contextual details. Suleiman (2011) criticizes the uncritical application of the "correlationist-variationist approach" to the Arabic context because, according to him, it downplays the importance of politics, history, and ideology, which are germane to identity politics in the Arab region. Suleiman's argument may be extended to other "borrowed" theories, approaches, and methods. Undeniably, several of these models and approaches have played a critical role in shaping the field of Arabic sociolinguistics. However, many others may not hold contextual relevance to the Arab contexts or may apply to one Arab speech community but not another. In other words, these approaches and methods should be scrutinized for their contextual suitability. Finally, a detailed description of context may help readers build their own readings of data and results, which may or may not coincide with that of the author. With the absence of contextual details, the researcher squelches the possibility of multiple readings of his or her work.

3.4 PARTICIPANTS AND PARTICIPATION

In this book, the term *participants* is used to refer to informants in a given study, whereas *participation* denotes the role of the researcher in the study. In every research project, a decision has to be made concerning the participants and the criteria for participant inclusion and exclusion. Selection of participants should consider candidates against five criteria: (1) are they the best candidates for studying the phenomenon under exploration? (2) May they provide relevant and rich information about the phenomenon under study? (3) Do they represent a larger population about which the researcher may seek to make generalizations (if any)? (4) Are they accessible? And (5) can they be selected in such a way that selection bias does not influence the research findings? It is not always possible to observe all of these details, and therefore it is important to find a compromise between an "ideal" group of participants and a group that shows clear selection bias. The most important criterion in selecting participants is their potential to provide relevant and rich information to address the research questions (Patton, 1990). The number of participants becomes an issue only when broad generalizations are sought (Gay & Airasian, 2000). This explains why quantitative designs, such as correlational, questionnaire-based studies, require more participants than qualitative designs, because the former often seek to establish generalizations about the population, whereas the latter type, such as those involving interviews and focus groups, are less inclined to do so.

Another consideration is participant sampling procedure. Random sampling techniques are far less common than purposeful sampling strategies in sociolinguistic research. Patton (1990) identified sixteen common types of samples that serve particular purposes:

- extreme case (exceptional representatives of the phenomenon of interest),
- intensity (information-rich representatives of the phenomenon),
- maximum variation (widely diverse group),

- homogeneous (focused or less variant group),
- typical case (average participants),
- stratified purposeful (comparison subgroups),
- critical case (one that is generalizable to other cases),
- snowball or chain (participants who know other participants),
- criterion (participants who meet a certain criterion),
- theory-based construct (cases that can elucidate a theoretical construct),
- confirming or disconfirming (cases that may verify initial analyses),
- opportunistic (selecting participants as they come),
- random purposeful (participants selected systematically, but without previous knowledge, from target population),
- politically important cases,
- convenience, and
- mixed purpose samples.

These sampling procedures are not equally appropriate for all circumstances. For example, a random purposeful sample may add more credibility to the results, but it may not be the best option in cases where a certain criteria is pursued, in which case criterion sampling is preferred. In sociolinguistic research, there is no "best" option in terms of sample selection. However, researchers need to justify their choices and explain how and why such choices do not bias the findings or limit the transferability of results.[2]

One important consideration in participant selection concerns the forum or media within which participants' language behavior, attitudes, or identity practices are studied. This can be face-to-face interaction or observation, internet-mediated interaction (e.g., Skype interviews), publically available recorded or videotaped data (e.g., songs), televised interviews or speeches, corpora (e.g., transcribed debates on Aljazeera website), printed texts (e.g., novels), and so on. The question here is whether language behavior is influenced by the framework within which it is contextualized or presented. This depends on the extent to which the media influence language behavior. For example, videotaped religious lessons may not differ greatly from religious speeches in a mosque setting because in each case, the speech is monitored and a relatively large audience is expected. However, speakers' language use in, say, text-based chatroom interactions is expected to be different from the patterns of language use in face-to-face interactions because various contextual factors are absent from the interaction, sometimes including the identity of the speakers. The media through which language behavior is carried out is an important participant factor because it has been found that participants' language behavior is influenced by the physical environment and media in which it occurs (Keating & Mirus, 2003; Labov, 1972).

One concern that occasionally arises with respect to participants is the incompatibility between their *reported* and *actual* language behavior. This is not a rule, but it has been sometimes been reported, particularly in language attitude studies (Lawsan-Soko & Sachdev, 2000; Murad, 2007). Gaining an awareness of this phenomenon may assist researchers in evaluating data sources to resolve this concern. A possible strategy is the use of multiple methods to elicit the desired data. For example, a study of language attitudes may implement surveys, interviews, and observation of attitudinal statements and attitudinal acts. This form of triangulation may add to the trustworthiness of the results (Creswell, 2003; Glesne, 2010). Another concern is whether participants should be made aware of their role as subjects of study, which may affect the "naturalness" of their verbal behavior. Based on my fieldwork experience in the Arab region, I believe that making the participants aware of their participation could add to the trustworthiness of the results in two ways. First, when the researcher succeeds in building trust and rapport with the participants, they become more inclined to cooperate and act unpretentiously. Second, when the participants recognize that they are treated ethically and humanely, they become more candid about their feelings and thoughts, especially when they see their participation as an act of "having voice" or making a contribution. In fact, one of the most striking patterns observed in collecting the data for this book is the extent of collaboration the participants displayed; they were enthusiastic to convey their opinions, especially when they knew that their anonymous voices would be heard by a wide audience. In short, concerns over participants' propensity to change their behavior or to produce discordant reports and actions can be reduced where research is made as much about "advancement of profession" as about human relations.

Turning to the researcher's role in research, a number of questions arise. First, the role a researcher plays in the research may impact research activities, participants' behavior, and research outcome. The researcher may be the subject of research, one of the participants, a participant-observer, an observer, a coordinator, a reporter, or an investigator. Not all of these roles are appropriate for all types of research. Each has its own advantages and disadvantages, which differ based on other components of the research. For example, in the context of discussing the relationship between self, identity, and displacement, Suleiman (2011) examined his experience as a name giver. Because the topic was about the Self, the role of the researcher as subject enriched the topic and added a personal tone. In his studies on CS, Holes (2004) assumed the role of a reporter as he listened, analyzed, and wrote on a broadcast interview between two Bahraini speakers. Parkinson (1996) assumed the role of an observer as he examined the language behavior of a lecturer at an Egyptian university. Belazi (1991) was both participant and observer as he examined the language choices that Tunisian participants made in informal social gatherings. Abu-Melhim (1992) coordinated informal conversations among Arab nationals from Egypt, Jordan, Iraq, Morocco, and Saudi Arabia to examine the dynamics of their CS behavior. In each of these examples, the researchers assumed roles pertinent to their goals, topics, informants, and data sources.

Regardless of the role the researcher assumes, three important points need to be considered. First, how does that role influence or guide his or her informants' language behavior, reactions, or responses? Second, how does the researcher's role impinge on his or her relationship with the informants and might this relationship impact the patterns observed? An informant who sees the researcher as a friend or colleague may behave differently from when the latter is seen as an investigator. Along the same line, a researcher who is seen as an insider may receive different responses from one who is seen an outsider. This is why the role a researcher undertakes should be explained and justified in detail. A third caution note concerns the researcher's authority and voice. The investigator may become the main "speaker" in qualitative research in the sense that sociolinguistic patterns are detected, analyzed, interpreted, and reported through the lens of the researcher's own point of view. It is true that, as Stanley and Wise (1993, p. 157) argue, "There is no method or technique of doing research other than through the medium of the researcher." However, the risk involved in this practice lies in stripping the informants of their voices and their definitions of their own social actions – which is supposed to be the main purpose of qualitative research (Peacock, 2001) – and enforcing the researcher's own interpretation. This point is particularly important in the Arabic sociolinguistic context because of the notable diversity in the Arab informants' cultural and socioeconomic backgrounds and their ideological and political orientations. When the informants' social meanings and voices are shirked, the reported patterns may simply represent a single narrow perspective on the sociolinguistic area under investigation.

A final remark in this section concerns the notion of researcher subjectivity. There is a growing sense among social scientists that subjectivity and ideological orientation are inevitable in the study of social phenomena (Bourdieu, 1999; Lather, 2003; Lincoln & Guba, 2000). Subjectivity may affect the research at different stages or in various components such as the selection of topic, research questions, approach, population, sampling procedure, data-collection method, analysis, and reporting of the data. Lather (2003, p. 186) argues that ". . . scientific 'neutrality' and 'objectivity' serve to mystify the inherently ideological nature of research in the human sciences . . ." In fact, Phillips (1990) argues that objectivity is dead and *all* research endeavors are subjective. Assuming that subjectivity is inescapable in sociolinguistic research, whenever possible, researchers need to reflect on and explicate their role, position, and voice in the research (Bourdieu, 1977; Spencer, 2001; Suleiman, 2011). According to G.L. Anderson (1989, p. 14), self-reflection or "reflexivity" should consider the interaction of five elements: (1) the researcher's constructs; (2) the informants' common sense; (3) research data; (4) the researcher's personal biases; and (5) the structural and historical forces informing the social construction under study. Finlay (2002) contends that researchers may follow different routes in demonstrating reflexivity, such as (1) introspection; (2) intersubjective reflection; (3) mutual collaboration; (4) social critique, and (5) discursive deconstruction. These steps could alleviate concerns about the role of subjectivity in biasing the results. Moreover, once the researcher's role and position are clarified, it becomes then the reader's responsibility to discern whether and how the researcher's subjectivity has influenced the findings, and to create their own readings accordingly.

3.5 DATA AND DATA COLLECTION

The questions of what counts as data and how we obtain and use it in research are central to the study, description, and explanation of social language-related phenomena. Assuming the appropriateness of all other theoretical and methodological components of research, a study can fail to attain its projected goals and may turn into mere speculations without relevant, adequate, and reliable data. As Wolfson (1986, p. 689) correctly argues, "No matter what else we do, we must remember that if data are inadequate, there is always the danger that the theory and conclusions drawn from them could be unreliable and misleading." This may explain the notable attention paid to data and data collection in sociolinguistic research.

One of the central questions in addressing the topic of data collection is which data sources are considered *acceptable* in sociolinguistic research. According to Labov and several other variationist sociolinguists, *authentic* data comes from the *naturalistic* vernacular. Labov asserts that "the most systematic and regular form of language is that of basic vernacular" (Labov et al., 1968, p. 167). Coupland (2007, p. 181) reflects this predilection by suggesting that ". . . variationist sociolinguistics has taken an ideological stance in favour of vernaculars, and that it has assumed that vernaculars are authentic speech products."[3] The presumption that authentic data comes from the vernacular implies that the non-vernacular is a less naturalistic and a less authentic form of data. In the Arab context, this claim would leave out many SA-delivered religious speeches, political speeches, university lectures, news reports, etc. from the "authenticity" matrix. To many Arabic speakers, however, SA is the expected and "natural" language variety in such contexts (Saeed, 1997). Some public performances, such as songs, are sometimes delivered in QA and other times in SA. Can we consider the ones rendered in QA to be more authentic than their SA counterparts simply because they are rendered in the vernacular? The issue of language authenticity becomes even fuzzier when we consider language use in digital media, where SA, QA, and English appear side by side or intermingle in a single message, comment, or text. It is true that Labov's argument focuses on oral language in everyday use. However, this raises the point of what can be subsumed under everyday language use. Can we, for example, exclude news reports or religious sermons from daily language use? Such patterns of language use demonstrate that the concept of authentic data is relative and often context-dependent.

Returning to the basic question of what constitutes data, it is possible to differentiate between four forms of data that are used in sociolinguistic research: naturally produced speech, elicited speech, retrospective and introspective data, and written texts.[4] Generally speaking, naturally produced speech covers every form of language use not particularly intended for research purposes, such as daily interactions, political speeches, religious sermons, news reports, and university lectures. The concept of research participant, in the literal sense of the word, does not apply to this form of data. Unlike naturally produced discourse, elicited speech is a speech derived from study participants for research purposes. Typically, the participants are aware of their participation and the tasks required, which may be whole narratives, descriptions, arranged interactions, or responses to stimuli. This form of speech is considered less natural. However, it is possible to increase the *naturalness* of elicited speech by embedding it in implicit tasks (e.g., narrating a story, talking about a meaningful experience, describing a set of pictures). Retrospective and introspective data is gathered through question-naires, one-on-one and group-based interviews, journalist-type questions and answers, auto-ethnographies, and self-reflections. Again, the data obtained is often based on conscious knowledge of the end to which it is put, which could make this type of data less natural. Lastly, written texts are a highly monitored form of discourse that encompasses everything from official documents and liter-ary and non-literary texts, to letters, newspaper reports, and other forms of written discourse. Electronic texts, such as emails, text messages, commentaries, blogs, wallpaper posts, and other forms of online writing will be discussed in Chapter 8 because of their unique features, which combine spoken and written discourses.

Each of these data forms has advantages and disadvantages. In general, spontaneous, naturalistic speech is the preferred form of data in sociolinguistic research because it represents speech as used in daily communications (Bucholtz, 2003; Coupland, 2007; Labov, 1972). Labov considers this type of speech as the only real form of data because it reflects the structure, organization, and flow of speech in everyday life. A main disadvantage of this type of data is that it may not always contain adequate instances of the examined phenomenon (e.g., bilin-gual CS), especially given the unpredictability of naturalist speech. This limitation to naturalist speech as a source of data may instigate researchers to resort to elicited speech, the main advantage of which is that it allows the researcher to exercise more control over the data and target specific forms. Elicited data may or may not emulate naturally produced data depending on the level to which the participants are aware of their role as research subjects and the extent to which the researcher is in control of the data-elicitation process. For example, lengthy narratives that are embedded in implicit tasks are closer to real-life speeches than, say, sentence-level responses to particular stimuli in controlled production tasks. A main advantage of retrospective and introspective data is that they per-mit the probing of mental or internal constructs, such as language attitudes and identity feelings, which may not always be observable, or which may need to be externalized through careful elicitation. However, when employed to examine lan-guage use, they become "secondary responses to the language" (Labov, 1972, p. 247). In other words, they do not represent participants' actual speech, but rather what they think their actual speech is. Written texts are useful for examin-ing monitored and editable language use or for studying written language norms. However, they are rarely used in researching the norms or practices of everyday language use.

Different types of data are relevant to diverse research questions, method-ologies, and theoretical frameworks. One researcher may use self-reflection as background information, while another may use self-reflection as a form of evidence. A questionnaire may be employed for collecting data on participant demographics, but it may be used as the sole research instrument as well. An interview may be utilized for answering attitudinal and ideological questions, but it may also be used as an object of discourse analysis. Ideally, using more than one form of data adds to the trustworthiness of the results (Creswell, 2003; Glesne, 2010). In researching language attitudes to CS, for example, observation, introspective data, and actual behavior may be used to probe the participants' attitudes to this social phenomenon. As a final remark, data needs to be systematically examined and reexamined before it can become presentable information. Revisiting the data often and examining it from different perspectives may help achieve this goal (Lincoln & Guba, 2000). For example, the interview questions used in this book were largely based on preliminary work in 2012 and pilot interviews with two students at Utah State University (see the following section). Although not all of these questions were posed to the participants in my pilot work, they emerged as interesting areas of investigation after I visited the transcribed data a few times. This suggests that the researcher variable is involved before, during, and after data collection.

3.6 RESEARCHING DIGLOSSIA, ATTITUDES, IDENTITY, VARIATION, AND CODESWITCHING

The previous sections have dealt with methodological issues that are general to Arabic sociolinguistic research. In this section, I will outline a few methodological remarks that address more specifically the five areas of interest in this book, namely, diglossia, attitudes, identity, variation, and CS. The aim is to discuss how these five areas have been and can be approached and investigated empirically through data-driven analyses.

3.6.1 Diglossia

Diglossia is a social and linguistic phenomenon that is subject to change, just as language itself and social realities are amenable to development and adaptation. The question of how to verify, capture, and represent this type of change is key for sociolinguists interested in or working with diglossia, regardless of their frame of reference as to the starting point of change or the theoretical model against which it is gauged. The question is both empirical and theoretical. It is empirical because it implicates methods to detect the indices and features of change in this social condition, and it is theoretical as it may formulate some generalized framework that captures any potential regularity in this process of change. The empirical side does not need the theoretical, while the reverse is not true. In other words, studies may be able to trace and point out sociolinguistic changes without the need to devise theoretical models that depict the change. On the other hand, proposing a theoretical conceptualization of these changes demands empirical evidence. Empirical data is therefore needed irrespective of which goal one sets out to achieve in researching diglossia.

Diglossia manifests itself through various situational, behavioral, verbal, and attitudinal variables. For example, according to Ferguson (1959a), Arabic diglossia is marked by the dissimilar values, distribution, and acquisition of SA and QA. Investigating just these three features of diglossia empirically requires a number of independent research endeavors. Thus, research aiming at assessing the relative statuses of SA and QA needs to examine whether and how these statuses are preserved in the community. Status here is not determined merely by speakers' attitudes, but also by actual use. For example, the High variety is often associated with the tradition of writing and literature, while the Low variety is not (Ferguson, 1959a). Changes in these writing conventions, especially when QA becomes part of this convention, could mean changes in the statuses of the two varieties (Hudson, 2002). In fact, changes in writing systems have often formed the basis of modern linguistic reforms (Coulmas, 1997; Haugen, 1966; Hudson, 2002; Kahane, 1986). Similarly, examining the potentially changing distribution of SA and QA requires data taken from a number of contexts that vary in their level of formality (e.g., mosque/church, university, café). This is because the perceived (in)formality of context may be implicated in the distribution of SA and QA (Hudson, 2002). Thus, the use of QA in domains or functions that are normally reserved to SA may indicate a change in the diglossic situation. This is particularly relevant for digital communication where QA use has become the norm (Al-Saleem, 2011; Gully, 2012; Haugbolle, 2007; Khalil, 2011; Panovic, 2010; Warschauer, El Said, & Zohry, 2002). Likewise, studying the acquisition of the High code and the Low code demands socio-psychological studies on the development of SA and QA in young Arab children. Such studies may pave the way for understanding whether and how SA are QA are acquired differently.

Hudson (2002) provides a detailed list of features that may mark a "language shift" in diglossic communities. In the Arab context, for example, the realization of the High and the Low codes does not index "inequality of social standing" among the interlocutors (p. 4). A change in the relationship between language use and social standing may reflect a shift in the functions of these two varieties. Another feature of diglossic communities is that the High code is never fully utilized for conversational purposes. When the High code appears fully in dialogue, especially when adults use SA with their children (Ferguson, 1959a a language shift may be underway (p. 6). A third aspect concerns "the linguistic affinity" between the two varieties (p. 9). Again, a language shift may be happening when the linguistic distance between the two varieties becomes so wide that they are mutually unintelligible or so narrow that they become almost identical. Hudson predicts that, "As the linguistic varieties become more divergent, more extensive training is required for the mastery of the literary variety." It is interesting that mastery of SA – the literary variety – is currently a main concern in the Arab region (Abdulaliim, 2012). A further sign of language shift concerns the emergence of intermediate codes that "connote sociological intermediacy as well" (p. 10). Sociolinguistic intermediacy here refers to well-defined socio-linguistic functions for the intermediate code. Moreover, when SA cannot cope with its literary function as a written language, then QA and other language forms may replace it in key societal functions. The use of so-called "Arabizi" due to the spread of English technology-related terms may fall under this trend. Lastly, a diglossic situation may change when a society is broken down, which is often accompanied by a disintegration of the classical variety associated with it (p. 34). From this standpoint, the political fragmentation of Arab societies may contribute to the functional deterioration of SA in the Arab communities – an observation that reverberates throughout the literature on diglossia in the Arab region (Abdu-laliim, 2012; Al-Dabiib, 2001; Al-Muusa, 2003; Al-Saḥmaraani, 2002; Bayyoumi, 2005; Bishr, 2007; Hamaada, 2012; Nourddiin, 2012).

An impressionistic mapping of these details on the current Arabic sociolin-guistic situation may underscore notable linguistic changes in the nature of its diglossia. However, as noted above, impressionistic evaluations of diglossia, which have characterized much of the discussion surrounding this topic, may not be the best method to approach this social phenomenon. Arabic sociolinguistics is in need of a more empirical assessment of the various manifestations of language change, which is practically impossible to carry out in a single study. Therefore, various studies may add different pieces to complete the picture of the whole. However, no matter how broad the perspectives drawn from these studies may be, the general framework that we may formulate for understanding the social workings of diglossia in language use is always a matter of inference derived from common patterns. Natural language interactions are filled with irregularities and individual variation, which renders impossible any framework capturing all potential patterns of language use in a given speech community. As diglossia manifests itself in language acquisition, historical background, writing traditions, language attitudes, social influences, and situational variables, the question is what data may be used to assess and reassess the use, values, distribution, and acquisition of the language varieties involved in the diglossic situation. An easy answer to this question does not exist. While some diglossic variables may be more suited for corpora of naturalistic speech or elicited recordings, others may be well-adapted to literary or non-literary texts, observation of language behavior, or logs of language use. Regardless of the data used, the specifics of the diglos-sic variable of interest need to be accounted for when attempting an explanation of any change in that particular variable.

3.6.2 Language attitudes

Language attitudes are a theoretically and methodologically knotty topic. They are theoretically problematic because of their multipronged nature. Ryan, Giles, and Sebastian (1982, p. 7) suggest that language attitudes embody "any affective, cognitive, or behavioral index of evaluative reactions toward different varieties or their speakers." According to this widely cited definition, language attitudes incorporate at least three facets: affect, cognition, and behavior. The affective component represents an individual's emotional response or liking to a language or its speakers. The cognitive aspect consists of a person's factual knowledge about that language or its speakers. The behavioral component involves a person's overt behavior directed toward the attitudinal object (Zimbardo, Ebbesen, & Maslach, 1977). According to Ajzen and Fishbein (1980, p. 20), "a complete description of attitude requires that all three components be assessed by obtaining measures of all three response classes". The methodological difficulty lies in identifying ways to *approach* language attitudes. For example, researchers disagree as to whether language attitudes should be approached atomistically or holistically. The atomistic approach views language attitudes as an autonomous construct that stands by itself. Hence, there is more focus on in-depth probing of language attitudes through individual members of the community. The holistic approach views language attitudes as intricately related to a wide range of contextual, social, demographic, and speaker variables (Agheyisi & Fishman, 1970; Baker, 1992; Bentahila, 1983a; Garrett, 2010; Haeri, 2003). This means that studying language attitudes in isolation may give only a partial picture of the complex social variables that may be involved in people's perceptions of language varieties and their speakers. This approach therefore aims to explain language attitudes in reference to other social factors, such as gender, age, socioeconomic status, and religion, among other things.

The methodological complexity of language attitudes also appears in the wide disagreement about the best way to *assess* language attitudes empirically. The debate centers on whether attitudes are externalized through elicited introspective responses, verbalized as overt judgments of language varieties or speakers, or enacted through language use in natural everyday life communications. After all, this depends upon the epistemological assumptions one brings to the table in studying this theoretical construct. Fasold (1991; also Appel & Muysken, 1987) distinguishes between the *mentalist* and *behaviorist* approaches to language attitudes. The mentalist perspective claims that language attitudes are internal, mental states that prompt one to act in a specific way. These internal states need to be reported and elicited through such methods as interviews and surveys. For example, Kachru (1982) developed a list of dichotomous evaluative terms that can be used to describe/judge linguistic codes: aesthetic/unaesthetic, correct/incorrect, cultivated/uncultivated, developed/undeveloped, effective/ineffective, proper/improper, religious/non-religious, etc. On the other hand, the behaviorist perspective assumes that language attitudes should be observed in actual conversations or samples of actual speech. For example, Saville-Troike (1989) suggests that language attitudes transpire in people's evaluative judgments of the speech of language users or in their language acts, such as complaints about certain features of the speakers' language. The epistemological assumptions of mentalists and behaviorists engender different methods for tapping into language attitudes, some focusing on judgments, both covert and overt, and others more inclined to study attitudes in language use. Societal treatment studies, like those focusing on content analysis, fall under the latter category (Garrett, 2010).

Another challenge in studying language attitudes is the mismatch between attitudes reported through psychometric scales and those observed in verbal behavior. For example, Lawson-Soko and Sachdev (2000) examined the attitudes and self-reports of twenty-eight Tunisian students toward CS. The study showed that students had negative evaluation of CS. However, the researchers found that these negatives attitudes disappeared in actual behavior. This underscores the difficulty and intricacy of assessing language attitudes. As noted above, a combination of two or more data-collection methods would allow the researcher to cross-check the validity of the different pieces of data. A challenge even more relevant to the diglossic and multilingual contexts concerns the existence of multiple language varieties, rendering incomplete the study of attitudes toward any single language or variety on its own. In such contexts where multiple language varieties coexist, language attitudes operate through a dynamic of checks and balances. For example, Benmamoun (2001) convincingly argues that some Moroccan Berbers have positive attitudes toward French because it balances the influence of Arabic and its accompanying political discourse of pan-Arabism. Thus, the study of language attitudes in the Arab context should incorporate the different language varieties in chorus. This may help exhibit the speakers' comparative perceptions of the respective varieties.

It is important to draw a distinction between assessing language attitudes and evaluating language attributes, such as beauty, richness, eloquence, and so on. Language attributes may be assessed by speakers based on factual or ideological groundings. For example, many Arabic speakers may rate English highly against the attributes of internationality, power, prestige, and practicality. However, this does not necessarily denote positive attitudes toward English. Language attributes are an independent theoretical construct, which may or may not impact speakers' attitudes to a given language or to those who use it. A concluding point in this section is that language attitudes are not stable (Baker, 1992; Romaine, 1995); they change both in relation to external circumstances in the sociocultural milieu and internal psychological developments in individual speakers. This means that a periodic or longitudinal assessment of language attitudes over time may be needed in tandem with other sociocultural and historical changes.

3.6.3 Social identities

Like language attitudes, identity is a complex socioaffective construct simply because identity is not a monolithic entity. Social identity can be defined and redefined across national, ethnic, and religious lines, and also in terms of geography, age, gender, education, and culture or even at the level of organizations, institutions, or persons (Hecht, 1993; Loscke, 2007; Somers, 1994). Different forms of identity are created and sustained by distinct classifications, narratives, and discourses (see Chapter 5). Social actors generally do not have a single form of identity, but "repertoires of identities" (Kroskrity, 1993). Therefore, they may linguistically mobilize different identity forms for varying purposes, and they may construct and reconstruct various identity forms based on changing contextual factors. Joseph (2004) shows that Lebanese people may linguistically emphasize their dissimilar religious identities over their common ethnic and national identities at times of sectarian tensions. The existence of multiple forms of identity stipulates the need for researchers to operationalize the specific forms of identity they are examining. Identity forms are not always categorical or non-overlapping (Somers, 1994). However, even when different identity forms conflate, researchers need to demystify this complex construct and possibly explain how any overlap plays out in their specific context.

The study of the identity dynamics and identity sentiments may be approached from different perspectives. For example, identity has been examined from historical, political, sociological, anthropological, and psychological perspectives, and it has involved an examination of discourse dynamics, power factors, ideologies, dominant social narratives, indexicality, iconization, and other identity-construction mechanisms (Bourdieu, 1999; Eckert, 2000; Fairclough, 1989; Fowler, 1985; Goodwin, 2003; Hall, 1996; Rampton, 1995; Suleiman, 2003, 2004). Irrespective of the subject, focus, or frame of analysis, it is generally accepted that the symbiotic relationship between language and identity is governed by, or embedded in, a larger social context (De Fina, 2007; Fairclough, 1989; Hall, 1996; Pennycook, 2004; Suleiman, 2011; Zimmerman, 1992). Thus, the study of identity should be approached with an eye tuned on the context-specific factors involved in the social construction of identity. For example, the dynamics of national identity construction in the Arab region differ from those found, say, in the United States. In the Arab region, national identity involves more emphasis on historical and ethnic commonalities, whereas in the United States it rests more on political, economic, and ideological factors. Therefore, an examination of these dimensions is essential for understanding identity dynamics in the Arab region versus the United States. In general, it is important to situate the study of identity within the unique historical, political, ideological, and socioeconomic context in which it is studied (Suleiman, 2011).

A third consideration in the study of social identities concerns the methods used in assessing or collecting data about this construct. The vast majority of existing studies, especially those published in the Arab region, have based their findings on historical narratives. Historical narratives are instrumental to identity practices because history works in the present as well as in the future. However, historical narratives are continually being constructed, reconstructed, and revised, as is the case of historical narratives about Berber and Kurdish ethnic and linguistic identities (Keita, 2010; O'Shea, 2004; Sheyholislami, 2008). Thus, these narratives may not always reflect current identity dynamics. Moreover, historical narratives are often created by the intelligentsia, and by the wealthy and politically powerful. Therefore, they may not necessarily resemble the prevalent identity feelings in the community. Based on my limited fieldwork experience in Morocco, I assume that the overtones of Berber *national* identity are not as widely spread among the aver-age Berber speakers as the historical narratives articulated in some of the relevant literature may suggest.[5] This means that researching identity practices among the Berber community in Morocco requires more than relying on historical discourses. The same applies to *nationalist* pan-Arab narratives, which lost much of their cre-dence among the young Arab generation (see Chapter 5). A distinction therefore must be made between identity as constructed through social and institutional discourses (i.e., often created by individuals in power, by intellectuals, or by the wealthy) and identity as reflected in sentiments among ordinary people.

As was the case with language attitudes, identity feelings are internal, and therefore researchers often use psychometric measures, such as questionnaires and interviews, to collect data about these identity feelings. Cummins (2000, p. ix) argues that, when verbalized, language ideologies are "Statement[s] of iden-tity." Thus, another method for collecting data about social actors' sense of iden-tity is by observing or eliciting explicitly stated ideological expressions. Identity is also performed, enacted, and iconized through different oral activities (Irvine & Gal, 2000; Pennycook, 2004). Pennycook (2004) argues that, rather than being considered a given, identity is built up through an ongoing series of social and cultural performances, including talk. Likewise, Irvine and Gal (2000) suggest that identity iconization occurs when particular characteristics of a speaker are observed in their use of certain linguistic features. Therefore, acts of identity are also possible venues for collecting data on identity. The appropriateness of one data-collection method or another depends on the context and purpose of the study. However, a combination of more than one method is always advantageous.

3.6.4 Language variation and change

From a sociolinguistic perspective, the study of language variation and change involves two main tasks: (1) to pinpoint the exact linguistic aspects of varia-tion and change within a given social setting or speech community and, (2), to identify the underlying social causes and motivations of this linguistic variation and change.[6] These two aspects lie at the heart of the sociolinguistic study of variation, irrespective of the theoretical frameworks sociolinguists adopt or the methods and techniques they undertake to accomplish these tasks (see Hazen, 2007 for a review for the different approaches).

The task of pinpointing the linguistic aspect of variation has not been partic-ularly challenging in sociolinguistic research. The common approach is to use the construct of *linguistic variable* (Labov, 1972).[7] A linguistic variable is "a structural unit that includes a set of fluctuating variants showing meaningful co-variation with an independent set of variables" (Wolfram, 2006, p. 333). The "fluctuations" or variants of a given linguistic variable could be phonemes, morphemes, func-tional categories, lexical items, grammatical rules, contractions, etc. Since fluc-tuation can be observed in the speech of both individuals and social groups, a distinction needs to be made between significant and insignificant fluctuation

(Wolfram, 2006).[8] Based on her study of variation in an East Sutherland Gaelic community, Dorian (1994) reports that the target variants are sometimes used by a single speaker in a single stretch of discourse and in the same setting. Hence, she comes to the conclusion that variation, as an inherent attribute of human languages, may not necessarily be related to social factors.[9] If the aim of research is to explain language variation from a social viewpoint, Dorian's conclusion raises the question of "what to include and what to exclude in the study of orderly variation" (Wolfram, 2006, p. 333). The question of selection is relevant to both linguistic variables and social variables.

Methodologically, the task of identifying the linguistic aspect of variation raises the question of how to document language variation and change. This question is multifaceted because it has to do with sampling, data, and data-collection techniques. To begin with, how many participants are needed to detect language change in a speech community? For example, is it possible to claim linguistic change based on a sample of, say, twenty participants? Moreover, how inclusive should the sample be if generalization about variation among different groups is sought? There is no definite answer to these questions because sampling depends on the size of the population as well as on the data-collection methods. With respect to data, a central question is what sort of data is needed to document the occurrence, scope, and depth of change. In studying language change over time, for example, what data may serve as a starting point of change? In her survey of urbanization in a number of Arabic cities, Miller (2004, p. 189) maintains, "When comparing the linguistic impact of various migrations on urban vernaculars, it is not easy to establish what have been the more relevant factors of differentiation between the different cities: is it the 'ethnic' origin of the migrants ... or the political context ... or the pre-existing social structures of the cities?" Miller argues that even when linguistic data is available, this data may not be interpreted without a clear understanding of the sociohistorical situation. The situation becomes more complicated when even linguistic data is missing. As Owens suggests (1995, p. 306), "The researcher in this situation has no fixed starting point by which to orientate himself, so criteria established by the linguist play a crucial role in the search for communal norms."

In terms of data-collection techniques, most of the existing studies adopt one the following seven methods to gather linguistic information pertinent to language variation and change (Labov, 1981; Milroy & Gordon, 2003):

- Sociolinguistic surveys (anonymous or fieldwork-based),
- Individual interviews (as speech events, techniques for elicitation of casual speech; or methods for collecting participant background information),
- Group interviews,
- Participant observation,
- Telephone interviews,
- Existing recorded data (e.g., electronic corpora),
- Specific data elicitation tasks (e.g., based on word lists).

Each of these methods has its strengths and weaknesses. For example, anonymous surveys may ease concerns about what Labov calls "observer's paradox" (Labov, 1981, p. 30), that is, the tension stemming from the need to observe naturalistic language behavior in context yet the potential influence of the observer's presence on the naturalness of the data. At the same time, however, the use of surveys does not warrant the compatibility between "reported data" and "actual speech." Since oral speech has historically been the hub of sociolinguistic variation research, data-collection techniques should provide large samples of recorded speech that may contain sufficient instantiations of the target linguistic variables (Labov, 1981).

The second component of the study of language variation and change involves investigating the social meaning of linguistic change. This component raises a number of interrelated questions. First, should researchers identify discrete social variables a priori based on speculations of what may influence language variation? We know that language contact situations, for example, involve different linguistic processes and may sometimes generate unpredictable outcomes (Al-Wer, 2007). Second, what criteria or mechanisms should be used to identify potentially consequential social variables? For example, should the selection be based on the researcher's judgment, previous findings, preliminary fieldwork in the speech community, or some other criteria? Third, how can social variables be assessed empirically? Some social variables (e.g., power) are more of social processes and negotiable relationships than dichotomized categories, and therefore it is not always easy to assess such social variables empirically. Thus, whereas some social variables may be assessed by rapid and anonymous surveys, others may requires multiple assessment techniques, such questionnaires, interviews, observations, historical records, and archival documents and artifacts. These questions are relevant for planning variationist research because whether social saliency is meaningful to language change rests heavily on what social variables are selected and how these variables are assessed in relation to the linguistic variables.

Another point that bears on the study of language variation and change is data interpretation, especially given the fact that language change is an ongoing process (Labov, 1981). The existing studies suggest that language variation implicates a host of historical, political, social, and demographic factors (Al-Wer, 2008; Haeri, 1991; Miller, 2004; 2007). Social variables do not usually operate autonomously but interdependently, and this is part of the complexity and fuzziness of social reality. For example, several variationist studies in the Arab region show that gender, age, social class, education, and locality interact in significant ways (e.g., Al-Essa, 2009; Al-Wer, 2007; Daher, 1999; Haeri, 1991; Ismail, 2007; Miller, 2003; Walters, 1991). Haeri (1991) suggests understanding gender-based variation necessitates, among other things, examining women's participation in the public sphere, their access to multiple dialects, and their attitudes toward modernization. Social variables are dependent not merely on one another but also on the social, historical, and political context in which linguistic variation occurs.

Data interpretation should therefore focus on deriving the social meaning of language variation locally and without losing sight of the complexity of social reality. For example, the study of sociolinguistic variation and gender in the Arab context has relied heavily on approaches, methods, and sometimes interpretations that are not based on the Arab context (see Chapter 6). Gender relations in the Arab world are intricate and vary across place, time, communities, and individuals. They also interact in complex ways with other social variables, such as education, age, and social status. To claim that these networks of relationships are the same cross-culturally, one has to negate the social nature of gender and the role of social context in defining gender roles.

Before concluding this section, it is necessary to recall the importance of diglossia, the dominant language attitudes, and identity factors for properly contextualizing and understanding language variation. These factors have been found pertinent for understanding the social dimensions of language variation and change in the Arab region (e.g., Al-Wer, 1999; Holes, 1983; Miller, 2007; Owens, 2001; Taine-Cheikh, 2012). Besides, language variation and change is a consequence of constant interactions between different social actors. It is therefore critical to examine the social and political relationships (e.g., power asymmetries) that govern social actors and their interactions. The inclusion of these factors may add depth to the social meaning of language variation within its immediate and broad sociohistorical contexts.

3.6.5 Codeswitching

The study of CS poses methodological questions that differ from those raised in researching language attitudes and identities for two reasons. First, there is a general agreement that CS refers to the alternation between, or the mixing of, two or more language varieties at some level in the discourse. Second, CS is not a mental or internal construct, like language attitudes and identity feelings, but rather it transpires in discourse through morphemes, words, sentences, and longer stretches of discourse. From this perspective, CS is relatively easy to capture compared to language attitudes and identity. In this section, I will highlight three main issues concerning the study of CS in the Arab context.

A first consideration concerns the lines between the distinct codes of interest. For example, in bilingual CS between Arabic and typologically distinct languages, such as English and French, how can one demarcate the start of a switch between Arabic and English/French? It is well known that many English and French words have become part of the Arabic language, and therefore it is necessary to set clear criteria for what constitutes a switch. Callahan (2004), for example, suggests that single "borrowed" words or expressions that have become part of the borrowing language and are phonologically adapted to its rule without having a clear discourse function may not be considered forms of switching. This becomes a major issue in studying internet-mediated interactions where many borrowed words (e.g., internet, message, net, email, computer, etc.)

have become an integral part of online communication (Al-Khatib & Farghal, 1999; Siraaj, 2013). The picture becomes even more nebulous in bidialectal CS between SA and QA because of the many similarities between SA and QA at the phonological, morphological, and lexical levels. Eid (1988), for example, provides detailed criteria for what distinguishes switches to QA or SA, including clear SA or QA forms, ambiguous forms (e.g., words that are shared by SA and QA), and intermediate forms (e.g., words modified phonologically or morphologically). Regardless of the criteria used, these should be clearly delineated in the study of bilingual and bidialectal CS.

A second consideration in studying CS is the mechanisms used to determine the social or pragmatic function of a switch to a given variety. From everyday experience, we know that some types of switches do not have a clear social function and may be triggered by retrieval issues (Saeed, 1997). In the case of CS between SA and QA, proficiency in SA becomes another issue because some speakers of Arabic may not be able to sustain conversations in SA and therefore have to shift to QA to fill in a proficiency gap (Hudson, 2002). This may explain why some of the early studies on bilingual communities have presented CS as a language deficiency resulting from certain gaps in the lexicon or morphosyntax of bilinguals (Bloomfield, 1927; Weinreich, 1968). In my view, determining the function of CS ultimately has to do with the issue of systematicity. When speakers consistently shift to QA to make jokes, then one may conclude that CS to QA is associated with joking. Retrieval and proficiency-based switches are often not systematic and do not operate at the sentence or discourse level, which is where CS acquires most of its social functions. However, this scenario may not be applicable to all contexts or types of discourse. For example, some studies on bilingual CS have shown that speakers may shift at the word level for technical and academic terms (Al-Enazi, 2002; Bentahila, 1983b; Bentahila & Davies, 1995, 1998, 2002; Davies & Bentahila, 2006b, 2008). Thus, what constitutes a social or pragmatic function of CS should be determined locally by the researcher and explicated clearly in his/her methodology.

A third consideration with respect to the study of CS is the type of data needed to analyze the social and pragmatic functions of CS. An examination of the relevant literature shows that the data used in studying this phenomenon falls under three main categories. First, a number of studies use actual speech or written data produced naturally, the speakers being ignorant of the purpose of the study. This is the most common form of data in CS research, and the one that may reflect CS patterns best in everyday speech. Examples of this type of data include everyday interactions, political speeches, religious sermons, and sports commentaries. Arranged interactions fall under the second category of data in researching CS, along with elicited speeches, narratives, or descriptions that emulate real-life interactions with the main difference being the researcher's control over different variables of the discussion (the participants, the topics, the contexts, etc.) and the speakers' awareness of being the subject of study. This type of data represents a compromise between the norm of natural speech and the need to produce speech that is prone to analysis. Arranged CS-deriving interactions also target social phenomena that are rare in naturalistic settings (e.g., CS in interactions among different Arab nationals). However, generalizations emanating from elicited data should be presented with caution when the language behavior is influenced by the arrangement. The third and last type of data is reported patterns of CS based on interviews, questionnaires, or other techniques of introspective or retrospective data elicitation. This measure is commonly used for collecting data regarding online CS, as in emails and personal messages, possibly because of issues of access and privacy. Data obtained through this method conforms to what Labov describes as secondary data because it does not involve tokens of actual speech.

A final remark in this section concerns case studies on CS, which involve, for example, the study of CS in a single text or by a single speaker/writer. These types of studies are useful in identifying new patterns of CS that have not been studied or noticed before. For example, in his study of CS by former Egyptian president Jamal Abulnasser, Holes (1995) draws attention to novel CS patterns and functions of CS in the speech of this politician, an area that was not studied extensively before. Abdel-Malek (1972) provides pioneering work on CS in the novels of a single author, namely Yousef Al-Sibaa'i. The importance of such studies lies in uncovering newly emerging trends that have rarely been examined in the existing literature, such as the use of QA in political speeches and literary genres. They may also point to sociolinguistic phenomena that are not widespread, as in the use of mixed language varieties in songs (Davies & Bentahila, 2008). The problem arises when similar studies are brought to the scene after this trend has been established in the literature. In such a case, studies may consider broader sets of data that allow the detection of general sociolinguistic patterns about the phenomenon of interest. Thus, different data may be useful for different research purposes.

3.7 METHODOLOGY IN THIS BOOK

This book is meant to serve as a reference for scholars and students with interest in the Arabic language, sociolinguistics, pragmatics, anthropological linguistics, social psycholinguistics, cultural studies, and communication studies. The book also engages in scholarly discussion on a number of topics in Arabic sociolinguistics through empirical work. The part of this book that seeks to provide a reference should be clear from the topics surveyed in the second chapter and will be clearer in the coming chapters, where I provide a critical review of the existing literature, analyzing, synthesizing, assessing, and deriving conclusions about previous patterns, current trends, and prospects for the future. The book approaches the topics under investigation from a sociohistorical perspective (Heller, 1988). A sociohistorical approach seeks to offer a contextually situated understanding of the various social, political, and historical factors that may influence language attitudes, identities, variation, and behavior. It also views language users as social actors that influence and are influenced by these social, political, and historical dynamics. Almost every chapter of the book starts with a historical sketch of the main issues discussed. Historical background is necessary to understand the present Arabic sociolinguistic situation since, as noted earlier, history works in the present and the future. This approach also allows for comparing previous sociolinguistic trends with more recent ones. The book tries to strike a balance between theoretical discussions and formulations and empirical data-based studies in support of or against these theoretical debates. I attempt to be comprehensive rather than selective in covering the relevant literature so that the readers can gain a relatively broad picture of the examined areas. This does not mean that many important works are not left out as it is practically impossible to cover every important work in a single book.

Other than the case study on social media, which is reported in Chapter 8, the empirical data reported in this book was mostly collected during my fieldwork in Egypt, Jordan, Morocco, and Saudi Arabia.[10] The idea behind fieldwork developed in summer 2012 during a four-week-long study-abroad program in Jordan. During the program, I carried out a pilot study on the acquisition of plural morphology by Jordanian children (see Albirini, 2015). This experience encouraged me to collect data for another main area of interest, namely language attitudes. I started with informal discussions with a number of colleagues in the host university about their attitudes toward SA, QA, and English. I also had the chance to interact with a number of Jordanian students, some of whom were planning to come to the United States to continue their education. After I returned to the United States, I reconsidered the insights gleaned from these encounters, and decided to expand them through dedicated fieldwork. Two criteria were used for selecting Egypt, Jordan, Morocco, and Saudi Arabia as sites for fieldwork. First, each of these four countries represents a main region in the Arab World respectively, including Egypt, the Levant, the Maghreb, and the Gulf. Second, my selection was based on the number of contacts in the target countries and the feasibility of collecting adequate data for the studies reported in this book. I should note that my visit to Saudi Arabia was an extension of a conference presentation in Riyadh. The interview questions were developed based on my 2012 study-abroad experience in Jordan and were expanded after conducting pilot interviews with two students at Utah State University in the spring of 2013.

In all my fieldwork, university campuses formed the hub of my research activities. In each of the four countries, I worked on two or more campuses to collect the projected data. At least one of the visited universities in each country was private, except in Saudi Arabia where this was not possible. My access to these campuses was facilitated by acquaintances from the local communities. University campuses contain an interesting population—young, educated Arabic speakers who may reflect the current trends in language use, language attitudes, and identity sentiments in the region. University campuses are a place where a high concentration of this population exists, and sampling is more convenient but less biased, given the fact that I do not know the students. In other words, university campuses were the sites that made my accessibility to the target population easy and practical. From mid-May to early June 2013, I made a single trip to Jordan and Egypt to do fieldwork there. In late November and early December, 2013, I made a nine-day trip to Morocco. My fieldwork in Saudi Arabia was realized through a nine-day visit to Saudi Arabia for a three-day conference at a university in Riyadh. Throughout my visits, I spent my time mainly on university campuses, but sometimes on the streets talking to taxi drivers, copassengers, pedestrians, hotel receptionists, shoppers and shopkeepers.

The three primary types of data collected in the trips were: (1) questionnaires focusing on language attitudes, Arab identity, and their relationships to other social variables, (2) in-depth semi-structured interviews focusing on a wide range of topics, and (3) narratives in SA to assess educated Arabic speakers' ability to sustain conversations in SA (see Appendices). The interviews and narratives were recorded with a digital recorder. The data obtained from the interviews and the recorded narratives was transcribed verbatim on Word documents. As for the questionnaire, it was transcribed into an Excel spreadsheet. All of the transcriptions were done by two graduate and four undergraduate students at Utah State University, and all were checked for accuracy. In addition to these main types of data, I used short question-and-answer interviews, which were always recorded except when carried out on the street. I conducted these types of interviews, for example, as I was on the train (in Morocco), in "shared" taxis (also in Morocco), train station (Morocco), shops (in all four countries), and the hotels where I stayed (in all four countries). The goal was to obtain input from diverse members of the community. These interviews will be published in a separate work because this book will focus mainly on "educated Arabic speakers," which may or may not apply to some of these participants. Only aspects of the collected data that are relevant to the book will be included in the discussions below. Last, I jotted down observations on settings and verbal and non-verbal behavior on a jotter that I used for this particular purpose. These rough notes were then turned into more detailed notes on my laptop.

It is impossible to simultaneously present all of the patterns found in the fieldwork data and do justice to the other themes of the book. A full analysis of the data requires more space than this book allows. In this book, however, I present the general trends in the data without getting into much detail. For example, the data presented in the next chapter about language attitudes does not include by-item or by-subject analyses of the language attitudes scale, which are typically reported in these types of studies. Moreover, language attitudes are presented in a relatively atomistic manner, which in my opinion is not the best approach for understanding language attitudes. However, presenting the overall patterns rather than the minute details is compatible with the overall purpose of the book, which is to provide a *survey* of the existing and emerging literature on a number of topics. Though the data adds an empirical dimension to this work, it does not change the main thrust of the work as a reference book. Rather, it adds to the wealth of existing data in the areas under investigation and highlights some developing trends.

Several reasons motivated my choice of fieldwork as a general methodology for data collection. A first obvious motive for fieldwork is to collect data that is pertinent to the themes of the book, which include mainly the questionnaire, in-depth interviews, SA-based narratives, and question-and-answer street interviews. Collecting the questionnaire in face-to-face environment was needed to explain the questionnaire completion process to the participants and to answer any questions that arose in the meantime. Similarly, interviews are more personal and less anonymous when conducted face-to-face than on the phone or electronic media, which reflects on the quality of the data obtained. Some researchers dismiss interviews done over the phone or other media because quality interview data rests on the personal aspect of the interview, which is often lacking in phone and digitally mediated interviews (Irvine, 2011; Rubin & Rubin, 2005). Irvine (2011) argues that when interviews are not carried out face-to-face, responses may lack in depth of meaning due to the absence of visual cues. The narrative task, which required the participants to narrate in SA about three different topics (see Chapter 7), involved "testing" the participants on the spot (i.e. without preparation). This task demanded my physical presence at the data-collection site. The goal was to ensure that the participants' narratives were as natural and spontaneous as possible. Moreover, when an informant stopped before the time allotted to each narrative, I had to pose questions to prompt them to carry on the narrative.

Familiarizing myself with the context was a second motive in choosing fieldwork. As noted above, knowledge of context is part of understanding the participants and interpreting the data they provide (Gumperz, 1993; Wolfson, 1986). Appadurai (1986, p. 360) notes, "place is not just a trivial contingency associated with data gathering, but a vital dimension of the subject matter...." Reading scholarly articles about French-Arabic CS in Morocco is different from experiencing it several times in daily conversation and in real social settings. Through fieldwork, I was able to experience firsthand the deep spread of English in Egypt, Jordan, and Saudi Arabia; English appeared visually on street signs and shop names and verbally in the speech of people at different sites. Fieldwork allowed me to hear pidginized Arabic in a conversation between a Saudi man and a South Asian driver at the hotel in which I was staying. In the experience of living in Egypt, Jordan, Morocco, and Saudi Arabia, one learns so much just from observing people's verbal and non-verbal behavior. Through fieldwork, a researcher gets a feel for the general sociolinguistic situation and may observe tokens of language use, attitudinal statements, identity acts, and CS (see Chapters 4 and 5). In Morocco, for example, I was able to obtain newspapers discussing the introduction of QA into the early stages of education. I also watched a televised debate between Abdullah Al-'Arui and Nouriddin Ayyoush, two well-known figures in the Moroccan sociocultural scene, concerning this same topic. I was also able to interview speakers of Berber. These types of unplanned data provided additional insights that were not part of my research agenda, but turned out to be very informative.

Third, one of the main advantages of fieldwork is that sociolinguistic patterns arise from the process of collecting and analyzing data (Wolfson, 1986). As Wolfson suggests, some of the patterns that a researcher finds may seem counterintuitive before working in the field and observing the participants, their verbal and non-verbal behavior, and the context in which they operate. The concept of interpretation is not as straightforward or simple as it may seem, particularly when the researcher's preconceived notions are left unchecked. Fieldwork allows the researcher to check his/her preconceived notions and interpretation against the informants' social meanings and the realities of the social context. For example, my hunches about Jordanian speakers' attitudes toward English, especially given the generally reported negative attitudes toward the spread of English, were disconfirmed in the data obtained from the questionnaire and from interviews. The justifications that the interviewees provided for the indispensability of English in their communication – such as to use it online, to travel abroad, or to acquire an edge in the local job market – were largely unexpected to me.

Fourth, fieldwork is one of the most effective ways in which to interact and build relationships with speakers within their speech communities. The idea of establishing face-to-face contact and rapport with these speakers is key to obtaining unaffected, candid, and heartfelt responses (Glesne, 2010). Some of the questions asked in face-to-face interactions could not be posed otherwise. For example, in the course of the interviews, I asked some participants personal questions about their identities or their views of others, which, I think, the respondents answered directly and candidly. In non-face-to-face environments, answers to such questions would be avoided, either directly or indirectly. Moreover, speakers' attitudes, views, and reactions may change based on whether they are inside or outside their speech communities. Milroy (1987, p. 35) points to the importance of examining "pre-existing social groups," where speakers' language behavior is observed in a "group/community" setting. Apart from the issue of naturalness and contextualized understanding of language behavior, face-to-face contact with the participants adds a human-relation dimension to the interaction.

Last, fieldwork can empower the young participants. Empowerment may take different forms and may occur at different levels. First, the research process with its attendant protocols and conventions (e.g., consent letters, participation details, recording, etc.) is a learning experience for many Arab college students. Second, the participating students generally appreciate the interest one shows in learning about their opinions and thoughts, especially when the value of their opinions is emphasized. Last, given the general sociopolitical situation in the Arab region, the speakers' ability to express their opinions, and the knowledge that these opinions will be anonymously heard, gives them a sense of power once they recognize that their voices can make a difference in the community of researchers and readers.

3.8 SUMMARY AND CONCLUSION

This chapter has focused on a number of methodological issues that are pertinent to the Arabic sociolinguistic situation and to the five main areas covered in this book. One of the principle issues addressed in this chapter is the importance of methodology as the bridge between theory and practice. Since linguistic practices are bound by specific contexts, theory and methodology should better emanate from the same contexts as well. When "borrowed," theory and methodology should map on the key parameters of the borrowing context, which are ultimately responsible for defining the social meaning of language practices. In selecting and dealing with participants, the issues of selection bias, ethical and human treatment, rapport and trust, voice, and mismatch between reported and actual language use were highlighted. On the researcher's side, the chapter has drawn attention to the importance of defining the researcher's role in the study, his/her relationship to the participants, and his/her authority and position with respect to conducting, interpreting, and reporting research. As for data collection, it has been noted that the sources, functions, and forms of data as well as the methods of data collection may impact the validity of any conclusions that may be derived from research.

The chapter also discussed a number of methodological concerns with respect to studying diglossia, language attitudes, social identities, language variation, and CS. Concerning diglossia, the discussion centered on the need to examine and reexamine the manifestations of this sociolinguistic condition in the Arabic-speaking communities due to the changing nature of language and social reality. The formal study of diglossia needs to take into account its social, linguistic, psycholinguistic, interactional, socioaffective, and contextual aspects. The goal of formulating or reformulating a theory of diglossia is reliant on empirical analyses of any emergent trends. As for language attitudes, the chapter discussed the implications of the paradigmatic (e.g., mentalist vs. behavioral) and methodological (e.g., atomistic vs. holistic) choices on capturing this complex construct. With respect to language identities, it has been argued that social identities should be examined based not only on historical narratives but also on reported identity feelings as well as identity statements and identity acts. The chapter examined some of the main challenges surrounding the process of selecting and empirically capturing the social antecedents of language variation and change. The chapter also highlighted the need to clarify the mechanisms used to demarcate mixed codes and define their social functions. It has been noted that studying speech tokens rather than reported language choices is critical for avoiding the pitfall of mismatch between reported and actual language choice.

Finally, the chapter provided a brief overview and justification of the methodology adopted in conducting the research for this book, particularly the selection of fieldwork as a general methodology for examining a number of sociolinguistic patterns in Arabic-speaking communities. A more detailed description of research methods appears in the course of presenting the empirical data in the remaining chapters.

NOTES

1 Positivism and post-positivism are dominant paradigms in social sciences, but they do not figure predominantly in sociolinguistic research (Wolfson, 1986). Although variationist research relies on quantitative data, the numbers are often interpreted in relation to social variables and with reference to a range of contextual, historical, political information (Gumperz, 1992; Johnstone, 2000). A wide range of terms, such as "pragmatic," "advocacy," "participatory," "emancipatory" paradigms have been used. However, these terms and concepts have similar assumptions (Creswell, 2003; Crotty, 1998; Lather, 2003; Lincoln & Guba, 2000; Mertens, 2010).

2 It should be noted that sampling is not restricted to people, but also covers contexts, places, timeframes, events, media, and dates. I focus on participant sampling because it is the most common form of sampling in sociolinguistic research.

3 See also Coupland (2001) for different types of "authentic" language.

4 Oral tradition and literature may be categorized under naturalistic data or may be seen as an independent category by itself.

5 Berber speakers with whom I interacted might have expressed their thoughts on Berber national identity taking into account that I am an Arab. However, I doubt this is the case because my hunches were confirmed by a Pakistani professor who has been working in Morocco for several years now.

6 Not all researchers agree on the social foundations of language variation change (see Hazen, 2007; Wolfram, 1991, 2006). However, in keeping with the themes of this book, I focus here on the sociolinguistic approach to variation.

7 See Coupland (2007) and Gordon (2013) for a critique of this technique and the Labovian paradigm in general. A number of researchers (e.g., Croft, 2000, 2006) have also problematized the link between linguistic variants and social factors as represented by speakers' demographics (e.g., social class, age, etc.).

8 See Wolfram (1991) for a discussion on linguistic rules that may be largely explained by independent linguistic constrains.

9 Dorian (1994) distinguishes personal-pattern variation from social, geographic, stylistic, and proficiency-based types of variation.

10 I refrain from describing my fieldwork as ethnographic, although it does have an ethnographic nature, because my stay in the four countries was not long enough to characterize my work as "ethnographic."

CHAPTER 4

Language attitudes

Language attitudes are an integral part of the study of language and key to understanding an important dimension of its sociolinguistic context, namely the common beliefs about the language varieties used by speakers in a given speech community. Language attitudes may tentatively be defined as the socio-psychologically evaluative reactions to a certain language or to the speakers of that language. Language attitudes permeate our personal and social lives on a daily basis. Whether they are expressed overtly, kept latent, or enacted in our speaking and attitudinal *acts*[1] language attitudes determine how languages, speakers, and language behavior are construed. Baker (1992, p. 10) argues that "The status, value and importance of a language is most often and mostly easily (though imperfectly) measured by attitudes to that language." This is important in the Arab context because language prestige hinges mostly, but not solely, on Arabic speakers' attitudes toward SA, QA, and the local and global languages that exist in the Arabic sociolinguistic arena. For example, several studies have shown that non-urban speakers tend to have positive attitudes toward the urban dialects because of certain features, such as the replacement of /q/ with /ʔ/ (Sawaie, 1994). In fact, Labov (1972) contends that a speech community may be defined by the collective attitudes of its members toward a language variety. Moreover, speakers may be judged on the basis of the language varieties they speak. In the Arab context, for example, speakers of the Maghreb dialects are often viewed as "westernized" partly because their dialects involve words borrowed from various languages (Shiri, 2002).

Language attitudes are an essential element of language policy and planning and are benchmarks against which language-related policies and practices may be assessed and reevaluated (Baker, 1992; Cooper & Fishman, 1974; Ferguson, 1996; Schiffman, 1996). For example, the success of second-language programs may be partly measured by whether the students, parents, teachers, and administrators have developed positive or negative attitudes toward them. A number of studies in the Moroccan context have proposed that the "Arabicization" policy that sought to replace French with Arabic "failed" based on the attitudes of pro-Moroccan Arabic, pro-French, and pro-Berber linguists, activists, opinion-leaders, policymakers, and ordinary people in the Moroccan society. Moreover, language attitudes are integral to language maintenance, change, and development (Crystal, 2000; Fasold, 1991; Garrett, Coupland, & Williams, 2003; Schiffman, 1996; Williams, 1991). The revival of the Kurdish language, its embracement by the Kurdish people, and its evolution into a national language has been foregrounded by attempts to cultivate positive attitudes toward this language (Blau & Suleiman, 1996). Likewise, Classical Arabic (CA) has survived hundreds of years of marginalization (in terms of usage) partly due to the positive attitudes of ordinary Arabs and Muslims toward CA as a symbol of Arab and Islamic tradition.

Language attitudes are related to language behavior. Several attitude theorists have emphasized the strong connection between attitudes and behavior. Ajzen and Fishbein (1980) propose that attitudes impact behavior indirectly by guiding the formation of behavioral intentions, which themselves prompt behavior. According to Ajzen and Fishbein's Model of Reasoned Action, people's actions are mostly rational and based on a systematic evaluation of the information available to them. Any action or behavior is determined by one's intention to perform that behavior. However, intentions themselves are a result of an individual's attitude toward the behavior – i.e., his/her positive or negative judgment of performing the behavior – as well as the social pressures put on him/her to perform or not to perform the behavior. Some theorists have gone a step further by emphasizing the possibility of changing individuals' behavior once their attitudes are pinpointed (Zimbardo et al., 1977). Zimbardo and his associates (1977) emphasize the interrelationship between behavior and attitude in that each affects the other. They suggest that "even though we cannot predict the behavior of single individuals, we should be able to predict that people (in general) will change their behavior if we can change their attitudes . . ." (p. 52). The link between language attitudes and language behavior may explain the wide interest in studying this socio-psychological aspect of language and language usage.

As an important socio-psychological construct, language attitudes interact with a number of social phenomena (Baker, 1992; Cooper & Fishman, 1974; Fasold, 1991; Garrett, 2010; Labov, 1966, 1972; Walters, 2006). In the Arab context, language attitudes have been found to be a major vehicle of sound change; a basis of interdialectal (un)intelligibility; a determinant of language resilience and maintenance; a catalyst of transformations in language use and function; a yardstick of linguistic convergence and divergence; a marker of functional status and code choice, an index of tribal, local, national, religious, ethnic, and global identities; and a predictor of second language achievement (Albirini, 2011, 2014a; Al-Wer, 2007; Amara, 2005; Blanc, 1964; Gibson, 2002; Hachimi, 2007, 2012, 2013; Lori, 1990; Miller, 2003, 2007; Rosenbaum, 2011; Saeed, 1997; Sawaie, 1994; Shiri, 2002; Suleiman, 1993, 2003). In this chapter, I discuss language attitudes only as they relate to three areas under study, namely diglossia, social identities, and CS. I will start with a brief overview of the historical background of language attitudes in the Arab context, focusing on their relationship to the language varieties at play in Arabic speakers' social lives.

4.1 HISTORICAL BACKGROUND

Some of the earliest available attitudinal statements about the Arabic language are contained in the Muslim holy book, the Qur'an. In at least ten different locations, spread across ten separate chapters,[2] the Qur'an repeatedly emphasizes the "Arabness" of its language. Through this linguistic aspect, the Qur'an builds the connection between its "perspicuous" language and its "unperverted/uncrooked" message (Chapter 39: 28). Since the Qur'an was believed to be revealed and written in SA, the Qur'an commentators and exegists understood the Arabic language as referring to SA. The link between SA and the Qur'an has fostered positive attitudes toward SA, which have been expressed in the writings of many early scholars in religious sciences, Arabic grammar, and Arabic literature (Chejne, 1969). For example, Ibn Katheer (AD 701–774), author of the famous commentary on the Qur'an *Tafseer Ibn Katheer*, attributed the selection of Arabic to be the language of the Qur'an to the notion that "It is the most eloquent, articulate, profuse, and suitable to convey meanings that can be understood" (Ibn Katheer, 1999, p. 365). Likewise, Ibn Mandhoor (1232–1311 BC), author of the renowned *Lisaan Al'arab* dictionary wrote, ". . . He [God] honored this Arabic speech over every other speech. It is enough honor for the Arabic speech that the Qur'an was revealed in it and that it is the speech of the people of heavens" (p. 11). Given the elevated style of the Qur'an, SA came to be perceived as a superior and sacred language, and its command turned into a mark of distinction, eloquence, and piety.

However, religion is not the sole basis of the positive attitudes held by Arabic speakers toward SA. As noted in Chapter 2, classical Arabic literature, which occupies a special place in the Arab heritage and culture, was encoded in SA. Classical Arabic poetry in particular has enjoyed a remarkable esteem in the Arab culture not only because of its beauty, wisdom, and eloquence, but also because it was the second most important source, after the Qur'an, in the codification and standardization of SA (Chejne, 1969; Walters, 1996). The high standing and power of classical poetry is evidenced by the fact that classical Arabic poetry continued to thrive centuries after the emergence of Islam, even though the Qur'an criticized poets and poetry explicitly (Chapter 26). Today, classical poetry is a staple of Arabic language curricula across the Arab region. The attitudes of many educated Arabic speakers toward SA as an elevated language are often reinforced by the contrast customarily made between the lofty classical poetry and the "degenerate" colloquial prose poetry, which finds little appeal among many educated Arab speakers.[3] A third aspect contributing to the positive view of SA is its status as the repository of a broad cultural knowledge in important disciplines and fields. Many of the major cultural artifacts and historical traditions are written in SA, which has in itself become part of this treasured heritage. Moreover, as a code mutually intelligible across the Arab region, SA is viewed as a primary symbol of Arab unity, history, and heritage, which reminds many Arabs of their glorious past (Al-Husari, 1985). As Fishman (1971, p. 31) argues, SA has come to "be associated with the mission, glory, history, and uniqueness of an entire 'people' . . ." This is why many Arabic speakers consider SA as an integral part of their identity. According to Chejne (1969), both the revival of SA and the surge of Arab nationalism in the nineteenth century went hand in hand to assert the unity of the Arab land, people, and destiny. Chejne further suggests that the renaissance manifests itself best in the Arabs' interest in the reactivation of SA and Arab history. Last, many Arabs often associate SA with education, linguistic sophistication, and knowledge (Haeri, 2003). This is unsurprising if one considers the status that SA enjoys as the official language of Arab governments, education, print publications, and formal and semi-formal spoken discourse.

Despite the ages of political and economic decline in the Arab history, the belief in the superiority, beauty, and elegance of SA is still accepted by many Arabs. This belief is reflected in the writings of several modern-day Arab intellectuals and writers. Mustafa Saadeq Al-Rafi'i (2002, p. 17), for example, writes, "The attribute of eloquence in this language [SA] is not in its vocabulary but in its structure, just as the ecstasy and joy are not in the tones but in the ways they are composed." Likewise, Taha Hussein states that "The educated Arabs who could not command their language [SA] lack in their education, and their manhood is incomplete and low" (cited in Mubaarak, 1985, p. 17). Such overtly expressed beliefs about the supremacy of SA and the need to acquire it have an undeniable effect on its enduring role as the High variety in the Arab speech communities. The positive attitudes toward SA are also widespread among the lay Arab public, who admire its beauty, logic, symmetry, complexity, and rich vocabulary. Ferguson (1968, p. 376) observes, "For many purposes even the illiterate peasant will prefer a classical-sounding, highly literary Arabic which he only half understands to a pure conversational Arabic which he understands perfectly". This suggests that the notions of the refinement and sophistication of SA are not confined to a particular socioeconomic class, educational level, or other factors, but are widespread in the Arabic-speaking communities.

Unlike SA, the QA varieties have traditionally been considered as a distorted, debased, and deficient form of SA – a form that necessitates consistent rectification (Versteegh, 2001). As a *Lahn* "eccentric accents," QA varieties are often viewed as a mark of ignorance. Salama Bn Abdulmalik is reported to have said "The lahn in the speech is uglier than the chickenpox on the face" (in Ibn Qutayba' *ʕuyuun Al-Akhbaar*, 1996, p. 197). Similarly, most of the early Arab grammarians depicted QA forms as deviations from SA (Chejne, 1969). The description of QA as a deviation from SA underlines two important facts about the relationship between SA and QA. First, SA and QA were perceived as different varieties of the same language with QA being a distorted form of the pure and accurate SA model. Second, the negative attitudes that some Arab intellectuals and laymen have toward QA seem to be deep-seated in the Arab consciousness and history. These negative attitudes to QA continue to persist in current Arabic-speaking communities. QA is still largely considered as a simplified yet jumbled version of SA with many borrowed words and with no underlying system, logic, or rules.

Although it is used in everyday interactions, QA has a lower status and is often associated with "colloquial," "slang," and the language of the uneducated masses. As Al-Toma (1969, p. 3) observes:

> In spite of its use as the dominant medium of the spoken word in conversation, and in various cultural or artistic contexts such as songs, stage and movies, the colloquial lacks the prestige enjoyed by the Classical and is looked upon, often with a considerable degree of contempt, as a stigma of illiteracy and ignorance.

The QA dialects are not typically written, although a certain amount of literature exists in some of them (Eid, 2002; Mejdell, 2006; Rosenbaum, 2011). However, as Semah (1995, p. 81) suggests the QA-based literature has often been seen as "a means of entertainment for the uneducated masses." According to Versteegh (2001, p. 132), "It remains difficult in the Arab world to arouse interest in the dialects as a serious object of study. Many speakers of Arabic still feel that the dialect is a variety of a language without a grammar, a variety used by children and women, and even in universities there is a certain reluctance to accept dialect studies as a dissertation subject". Further, QA is stigmatized for its divisive influence (Suleiman, 1994, p. 12). For this reason, several Arab intellectuals have frequently suggested that QA is a language variety unworthy of learning or serious study. Based on my research experience in the Arab region, many educated Arabs look suspiciously at studies that focus on the dialects. These studies are viewed as part of a Western agenda to further fragment the Arab region and further detach Arab countries and peoples by creating communication barriers among them.

In addition to SA and QA, a number of global (particularly French and English) and local languages (Berber and Kurdish) are part of the language repertoires of some Arabic speakers. Therefore, it is necessary to have a brief overview of their historical roots in the region as they relate to the study of language attitudes. As noted in Chapter 2, French was introduced into the Arab region (particularly Morocco, Algeria, Tunisia, Mauritania, Lebanon, and Syria) through colonization, and it is still associated with the colonial experience in the writings of the overwhelming majority of Arabic-speaking scholars and intellectuals, particularly in the Maghreb where French has a notable presence (Abbasi, 1977; Bentahila, 1983a; Chakrani, 2010; Ennaji, 2007; Sadiqi, 2003; Suleiman, 2003, 2004; Walters, 2011). French was diffused into the social, educational, economic, political, administrative, technical, and commercial realms through a carrot-and-stick approach in which the forced imposition of French on the local people was reinforced by claims of modernity, prestige, enlightenment, and global influence. Arabization was the sociolinguistic reaction to French presence in the Maghreb countries soon after they gained their independence. The Arabization policies, however, failed to loosen the grip of French on key educational and economic domains for three main reasons. First, many of those who were educated in the elitist French educational system or those who studied in France have refused to exclude French from the Maghreb linguistic map (Benmamoun, 2001). Second, there seems to be no political will to make real changes in the current sociolinguistic situation in the Maghreb (Sadiqi, 2003). Last, the association between French and modernity, prestige, and enlightenment still has currency among a sizable number of Maghreb speakers (Chakrani, 2010; Ennaji, 2007).

Although the Arabs' early contacts with English were through colonialism, English is not generally approached as a colonial language in the same sense as French. English was taught in schools as early as the 1920s, when Britain was occupying different parts of the Arab region. However, it was rarely used as a means of daily interaction by the Arab people (Al-Khatib, 2007). Moreover, after the British-colonized Arab countries gained their independence, English was no longer a main contender of the local languages, as is the case in the Francophone countries. Rather, English has gained popularity in the Arab region since the 1990s due to the rising political and economic prowess of the United States. English has dominated in the areas of international business and commerce, and the diffusion of modern technologies into the Arab region has borne the trademark of the international lingua franca, namely, English. Nowadays, English is taught as a second language from elementary school up to college in most Arab countries.[4] While the official position on English is that it is instrumentally and educationally necessary for national economic development and workforce preparation, there is much ambivalence in the intellectual and professional Arab circles and among the public in general concerning the role and status of English. The main apprehension is that English may become one facet of the Anglophone cultural hegemony that is sweeping across many parts of the world, particularly in the areas of technology, media, business, and education. English is by far more prevalent than French in the countries of the Middle East – except Lebanon where both French and English are popular – whereas French has its stronghold in the Maghreb but is gradually losing ground to English (Battenburg, 2006; Walters, 2011).

Last, the local languages (Berber and Kurdish) have a unique position in the Arab sociolinguistic situation. These languages have been, until recently, marginalized and hidden from the dominant cultural and sociolinguistic discourse (Benmamoun, 2001; Blau & Suleiman, 1996; Chakrani, 2010; Ennaji, 2007; Miller, 2003; Sadiqi, 2003). According to Ennaji (2007, p. 247), Berber has traditionally been viewed as "'a dialect' which is not worth introducing in schools because it is neither standardized nor codified and is neither a language of wider communication nor a language with a rich written literature." The same applies to Kurdish in Iraq prior to the second Gulf War. However, due to changes in the sociopolitical climate in the Arab region and the notable activism by proponents of these languages, Berber and Kurdish have recently gained recognition as national and/or official languages in a number of Arab countries, including Algeria, Morocco, and Iraq. These languages are no longer confined to the home and street domains, but are used in such areas as music, magazines, digital media, television programming, and education. In fact, Kurdish enjoys social, legal, and political recognition on par with Arabic and is used as a means of communication and intellectual discourse (Hassanpour, 2012; Sheyholislami, 2008). The following section will outline some of the recent studies and the empirical findings addressing Arabic speakers' attitudes toward SA, QA, English, French, Berber, and Kurdish.

4.2 LANGUAGE ATTITUDE STUDIES IN THE ARAB CONTEXT

One of the most important assumptions about language attitudes is that they are part of the deep-seated norms, orientations, and beliefs in a given speech community. As Saville-Troike (1989, p. 181) notes, "individuals can seldom choose what attitudes to have toward a language or variety. Attitudes are acquired as a factor of group membership, as part of the process of enculturation in a particular speech community, and are thus basic to its characterization." Saville-Troike's assertion underlines three important properties of language attitudes. First, they are rarely individualistic because speakers are influenced by the dominant sociolinguistic order in their sociocultural milieu. Second, language attitudes are one of the sociolinguistic constructs that may define a speech community. This entails that one may draw on language attitudes in a given speech community to make some generalizations about other aspects of language behavior. Last, the methodological implication of this contention is that data collected from a selectively small yet representative sample may provide a good basis for describing general language-related trends in the speech community. This assumption seems to underlie much of the *discussion* on language attitudes in the Arab context, which are important because they are often tied to the perspectives and dispositions of rational individuals who are part of the community or who have extensive contacts with some of its members. The value of language attitude studies is to provide empirical validations of these discussions.

Much of the existing research on language attitudes confirms the long-standing positive attitudes toward SA and the negative attitudes toward QA. For example, Hussein and El-Ali (1989) surveyed the attitudes of 303 Jordanian students toward SA and three QA varieties in Jordan (Bedouin, Madani "urban," Fallahi "rural"). The findings indicate that the students view SA in a greater reverence and admiration compared to the three colloquial varieties. Also focusing on the Jordanian context, Saidat (2010) used a questionnaire, interviews, and observation to examine the language attitudes of 119 participants who were of different ages and genders and came from different Jordanian cities. Saidat found that, although the subjects reported having a limited fluency in SA, they appreciated SA more than QA. Al-Muhannadi (1991) found that Qatari speakers have more favorable attitudes toward SA than their own dialect. In a study on attitudes toward SA and the Egyptian variety, Haeri observed that the "language of the Quran separates the sacred from the profane, writing from speaking, and prescribed religious rituals from personal communication with God" (Haeri, 2003, p. 1). Ennaji (2007) reports that 73% of his 124 participants viewed SA a school language, compared to 2% to Moroccan QA and 51% to French. Further, the respondents viewed Moroccan QA as "a corrupt form of Arabic [SA] which is associated with everyday life and which is useless in formal settings or domains" (p. 274). Moreover, the majority of the respondents disagreed with the statement that SA should be replaced by the Moroccan dialect. Most of these studies attribute their subjects' positive attitudes toward SA to the Muslim faith and Arab unity and ascribe the negative attitudes to QA to the colonial advocacy of QA and the lack of systematicity in QA. Interestingly, Saidat (2010) found that SA is regarded highly by the participants for its *ease* of use, which contradicts the common beliefs about this variety.

The positive attitudes toward SA seem to increase in accordance with higher levels of education. This is anticipated because education provides Arabic speakers with an extensive exposure to SA, which often leads to a greater command, fluency, and possibly an appreciation of SA. Al-Abed Al-Haq (1998) assessed the language attitudes of faculty members at Yarmouk University in Jordan. The 211 participating faculty displayed highly favorable attitudes to SA and considered it as a mark of prestige and knowledge. At the same time, the participants underlined the instrumental role of QA for daily conversations. Haeri (2003) indicated that highly educated Egyptians, such as writers and journalists, regard SA as the language of intellectual activity, creative works, science, political discourse, and religious preaching. In contrast, the Egyptian QA is viewed as a mark of "backwardness," ignorance, and mundane activities. Al-Muhannadi (1991) discovered that educated Qatari speakers viewed SA more favorably than the less-educated speakers. In Iraq, Murad (2007) surveyed 107 college students and 89 individuals with no post-secondary degree. The results point to a significant difference between the language attitudes of the two groups; the former showed more favorable attitudes to SA compared to the latter, who preferred Iraqi QA.

While SA seems to have a clear attitudinal edge over QA, the picture becomes blurry when SA is attitudinally compared to languages such as French and English. El-Dash and Tucker (1975) examined the attitudes of college and high school students in Egypt toward SA, Cairene QA, American English, British English, and Egyptian English (i.e., English spoken by Egyptians). In reaction to a matched guise test, the participants showed more favorable attitudes to SA in general and to QA in the home domain and less toward the three English varieties. Shaaban and Ghaith (2002) examined the language attitudes of 176 Lebanese college students toward Arabic, English, and French. The findings indicate that each of these varieties is valued for different purposes. For example, English is associated with science, French with culture and education, and SA with news media, education, and regular interactions. Overall, however, the students saw English as the language of potential and future because of its global position. In his study of high school students' attitudes toward the language varieties in

Morocco, Chakrani (2010) found that French is contending the solidarity traits of SA and QA as local varieties. On the other hand, SA is challenging French as the variety of status. Chakrani also reports of favorable attitudes to the inclusion of English, particularly in business and education. Based on his findings, Chakrani maintains that the promotion of SA in Moroccan education carries insignificant symbolic capital relative to the discourse of modernity and overt prestige ascribed to French and English. In general, recent studies seem to suggest that the status of SA is increasingly challenged by English (across the Arab region) and French (particularly in the Maghreb).

When the different QA varieties are concerned, attitudes become more difficult to pinpoint because they become intricately related to different contextual and speaker variables. For example, Ferguson (1968, p. 379) remarks "Sedentary Arabs generally feel that their own dialect is best, but on certain occasions or in certain contexts will maintain that the Bedouin dialects are better." Ferguson attributes this trend to the speakers' attempt to enhance the status of their respective dialects in comparison to other dialects. Similar findings were reported by Nader (1962), who notices that her informants would defend their dialects if they were outside their towns because this is a form of loyalty to their own dialects and towns. However, in their own towns, they would state that the Bedouin dialect was the best. For Nader (1962), however, the situation is much more complicated because such factors as the context of the speech, social appropriateness, personality, group membership, and cultural influences may shape speakers' attitudes toward a given dialect. For example, even when in their towns, the upper-class and middle-class Christians in Beirut and Zahle would show positive reactions to the dialect of the socioeconomically disadvantaged Shi'is in a small village in the Bekka Valley. On the other hand, "A Zahle dialect would be imitated if one were telling a joke" (p. 26). Similar findings were reported by Hussein and El-Ali (1989), who found that, although they come from a sedentary center and usually have a higher socioeconomic status than the Bedouins, their 303 participants displayed more favorable views to the Bedouin dialect over their own. Sawaie (1994) probed the attitudes of 321 university students toward SA and three dialects in Jordan, which are marked by the use of /q/, /k/, /g/, and /ʔ/. Apart from SA, which received the most favorable ratings, the participants reported more positive attitudes toward the /ʔ/ variety (urban variety) as a marker of social status, but many male informants viewed it less favorably than the other two varieties because of its feminine /ʔ/ sound. Such ambivalent attitudes toward the local QA dialects are well documented in the literature (Abdel-Jawad, 1986; Al-Wer, 2002, 2007; Amara, 2005; Behnstedt, 1997; Habib, 2010; Hussein, 1980; Wahba, 1996).

A number of patterns emerge from these studies. First, generally speaking, SA seems to fare attitudinally better than QA in terms of status, role, and functions. The auspicious position of SA stems from a number of interrelated factors, particularly its relation to Arab history and traditions, Muslim religion, and Arab identity. Second, SA competes with English and French not only in terms of relative standing in the Arabic-speaking communities, but also in domains of use. For example, some studies point out the participants' preference for a multilingual reality where SA and French and English may exist in education and other social domains (Chakrani, 2010; Marley, 2004; Shaaban & Ghaith, 2002). Third, the Arabic speakers' attitudes toward the QA varieties are difficult to generalize because they depend on many factors. While the existing studies provide a rich and complex picture of language attitudes in different speech communities, what is missing is a study that compares the attitudes of different Arabic-speaking communities toward SA, QA, English, French, and local languages (e.g., Berber). This is important because language attitudes are largely shaped by the social context and speech communities in which they develop, and therefore a comparative study on this topic may reveal important patterns about the role of contextual factors in shaping speakers' beliefs toward different language varieties and their speakers. The study presented in the following section addresses the need for a comparative assessment of language attitudes in the Arab region.[5]

4.3 CASE STUDY

The study focuses on the attitudes of Egyptian, Jordanian, Moroccan, and Saudi college students toward SA, QA, English, French, and *Other* languages, such as Berber. The inclusion of the "Other languages" category was particularly necessary to represent local languages that are spoken by some of the participants. As noted in the previous chapter, the selection of participants from these four countries aimed to represent four different areas in the Arab region that differ in their historical (e.g., colonialism) and sociocultural (e.g., multilingualism in Maghreb) experience. Language attitudes are investigated using three research techniques – a questionnaire, interviews, and language behavior – which may allow us to assess the weight of different methodologies on the patterns observed.

4.3.1 Questionnaire data

The purpose of the questionnaire was, first, to collect data on the attitudes of college students in Egypt, Jordan, Morocco, and Saudi Arabia toward the varieties that they may speak or hear in their lives and, second, to explore the relationship between the participants' attitudes and their demographic and linguistic background. Fetterman (1989, p. 65) suggests that surveys are "an efficient means of large-scale data collection". The questionnaire included 107 items, which were created based on the review of the relevant literature, existing psychometric scales on attitudes in general, studies on language attitudes in the Arab context, and the researcher's own experience. Some of the items in the attitude scale were borrowed or adapted from Chakrani's (2010) study (see Appendices). A full analysis of the questionnaire data is far beyond the scope of this chapter. In keeping with the nature and goals of the book, the data presented here focus

on the attitude scale in the questionnaire and the relationship of language attitudes to a number of demographic variables, including *income, gender, ethnicity,
religion, major or specialty,* and *number of spoken language.* This set of demographic variables was selected based on their potential relevance to attitudes as
indicated in previous research (e.g., Bentahila, 1983a; Chakrani, 2010; Sawaie,
1994).

A convenience sample of 691 college students completed the questionnaire,
and these were distributed as follows: 188 Egyptians, 169 Jordanians, 180
Moroccans, and 154 Saudis. The target sample for each of the four countries
was 150. However, the data was collected from a larger number of participants
in case some questionnaires were not usable, especially given the fact that most
of the data was collected from whole classes. Out of the collected questionnaires, forty-four were unusable because they were missing whole scales (e.g.,
attitudes scale), subscale (e.g., affective subscale), or half of the items in any
single scale or subscale. The literature lacks any definitive criteria for excluding or including partially completed questionnaires, and therefore a subjective
decision had to be made as to when the missing items may bias the findings.
The unusable questionnaires were distributed among the participants as follows:
eleven Egyptians, six Jordanians, fifteen Moroccans, and twelve Saudis. In the
data collected in Jordan, seven questionnaires were completed by students who
claimed a country other than Jordan, and these were also excluded.[6] Similarly,
in Egypt, a single questionnaire was completed by a participant who reported a
non-Egyptian origin, and this questionnaire was not included in the analysis for
consistency purposes. The number of the questionnaires analyzed in this study
was 639 (92.47% response rate) including 176 completed by Egyptians, 156 by
Jordanians, 165 by Moroccans, and 142 by Saudis. The majority of the questionnaires were completed inside classes offered by a minimum of two universities
in each host country. A few questionnaires were collected from smaller groups of
informants on the host campuses. In Egypt, the data-collection process occurred
in four different universities in Cairo and Al-Ismailia. In Morocco, data was collected from three campuses in Al-Jadida, Casablanca, and Ifrane. In Jordan, data
collection was undertaken on two campuses in Amman and Irbid. Saudi Arabia
was the only country where the data was collected from two different universities
in a single city, Riyadh.

The questionnaire data was transcribed into an Excel document and then
analyzed using the SPSS.21 program. The demographics of the participants
appear in Table 4.1. The items used to characterize the college students' demographics were income, gender, ethnicity, religion, specialty or major, and number
of spoken languages. The selected variables were quantified by individual scores
on six items (see Appendices). The responses to all six items were treated separately as descriptive information that was correlated with the attitudes. *Income,* as
a mark of socioeconomic status, was excluded because this item was not completed by many participants. Therefore, its inclusion based on partial information
may bias the results.

Table 4.1 Summary of relevant participants' demographics

Variable		Egyptian	Jordanian	Moroccan	Saudi
Gender	Male	90	72	68	142
	Female	86	84	97	0
Ethnicity	Arab	167	150	123	142
	Non-Arab	9	6	42	0
Religion	Muslim	168	152	163	142
	Non-Muslim	8	4	2	0
Major or specialty	S. Sciences	122	114	94	95
	P. Sciences	54	42	71	47
No. of languages spoken	SA	56	76	132	64
	QA	166	151	157	122
	English	88	110	71	67
	French	26	25	127	4
	Other	14	16	45	6

As Table 4.1 shows, the female/male ratio was relatively balanced among the participating groups except in the Saudi case where all the participants were males; the ban on gender mixing did not permit the collection of data from both genders. In terms of ethnicity, the participants who claimed a non-Arab ethnicity were nine Egyptians, six Jordanians, and forty-two Moroccans. None of the nine Egyptian participants who claimed non-Arab ethnicities stated their ethnicities in the questionnaire. On the other hand, the six Jordanians who had non-Arab ethnicities were Circassian (five) and Turkoman (one). Thirty-six of the Moroccan participants who claimed a non-Arab origin indicated their Berber origins and the remaining six did not declare their ethnic origin. All of the Saudi participants reported an Arab ethnic background. Similarly, all Saudi participants reported to be Muslim, whereas eight Egyptians, four Jordanians, and two Moroccans declared their non-Muslim affiliation. The eight Egyptian participants reported a Coptic/Christian background and the four Jordanians reported a Christian background. The two Moroccan participants did not state their non-Muslim affiliation.

The *Specialties* under question 11 in the questionnaire were grouped into social sciences and physical sciences for ease of analysis. Computers, medicine, engineering, and commerce were included under physical sciences, and the remaining categories fell under social sciences. In each of the four groups, the participants majoring in the social sciences outnumbered those in the physical sciences. With respect to the number of languages spoken by the participants, the vast majority indicated that they speak their colloquial dialects. Fewer participants in each group indicated that they spoke SA. The second most frequently spoken language is English in the case of the Egyptians, Jordanians, and Saudis. French figured predominantly in the language use reported by the Moroccan participants, but not the remaining three groups. For the Egyptian participants, the

"Other languages" category included German (six), Korean (two), and Spanish (six). The Other languages spoken by the Jordanian participants included Circassian (five), German (three), Hebrew (two), Italian (one), Spanish (three), and Turkish (two). The Moroccan participants spoke a wide variety of languages including, Berber (twenty-eight), Dutch (two), German (one), Italian (two), Japanese (two), Spanish (nine), and Turkish (one). The Saudi participants reported speaking the German (two), Italian (one), and Spanish (three) languages.

Thirty-six attitude-related statements comprised the Language Attitude scale. The statements were divided equally among three subscales: Affective (items 1–12), Cognitive (items 13–24), and Behavioral (items 25–36).[7] Language attitudes were quantified using a 5-point, rank-order scale, ranging from *favorable choice (4)*, through *second favorable choice (3)*, *third favorable choice (2)*, and *fourth favorable choice (1)*, to *least favorable choice (0)*. The range of possible mean scores was between 4 and 0, with higher scores indicating more favorable attitudes to a given language variety. The face and content validity of the Arabic version of the instrument was tested by a representative group of undergraduate Arab students at Utah State University (n=4) for comprehensibility and clarity. Based on this pilot study, minor changes were made to increase the clarity of some items. The Arabic version of the questionnaire was used in the main study. Before the students completed the questionnaires, I explained to them as a group the purpose and significance of the study and how to complete the questionnaire. The students were instructed that they could give the same rating to any of the evaluated languages. They were also informed that they could ask questions before and as they completed the questionnaires.

As noted above, it is impossible to do justice to the questionnaire data, and, therefore, the information presented in this section only summarizes the general trends in the attitude scale illustrated in the tables below. As Table 4.2 demonstrates, the Egyptian participants' attitudes toward SA (2.85 out of 4.0) were more positive than their attitudes toward English (2.61), QA (2.57), and French (1.29). Their positive attitudes toward SA were particularly visible in the affective domain (3.26), unlike QA, which was favored in the behavioral domain (2.97) and English, which was preferred in the cognition domain (2.82). The Jordanian group was overall more favoring of English (2.91) than SA (2.68), QA (2.53), and French (1.12). Their positive attitudes appeared particularly in the cognitive (3.01) and behavioral (2.80) domains and less so in the affective domain

Table 4.2 Distribution of the overall mean rankings by the Egyptian speakers

Scale	Standard Arabic	Colloquial Arabic	English	French	Other
Affective	3.26	2.51	2.37	1.20	0.47
Cognilive	2.79	2.22	2.82	1.53	0.44
Behavioral	2.51	2.97	2.64	1.13	0.51
Overall attitudes	2.85	2.57	2.61	1.29	0.47

(2.94), where SA was favored (3.42). Unlike their Jordanian but like their Egyptian counterparts, the Moroccans perceived SA (2.90) more favorably than QA (1.99), English (2.64), and French (2.25). Their favorable attitudes to SA were relatively consistent across the affective (3.24), cognitive (2.95), and behavioral (2.47) domains. Similarly, SA received the most favorable ranking (2.89) by the Saudi participants followed by English (2.83), then QA (2.55), and French (1.10).

A comparison of the language attitudes in the four groups reveals a number of patterns. First, the respondents in all four groups reported a high *affection* to SA, thus identifying SA as their preferred language with respect to official status, language maintenance, and use in different domains, such as religion, business, literacy, media, education, government offices, and conversation (see Appendices). This pattern is consistent with previous reports on Arab-speaking people's attitudes to SA (Al-Muhannadi, 1991; Chakrani, 2010 Ennaji, 2007; Haeri, 2000; Hussein & El-Ali, 1989; Murad, 2007; Saidat, 2010). Cognitively, SA was contested by English in terms of its utility and importance. While SA was still rated highly on questionnaire statements related to culture, education, richness,

Table 4.3 Distribution of the overall mean rankings by the Jordanian speakers

Scale	Standard Arabic	Colloquial Arabic	English	French	Other
Affective	3.42	2.42	2.94	1.38	0.68
Cognitive	2.80	2.45	3.01	1.51	0.71
Behavioral	1.82	2.71	2.80	0.47	0.42
Overall attitudes	2.68	2.53	2.91	1.12	0.60

Table 4.4 Distribution of the overall mean rankings by the Moroccan speakers

Scale	Standard Arabic	Colloquial Arabic	English	French	Other
Affective	3.24	1.90	2.75	1.91	0.65
Cognitive	2.95	1.92	2.79	2.39	0.71
Behavioral	2.47	2.16	2.40	2.46	0.82
Overall attitudes	2.90	1.99	2.64	2.25	0.71

Table 4.5 Distribution of the overall mean rankings by the Saudi speakers

Scale	Standard Arabic	Colloquial Arabic	English	French	Other
Affective	3.57	2.47	2.69	1.31	0.51
Cognitive	2.98	2.48	2.96	1.48	0.46
Behavioral	2.13	2.69	2.85	0.53	0.22
Overall attitudes	2.89	2.55	2.83	1.10	0.40

eloquence, and Arab belonging, English received higher ratings on statements focusing on modernity, liberality, science and technology, professional careers, and general usefulness in everyday life. With the exception of the Moroccan group, all of the groups viewed QA as the variety most reflective of their behavioral intentions, which is not surprising given the fact that QA is used on a daily basis through social interaction and media. English, however, was favored behaviorally in terms of the websites visited and the movies watched by the participants. Both QA and English fared better than the other language varieties with regard to email usage and text messaging. However, SA was the preferred code for reading books. All the groups had less favorable attitudes toward French and least favorable attitudes to "Other" languages compared to SA, English, and QA.

Apart from these similarities, the four groups differed in a number of respects. First, in comparison to their Egyptian, Jordanian, and Saudi counterparts, the Moroccan participants displayed the most positive attitudes to SA (2.90) and the least positive attitudes to QA (1.99). This attitudinal disparity between SA and QA is due to various historical and sociopolitical factors. Historically, SA was presented in the post-colonial Morocco as a substitute to the French language and as a means of regaining the cultural identity of Morocco within the larger Arabic-speaking communities (Benmamoun, 2001; Bentahila, 1983a; Chakrani, 2010). Moreover, due to its link to Islam, SA is a main unifying factor among the ethnically divergent Arab and Berber Moroccans, unlike Moroccan Arabic, which, for many Berber speakers, instantiates the divisions between Arabs and Berbers in the Moroccan context. Like their Moroccan peers, the Egyptian participants held positive attitudes toward SA (2.85), but they also comparatively exhibit the most favorable attitudes to QA (2.57). For many Egyptian speakers, the Egyptian dialect derives its value from its versatile uses as a spoken and written language, its popularity in the Arab region, and/or its association with the Egyptian identity (Haeri, 2003; Mejdell, 2006; Rosenbaum, 2011; Suleiman, 2003). All these factors combine to give the Egyptian dialect an attitudinal edge in comparison to the other Arab dialects.

The Jordanian participants held the most positive attitudes to English. This may be due to the socioeconomic and political influence of the United States in Jordan, the increasing demand for English in the job market, and the widespread desire among the Jordanian youth to study, live, and work overseas – a pattern that materialized in my interactions with several Jordanian college students in the host universities. Although they conferred their most positive attitudes to SA, the Saudi participants still demonstrated positive attitudes toward English. Comparatively, the Moroccans held the most positive attitudes to French and to Other languages. This is not surprising given the exposure of many Moroccans to European languages due to their proximity to Europe and the continuous influx of people, materials, and communication between Morocco and Europe. French is also associated with business, mobility, modernity, and technology in the Moroccan context (Bentahila, 1983a; Chakrani, 2010; Ennaji, 2007; Marley, 2002). However, as previous studies have shown, French is gradually losing ground to

English in the Maghreb region (Chakrani, 2010; Lawson-Soko & Sachdev, 2000), which is evident in the speakers' more favorable attitudes to English. This attitudinal change may have to do with different sociopolitical factors (e.g., colonialism), and it may also reflect the youth's recognition of the importance of English as the global lingua franca, especially in the areas of global business, technology, and digital communication.

The relationships among the participants' attitudes toward each of the language varieties under study and their demographic variables were investigated through Pearson and Spearman correlations. Pearson product-moment correlations were used to examine relationships in language attitudes toward SA, QA, English, French, and Other languages, while Spearman's Rho correlations were utilized for examining associations between languages attitudes and demographic variables. A summary of the groups' correlation matrices is presented in Tables 4.6 through 4.9.

The correlation matrices revealed a number of general patterns. First, there was a negative relationship between the participants' attitudes to SA and their attitudes to English, French, and/or Other languages across the four groups; their positive attitudes toward SA generally corresponded to less positive attitudes toward English, French, and/or Other languages. By the same token, participants who rated English, French, or Other language favorably held less positive attitudes toward SA. Moreover, informants who had positive attitudes toward English usually had positive attitudes toward French and/or Other languages and vice versa. The negative relationships between SA and non-Arabic languages indicate that a significant number of the participants deem SA to be in competition with English, French, and Other languages with the acceptance of these languages being perceived as a threat to the status of SA. Attitudes such

Table 4.6 Summary of the correlation matrix of the Egyptian participants' attitudes and demographic variables

	SA attitudes	QA attitudes	English attitudes	French attitudes	Other attitudes
SA attitudes	1				
QA attitudes	.076	1			
English attitudes	−.453**	−.256**	1		
French attitudes	−.272**	−.325**	.246**	1	
Other attitudes	−.263**	−.310**	.038	−.220**	1
Ethnic membership	.407**	−.020	.033	−.138	−.102
Religious membership	.422**	−.035	−.004	−.202**	−.136
Gender	.009	−.010	−.022	.066	−.040
Specialty	.080	.123	−.014	.019	−.125
No. of languages	−.207**	−.007	.265**	−.093	.049

** = Correlation is significant at the 0.01 level; * = Correlation is significant at the 0.05 level

Table 4.7 Summary of the correlation matrix of the Jordanian participants' attitudes and demographic variables

	SA attitudes	QA attitudes	English attitudes	French attitudes	Other attitudes
SA attitudes	1				
QA attitudes	−.096	1			
English attitudes	−.309**	.305**	1		
French attitudes	.500**	.037	.238**	1	
Other attitudes	−.061	.054	.512**	.497**	1
Ethnic membership	.135	.019	−.110	.043	−.142
Religious membership	.250**	−.032	−.073	.090	−.033
Gender	−.093	.077	−.058	−.015	−.018
Specialty	−.027	−.026	.009	−.078	.084
No. of languages	−.040	.033	−.009	.083	.086

Table 4.8 Summary of the correlation matrix of the Moroccan participants' attitudes and demographic variables

	SA attitudes	QA attitudes	English attitudes	French attitudes	Other attitudes
SA attitudes	1				
QA attitudes	.110	1			
English attitudes	−.230**	−.101	1		
French attitudes	−.160*	−.003	.297**	1	
Other attitudes	−.008	.016	−.015	.006	1
Ethnic membership	−.021	.100	−.073	−.011	−.151
Religious membership	.202**	−.069	−.025	−.021	.070
Gender	.114	.148	.031	−.069	.049
Specialty	.128	.115	−.049	.107	.094
No. of languages	−.130	−.115	.093	.228**	−.049

as these may underline precarious situation of SA in the face of English, French, and Other languages. They may also explain the ardent calls across the Arab World for strengthening the position of SA relative to English (Abdulaliim, 2012; Hamaada, 2012; Nourddiin, 2012).

Participants who claimed an Arab background were more positive about SA than those who did not, only in the Egyptian situation. To understand this type of attitudes, it is important to consider the fact that Egyptian speakers who claim a non-Arab origin also view SA as an intruding language that has been imposed on the Egyptian people (Suleiman, 2011). For these speakers, SA is neither practically nor emotionally related to them, which may explain their less favorable attitudes toward SA. By contrast, the positive attitudes toward SA were not

Table 4.9 Summary of the correlation matrix of the Saudi participants' attitudes and demographic variables[i]

	SA attitudes	QA attitudes	English attitudes	French attitudes	Other attitudes
SA attitudes	1				
QA attitudes	.055	1			
English attitudes	.030	.087	1		
French attitudes	−.066	−.009	.222**	1	
Other attitudes	−.180*	.005	.307**	.475**	1
Specialty	−.112	.029	−.131	.070	−.056
No. of languages	.010	.019	.030	.011	.086

[i] Gender, Religion, and Ethnicity do not apply to the Saudi participants because there was no variation among the participants with respect to these variables.

affected adversely by the participants' ethnicity in Jordan and Morocco. Most of those who claimed a non-Arab origin in Jordan (Table 4.1) are Circassian and Turkoman, and those who claimed a non-Arab origin are mostly Berber in the Moroccan context. Although these speakers do not share ethnic membership with the Arab participants, they do share their religious affiliation, which provides a cushion for their positive attitudes to SA. It is for this reason that religious membership was also positively related to SA attitudes; informants who claimed a Muslim faith had more positive attitudes to SA than those who did not. This has to do with the link between SA and Islamic texts, scholarship, and important historical figures.

Another important pattern concerns the absence of a significant relationship between the participants' attitudes to SA and their attitudes to QA. The lack of mutual interplay between attitudes toward SA and QA suggests that participants who express favorable attitudes to SA do not necessarily have unfavorable attitudes to QA and vice versa. This finding points to a possible change in the attitudes of many educated Arabic speakers toward QA, which is probably no longer seen as a competitor to SA, as some of the recent literature in the Arab region suggests (e.g., Al-Muusa, 2003; Al-Sa'di, 2012; Hashimi, 2012). In other words, the relationship between SA and QA is possibly perceived as less frictional and more complementary in nature. This may explain why diglossia is not viewed as a social problem by many educated Arabic speakers (Kaye, 1975; also see section 4.5 below). As will be noted in the next chapter, this attitudinal pattern may also have to do with the rise of state-based nationalisms across the Arab region so that both QA and SA are needed to represent different forms of identity.

In general, the questionnaire data shows that SA enjoys a high affection among the Arab youth, whereas English is favored cognitively and, to a lesser extent, behaviorally. QA receives the highest attitudinal scores in the behavioral domain. This dichotomy between the affective and the behavioral and cognitive dimensions may explain the reportedly declining use of SA (Al-Sa'di, 2012; Rayhaan, 2012; Zuwaini, 2012), despite the participants' positive attitudes toward SA. It may also account for the rising use of QA and English, even though these two language varieties receive less favorable attitudinal ratings. Religious affiliation continues to be the major instigator of the positive attitudes to SA (Haeri, 2000). Ethnicity impacts language attitudes only in contexts where it implicates other sociolinguistic rifts, as is the case in Egypt, where a claim of a non-Arab ethnic group (e.g., Pharoanic origin) entails elevating QA at the expense of SA.

4.3.2 Interview data

The quantitative analysis was supplemented by face-to-face, semi-structured interviews (see Appendices). This qualitative element was employed not only to gather more in-depth information about the participants' language attitudes but also to ensure the trustworthiness of the results. As Glesne (2010) notes, the use of multiple data-collection methods contributes to the trustworthiness of the data. The use of qualitative measure was in response to current calls by many researchers to triangulate methods, particularly when studying constructs that call for greater consideration than quantitative methods can afford (Creswell, 2003; Glesne, 2010).

Interviews were arranged after the completion of the survey. In each of the classes visited, I asked if there were volunteers to participate in a twenty-minute interview about their opinions toward the language situation in the Arab region and their respective countries in particular. The number of interviewees was as follows: twenty Egyptians, twenty Jordanians, twenty Moroccans, and sixteen Saudis. The target number of interviewees was twenty per country. However, due to time limitations and feasibility issues, I was only able to conduct sixteen interviews in Saudi Arabia. The interviews were analyzed using an interpretive qualitative approach in which "it is possible to understand the subjective meaning of action (grasping the actor's beliefs, desires and so on) yet do so in an objective manner" (Schwandt, 2000, p. 193). Interviews were transcribed verbatim and then coded using analytic and thematic categories (i.e., categories that go beyond the literal meaning of words, phrases, and sentences to their larger contextual, social, and symbolic representation). The relationships among these categories were sought and then assembled into themes. Relevant quotations were grouped with their related themes.

The interviews probed the attitudes of the informants toward the various QA dialects in relation to SA and to each other (see Appendices). One of the questions asked is "in general, which do you *like* or *prefer* more: Al-Fusħa or Al-ʕaamiyya?" The majority of the respondents (44.7%) favored SA. They explained that SA is "a rich and beautiful language," "the language of the Qur'an," "the language of Arab heritage and civilization," "the language of Arab literature, and poetry, and politics," and "the language of news." To some interviewees, Arabic "enables [Arabic speakers] to communicate even when they live in different Arab countries," "brings Arabs together," "has an official status and . . . is acknowledged in the United Nations and worldwide." On the other hand, 22.4% of the interviewees preferred QA because it is "easier," "simpler," "natural," and "used by everyone." Five interviewees (two from Egypt, two from Saudi Arabia, and one from Jordan) indicated that this was a personal preference because they were not good at SA or because SA is "difficult" for them. The remaining interviewees (32.9%) indicated that they had an equal preference for SA and QA because each is important and is needed in some way. It should be noted that the Moroccan interviewees showed a notably stronger positive attitudes to SA and less favorable attitudes to QA than their Egyptian, Jordanian, and Saudi counterparts. Thus, out of the twenty Moroccan interviewees, twelve favored SA to QA, compared to eight Egyptians, seven Jordanians, and seven Saudis.

When asked about their favorite colloquial Arabic dialect and the rationale for their choice, the majority of Egyptian speakers favored their own Egyptian dialect because it "is understood by all Arabs" and "is the closest dialect to Al-Fuṣħa." The same applies to the Jordanian and Saudi speakers, who maintained that their own dialects are close to SA, and some indicated that they are "intelligible" and "lucid." A few Jordanian and Saudi participants cited their use of interdentals /ð/, /θ/, and /ẓ/ to assert the clarity of their dialects. Two Saudi participants invoked the link and proximity of the Saudi dialect to the dialects of "old Arab tribes in the Arabian Penninsula." The Moroccan interviewees diverged from their Egyptian, Jordanian, and Saudi counterparts because only two Moroccan interviewees viewed the Moroccan dialect as their preferred dialect. The majority of them favored the Syrian dialect, followed by the Egyptian dialect. What is intriguing, however, is that their liking of these dialects was not merely based on "linguistic" aspects, but social aspects as well. Thus, the Syrian and Egyptian dialects were identified as "beautiful," "easy to understand," and "close to SA." However, a number of participants also indicated that the Syrian people are "nice," "good," "close to us," and that the Egyptians are "good," "witty," and "likable." This shows that language attitudes are affected not only by the linguistic aspects of the dialects themselves (e.g., closeness to SA), but also by the perceptions of their speakers as well. When asked about the most difficult dialect, the majority of the Egyptian, Jordanian, and Saudi participants pointed to the Maghreb dialects. On the other hand, the majority of the Moroccan speakers indicated that the Tunisian, Iraqi, and Gulf dialects were the most difficult. Follow-up questions revealed that these attitudes were not due only to "linguistic factors" but also due to sociocultural factors (certain aspects of behavior) that are related to the speakers of these dialects. For example, three of the Moroccan participants who affirmed the difficulty of the Gulf dialect also expressed their disapproval of the behaviors of "many Gulf tourists" in Morocco.

In response to the question "if we were to replace Al-Fuṣħa with one of the colloquial dialects, which one would you personally choose?" the majority of the respondents disapproved this idea, again recalling the historical, religious, and cultural importance of SA. In fact, this question provided insights into one of the reasons for the importance of SA for many Arabic speakers, which may be summarized in the following words by a Jordanian speaker: ". . . it is a strong and expressive language . . . there is no language in the world that can compete with this language in expression and in strength. . . . No one can learn it except if they were born as Arab . . . *And it reminds me of the ancient time that I always long to have lived in. . . .*" SA is part of some Arabs' nostalgia to the past, which is often associated with social, political, and economic stability and prosperity. Moreover, there seems to be an apprehension among some participants of losing their connection to the past by abandoning what would allow them to read the texts of Arabic civilization. In contrast, QA reminds them of "scattered Arab states," "political divisions and problems," "bad economy," and "colonialism." As for participants who chose one of the QA dialects, again, the Egyptian, Jordanian, and Saudi participants mainly favored their respective dialects for the same reasons mentioned above. On the other hand, the Moroccan speakers favored the Syrian dialect followed by the Egyptian dialect. Here again, language attitudes are intricately related to ideological, social, historical, and cultural factors, including past experiences with speakers of the evaluated languages or dialects.

Last, the participants were asked about their attitudes toward the spread of English in their respective countries. All of the participants saw the spread of English positively as long as it is restricted to "some specific spheres, like technology" and "it does not affect the culture and the behavior of people." The majority of the respondents, in fact, saw the mastery of English as "a necessary skill for many jobs nowadays." However, a few respondents were disappointed that there were no mechanisms for controlling the many new English words that have become in use in the Arabic-speaking communities: "the Arabic governments should have ways to control the flow of foreign words . . . flow of English words in particular . . ." Moreover, the majority of the respondents criticized people who use English in everyday speech because "they are trying to show off" or "they are trying to be stylish." Some interviewees described this practice as "disrespect to the self and to the others," "unacceptable," "weird," or "disturbing." To many of them, the use of English with people who speak Arabic is "unjustifiable." As for attitudes toward French, the majority of the Moroccan participants viewed the existence of French and the learning of French in the Moroccan sociolinguistic landscape positively. They explained that "many jobs here in Morocco require French," "French increases one's opportunities to study abroad and find opportunities for work," and "science subjects are taught in French," and "it is good to learn many languages. . ." Likewise, the majority of the interviewees viewed the use of French in daily interactions as "bad behavior," although most of them acknowledged its prevalence in the Moroccan context (see Bentahila, 1983a; Walters, 2011 for similar findings). Again, most Moroccan interviewees indicated that they support the persistence of French in the Moroccan context, but would like to see the influence of the French culture diminish. Overall, the attitudes toward English and French seem to be driven by pragmatic purposes, which is quite different from how SA and QA are approached.

4.3.3 Language behavior

Language behavior is an important indicator of language attitudes. As noted above, language attitudes usually guide language behavior through the formation of behavioral intentions, which in turn become the basis of language behavior (Ajzen & Fishbein, 1980; Zimbardo et al., 1977). I will restrict my description here to observations that I noticed during my fieldwork. Whenever relevant, I will relate them to previous experiences or studies on the same topic.

In my interactions with academicians, acquaintances, and ordinary people in Egypt, Jordan, Morocco, and Saudi Arabia, I tried to alternate between SA and the Syrian dialect to see how they would react to my choice of language variety. In general, the Jordanian and Saudi participants used their respective dialects when I conversed with them in the Syrian dialect. When I spoke to them in SA, however, they often alternated between their dialects, a mixture of SA and their respective dialects, or SA. The Egyptian speakers mostly used their Egyptian dialect in both cases, and some used a mixture of their dialects and SA when I spoke to them in SA. Only one Egyptian professor responded in SA irrespective of whether I used my Syrian dialect or SA. This professor taught in the college of agriculture at one of the host universities, but he indicated that he always used SA in his lectures and when interacting with students outside and inside the classroom. He justified his choice by stating that "the language of teaching and education should be different from the language of the street . . . I personally do not prefer . . . or in fact I cannot speak the language of the street in my classroom." Unlike the Egyptian, Jordanian, and Saudi participants, the Moroccan speakers mostly used SA when I interacted with them in SA. However, when I spoke with them in the Syrian dialect, some of them used SA, others relied on the Moroccan dialect, and still others shifted to a Syrian-like or Egyptian-like dialect or mixed SA with Moroccan. In other words, the Moroccan speakers were the only group that used a dialect different from their own in their interactions with me.

These different patterns of behavior reflect the speakers' attitudes toward SA and QA. When I spoke in SA, most of the informants tried to approximate my SA speech, except for the Egyptian informants. This is because many Egyptian speakers assume that their dialect is accessible to non-Egyptian Arabic speakers, and therefore they do not need to accommodate their interlocutors or to use a *common* variety to communicate with them. The assumption is that the Egyptian variety is understood by the majority, if not all, of the Arabic-speaking people (Hammond, 2007). When I resorted to my Syrian dialect, two patterns emerged. First, the Egyptians, Jordanians, and Saudi interviewees did not shift away from their dialects. This may be related to their pride in or loyalty to their dialects or simply based on their assumption that their dialects are intelligible (see Ferguson, 1968; Ibrahim, 2000; Nader, 1962 for a similar observation).

The Moroccans displayed an inconsistent linguistic behavior. Some of the Moroccan speakers used SA, possibly because it is a common variety among all Arabic speakers. Some (especially male participants) used their Moroccan dialect possibly to assert their Moroccan identity or to express their loyalty to their dialect. However, one group (mostly female participants) shifted mostly to a Syrian- or Egyptian-like dialect. This has to do with the Moroccans' attitudes toward their dialect as less *Arabicized* (due to foreign words and expressions) than the other dialects (Shiri, 2002).

In Chapter 2, I introduced an episode that is relevant to the discussion here. As I was in a train station in Casablanca waiting for my train to Fes, I had a chance to interact with a lady who started her conversation with me in Moroccan Arabic, but shifted to the Egyptian dialect when she recognized that I spoke the Syrian dialect. When I inquired about her use of the Egyptian dialect, she maintained that the Egyptian dialect is better understood to most Arabic speakers. I asked her about the Moroccan dialect, she said that it is a "difficult" dialect because it is a mixture of different languages. Similarly, on my way between two nearby Moroccan cities, I was in a shared taxi with three police trainees. At one point during the trip, I started a conversation with them using SA. The first trainee to respond to me used a Gulf-like dialect. When I asked him if he was from the Arab Gulf, he indicated that he was a Moroccan. He attributed his use of a Gulf-like dialect to the fact that he thought that I am from the Gulf, and assumed I would understand his Gulf-like accent more than his Moroccan accent. He confirmed that the Moroccan dialect is a "difficult" dialect because it does not have clear rules, and it contains many foreign words. This reflects the general attitude of many Moroccans toward their dialect, and how these attitudes of linguistic insecurity impact their linguistic behavior. Linguistic insecurity refers to the negative attitudes that a speaker may have regarding his or her own dialect or language, especially when this dialect or language is perceived to be different from other dialects or languages that are perceived as being "easier," "more correct," or "more acceptable" by other speakers.

A third observation involves an interaction with three Berber speakers, whom I accompanied on a trip (see next chapter). The speakers used a mixed SA-Moroccan Arabic speech in our informal conversation and then shifted to SA in the course of a formal interview with them. At the end of the interview, I asked the informants about their use of SA, to which one of them replied that he only speaks in SA, elaborating that SA is the language that is "fitting . . . for the development of Moroccans and Arabs in general" and "part of the Islamic belonging of the majority of Moroccans." On the other hand, the Moroccan dialect did not have the same value for him because it was not his mother tongue. Again, language attitudes and issues of identity are materialized behaviorally through language choice in this case. This pattern has been observed in contexts where religious affiliation, rather than ethnic membership, constitutes the shared grounds between speakers of minority and majority languages. In such contexts, speakers of the minority language have been reported to display more favorable attitudes to SA because of its religious attachments, unlike the QA dialects that index ethnic or political affiliations that are not necessarily shared by speakers of the minority and majority languages (Chakrani, 2010; Murad, 2007).

A last observation concerns the use of English words by the interviewees in Jordan, Saudi Arabia, Egypt, and Morocco. The interviewees from the four different countries used English words and phrases in their speech (see also Chapter 6). The use of English was more salient in the speech of the Jordanian and Saudi informants in terms of number of shifts and the type of shifts than in the discourse of the Egyptian and Moroccan informants. For example, the Jordanian and Saudi participants deployed words that are technical and circulated in their English forms as well as words that are non-technical and have common Arabic equivalents (e.g., *math*). On the other hand, the Egyptian and Moroccan participants restricted their use of English mainly to technical terms, whereas words that have Arabic equivalents were rendered in Arabic. It is possible that the interviewees shifted to English because of my background, but the fact the several of them displayed this tendency shows that this is possibly a common pattern among educated speakers in these countries. It is important to note that the extent of English usage by the interviewees seems to correlate with their attitudes toward English; Jordanian and Saudi participants generally have more favorable attitudes toward English than the Egyptian and Moroccan participants, which may explain their frequent shifts to English.

Overall, the behavioral patterns reported in this section exhibit the informants' attitudes toward the languages and language varieties in question. The Moroccan participants were the only group to shift away from their colloquial dialect to a different colloquial dialect. As I will explain in Chapter 7, the Moroccan participants have a better grasp of SA than the other groups. This means that their shift to the Syrian and Egyptian dialects was not motivated by lack of proficiency in SA, but rather a reflection of linguistic insecurity that externalizes their attitudes toward the Moroccan dialect versus the other Arabic dialects. In other words, language use is motivated by perceptions of the presumed acceptability of a certain variety to the interlocutors, rather than by language prestige issues.

4.4 LANGUAGE ATTITUDES AND LANGUAGE STANDARDIZATION

Standardization is one of main factors contributing to differences in the statuses and functions of language varieties in a speech community. Standardization may historically be seen as a sociopolitical and linguistic process that deliberately seeks to distinguish a particular variety from others in terms of position and use in a given speech community. Ferguson (1996, p. 43) defines standardization as "the process of one variety of a language becoming widely accepted throughout the speech community as a supradialectal norm – the 'best' form of the language – rated above regional and social dialects." According to Ferguson's definition, the standard variety is marked by its prestige relative to the other dialects as well as its acceptance by the speech community as the linguistic norm. Similarly, Trudgill (2004) maintains that the most important criterion of a standard variety in multidialectal speech communities is that it is recognized by speakers of these varieties as such. Trudgill suggests that multidialectal speech communities are marked by the existence of a standard variety to which other dialects are related. Once the standard is absent, the dialects become distinct languages. Other researchers have given more prominence to multifunctionality as the main feature of a standard variety, particularly in the areas of written norms, literacy, business, and politics (Garvin, 1993; Haugen, 1994; Milroy, 2001). Still others argue that socioeconomic power and indexation of social status are two main characteristics of a standard variety (Bourdieu, 1999; Giles & Billings, 2004).

The phenomenon of language standardization is inherently related to language attitudes because most of the criteria associated with the standard variety, such as prestige, formality, and carefulness, are "evaluative" (Milroy, 2001, p. 533). Language attitudes are also a fundamental component of standardization because, as the definitions above indicate, the standard variety has to be accepted by the community of speakers in a given context. This is not a one-time decision but an ongoing process that is liable to change and adaptation. Scots is an example of a language that lost its status as standard due to different reasons, including its speakers' acceptance of (British) English as the standard (Trudgill, 2004). In contrast, Maltese Arabic was a dialect that evolved into a standard language. The implications for the Arabic sociolinguistic situation is that, because they are typically involved in the mutable process of standardization, language attitudes may play a critical role in defining the future of SA as the standard variety in the Arab context, especially with the emergence of new forms of authority, identity, and communication. As Mansour (1993) suggests, even when it is dictated by a higher authority, standardization may not proceed smoothly when it is challenged by local social and linguistic loyalties.

The Arabic situation is particularly intricate because the present status of SA as a standard variety is mostly based on ideological rather than an instrumental basis, especially considering the diminishing realms in which SA is put to use at the individual and societal levels. In fact, it is still debated whether the standardization of SA was initially built on an instrumental or an ideological basis. According to one account, the standardization of SA was motivated by a mixture of instrumental and ideological reasons (Chakrani, 2012; Chejne, 1969; Mansour, 1993; Versteegh, 1997). For example, according to Chejne (1969, p. 38), the standardization of Arabic "arose first in relation to Islam, and then was furthered by national, political, administrative, commercial, and economic motives." Similarly, Chakrani (2012) attributes the codification of SA to efforts to maintain religious, linguistic, and cultural unity in the multiethnic, multicultural, and mutilinguistic Arab-dominated state. Another account, however, attributes the standardization of SA mainly to ideological reasons. For example, Suleiman (2012) maintains that the general principle that guided the standardization of SA was maintaining the purity of the Arabic language, which led to concerns about the correctness of the language of the Qur'an. Correct language use was then linked to ethics, i.e., language behavior can be judged as ethical or unethical based on its adherence to specific standards. Suleiman further argues that the standardization of SA after the Islamic conquests was initially meant to keep the distinction between Arabs and non-Arabs through socially constructed concepts, such as ḥikmatu al-Arab "wisdom of Arabs," that were related to the purity of language. Hence, standardization was not merely a linguistic, social, or political process, but an ideological one as well.

The status of SA as the standard variety has raised a number of questions in the Arabic sociolinguistic scene. The first question is whether SA is indeed a typical standard variety. Mejdell (2008a) argues that SA shares a number of features with modern standard languages in Europe, including its codification and norms of correctness. However, its status as the standard language is challenged by the increasing spread of English terminology, its limited use in oral interactions, and its neglect by a significant portion of the Arabic-speaking populace. The second question is whether SA is related to prestige, which is often a distinctive feature of standard language varieties. As noted in Chapter 2, Ibrahim (1986) argues that, although SA is generally accepted by Arabic speakers as a standard variety, it does not index prestige in the same way modern standard languages do. Ibrahim maintains that prestige is associated with power and socioeconomic status, which are not reflected in the use of SA in the Arab context. This argument, however, is valid only if it is based on a specific definition of the standard variety that posits a definite link between the prestige of the standard variety and social status. The last question to be raised here is whether the positive attitudes that Arabic speakers have toward SA are due to its status as the standard variety. It has been found that multidialectal speakers would typically have more positive attitudes toward the standard variety than the colloquial varieties (see Pavlou & Papapavlou, 2004). Therefore, the question is whether the status of SA as the standard variety may explain the Arabic speakers' positive attitudes toward it.

In answering this question, it is important to consider a level of analysis that goes beyond socioeconomic and power-related factors. Issues of local loyalties and identities may act against the approval of the standard variety in a given context. For example, Montgomery (2008) notes that working-class loyalty to a non-prestige, non-standard variety sometimes result in negative attitudes toward standard varieties and forms. However, even if we accept the assumption that standard is associated with positive attitudes, the case of SA is still somewhat unique. As the study above shows, the status of SA among Arabic-speaking people is based on linguistic, historical, cultural, and religious reasons. These complex relationships may explain the Arabic speakers' positive attitudes toward SA as well as their negative attitudes toward past and present efforts to codify or standardize any colloquial dialect. For example, the move to standardize and instate the Egyptian dialect as the official language of Egypt in the 1930s was met with staunch resistance by many prominent Egyptian figures (Suleiman,

2003). This move eventually did not come to fruition due to many factors, but mainly because it was considered as a threat to the status of SA as a standard variety across the Arab region. In other words, the Egyptian speakers' attitudes were influenced by concerns that went beyond the local realities and boundaries to the pan-Arab sociocultural scene. This attitudinal pattern is still involved in shaping the debates about the future of SA as the standard variety in the Arabic sociolinguistic situation.

During my visit to Morocco, I had a chance to examine firsthand the reaction of several Moroccan speakers to the call for codifying the Moroccan dialect (which complements the call for entering QA in education). I also had the opportunity to collect issues of newspapers published over three days of my stay there, including *Al-Akhbaar, Al-Massa', Al-Ittihad, Al-Ahdaath Al-Maghrebiyya*. Below are some of the headlines that appeared around this period in these newspapers and in another online news site that focuses on language issues:

(1) أرفض الاتجاه الذي يسعى إلى أن تصير ثقافة المغاربة فولكلورية

"I am against the trend that seeks to turn the Moroccan culture into a folk culture" (*Al-Ahddath Al-Maghribiyya*, No. 5135, 23–24 November 2013).

(2) عليك أن تعثر على سيبويه جديد قادر على دراسة الدارجة

"You have to find a new *Sibawayeih* who is able to study the colloquial" (*Al-Ahddath Al-Maghribiyya*, No. 5135, 23–24 November 2013).

(3) اللغو في وضع اللا لغة

"The gibberish over the situation of non-language" (*Al-Ittihad*, No. 10.561, 27 November 2013).

(4) موسم انقراض اللغة العربية

"Season of the extinction of Standard Arabic" (*Al-Ra'i*, No. 319, 28 November 2013).

(5) أسمعتم عن وأد اللغة؟

"Have you heard about language infanticide?" (*Al-Akhbaar*, 24. No. 317, 26 November 2013).

(6) الحرب على اللغة العربية الفصحى. . . . إلى أين؟

"War on Standard Arabic.... Where to?" (Elaphblog.com, 7 November 2013).

(7) الدعوة للعامية في التعليم إهانة للشعب

"The call for vernacular education is an insult to the [Moroccan] people" (*Al-Khabar*, 13 November 2013).

These headlines underscore Moroccan intellectuals' negative attitudes toward the notion of the codifying QA or its adoption in education. There are four main issues outlined in the headlines: (1) the association of QA with "folk" or popular culture; (2) the difficulty of standardizing QA based on the notion that it does not have rules or uniform system; (3) the dissociation between QA and prestige, which seems to underline the notion that QA is not a language; (4) the repercussion of QA standardization on the status of SA as a standard variety. These concerns were reiterated during my interviews. When I asked the interviewees about their attitudes toward the idea of using QA in writing after developing QA-based grammar books and orthographies, they raised four main concerns about the possibility of codifying QA. The first concern is that QA does not have agreed-upon rules. The second concern is whose dialect is to be standardized; standardizing a given local variety may not be accepted by speakers of other varieties. Third, the standardization of any Moroccan dialect will sever Moroccans from the wider Arabic-speaking community. Last, QA cannot replace SA because the latter is more than a means of communication; it is "language of our heritage," "language of our prayers and acts of worship ... of our religion," "language of Arab history," and "language of Arabs from old time."

In general, language standardization is a complex topic in the Arab context because the relationship between SA and the notion of standard is not merely instrumentally based, but is grounded in history, culture, identity, and ideology. Language attitudes may be seen as both a mark of the prestige of SA in the Arab context as well as a safeguard against attempts to change its present role as the standard variety in the near future. However, the fate of SA is still far from settled by the fact that many Arabic speakers use it on a limited scale. Thus, the attitudinally–ideologically supported status of SA as a standard variety may eventually give way to pragmatic realities, that is, when SA usage in Arabic speakers' social lives diminishes to the extent that it is no longer a living language.

4.5 LANGUAGE ATTITUDES AND THE "PROBLEM" OF DIGLOSSIA

The notion of diglossia in the Arab region is interwoven with a number of social and socio-psychological constructs, including language attitudes. Language attitudes are needed to understand diglossia in the Arab region because they are involved in the unequal statuses of SA and QA and they influence how speakers of Arabic perceive and sometimes use these two varieties. Moreover, although diglossia is partly dictated and reinforced by the language attitudes and language behavior of Arabic speakers, it is often presented as a social or linguistic problem. The problematicity of diglossia is often attributed to its disruptive effects on communication among Arabic speakers, its negative influence on the education of young Arab children, its repercussion on socioeconomic and cultural advancement, and its role in the political fragmentation of the Arab World (Al-Toma, 1969; Maamouri, 1998; Suleiman, 2003; Versteegh, 2001; Walters, 1996). The challenge of diglossia is sometimes seen as stemming from practical, real-life concerns, but almost always implicates an attitudinal dimension. Given the focus of this chapter, I will restrict the discussion here to Arabic speakers' *perceptions* of diglossia as a sociolinguistic phenomenon.

The notion of the "problematicity" of diglossia recurs frequently in the writings of many contemporary scholars, writers, and intellectuals both inside and outside the Arab region. For example, the renowned and influential advocate of Arab nationalism, Saatiʕ Al-Husari (1985) writes, "The question of Al-Fuṣḥa and Al-'Aamiyya is one of the most important problems that raise debate and discussion among the intellectuals and writers, in the various Arab countries, for a while ago." Al-Toma (1969, p. 112), who carried out a comparative study between SA and Iraqi QA, concludes, "the problem [of diglossia] is too complex to lend itself to practical solution". In a lengthy report delineating the linguistic challenges facing the Arab educational systems, Maamouri (1998) identifies "the problems caused by diglossia in school or pre-school" as a major hurdle facing education in the Arab region. Likewise, Abu-Rabia (2000, p. 147) argues, "Reading difficulties in Arabic in elementary school are usually attributed to the diglossia of the Arabic language, whereby the spoken language is totally different from literary Arabic, the language of books and school instruction." However, an alternative view depicts diglossia not a social problem, but rather a linguistic problem when approached analytically. Kaye (1975, p. 335) argues, "The word 'problem' is to be understood in the light of the linguistic analyst, for whom it does offer many problems of a descriptive nature . . . and not in the sense that it is a problem for the Arab world." Kaye, like Ferguson, asserts that some Arabic speakers do not realize or acknowledge that there are two varieties in their sociolinguistic milieu and that the only language that they know and speak is SA. This claim, undoubtedly, addresses an attitudinal rather than a behavioral concern, and therefore it should be explored attitudinally.

One of the questions that I asked my informants during my fieldwork is "Do you see the existence of SA and QA in the Arab word as something positive or negative?" Three patterns of responses could be observed among the 76 interviewees. The first group of interviewees, consisting of thirteen Egyptians, fourteen Jordanians, ten Moroccans, and fourteen Saudis (67.1%), saw no problem in the coexistence of the two varieties as they are now. The interviewees explained that SA and QA have coexisted for a long time, are significant to different groups of people, and are a form of linguistic richness (particularly to distinguish different communities). A second group of interviewees, represented by five Egyptians, four Jordanians, nine Moroccans, and two Saudis (26.3%) considered diglossia as a problem and blamed it on QA. For them, the Arabs should use a single common language (i.e., SA) because the existence of QA "weakens" SA, dilutes one's affiliation to the Arab and Muslim communities, creates new affiliations and new barriers between Arabs, and severs new Arab generations from their heritage. As one of the interviewees indicated, "Every nation should be represented by one language. The existence of the colloquial varieties weakens the Arabic language and creates unreal . . . creates artificial barriers between the Arabs." The third and last group (6.6%) also saw diglossia as a problem, but related this problem to the fact that SA is used in areas where QA should be used (education, TV programming). For them, QA is the code used in everyday interactions and is therefore more accessible to ordinary people. As one of the interviews mentioned, "al-Fuṣḥa is something from the past . . . I do not see a need to stick to it because people do not use it in their everyday life . . ." Only two Egyptians, two Jordanians, and one Moroccan held this point of view.

The challenge of Arabic diglossia has been accentuated in the area of child education in the Arab region (Abu-Rabia, 2000; Al-Husari, 1985; Al-Kahtany, 1997; Al-Toma, 1969; Ayari, 1996; Ibrahim, 1989; Khamis-Dakwar & Froud, 2007; Maamouni, 1998; Saiegh-Haddad, 2005; Schiffman, 1997; Zughoul, 1980 among many others). Two main interrelated arguments have been put forward concerning the adverse impact of diglossia on child education. The first argument concerns the assumption that the difficulties in acquiring SA stem from the notable disparities between SA and QA (Abu-Rabia, 2000; Ayari, 1996; Eviatar & Ibrahim, 2000; Ibrahim & Aharon-Peretz, 2005; Maamouri, 1998). The second argument relates to the role of the "complexity" of SA in the low educational attainment of Arab children in schools. This argument is summarized by Maamouri (1998, p. 1) as follows:

> There is a growing awareness among some Arab education specialists that the low levels of educational achievement and high illiteracy and low literacy rates in most Arab countries are directly related to the complexities of the standard Arabic language used in formal schooling and non-formal education. The complexities mostly relate to the diglossic situation of the language, which is making reading in Arabic an overly arduous process.

Irrespective of the nature of the relationship between SA and educational achievement, the problem seems to be more attitudinal than educational because of the lack of any empirical studies on the impact of language choice on educational attainment in the Arab region. Such studies would be difficult to conduct not only because educational achievement is a complex construct to measure but also because measuring this construct empirically would require controlling for many factors, such as the learning environment, teaching materials, teachers' instructional skills, teaching methodologies, and parents' involvement in exposing the child to the language at home. Interestingly, a number of studies have recently shown that these "extraneous" factors are, in fact, an integral part of the "problem." For example, it has been found that home literacy activities (e.g., using children's books) enhance children's reading performance at school (Aram, Korat, & Hassunah-Arafat, 2013; Hassunah-Arafat, 2010). Likewise, studies report that children's reading comprehension skills may be predicted by their early exposure to SA orthography (Abu-Rabia, 2000). These studies show that, even if we accept the relationship between SA and children's educational attainment, the educational challenges that face Arab children may not necessarily be attributed to SA, but to contextual and human factors surrounding SA usage inside and outside of school. Two lines of research may be needed to lay the ground for a fruitful discussion on this topic. One line focuses on the relationship between scholastic achievement and SA usage inside and outside of school. Another centers on the potential role of QA in accelerating and facilitating the acquisition of SA, particularly its role in enhancing skills that have traditionally been associated with SA, such as reading and writing.

Another area where the relationship between diglossia and speakers' attitudes materializes is teaching Arabic as a foreign language (e.g., Abboud-Haggar, 2005; Al-Batal & Belnap, 2006; Alosh, 1997, 2009; Brosh & Olshtain, 1995; McLoughlin, 2009; Palmer, 2008; Ryding, 1991; Trentman, 2011; Wilmsen, 2006; Younes, 2006, 2009). The "problematicity" of the diglossic situation has given rise to the three approaches to teaching Arabic as a foreign language, namely the SA approach, the QA approach, and the integrated approach (see Alosh, 1997, 2009 for a summary of the main arguments). These approaches call for the prioritization of SA, QA, and SA–QA combination in terms of sequence of acquisition. My aim here is not to critique the arguments put forth by proponents of each of these approaches, but to point out that these approaches emanate largely from attitudes toward the main parameters of the Arabic diglossic situations, namely SA and QA. An examination of the arguments for or against the teaching of SA, QA, or the mixture thereof show that, although they are largely grounded in perceptions of the benefits associated with teaching one variety or the other, they are only valid based on certain assumptions and values associated with these varieties (e.g., SA is not "proper" for daily interactions, QA is not suitable for literacy skills, etc.). These arguments can be entertained in a more systematic way once one exposes the values that underlie support for one variety of another, which again depends on preconceived notions about each variety and its role in the Arab diglossic situation (in daily communication, on the media, in reading history documents, etc.).

In general, diglossia as a sociolinguistic situation may *analytically* be viewed as a social and linguistic problem. The uneasy coexistence of SA and QA in the same environment may be explicated by representational, educational, and identity-related factors. Regardless of how defensible the arguments about the "problem" of diglossia are, however, they do not match well with Arabic speakers' attitudes toward this social phenomenon or establish the existence of a real problem in their linguistic behavior.

4.6 LANGUAGE ATTITUDES AND ARABICIZATION

Arabicization is one of most controversial aspects of language policies in the Arab region (see Chapter 5) because of the complex nature of the Arabic multidialectal, multinational, and multiethnic sociolinguistic situation.[8] The term Arabicization has been used widely in a number of disciplines, such as sociolinguistics, translation, education, communication, politics, and gender studies. It is not surprising to find that Arabicization has been defined differently in different fields. Al-Abed Al-Haq (1994), for example, identifies twelve distinct definitions of Arabicization based on his review of the relevant literature. In the field of sociolinguistic, the term often refers to two interrelated concepts: (1) language policies that promote the use of the Arabic language, particularly in the public sector (e.g., education) in the post-colonial era, and (2) the *linguistic* and *sociocultural* process of incorporating new foreign words and terminology into the Arabic language (Al-Abed Al-Haq, 1994; Al-Asal & Smadi, 2012; Ayari, 1996; Benmamoun, 2001; Ennaji, 2007; Faiza, 2013; Marley, 2002; Sayadi, 1982; Sirles, 1999; Spolsky, 2004; Wright, 2004). These two concepts have sometimes been referred to in the literature as status and corpus planning because the former seeks to interfere with the statuses and distribution of languages in different domains whereas the latter seeks to define the form and structure of languages (Faiza, 2013; Reagan, 2009). Like any language policy, Arabicization may be seen as a problem-solving endeavor that attempts to "direct, change, or keep the linguistic norm or the social status and communicative function of a given variety of language" (Faiza, 2013, p. 25).

A distinction needs to be made between Arabicization and Arabization, which, although often used interchangeably, describe two related but distinct processes (Al-Abed Al-Haq, 1994; Ibrahim, 1989). Generally speaking, Arabicization is a language policy that has been applied on a limited scale in different Arab countries, whereas Arabization is a linguistic and sociocultural process that has never been implemented in the modern Arabic sociolinguistic context. Arabization refers to plans aiming to regain the cultural, historical, and political identities of the Arab societies. According to Ibrahim (1989), Arabicization as a language policy has "failed" because it was not attended by earnest official efforts to Arabize the post-colonial societies of the Middle East and North Africa. Ibrahim's postulation insinuates that Arabicization cannot succeed single-handedly in de-colonizing the Arab sociolinguistic scene linguistically and socioculturally; broader sociocultural transformations need to concur with changes in language policies. Arabicization is a complex social process that interacts with a host of political, economic, and sociocultural factors. This chapter will focus mainly on the attitudinal aspect of Arabicization. Before exploring the attitudes of Arab speakers toward Arabicization, it is important to outline some of the arguments for and against Arabicization as well as the approaches that different scholars have undertaken in analyzing this language policy.

Attitudinal studies on Arabicization suggest that Arabic speakers' views of this language policy follow three main patterns: (1) pro-Arabicization position, (2) anti-Arabicization position, and (3) critical position of Arabicization. The first position is embraced for cultural, nationalist, religious, and historical factors. Representatives of this position see in Arabicization a venue for decolonizing the Arab World from the linguistic and cultural hegemony that characterized the colonial period. Thus, it serves to assert the Arab unique identity through the medium of language, and to recognize the religious roots of the majority of the population in the Arab region (Al-Abed Al-Haq, 1994; Benmamoun, 2001; Benrabah, 2007; Chakrani, 2010; Ennaji 1988; Suleiman, 2003). Al-Abed Al-Haq (1998) assessed the language attitudes of faculty members at Yarmouk University in Jordan toward the Arabicization policy. The participating faculty members were in favor of *Arabizing* (i.e., using SA only) education at all levels. The respondents rationalized that Arabicization is essential for Arab "unity" and for continued communication among Arabs from different regions. In his study on language attitudes in the Moroccan context, Chakrani (2010) reported similar results; students saw Arabicization as a means of restoring Morocco's national and cultural uniqueness and to reverse the linguistic and social inequalities created by French colonization.

The anti-Arabicization position is upheld by those who view languages through either instrumental or identity lenses (Al-Abed Al-Haq, 1994; Bentahila, 1983a; Chakrani, 2010; Faiza, 2013). Some proponents of this position suggest that Arabic cannot compete universally with English or French or satisfy the projection of progressive or modern identity for individuals and states. The "utilitarian" approach favors English (in the Middle East) or French (in North Africa) because of their indexicality of global communications, progressiveness, and modernity. According to Al-Abed Al-Haq (1994), this approach is espoused mostly by "westernized" people who perceive language choice from a personal, rather than a communal, perspective. For example, Mouhssine (1995) reports that, although his respondents had positive views of the Arabicization policy, they associated French with modernity and viewed English even more positively for its global influence, lack of colonial-era legacy, and link to modernity and science. In some cases, however, anti-Arabicization involves speakers of local languages (e.g., Kurds and Berber) who see in the Arabicization policy as a threat to their linguistic and ethnic identities as non-Arabs. Benmamoun (2001) cites the Berbers' protests against Arabicization policies in Algeria to argue that some Moroccan and Algerian Berbers were not in support of this language policy for ethnic/cultural/nationalist reasons. According to Benmamoun, some Moroccan Berbers were in favor of the continued presence of French in the Maghreb sociolinguistic scene because it balances the influence of Arabic and counteracts the discourse of pan-Arabism.

The critical position of Arabicization generally favors Arabicization as a language policy, but scholars who adopt this approach are critical of the way Arabicization has been applied, particularly in the Arab educational systems. Critics of Arabicization often start with the assumption that Arabicization was unsuccessful in attaining its projected goals, and therefore try to explain why this is the case. For example, Ibrahim (1989) suggests that Arabicization is not and cannot be successful because it is not attended by Arabization, which is a more comprehensive sociocultural process of change. Ennaji (1988) contends that Arabicization has not succeeded because it is directed toward the past instead of the present, the modern, and the future. Gill (1999) maintains that the system that was built by the colonial powers (particularly with reference to France in the Maghreb) does not allow for the success of Arabicization because French is projected to be indispensable for the Maghreb societies for many years to come. A major question that this position raises is how to define the "failure" of Arabicization. A main criterion for the "failure" proposition is that Arabicization has been applied selectively in Arab countries, such as Morocco and Algeria. The use of SA has been restricted to the humanities and social sciences, whereas the domains of business, science, technology, and media have witnessed a strong presence of English and/or French. While this is an important criterion, what is needed is an empirical investigation of the social, economic, and political factors behind the limited diffusion of SA into such domains. More importantly, assessing "failure" requires a more systematic and comprehensive evaluation of the different actors and variables involved in the Arabicization policy. In education, for instance, these could be policymakers, administrators, students, teachers, parents, textbooks, job demands, career opportunities, and so on.

The controversies surrounding Arabicization in its first meaning as a promotion of the Arabic language in official and public spheres may be extended to the second meaning of Arabicization as the process of transferring non-Arabic words into the Arabic language. Again, there are three approaches to this process. One approach is represented by language purists in the Arab regions who oppose Arabicization out of concern for "an overflow of foreign words that ultimately do violence to the language and overwhelm it" (Chenje, 1969, p. 151). These purists call for following the traditional methods used by Arab philologists in deriving new words from Arabic roots. One of the main proponents of this school of thought is Abd Al-Qadir Al-Maghrebi, author of *Al-Ishtiqaaq wa-Ta'riib* (1947), who warns that Arabicizing words without following the Arabic root and pattern system may lead to the loss of the purity and integrity of the Arabic language. A similar argument is advanced by Anis Salloum, who cites the richness of the Arabic language and its ability to absorb many new foreign words throughout history to assert the need to coin new words based on the traditional derivational methods of the Arabic language (Al-Dibs, 1934). A second approach supports the use of borrowed words as they are because replacing these words with "old" Arabic terms would lead to the loss of their original meanings. For example, Yaacoub Sarrouf (1929) questions the need to rummage the Arabic language for words that may strip the borrowed words from their intended meanings in the source language. Similarly, Jurji Zaidan (1988) argues that the proposed filtering of foreign words through Arabicization limits people's ability to cope with the needs of the modern world and their growing exposure to new terms and expressions. A third approach advocates following the classical rules of word derivation, but shows less reservation about the use of foreign words when these rules cannot accommodate the composition of the borrowed words. This attitude resembles the opinion of many Arab intellectuals and falls in line with the guidelines of most Arabic language academies. Regardless of the approach, the root of the controversy over borrowed words is the lack of coordination among the different Arab countries or among their Arabic language academies concerning the establishment of accepted mechanisms and guidelines for Arabicizing such words.

In my fieldwork, I asked the interviewees about their opinions on the Arabicization policy in education. With the exception of two Egyptians, four Moroccans, and two Jordanians, all of the interviewees were in support of this policy. The main rationalization is that Arab children should learn the Arabic language because it is the language of their heritage, history, and culture. Moreover, the Arabicization policy, as one of the interviewees indicated, ". . . gives strength to Arabic to compete with other world languages." By strengthening the position of Arabic, another interviewee argued, "Arabicization enables future Arab generations to relate to their peers in other Arab countries." At the same time, more than half of the participants were not content with the progress of the Arabicization policy. Put in the words of one of the interviewees, the Arabicization policy "did not achieve much . . . I mean . . . many students . . . including myself . . . cannot speak Al-Fusḥa well." Most of these informants saw that SA still plays a marginal role even in the official and public spheres: "the kids may hear Al-Fuṣḥa for a few minutes in the class . . . maybe the Arabic language class . . . that is it." All of the interviewees emphasized the need to retain the use of "foreign" languages, especially English, for its instrumentality in technology, science, business, foreign relations, and general job competencies. This falls in line with previous studies showing Arab students' favorable attitudes toward global languages in general. Marley (2004) surveyed the attitudes of Moroccan high school students and teachers toward SA, French, bilingualism, and the policy of Arabicization. The participating teachers and students held both SA and French in similarly positive regard, and saw their coexistence in the Moroccan landscape as an advantage. Al-Abed Al-Haq and Al-Masaeid (2009) examined the attitudes of students from four Jordanian universities toward language Arabicization in Jordan. While the respondents expressed positive views of this policy, they also regarded English as the language of future opportunities in education, business, and trade.

While the Arabicization policy aimed to promote the use of "Arabic" (resembled by SA) in official and public spheres, a more recent trend places an increased emphasis on implementing QA in education, especially in the early stages of education. One of earliest research-based reports concerning the need to introduce QA into the Arab educational system came from the UNESCO (1956 as cited in Ayari, 1996). The report indicated that the gap between SA and QA necessitates the use of QA in early education (Ayari, 1996). This line of reasoning instigated a considerable amount of discussion about the need to reorient the Arabicization policies toward the integrative approach where SA and QA are employed at different stages of education or cotaught in the same educational milieu. There is abundant variation in how different Arab countries deal with this topic. For example, Arabicization is not discussed in Saudi Arabia as it is considered a matter of fact. In Jordan, Arabicization is almost always associated with SA and therefore the SA–QA debate is hardly relevant (Al-Abed Al-Haq, 1998; Al-Abed Al-Haq & Al-Masaeid, 2009; Al-Oliemat, 1998; Mizher & Al-Abed Al-Haq, 2014). In Egypt, the discussion is informal, mainly occurring between academicians and sometimes in the media. In Morocco, however, the discussion has become formally disseminated, and this is reflected in the headlines of a number of Moroccan newspapers, such as the ones listed below:

(8)   إرجاع فشل التعليم المغربي إلى لغة الضاد هي مغالطة إيديولوجية وليست نقاشا علميا

"Attributing the failure of Moroccan education to Standard Arabic is an ideological fallacy, not a scientific debate" (*Al-Akhbaar*, No. 317, 26 November 2013).

(9)   ضد الدارجة في التعليم. ضد إفقار الذات المغربية

"Against the colloquial in Education . . . Against the impoverishment of Moroccan identity" (*Al-Ittihad*, No. 10.561, 27 November 2013).

(10)   اعتماد الدارجة حط وتبخيس من قيمة المغرب والمغاربة

"Embracing the Moroccan dialect [in education] degrades and understates the value of Morocco and the Moroccans" (*Al-Ahdaath Al-Maghribiyya*, No. 5135, 23–24 November 2013).

(11)   التلميذ بين لغة التدريس و تدريس اللغة

"The student between the language of teaching and the teaching of language" (*Al-Ittihad*, No. 10.561, 27 November 2013).

(12)   ندعو إلى اعتماد اللغات الأم في التعليم الأساسي لنساعد التلميذ على اكتساب المعرفة الأساسية.

"We call for adopting the mother tongues in primary education to help the student acquire the basic knowledge" (Al-Ittihad, No. 10.561, 27 November 2013).

While a few of the reporting titles presented the rationale for the QA-in-education argument, the vast majority of the opinion and reporting headlines presented the argument against the incorporation of the Moroccan QA in education. The arguments put forward by proponents of QA integration in education can be summarized by three interrelated points: (1) QA is the mother tongue of Arab children; (2) it is easier and more accessible to children and, therefore, it may facil-itate the learning process; and (3) it allows children to start learning the subject matter without the need to learn a "new" language. On the other hand, according to Abdullah Al-'arwi, a prominent Moroccan scholar and historian, selecting QA would turn the Moroccan culture to a "folkloric culture," "demote the value of Morocco and Moroccans," strip the Moroccan society from its written tradition, sever Moroccans from their heritage and civilization, separate Morocco from the Arab culture, create a system that has no clear rules, construct a language from a "crude material," confuse children in the process of shifting between dialects, and cut off the "daughter [Moroccan QA] from the mother [SA]" (*Al-Ahdaath Al-Maghrebiyya*, 21/22/23/24/25 November 2013; No. 5135).

While in Morocco, I asked the twenty student interviewees as well as a num-ber of faculty in the host universities about their attitudes toward the introduc-tion of QA into education. With the exception of one, all of the respondents had highly negative attitudes toward this step, arguing that QA "may not accepted by all Moroccans," "cannot compete with foreign languages," "creates generations with no connection with their past," "strips Moroccan children from the ability to communicate with other Arabs," "is a means to destroy the Moroccan culture," and "creates ill-educated generations." These responses replicate previous findings in the Moroccan context that show little support for the introduction of QA into education. For example, Ennaji (2007) found that only 2% of his respondents were in favor of introducing QA into education. Likewise, Chakrani (2010) found that the majority of his respondents were supportive of the continued use of SA as a medium of Arabicization. Similar patterns were reported in other Arab coun-tries (Mizher & Al-Abed Al-Haq, 2014). Needless to say, although the attitudinal dimension may play a role in the eventual success or failure of the Arabiciza-tion policy, policymakers may not necessarily take it into account in deciding the future direction of this policy.

4.7 LANGUAGE ATTITUDES AND CODESWITCHING

In the Arabic diglossic communities, SA and QA are assumed to have different statuses and roles. According to Ferguson (1959a), these statuses and roles are pinned down by what is sociolinguistically appropriate or inappropriate in the Arab speech community. For example, Nader (1962, p. 26) explains, " . . . classical Arabic and scolding a child would be mutually exclusive . . ." If this pattern is still relevant to language use in the present, then one would expect negative attitudes toward CS because it resembles a violation of an unwritten, yet accepted rule of sociolinguistic appropriateness – a supposition that is supported by empirical evidence.

The negative attitudes toward CS appear particularly in written discourse. This is a domain that has traditionally been reserved to SA, and, therefore, incorporating QA in this domain violates the sociolinguistic conventions of the literary tradition and may be seen as a sign of disrespect to a readership composed mostly of educated speakers. In his work on CS in the literary work of the Egyptian novelist Yuusif Al-Sibaa'i, Abdel-Malek (1972, p. 134) reports the author's attempt "to erect an impregnable fence which would prevent colloquial expressions from sneaking in". As the author and Abdel-Malek also note, the author's abidance by SA stems from his apprehension of the rejection of his work, especially by the language purists in Egypt. Moreover, although he resolved to use a heavily QA-saturated style at one point in his literary career, Al-Sibaa'i was forced later to implement a style that is acceptable to the language purists and yet appeals to a larger audience. Similar observations about the negative attitudes toward CS in literary genres were made by Eid (2002) in her study of feminine short-story writers in Egypt. Rosenbaum (2011) discusses how the majority of Arabic speakers and literary figures across the Arab region disapprove the coexistence of QA with SA in literary genres. Rosenbaum, however, observes that this attitude is changing slowly, particularly in Egypt where it is common to use QA in a number of literary genres, such as novels and short stories (see also Mejdell, 2006).

Even when it appears in oral interactions, CS is not received favorably by most Arabic speakers. In his study of language attitudes in Morocco, Bentahila (1983a, p. 37) describes the common attitudes toward bilingual French-Arabic CS as "one of the unfortunate consequences of colonization, and as something to be deplored." According to Bentahila, this common attitude toward bilingual CS makes it a topic unworthy of study for many scholars and researchers. Bentahila reports that around 75% of his 109 participants disapproved CS, with attitudes "ranging from pity to disgust" (p. 37). The respondents viewed speakers who switch codes negatively, suggesting that they are ignorant, poorly educated, lacking in confidence and sense of identity. In another work focusing on rai music, Davies and Bentahila (2008, pp. 18–19) argue that "The general public, who may or may not enjoy rai music themselves, often tend to denigrate its lyrics as being banal, clumsy, or not elevated enough, sometimes precisely because of the mixture of languages they contain." Likewise, Caubet (2002) reports how the very act of mixing languages in Algeria becomes a subject of humor. Belazi (1991) suggests that language attitudes are one of the major sociolinguistic constraints on when a speaker can or cannot switch codes. Lawson-Soko and Sachdev (2000) indicate that CS is viewed negatively by French-Tunisian Arabic bilinguals and is bound by contextual factors. In his study of language attitudes in Jordan, Hussein (1999) found that the majority of respondents viewed the introduction of *foreign* words in Arabic discourse as a form of linguistic "pollution" rather than enrichment to the language and that much of foreign-language use is motivated by lack of equivalents to scientific words found in other languages. Saidat (2010, p. 237) describes switching between QA and foreign words as "a form of Arabic that is considered by many Arabs a language that has no roots and grammar." The negative attitudes to bilingual CS are not unique to the Arab context, but are confirmed in different speech communities (Garafanga, 2007; Gumperz, 1976; Kachru 1977; Stavans, 2000; Tollin, 2012; Valppu, 2013).

While numerous studies have focused on Arabic speakers' attitudes toward bilingual CS between Arabic and other typologically distinct languages, speakers' attitudes to bidialectal CS between SA and QA has received little scholarly attention. The existing reports on CS between SA and QA are largely based on general observations about this type of CS. These observations indicate that diglossic CS is also surrounded by negative attitudes, which seem to transpire only when the situation or the function to be performed call for the use of SA. Hashimi (2012) criticized Arabic public speakers, teachers, and professors who mix their SA speech with colloquialisms, highlighting their negative influence on the language of the *special/educated ones* "lughat al-xaaṣṣa." Although Hashimi focused mainly on the quality of the speakers' use of SA, he was implicitly criticizing the speakers for lowering the standards of their discourse; they merge QA elements into their SA-based discourse. Versteegh (2001) observes that President Nasser would shift gradually from SA to an SA–QA mixture to avoid the direct use of QA "since this would be regarded as an insult to [the] audience" (p. 196). Language attitudes on CS among national or local Arabic dialects have rarely been studied systematically possibly because this practice is so unmarked in everyday interactions to the extent that it does not draw much attention.

In my fieldwork in Egypt, Jordan, Morocco, and Saudi Arabia, I asked the interviewees about their opinions of mixing Arabic with other languages as well as their perceptions of those who mix. I asked the interviewees to select one of three possible answers (positive, neutral, or negative) and explain their choice Out of the seventy-six participants, 65.8% expressed negative attitudes toward bilingual CS, 26.3% accepted CS with no positive or negative evaluations, and 7.9% saw it as a positive social phenomenon. The explanations provided by the interviewees largely replicated those found by Bentahila (1983a); some of the reactions described CS as "an indication of bad education," "a show of disrespect to oneself and to others," and "careless feelings about one's language and identity." The respondents described those who use this type of CS as "spoiled youth," "uneducated generation," and "people who hang on to the peels of civilizations." Overall, the majority of the interviewees saw bilingual CS as a sign of unhealthy language behavior and attitude toward one's own language. The informants were also asked about their opinions of the occurrence of CS in religious and political speeches and in everyday discourse. In response to this question, 50.0% of the interviewees disapproved the use of QA in religious speeches, 32.9% were neutral, and 17.1% had favorable attitudes to this practice. Similar patterns were reported with respect to political speeches with 47.4% expressing negative attitudes to the use of QA in this domain, 43.4% neutral, and 9.2% positive. A completely different pattern emerged with respect to the use of SA in everyday speech because only 14.5% expressed negative attitudes toward this practice, 44.7% were neutral, and 40.8% were positive.

Participants who were against the use of QA in religious and political speech commented, "People are used to hearing speeches in Al-Fuṣḥa"; "the speech [khutba] becomes tasteless when the speaker speaks in 'Ammiyya"; "I don't think that this is the place of Al-'Ammiyya . . ."; and "this is what happens when people who do not know how to speak become religious leaders and politicians." Those who use QA in their religious speeches and political speeches were described with such labels as "intruders in this profession" and "contribut[ing] to the deformation of the Arabic language." However, the few informants who were in favor of using QA in religious and political speeches pointed to its "ease to the ordinary people," arguing that "this is what people hear and speak with one another" and that "using Al-'Ammiyya attracts more ordinary people." The third group, the neutralists, were mostly not keen on this "unimportant" issue in the first place, and some indicated that "what is important is what is being said not how it is said." As for the use of SA in everyday speech, the interviewees who advocated this practice suggested, "this is what Arab governments should try to encourage"; "the use of Al-Fuṣħa in common life makes it circulated among people"; and "this would lead to the spread to Al-Fuṣħa, which is good." On the other hand, those not in favor of SA use in everyday speech rationalized that it would be "funny to hear . . . ," "simply not acceptable by everyone . . . by the ordinary people . . . ," and "difficult to use for many people." The neutralists were neither in favor nor against SA use because, for most of them, "it is a personal matter . . . a matter of choice."

In summary, the negative attitudes toward CS stem from two interrelated factors. First, in the minds of many Arabs, SA and QA have different statuses, functions, and roles, and so it is important to separate these two varieties not only linguistically, but socially, contextually, and functionally (which is not often feasible). One may argue that the Arab academies, though set to maintain the linguistic distinction between SA and QA, also sought to preserve their functional distribution. This explains why the mixing of the two varieties is stigmatized, especially when SA is expected because this means lowering the standards of the discourse. It should be noted that, to date, no studies have documented CS between SA and typologically distinct languages (see Chapter 7). Therefore, it is difficult to speculate about the attitudes of Arabic speakers toward this type of CS.

4.8 CHANGES IN LANGUAGE ATTITUDES

Interest in the study of language attitudes stems not only from the need to understand individuals' beliefs about the language repertoires in their communities at a fixed point in time or how they impinge on the sociolinguistic reality of a given community, but also from the necessity of investigating how attitudes may change, or should be changed, in a particular direction. This change in speakers' language attitudes is assumed to have an impact on other aspects of their behavior. According to Katz (1960), understanding changes in attitudes necessitates understanding the functions of attitudes for a given individual or community. Katz classifies the functions of attitudes into four categories: (1) instrumentalist, adjustive, or utilitarian; (2) ego-defensive; (3) value-expressive;

and (4) knowledge functions. The *instrumentalist* function of attitudes revolves around the notions of gain and loss based on language choices; attitudes toward a certain variety stem from conceptions of certain gains associated with it. The *ego-defensive* function operates in cases where self-protection against threats, embarrassment, or anxiety is at play. The *value-expressive* function allows an individual to derive satisfaction for expressing attitudes that are compatible with his or her own values and self-perception. The *knowledge* function stems from the need for social actors to give meaning to what is happening in their narrow and broad social environments.

More often than not, the sought attitudinal change has broader political, economic, and social objectives. It is reported that Napoleon Bonaparte's first proclamation to the Egyptian people following the occupation of Egypt in 1798 was written in Arabic and contained praise of SA and the Qur'an. This act was to sway the Egyptian populace's attitudes toward accepting the French occupation as a better substitute to the Mamluk rule. In his famous history of Egypt, Al-Jaberti (1756–1825) notes that, because this proclamation was written in crude Arabic, it became a source of suspicion among the population and led to major criticisms and subsequent resistance to the French military and cultural occupation (Cole, 2007; Suleiman, 2013). Contrastingly, the French incursion into Lebanon during the same period was largely well-received because most of the educational institutions that they established promoted SA and produced graduates who led the revival of SA in the nineteenth century (Makdisi, 1996, 2002; elaboration on this point is presented in the next chapter).

A survey of the pertinent literature reveals four general patterns of attitudinal language change in the Arabic sociolinguistic context. These patterns may be detected by comparing the trends reported in previous studies with the relatively more recent ones. An important pattern of change concerns the attitudes of Arabic speakers toward the status and role of SA in domains and functions that are supposed to favor it most, such as religious and political speeches. This attitudinal aspect is not only reflected in the language behavior of Arabic speakers who sometimes shift away from SA in domains or for functions that have traditionally been reserved to SA (e.g., Albirini, 2011; Bassiouney, 2013; Holes, 2004; Mejdell, 2006; Rosenbaum, 2011), but also in their overtly favorable language attitudes toward this practice. Soliman (2008) investigated the attitudes of Egyptian speakers toward the use of Egyptian QA in religious discourse. His findings point to the participants' positive attitudes toward the use of Egyptian Arabic in religious discourse, contending that "the Egyptian public opinion nowadays regards the use of Egyptian Arabic to be 'more practical' 'simpler', and 'more influential' than Classical Arabic" (p. iv). In literary genres, such as short stories and novels, there is an increasing acceptance of a style in which SA is accompanied by QA (Eid, 2002; Mejdell, 2006; Rosenbaum, 2000, 2004). The responses to the interview questions reported above also point to increasingly "accepting" attitudes toward the mixing of SA and QA in social spheres that were traditionally allotted to SA.

A second pattern of change concerns the increasing recognition of QA as an integral part of the Arab sociolinguistic scene. Some of the early studies on Arabic speakers' attitudes toward QA suggest that some speakers of Arabic did not even acknowledge the existence of this variety or realize that they speak it on daily basis (Ferguson, 1968; Kaye, 1975; Nader, 1962). However, most of the more recent studies on language attitudes in the Arab context suggest that Arabic speakers value the "instrumental" role of QA in everyday communications (Al-Abed Al-Haq & Al-Masaeid, 2009; Chakrani, 2010; Murad, 2007; Saidat, 2010). In fact, Mizher and Al-Abed Al-Haq (2014) report that their respondents (faculty and staff representing four colleges in a Jordanian university) displayed more enthusiasm to QA than SA in general social interactions, although they generally had more positive attitudes toward SA. Apart from recognizing the important role of QA, the literature underscores the mounting pressure from pro-QA intellectuals and constituencies to accommodate QA in key SA domains, including education and media. This trend has been more visible in some Arab countries than others because of the specifics of their sociohistorical experience. As noted above, Morocco is now at the forefront of this line of change. These two patterns of change seem to be compatible with the *value-expressive* function of attitudes because they underline the orientations and values that stand behind the speakers' support of SA or QA (Katz, 1960).

A third form of change is the recognition of languages that have historically been stigmatized, such as Berber and Kurdish (Blau & Suleiman, 1996; Chakrani, 2010; Ennaji, 2007; Sadiqi, 1997). After years of marginalization, both Berber and Kurdish, as the two main local languages in the Arabic sociolinguistic sphere, have gained formal or official status in a number of countries (Iraq, Algeria, and Morocco). This is anticipated and attended by developments of positive attitudes toward these languages, particularly among their speakers (Blau & Suleiman, 1996; Ennaji, 2007). This recognition has various implications for the dissemination of these two languages in the public sphere. For example, Ennaji reports that 72% of his Berber respondents were in favor of using Berber in Moroccan schooling. In summer 2013, I had a chance to meet with Iraqi scholars who were visiting the United States. In our discussion on the language situation in Iraq, I came to realize that the Kurdish language is concurrently gaining sociopolitical capital and more favorable attitudes in the Iraqi sociolinguistic sphere. This was asserted by all scholars, including one of a Kurdish descent. For speakers of the Berber and Kurdish languages as mother tongue, these positive attitudes toward their languages have a value-expressive function, which reflects their beliefs about the importance of these languages. For non-Berber and non-Kurdish speakers, the attitudes toward these languages are knowledge based; these languages are increasingly interwoven into the sociolinguistic fabric of the Arab region.

A last pattern of language attitude change concerns the growing espousal of English in key social domains and functions, including education. This attitudinal pattern does not seem to be restricted to a single Arab country, region, community, or social class. For example, even in countries where French is well-established,

English is receiving more favorable attitudes than French and is proliferating in areas formerly dominated by SA and French (Battenburg, 2006; Chakrani, 2010). This type of change may be seen as a reflection of broader sociocultural values, which favor the instrumental view of language. However, because of its wide infiltration and spread, English is sometimes viewed as a threat to the local languages and culture (Mizher & Al-Abed Al-Haq, 2014). The value-expressive function of attitudes is manifest in the reactions that resist the increasing influence of English on the modes of thinking and communication across the Arab region.

4.9 SUMMARY AND CONCLUSION

Language attitudes are an integral part of Arabic diglossia as they contribute to the value asymmetry between SA and QA. SA is held in high regard not only because of its own qualities as a "beautiful," "expressive," "strong," "sophisticated," and "pure" language, but also because of its link to the Arab tradition, Arab identity, and Islam. Unlike SA, QA has lower esteem among many Arabic speakers because of its "randomness," "unsystematicity," "weakness," "inexpressiveness," "simplicity," and "impurity." Moreover, QA is unappreciated because of its presumed role in the socioeconomic and political weakness of the Arab region and its ostensibly adverse impact on the Arab collective identity. Given this value disparity between SA and QA, it is not surprising that SA and QA have dissimilar statuses and roles in the Arab speech communities. This functional inequality may also explain the attitudinal resistance to the codification and standardization of QA as well as the negative attitudes to CS in domains where SA is expected.

English is viewed favorably due to its link to globalization, power, versatility, practicality, and prestige. The positive attitudes toward English are well documented in previous publications and are confirmed in the study reported in this chapter. These positive attitudes are more visible in the responses of the Jordanian participants, possibly because of the social and economic influence of the United States in Jordan. Thus, the emulation of the American model in business and technology is reflected in language attitudes as well. The notably positive attitudes to English may reflect a change in language attitudes from a value-expressive perspective to an instrumentalist one; English is gaining attitudinal mileage because of its global prestige and utility. Compared to English, French receives less favorable attitudes because of its receding global presence, lower prestige, and limited practical uses in the international arena. Nonetheless, based on the interviews, French is still viewed favorably by the majority of the Moroccan participants for its association with modernity, science, and business. The presence of French in the Maghreb is not merely sustained by practical reasons: French is embraced by *active* speakers who see French as an integral part of the Maghrebi socioeconomic and sociolinguistic scene.

One of the ongoing debates in a number of Arab countries concerns the Arabicization policies that sought to regain the linguistic and cultural independence of the Arab states from their former colonizers, particularly in official domains. This policy, however, has led to the marginalization of minority local languages, including Berber and Kurdish. It is not surprising that many minority-language speakers have stood against this policy. Moreover, because of the weak representation of Arabic in international business and technology, which could be a corollary of the fragmented Arab polities, English and French are taking the lead in the teaching of science and technology across the majority of Arab countries. The Arabicization policy has been and is still under criticism by pro-QA intellectuals, who seek to introduce QA into education. This chapter explored the ambivalent attitudes toward Arabicization, which, although still favoring this policy, are also critical of the practices surrounding its implementation in different Arab states. It should be noted that the Arabicization policy has been motivated primarily by identity-related considerations and is still at the heart of identity dynamics in the Arab region.

NOTES

1 Speech and attitudinal acts are used in general sense here without reference to a particular theoretical framework.
2 The chapters and verses in the Qur'an that contain direct reference to the Arabness of the Qur'an are: 12 (2), 13 (37), 16 (103), 20 (113), 26 (195), 39 (28), 41 (3), 42 (7), 43 (3), and 46 (12).
3 This observation is based on my personal experience.
4 French is also taught as a third language in a number of Arab countries (e.g., Syria), but comparatively many more Arab students learn English than French.
5 The study will be published separately in a different venue. What is presented here are overall patterns that are relevant to the themes of this book.
6 In Jordan, seven questionnaires were completed by four Iraqi and three Syrian students. Participants who claimed a Palestinian origin in the questionnaire were still considered as Jordanians because a significant Palestinian population are settled in Jordan and are Jordanian citizens. In Egypt, one questionnaire was completed by a student who reported a Palestinian background.
7 See definitions of these terms in Chapter 3.
8 According to Maamouri (1998), Arabization started with the Islamic conquests in the Middle Ages, has receded during the Western colonial period, and reemerged after the independence of many Arab countries (see also Faiza, 2013).

CHAPTER 5

Social identity

The Arabic language has been the soul and the substance of identity dynamics in the Arabic-speaking world. It is difficult to fully understand the polemics of identity in the Arab region without considering its linguistic dimension. The language–identity link has recently become one of the most widely discussed topics in Arab politics, literature, education, and other social sciences. Joseph (2004, p. 12) argues that "the entire phenomenon of identity can be understood as a linguistic one." Joseph justifies his assertion by arguing that the language–identity nexus is integral to a number of sociolinguistic phenomena. For example, our attitudes toward other speakers and our perceptions of who they are depend partly on how they speak. Our views of languages are influenced by the way we view their speakers. Our language use and accommodation reflect our consideration of the identity of the people with whom we interact. The development of national languages is connected to national identities just as national languages are involved in shaping national identities. The inseparability of language and identity is particularly relevant here because the "Arab World," as a sociopolitical entity that has never been materialized in modern history, rests heavily on the existence of a shared language among its inhabitants. The Arab League defines an Arab as "a person whose language is Arabic, who lives in an Arabic- speaking country, and who is in sympathy with the aspirations of the Arabic-speaking peoples."[1] As the definition suggests, language is the foremost criterion of identifying who an Arab is. Moreover, the various state-based and local identities are largely dictated by factors related to linguistic diversity.

Research within the framework of social identity theory has demonstrated the critical role of language in the construction of social and personal identities and, conversely, the impact of identity dynamics on social actors' language behavior in daily communication and interaction (Bucholtz & Hall, 2004; Hall, 1996). While social identity can be defined across national, ethnic, racial, religious, linguistic, geographical, historical, and ideological lines, it often involves "self-definition as a group member in terms of ingroup–outgroup differentiations" (Simon, 2004, p. 37). On the other hand, personal identities are "based on one-on-one relationships with others" (Holmes, 2006, p. 167). Diverse disciplines, such as sociology, anthropology, social psychology, history, communication studies, political science, and linguistics have contributed to the growing body of literature detailing the relationship between language and identity. This explains why the interaction of identity and language has been approached from different perspectives and frameworks, such as social constructionism (Hall, 1996; Kroskrity, 2000), anti-essentialist view of the self (Bucholtz et al., 1999), categorization and membership definition (Antaki & Widdicombe, 1998), social and discursive practice (Fairclough, 1989), and indexicality (Blommaert, 2010; Silverstein, 2003).

Identity is a dynamic construct that is negotiated among social actors within immediate situational elements such as time, place, event, and occasion as well as in larger social norms, power relationships, cultural traditions, ideological concepts, and discursive practices (Bourdieu, 1999; Eckert, 2000; Fairclough, 1989; Fowler, 1985; Goodwin, 2003; Hall, 1996; Rampton, 1995). Since the dimensions of context are not uniform cross-culturally, the semiotic relationship between language and identity may be realized differently in different sociocultural contexts. This means that the relationship between the Arabic language and the multiple forms of identity in the Arab region should be considered within its unique sociohistorical environment (Suleiman, 2003). The Arab social and political systems with their historical roots, norms, structures, organizations, networks, expectations, power relationships, and systems of meaning provide the framework and boundaries within which Arabic speakers construct their identities and define themselves in relation to others. The social system, however, does not preclude the role of social agency, which is used here to refer to speakers' ability to exercise their choices and make decisions based on their membership in the social system and their understanding of different contextual factors (Bucholtz & Hall, 2004; Elster, 1979; Myers-Scotton & Bonlonyai, 2001).

Individuals living within the same politically or geographically defined region in the Arab World may have different sociocultural environments, historical roots, lifestyles, political affiliations, religious beliefs, ethnic origins, and individual dispositions. They are therefore expected to differ significantly in how they define themselves in relation to others. This means that they may simultaneously have convergent and divergent forms of identity. A Berber-speaking Moroccan, an Arabic-speaking Moroccan, a Kurdish-speaking Iraqi, and an Arabic-speaking Iraqi may have a common religious identity, but may have divergent political, tribal, ethnic, cultural, and historical identities. Similarly, a Christian Lebanese and a Muslim Lebanese may have the same national identity, but they may differ in other forms of identity. One question then is whether and how language is involved in speakers' internalization or display of particular identities. This question is at the heart of research on identity worldwide as well as in the Arab context, and it is the subject of the discussion in this chapter. A second question that is pertinent to the Arab context concerns the impact of diglossia on identity formation and the role of SA and QA in indexing different social and personal identities. A third question relates to the implications of the coexistence of a number of competing local and global languages, sometimes in the same social spheres, for Arabic speakers' view of themselves as members of certain social groups and as individuals.

This chapter examines these questions with particular emphasis on three identity forms: national, ethnic, and religious. These identity forms overlap in various ways, but this does not mean that they are inseparable or that their interrelationship with diglossia, language attitudes, and language use would play out similarly throughout the Arab region. The relationship between language and identity is complex and multifaceted, and it has been approached from different perspectives. The bulk of research on identity dynamics in the Arab region has focused on historical narratives; much less has investigated identity statements and identity acts in diverse Arabic-speaking communities. The chapter focuses on historical narratives as well as identity statements and identity acts. Before I discuss these topics, I briefly outline the historical conditions that contributed to the development of various identity forms in the current political map of the Arab region.

5.1 INTERPLAY OF IDENTITY AND ARABIC LANGUAGE: A BRIEF HISTORICAL SKETCH

Although the historical origins of Arabs predates any existing records, the situation of the Arab tribes before Islam indicates their awareness of their common ethnic or cultural background, given the occurrence of the term "Arab" in pre-Islamic poetry, its frequent use in the early Islamic writings, and its contrast to 'Ajam "non-Arabic-speaking people" (Aldawri, 1984; Chejne, 1969; Hourani, 1991; Versteegh, 2001). Hitti (1996) suggests that, even before Islam, Arabs shared a range of customs and traditions, such as tribal structure, blood relationships, and literary traditions. According to Hitti (1996), Arabs were also very proud of their free lifestyle, their *pure* origin, and their unique and eloquent language. However, it is difficult to conceptualize what "Arabness" meant before Islam without considering the Arabic language as a common denominator among the various warring tribes in the Arabian Peninsula. Arabs did not form a coherent religious group or a unified political entity, and therefore the Arabic language was possibly one of the main shared resources linking the various Arab tribes. The Arabic language could have been the single most important foundation upon which Arab consciousness before Islam was built. This means that *Arabness* as a form of ethnic identity was independent of religious and national identity before Islam. The language of the Meccan Quraysh tribe in particular was significant because Mecca was a meeting place for many Arab tribes due to its religious, commercial, and literary position; Mecca was the host of Ka'ba, the main trade center between Yemen and Syria, and the pivot of intertribal literary activity (Chejne, 1969; Versteegh, 2001).

The rise of Islam in the seventh century AD increased the Arabs' consciousness of their unique identity, mainly because Arabic was the *conspicuous* language of the Qur'an and the language of Prophet Muhammad. However, the Arabs' sense of collective identity as a group ethnically distinct from the 'Ajam started to take clearer shape after the Islamic conquests, many years after the death of the Prophet (Aldawri, 1984; Al-Jaabiri, 1989; Suleiman, 2012). The antecedents of the externalization of Arab identity in this period are far from clear. Aldawri (1984, p. 50) argues that the conquests may have created a sense of "common fate" among the Arabic-speaking people and an awareness of their "eminent historical role." The development of the unique Arab identity might also have been a corollary of their linguistic and cultural contact with ethnically, cultur-ally, and linguistically diverse communities outside Arabia, such as the Persians and the Byzantines. Language was just one parameter of multiple disparities between the Arabs and non-Arabs, but it was an important one because it was a distinctive feature of the conquerors and the bearers of the message of Islam. The Arabic language was not simply a container of the Islamic message or a means of communication, but an identity marker of a group of people who saw in their eloquent language a point of an identity difference from the non-Arabic-speaking communities. One may also speculate that Arabs started to develop a sense of pride in their language and then their identity as a reaction to the expan-sion of the Arabic language and culture at the expense of the existing linguistic and cultural traditions.

A number of researchers have argued that the Arabs paid much attention to the Arabic language in their quest to set themselves apart from other ethnic groups with which they came into contact after the expansion of the Muslim state. This explains their efforts to codify and standardize it (Nassar, 1956; Sulei-man, 2012). Nassar (1956) further argues that the Arabs' sense of superiority after the conquests prompted them to cultivate this edge by highlighting aspects of their heritage that bolster this superiority – the Arabic language and the Arabic literature being the two main ones (see also Suleiman, 2012).[2] Hamad (1913) argues that the Umayyad rulers initiated the first attempt to draw identity lines between Arabs and non-Arabs based on language factors. Identity politics at this stage focused on the implementation of the Arabic language in administration, the policy of assigning key administrative posts to the Arabs, and the institu-tionalization of Arabic in official circles. The Arabs who were settled in Greater Syria and Iraq before the Islamic conquests were as involved in the Umayyad administration as those who came from the Arabian Peninsula during the Islamic conquests. The Arab grammarians who codified Classical Arabic considered the language of the Arab tribes in the Syrian and Iraqi deserts as a main source of what constituted correct Arabic (Aldawri, 1984). It is reported that Abdulha-mid Al-Katib, the secretary of the last Umayyad Caliph Marwaan bn Muhammad, referred to the Umayyad caliphate as an "Arab state," although he himself was not an Arab (Kurdali, 2010). Aldawri (1984, p. 50) maintains that the Arabic lan-guage "drew the demographic and geographical parameters of the Arab nation" at that time. However, the Umayyads were successful in interweaving the Ara-bic language and identity within Islam so that it was difficult to disentangle this triplex. Unsurprisingly, their policy triggered the resentment of many non-Arab Muslims, especially the Persians (Kurdali, 2010).

Unlike the Umaayyads, the succeeding Abbasid dynasty favored the Persians and the Turks in most military and administrative positions. Aldwari (1984) examined some of the main treatises written in the Abbasid period, when notable cultural, intellectual, and political tensions between Arabs and non-Arabs (particularly Persians and Turks) started to transpire. He observed that many of the treatises that were written by Arab intellectuals in this period focused on the unique *ethnic* identity of the Arabs by highlighting their eloquent language and their "pure" ancestry. Among these treatises are *Al-Bayaan wa Al-Tibyaan* "Eloquence and Clarity" by Al-Jaahiẓ, *Al-Taariix* "History" by Al-Ya'quubi, and *Muruuj Al-Dahab* "Meadows of Gold" by Al-Mas'uudi. The term "Arab nation" recurred during this period, but always in connection with the Arabic language. For example, in his *Al-Imtaa' wa l-Mu'aanasa* "Entertainment and Sociability," Al-Tawhiidi distinguished the Arabs from other *nations*, such as the Persians, the Byzantines, the Africans, the Indians, and the Turks, by "succor, generosity, trustworthiness, fighting skills, leadership, oration, and eloquence" (2002, p. 44). Similarly, Al-Jaaḥiẓ (1983, p. 10) argues, "when the Arabs were united, they were similar in upbringing, in language, attributes, mettle, pride, and ardor . . .". Moreover, the Arabic literature during the Umayyad and Abbasid dynasties abounds with statements concerning the superiority, sacredness, eloquence, and distinctiveness of the Arabic language that are sometimes directly linked to the Arabs as an ethnic group (see Chejne, 1969 for a review). Further, travelers' accounts of their journeys in the Arab region suggest a sense of a common identity, given the uniform means of communication (Hourani, 1991). Toward the end of the Abbasid period, however, the Arabs' sense of pride in their identity started to fade away as they were overpowered by the Mongols, Crusaders, and a number of Turkic and Persian dynasties (e.g., Seljuks, Ghaznavids, Buyids, and eventually the Ottoman Turks). This identity devaluation led to the withdrawal of SA from public life (except for religion-related purposes) and the predominance of the dialects (Chejne, 1969). These historical coincidences provide insights into the interdependence of Arab identity and the Arabic language.

This situation persisted throughout the Ottoman rule of the Arab region, which lasted for about four centuries (1516–1919). Despite the relegation of Arabic mainly to the religious domain, many Arabs felt no threat to their identity because the Ottomans implemented no anti-Arabic policies, as they recognized the value of the language to the Arab people and Muslims (Chejne, 1969). Moreover, the Muslim Arabs considered the Turks as their associates in faith (Makdisi, 1996, 2002). However, several factors eventually led to the rupture of this religious link. Among these factors are the Ottomans' move to a European-style nation-state and their implementation of the Turkification policy, the Arabs' contact with the European civilization, and the active role of many Arab intellectuals in rebuilding relationships between the Arabs based on shared ethnic heritage and language. Antonius (1938) argues that the Arabs' revolt against the Turks was mainly a reaction to the Turkification policy, which raised their sense of their ethnic (not religious) disconnection from the Turks. In response to the Turkification move, a number of Arab intellectuals,[3] especially in Greater Syria and Egypt, invoked the Arabs' glorious history and language to assert the Arabs' unique identity. This sociocultural movement went hand in hand with an attempt to revitalize the role of Arabic (SA) in literary and public domains, in what is called Al-*Naḥḍa*, i.e., the renaissance period (in the nineteenth century). Aldawri (1984) maintains that, before the 1914 Arab revolt, Arabism was promoted primarily upon ethnic grounds (shared language, history, and heritage) and not based on well-defined political or territorial imperatives. Thus, its proponents lacked a clear vision of post-independence political order. However, it acquired a political identity when the British participated in the campaign against the Turks and presented the prospect of an Arab nation based on territorial boundaries and a type of governance that was grounded in the Arab history, namely, the kingdom.

The Arabic language was brought to the scene again when the leaders of the Arab revolt were negotiating with the British and the French governments concerning the prospective Arab *nation*.[4] For example, during a 1919 conference with British and French delegates, the *representative* of the prospective Arab nation, Faysal bn Hussein, submitted a memorandum in which he asked "that the Arabic-speaking peoples in Asia, from the line Alexandretta-Diarbekir southward to the Indian Ocean, be recognized as independent sovereign peoples" (cited in Zeine, 1977, p. 568). However, the Arab nationalist movement, the Arabs' sense of collective identity, and the prospect of building a "nation" for Arabic speakers soon evaporated when the British and the French divided among themselves much of the land that was under the Ottoman control. This started a new chapter in Arabs' quest for a frame of identity – a quest in which language played a critical role in mobilizing social and political movements against the new colonizers. The Arabs have different experiences with Western colonialism with some barely affected by it (e.g., current Saudi Arabia) and others falling under its direct control for longer (e.g., Algeria) or shorter (e.g., Iraq) periods of time and under colonizers who followed diverse approaches to Arabic language and Arab identity. Thus, the relationship between language and identity played out differently in separate communities across the Arab region.

With this very brief historical background, I will now turn to the main topic, namely the dynamics of identity in the contemporary Arab region as it relates to the Arabic language. Three main types of identity will be discussed: national identities, ethnic identities, and religious identities. As noted above, although they overlap in significant ways, these forms of identities have their distinctive characteristics, and they interact with the Arabic language in some unique ways, as the following sections illustrate.

5.2 NATIONAL IDENTITIES: PAN-ARAB AND REGIONAL IDENTITIES

National identity, in its modern sociopolitical sense, is a relatively new concept in the Arab history. It evolved under the influence of the European nationalist movements, particularly in the nineteenth century. The European concept of nationalism was transferred to the Arab region through three main channels: (1) students who studied in Europe and returned to their home countries afterwards; (2) colonialism, especially after the French occupation of Egypt between 1798 and 1801; and (3) the European missionary and religious schools in Lebanon (Kedourie, 1993). Moore (1997, p. 906) defines the concept of *nation* as "a group of people who identify themselves as belonging to a particular nation group, who are usually ensconced on a particular historical territory, and who have a sense of affinity to people sharing that identity." Smith (1981, p. 187) defines the nation, in its modern meaning, as "a sense of historic community associated with a unique 'homeland.'" He differentiates *nation* from *state*, which refers to "a set of autonomous and abstract institutions within a given territory." Smith argues that all nations seek to establish statehood just as state leaders strive to construct a national identity that gives unity and coherence to the population and legitimacy to the state's authority. Regardless of which definition one adopts, neither the concept of nation nor nationalism is globally uniform. As Conversi (1995) argues, the lack of a universal definition of nationalism is due to the fact that "the nation is itself a tool of definition" (p. 77). This is particularly relevant in the Arab region because the meaning of nationalism has been constantly changing, and with this change comes new forms of national identity.

Although the denotation of national identity has been changing in the Arab region relative to global and local sociohistorical and political circumstances, it has often involved a linguistic dimension. This is not surprising as the Arabic language is implicated in the very definition and possibly evolution of who Arabs, as a political or ethnic group, are. The concept of *qawmiyya*, which is derived from the Arabs' identification with their tribe as *qawm* "folk," has been widely used in the literature to reflect the Arabs' increasing sense of their common ethnic and linguistic heritage (Kallas, 2007). The other necessary component of a modern nation, namely homeland, has been fluid with its boundaries sometimes confined to a geographical region (Mount Lebanon), a historical region (Greater Syria), or the whole Arab Middle East and North Africa (i.e. often captured by the cliché *from the Ocean to the Gulf*). However, as Conversi (1995) argues, the boundaries of nations have not always been defined by territorial borders in the pre-modern era. Dawisha (2002) suggests that, up to the collapse of the Ottoman Empire, the Arab nationalist movement focused mainly on pan-Arab nationalism, with the exception of the Egyptian and Lebanese experiences. The pan-Arab nationalist movement was led by intellectuals, professionals, and literary figures, such as Ibrahim Al-Yaziji (1847–1906), Butrus Al-Bustani (1819–1883), Sati' Al-Husari (1880–1967), Zaki Al-Arsuuzi (1899–1968), Shakiib Arsalaan (1869–1946), and Abdulhamid Zahrawi (1871–1916), who considered the Arabic language as a mainstay of the Arab identity because of its link to the Arabs' glorious past, heritage, and traditions. As Chejne (1969, p. 18) argues, the "Revival of the language [SA], along with the study of Arab history, has long been regarded as the most important means for establishing the identity of the Arabs as people capable of attaining as important an intellectual and creative position in the world today as the one they enjoyed in the past." Arab nationalism therefore falls under what Smith (1986) calls the "essentialist" view of the nation, in which the nation is materialized or theorized through political myths of common descent, history, culture, territory, sense of solidarity, and other sociocultural symbols. In this approach, language is often a key component of national identity construction.

The revival of Arab nationalism in the nineteenth century was accompanied by the restoration of 'uluum al-lugha al-'arabiyya wa 'aadaabuha "sciences and literatures of Arabic." Thus, this period witnessed the development of the so-called neoclassical tradition, which focused on Classical Arabic and its literary uses, and the production of many important Arabic-language-related works, such as *Muħiiṭ Al-Muħiiṭ* dictionary "Encompasser of the Ocean, 1870" by Butrus Al-Bustani, *Al-Jassus 'ala Al-Qaamuus* dictionary "Spy of the Dictionary, 1881" by Ahmad Fares Al-Shidyaaq, *Majma' Al-Baħrain* "Meeting Point of Two Seas, 1800" by Nasif Al-Yaziji, *Ħayaat Al-Lugha Al-'Arabiyya* "Life of the Arabic Language" by Ħafni Naasif, and *Al-Wasiila Al-'Adabiyya li-'Uluum Al-'Arabiyya* "The Literary Means for the Sciences of Arabic" by Hussein Al-Marsifi. The pan-Arab nationalist movements have often been associated with SA, whereas QA has been considered "unworthy of marking the Arab national identity" (Suleiman, 2003, p. 9). According to Suleiman (2003, p. 10), "Relying on standard Arabic, nationalism in the Arab Middle East can define for itself a usable past, a source of tradition and authenticity that can enable it to stand its ground in relation to other nationalisms inside and outside its immediate geographical context." SA was, and still is, one of the main emblems of Arab common ethnicity and unity, unlike the colloquial varieties that are often associated with particular states or regions. The denunciation of QA as a symbol of Arab identity externalizes the Arabs' belief in the intricate relationship between QA and the period of Arab decline in the historical, political, and economic senses.

Alongside the pan-Arab nationalist movement, there developed a number of state-based nationalist movements, particularly in Egypt and Greater Syria. One of the earliest Arab theorists of state-based nationalism was Rifaa'a Al-Ṭahṭaawi (1801–1873), an Egyptian teacher, translator, and writer. Al-Ṭahṭaawi was delegated to lead a group of Egyptian students in France by Muhammad Ali, one of the most powerful leaders in modern Egyptian history whose powerful reign invigorated the Egyptians' sense of unique identity. Al-Ṭahṭaawi maintained that loyalty should not be directed to ethnic background or religion, but to the "homeland." Although heritage and history are important, the homeland is the space where members of the *nation* belong, live, and acquire their rights. Al-Ṭahṭaawi particularly focused on Egypt due to the influence of his European education and the European model of nationalism on his views of the nation. Many Egyptian writers followed his lead. For example Abdullah Al-Nadiim (1845–1896), an Egyptian writer and poet, called for the unity of the Egyptians based on the interests of the "nation," and not based on ethnicity or religion. Al-Nadiim theorized that all Egyptians are brothers because they share the same homeland, unlike the British and the non-Egyptian Arabs (e.g., Syrians). Proponents of Egyptian nationalism gradually summoned up their Pharaonic origins, history, and cultural heritage to substantiate and legitimize their claim to a unique national identity. As Hawkins (2010, p. 229) argues, "The construction of a national identity depends on the construction of a historical narrative: a chain of events, people, and practices that authenticates and helps define contemporary national identity." This localized nationalist movement was further sustained by mass media, including newspapers and music, which used the colloquial Egyptian dialects on a wide scale (Fahmy, 2010).

The promotion of Egyptian nationalism generated much controversy among the Egyptian intelligentsia concerning the language of the "Egyptian nation." Some, such as Rifaa'a Al-Ṭahṭaawi, Taha Hussein, and Mohammad Abdu, maintained their support to standard Arabic because it was still part of the "culture," even when they called for modernizing it along with other aspects of the Egyptian society. Others, like Aḥmad Luṭfi Al-Sayyed (1872–1963), Ahmad Husein Haykal, and Louis 'Awwad, maintained that only the Egyptian colloquial dialect can represent the Egyptians and reflect the Egyptian culture and literature. A third group, represented mainly by Salaama Musa, called for the development of a unique Egyptian language that adopts the Roman alphabet (Musa, 1958). The last position meant parting completely with the Arab identity through redefining what the "national" language is. The call for using non-Fusha forms was most vehement under the British tutelage and was pioneered by British writers, such as John Selden Wilmore (1856–1931) and William Willcocks (1852–1932). Thus, it was, and still is, considered by many Egyptians as part of a Western agenda aiming to detach Egypt and Egyptians from their larger Arab and Muslim identity (Suleiman, 2011). Later scholars, such as Muhammad Fareed Abu Ḥadiid (1893–1967) and Amin Al-Khuuly (1895–1966), tried to reconcile these incompatible positions by proposing to bridge the gap between the Egyptian QA dialect and SA by "elevating" QA and "purifying" it from foreignisms and/or by simplifying the grammar of SA.

The Egyptian nationalist movement lost much of its momentum after Egypt's independence and the reemergence of pan-Arab identity, especially after the ascendance of Jamal Abdulnasser to power. However, the failure of Nasser's pan-Arab agenda after the collapse of the Egyptian-Syrian United Arab Republic and the loss of the 1967 war to Israel, brought to surface a new form of Egyptian nationalism. Instead of being a widespread *intellectual* movement, as was the case in the early twentieth century, the new form of Egyptian nationalism developed into a covert social process, in which the linguistic dimension is still critical.[5] The widespread use of the colloquial Egyptian dialect in formal and informal domains, including major literary works, is one manifestation of this phenomenon. As Rosenbaum (2011, p. 328) observes, "A different type of demand to write in CEA [Colloquial Egyptian Arabic] comes from some Egyptians who want to culturally detach themselves from the Arab World and to emphasize the unique and separate local, even Pharaonic, identity of Egypt." Egyptian nationalist voices reverberate in media outlets as well (Abdulaliim, 2012). However, in most cases, this trend is grounded in social tensions (e.g., the work conditions of many

Egyptians in the Gulf region), and therefore the detachment from the Arab World appears to be political rather than cultural or linguistic. For example, under the title "Isis shines with her tears," the well-known Egyptian playwright Usama Ukaasha dramatizes in the daily Ahram (28 November 2013) the connection between the ancient Egyptian "homeland" and "Egyptian nation," although he still contends that he is an Arab culturally and linguistically. The indirectness of these calls for the Egyptian nation is due to the sensitivity of this topic to other Egyptians who self-identify with different forms of nationalism.

Another notable case of state-based nationalism is that of Greater Syria, which included Syria, Lebanon, Jordan, and Palestine. The idea of the "Syrian nation" was first proposed by Butrus Bustaani as a response to the 1860 violent conflict between the Christian Maronites and the Druze in Mount Lebanon, the role of the European missionaries in feeding sectarian tensions between the Maronites and other Christian groups, and the Ottomans' mishandling of the sectarian tensions in Greater Syria (Makdisi, 2002). Bustani called on his Syrian compatriots or *Abnaa' Al-Watan* to work together to attain secular liberal citizenship that would allow all Syrians to live in harmony. According to Bustani, the Syrians have a common history, homeland, and language, which justify their unity and exclusive identity. Unlike Bustani, who focused on the homogeneity of the Syrian people, Antuun Sa'aada (1904–1949) embraced the notion of "the Syrian homeland," which included the countries of the Fertile Crescent, namely Syria, Lebanon, Jordan, Palestine, Iraq, Kuwait, Cyprus, and regions in Turkey and Iran that have historically been part of the "Fertile Crescent." According to Sa'aada (2014), the Fertile Crescent constitutes a geographically well-defined area, and its inhabitants have shared a long historical coexistence. Sa'aada established the Syrian Social Nationalist Party, whose main dogma is "Syria is the homeland of the Syrians and the Syrians are a complete nation." However, Sa'aada denied any important role for language in the creation of the Syrian nation because, according to him, it is societies that give birth to languages and not vice versa. According to Zisser (2006), the Syrian nationalist movement is still alive, and it inspires much of the Syrian governments' politics and its relationship with the other Arab states. For example, Zisser (2006) examines how the loyalty to Syria and to the Syrian national identity figures predominantly in the speeches of Bashshar Al-Assad and other Syrian officials.

The pan-Arab and state-based types of nationalism wax or wane depending on different sociopolitical circumstances, and the fluctuation typically moves from politics to language. During the colonial period, the political strife against the foreign forces was often complemented by a cultural and linguistic struggle to assert the Arabic language and Arab-Muslim identity. For example, the French policies to exclude SA from public domains in the Maghreb were faced with notable activism from the local people to revive the role of the Arabic language in non-official domains (Benmamoun, 2001; Benrabah, 2013; Grandguillaume, 1990). This was a form of cultural and linguistic resistance aiming to assert the local people's Arab-Muslim identity. Similarly, language was a main player in cases where local identities were projected against pan-Arab nationalist sentiments, as was the case of Egypt in the 1920s and Lebanon in the 1930s. The resurgence of pan-Arab nationalism in most post-independence Arab countries was reflected in the language policies that the Arab states followed. The establishment of several language academies to protect, regulate, and modernize SA is another manifestation of pan-Arab nationalism. The first Arabic language academy was established in Damascus in 1919, which was followed by others in Amman, Cairo, Baghdad, and Rabat (Sawaie, 2006). This also was manifest in the proliferation of many pan-Arab nationalist parties in this period, such as Al-Ba'th Party and the Democratic Arab Nasserist Party, which invoked the socio-historical status of SA among its speakers as a justification for their pan-Arab nationalism and simultaneously identified the promotion of the SA as a priority on their political agendas.

However, the various setbacks that pan-Arab nationalism has suffered since the 1948 Arab–Israeli war and the contradiction between the rhetoric of pan-Arabism and the reality of the fragmented Arabic polities led to an identity crisis in the region and the emergence of neoteric forms of nationalism (Barakat, 1993; Barnett, 1995). For example, Habib Bourguiba called for the Tunisization of Tunisia linguistically by adopting the Tunisian dialect and culturally by aligning the country with the West and denying common roots with the Arabs. Other Arab states abandoned the Arab nation as a unifying factor despite their professed commitment to the sponsorship of the Arabic language. According to Zisser (2006), since the ascendance of Hafiz Al-Assad to power in 1970, Syria has been carving its niche in the region away from the Arab nation, and its top officials have expressed the distinctiveness of the Syrian state from the other Arab nations. At the same time, the state is well known for its support of the Arabic language because of its link to Syria's history since the Umayyad rule (Zisser, 2006). Yemeni nationalists define themselves in relation to their pre-Islamic history, but do not linguistically or ethnically distance themselves from Arabs in general (Hawkins, 2010). In Saudi Arabia, Arab nationalism is bartered for loyalty to the ruling family and expression of religious identity, whereas the Arabic language is still promoted for religious and cultural reasons. The Saudi support for the Arabic language materializes, for instance, in the establishment of Arabic language centers, the creation of different international awards related to the Arabic language, and the establishment of a number of scholarships awarded to students from Africa and Asia to study the Arabic language in Saudi Arabia (Al-Salem, 2012).

Since the 1990s, particularly after the first Gulf War, Arab nationalism has become basically a historical subject that Arab students learn at school rather than a social reality that they live. While the politically charged term *al-qawmiyya al-'arabiyya* "Arab nationalism" has become a taboo among various groups in the Arab societies (e.g., some religious groups), the more culturally oriented concept of *al-'umma al-'arabiyya* "Arab nation" has been used fluidly to refer to the common *cultural* and historical heritage of the Arab people. The coercive statisms that have been enforced by the repressive Arab regimes and the inter-Arab conflicts made Arab nationalism an ideation that has furthered demands for alternative nationalisms. This has resulted in the spread of localized movements whose priorities are (1) to mitigate coercive statism by civic activism and (2) to secure the basic rights of citizens, such as democracy, dignity, religion, and citizenship. The Arab Spring may be considered a manifestation of this emergent form of civic nationalism. The Tunisian, Libyan, Egyptian, Yemeni, Bahraini, and Syrian uprisings demanded freedom, democracy, and other basic human rights. The focus on the basic civil rights has left the issue of language in the background. During my fieldwork in Egypt, I asked a number of acquaintances and colleagues in the host universities about the liveliness of the QA–SA controversy. Most of them indicated that, given the sociopolitical situation in the country, language was no longer a substantive issue at the time. The same applies to Syria and Libya, where the struggle for civic nationalism overshadows any language considerations at this point in the history of these countries.

This does not mean that pan-Arab nationalist sentiments and their related language-identity link are outworn; rather, they are mostly immobilized by the sociopolitical atmosphere in the region. The reactions of the ordinary Arab to the events in Syria, Libya, Egypt, Tunisia, and Yemen show that pan-Arab identity is still alive among a sizable sector of the Arab populace. The spread of the modern means of communication and transportation has increased Arabs' awareness of their linguistic similarities as well as the similarity of their sociopolitical challenges. There is no doubt that the new technologies have also brought consciousness of cultural diversity among Arabic speakers, but these sociocultural disparities are counterbalanced by various similarities as well, including SA. For many Arabs, the use of SA by different Arab nationals on information and communication technologies revives the prospect of a relationship between the culturally diverse Arab populations based on shared language and history.

5.3 ETHNIC IDENTITIES: ARABS AND NON-ARAB MINORITIES

Ethnicity refers to "a collectivity or community that makes assumptions about common attributes related to cultural practices and shared history" (Phoenix, 2010, p. 297). Ethnic identity refers to "a person's knowledge of belonging to an ethnic group and pride in that group" (Aboud & Doyle, 1993, p. 47). Conversi (1995) argues that ethnic identity is not only the result of interaction between different groups, but also a feeling of "otherness" or "opposition" with respect to cultural details. Ethnicity may overlap with nationality, race, and religion, but it has its unique properties and role in an individual's and a group's life; it involves factors related more to cultural and historical heritage and attitudes and less to religion or political affiliations. This distinction is necessary to include individuals who claim an Arab ethnic background, though they may have different nationalities (e.g., Iranian Arabs in Al-Ahwaz), races (e.g., Arabized Turkomans in Syria), or non-majority religions (e.g., Druze in Lebanon).

The notable decline in the Arab nationalist rhetoric since the 1990s has given way to greater emphasis on ethnic and religious identities; the latter will be discussed in the next section. In fact, by and large, the term Arab identity has recently been used to denote cultural or ethnic identity, which has become the focus of many new conferences and studies across the Arab region, particularly in the light of the growing sense of identity threat due to the effects of globalization and the spread of English in the Arab region. The *International Conference on the Arabic Language* in its first and second meetings (2012 in Beirut and 2013 in Dubai) involved 607 papers, twenty-four of them focused primarily on the relation between the Arabic language and the Arab identity, and several others discussed the language–identity link in some detail. The *Arabic Language and Arab Identity* conference in Amman 2012 proclaimed as its first area of focus the relationship between language and identity. The *Fourth Forum for the Arab Youth* in Cairo (2009) adopted as its title *Arab Youth and Arab Identity in the Age of Globalization*, with the aim of exploring the impact of globalization and the spread of English on the identities of the Arab youth. In the same year, the *Arabic Language and Identity Symposium*, which was held in Doha (2009), focused on the challenges facing the Arab language and their repercussions on Arab identity. In (2007), a conference titled *Arabic Satellite Channels and Cultural Identity* was held in Sharja, with the main focus being the role of the language used on satellite television channels in the development of "cultural identity." The *Symposium of the Arabic Language and Identity* in Riyadh (2006) focused on the competition that the Arabic language receives from English and other languages and the impact of this competition on the status of Arabic and its ability to safeguard Arab identity. It is important to note that most of these conferences and the papers presented in them focused on the SA-Arab-identity bond, rather than QA-related identities, even when the emphasis was on state-based identities.

The bond between the Arabic language and Arab identity has been reviewed along external and internal dimensions. The external dimension concerns globalization and the dominance of English in critical social spheres, such as higher education, technology, and sciences. The cultural-linguistic incursions into the Arab region are manifest, for example, in (1) the widespread use of English names for shops, companies, and people, (2) the use of English words on clothes and decorations, (3) the proliferation of English language centers, schools, and universities, (4) the reliance on English in tourism and commerce, and (5) the use of common English expressions (e.g., "hi," "bye," "okay," etc.) in daily interactions by young Arab people (Abdulaliim, 2012). The spread of English presents a serious threat to SA because the dominance of English internationally makes it appealing to young Arab generations, who may embrace it for instrumental and ideological reasons (Siraaj, 2013). The apprehension in the Arab region is that, with the spread and adoption of English, the Arab youth may disconnect themselves from their Arab belonging, heritage, and history and assume a globalized identity (Al-Sa'di, 2012; Rayhaan, 2012; Siraaj, 2013). This is a likely scenario because "modernity" and "sophistication," which are desirable societal traits, are associated more with English than with SA. The youth's detachment from their language, as an anchor of cultural and historical belonging, may eventually jeopardize the survival of SA itself (Zuwaini, 2012). Abdulaliim (2012, p. 12) suggests, "Our way of escape from the trap of globalization is by supporting our Arabic and Islamic identity through realizing our unity in different spheres, particularly the linguistic one." To preserve the Arab identity, Abdulaliim argues, the Arabs should focus on strengthening the position of SA in education, media, and society at large. According to him, SA can compete with English if earnest efforts are made by the Arab governments and responsible institutions to promote SA.

The internal dimension has to do with the deployment of QA varieties in domains that were mostly allocated to SA, such as poetry, radio, television, and the internet. The dwindling presence of SA in these domains threatens to weaken the position of SA, diminishes common ties between its speakers, and creates local identities that do not realize the common Arab history and heritage. Hashimi (2012, p. 10) summarizes the problem by suggesting that ". . . if Al-Fuṣħa becomes extinct . . . , the Arab nation will lose its identity." Hashimi (2012, p. 2) describes SA as the "mother tongue that distinguishes the intellectual, scientific, literary, and cultural identity of the nation which an Arab who belongs to this nation has to be aware of." QA, however, "represents an alien, beastly body that is unintelligible among speakers of the different dialects" (Al-Sa'di, 2012, p. 10). This line of argument is not very different from the contentions put forth by pan-Arab nationalists against the calls for adopting QA varieties as national and official languages (see Zughoul, 1980). However, the more recent arguments take an ethnic rather than a political form; instead of invoking the *political* unity of the Arab "nation," it is now more common to invoke the *cultural* and *historical* unity of Arab people. It is noteworthy that the QA varieties are still mostly treated not only as non-representative of the Arab identity, but also as a threat to this collective identity. Hence, they have to be blocked from the official and formal domains. However, this position, which is upheld by most Arab intellectuals, is not shared by many young Arabs and does not account for their changing sentiments toward QA (see below).

However, the Arabs are not the only ethnic group whose sense of unique ethnic identity has been marked by language; the Berbers and Kurds have drawn the boundaries of their ethnic identities through language. From linguistic and historical perspectives, both groups possess distinct ethnicities. The majority of Berbers and Kurds are Muslims, and, therefore, they share with the Arab majority their general religious membership. They also share a wide range of cultural practices and traditions. The Arab national states, like other states in the world, have strived to erase "ethnic" differences within their geopolitical borders and to reinforce these differences outside their geopolitical borders (Conversi, 1995).

This has been achieved through underrepresenting minority groups, excluding their languages, or repressing movements that represent their unique identities (Benmamoun, 2001; Benrabah, 2013; Ennaji, 2005; Vali, 2003). The politicization of ethnolinguistic identity by some Berber and Kurdish groups may be seen as a reaction against such state-backed assimilation efforts. Although Berber and Kurdish ethnic groups are similar regarding the basis of the language–identity relationship, they differ with respect to how this relationship is expressed and mobilized within the larger Arabic-speaking communities. This has to do with the specific historical circumstances through which these two populations have gone and the divergent historical narratives that have undergirded their identity construction in relation to the Arab majority.

As noted in Chapter 2, members of the Berber communities speak numerous distinct language/dialects that are often mutually unintelligible (Ennaji, 1997; Maddy-Weitzman, 2001; Maddy-Weitzman & Zisenwine, 2013). Berber speakers had inhabited various parts of North Africa before the Arabs arrived there in 682, carrying the message of Islam to this region. The Berbers embraced Islam as their religion together with the Islamic laws and ethical codes. The Berber also adopted SA because it is the language of the Qur'an and worship. The strong bond between SA and Islam has permitted Arabic to overshadow the Berber languages in the linguistic landscape of the region (Asker & Martin-Jones, 2013; Benrabah, 2013). The Arabic colloquial dialects have accumulated more prestige than their Berber counterparts because they were linked to SA and eventually came to represent the Arab majority (Keita, 2010). According to Benmamoun (2001), many Berber speakers became Arabized due to the prestige of SA and its use in education and religious preaching, the migration of Arab tribes to the region (e.g., Banu Hilal and Banu Maqil in the twelfth century), and the influx of Arabs from Andalusia in the late fifteenth century. However, many Berber speakers retained their mother tongues, which could explain the survival of the various Berber languages till our present day, despite the fact that none of these languages was codified or standardized. The importance of language in the distinction between the Berbers and the Arabs becomes manifest when one considers their similar cultural and religious traditions, their coexistence in the same geographical space, and their intermarriage. The Berbers and the Arabs collaborated in disseminating the message of Islam to Europe (Andalusia) and parts of Africa. Tariq Bn Ziyaad (670–720), the famous leader who headed the conquests in Spain, was a Berber, and so were a number of the Moroccan ruling dynasties, including the Almoravids (1056–1147), the Almohads (1130–1269), and the Marinides (1196–1464) (Benmamoun, 2001).

The politicization of the Berber ethnolinguistic identity became visible in the light of the Arabicization policies that aimed to promote the "Arab identity" of the post-independence North African countries and to build connections with the Arab east (Benmamoun, 2001; Miller, 2003; Sirles, 1999). Many Berber speakers saw the Arabicization policy as a threat to their identity as a minority group because it does not recognize their ethnic and linguistic background. This threat, however, was presented through the colonially promoted notion of eth-nic and linguistic "opposition" of Arabs and Berber (Maddy-Weitzmann, 2001). Commenting on the Algerian case, Silverstein (1996) argues that the challenge to the Arab identity is "rooted in the colonial 'Kabyle myth' which conceptualizes Arab/Berber ethnic differences in Algeria as primordial." The construction of the Berber identity necessitated the need to recognize the Berber languages in the social lives of the Berber-speaking population and in society at large. The demands for the recognition of the Berber language and identity took a critical turn after being adopted by the Berber Academy in France in 1967 (Ennaji, 2005). These demands were adopted by many Berber intellectuals who saw in the Berber languages a main mark of their identity and heritage. According to Ennaji (2005), about fifty Berber organizations in Morocco alone have called for the codification of the Berber languages. These calls were framed within historical narratives concerning the "nativeness" of the Berber community to the region, their political dominance before the Arab–Islamic conquests, and their distinctive origins, languages, and culture (Keita, 2010). However, the politiciza-tion of the Berber movement has instigated retaliatory political measures by the governments in Algeria, Libya, and Morocco. The Algerian government imposed sanctions on the use of Berber in official documents, in schooling, and even in singing (Kallas, 2007). The Libyan authorities issued legislations that banned the use of non-Arabic languages in public spaces (Asker & Martin-Jones, 2013).

The tenacity of the Berbers' activism and the internationalization of their "cause," however, have forced the Moroccan and Algerian governments to rec-ognize the Berber language as an official language in Morocco and as a national language in Algeria. Along with the recognition of the Berber language came the recognition of *Amazighity* as the identity of the Berber community in Morocco and Algeria (Benrabah, 2013; Ennaji, 2007; Miller, 2003). This was followed by the adoption of the Berber languages in Moroccan schools and in Berber-dominant Algerian schools (Benrabah, 2013; Hoffman, 2006). More recently, there has been a shift in the Berbers' identity assertion, with more focus being placed on the Berber "nation," as opposed to the Arab or Moroccan nations. For example, one of the objectives of the Amazigh World Congress is "the defense and promo-tion of the cultural identity of the Amazigh [Berber] nation" (cited in Benmamoun, 2001, p. 105). The national–political dimension of these calls may require new historical narratives that situate the ethnolinguistic character of the Berber iden-tity within a historically or geographically unified state or national entity. It may also require redrawing the identity lines between the Berbers and the Arabs not based solely on language, but also other experiences that could break the cul-tural, religious, and state-based commonalities that sustain their shared Moroc-can and Algerian identities.

The Kurdish ethno-nationalist movement emulates its Berber counterpart in various respects. For example, the Kurdish identity is founded mainly on ethno-linguistic grounds, which include languages, heritage, and history. The Kurdish people speak many distinct languages and dialects, which fall under four main language groups: Kurmanji, Sorani, Gorani, and Kirmashani (Hassanpour, 2012; Vali, 2003). The languages are written in three different scripts: Arabic, Roman, and Cyrillic (Ghazi, 2009; Hassanpour, 2012). These linguistic differences are often ignored in the face of the need to construct a unified identity in relation to "others" (Sheyholislami, 2008). Like the Berber, the Kurds embraced Islam and the Arabic language shortly after the Arab–Islamic conquests. Like the Berbers, too, many Kurds soon assimilated into the Arab–Islamic culture for purposes of religious cohesion, although many retained their mother-tongue languages (Blau & Suleiman, 1996). Arabized Kurds figure predominantly in the Arabic–Islamic history, contributing such important names as Abu Ĥanifa Al-Daynawari (828–896), Ibn Salaah Al-Shahrazuuri (1181–1245), Shams Al-Diin Ibn Khallakaan (1211–1282). The acclaimed Ayyoubi dynasty and their prominent Saladdin leader have a Kurdish descent. As was the case with the Berber–Arab relationship, the religious bond between the Arabs and Kurds overshadowed their ethnic differences. Likewise, the language of the Qur'an was accorded a high status by the Kurdish people, whereas the Kurdish languages were seen as inferior and ill-suited to literary and official uses (Blau & Suleiman, 1996).

According to Blau and Suleiman (1996), the Kurds were largely an invisible ethnic group because they assimilated culturally and linguistically into the dominant cultures in which they lived. Thus, they adopted the Persian, Arabic, and Turkish languages when these groups were in control of the territory heavily populated by the Kurds. Blau and Suleiman (1996) trace back the development of Kurdish ethnic identity to the eighteenth century when a number of Kurdish literary figures ventured into cultivating a sense of pride in the Kurdish languages, which eventually raised their sense of identity as a distinct ethnic group. However, the Kurdish ethnolinguistic movement was largely influenced by the Turkification policy, which sought not only to enforce the Turkish language in Kurdish-dominant provinces in southeastern Turkey and northern Iraq, but also to suppress any presence or expression of the Kurdish languages in the public domain (Vali, 2003). Like its Arab counterpart, the Kurdish movement soon shifted from a focus on recognition of ethnolinguistic identity to a nationalist-separatist movement due to the support of the British. According to Conversi (1995), *separatism* typically emerges in historical moments when a social group seeks to preserve its identity in the face of a state-enforced order. When language is the hallmark of a group's identity, a threat to language may end in a loss of the community or culture. This may explain the Kurds' unwelcoming reaction to Turkification.

The British fostered the Kurdish sense of national–ethnic identity by promising the establishment of a homeland to what is often called "stateless nation." International politics among the British, French, and Turks, however, stood in the way of establishing the promised state. In 1932, the Kurdish language was recognized in the Iraqi constitution, and in 1958, Kurdish was designated as the second language of the country and was used in schools and universities (Meho & Maglaughlin, 2001). In 2001, the American-appointed Iraqi government opposed a proposal to institutionalize Kurdish in all official and government bodies, which, according to Meho and Maglaughlin (2001), was a resistance to "ethnic federation" in Iraq. Eventually, however, the Kurdish language attained an official status on a par with Arabic.[6] Along with Arabic, the Kurdish language is used in all government-issued documents, legal constituencies, and official circles. In the northern Kurd-dominated areas of Iraq, Kurdish is used as a main means of communication, education, print, and media. It is increasingly used among Kurdish people as a marker of their ethnic and national identities. Kurds who know Arabic may refrain from using it with non-Kurds whenever a third language is possible. In summer 2013, I was invited to lead a discussion on the sociocultural and linguistic situation of Arab Americans with a group of Iraqi scholars who were visiting the United States. When I asked whether the lecture was to be given in Arabic or English, I was informed that a Kurdish scholar, who was in the group, favored English over Arabic in this context. English here is a neutral language that does not belong to Arabs or Kurds and may not create identity tensions between the two groups. This is not different from the situation in the multilingual countries of Africa, where English often assumes the role of the *neutral* language (Appel & Muysken, 1987; Heugh, 2002).

In recent years, there have been intense debates concerning the official language for Iraqi Kurdistan, the language rights of the different Kurdish communities, and the potential impact of the linguistic plurality of Kurdish on the fragmentation of the Kurdish political and ethnolinguistic unity. For example, a 2008 petition signed by fifty-three intellectuals, academicians, and literary figures to make Sorani the official language of Iraqi Kurdistan was opposed by speakers of other languages, who also sought to have their languages recognized officially by the Kurdistan Regional Government (Ghazi, 2009; Hassanpour, 2012). While the Sorani dialects are spoken by the majority of Iraqi Kurds, the Kurmanji dialects represent the dominant group of dialects in terms of overall speakers worldwide. Thus, one aspect of the tension centers on whether to adopt the language of the local or global majority. Another aspect of the tension concerns speakers of the less dominant languages, such as Hawrami, who also petitioned with the Kurdistan Regional Government to recognize Hawrami as a distinct language and to grant full linguistic rights to its speakers, especially in education. These calls have been dismissed by the Kurdish authorities because they have been perceived as a potential source of disunity among the Kurdish people. O'Shea (2004) attributes these tensions to the failure of the Kurdish nationalist narratives to acknowledge the linguistic and ethnic diversity of the Kurds. In other words, these narratives have primarily attended to the ethnic homogeneity of the Kurdish people in relation to other ethnic groups. This is not different from the practices of various Arab states that often turn a blind eye to the linguistic and ethnic heterogeneity of their populations.

The Berber and Kurdish cases are similar in that the Berber and Kurdish languages have been used effectively as "othering" mechanisms, which have become a typical process in the construction of social and political identities in the post-colonial era (Critchfield, 2010; Genoni, 2010; Said, 1978). The politics of constructing the *external* "other" have played a major role in bridging the linguistic fragmentation of the various Berber and Kurdish communities. The Berber and Kurdish ethno-political movements have depended on historical narratives that justified the need for members of these two ethnicities to redraw their identity borders with the Arabic language and ethnicity being the "other." At the same time, they have challenged nation-state ideologies with ethnocentric identities in which language becomes the most critical grouping factor. This suggests that, as Bucholtz and Hall (2004, p. 371) argue, national and ethnic identities "do not coexist in the kind of multicultural harmony marketed in the mass media and promoted by liberal education. . . ." However, the Berber and Kurdish experiences differ in an important respect. In the Berber case, the religious and cultural bonds between the Berbers and the Arabs have played a major role in withholding the move for an autonomous political entity. This explains why separatist nationalism has not featured predominantly in the Berber identity discourses. In contrast, in the Kurdish case, the politics of identity construction relies on nationalist and ethnic discourses.

The current tensions between the Gulf countries and Iran are feeding the Arabs' sense of ethnic identity in the face of the so-called "Iranian threat" (Al-Nafisi, 1999). According to Al-Nafisi, the hidden war between the Gulf countries and Iran is not only ideological or political, but also ethnic and linguistic. Al-Nafisi traces the origins of the tensions between the Persians (*Al-Furs*) and the Arabs to the early Islamic conquests when the Arabs imposed their language, religion, and even culture on the Persians. According to Nafisi, the Iranians seek not only to reinstate their ethnolinguistic identity or recover their pre-Islamic edge over the Arabs, but also to fragment the Arab unified identity. The "Iranian Threat" is materialized, for example, in the Iranians' linguistic policy against the Arab Iranians in Alahwaz, its divisive policies in Iraq, Bahrain, Syria, Lebanon, Yemeni, and its *antagonistic* policies toward the Arabs in general and the Arab regimes in particular. The linguistic aspect of this threat is that the Iranians are engaged in dissolving the Arabs' authority over SA (as an Islamic symbol) by creating Arabic language centers and scholarships for non-Arab Muslims worldwide. Although not entirely new, these arguments have been echoed widely by Arab politicians, news channels, print media, and among the Arab populations. They are also widely circulated in the new media technologies. For example, the Al-Arabiya Channel website has a whole section for news on Iranian politics, which often highlights the Iranian government's "anti-Arab" policies. The new technologies are creating a heightened sense of ethnic identity among the different ethnic groups in the Middle East and North Africa by exposing their ethnic heterogeneity, their notable cultural and linguistic differences, and their conflicting self-projections in relation to one other.

5.4 RELIGIOUS IDENTITIES: MUSLIMS AND NON-MUSLIM MINORITIES

Religious identity refers to "belonging based on beliefs held in common" (Fox, 2013, p. 25). Religion becomes a main marker of identity when it incorporates spiritual beliefs and religious practices that influence a person's perceptions of him/herself in relation to others who have similar or different spiritual beliefs and religious practices. However, religion may also be part of an individual's cultural belonging (Webber, 1997). For example, some Arabs may identify themselves as Muslims because they were born to a Muslim family and because Islam is the dominant religion in the Arab culture, while they would not necessarily consider Islam as a main marker of their identity. This means that religious identity may not be relevant to every individual, speech community, society, or political entity. In the Arab region, however, religion has been an important facet of Arabic speakers' self-identification as individuals and communities, and it often interacts with language in complex ways; the Arabic language is interlinked to the religion of the majority group and it is involved in creating a sense of cohesion in the Muslim communities (Jaspal & Coyle, 2010; Rosowsky, 2007; Ward, 2000). Religious identity may not necessarily overlap with ethnic and national identities, although it may be part of either or may work against either.

Aldawri (1984) argues that, within the Arab context, different languages were relevant for different religious groups long before Islam. For example, the Jewish communities in Yemen used the Hebrew language in their rituals. With the rise of Islam in the seventh century AD, religious affiliation became intricately related to language because Arabic was the language of the Qur'an, the Prophet, and Islamic liturgy and scholarship. The main Muslim sources (the *Qur'an* and the *Hadith*) lack clear indication of the relationship between language and the Islamic faith.[7] However, the dominant voices of Islamic scholarship during the Umayyad and Abbasid reigns emphasized the superiority of Arabic, its unique aptness to encode God's last message to humanity, and its importance for understanding Islamic teachings. This is the main purport of celebrated works such as *Bayaan I'jaaz Al-Qur'an* "Explaining the Miracle of the Qur'an" by Al-Khattaabi (931–988), *I'jaaz Al-Qur'an* "Miracle of the Qur'an" by Al-Baqillani (950–1013), and *Al-Balaagha* "Eloquence" by Al-Zamakhshari (1074–1143). Islamic *fiqh* scholarship presented the rule that an obligation that cannot be fulfilled without a given means makes the means an obligation. This rule may have been derived from the second Caliph Umar Bn Al-Khattab's saying, "Learn Arabic because it is part of your religion." Thus, Muslims, regardless of their ethnic backgrounds, had to learn Arabic in order to perform the basic acts of worship. Arabic was also needed to obtain Islamic education, given the fact that most of the Islamic scholarship was written in Arabic. This allowed Muslims, regardless of their ethnic and linguistic backgrounds, to learn the Arabic language and sometimes to assimilate into the Arab–Islamic community. Arabic gradually became not only a common language among the diverse communities of Muslim adherents, but also a major symbol of Muslim identity (Chejne, 1969).

One of the key social transformations that Islam introduced was the concept of *ummah*, which joined all Muslims in a single community. This concept remains vague till our present day, mainly because the Qur'an does not specify the boundaries and the parameters of this community. However, it was the foundation of the early Muslim community in Madina that set an example of what an ummah may look like − a community of diverse racial, ethnic, cultural, and tribal backgrounds whose members are bound by a common religious, legal, and moral code. Language was not a defining factor in this community. However, by virtue of its link to the Qur'an and to the early Muslims in Madina and Mecca, Arabic came to be associated with this community. The concept of ummah has mistakenly been treated as synonymous with "nation" in the modern political sense. However, as Piscatori (1986) suggests, the concept of ummah is not grounded in politics. The concept is introduced in the Qur'an several times in reference to individuals (Chapter 16: 120), factions of a larger group (Chapter 3: 104), previous nations (Chapter 2: 134), human communities in general (Chapter 7: 34; 10: 47), and the community of believers since the time of Adam (Chapter 21: 92). This does not mean that Muslims and Islamic groups have not used this term to politicize their religious identities. What is important here is that, as Khan (1958) suggests, Islamic identity and the Arabic language have become inseparable from the concept of *religious* ummah.

Under the Ottoman rule, the Muslim Arabs' religious identity was couched within the caliphate, which, for many Muslim Arabs, then represented the Muslim ummah (Dawisha, 2002; Patel, 2013). The Ottomans presented no threat to the Muslim Arabs' sense of religious identity because, besides being Muslims themselves, they (1) recognized the status of the Arabic language at least in the religious domain, (2) used the Arabic script in writing the Turkish language, and (3) permitted the teaching of Arabic in the Turkish religious schools as a school subject. This explains the reluctance of most Muslim Arab intellectuals to agitate the prospect of the Arabs' separation from the Ottomans, even when these intellectuals criticized the Ottomans' policies in the Arab provinces and called for extensive reforms. Arab reformers, such as Abdulraħman Al-Kawaakibi (1855–1902), Abdulħamid Al-Zahrawi (1871–1916), Rafiq Al-'Aẓm (1867–1925), Shakib Arsalaan (1869–1946), called for ameliorating the status of Arabs and their language in the Ottoman state. This reformist approach also appeared in the publications of Arab associations and organizations (tanẓiimaat). For example, the first manifesto of the Arab-Ottoman Association (established in 9 August 1908) called for the self-governance of the Arabs "who possess the noble Qur'anic language and the glorious past." The manifesto also declared that the Association aimed to "elevate the status of the Arabs and the Arabic language within the Ottoman union" (cited in Aldawri, 1984, p. 198). Similarly, among the declared aims of the Arab Renaissance Association (founded in 1906) was "to revive the historic role of the Arabs by reviving the Arabic language" (cited in Aldawri, 1984,

p. 198). It seems that, to many Arabs at that time, the elevated religious status of Arabic should warrant a better recognition of the Arabs themselves.

The Europeans used religious affinity to penetrate Mount Lebanon, first, to protect the Christian communities against Druze and Shia "hostilities" and, second, to "civilize and reform the 'fanatical' and 'Mohemmedan' Ottoman Empire" (Makdisi, 1996, p. 24). Makdisi (1996) argues that some of the Christian Maronite elites appealed to the Europeans, along religious lines, to strengthen their position in the volatile Mount Lebanon. While the Maronite elites were highly skilled in Arabic, many of them embraced French as a mark of their modern Europeanized identity. In return, the French mobilized the Christian–Muslim rift to carve Lebanon out of the Syrian map, combining the religion argument with a claim of a pre-Islamic, pre-Arab Phoenician origin of Lebanese people – an argument that was then adopted and propagated by some Lebanese intellectuals. The construction of the Phoenician identity may be seen as part of the West's scheme to redefine the East (Said, 1978). Arabic was presented as an interposing language that is neither rooted in ancient Lebanon nor germane to "modern" Lebanon (especially among some of the elites who already knew the *prestigious* and *modern* French language). This pro-French position was key to the formation of Lebanon with its religion-based division of power and its secular and multilingual character. The 1943 "National Pact" allocated the presidency to Maronites, the cabinet to Sunnis, and the parliament to Shi'is, while still noting the sectarian and multilingual nature of Lebanon. The Sunnis' aspiration to align Lebanon with the pan-Arab or Greater Syrian schemes was hampered by their lack of political power, and they eventually had to learn French to be able to function in "modern" Lebanon.

During Western colonialism, localized nationalist, anti-occupation sentiments were the main umbrella under which different religious (Muslims, Christians, Druze, etc.) and ethnic (Arabs, Berbers, Kurds, etc.) groups operated against the occupying forces. This explains why religious movements were either nonexistent or largely invisible,[8] despite the colonizers' attempts to employ the rule-and-divine strategy along religious lines. In Morocco, for example, the French's attempts to privilege the Berber languages at the expense of the Arabic language were met with resistance from both the Berber and the Arab Muslims (Benmamoun, 2001; Holt, 1994). Both considered the marginalization of Arabic as an assault on their identity as Muslims. Similarly, the calls to adopt the colloquial Egyptian dialect as the national language of Egypt was seen by many educated Egyptian Muslims as a Western attempt to dismantle Egypt's Islamic identity (Suleiman, 2003). These religiously motivated reactions were not embedded within structured religious movements or organizations. Even Muslim scholars, such as Jamal Al-Diin Al-Afghani (1938–1897), who called for the adoption of the Arabic language as a marker of religious identity and a unifier of the Muslim ummah, prioritized the localization of the anti-occupation efforts in Egypt. Religious identities were quelled by the post-independence secular–nationalist discourses that insinuated the need for "citizens" to forego religious and ethnic loyalties that may inhibit Arab unity. This is not surprising because nationalist discourses have always tried to eliminate the ethnic and religious frontiers within the nation-state (Bucholtz & Hall, 2004). The power of the nationalist sentiments explains the popularity of the nationalist Abdulnasser, who silenced or eliminated every dissenting voice, including Islamic opponents like Sayyed Qutb, one of the most influential Islamic scholars in the twentieth century.

However, the failure of the secular–nationalist movements on the political and economic fronts, especially after the Arabs' 1967 defeat to Israel, gave way to the emergence of a new framework within which the Arabs' identities can recuperate, namely Islamic movements. Islamic movements (e.g., Muslim brotherhood) became increasingly politicized due to the sense of "otherness" that the secular Arab governments nurtured in these movements. As a representative of this trend, Sayyed Qutb (1906–1966) in his book *Ma'aalim Aṭ-Ṭariiq* "Milestones" argued that Arab nationalism had "lost its credibility" and called for "bringing the ummah back into existence" (p. 3). The emergent religious discourses sought to provide a new identity framework beyond the frail Arab nationalism. Although the pan-Arab and Islamic movements were in disagreement regarding the nature and boundaries of the prospective political, geographic, or religious entity that holds together and represents the Arab people, both assigned a prominent role to the Arabic language in the formation of such entities. By default, Islamist movements promoted Arabic (i.e., SA) as the language of self-representation because of its religious value (e.g., in worship) and historical role (e.g., as a container of the Arab historical and religious heritage).

The emergence of the Islamist movements and their religion-based narratives has reinvigorated religious-sectarian sentiments among minority groups as well, particularly Christian Arabs (Eid, 2003, 2007). Eid traces the emergence of these sectarian sentiments to suppressive practices during the Ottoman rule and to the intervention of the European colonial powers in the region. This may explain why Christian intellectuals in Greater Syria took the lead in promoting Arab nationalism, which, although appealed to the Arabic language, history, and heritage, sought to untangle the religious bond between the Arabs and the Turks and restore the ethnic link between Christian and Muslim Arabs. However, the decline of pan-Arabism created the need to redraw the identity lines through religious–sectarian lenses. These sectarian identities, according to Eid, were bolstered by national narratives that gave salience to Islam while marginalizing other religious communities. The espousal of the worldview of the majority religion engendered a sense of exclusion among members of the minority religions and threatened their feelings of belonging in the mainstream community. Unsurprisingly, new narratives invoked language and history to set the boundaries of the *new* religion-based identities. Thus, a constructed Pharaonic identity supported by an ancient Coptic language has come to mark the Coptic identity (Jones, 2000). Many Coptic Christians identify with the Coptic language, rather than the Arabic language (i.e., SA), because Coptic is sometimes used in religious Coptic rituals, unlike Arabic, which is associated with Islam. The Phoenician, Lebanese, transnational, or even European identities in Lebanon were linked to the linguistic diversity of Lebanon and away from the Arab identity (Shryock & Lin, 2009;

Stiffler, 2010). Again, language has been mobilized directly or indirectly to legitimize the boundaries of the emergent forms of identity.

Since the second Gulf War, sectarianism has become the dominant mode of identity expression in the Arab region. According to Makdisi (1996, p. 24), sectarianism is "antithesis of nation" because it is "constructed against a territorially-bounded liberal nation-state." Sectarianism erases language-based identity borders and recreates new boundaries based on religious–political commitments to the sect. For example, the leader of the Lebanese Hezbollah party has occasionally announced his loyalty to the Iranian religious authority (Tabarani, 2008). Such a sect-based loyalty may discredit common language, nationality, and geography as markers of identity. The current conflicts in Syria, Lebanon, Bahrain, and Yemen between Shi'is and Sunnis are underpinned by sectarian intra-linguistic, intra-national, and intra-ethnic identities. The division of Christian polities in Lebanon across sectarian lines (e.g., Maronites vs Eastern Orthodox) is another manifestation of the sect-based identities. This sectarianism is slipping into a sectisim similar to the statism discussed above, where loyalty is to an individual, rather than a social or political group. This is certainly the case in post-2003 Iraq where loyalty to a religious leader becomes the whole mark of one's self-identification. The Saudi support of the military coup against the Muslim-Brotherhood-led Egyptian government in 2013 is another manifestation of this secticism; the Saudi state, which projects itself as a representative of the Sunni order, stands against Sunni religious movements that challenge its religious authority. The trajectory of the transformation of Islamic religious identities into sectarian identities is similar to the dissolution of pan-Arab nationalism into state-based nationalism and then into statism. In his renowned *The Clash of Civilizations*, Huntington (1996) presented Muslims as a monolithic, unified group with a universal worldview and religious identity. This conceptualization runs against the current sectarian-based identity politics, which may eventually exhaust pan-Arab, pan-religious, and pan-ethnic identity forms. This constant "identity breakup" may leave the Arabic language with no strong "sponsors" as was the case with the earlier pan-Arab and pan-Islamic movements.

In most of the conferences, meetings, and intellectual productions mentioned in the previous section, the link between SA, Islamic identity, and the concept of *ummah* is often stated as a side topic because of the negative implications of the concept of ummah on the authority of Arab statisms. There is often an emphasis on the need to maintain SA for its religious value. However, while these calls may encourage individual commitments to SA, the overall social reality of the fragmented Arab region may not be as supportive of SA. The new media technologies have played a critical role in exposing and reinforcing the sect-based, patronage-driven factionalism in the Arab region, thus breaking the common belief that religions are monolithic. Thus, it is no longer possible to view religious identity as homogenous. Nor is it possible to ascertain the role of language in defining religious identity in the social sense. As noted above, the link between SA and religious identity operates on a personal level rather than on the level of social groups or communities.

5.5 IDENTIFY POLITICS AND LANGUAGE PLANNING

Language planning has often been used interchangeably with language policy,[9] both of which refer to "deliberate efforts to influence the behavior of others with respect to the acquisition, structure, or functional allocation of their language codes" (Cooper, 1989, p. 45). Researchers disagree, however, as to whether language planning is confined to *governmental* efforts to manipulate language roles and uses. Fishman (1974, p. 79) argues that "language planning refers to conscious governmental efforts to affect the structure and function of language varieties." However, Tollefson (2000, p. 13) suggests that language planning is "a wide range of governmental and non-governmental actions designed to influence language acquisition and language use." Eastman (1983, p. iv) combines the two definitions by suggesting that "language planning is done through the cooperative efforts of political, educational, economic, and linguistic authorities." Similarly, Shohamy (2006) argues that the "overt" mechanisms deployed by official bodies are just one actor in language policy; "covert" mechanisms, such as language testing and research in the linguistics field, may have an even more enduring impact. Most often, language planning is governed by official bodies that operate within a preset national–political agenda, and therefore politics and ideology are always involved in language planning. Media outlets, professional organizations, and political activists may play a role in changing aspects of language policies, but their role is typically peripheral.

Language planning involves a wide range of political, social, economic, and educational considerations because it is generally embedded within national development plans. As Reagan (2002, p. 420) suggests, "Language planning can serve as a tool for empowering groups and individuals, for creating and strengthening national bonds and ties, and for maximising educational and economic development . . . However, language planning can also be used to maintain and perpetuate oppression, social class discrimination, and social and educational inequity . . ." In this section, however, the focus is on language planning only as it relates to identity dynamics. As Wright (2004) argues, identity politics are at the heart of language planning, and they may determine the success or failure of language policies. Language planning is an important indicator of identity dynamics in the Arab region for a number of reasons. First, the Arab region is diverse ethnically, culturally, and religiously, and, therefore, language planning may reflect how the relationships among the diverse groups are linguistically structured and perceived. Second, language planning is generally received differently by majority and minority social groups, and, therefore, it may demonstrate the attitudes of these groups toward the different community languages and the values that they assign to these languages. Last, language policies during the eras of Ottoman and European control of the Arab region were a primary motive of Arab political activism, particularly with respect to its emphasis on restoring the role of Arabic in the Arabic-speaking communities in the face of Turkish/English/French. Hence, language policies may underscore the projection of Arab identity in relation to "other" sociopolitical orders and languages.

Language planning in the post-independence Arab states sought to undo the culturally hegemonic policies of the colonial powers, to turn back the tides of French and English, and to assert the unique identity of the Arab people. These post-independence language policies were largely a reaction to colonial language policies that sought to exclude Arabic from the public domain in general and from official, political, and educational domains in particular.[10] Among the various languages and language varieties available in the Arab region (e.g., Berber and Kurdish), SA was particularly targeted because it is a main emblem of Arab unity and Islamic identity – two main paradigms that threatened to undermine the colonial presence in the Arab region. Speaking of the linguistic situation of Arabic in the Moroccan context during the French occupation, Benmamoun (2001, p. 100) suggests that "The linguistic dimension of this [French] educational policy was to avoid giving any prominent position to Arabic within the Berber community, since Arabic was the language of Islam, the faith of both Arabs and Berbers, and also the linguistic anchor that linked the Maghreb to the East." Although Arabic was designated as an official language along with French and English in most Arab states, these languages enjoyed more prestige than Arabic and prevailed in key domains, such as media, administration, technology, and higher education (Shaaban, 2006). Such a privileged position of French and English presented the risk of acculturating the Arab youth into Western values and lifestyles and enforced a linguistic reality that negates the national, ethnic, and religious identities of the majority of the local people.

In addition to privileging their own languages, the British and French led the initiative of promoting QA in education and Arab societies in general. The call to adopt QA in education and other formal spheres under the British and French occupations was inspired by three developments: (1) the establishment of various QA-focused programs across Europe starting from the eighteenth century (e.g., in Naples, Vienna, London, etc.), (2) linguistic studies on the structure of QA (e.g., those carried out by Wilhelm Spitta, Carl Vollers, Selden Willmore), and (3) publications explicating the advantages of adopting QA in reading and writing in the early twentieth century (e.g., Salama Musa, Qasim Amin, William Willcocks) (for a detailed review, see Al-Sa'di, 2012; Suleiman, 2003, 2011). The call to adopt QA was most vigorous in Egypt, but with implications far beyond the Egyptian borders. Given the sociopolitical status of Egypt in the Arab region, the Egyptian model would be followed by the Arab states. In Algeria, the French used QA-based textbooks in many Algerian schools (Dawood, 2012). The promotion of QA was based on the rationale that QA is easier than SA, capable of absorbing modern science, congruent with the modern nation, and reflective of the local thought and literature. For Arab nationalists, however, the mere fact that the colloquial dialects were promoted by the colonial powers made them unsuitable representative for national identity (Suleiman, 2003). Moreover, the prospect of Arab unity rests largely on the Arab linguistic homogeneity, which would be defied by the existence of several national varieties. Thus, the attempts to recognize QA were resisted resolutely by pan-Arab nationalists because of their weakening effects on counter-occupation and pan-Arab sentiments. They were also opposed by many Muslim scholars because of their harmful effects on SA. It is interesting that works focusing on QA are still often met with suspicion because they seek to legitimize a variety that is seen to have "no roots" in the early Arab history, no rules or standards, and no general acceptability among most Arab intellectuals (Al-Sa'di, 2012; Dawoord, 2012; Mejdell, 2006; Versteegh, 2001).

The post-independence language policies across the various Arab states adopted SA as the national and official language to be used in administration, education, and media. The selection of SA to be the official and national language of all Arab states reflects the post-independence governments' assertion of their linguistic independence from the colonial powers and their aspiration to maintain the linguistic link between the different Arab countries (Ennaji, 1997; Marley, 2004; Sulieman, 2003). As Sadiqi (2006b, p. 15) notes, this coordinated effort to institutionalize SA in the administration, education, and media "was needed for cultural unity and cultural identity of newly independent countries in a specific historical era where such unity made genuine political sense." Given its rootedness in the Arab consciousness, SA reflects the Arabs' long history and heritage, their linguistic unity, and their unique identity. Moreover, the Arabicization policies allowed the generally elevated SA to occupy domains formerly reserved to the prestigious English and French languages. Language planners hoped that, with the increasing literacy rates, speakers from different parts of the Arab World would be able to communicate using SA (Abdulaziz, 1986).

Although all the independent Arab states pursued Arabicization, they followed different routes in implementing this policy with the expected result that the outcome of this policy was dissimilar. In Syria, for example, the Arabicization policy started shortly after the Turks' withdrawal from the Arab region and before the French occupied Syria in 1920. Within this short period, two official institutions were established in 1919: the Knowledge Bureau and the Arab Academy. These two bodies undertook several tasks, the most important of which was "purifying" SA from Turkish words, "modernizing" SA, Arabicizing education, creating textbooks that conform to specific SA-based standards, and training teachers in SA (Shahiid, 2002). The Arabicization was halted during the French occupation, but resumed its course after Syria's independence from France in 1946. The period after independence witnessed the Arabicization of education from pre-school to college, the creation of several specialized dictionaries (e.g., the Arabic Medicine Dictionary in 1956), the use of Arabic in teaching all disciplines, including medicine, and the development of Arabic mathematical symbols and expressions (Shahiid, 2002). The Syrian Arabicization experience is generally considered the most pervasive and successful among all other Arabicization experiences because of its ability to Arabicize all disciplines and to produce graduates who can compete internationally. Al-Sibaa'i (2000, cited in Shahiid, 2002) examined the test scores obtained from medical exams in the United States. He found that the average scores of the Syrian physicians are higher than those of the international average, even though the exams were in English and the language of instruction in the Syrian medical schools was SA.

The Arabicization policy has been proceeding less smoothly in the Maghreb because of the complexity of the multilingual situation, the identity tensions, and the persistent influence of French in language policies. In Algeria, the Arabicization experience focused on SA because of its unifying influence after the French have used the colloquial Algerian dialect and Berber to rule and divide the country (Ager, 2001; Buziani, 2012; Dawood, 2012). Ager (2001, p. 21) notes, "Because the French had defined Classical Arabic as a foreign language in 1938, rejecting it for internal use, it became the sole official and national language in 1963." In other words, SA represented the identity of the unified Algeria state in opposition to the French identity of the colonized Algeria, which favored French, Algerian Arabic, and Berber. However, the deep-rootedness of French in the social system, the resistance of the pro-French Algerian elites who had political and/or economic ties with the French, and the lack of trained teachers and teaching materials were main obstacles to the full implementation of the Arabicization policy. This has necessitated the amendment of this policy more than once. Thus, in 1976, the Algerian government banned the use of "any foreign inscriptions in a foreign language" (Mostari, 2004, p. 28). In 1977, it reacted to the lack of SA-speaking staff by importing a large number of Egyptian teachers (Ager, 2001). In 1998, the Algerian government issued the General Use of the Arabic Language Law, which required the use of Arabic in all government and public spheres. While this policy was notably successful at the school level, it was not so at the college level because of the privatization of some Higher Level Institutions and the need to produce graduates who can function in companies owned by French businessmen or pro-French Algerians. Moreover, the colonially propagated notion that SA is incompatible with modern science still persists (Dawood, 2012). Thus, SA is now used for teaching subjects in the humanities and social sciences, whereas French is still used in teaching science, medicine, and engineering.

The Algerian Arabicization experience is not very different from its counterparts in the rest of the Arab states. SA is considered as a main marker of the Arab states' "national" identities (along with Berber in the case of Morocco and Kurdish in the case of Iraq). In most Arab countries nowadays, SA is taught at all school levels, while it is one of the languages used at the college level – together with English or French. The various pitfalls that have attended the experience of Arabicization within the various Arab states have rejuvenated the calls for the adoption of the local QA dialects in education and in other social spheres, and some have ignited the identity tensions already in place in the region. For example, Francophones in Algeria, Morocco, and Tunisia see the adoption of SA as a form of trading the "modern" Algerian/Moroccan/Tunisian identity for a more traditional, pre-modern national identity (Chakrani, 2010). Similarly, the Kurds in Syria look at Arabicization as a form of linguistic and cultural hegemony that negates the existence of the Kurdish language. The challenges posed by language diversity and identity dynamics in a number of Arab countries, particularly in view of the "incomplete success" or "failure" of the Arabicization policies, may in due course entail revising the existing language policies and giving more prominence to QA. The thrust in this direction is signaled by the intermittent calls and efforts to codify QA.

The call to codify QA, recognize its national status, and adopt it in education rests on a number of arguments, most of which were promoted earlier by the nation-state nationalists (Suleiman, 2003). A first rationale for adopting the QA varieties as official languages, written and spoken, is the prospect of canceling out the problem of Arabic diglossia and creating a situation where QA varieties become the norm not only in everyday speech but in formal domains (e.g., education). A second justification for espousing the QA varieties as official languages is the difficulty of learning SA, particularly for elementary-level students (Ayari, 1996; Maamouri, 1998). A third major reason is that the time that students use for learning SA can be utilized more fruitfully to learn school subjects through QA, their mother tongue, which is more accessible to them. Among the contemporary advocates of the adoption of dialects as national languages are Nour Al-Diin Ayyoush in Morocco and Said Akil in Lebanon, the latter has been using Roman letters in his later publications to encode the Lebanese dialect (Aqil, 1961). The proposals to adopt QA as an official language are often encountered by resistance at the official, intellectual, and public levels. As noted above, the adoption of QA is not merely a threat to the status of SA, as a symbol of common Arab heritage and history, but also a menace to the notions of Arab and Muslim identity.

It should be noted that, even among those who emphasize the integrity of SA and its inseparability from Arab and Muslim identity, there is an increasing recognition of the need to "modernize" or "simplify" SA to absorb technological and scientific terms and expressions, to cope with the demands of the technological age, and to be accessible to its learners, both children and adults (Haeri, 2000; Qaymasoon, 2013). Researchers have presented a wide range of modernization/simplification schemes, which affect lexical selection (e.g., using words that are shared between SA and QA), grammar (e.g., dropping case declensions), orthography (e.g., consistent use of diacritics), dictionary (coordinated efforts to standardize foreign words and neologisms), and uses (functions that are similar in SA and QA) (see Al-Toma, 1961; Maamouri, 1998 for a review). Although these changes are projected to maintain the general structure and character of SA, some religious traditionalists and Arab classicists insist on maintaining the "pristine" nature of SA because of the interdependency of the Qur'an and the Arabic language (Al-Sa'di, 2012; Chejne, 1969). Most advocates of this trend are classical literature enthusiasts and religious figures or groups, like most Wahhabi scholars. In this case, language planning is as much about communicative utility as about identity maintenance.

Another challenge to the Arabicization policies and to the link between the Arabic language and Arab identity concerns the influence of English and French in Arab region (Randall & Samimi, 2010; Zakharia, 2008). French and English are still used in teaching science, engineering, and medicine in most Arab countries. They are taught as "foreign languages" starting in elementary school, and sometimes they carry more weight than Arabic in the grading schemes in most private schools across the Arab region. A growing number of private schools use English/French as the medium of instruction. English and French are increasingly used in business and technology-related fields. Language planners who rejected the role of colonial languages (British and French) are now faced with the question of how to regulate the presence of English and French in schools, academia, media, and public domains. For language planners, the goal of redeeming the Arab states' linguistic and cultural identity through the post-independence language policies is no longer a realistic undertaking. Therefore, the main question is how language policies can strike a balance between maintaining the role of Arabic in education and society while still promoting English/French for national development, global communication, and international economic competitiveness. Language policies in the Arab region seem to lack a definite answer to this fundamental question. This may explain the absence of clear vision concerning the place and function of these languages in education. Language planners are also faced with another challenge concerning the Arabicization of English terms in science and technology disciplines. As Shaaban (2006, p. 703) suggests, "educational authorities claim that because of the need for modernization and technology and its fruits, they cannot afford to wait for academics to coin new terms; thus, they argue for retaining a major role for foreign language in education."

The expanding role of English, in conjunction with the spread of globalization, raises the question of whether Arabic can still be used as a marker of Arab identity. In their study of the status of Arabic and English in Dubai, Randall and Samimi (2010) found that English is replacing Arabic as the lingua franca at all levels of the society. Although Arabic is the official language of the United Arab Emirates, the question of official language becomes irrelevant because of the mismatch between the national language policy and the social reality. Al-Muhammadi (2013) argues that Arabic is the third or fourth spoken language in the Gulf after English, Hindi, and Urdu due to the notable presence of Asian workers. Tosco and Manfredi (2013) point to the emergence of pidginized forms of Arabic across the Arab region due to the contact of Arabic with other languages. The phenomenon is most transparent in the Gulf region where speakers of Arabic customarily adapt their speech to accommodate the Asian workers (Bakir, 2010; Næss, 2008; Smart, 1990). Zakharia (2008, p. iii) found that, despite the politicized promotion of Arabic in Lebanese education, "mundane school practices served to undermine the Arabic language" for the sake of French and English. Siraaj (2013) points out the emergence of the Arabizi dialect where English and Arabic are mixed in a systematic way in the Lebanese context in particular (see Chapter 8). Studies in the Gulf region also show that many parents are favoring schools that use English as the language of instruction to those that use Arabic (Al-Muhammadi, 2013; Randall & Samimi, 2010). The effects of globalization on the Arab societies have been felt at all levels, but its role in shaking an important anchor of Arabs' collective identity, namely the Arabic language, is becoming more and more tangible.

One of the main concerns recently raised in the Arab intellectual and educational circles is how to instill a sense of belonging and identity in Arab children and youth, given their daily exposure to non-Arabic languages in the educational systems, media, and societies at large. This concern has become the topic of much discussion in the Arab region in the past two decades or so (e.g., Al-Ḍabiib, 2001; Al-Jaabiri, 1995; Al-Muusa, 2003; Al-Saḥmaraani, 2002; Bayyoumi, 2005). It was also one of the main motives for the 2008 Damascus Meeting, which was attended by scholars from different Arab countries. The Meeting issued a statement titled, "My Homeland, My Identity, and My Pride," the essence of which is how to instate a sense of identity among Arab children and youth. It is interesting that the statement's title uses the word *watani* "my homeland," which refers to the independent Arab states. An important stream of research in this area centers on the question of whether education can undertake the role of upholding the Arab identity in the face of the failures of the Arab political and social systems to ensure that Arab children continue to have a sense of belonging to their specific countries or to the Arab *culture* (Abdulaliim, 2012; Nourddiin, 2012; Qaymasoon, 2013). This approach to the identity crisis narrows the scope of language planning to the educational realm, particularly educational curricula. The argument is that, because the new Arab generations are becoming "lost" in the sense that they feel no strong attachment to their Arab identity, the instructional curricula have to find innovative ways to reorient the Arab generations to their heritage. One of the main functions of education in this respect is to nurture Arab children's confidence in the Arabic language, its power, and its relevance for their identity. As Rayhaan (2012) suggests, the main dilemma nowadays is that the Arab generation have lost their faith in the importance of Arabic language for Arab unity and their own lives. It is possible that Arab children have come to depreciate the Arabic language due to their growing frustration with the political, economic, and social situation of the Arabs societies, which impacts their attitudes toward the language. This may explain the recurring calls in the Arab region to nurture children's sense of pride in themselves and their language (Qaymasoon, 2013).

Education is also called upon to preserve the identity of the Arabic language itself. Many Arabic speakers are no longer able to use SA effectively in their speech. This appears not only at the level of school children or university graduates, but also at the level of professional broadcasters, politicians, and teachers, who either infuse their SA-based speech with colloquialisms and foreign words or make mistakes in their speech (Hamaada, 2012; Nourddiin, 2012). Thus, the lack of SA model, which is supposed to be illustrated best in education and media, is absent. It is feared that, in the long run, the structure and form of SA will be "deformed" by the consistent erroneous use (Nourddiin, 2012). Zuwaini (2012, pp. 3–5) argues that the broadcasters' and journalists' "non-eloquent" use of SA, the use of foreign language over the internet, the lack of qualified teachers of SA, and the Arabic speakers' dominant use of the colloquial varieties even in educational settings "under the pretext of language simplification" will expose SA to "erosion" and "attrition" and will eventually change its established norms and character. According to Zuwaini, "Elementary and secondary education are the basic foundations for mastering the national language, and that is why language planning should start with these." A symposium titled "The Phenomenon of Linguistic Incompetence at the College Stage" was held in Saudi Arabia in 1994 to discuss the weak abilities of Arab college students in SA and the possible ways to overcome it. One of the main recommendations of the symposium was, "reforming the curricula for teaching the Arabic language at all educational levels as well as the teaching methods used in it in such a way to preserve its originality and purity and facilitate – at the same time, its understanding and use." What is interesting is that the status of SA, which was taken for granted after the Arab states' independence, is highly contested today. Thus, Arab intellectuals have to elaborately justify the importance of SA for the Arab and Muslim identity. It is also illuminating that the current discourse with regard to language planning has been narrowed down to focus on more realistic issues that reflect the current politically and linguistically fragmented conditions of the Arab region.

5.6 LANGUAGE ATTITUDES, IDENTITY STATEMENTS, AND IDENTITY ACTS

As noted above, the construction of social identities rests heavily on forging discursive narratives that claim a number of historical commonalities (e.g., origin, language, and shared territory) for a given group. These discursive narratives often seek to legitimize the group's constructed versions of history and its claim to political statehood. However, historical narratives are not the only way through which social actors create their social and personal identities. Cummins (2000) argues that social actors may enact their identity through "identity statements," which often articulate their language attitudes and at the same time establish their identities in relation to other speakers and social groups. Le Page and Tabouret-Keller (1985) describes speakers' *use* of language to mark their identities as "acts of identity," through which they *enact* their identities rather than describe them. Similarly, Pennycook (2004) maintains that, rather than being a pre-given, identity is constructed through social and cultural performances. Irvine and Gal (2000) suggest that speakers may *iconize* their identities by using language to draw their particular characteristics. Identity statements and identity acts are important tools for identity construction because they may index one's belonging to a given social group and reveal the pragmatic and sociolinguistic dynamics involved in identity creation and indexation. Since they are often realized in interactions, identity statements and acts may also reveal how speakers use their agency in "identity negotiation" with other interlocutors (Eckert, 2000; Fowler, 1985; Goodwin, 2003; Rampton, 1995).

One of the questions surrounding identity dynamics in the Arabic diglossic situation concerns Ferguson's definition of SA as "transposed/superposed" variety (Ferguson, 1959a; Kaye, 1972; Walters, 2003). This term has been used in bilingual contexts where a foreign language accruing power and prestige from a previous asymmetric, often colonial, relationship is superimposed on a local and low-prestige language (e.g., Appel & Muysken, 1987; De Fina, 2007; Heller, 1992; Heugh, 2002). In these contexts, the local variety is often employed strategically to resist the superposed variety and to assert the group's local identity. While previous studies suggest that the expression of identity is often carried out through the local variety, Albirini (2011) shows that Arab and Muslim identities are expressed by the so-called superposed variety, namely SA. Albirini observes that the participants used SA consistently to mobilize the concept of *ummah* "nation," which often has pan-Arab[11] and pan-Islamic connotations. The link between SA and Arab/Muslim identity suggests that this variety is viewed, not as a superposed, but a local language that represents the Arabic-speaking communities. Speakers externalize their belief in the *localness* of SA by creating a link between themselves, their Arab or Muslim identity, and the use of SA. Similarly, in her study of the accommodation strategies deployed by Tunisian participants in their interactions with their Middle Eastern Arab counterparts, Shiri (2002) found that Tunisian speakers index their membership in the wider Arab community through using linguistic forms that approximate SA. The use of SA in these studies may be seen as an act of identity that reveals the intricate relationship between SA and ingroup Arab identity.

The association between SA and pan-Arab or Muslim identity has also been observed among Arabs and Muslims in the diaspora. Rouchdy (2013, p. 143) argues that "the classical/standard form of Arabic creates a sense of ethnic identity among Arab Americans who belong to different speech communities." According to Rouchdy, SA is the variety that Arabs and Muslims learn together in religious institutions and use in religious and social gatherings, and it is the language through which they distinguish themselves from non-Arab speakers. Thus, SA erases ethnic and geographical boundaries between different Arab and Muslim nationals to create a sense of a unified Muslim or pan-Arab identity. In their study of non-Arab Muslims in Britain, Jaspal and Coyle (2010) and Rosowsky (2007) found that non-Arab Muslims associate SA, rather than their mother tongues, with their collective Muslim identity. Moreover, they prefer to index their religious identity through SA and not through their "ethnic languages." García-Sánchez (2010) also found that Moroccan immigrants in Spain maintain their ethnic and religious identity through learning and using of SA in their daily lives. Similarly, Ouassini (2013) observed that Spanish Moroccans rely on different cultural resources, including the Arabic language, to mark their Arab–Islamic identity in the face of the increasing "Islamophobia" that they face in Spain. Seymour-Jorn (2004) and Temples (2013) found that Arab Americans embrace SA as a marker of their religious identity and they enact this adoption by using Arabic within their families and communities. All of these studies suggest that SA may not be described as "superposed" but a local variety that is mobilized to mark or enact ingroup identity.

The relationship between SA and Arab or Muslim identity, however, is not always straightforward. For example, dealing with the topic of language accommodation between different Arab nationals, Abu-Melhim (1992) found that, when speakers try to pinpoint their distinct national identities, they retain their national dialects and resist acts of linguistic accommodation. Haeri (1997, 2003) observed that, although her participants associate SA with their Muslim and pan-Arab identities, their language behavior did not always reflect their assertions. Haeri's observation highlights the fact that language attitudes may not always reflect language behavior. This means that there is not always a definite link between identity statements and a certain code; the link is eventually enacted by social actors themselves. Zakharia (2008) contends that Arabic is ideologically accruing greater power as a marker of the unified Lebanese identity, though in practice French and English have a stronger hold of the sociolinguistic reality of the sectarian Lebanon. Bitar (2011) found that Palestinians in the diaspora affiliate with SA as a marker of their pan-Arab identity as well as with the Levantine dialect to mark their unique Palestinian identity. A similar finding is reported by Albirini (2014b), who argues that, for Palestinians, language may be one of the strongest links to their Arab and Palestinian roots in a world where many Palestinians feel strongly about the need to maintain those ties. This may also have to do with their attempts to foster a sense of community in the face of identity risks that they face as a displaced and minority group.

Identity construction in everyday interactions is often governed by pragmatic factors. Speakers may use their linguistic package to manage their self-representation in relation to other speakers and maximize their benefit from social interactions with different speakers. Albirini (2014a) reports that Bedouin speakers use their Bedouin dialects in Bedouin events and gatherings, whereas they resort to the urban/rural dialect in the workplace. In Bedouin-specific events, the Bedouin dialect becomes a valued linguistic and cultural resource because it helps Bedouins index their Bedouin identities, which in turn guarantees their positions in tribe-based networks. In the workplace, however, the Bedouins use the urban or rural dialect to build social relationships and networks with the urban and rural people. The use of urban or rural dialect helps the Bedouins to project themselves as insiders within the workplace social networks. Suleiman (1993) found that Bedouin speakers switch to the rural and urban dialects in the multi-ethnic Jordan to express common national identity with speakers of these dialects. Albirini (in progress) indicates that, in cases of identity conflicts, Arabs from different nationalities may use their language repertoires to revoke one form of identity and reconstruct another form that harmonizes with their goals. Similarly, Shiri (2002) shows that language accommodation may be the outcome of identity negotiation. Focusing on the Iraqi situation, Abu-Haidar (1996) found that her Sunni Muslim participants used fossilized borrowings from Turkish and similar naming techniques as part of their religious identity, unlike the Shi'a participants who did not subscribe to this practice. However, the Shi'a participants used Turkish forms in their interaction with the then-dominant Sunni group. Identity negotiation may thus result in linguistic convergence or divergence with the interlocutors (Giles et al. 1991).

In multilingual contexts, as in Lebanon and the Maghreb, different language varieties may be associated with different identities. For example, in Lebanon, French is often used as a marker of Francophone identity, whereas Arabic is used as a marker of Arab heritage and belonging (Abou, Kaspartan, & Haddad, 1996; Al-Battal, 2002; Daoud, 2012; Joseph, 2004, Nasr, 2010; Zakharia, 2008). More recently, English has become an important player in the Lebanese linguistic landscape, which is often used to project a modern transnational identity (Daoud, 2012; Nasr, 2010; Zakharia, 2008). Joseph (2004) indicates that, during the Ottoman rule, French was adopted mostly by educated Maronites and Roman Catholics, whereas English was embraced by Muslims and Orthodox Christians. Although French gained more popularity among all religious groups during and shortly after the French occupation, the eruption of the civil war in 1975 reinstated the French–English dichotomy. In particular, the Maronites and Roman Catholics came to emphasize their unique Lebanese Christian identity through the use of French, which also sets them apart from the Muslim community. Abou, Kaspartan, & Haddad (1996) found that, during this period, 50% of the French speakers were Maronites compared to 25% French-speaking Muslims. After the civil war, Joseph (2004) notes, Christian and Muslim groups became more inclined to use English as a second language. In his study of advertisements on Lebanon-based television channels, Nasr (2010) found that most television advertisements interweave Arabic with English and French to represent a hybrid Lebanese cultural identity that is sensitive to the linguistic and cultural diversity in Lebanon. Daoud (2012) examined the speeches of two politicians, a Shi'i and a Maronite, in the light of the current sectarian tensions in Lebanon. Daoud (2012) observes that language is used to define one's sectarian identity, to create ingroup cohesion, and to defile the "other," while still claiming representativeness of the Lebanese "nation." It is clear that identity statements and identity acts in Lebanon change according to the sociopolitical climate in the country.

Some of the early studies on the language–identity link in Morocco suggest that Moroccans associate SA with their religious, pan-Arab, and Moroccan identity, whereas French is linked to modern identities[12] (Bentahila, 1983a; Mouhssine, 1995). In some cases, however, French is presented as a threat to the local forms of identity. Redouane (1998), for example, asserts that SA is "the mother tongue" of Moroccans and one that represents their cultural identity, whereas the continued use of French presents the prospect of "loss of identity." Such statements were widespread after the Arabicization policy, and they sought to reaffirm the national identity of Moroccans in the face of their former colonizers (Bentahila, 1983a). However, more recent studies, especially after the official recognition of Berber language and the establishment of Institut Royal de la Culture Amazighe in 2001, suggest that language–identity ideologies focus more on issues of multilingualism, locality, modernity, globalism, and prestige. Sadiqi (2003) argues that Berber women in Morocco use various types of "loanwords" from Moroccan Arabic to form composite identities, which is a form of "prestige." Marley (2004) found that her participants saw SA as a representative of their religious identity, whereas Moroccan Arabic and Berber represented the local Moroccan identity. In contrast, Chakrani (2010) found that his participants associate French with the identity of the global modern citizen, even though they consider it as a "local" language. Similarly, SA contests French in terms of locality and modernity, although it is associated more with religious identity and Arab culture and traditions. Several recent studies point to a tendency among the Moroccan youth to embrace multilingualism – a pattern that coincides with the emergence of a new form of Moroccan-ness where Arab–Islamic identity is represented by SA and Berber identity is represented by the Berber language (Anderson, 2013; Todd, 2011). French and English, as global languages, are both accepted for their utilitarian uses (Anderson, 2013). For example, Marley (2004) found that, although participants saw SA as the "national language," they were still in favor of bilingualism, which merits openness to other cultures as an advantage for future success.

It should be noted that, when they employ identity statements or identity acts to construct their preferred identities, social actors are usually attentive to the dominant historical narratives running in their societies. Identity statements and acts often reproduce the grand narratives at a given historical moment and reflect the ambient political atmosphere. This pattern applies more to dominant groups than to minority groups. Members of the minority groups often use language to counteract the dominant narratives (Heller, 1988).

5.7 CASE STUDY

This case study focuses on identity sentiments as reported, conceptualized, and practiced in Egypt, Jordan, Morocco, and Saudi Arabia. In addition, the section examines the relationship between identity sentiments, on one hand, and, on the other, language attitudes, ethnic membership, religious membership, and other demographic variables. These relationships may provide insights into whether Arabs see themselves as one group, whether they see language as part of their shared Arabness, and which language variety is associated with their Arab identity. The data used in this section is collected from an identity scale in the questionnaire, in-depth interview questions, and observations of verbal behavior. A decision had to be made about the specific type of identity to be examined among the multiple forms of identity characterizing Arabic speakers' personal and social selves. In the questionnaire, the focus is only on *ethnic* identity because ethnicity cuts across a number of identity-related contrasts. For example, Arab ethnicity is partly involved in nationalist pan-Arab identities as well as in Muslim identity. Moreover, as noted above, ethnic identity is currently more active across the Arab region than pan-Arab and pan-Islamic forms of identity. The inclusion of multiple forms of identity would have made the questionnaire too long for the participants to complete in thirty minutes. However, the in-depth interview questions were dedicated to more specific issues about different forms of identity that the participants may claim in relation to the language varieties under study. Last, I report on the enactment of identity through verbal practices and performances. The use of multiple methods may provide a better understanding of identity practices in the Arab region. Unless specified otherwise, the terms "Arab identity" or "identity" are used in reference to the "ethnic" form of identity throughout this section.

5.7.1 Questionnaire

In the questionnaire, the identity scale assessed the extent to which the participants (1) felt positively about Arab ethnicity, (2) felt attached to members, groups, or organizations of this ethnic group, and (3) appreciated the sociocultural expressions and activities associated with Arab ethnicity. The identity scale consisted of twelve items, which were quantified using a 5-point, Likert-type scale, ranging from *strongly agree (4)*, *agree (3)*, *neutral (2)*, *disagree (1)*, to *strongly disagree (0)*. The range of possible mean scores was between 4 and 0, with higher scores indicating a greater sense of identity. Prior to conducting the analysis, the scoring of all negatively stated items was reversed. Tables 10 and 11 summarize the percent distribution, means, and standard deviations of the scores derived from the identity scale data.

As the percent distribution of the responses in Table 5.1 shows, the majority of the participants' responses fell under the "strongly agree" and "agree" categories.[13] Thus, the participants in the four groups had comparably very favorable or favorable views of the Arab identity in terms of feeling positively about the Arab ethnicity, associating with members or groups of Arab background, and valuing

Table 5.1 Percent distribution of responses on the identity scale

	Strongly disagree	*Disagree*	*Neutral*	*Agree*	*Strongly agree*
Egyptians	8.05	8.00	13.95	14.00	56.00
Jordanians	6.17	9.18	15.73	20.13	48.79
Moroccans	10.35	8.64	15.01	19.31	46.69
Saudis	4.11	8.98	14.15	21.14	51.61

Table 5.2 Mean and standard deviation scores on the identity scale

	Mean	*Standard deviation*
Egyptians	3.02	0.47
Jordanians	2.96	0.49
Moroccans	2.84	0.52
Saudis	3.07	0.30

the traditions and practices associated with the Arab culture. The participants' overall feelings toward their identity were close to positive with an overall mean score of 3.02, 2.96, 2.84, and 3.07 (out of 4) for the Egyptian, Jordanian, Moroccan, and Saudi participants, respectively. The participating Moroccans, Jordanians, and Egyptians showed greater variance in their responses than the Saudis because of the ethnic diversity in these countries compared to Saudi Arabia. As noted in the previous chapter, a notable portion of the participants in the Moroccan context were non-Arabs (mostly Berber). A smaller proportion of the Jordanian and Egyptian participants also identified themselves as non-Arabs (see Chapter 4).

With regard to the relationship between identity and other variables, the correlations in Table 5.3 point to a significantly positive relationship between identity sentiments and ethnic membership for all of the participating groups; unsurprisingly, participants who identified themselves as Arabs had higher Arab-identity sentiments than those who did not. Ethnicity is the foundation upon which many Arabs nowadays claim their common history and heritage. It is also the yardstick against which non-Arabs claim their distinct identities, which separates them from Arabs even when Arab and non-Arab groups may share national and religious identities. In the case of Egypt, a significantly positive relationship was also found between identity sentiments and religious membership ($r = .183$); Egyptian participants who identified themselves as Muslims had more favorable Arab-identity sentiments than those who did not. There is no doubt that some Muslim Egyptians do embrace a unique Egyptian identity and negate their affinity to the larger Arab World (Hammond, 2007; Kayyali, 2006). The data, however, shows that Muslim Egyptians are more likely to associate with the Arab ethnic

Table 5.3 Summary of the correlation matrix of Arab ethnic identity and other variables

| | Arab ethnic identity | | | |
	Egyptian	Jordanian	Moroccan	Saudi
SA attitudes	.405**	.230**	.188*	.475**
QA attitudes	−.074	.160*	.139	.194*
English attitudes	−.142	−.091	−.059	.107
French attitudes	−.063	−.048	−.126	.018
Other attitudes	.002	−.405**	−.129	−.147
Ethnic membership	.252**	.314**	.725**	N/A
Religious membership	.183*	−.003	−.099	N/A
Gender	−.020	−.068	.060	N/A
Specialty	.100	.039	−.013	−.006
No. of languages	−.145	−.027	−.064	.012

** = Correlation is significant at the 0.01 level; * = Correlation is significant at the 0.05 level

identity than non-Muslim Egyptians. An interesting area for future investigation is the impact of religious and ethnic backgrounds on state-based nationalism, and the individual and combined effects of these three forms of identity on language attitudes, language choice, and language use.

A significantly positive correlation was found between identity feelings and language attitudes toward SA across the four groups; participants who had positive identity feelings also displayed positive attitudes to SA. The connection between identity sentiments and SA attitudes across the four groups underscores the role of SA in the Arabs' sense of linguistic and ethnic fellowship. This function of SA is not new to many Arabs. What is novel, however, is that QA attitudes are positively related to Arab ethnic identity for two groups: the Jordanian and Saudi participants ($r = .160$; $r = .194$, respectively); Jordanian and Saudi informants with positive Arab-identity feelings have positive attitudes toward QA. To explain this, a number of sociohistorical factors need to be invoked. Starting with Jordan, this country has received steady waves of immigrants and refugees from other Arab countries, such as Iraq, Lebanon, Libya, and Syria. One of the distinctive features of the Jordanian society is that Arab nationals are generally identified by their state nationalities. For example, an Iraqi named Sami is normally called Sami the Iraqi rather than just Sami. The speakers' dialects become critical in identifying their Jordanian or non-Jordanian identity, and this may give salience to QA as a marker of Arab identification. Thus, QA is implicated in defining Arabness at a more refined level by marking the distinction between Jordanian Arabs and non-Jordanian Arabs. The Saudis also have a heightened sense of Saudi identity due to the socioeconomic conditions of many Saudis, especially in comparison to many Arab nationals who work in Saudi Arabia, and the fact that Saudi Arabia contains some of the holiest Muslim sites. From an attitudinal perspective, many Saudis believe that their dialect is close to SA. This is possibly based on the assumption that the current inhabitants of Saudi Arabia are descendants of old Arab tribes that inhabited Arabia before Islam. In fact, a significant portion of the Riyadh population still affiliate themselves with particular clans and tribes with long-held roots in the region. On these bases, the Saudi dialect(s) may be seen as being related to Arabness as an ethnic category.

The Egyptian and Moroccan participants diverge from their Jordanian and Saudi counterparts in that their identity sentiments are not related to QA attitudes. A possible explanation for the Egyptian case is that some Egyptians see no link between the Egyptian dialect and Arab ethnicity, that is, the Egyptian dialect is related only to their unique Egyptian identity (Suleiman, 2003, 2011). By the same token, other Egyptians may separate QA from the Arab ethnic identity as a reaction to calls for linking the Egyptian dialect to the Egyptian identity. For this group, it is SA, rather than the Egyptian dialect, that marks the Arabness of Egyptians. The Moroccan case is even more complicated. As Benmamoun (2001) argues, the fact that the Moroccan dialect was promoted during the colonial period makes it unsuitable candidate for the Arab ethnic and cultural affiliation. Moreover, many Berber speakers may readily embrace SA as part of their Muslim identity, but may not do so for the Moroccan dialect because it is the defining line between two communities that share their religious and national identities, but diverge in their ethnic identities. In short, in the Egyptian and Moroccan contexts, QA is associated with the colonial experience, with attempts to isolate Egypt and Morocco from the wider Arab context, and with ethnic divisions within the Egyptian and Moroccan societies. QA does not have these connotations in the Jordanian and Saudi contexts, which may explain its association with the Arab ethnic identity along with SA.

No significant relationship was found between the participants' identity feelings and their attitudes toward English or French. The fact that the participants' identity sentiments did not have an adverse impact on their attitudes toward English and French suggests that these languages are approached more pragmatically than socioaffectively. If we consider the reportedly declining use of SA among the young Arab generation (Al-Sa'di, 2012; Bishr, 2007; Rayhaan, 2012; Zuwaini, 2012), the dissociation between identity sentiments and attitudes toward English and French indicates that practical reasons are possibly as pivotal in shaping language attitudes and determining language use as identity factors. This pragmatic approach to language may also explain the expanding use of QA even in domains that were reserved to SA (Mejdell, 2006; Rosenbaum, 2011) despite the relatively less favorable attitudes that the Arab youth display toward QA – though these attitudes seem to be changing slowly. Overall, identity feelings seem to operate more at the affective level than at the practical plain, which may explain their weak connection to the realities of language use.

5.7.2 Interviews

The interviews were needed to provide possible *explanations* for the questionnaire data and to explore other forms of identities that the speakers may claim. In this study, the data collected from the questionnaire and interviews served as a mutually validating procedure since it satisfies the convention of triangulation (Gay & Airasian, 2000; Glesne, 2010). As Lincoln and Guba (2000) note, such a strategy also increases the trustworthiness of the findings. Seven identity-related questions were asked in the interviews, focusing on the symbolic value of SA, QA, and English and their relationship to different identity forms (see Appendices). The questions were meant to be broad for probing purposes, but they were supplemented by follow-up questions that elicited additional details about identity feelings. Instead of reporting all of the interview details, I report information that is relevant to theme of this section and the chapter as a whole.

The first identity-related interview question was: "What does Al-Fuṣḥa represent for you?" The question triggered little variance in the speakers' responses; with the exception of one Egyptian interviewee, all of the participants explicitly or implicitly associated SA with their Muslim and Arab identities. Comments such as "it resembles my identity as an Arab and Muslim," "it is part of the Arab history," "it is the most important language to me . . . as an Arab," and "it is part of the Arab civilization" were typical of the interviewees' responses. More than the other groups, the Saudi students highlighted the link between SA and their

Muslim identities, describing SA as, for example, "the language of Qur'an," "the language of the religion," or "the language of all Islamic sciences and texts." The link between SA and Muslim identity has also been reported in previous studies (Haeri, 2000; Saidat, 2010). In fact, Saidat (2010) found that SA is valued mainly for its link to Islam and Arabness. However, SA is not valued just for identity links in the present work. Some participants associated SA with "education," "reading and writing," "communicating with Arabs in other Arabs countries," and "Arab culture" in addition to its symbolic value. An Egyptian interviewee described SA as, "... an intruding language ... it is not the natural language ordinary people speak." The interviewee indicated that the Egyptians do not have an Arab background, and, therefore, SA is forced on them. This pattern exemplifies the tenacious interplay of language and state–national identity in the Egyptian context. In general, however, the interviewees saw SA as a mark of their membership in the larger Arab and/or Muslim communities as well as a means for communicating with others who claim the same background.

However, the participants varied in their responses to the question, "What does Egyptian/Jordanian/Moroccan/Saudi ʻAamiyya/Daarija represent for you?" Less than half of the participants saw their colloquial dialects as "the language of everyday communication with those around us," "the thing we use in daily life," or "the dialect circulated among people." The association between the interviewees' colloquial varieties and their state-based identities was brought up in the case of thirteen Egyptian, eleven Jordanian, eleven Saudi, and seven Moroccan participants. For example, one of the Egyptian participants stated, "The Egyptian dialect represents me as an Egyptian ... or as one who is living in Egypt." Another Egyptian participant reflected, "The Egyptian colloquial is the dialect that we grew up speaking as children . . . so it is part of my identity as someone who speaks this dialect." Similarly, a Jordanian interviewee indicated, ". . . the Jordanian colloquial represents me . . . and also represents Jordanians and distinguish them from other Arab countries." The Moroccan participants had the least fervor for the symbolic value of the Moroccan dialect as a representative of the Moroccan identity, with some depicting the Moroccan dialect as "the reason that other Arabs do not understand us we Moroccans," "it is not one thing . . . it is many dialects," and "it represents division and dispersion . . . dispersion among Arabs and among Moroccans." What was distinctive in the interviewees' responses about QA is the lack of consensus about its link to their state-based identities. However, the Egyptian informants were comparatively the group most positive about this symbolic value of their dialects and the Moroccans were least so.

To probe the identity–language link more directly, I asked the interviewees two separate questions: "Which language or dialect represents your identity as an Arab?" and "Which language or dialect represents your identity as an Egyptian/Jordanian/Moroccan/Saudi?" In response to the first question, all of the interviewees, with the exception of one Egyptian informant, indicated that SA represents them. What is interesting is that four of the Moroccan interviewees stated that they are not Arabs (i.e., they were Berber), but they still considered

SA as a representative of their identities. This trend has been reported in the previous literature (Chakrani, 2010). A single Egyptian interviewee stated that he did not consider himself as an Arab and that SA did not represent him. As for the second question, most of the Egyptian interviewees indicated that the Egyptian dialect represents their Egyptian identity. The Jordanian participants, however, were split, with the majority identifying the Jordanian dialect as a representative of their state-based identities and only a few self-identifying with the "dialect used in Amman." The Saudi interviewees were also split with some pointing out the "Saudi dialect" and a few others pointing to "the dialect of the Gulf people" as markers of their Saudi identity. The Moroccans were unique in that they were the only group in which seven out of twenty participants identified SA as the representative of themselves as Moroccans. Four participants indicated that Berber and SA represented their Moroccan identity, and the remaining nine assigned the Moroccan dialect to their Moroccan identity.

As for the question, "What does English represent for you?" all of the interviewees indicated that English represents a global language that is important to them, some for personal reasons, others for professional reasons, and most for both. Follow-up questions, such as "So which is more important to you, English or Arabic?" showed that the participants diverged with respect to the comparative symbolic values of English and Arabic. The difference may be captured by two statements made by two Jordanian interviewees. One interviewee indicated that, "The English language is the most important language in the world . . . nobody can deny that . . . it is used everywhere and it is understood everywhere one goes . . . I . . . in my opinion . . . English is more important these days than Arabic." The other Jordanian interviewee, however, stated that "English is necessary nowadays for many things . . . jobs or things like that . . . But, for me Arabic is more important because it represents me as an Arab and as a Muslim." In general, the Jordanian students' self-identification as Arabs, Muslims, or Jordanians had no adverse influence on their perception of English. The Saudi students were also positive about English, with only a few apprehending "the negative influence of the extra spread of English on the language of religion." Most of the Moroccan and Egyptian speakers viewed English as instrumentally useful, but symbolically remote from them. As one of the Moroccan interviewees stated, "To me, English represents the language of sciences, technology, and jobs, but it is not the language of culture, or history or ordinary dealings." Again, the importance of English to most of the participants seem to stem from its instrumental rather than symbolic, identity-based value, which is consistent with previous studies (Chakrani, 2010; Marely, 2004).

A last question with respect to the language–identity nexus was "Which language or dialect represents your identity in general?" The question did not name a specific identity or a language variety leaving it open to the interviewees' choice, which may reflect the saliency of certain identity form or language variety for them. The participants' responses fell under three patterns. A first group of interviewees, composed of seven Egyptians, six Jordanians, twelve Moroccans, and seven Saudis (42.1%), described SA as representative of their identity. Since SA is associated with pan-Arab and Muslim identities, respondents in this group probably viewed one or both of these two identity forms as most valuable to them. A second group, which consisted of five Egyptians, five Jordanians, two Moroccans, and three Saudis (19.7%), self-identified with QA, which indicates their prioritization of their country affiliations over other attachments. The last group (38.2%) remarked that both SA and QA are representatives of their identities. Respondents in this group may have identified with their state-based belonging as well as their pan-Arab or Muslim identities. When one compares these patterns with those reported in earlier studies (e.g., Haeri, 2000; Zughoul, 1980), where pan-Arab and Muslim identities are foregrounded, it becomes clear that more and more Arab young people are associating with their nation-state identities because of the current political atmosphere in the Arab region and the media-fed state-nationalisms across the Arab region. In other words, the pan-Arabist rhetoric is giving way to state-based nationalist realities, and this is reflected in the interplay of identity and language on the personal and social levels.

Finally, the interviewees were asked, "How often, when and where do you use Al-Fuṣħa, Al-'Aamiyya, and English?" This question aimed to investigate any links between the participants' identity feelings and their language usage. All of the participants indicated that they rarely use SA in their daily lives, but rather utilize it for specific purposes. For example, some, as one of the Saudi students explained, use it "only in reading the Qur'an and in the prayer . . . ," whereas others said that they use it "sometimes in the school." When summoned to comment on their SA usage in their college education, the majority of the participants indicated that SA occupies only a peripheral position. This declining use of SA may explain the growing Arab-World-wide dissatisfaction with educational practices that marginalize SA and its use in education (Al-Nassar, 2012; Zuwaini, 2012). Some of the participants maintained that they preferred to use SA routinely, but they cannot either because they do not command it well or because its use in everyday speech is not socially accepted. As one of the Saudi students indicated, "When I think of using Al-Fuṣħa, I know . . . of course . . . people will make fun of me . . . or they think of me as living in Al-Jaahiliyya era."[14] A Moroccan interviewee indicated, "I like to use Al-Fuṣħa everyday . . . but . . . you know . . . people will find this a little strange . . ." Generally, there is an apprehension among the young people to use SA either because of fear of making mistakes or because of the generally discouraging societal attitudes toward the use of SA in everyday speech. As for QA, the participants indicated that they use this variety regularly in their daily lives. English use is interesting because the majority of the respondents reported that they used English customarily, especially in their digitally mediated communications (see Chapter 8). However, others indicated that they use English because they see it as a must. As a Jordanian student indicated, "these days you cannot but learn English . . . this is the message you get in school and university . . . if you do not learn English, you will be a failure . . . I mean you will not get a respected job or continue your education." This pattern is not specific to the Jordanian context, but also to the Egyptian, Saudi, and Moroccan contexts as well. For example, a number of Egyptian, Moroccan, and Saudi participants indicated that they use internet-based discussion forums to practice their English skills.

Overall, the patterns gleaned from the interview data confirm those found in the questionnaire. SA is still a main marker of young Arabs' identities, but QA is gradually joining the identity link because of the rise of state-based nationalisms. English is not as involved on the symbolic front, but it is implicated in the functional front due its instrumental significance to the young Arab generations.

5.7.3 Identity in verbal behavior

In this subsection, I focus on identity as displayed in Arabic speakers' verbal behavior. The anecdotes reported here are based on observations made during my fieldwork, two study-abroad programs in Jordan in 2012 and 2014, a short visit to Lebanon in 2014, a visit to Syria in 2009, and a 2014 conference experience in Saudi Arabia. There is no claim of generalizability here, unless one accepts the idea that identity feelings are constructed more socially than individually or that they reflect what is accepted or unacceptable in a given speech community, which is open to discussion (Hall, 1996; Kroskrity, 2000; Saville-Troike, 1989). However, the insights offered by these anecdotes reflect some of the extant or emergent identity patterns and corroborate some of the trends reported above.

The first set of observations concerns the link between SA and Arab identity. A first observation occurred in 2009, during a summer trip to Syria. The observation took place during a feast to which I was invited in a suburb of Hims, the largest governorate in Syria. The feast was made by a distant relative in honor of his newly married son – a tradition that is widely practiced in the area. More than fifty men were in attendance, filling a spacious guest room called *maḍaafa*. In such feasts, it is customary for religious figures to give short speeches after the meal, often focusing on some societal, moral, or religious issues. Two familiar attendees gave the speeches, using SA, with intermittent switches to QA. Upon finishing his speech, the second speaker invited me to speak about my experience in the United States, an invitation that was seconded by the host. After some negotiation, the speaker and the host agreed that, instead of *lecturing*, I just recount a memorable story or event. Given the fact that the previous two speakers used SA and because the attendance included several educated members of the community, I chose to deliver my narrative in SA. The story was about a student of mine, who changed his attitudes toward the Arab people and culture after a study-abroad program, and eventually acquired a Bedouin nickname, which came to be associated with him while in Jordan. The story was based on a conversation I had with the student earlier that year. At the end of my story, I received a number of questions and comments. One of the striking comments came from another distant relative whom I met a few times before this event. The comment associated my use of SA with the observation that I still sounded like an

Arab. What is sociolinguistically remarkable is that my previous interactions with this person in the local dialect did not trigger the remark about my "Arabness," whereas my use of SA did.

The idea of judging an immigrant Arab's *Arabness* based on his/her ability to speak in SA recurred during a conference on Arabic as a second language in Riyadh in 2014 (February 2014). The conference was attended by a large number of scholars from the Arab region, Asia, North America, Europe, and Africa. As is the norm in such public speeches, all the speakers delivered their presentations in SA. The presenters stayed in the same hotel, and so we often met either in the hotel's lobby or restaurants. During these gathering, we discussed mostly issues related to scholarship on Arabic, the conference, and the presented papers. In one of these meetings, the group discussed the ideas presented by a colleague who lives and teaches outside the Arab region. The discussion centered on some of controversial topics that are of interest to language specialists and non-specialists. One of the interlocutors, however, indicated that he was struck less by the details of the paper, and more by the speaker's "pure" Arabic (*'Arabiyya quħħa*). Again, the interlocutor expressed his appreciation that the presenter had not assimilated in the new culture even though he may have stayed there for a long time. The notion of still being an Arab was again brought to the scene to characterize the presenter. One of the statements that caught my attention was the interlocutor's suggestion that the presenter "at least knows how to speak sound Arabic," contrasting him to many young Arabic people who live in the Arab region and still "cannot speak well."[15] The casualness of the comment reflects the commonplace nature of such judgments.

One of the most personally illuminating experiences with respect to the SA-identity link occurred during my fieldwork in Jordan. After I collected data from a professor in one of the host universities, she directed me to her Syrian colleague who works in the same department. What is special about this professor is that he speaks only in SA outside his home – a fact that raised my interest in meeting, interviewing, and getting data samples from him, even though Syrians were not part of my target population. In my meeting with this professor, I came to know that he speaks SA fluently and faultlessly (based on my short interaction with him). When I asked about his choice of SA, he indicated that it was not proper for him to use QA in public just as it was not proper for him to wear "sleeping pajamas" at work. He also indicated his keenness to present himself to people at work and elsewhere through SA rather than QA. He further asserted that he restricts his use of QA to interactions with his children. This informant rationalized that, "part of our problems today as Arabs is that we do not respect our language. . . . We do not respect what it represents to us as peoples and as a nation." For this informant, the use of SA is a way for preserving the language from becoming "dead." It is also a marker of his personal identity as an educated Arab and of his ethnic/national identity as a member of the "Arab nation," a term that he used frequently to describe the Arabic-speaking peoples.

The second set of observations deals with minority speakers' verbal enact-ment of their identities. In May 2014, I embarked on a study-abroad trip to Jor-dan. On my Royal Jordanian flight from Chicago to Amman, I found myself seated behind an old woman before a couple came to claim their seat. The middle-aged couple asked the women in English to leave the seat, and she responded to them in Arabic. They reiterated their right to the seat, and she again replied to them in Arabic. It was clear that the woman had limited proficiency in English. The couple could clearly understand her because their arguments were always a response to her speech. Eventually the couple called upon the flight attendant, who explained in Arabic to the woman that she had to be reseated because the seat belonged to the couple. After sitting in their seats, the couple started talking in Kurdish,[16] and they uttered a few Arabic sentences in the course of their discussion of the encounter. It seemed to me that the couple was reluctant to speak to the woman in Arabic even when they knew that she could not communicate in English; by insisting on using English, as the neutral language, they were possibly showing their unwillingness to compromise their identities as non-Arabs. This incident is revealing about identity dynamics because the situation of the Kurdish couple on the plane somehow mimics the situation of many Kurds in real-life encoun-ters, especially in areas where a Kurdish minority lives among an Arab majority.[17] Since Kurds are subsumed within larger Arab communities, many of them seek to emphasize their non-Arab identity, mainly through language.

In my stay in Morocco, I had to commute between a city where my hotel was and a nearby city where one of the host universities was located. On my first day of data collection at the host university, I was introduced to a professor who resided in the same city where I was staying. At the end of our short encounter, the professor offered to give me a ride to the host university. The next day, the professor, I, and two other persons whom he picked on our way drove to campus. On our hour-long trip to the university, I came to know that the three were speak-ers of Berber. The professor asked me a few questions about the purpose of my trip and subsequently about the end product of my research. I explained briefly the reasons for the trip and where it was to appear. The professor offered to help with the study and expressed his willingness to answer questions relevant to my topics. The professor conversed with me in a mixed SA-Moroccan speech up till his offer to help with the interview. However, once the interview started, he shifted to SA. The two other individuals, who also volunteered to answer questions about the Moroccan sociolinguistic situation, followed his lead insofar as the use of SA in the interview was concerned. The shift to SA was only interpretable to me once the informants explained the link between SA and their Muslim identity. The infor-mants also expressed their strong objection to introducing the Moroccan dialect into education, which, as indicated above, was a contentious topic in Morocco at the time. For Berber speakers, SA, as the language of Islamic texts and liturgy, is the main link that connects them linguistically to Arabic speakers. This may explain their attachment to it and their keenness to use it along with their local languages. The speakers' assertion of the link between SA and their religious identity was confirmed in the student interviews. All the Berber interviewees (the three professors and four students) considered SA as a major dimension of their shared identity with the Moroccan Arabs. This pattern diverges from previous studies that identify the local dialects with "national identity." For example, Sherazade (1993) found that Arab and Berber participants in her study have similar attitudes toward Algerian Arabic because it is the language that symbolizes "national unity" (p. 112). At the same time, the Berber participants were keen to preserve their mother tongue as a group whose ethnolinguistic identity is threatened – a pattern that is confirmed in this study.

The third set of observations relates to English and its role in changing the meaning of linguistic belonging to the Arab speech community. During my 2014 study-abroad experience in Jordan, I undertook a two-day weekend visit to Lebanon. On the way back from Beirut to Amman, I had a long wait before I could get onto the plane. As I stood in the line proceeding to the gate, I was intrigued by the verbal behavior of a couple with their toddler who were standing before me. What caught my attention is that the mother spoke to the baby in heavily-accented English. In the few occasions where the father addressed the baby, he also used heavily-accented English. However, when the father in particular addressed the mother, he used Lebanese Arabic and she responded using the same dialect. I had a chance to comment on the toddler's cuteness, which was followed by a short interaction with the father, mainly triggered by my curiosity. Through this interaction I came to know that he and his wife live in Lebanon and were leaving to Jordan just for a visit. However, they use English with their child so that he acquires it at an early age. Although this use may not be directly related to identity issues, it still implies that some Arab families seek to *instill* English in their children for practical purposes. From this perspective, language acquisition is motivated less by a sense of belonging and identity and more by pragmatic ends.

This pattern is not unique to an individual Arab country. In my 2012 study-abroad experience in Jordan, I had to a chance to meet with a number of students, as the Arabic program at Utah State University was looking for graduate teaching assistants to teach lower-division Arabic courses. I asked the Head of the Department of English in the host university for help identifying students who may be interested in pursuing their graduate studies in the United States. She referred me to a number of students, two of whom were female students who were born in the United States and moved with their families to Jordan toward school age (six and five years). The two students spoke English as well as native speakers in the United States. When I inquired about their notable proficiency and fluency in English, both indicated that, even after their relocation to Jordan, their parents continued to speak to them in English at home so that they retained the English language skills that they acquired as children in the United States. In fact, one of them had a subtle accent in Arabic, which is sociolinguistically interesting. The student's mother is American, and, therefore, the student did not have to use Arabic at home. However, according to the student, both of her parents instilled in her the importance of maintaining her English language skills so that, at one point, she, as an American citizen, could go back to the United States to complete her studies. The notion behind maintaining English in this particular situation may again be related to practical factors. However, when a member of a speech community does not fully acquire the language of the community in which he or she lives, especially when language is a major marker of one's belonging to the community, then this becomes an identity question as well. This social *pattern* suggests that identity considerations may be relegated to minor importance compared to practical ones.

In the 2012 study-abroad program, the group's residence was facing a small restaurant owned by a Jordanian who lived in the United States for several years before moving back to Jordan and establishing his own business in Amman. The restaurant is mainly a fast food restaurant with a few small dining tables. As I frequented this restaurant, the owner, who also sometimes worked as the cashier, came to recognize my face. On one of my visits to the restaurant, the restaurant owner started a conversation with me and eventually realized that I work in the United States and was visiting Jordan for the study-abroad program. In my next few visits to the restaurant, the owner started to converse with me mostly in English. This pattern recurred in different contexts. For example, in my communication with a number of students in the host university, several of them interacted with me in English, even when I initiated the conversation in Arabic. Since the speakers knew about my Arab background, this language behavior may not be viewed simply as a matter of language choice; the uncalled-for use of English in this particular setting perturbs the link between identity and language because it has to do with how these young people present themselves in relation to others.

The observations reported in this subsection may underscore personal identity practices, but they may also be part of existing or emerging identity patterns in the Arab region. The commonness of these patterns need to be verified through studies particularly dedicated for this purpose.

5.8 SUMMARY AND CONCLUSION

In the Arab context, multiple languages, ethnicities, religions, nationalities, and affiliations exist. Therefore, it is impossible to speak of identity as a monolithic concept. Arabic speakers have different forms of identity that converge, diverge, or even clash based on various factors. However, language has always been at the center of identity dynamics in the Arab region for three main reasons. First, the Arabic language is the single main denominator of the Arab people's ethnic identity, and thus it largely defines who an Arab is. Shared language(s) also index the ethnic identities of other speech communities in the Arab region, such as the Berbers and the Kurds. Second, Arabic is one of the foundations upon which claims of Arab political unity are based. This may explain the mobilization of the Arabic language as a mark of Arab unity by Arab nationalists and pan-Arab movements. Not only does the Arabic language geographically demarcate the distribution of Arabic speakers on the political map of the Arab World, but it also relates these speakers to a shared heritage and history. Last, the Arabic language is a main symbol of Islam, and therefore it is often invoked for constructing or reaffirming Muslim identity.

The ethnic, national, and religious forms of identity are constructed through discursive narratives that seek to naturalize historical accounts explaining a group's shared ethnic, national, and religious backgrounds. These historical narratives may become socially accepted, circulated, and shared to the extent that they eventually become axiomatic within the social group. In the case of minority groups, historical narratives also work through a dynamic of "othering" where the discursive construction of the self necessarily implicates the creation of the "other" (Said, 1978). These historical narratives may eventually translate into identity statements and identity acts by which social actors aver, display, and enact their shared social identities. Social actors' identity statements and acts may simply be byproducts of historical narratives; they transpire when the historical narratives succeed in creating a sense of shared social identity in a given speech community. However, identity relationships become complicated when the historical narratives are not supported by sociopolitical realities on the ground. For example, the current state of Arab disunity, political squabbles, and state-based nationalisms runs counter to the historically based pan-Arab narratives.

The incompatibilities between identity-constructing discursive narratives and sociopolitical realities may eventually lead to the dissolution of the traditional forms of identity and the evolution of multiple new identities. The spawn of state-based and sect-based identities across the Arab region are examples of the fragmentation of the *traditional* national and religious forms of identity. Historically, the status of SA in the Arab region has been closely tied to pan-Arab and pan-Islamic identities. However, the symbolic, identity-saturated value of SA is no longer supported by the social realities surrounding the concepts of *pan-Arabism* and *ummah*. Hence, SA is gradually losing its currency among the younger Arab generations as a politically and religiously unifying factor. Although many Arabs still associate SA with their Arab identities, the link between SA and Arab identity is mostly structured along cultural and ethnic – rather than political or religious – lines. The emphasis on the Arabs' unique culture and language is what may also characterize several intellectual works produced in the Arab region since the 1990s. The conceptualization the Arab identity as a form of cultural identity (*al-huwiyya al-thaqaafiyya*) focuses mainly on the identity risks to which the new Arab generations are liable because of globalization, the spread of English, the deteriorating use of SA, the borrowing of many English words, and the growing use of the colloquial dialects (Musa, 2013). These concerns have been underlined in intellectual efforts seeking to revive the role of SA in the Arab community. QA is still associated with state-based nationalisms, but it is increasingly related to Arab identity as well. Once again, this is due to the fact that "Arab identity" is more of a cultural belonging than a political one.

NOTES

1 Obviously, this definition does not cover many people who reside in the Arab region. For example, some people who identify themselves as Arabs may not speak Arabic, as is the case in Somalia.

2 An additional explanation that Aldawri (1984) provides is that the Ummayads' policy of assigning important government posts to Arabs raised the Arabs' sense of pride in their identity.

3 Many of these intellectuals (e.g., Rashiid Riḍa [1865–1935], Ahmad Fares Al-Shidiyaq [1804–1887], Ibrahim Yaziji [1847–1906], and Adiib Ishaaq [1856–1885]) did not have well-defined political agenda, and, therefore, their focus was mainly on the Arabs' linguistic and cultural distinctiveness, which became the major mark of their distinct ethnic identities.

4 The prospective *nation* mainly included the Levant, Iraq, and the Gulf.

5 Although there are still Egyptians who advocate the use of the colloquial Egyptian dialect, they often stand as individual voices and do not constitute an intellectual or sociopolitical movement.

6 The situation of the Kurdish language is completely different in Syria, where Kurdish, till recently, had been banned in schools, published materials, and business. Since the 1990s, however, the Kurds' display of their identity and their "official" use of their language have been kept in check by means of either intimidatory force or political settlements (e.g., hosting anti-Turkish activists). The start of the 2011 Syrian Revolution against the Syrian regime has given the Kurds the momentum to replicate the Iraqi experience. In 2013, the Syrian Kurds indeed declared Qamishli as a self-governing province – a step that may come to full fruition depending on the outcome of the struggle.

7 Many forged Ahaadiith (Prophetic sayings) have been fabricated to support the superiority of Arabic (Lo, 2009).

8 Muslim Brotherhood, which was established in Egypt in 1928 and then spread to the other Arab countries, was not politically active till after Egypt's independence.

9 See Kaplan and Baldauf (1997) for a fine-tuned distinction between language planning and language policy.

10 Based on their study of the Arabicization policy in Sudan, Abdelhady et al. (2011) argue that the Arabicization language policy of (northern) Sudan was built on British colonial narratives. It is also generally accepted that the French language policies in the colonized Maghreb still impact the Arabicization policies in the post-colonial Maghreb (e.g., Benmamoun, 2001; Benrabah, 2013; Chakrani, 2010; Ennaji, 2005; Walters, 2011).

11 Pan-Arab here carries cultural/ethnic rather than political connotations.

12 It should be noted that French is used in Muslim schools as well.

13 These percentage are calculated after reversing the polarity of negative items.

14 Al-Jaahiliyya refers to the pre-Islamic era.

15 I jotted down this note upon hearing it due to its importance.

16 I have some basic knowledge of Kurdish, and the couple also indicated that they were going to Al-Suleimaniyyah in Iraq.

17 This does not apply to Iraqi Kurdistan where Kurdish is the majority language.

CHAPTER 6

Language variation and change

Variation is an intrinsic attribute of all human languages. It has been observed in individual speakers, among members of the same speech community, and naturally, across different social groups. *Intra-speaker* variation refers to stylistic variation in individual speakers (Schilling-Estes, 2013). This type of variation, in the Arab context, is considered CS because the shift between High and Low registers falls under diglossic CS (see next chapter). *Interspeaker* variation refers to language differentiation among speakers within a single speech community or particular geographic area. Language variation and change are realized through speakers' linguistic practices in a given social setting, and they are often influenced by speakers' language attitudes or ideologies. Moreover, these variations and changes interact with social categories that mark the personal and social identities of speakers as individuals and members of social groups. Gender identities, for example, have been found relevant cross-culturally for understanding language variation and change (Holmes & Meyerhoff, 2003). Language variation and change is typically related to relations of power between different social groups. By studying the mechanisms of language variation and the direction of language change, we can obtain a better understanding of social dynamics and power relationships among different social groups. Like other language phenomena, variation and change may mirror social structures, processes, and relations. The reverse is true; language variation and change may not be completely understood without regard to the social, political, and historical dimensions of the context in which they occur.

We see reference to language variation in the writings of the early Arab grammarians, lexicographers, etymologists, and language scholars (Ibrahim, 2007; Owens, 2005; Palva, 2013; Versteegh, 2001). One aspect of this variation is described as a deviation from the prescriptive linguistic norms of Classical Arabic (CA). As noted in Chapter 2, Sibaweih observed various morphosyntactic differences among Arabic speakers in his analytic study of Arabic grammar (Owens, 2005). As he observed these variations, Sibaweih provided evaluative judgments concerning the "deviating" features and their comparability to their CA counterparts. Ibn Jinni (AD 937–1002), one of the founders of the science of etymology, has a whole chapter about variation in his book *Al-Xaṣaa'iṣ* "The Attributes" (Ibrahim, 2007). Palva (2013) refers to phonological variation in Ibn Manzuur's renowned thirteenth-century dictionary, *Lisan Al-'Arab* "Arabic Tongue," and Al-Suyuuṭi's *Al-Muẓhir fii 'uluum al-luɣa* "The Illustrator in Language Sciences" (AD 1445–1505). Among the aspects of variation recorded in these works were *'an'ana, Al-kaškaša, kaskasa*, and *ɣamɣama*, each of which were attached to particular tribes or social groups. Phonological and lexical variation is widely documented in the pre-Islamic and early-Islamic Arabic dialects (Holes, 1995; Versteegh, 1997). This variation appears even in Islamic scholarship, particularly in treatises dealing with the Qur'an and its interpretation. Most of the early commentators on the Qur'an, particularly Al-Tabari and Al-Qurtubi, explained Qur'anic words and expressions by referring to their unique use by different individuals (e.g., poets) or tribes (e.g., Quraysh). However, variation was not studied as a topic in itself, nor were its social motivations investigated. Rather, language variation was examined mostly for religious and prescriptive purposes.

The systematic study of variation as a socially conditioned phenomenon can be traced back to the 1960s. William Labov carried out a number of studies on the relationship between linguistic features and social variables such as class, age, and gender (Labov, 1963, 1972). Labov not only linked differences in linguistic forms to social factors and influences, but he demonstrated that time also affects language processes. In a sense, Labov is credited for developing two interrelated areas in sociolinguistics: *language variation* and *language change*. While *language variation* often involves a synchronic approach to varying linguistic forms and their social antecedents, *language change* focuses on the emergence and spread of linguistic forms diachronically. Language change always involves variation, but not all variation can be defined as change (Chambers, 2013). In addition, Labov drew attention to stylistic variation, which gradually developed into a somewhat autonomous subfield of sociolinguistics. Labov's work departed methodologically from previous sociolinguistic research in that he incorporated statistical techniques in approaching the interplay of linguistic forms and social phenomena. Many subsequent studies followed the Labovian sociolinguistic approach, challenging the homogeneity of language and linking linguistic processes to broader historical and social mechanisms (see Chambers & Schilling, 2013 for a review).

Arabic sociolinguists were quick to make their contribution to this burgeoning field. The Arabic-speaking world is linguistically and culturally heterogamous, and this diversity has become the subject of intense interest in the past few decades. Variationist research rests on a number of assumptions, and in the Arab context these have all been widely embraced in variationist studies.[1] First, variation is characterized by "orderly heterogeneity" (Weinreich, Labov, & Herzog, 1968, p. 100). Weinreich and his associates list two types of constraints on variation – internal and external. Internal constrains involve the linguistic environment, which either permits or prevents the occurrence of a specific linguistic form. For example, the aspectual marker in the Palestinian dialect spoken in Amman may be phonologically realized as [bi] or [byi] depending on the structure of the following syllable – [bi] appears after open syllables (e.g., *biruuħ*) and [byi] surfaces after closed syllables (e.g., *byidrus*) (Al-Wer, 2008). External constraints may deal with social, geographical, psychological, or stylistic factors. For example, the use of certain linguistic forms may be constrained by the gender of the speaker. A second assumption in variationist research is that language is always mutable, which necessitates the investigation of factors that affect language evolution and change. Third, language is not merely a means of communication, but a mirror of broader social and historical processes. Linguistic variation in the Arab region is the outcome of various historical, social, political, and demographic factors. Because these factors vary from one context to another, the same social category (gender, for example) may not affect linguistic forms and processes in the same way in different social settings (Miller, 2007).

In the Arab context, variation has been recorded across regions, social parameters, time, and even among individual speakers. These influences correspond to the distinctions commonly made between four interrelated areas in the study of language variation and change: regional variation, social variation, temporal variation, and stylistic variation, respectively. The first three aspects of variation will be the subject of this chapter. Stylistic variation, which involves the shift between a Low and a High style/register/dialect, will be discussed in the next chapter as an aspect of CS.

Before delving into these topics, it is important to shed some light on some of the main approaches used in addressing language variation. These are by no means the only approaches to analyzing the phenomenon, but each of them has been used frequently in researching variation in both the Arabic sociolinguistic scene and worldwide.

6.1 APPROACHES TO LANGUAGE VARIATION AND CHANGE

Prior to Labov's work in the 1960s, the study of linguistic variation focused mainly on regional and contextual variation. The study of regional and contextual variation typically followed an ethnographic approach, wherein fieldwork constituted the staple method of data collection, analysis, and reporting. Qualitatively oriented descriptions of variation were the norm. This approach is still in use, sometimes in combination with a quantitative component. Two main lines of research followed this approach to variation. One focused on the geographic boundaries of different dialects. Descriptive studies sought to draw lines between different dialects based on the geographical distribution of their speakers. Another line of research focused on language diversification over a territory due to language contact. The drive behind the latter type of studies was to investigate the impact of language contact phenomena – such as immigration and urbanization – on language differentiation. Researchers in this line attributed non-regional and non-contextual differentiations either to dialect mixing or free variation (Mesthrie & Swann, 2009). This approach still inspires variationist research in the Arab region and worldwide, as will be explained below.

Beginning in the 1960s, variationist studies started to approach language variation in terms of a correlation between specific linguistic forms and static social categories, particularly demographic variables such as social class, gender, and age. In his classic study of Martha's Vineyard, Labov (1963) found a correlation between conservative fishermen's tendency to exaggerate vowels already existing in their speech – e.g., the use of the centralized /əi/ diphthong instead of /ai/ – and their attempt to display their identity as authentic Vineyarders who rejected the values of the mainland and the incursion of rich summer visitors. This innovative use of language came to be displayed by young speakers who used the same linguistic means to cultivate their identity away from the "outsiders." In a similar fashion, in his New York study, Labov (1966) showed a correlation between the extent to which sales assistants in three department stores articulated or dropped the prestige final or pre-consonantal /r/ sound and their social class. Participants from the classiest store (Saks) enunciated the /r/ sound more frequently than those in the less classy stores (Macy and Klein). Labov maintained that the driving force behind language variation is social class. Labov's research inspired many subsequent works on language variation and change, and his approach featured strongly in variationist studies in the Arab context.

Milroy departed from Labov's notion of social variables and presented an alternative view of social reality. Based on her research in three Belfast inner-city communities, Milroy (1987) explained language variation and change in terms of social networks between individuals in a speech community. Milroy (1987) and Milroy and Milroy (1992) argued that an understanding of the structure of the relationship between community members and the content of ties between them is key in comprehending linguistic variation and change. For Milroy, social networks may be defined both structurally and interactionally. The structural property of a social network is defined mainly by that network's density, that is, the proportion of existing links among community members relative to the potential links. The interactional feature of networks can be identified by examining the multiplexity, durability, and intensity of the relationships that bind community members. These features define the nature and strength of the ties. Milroy (1987) stratified social networks into different order zones. A first order zone includes friends who are bound by direct and strong ties. A second order zone involves "friends of friends," whose relationship ties are usually not as strong nor as direct. The third order zone deals with distant or indirect relationships between community members. Speech communities characterized by close-knit relationships act as "a conservative force, resisting pressures for change" (Milroy & Milroy, 1992, p. 5). By contrast, communities lacking these strong relationships are more prone to language variation and change.

Eckert (2000, 2012) argues that language use in the social world involves constant consideration and evaluation of people, settings, social categories, and language forms. Linguistic variation is the outcome of speakers' attempt to index different social meanings through language. For example, through their varied speech, speakers may mark their group membership, their social class, and their gendered identities. In particular contexts, certain linguistic features become attached to particular social meanings, and these meanings vary from one context to another. Social actors are capable of invoking their desired social meanings based on understandings of the semiotic relationship between language and social forms. In this sense, "Variation constitutes a social semiotic system capable of expressing the full range of a community's social concerns" (Eckert, 2012, p. 94). In addition, variation allows speakers to position themselves within a larger social order. In essence, then, language variation is a *social practice* that materializes through "social-semiotic moves" (p. 94) with specific social meanings. Eckert's approach is, therefore, to view language variation not only in terms of linguistic processes and discrete social variables, but also through the lens of the implications of its broader social significance.

A number of researchers view language variation and change as evolutionary processes (e.g., Croft, 2000; Keller, 1994; Ritt, 2004). According to Croft (2000, 2006), language may be seen as a "historical entity," and therefore it is susceptible to the laws of life, evolution, and extinction (Croft, 2006, p. 98). The tenacity of language forms often implicates new speakers' ability to replicate the previous generation's model of linguistic competency. Language variation may evolve in the process of replication or as a result of interactions among speakers. Young speakers' ability to replicate the competencies of an existing model depends upon their opportunities to be exposed to language use in context. When multiple linguistic models or options are available, young speakers will usually choose among linguistic forms depending on their interactional objectives. As part of the selection process, speakers may break a linguistic "convention." Linguistic choices may lead to large-scale linguistic changes when particular forms are adopted by many individuals. Thus, social, attitudinal, and identity-related factors become secondary to actual language use and individual choice. Croft refers to this type of variation and change as "usage-based." According to Croft (2006), language variation may appear in any of three different forms. First-order variation affects language utterances or forms. Second-order variation involves "socially-valued variants" and is motivated by sociolinguistic variables, such as social identity. Third-order variation occurs across dialects and languages and affects language typologies. Croft also distinguishes between "internal" and "external" causes of language change, the former being the outcome of innovations in the speech community, whereas the latter is the result of language contact (p. 123). In either case, however, language use is still the main trigger of variation and change.

These various approaches to language variation reflect differences in conceptualizing the nature of language and the role of society in shaping language development and change. Even when social factors are deemed a main catalyst of language variation, researchers disagree on the best way to assess the role of a given social variable.[2] For example, accounts of gender-motivated language variation have adopted approaches that may not be strictly considered *variationist* in the Labovian sense, as they incorporate insights from various semiotic, pragmatic, and historical perspectives.

6.2 REGIONAL VARIATION

Regional dialectology refers to the study of language variation within a given geographical area or among distinct geographical areas. Thus, it involves both descriptive regional dialectology as well as the sociolinguistic study of phenomena related to language contact, such as koineization and pidginizaton. Descriptive regional dialectology is sometimes referred to as *traditional dialectology* in the literature. Chambers (2013) describes "traditional dialectology" as the precursor of sociolinguistics. This kind of research involves "the collection of linguistic features in a given geographical area and the study of these features with regard to their distribution in this area to establish dialectal border lines, transitional areas, core areas, and dialectal continua" (Behnstedt & Woidich, 2013, p. 301). As the definition suggests, descriptive regional dialectology helps both identify the linguistic features of different dialects and map those features onto geographical areas.

Research on regional dialectology also describes contact-induced variation and change.[3] Two outcomes of language contact particularly relevant to the Arab context are examined: (1) koineization and (2) pidginization and creolization. These two processes are responsible for much of the variation found among the different varieties of Arabic, including both the variances in regional and local colloquial varieties, as well as the differences between SA and QA. They also explain some of the main changes that overtook the Arabic language in the past and in recent history with the emergence of new Arabic-based language varieties.

6.2.1 Descriptive regional dialectology

Interest in Arabic dialectology emerged in the nineteenth century, not long after the development of dialectology as a new discipline in Europe and the quest for dialect atlases in a number of European countries (Behnstedt & Woidich, 2013). Prior to the nineteenth century, linguistic interest in Arabic centered on the language of reading and writing, i.e., SA, because of its importance to understanding historical documents and religious texts. The Arabic dialects were not within the radar of early dialectologists because of the generally negative attitudes toward the dialects among Arabs themselves (Behnstedt & Woidich, 2013). Moreover, as a geographical entity, the Arab world did not have the political weight it later achieved after most Arab countries gained their independence in the wake of World War II. The nineteenth century witnessed the birth of Arabic dialectology in its modern sense, but not in its social variationist sense. In other words, the study of variation was an end in itself at that time rather than a means for understanding the social meaning of language variation.

Among the earliest empirical works on Arabic dialectology were those by Wallin (1851). In Egypt, Wallin collected, transcribed, and analyzed samples of Bedouin poetry. These data samples became the basis of his analysis of the Bedouin dialects, particularly their morphological features (Palva, 2013). Expanding on Wallin's work, Wetzstein (1868) provided examples of phonological variation in the Bedouin dialects in Syria and the northwestern part of the Arabian Peninsula, including the variants /y/ and /dʒ/. These early works inspired much of the later research on other varieties of Arabic across the Arab region (see Behnstedt & Woidich, 2013 for a review). The early studies were relatively limited in terms of scope and depth because the task of data collection and analysis was rendered arduous by limitations in transportation and modern technologies. Toward the end of the nineteenth century and the beginning of the twentieth, most of the works in Arabic dialectology aimed to develop grammar books and dictionaries (e.g., Spitta, 1880). They focused mainly on more widely spoken dialects with well-established linguistic features, such as the Cairene dialect.

More recent studies on language variation in the Arab region sought to provide detailed and systematic analyses of regional dialects with an effort to bring less-researched dialects to scholarly attention. Features of these varieties are often compared to SA or regional dialects whose features are well-established (see, for example, the collection in Al-Wer & De Jong, 2009 and in Haak, De Jong, & Versteegh, 2004). For example, Eades (2009) examined the Šawaawi dialect in northern Oman, which up to the time of this publication had not found its way into the dialectology literature. The author describes in detail distinct phonological, morphological, syntactic, and lexical features of this dialect, and places these features within the broader Omani multidialectical context. Similarly, Ingham (2009) provides a detailed description of a dialect spoken by *Badu Al-Furaat* "the Bedouins of the Euphrates." She compares the linguistic features of this dialect to corresponding features in the Southern Iraqi dialects, Northern Najdi dialects, and general Najdi features. Descriptive studies on Arabic dialectology often discuss the status and development of these dialects in relation to geographic, historical, and contextual factors. In Eades's (2009) study, for example, geographical isolation becomes a critical factor in understanding the features of the Šawaawi dialect. Ingham's study invokes the historical link between the dialects of the Euphrates Bedouins and their Najdi ancestors, as well as their interactions with neighboring dialects. These scholars have contributed hugely to the field of Arabic dialectology not only in that they documented linguistic diversity, but that they explained the historical and contextual mechanisms underlying dialect variation.

Descriptive regional dialectology has been used in typological analyses and classifications. They have also been used to refine dialectal divisions that were based on earlier impressionist accounts, such as the division between urban, rural, and Bedouin dialects. In addition, they have informed linguistic geography, particularly the construction of dialect maps and atlases. While several other atlases target particular regions or countries in the Arab World (see Behnstedt & Woidich, 2013; Taine-Cheikh, 2012 for details), the *Wortatlas der arabischen Dialekte* (2011, 2012, 2014) by Behnstedt and Woidich represents the only available atlas that covers the entire Arab region. One of the central concepts used in descriptive regional dialectology is *isogloss*. An isogloss is a line drawn between geographical areas that marks their distinction based on a single linguistic feature. The feature's binary division is sometimes specified intuitively and then verified empirically through a process of measuring its homogeneity and consistency in a given area (Labov, Ash, & Boberg, 2005). Instead of being defined by a single isogloss, dialect borders may be delineated by a bundle of isoglosses (sometimes called a *heterogloss*; Kurath, 1972) that demarcate the core area of a given dialect as well as transitional areas where a number of isoglosses overlap between one dialectal region and another.

Behnstedt (2006) identifies a number of challenges facing the prospect of developing accurate dialect geographies in the Arab region. Among these factors is the difficulty of establishing clear-cut boundaries between dialects; within regional dialects are transition zones where members of a speech community may mix or alternate between two or more linguistic features. Another challenge concerns selection criteria for the isoglosses to be used in marking regional dialects. It is well-known that Arabic dialects display similar and dissimilar features, and therefore isogloss selection may sometimes become the defining criterion in how dialect borders are drawn. A third challenge concerns speakers' perceptions of dialect borders, often named "mental maps" (Behnstedt, 2006, p. 585). When used as supplementary material for dialect geographies, these mental maps do not always mirror geographical maps, which are based on recorded data of actual language use. Computational linguists have recently joined efforts to examine the linguistic distance between dialects spoken in both geographically close and distant regions (Abu Nasser & Benmamoun, in press). Dynamic online surveys and automated isogloss generators have recently been used to map linguistic variation on geographical areas (e.g., Cambridge survey, 2007; Harvard dialect survey, 2003), but these techniques have yet to be developed in the Arab context.

A relatively recent trend in descriptive regional studies to base dialect divisions not merely on linguistic features, but also on language use, social factors, and contextual factors, has made descriptive regional dialectology an integral part of sociolinguistic research (Taine-Cheikh, 2012). Thus, dialectal classification has become more intertwined with sociolinguistic research. As a leading figure in this trend, Cohen and his associates (Cohen, 1973; Cohen & Caubet, 2000) proposed complementing data-collection techniques focused on linguistic features with techniques that focus on the social and historical backgrounds of the dialects and their interaction with other dialects. For example, Cohen and Caubet (2000) propose using three questionnaires to identity dialect boundaries: one for lexical items, another for morphosyntactic and phonological features, and a third for sociohistorical background and language usage. This new, integrated approach has been used by Cohen in his studies on language variation in the Maghreb and has been adopted by a number of other researchers (see Taine-Cheikh, 2012). This interdisciplinary approach adds a new dimension to the study of language variation.

Although descriptive regional dialectology continues to feature strongly in Arabic variationist research, more recent studies have drawn attention to language contact situations and the sociolinguistic processes emanating from these situations. Among the most researched processes are koineization and pidginization, which will be covered in the following two subsections.

6.2.2 Koineization

Koineization is the sociolinguistic process through which a new linguistic variety emerges in language contact between speakers of mutually intelligible varieties (Trudgill, 1986). As Palva (1982, p. 18) suggests, "Koineization involves elimination of specific isoglosses between different dialects." A koine typically appears with the migration of speakers of mutually intelligible varieties to new settlements (Kerswill, 2013).[4] This involves, for example, the migration of rural and Bedouin workers into the city. Koineization involves a number of related sociolinguistic phenomena including dialect mixing, accommodation, and leveling, among others.[5] Mixing refers to the coexistence of features from two or more dialects. Accommodation occurs when one dialect undergoes long-term changes under the influence of another. This includes *diffusion*, which is the spread of linguistic features from one dialect into another (Kerswill, 2013). Accommodation, in this sense, differs from accommodation as a discursive strategy employed under special circumstances to achieve particular communicative goals. Such circumstantial accommodation does not affect the internal structure of the speakers' dialect or language. Leveling refers to sociolinguistic processes whereby linguistic convergence or borrowing from another variety, such as SA, minimizes the differences between two or more dialects (Siegel, 1985). According to Trudgill (1986), leveling often affects marked linguistic forms. While it is theoretically possible to tease apart these processes for descriptive purposes, no attempt will be made to do so in this work because they often operate together or complement each other.

Researchers have frequently invoked koineization to account for the development of the different varieties of Arabic, including Classical Arabic (CA). According to Anis (1959), CA was "a common language" that grew out of contacts between speakers of different Arabic dialects. Mecca, which was an important religious, commercial, and literary center in the pre-Islamic era, was the site of this koineization process. As a koineized variety, CA developed as a mixture of features from various dialects representing distinct tribes or groups of neighboring tribes when speakers of these groups met and interacted. Some of the surviving pre-Islamic literature indicates that this variety was used in poetic contests and intertribal communication. It should therefore have been well-known both to its users (e.g., poets) and to those who participated in intertribal activities.

Koineization also seems to be implicated in the formation of the modern colloquial dialects. Ferguson (1959b) suggests that a single urban *koine* was used in speech throughout the Muslim world in the early centuries of Islamic expansion. The urban koine evolved in garrison towns and was used side by side with CA as a spoken variety. Ferguson argued that this koine developed as a result of "mutual borrowing and leveling among the various dialects" (p. 53). The modern dialects are a continuation of this koine with the differences attributed mainly to borrowings and innovations. Ferguson rationalizes his hypothesis by arguing that "The modern dialects agree with one another as against Classical Arabic in a striking number of features" (p. 52). Ferguson identifies fourteen features of the koine that converge with the modern dialects and diverge from SA.[6] He further argues that these features cannot be ascribed to an analogous evolutionary process by the different dialects, but rather to a single ancestor. While Ferguson explained the common origin of the dialects by focusing on such similarities, he also suggested that the differences are due to independent processes of development. Cohen (1962) advanced a similar view, but pointed to multiple urban koines instead of one. Corriente (1976) suggested that the modern dialects evolved from a pre-Islamic commercial urban koine, which was modified due to language contacts in several influential sedentary centers.

Koineization has possibly been the most significant process in dialect formation and re-formation across the Arab region. At least since the Arab-Islamic conquests, cities and towns have often been the center of the koineization processes as they have historically been the common meeting place of sedentary and Bedouin populations.[7] Given their coexistence in the same geographical area, Arabic dialects have developed conjointly rather than autonomously, which explains why several regional and local dialects contain features from both sedentary and Bedouin dialects (Holes, 1995; Miller, 2006; Palva, 1982, 1994; Versteegh, 1997, 2001). The idea of koineization in the Arab context assumes that there are specific features associated with Bedouin dialects and others related to the sedentary (urban and rural) dialects. However, as Miller (2007, p. 4) correctly observes, dialect categorization derives its legitimacy from "theorization of the origin(s) of the Arabic vernaculars." Moreover, the labels "Bedouin," "sedentary," "rural," and "urban" are not used as *social* categories because that would implicate ideological and identity-based factors. These factors may not only shift over time across and within communities, but may also be viewed differently by individuals within a given community at any given time. This does not mean that these labels have not been studied as social categories, but that the regional variationist approaches have focused more on their characteristic linguistic features and forms.

The common assumption that the language variety (or varieties) brought by the Arab conquerors is *Bedouin* in type is key for understanding the koineization of Arabic dialects (Fück, 1950; Zwettler, 1978). A second and related assumption is that most of the peoples with whom the Arabs interacted in the conquered territories were sedentary. Bearing these two assumptions in mind, it is no surprise that Bedouinization was the norm in the early stages of the Islamic era. In fact, the existing studies suggest that Bedouinization was the chief propeller of language change in most Arab cities until the emergence of centralized Arab states in the second half of the twentieth century (Miller, 2004). Three interrelated factors may explain this phenomenon. First, from a sociopolitical perspective, Bedouins were generally more militarily and politically powerful than the sedentary populations, and they were until recently more recalcitrant to state authority (Chatty, 2010; Hitti, 1996). The impact of Najdi tribes on the sociolinguistic landscape of eastern Syria and western Iraq, and the influence of the Banu Hilaal and Banu Sulaym on the local Maghrebi dialects are two well-documented examples of language change driven by an imbalance in power (Cantineau, 1937; Cohen, 1973; Zakaria 1983). Second, from a socioaffective standpoint, Bedouins were generally more attached to their dialects as emblems of their heritage and history (Abdel-Jawad 1981; Sawaie 1994; Suleiman 1993).[8] Therefore, they were less disposed to give up or change their dialects than the sedentary people. Last, from a social perspective, their societal organization into clans and tribes with strong social ties made Bedouins resistant to linguistic assimilation in the sedentary centers. This interpretation is compatible with Milroy's social network framework, which emphasizes the role of close-knit relationships in language maintenance.

That the regional dialects were Bedouinized does not mean that the dialects of the immigrant Bedouins remained intact, but that the features of the Bedouin dialects became more visible in the process of mixing between the sedentary and Bedouin language varieties. From this perspective, Bedouinization may be seen as a pervasive sociolinguistic phenomenon that spread throughout several Arab urban centers. One of the earliest studies to document this process was carried out by Cantineau (1937), who traced the spread of the Šaawi dialects in eastern Syria and western Iraq to the arrival of the Najdi tribes from current Saudi Arabia. Palva (1994) shows how the previously sedentary dialect of the Sult in Jordan was influenced by the neighboring Bedouin dialects, particularly in terms of phonology (e.g., realization of /k/ as /tš/). Palva suggests that the Sult variety could be characterized as a Bedouin dialect before it was re-sedentarized beginning in the nineteenth century.[9] Procházka (2003) reports a similar Bedouinization process in the Urfa dialect in southern Turkey. The sedentary dialect was superseded by a Bedouin-type dialect due to the influence of Bedouin groups. Pereira (2007) describes the Bedouinization of the urban dialect of Tripoli (Libya) due to immigration movements to the city and the general positive attitudes toward Bedouin values and traditions at the state level. Hachimi (2007) reports of immigrant speakers of Fessi urban dialect in Moroccan converging to the Casablancan Bedouin dialect. Sawaie (1994) points to the adoption of the Bedouin dialectal features by Palestinians in Jordan, which he attributes to identity-related factors.

In a number of sedentary centers, the koineization process has led to the formation of mixed varieties. One striking modern case of mixed varieties occurred in Cairo in the nineteenth century. Woidich (1994) attributes this koineization process to the influx of many Egyptians from areas surrounding Cairo in the wake of the 1835 plague. He suggests that the present Cairene dialect is a product of the mixing of several dialects from areas surrounding Cairo. Similarly, Woidich (1996) provides several examples of mixing and leveling in the rural dialects of Egypt, such as those in northern Egypt and Upper Egypt. Dialectal mixing and leveling occurred with the contact between the sedentary centers and the

Bedouin tribes that settled in these areas. For example, unlike the Cairene dialect, some of these areas use /g/ for the Cairene /ʔ/. They also retain the plural feminine pronouns (e.g., *intin* "you.FP") and affixes (e.g., *yimšan* "walk.3FP"). In addition, they use the *n-* prefix in the first person singular form of imperfect verbs (e.g., *niktib* "I write"). Besides these features, certain plural forms are derived from Bedouin forms (*bnitta* "girls"). The koineization of these dialects also appears in lexical choice, which integrates several Bedouin words, such as *kiif-keif* "how?," *zein* "good," *šein* "bad," *daħya* "egg," etc. Woidich argues that most of the rural dialects in Egypt are koineized varieties resulting from the interaction of the sedentary peoples and the Bedouin peoples, as well as from the influence of the Cairene dialect. The koineized varieties appear clearly in areas on trade routes where there is constant contact between the sedentary and Bedouin populations.

A more recent example of dialect mixing is provided by Al-Wer (2007). Al-Wer examined language variation in speech elicited from speakers representing three generations in the city of Amman: grandparents, parents, and children. The participants were first-, second-, and third-generation "immigrants" to the city. They came from Palestinian and Jordanian backgrounds and ranged in age from twelve to seventy-eight years. The author used this synchronic cross-sectional data-collection method to project a diachronic development of the Ammani dialect. Based on the patterns of mixing in the speech of the study's participants, she suggests that their native dialects endured three stages of change. In the first stage, the dialects of first-generation immigrants "underwent rudimentary leveling, as part of a koineization process" (p. 73). The second stage marks the unsystematic mixing of the linguistic forms between speakers of different dialects, which appears in the speech of second-generation, Amman-born speakers. The last stage is characterized by the emergence of a new, stable and regularized variety, that is, the Ammani variety. This variety is spoken by third-generation, Ammani-born immigrants. The development of the Ammani dialect may therefore be seen as a more recent case of koineization induced by language contact.

Miller (2004) suggests that most of the language varieties spoken in Arab cities are mixed varieties that have been koineized over time. The old sedentary-based dialects seem to be restricted in their use to certain social classes or groups (e.g., old women). By contrast, the koineized urban varieties have become national or regional standards, bestowed with prestige by virtue of the socioeconomic power of their speakers. The rise of the Arab nation-states, and the subsequent decline in the power of Bedouin tribes, have caused these koineized urban language varieties to spread and replace rural and Bedouin varieties. Big cities, such as Cairo, Damascus, Amman, and Algiers, have become the seats of learning, working opportunities, and wealth. The better infrastructure and higher overall quality of life offered by the cities may explain the increase in the Arab urban population from 10% in 1900, to 40% in 1970 and to 58% in 2014 (Barakat, 1993; World Bank, 2014). Rural and Bedouin people who seek better education, positions, and social amenities may find these in the city, and as these individuals relocate to the city, many choose to integrate socially into city life (Habib, 2010; Jabeur, 1987; Messaoudi, 2001). An important part of this social integration is the adoption of the urban dialects.

Some studies have ascribed the linguistic assimilation of rural and Bedouin immigrants living in the city to the prestige of the koineized urban dialects (Abdel-Jawad, 1981, 1986; Al-Wer, 2002, 2007; Amara, 2005; Habib, 2010; Sawaie, 1994). For example, Abdel-Jawad (1981) examined the dynamics of language variation and change in two Jordanian cities: Amman and Irbid, both of which host speakers of three main dialects, including the urban Palestinian, rural Palestinian, and rural and Bedouin Jordanian varieties. Recorded materials were obtained from 200 families in each city. The family members represented two age groups (or two generations): parents and children. The author found that the rural and Bedouin groups converged linguistically with the urban group. For example, all of the three groups have adopted the urban variant /ʔ/ and dropped the /k/ and /g/ variants, which are characteristic of the speech of the rural Palestinians and rural and Bedouin Jordanians, respectively. Abdel-Jawad attributes this type of language convergence to the prestige of the urban dialects. Habib (2010) also interpreted language shift among rural immigrants in the city of Hims (Syria) in terms of the prestige associated with the urban Himsi dialect. Holes (1996) reports of a similar urbanization pattern in Oman, where the distinction between the Bedouin and sedentary dialects has been reduced significantly in the wake of urbanization and modernization.

The increasing stigma associated with the Bedouin and rural dialects represents another factor that may explain the shift to the urban varieties. Versteegh (2001) observes that people who move to Cairo almost always adapt their speech to the Cairene dialect. This also applies to the Syrian situation, as a number of scholars have observed (Daher, 1999; Habib, 2010; Ismail, 2007; Palva, 1982). Palva (1982) documents the spread of the glottal stop /ʔ/ at the expense of alternative variants, such as /q/ and /k/, in a number of Syrian cities and towns. According to Palva, though the variant /k/ was predominantly used by Muslims in the city of Aleppo, the /ʔ/ sound became uniformly used by all urbanized inhabitants of Aleppo due to the influence and prestige of the urban dialects spoken by the Christian and Jewish communities. Similarly, in Mechrefe, the /q/ reflex is dropped and replaced by /ʔ/ due to the prestige associated with this urban feature. This type of koineization is not motivated by religious factors, but by issues of prestige. It should be noted that stigmatization may not always be associated with the dialects themselves, but with certain social indices and stereotypes associated with their speakers. These social stereotypes may eventually become part of the social, personal, and linguistic profile of speakers who use these dialects. For example, many Bedouins are socioeconomically less advantaged and less educated than the urban population. Thus, their dialects may index poor education and poverty compared to the urban dialects (Albirini, 2014a).

In general, the existing studies reveal a host of social, historical, and political factors exerting their influence on koineization. Power relationships between speakers of different varieties are critical for understanding the outcome of the koineization process, though the dynamics of koineization may also be influenced by prestige, identity, and attitudinal factors.

6.2.3 Pidgins and creoles

Arabic-based pidgins and creoles are particular outcomes of language contact between Arabic speakers and speakers of other languages. A pidgin is a new language developed by speakers who do not have a common language but need to communicate, usually in long-term contact situations. A creole is a pidgin that has been nativized and stabilized by children who acquire and use it as a primary means of communication. According to Trudgill (2009, p. 174), "pidgin and creole languages have no irregularity, high transparency, no morphological categories, and no syntagmatic redundancy." The most distinctive feature of pidgins and creoles is linguistic simplification, which is marked by the regularization of irregularities, increase in lexical and morphological transparency, and the loss of redundancy (Britain, 2009; Trudgill, 2009).

Versteegh (1984, 2004) suggests that the Arabic colloquial dialects developed through a process of pidginization and creolization, followed by an ongoing process of decreolization. According to Versteegh, the development of the modern colloquial dialects was motivated by the need for communication between Arabs and non-Arabs; Arabic was learned as a second language by people who needed to communicate with native Arabic speakers in post-diaspora contact situations. In particular, Versteegh speaks of mixed marriages between Arabs and non-Arabs in the new territories making spouses second language learners. These learners were compelled to employ "universal strategies of second language learning" in the process of undirected/untutored second language acquisition (Versteegh, 1984, p. 77). This gave rise to a pidginized form of Arabic, which was then acquired and naturalized by children. The new creolized variety was then decreolized over time due to a number of factors, particularly the spread of literacy and formal instruction in CA. The process of decreolization followed different paths as it occurred in geographically distant areas, and the decreolized varieties have retained some of the features of the creolized varieties and dropped others. In this view, Versteegh's proposition accounts for the similarities and differences among the Arabic colloquial dialects, as well as those occurring between the colloquial dialects and SA.[10]

Working within the pidginization and creolization hypothesis, Aune (2003) argues that the sociolinguistic conditions surrounding the development of Moroccan Arabic provide a case for pidginization, creolization, and decreolization. Aune examined a number of constructions that point to this process of pidginization and creolization, including the tense, mode, and aspect systems, word order, question formation, genitive forms, and the indefinite articles. According to Aune, evidence for the pidginization and subsequent creolization of Moroccan Arabic appears in the dialect's simplified and severely reduced tense, mode, and aspect morphology, as well as by the absence of embedded clauses, unmarked SVO word order, and polymorphemic interrogatives. Moreover, Moroccan Arabic employs analytic genitives and an indefinite article derived from a lexical item meaning "one." Aune states that all of these features are identified in the literature as characteristic of Arabic pidgins and creoles. The author also argues that Moroccan Arabic is currently undergoing a process of decreolization in the sense that it is shifting closer to SA as speakers of the Moroccan dialect are constantly exposed to SA in its spoken and written forms. The decreolization of the Moroccan dialect will, in due course, bring the reclassicization process to full fruition. Aune describes Morrocan's common perception of their dialect as a simplified version of SA as evidence for the pidginization and creolization of Moroccan Arabic.

Moving outside the political map of the Arab world, the four most established Arabic-based pidgins and creoles are Turku, Bongor Arabic, Kinubi, and Juba Arabic (Tosco & Manfredi, 2013). These languages are referred to as Sudan-based pidgins both because they originated in South Sudan and grew out of contacts between Sudanese and Egyptian Arabic speakers and speakers of African languages (e.g., Heine, 1982; Luffin, 2007; Mahmud, 1979; Miller, 2002, 2006; Owens, 1985, 1991; Tosco, 1995; Versteegh, 1993; Wellens, 2005). Arabic served as the superstrate in the development of all of these languages both because of its relative prestige compared to the substrate languages, and also because of the asymmetries in power that characterized the relationship between Arabic speakers and those who spoke native African tongues at the time of language contact. The four languages emerged from the relationships between Arabic-speaking soldiers and traders and the local African peoples, who spoke any of several Nilotic languages (Tosco & Manfredi, 2013). This explains why these languages are sometimes called *military lingua franca* (Miller, 2006; Tosco & Manfredi, 2013). Like all pidgins, each of these grew out of the need for communication between speakers of languages not mutually intelligible. None of these languages are currently understood by Sudanese speakers of Arabic, though they were originally simplified versions of Sudanese Arabic dialects (Owens, 2001; Tosco & Manfredi, 2013). Turku and Bongor Arabic are spoken in Chad, whereas Kinubi Arabic is spoken in Kenya and Tanzania and Juba Arabic in Juba, South Sudan.

Tosco & Manfredi (2013, p. 499) list a number of linguistic features that are common to all of these pidginized varieties of Arabic. First, in terms of phonology, the following features are observed:

- Loss of pharyngealization,
- The velar fricatives /x/ and /ɣ/ usually merge with /k/ and /g/,
- Gemination and vowel length are lost,

- Interdentals /θ/ and /ð/ are changed into dental stops /t/ and /d/ or into fricatives /s/ and /z/.

In morphosyntax, the following changes are reported:

- Root and pattern morphology is lost as a productive derivational and inflectional system,
- The definite article al/il is lost,
- The construct state is lost and is replaced by the analytic genitive,
- Only independent pronouns are preserved, whereas possessive and object pronouns are lost,
- SVO is the dominant word order.

The lexicon is severely reduced, and semantically transparent compound expressions are used to compensate for the lack of specific terms.

One less-conventionalized Arabic pidgin is Gulf Pidgin (Bakir, 2010; Næss, 2008; Smart, 1990). The emergence of this pidginized variety may be traced to the 1970s following the economic boom that the Gulf States witnessed with the emergence of oil industry.[11] A continuous influx of expatriate laborers from different parts of the world, particularly Iran and South Asia, accompanied this socioeconomic boom (Bakir, 2010), and Gulf Pidgin surfaced as a way to facilitate communication between these immigrants and Gulf Arabs. Gulf Pidgin may be described as an inchoate pidgin because its linguistic features are marked by variation and instability (Bakir, 2010; Næss, 2008). According to Næss (2008, p. 94), Gulf Pidgin is based on "immigrant talk," which is a simplified form of Arabic tailored to target learners. Although this pidgin originated as a means of communication between speakers of Gulf Arabic and non-Arab speakers, it is also used by immigrant workers who speak different languages, such Farsi, Panjabi, Urdu, Hindi, Bengali, Thai, Tagalog, Indonesian, Nepalese, Tamil, and Sinhalese (Bakir, 2010). Reduction and overregularization are some of the most salient traits of this pidginized variety of Arabic. Næss (2008) reports that out of the twenty-nine consonant phonemes found in Omani Arabic, only eighteen exist in Gulf Pidgin Arabic. Negation is always expressed with *mafi* "there is not" and possession is realized through the analytic genitive construction. Bakir (2010) found that verbs in the Gulf Pidgin spoken in Qatar are not inflected for tense, aspect, or modality. Verbs are mostly used in their third person singular masculine form. In terms of negation, only two forms are used, namely, *ma* "did not" and *mafi* "there is not."

Avram (2010) and Bizri (2010) document two other cases of unconventionalized Arabic pidgins. Avram (2010) reports of a pidgin Arabic that was used in Iraqi oil camps before the eruption of the first Gulf War, though it is no longer in existence due to the political conditions in Iraq. Bizri (2010) describes a "Pidgin madam" variety burgeoning between Lebanese Arabic speakers and their Sri Lankan housemaids. However, this latter means of communication might not eventually develop into a real pidgin because housemaids interact with their Lebanese employers independently and possibly on only a very limited basis among themselves, minimizing the possibility of establishing common norms for this variety.

6.3 SOCIAL VARIATION

Following Labov's work, a large number of studies have focused on the relationship between the formal aspects of language and social variables. A survey of the dissertations produced during the 1980s and 1990s reveals that perhaps only diglossia received as much scholarly attention as the study of the social antecedents of language variation (e.g., Abdel-Jawad, 1981; Abdul-Hassan, 1988; Al-Ahdal, 1989; Al-Dashti, 1998; Al-Jehani, 1985; Al-Khatib, 1988; Al-Muhannadi, 1991; Al-Shehri, 1993; Al-Wer, 1991; Daher, 1999; Haeri, 1991; Jabeur, 1987; Khatani, 1992; Walters, 1989). Most of these studies have adopted a quantitative approach to language variation and change, exploring possible correlations between language variants and social variables, such as gender, social class, age, ethnicity, religious identity, and locality. This section provides an overview of some of the social variables that have been invoked in Arabic studies to explain variation. These are by no means the only social factors influencing variation, but they received the lion's share of variationist research in the Arab region.

Social factors operate in concert and not independently, and therefore it is not always easy to untangle and isolate the influence of one variable from the others. In fact, it is sometimes misleading to predict social variation and change through discrete or isolated social variables, and this is simply because social reality is complex, dynamic, and nuanced. Therefore, a contextualized understanding of language variation depends largely upon uncovering the historical, social, political, and socioaffective factors surrounding language development and use. Indeed, many sociolinguists have illustrated that some of these variables may not operate separately and are often confounded by other social factors (Al-Wer, 2007; Haeri, 1991; Holes, 1995; Miller, 2007; Taine-Cheikh, 2012; Owens, 2001). For ease of presentation, however, the following subsections will be dedicated to four social variables: (1) gender, (2) social and educational background, (3) ethnicity and religion, and (4) time and locality.

6.3.1 Variation in relation to gender

Gender is the most widely researched social variable in relationship to language variation and change. Gender is a socially and culturally developed construct, distinguishable from sex, which refers to biological characteristics. Cameron (2006, p. 724) defines gender as "the cultural traits and behaviors deemed appropriate for men or women by a particular society". As a social construct, gender is created through various discourses, practices, and relations. There is a growing tendency in sociolinguistic research to avoid describing gender as a single or fixed social category and to describe it instead in terms of gendered identities.[12] In other words, gender is no longer seen as a dichotomy, but as a continuum of identities and roles. The term "gender identities" postulates the possibility of accepting or rejecting certain social expectations, roles, and behaviors associated with one's sex. However, in the vast majority of variationist studies – and in Arabic variationist research – the distinction between gender and sex disappears; the male/female binary refers to fixed categories that pinpoint biological sex and gendered identities simultaneously. *Gender* is used merely as a euphemism for sex, and these two terms are used interchangeably in this work.

As a social category, gender has been approached from three main perspectives.[13] One perspective focuses on gender as a *grammatical category*, examining the social meanings of grammatical gender markings. A second perspective deals with *language practices* by men and women, focusing on distinctions in conversation styles, speech acts, communicative practices, dominance tactics, discursive politeness, speech performances, gender positioning, and ideological articulations (Eckert & McConnell-Ginet, 2003; Holmes & Meyerhoff, 2003; Sadiqi, 2003, 2006a). Not all of these topics have been studied in the Arab context, partly because the study of gender as a social construct is relatively new to Arabic sociolinguistic research (Sadiqi, 2003, 2006a; Vicente, 2009). A third and last perspective deals with the distinction between the *linguistic features* of men's and women's speech. Within this perspective, language is seen as a symbolic system that is amenable to variation and change under the influence of speakers' gender. Therefore, this line of research focuses mostly on the distinctive linguistic features in the speech of women and men (Al-Wer, 2008; Sadiqi, 2003, 2006a). Most quantitative variationist studies on gender-based language differences adopt this approach, typically with the goal of discovering correlations between certain linguistic features and speakers' gender. The following subsection will briefly outline the first two perspectives before moving to the main topic: gender-based variation in relation to linguistic features.

Gender and variation in grammatical categories and in language use

One trend in research on language and gender deals with grammatical gender and its origin, function, and variation (Hachimi, 2007; Sadiqi, 2006a). This perspective problematizes grammatical gender as an ideologically charged system. It is well-known that Arabic works with masculine and feminine genders, but lacks a neutral gender, and the assignment of gender markings is seen as biased in several respects. Citing a number of classic treatises on Arabic grammar, Sadiqi (2006a) maintains that the masculine–feminine dichotomy originates in sexist ideology that favored masculine traits over feminine traits and used grammar to index this cultural preference. However, we still do not know whether these classic treatises were themselves involved in dictating the social meaning of grammatical gender, were descriptions of patterns already in use, or simply expressed the personal opinions of their authors. Feminine gender is seen as a *marked* form because feminine words are generally derived from masculine counterparts (Hachimi, 2007). In Arabic, a word like *muhandisah* "female engineer" is derived from *muhandis* "male engineer" by adding the singular feminine marker − *ah*. The fact that the derivation is realized through addition rather than subtraction is taken as a sign of "formal androcentricity" (Sadiqi, 2006a, p. 642). Another aspect of gender bias concerns the fact that most generic or default forms are masculine (Sadiqi, 2006a). Sadiqi gives the example of *marʔ* "a person," which encompasses both genders and yet may also refer to males, whereas *marʔa* "women" is a derivation. This feature exists in many gendered languages through-out the world, but its historical background is far from clear (Vicente, 2009).

A second line of research focuses on the differential *language practices* among men and women. This approach may not be considered variationist in the Labovian sense; in fact, some studies simply focus on women's language behav-ior. However, as Sadiqi (2006a) notes, these studies are undertaken with male speakers' language behavior positioned as the major point of reference. Prob-lems sometimes emerge when the sociolinguistic norms of this point of reference are not well-established, which makes the comparability of men's and women's language behavior challenging. To establish a comparative perspective, men's and women's linguistic behavior should be compared and contrasted with respect to a given sociolinguistic phenomenon under the same circumstances. For exam-ple, the common assumption that women use more polite forms than men is not substantiated empirically, but based on generalizations derived from research in non-Arabic speaking communities. Moreover, the idea that Arab men's and wom-en's language practices are dictated by social norms and expectations ignores the role of their gendered agencies (Abu-Lughod, 1990; Bassiouney, 2010; Hachimi, 2001, 2012; Sadiqi, 2003, 2006a). Gender studies therefore need to explain women's language use in the light of contextual and social factors con-ditioning their language behavior as well as their own personal, professional, and social experiences.

One aspect of the difference between men and women concerns the dis-similar language ideologies underlying their language use (Abu-Haidar, 1991; Bassiouney, 2010; Hachimi, 2001, 2012; Sadiqi, 1995, 2003, 2006a). Based on a number of previous analyses (e.g., El Saadawi, 1980; Mernissi, 1997), Sadiqi (2003, 2006a) proposes a "space dichotomy," which allocates men to public space and women to private space, a dichotomy "not only spatial but also linguis-tic and symbolic" (Sadiqi, 2006a, p. 645). The outside space is the site of power, whereas the inside space is the place of subordination. Women's inability to access the public domain of men restricts their language choices in such venues as religion, politics, law, and literacy. For example, certain religious terms, such as *imama* "female religious leader" or *muftiya* "female religious legislator," are absent in women's everyday language use. With respect to politics, women are rarely competent public speakers because they principally use oral languages. In terms of law, Sadiqi points to "the legal power associated with Arabic," and explains the shift of many feminist writers and activists from French to Arabic since the mid-1980s as an effort to make their voices heard in the legal space. Lastly, Sadiqi cites high illiteracy rates among women as the cause of women's exclusion from using Arabic, which has traditionally been associated with literacy. In general, women's lack of access to the spaces of power limits their linguistic choices or dictates upon them particular language usage, especially considering that SA is seen as a male language; SA is associated with the public domain (religion, politics, law, education, etc.), which is less accessible to women.

Gender has been employed as a mediating lens for analyzing language choice (Bassiouney, 2009a, 2010; Sa'ar, 2007; Sadiqi, 1995; 2003). Sadiqi (1995), for example, surveyed 100 Moroccan women, including twenty-five students, twenty-five teachers, and fifty women with different professions. In addition, she conducted interviews with ten women from each group. She found that house-wives used Moroccan Arabic more predominantly at home than working women did. By contrast, working women spoke more French. Berber was used less than Moroccan Arabic and French in the home and work domains. The author ascribes this tendency to the better utility of Moroccan Arabic and French compared to Berber. According to Sadiqi, working women adopt French to "assert them-selves, given their social status" and the need to make recourse to a language that is perceived as more prestigious (p. 69). Similarly, working women switch codes more often because of factors of prestige. Regardless of their occupa-tion, however, women avoid non-standard language features because these are perceived as "tough," "uncivilized," and "uneducated," compared to the standard forms, which are seen as "intelligent," "independent," and "sophisticated" (p. 69). Women are selective in their word choice. For example, women's language is described as replete with euphemisms, emotions, intensifiers, and diminutives. That being said, we still do not know whether female speakers' language choices converge or diverge from male speakers' linguistic practices in the same settings and circumstances.

Several studies have focused on the discourse strategies employed by women. One interesting pattern noted in these studies is Arab women's adop-tion of "masculine talk." Some scholars argue that women switch to "masculine talk" as a purposeful act to sidestep patriarchal sociolinguistic norms and partic-ipate fully in the public domain (Abu-Haidar, 1991; Barontini & Ziamari, 2009; Rosenhouse & Dbayyat, 2006; Sa'ar, 2007). Barontini and Ziamari (2009) used audio recordings and a survey to examine language choice among six urban girls from the city of Meknes, ranging in age from seventeen to twenty, and one rural woman of forty-five years from a neighboring village. The rural woman worked in agriculture, mostly with men, and therefore she had adapted her speech to mas-culine style. Barontini and Ziamari describe the woman's choice as emanating from a need to cope with the dominantly male environment and to protect herself against abusive and dominant male language. By contrast, the young girls alter-nated between male and female talk, the former to show toughness and playful-ness, and the latter to display politeness, employing strategies such as indirect language, diminutives, euphemisms, and supplications (p. 164). In a slightly different study, Sa'ar (2007) showed how the use of "masculine talk," particularly with respect to grammatical gender, pervades female speakers of Hebrew and Arabic. For example, speakers avoid feminine grammatical forms in favor of masculine forms both in reference to themselves and in generic or gender inclusive reference. According to Sa'ar, this practice is part of the construction of cultural gender and makes the speaker less offensive to cultural norms. Moreover, women use this strategy to achieve "fuller cultural participation" (p. 408).

Research on gender-based asymmetries in language use points to differences in the practices of naming and addressing men and women. Often, researchers attribute the differences to the unequal positions of men and women in terms of status and power (Abdel-Jawad, 1989; Eid, 1994; Hachimi, 2001; Jebra, 1980; Muñoz-Cobo, 2008). For example, in her study of Egyptian obituaries in the daily *Al-Alhram* newspaper, Eid (1994) found that the omission of a deceased person's name is predicted by his or her gender. Most women's names are omitted and related to a relative, whereas most male obituaries state the man's name explicitly. Based on her study of terms of address in Morocco, Muñoz-Cobo (2008, p. 99) divides terms of address into two categories: neutral and connotative. She associates neutral forms of address with stable, denotative attributes, such as *hajj* for someone who has performed pilgrimage. However, this same term may also be used connotatively to reflect respect to an older person regardless of whether he/she has performed pilgrimage. The connotative use of terms of address is influenced both by disproportionate power and by the type of relationship binding the interlocutors. Thus, it may mark identity negotiation between different interlocutors either vertically or horizontally. Muñoz-Cobo observes that gender, among other social variables such as age, origin, and occupation, is involved in the negotiation process because some terms associated with men and women reflect their allocation to different spaces. Citing Mernissi (1990), Muñoz-Cobo notes that whereas men rarely use their wives' names or refer to their relationships with them in the public space, women do. For example, a man may refer to his wife as *əl-mra* "the woman" or *əd-daar* "the house," whereas a woman would use the terms *raajli* "my man" or *muul əd-daar* "owner of the house" (see also Hachimi, 2001; Sadiqi, 1995, 2003). As noted earlier, these differences are attributed to gender inequality in power relationships.

However, a number of studies have shown that gender is not a major determinant in the selection of terms of address (El-Anani, 1971; Parkinson, 1985; Yassin, 1975). For example, Parkinson (1985) examined terms of address used with family members, relatives, employees, supervisors, foreigners, elderly, Muslim fellows, etc. Based on a wide range of interviews and various recorded data, Parkinson found that speakers change their terms of address based not only on the sex, age, occupation, and social class of the addressee, but also on the relationships between the interlocutors. However, terms displaying power and deference or intimacy and solidarity were not influenced by the sex of the interlocutors. In his study of Kuwaiti terms of address, Yassin (1975) reports that terms of address are largely unaffected by gender. For example, a father would call his son and daughter by the same title *yuba* "my father," and a mother would address her children, using the term *yumma* "my mother," regardless of their gender. El-Anani (1971) argues that terms of address cannot be understood without understanding the interlocutors' backgrounds and relationships. For example, the term *ya xaayse* "you loser" may be used as a term of endearment among closely related women in some rural areas in Jordan, whereas the same vocative phrase could be offensive among distantly related women or in another context.

A group of studies have examined the politeness strategies employed by men and women with the expectation that these strategies may reflect their social status or position (Muñoz-Cobo, 2008; Sadiqi, 1995). In particular, it is predicted that women's want for power and their low social status may force them to address their interlocutors more politely and less forcefully. Several researchers have challenged this assumption both theoretically and empirically. Farhat (2013) argues that the idea of relegating women to subordinate positions and less power ignores the fact that women enjoy a great deal of respect in Arab societies, because of religion and culture, and sometimes for their family status and age. Kharraki (2001) examined more than sixty bargaining exchanges involving men and women in eastern Morocco. Kharraki compares the different politeness-based strategies men and women utilize leading up to and during the bargaining process. He suggests that bargaining is a "negative politeness act since it impedes the freedom of the bargainee" (p. 629). Since the buyer is in need of the commodity, he/she must initiate and sustain the bargaining process in order to attain the desired price reduction. The findings indicate that men and women rely upon different strategies in the bargaining process. Men are more prone to depreciate the quality of the goods, whereas women are less inclined to do so as this threatens the reputation of the vender. Moreover, women are more assertive and more insistent in their bargaining, and they deploy more direct strategies and strive less for intimacy with the vender than men. Kharraki's findings indicate that understanding the dynamics of politeness requires first and foremost paying attention to societal norms and expectations. For example, women try to display distance from venders in compliance with the cultural honor system. Likewise, men refrain from strategies of insistence because such communication styles could come across as "an affront to their dignity" (p. 629).

An important trend in gender research deals with the analysis of women's discourse, particularly with respect to the issues of "voice" and authority. Voice refers to "the capacity to make oneself heard" and therefore is connected to the issues of authority, power, and inequity (Juffermans & Van der Aa, 2013, p. 112). In a pioneering work, Abu-Lughod (1986, 1990) examined the discursive practices of Bedouin women in Egypt's Western Desert. In particular, the author focused on forms of resistance that women use to undermine "the ideology of sexual difference . . . as a form of power" (1990, p. 46). Abu-Lughod identified a number subversive discourses among Bedouin women, including folktales, songs, jokes, and oral lyric poetry. For example, women use songs to resist arranged marriages, and they mobilize jokes and folktales to make fun of men and manhood. In addition, they violate the two codes by which the Bedouin society abides, namely honor and modesty, by reciting oral poetry highlighting their romantic relations and ventures. Al Natour (2012) examined the forms of resistance to repressive authority in three literary works: *The Shell* by Mustafa Khalifa, *Girls of Riyadh* by Rajaa Alsanea, and *Absent* by Betool Khedairi. These novels deal with dissimilar types of oppression, including political, social, domestic, and gendered violence and suppression. Al Natour shows how women in these novels use diverse resources to express their voice, assert their authority, and challenge the mandates of the societies in which they live. In *Girls of Riyadh*, for instance, the four female protagonists resort to the internet and cell phone technologies to break the restrictions imposed upon them by societal norms. Through the new media, women create their own discourses and affirm their individualism and independence.

As this short review demonstrates, the existing patterns depict a complex picture of the linguistic behaviors of men and women. Hachimi (2001) correctly warns against generalizations with regard to language use and gender. Such generalizations have the potential to incorrectly create or reinforce stereotypes that apply to certain settings but may not extend to others. Sadiqi (2003, 2006a) notes that this area of research is still in its infancy, and therefore the findings should be interpreted locally or within their immediate context. While power imbalances provide an important lens in approaching the relationship between language and gender, it may also be fruitful to examine some communication patterns in terms of cultural differences and uniqueness. The use of multiple approaches is conducive to a richer and more comprehensive assessment of social factors that may be involved in the various languages practices of men and women.

Gender and variation in linguistic features

Linguistic variation originating in gendered categories has been widely documented in the literature (e.g., Abdel-Jawad, 1981, 1986; Abdul-Hassan, 1988; Abu-Haidar, 1989; Al-Essa, 2009; al-Rojaie, 2013; Al-Wer, 1991, 1999, 2007; Daher, 1999; Hachimi, 2007, 2011; Haeri, 1991; Ismail, 2007; Jaber, 2013; Jabeur, 1987; Miller, 2006; Royal, 1985; Taqi, 2010; Trabelsi, 1991; Walters, 1989). Most of the existing studies reveal that gender is intertwined with other social variables, such as age and education, in affecting language variation. Considering the results of these studies, not every instance of variation reported in this subsection may be attributed to gender alone. In fact, the findings about the role of gender should be interpreted with caution because gender seems often to work in tandem with other social variables in producing certain types of language variation or change.

The study of gender and language variation in the Arab region has been framed and interpreted within generalizations gleaned from worldwide research on the same phenomena. Among several common generalizations, four stand out (Cheshire, 2002; Labov, 1972; Tagliamonte, 2011; Trudgill, 1986; Wolfram & Fasold, 1974):

- Compared to men, women are more attentive to socially evaluative linguistic forms because they are often under greater social scrutiny.
- Women are more likely to use linguistic forms that reflect social class because they have historically been deprived from access to high-ranking positions.
- Women tend to converge on overtly prestigious varieties or features – regardless of whether these are represented by standard, national, supralocal, or local varieties.
- Compared to women, men are more likely to opt for stigmatized varieties and features that are associated with covert prestige as these also often mark masculinity.

These assumptions have generally constituted the starting point for research on the relationship between gender and language variation in the Arab region.

Most of the early studies on gender-based language variation and change have investigated the extent to which men and women converge on SA. As noted above, this line of research was motivated by the general claim that, cross-culturally, women are more inclined to approximate standard and prestigious linguistic forms in their speech (Labov, 1972; Trudgill, 1974). Studies on language variation in the Arab region have provided conflicting evidence as to whether gender plays a role in the frequency and nature of SA features occurring in the speech of men and women. One group of studies has confirmed the "universal" trend wherein women favor standard forms (Abu-Haidar, 1989; Holes, 2004; Jaber, 2013; Mejdell, 2006; Walters, 2003). Abu-Haidar (1989) investigated the use of six linguistic variables by fifty Iraqi men and women in Baghdad. The six SA linguistic variables were compared to their counterparts in the Baghdadi dialect, and these included: (1) passive forms, (2) ordinal numbers for months of the year, (3) the adverb *lamman* "when," (4) the adjective ṣaɣiir, and (5, 6) lexical items whose equivalents are either borrowed or well-established in the colloquial dialect. The participants were the investigator's friends or colleagues. To ensure that the potential difference between the male and female groups may be attributed to gender alone, the researcher controlled for a number of extraneous variables, such as age, level of education, and socioeconomic background. She collected her data through both formal interviews and informal observations of language behavior. Abu-Haidar reports that women in her study generally tend to use SA features more often than men. Jaber (2013) examined lexical choice among speakers of Baghdadi Arabic and correlated these choices with age and gender. The author also found that women lean more often toward the use of SA words than men. Jaber attributes this disparity to women's awareness of SA's prestige. Other researchers have corroborated these findings, reporting that educated women, more often than men, mark their education or the elevation of their discourse through the use of SA variants in formal speech (Mejdell, 2006; Walters, 2003).

Another group of studies, however, has concluded that men are more prone to use SA features than women (e.g., Abdel-Jawad, 1981; Abdul-Hassan, 1988; Al-Wer, 1999; Daher, 1998; Ibrahim, 1986; Kojak, 1999; Schmidt, 1986). For example, Abdel-Jawad (1981) reports that men use the standard /q/ phoneme more frequently than women, regardless of their age, education, place of origin, or the formality of their speech. By contrast, most women prefer the urban /ʔ/ variant. Abdul-Hassan (1988) found that Iraqi men produce the standard /k/ with more frequency than the Iraqi colloquial variant /tš/, whereas the opposite is true of Iraqi women. Al-Wer (1999) also reports that Jordanian men tend to use the SA [q] or Bedouin [g] in their speech, while women are more inclined to use the urban Palestinian [ʔ]. Al-Dashti (1998) found that Egyptian women in Kuwait were more successful than Egyptian men in acquiring the Kuwaiti variants /y/ and /dʒ/, which correspond to the variant /dʒ/ and /q/ in SA. All of these findings depart from the general assumption that women lean toward the standard and prestigious variety more often than men do (Labov, 1972). Such a disparity in conclusions explains why researchers have argued that the relation between SA features and gender cannot be seen as fixed, calling rather for a case-by-case analysis (Mejdell, 2006; Walters, 1989). Bassiouney confirms this conclusion (2010), as she found no relationship between the sex of the speaker and the frequency with which Egyptian men and women deploy SA or QA features in talk shows.

One interesting interpretation of the distinct linguistic behavior of men and women with respect to SA and QA features is the association of SA with traditional values or professions that men cherish, and the similar linking of QA to modernization and progress, things often favored by women (Abdel-Jawad, 1981; Daher, 1998; Haeri, 1991; Ibrahim, 1986). An illustrative example of this pattern is Daher's (1998) study on language variation in Damascus. Daher (1998) investigated the distribution of the SA phonemes /θ/, /ð/, /q/ and their Damascene variants /s/, /z/, and /ʔ/ in the speech of twenty-three men and twenty-three women in Damascus. In addition to their variance in sex, the participants differed in terms of age group (15–24, 25–39, and 40–70) and educational level (elementary school, high school, and college or higher). Daher used sociolinguistic interviews to explore whether the use of the three linguistic variables was correlated to the social variables of sex, age, and education. The findings indicate that the use of the SA variants /θ/, /ð/ is restricted mainly to educated speakers – principally men – whose profession requires the use of SA in its written form. As for the phoneme /q/, Daher found that men use the SA variant more frequently than women because it is associated with the "traditional values" represented by SA, and it indexes the identity of the educated, literary, or religious male. On the other hand, women lean toward the Damascene variant /ʔ/ because it marks urbanization, modernization, and progress – values that women often hold in higher regard than men do.

Several interesting discussions have arisen around a possible reconciliation of these contradictory findings. These discussions explored potential reasons underpinning Arab women's divergence from the "universal" norm concerning women's tendency to deploy standard and prestigious language forms in their speech. Ibrahim provided one explanation, which was subsequently adopted by many researchers working on Arabic. Ibrahim (1986, p. 124) maintained that "All available data indicate that Arab women in speaking Arabic employ the locally prestigious features of L more than men. This is in perfect conformity with patterns of language use in other language communities investigated for sex differentiation . . .". For Ibrahim, then, women do tend to adopt features of the prestigious dialects. However, prestige is not necessarily associated with SA, but with regional standards or supralocal varieties, such as the varieties of the capital cities in most Arab countries (see also Miller, 2007; Taine-Cheikh, 2012; Vicente, 2009). Ibrahim's proposition reinstates prestige as a main motif of language variation and change, but assigns it to varieties that have not traditionally enjoyed much esteem in the Arabic-speaking communities.

Several subsequent studies have interpreted their findings along these lines. Researchers have invoked the connection between language variation and prestige in scenarios where women have been found to favor urban or "supralocal" features compared to men, who tend to lean toward features of local Bedouin or rural dialects. Haeri (1991), among others, suggested that the urban dialects, particularly those of the capital cities, function as the national standards in most Arab countries (see also Miller, 2006; Vicente, 2009). According to one account, some features of the urban dialects (such as the glottal stop /ʔ/) are marked with "prestige." Al-Ali and Arafa (2010) found that men and high schoolers in Irbid (Jordan) are more likely to utilize the local /θ/, /dʒ /, and /ð/ sounds, whereas women and university graduates tend to use the prestigious supralocal variants of these sounds. Al-Rojaie (2013) examined the impact of age, gender, and level of education on the patterns of variation in the distribution of the variant [tš] for [k] in the speech of seventy-two speakers of Qasiimi, a local dialect of Najdi Arabic. Findings indicate that older less educated speakers, regardless of their sex, tend to maintain the use of the local variant [tš], whereas younger, educated speakers, particularly women, favor the use of the supralocal variant [k]. Similar results are reported by other researchers (Abdel-Jawad, 1981; Habib, 2010; Sawaie, 1994). According to Al-Wer (2014), this pattern shows that Arab women follow the global pattern of women leaning toward the linguistic features considered prestigious, especially if one sees the urban varieties as the "national" prestige varieties.

Apart from prestige, some accounts have attributed men's and women's linguistic choices to the masculinity or femininity associated with certain varieties or linguistic features. In the Arab culture, like in several other cultures, it is inappropriate for women to act like men or for men to act like women. The adoption of feminine (usually urban) features helps women index their feminine identities. The same may be said of men, who may resort to "masculine" linguistic features to mark their masculinity. As women generally live under more social pressure to conform to societal norms, they are often more likely to espouse the feminine features in their speech. For example, women often favor urban varieties that feature the [ʔ] sound over varieties with alternative forms, such as [q] and [g]. This phenomenon has been observed among women in Algeria, Egypt, Jordan, Syria, and Tunisia (Abdel-Jawad, 1981; Al-Wer, 1991; Daher, 1998; Dendane, 2007; Miller, 1997; Royal 1985; Wahba, 1996). Men diverge from women in this respect in that they favor Bedouin and rural dialects, which are often marked with masculinity. In Tlemcen (Algeria), Dendane (2007) found that women maintain the use of the old Tlemceni variant [ʔ], unlike men who shift to the newer koineized [g], which has to do with the perception of the old urban [ʔ] as a mark of femininity (see also Belhadj-Tahar, 2013). Abu-Haidar (1989) attributes men's display of strongly pharyngealized phonemes to their masculine associations. Miller (1997) observes that male rural immigrants in Cairo retain the use of [g] and refrain from shifting to the Cairene [ʔ] because the latter is a salient feature of the Cairene dialect's perceived softness and femininity. Daher (1999) similarly found that women are more likely to use the Damascene [ʔ] than the [q] because the latter is associated with education and masculinity.

On the other hand, a number of studies have challenged the idea of aligning the use of feminine or masculine linguistic features with gender roles, demonstrating that, in certain contexts, women may opt for "masculine linguistic features" in their speech. Women assert their agency through the selection of particular language features, which help them convey specific social meanings or index their preferred identities in social interactions and relations (Al-Wer, 1999; Rosenhouse & Dbayyat, 2006; Sa'ar, 2007; Walters, 1991). As an example, in his study of the speech of female and male speakers in Korba, Tunisia, Walters (1991) found that many young educated women tend to use the local /z/ variant instead of /ṣ/ variant, even though the former is generally associated with male speech. The use of the local variant, according to Walters, is a way for these female speakers to express loyalty to their local variety and identity. Al-Wer (1999) shows that women in three different Jordanian towns prefer to use the local /g/ sound to non-local alternatives (including the urban /ʔ/ sound), thereby expressing "a local and ethnic identity" (p. 54). These findings suggest that rather than being governed by any hard rule, the use of feminine or masculine linguistic features is liable to vary based on context and is influenced by several social factors.

Similar controversy surrounds the generalization that women tend to adopt novel linguistic forms compared to men, who seem to prefer traditional forms. A number of studies have found that women, particularly younger women, embrace novel linguistic forms more quickly and pervasively than men. As noted above, Haeri (1991) found that middle-class women lead new phonological change in the Cairene dialect. Al-Wer (1991) found that women – not men – shifted between four phonological variants representing the local dialects in Sult, Ajloun, and Karak, as well as variants of the non-local urban Palestinian dialect. In Amman, Al-Wer (2007) also reports that women were ahead of men in adopting novel non-local features. Alghamdi (2014) shows that Saudi women consistently use more foreign-borrowed words than local Saudi Arabic words to identify colors. The same pattern was reported by Lawson-Sako and Sachdev (1996) in the Tunisian context. Lawson-Sako and Sachdev suggest that young middle-class women tend to deploy foreign words in their speech because such words index modernity, which is a favorable social attribute in Tunisia. Al-Essa (2009) examined language variation among a Najdi community in the city of Jeddah, whose majority dialect is a Hijazi dialect. She found that older Najdi women have maintained their Najdi dialect to a greater extent than Najdi men did. The author attributes this trend to gender segregation and lack of access to the majority dialect. Younger women, however, were found to accommodate the Hijazi features in their dialects more frequently than men do. For example, women mark feminine gender in the second person less by using the Najdi variant [ts] and more often with the Hijazi variant [-k]. According to Al-Essa, the younger generation has greater access to the Hijazi dialect and is less affected by gender segregation.

However, most of these studies reveal that gender interacts with age in explaining language variation; only younger women seem to be involved in this linguistic innovation and change, whereas older women do not (see the following section). Moreover, some studies have shown that men are sometimes ahead of women in linguistic change. Hachimi (2011) examined gender-based differences in the use of the Fessi postalveolar approximant [ɹ] and the Casablancan alveolar trill [r]. Hachimi conducted interviews with first-, second-, and third-generation Fessi immigrants in Casablanca. Immigrant Fessi men were found to be ahead of the Fessi women in terms of using the Casablancan alveolar trill /r/. Similarly, Belhadj-Tahar (2013) investigated the linguistic behavior of men and women in the Tlemcen speech community (Algeria). In particular, the researcher investigated the realization of a single phoneme, /q/, in its traditional and local /ʔ/ variant and in its novel, non-local /g/ variant. Using a questionnaire, participant observation, and audio recordings, Belhadj-Tahar discovered that women were significantly more conservative in their linguistic choices than men. Whereas women tended to use the traditional /ʔ/ form, men were more inclined to adopt the new /g/ form. In fact, educated women tended to infuse their speech with French elements, which indexes prestige and modernity. The use of the /ʔ/ variant was triggered by its association to femininity, although it is a "traditional" feature. This suggests that men's and women's linguistic preferences are often determined by a complex network of social factors, including gender and age, rather than by a single factor considered alone.

In general, the existing findings about the relationship between language variation and gender seem to defy any broad generalizations. The Arab region is socioculturally diverse, and this diversity may change the meaning and weight of any single social factor from one setting or community to another. For example, Sadiqi (1995) found a correlation between Moroccan women's shifts between

Moroccan Arabic and French and their concept of which language variety carries more prestige. For Moroccan housewives, Moroccan Arabic is the prestigious variety, whereas French is the language of prestige among working women. Walters (1989) examined linguistic variation in the Arabic dialect spoken in Korba, a small town in northeastern Tunisia. A sample of twenty-four speakers who varied in gender, education, and age were interviewed by a male interviewer and a female interviewer in order to examine whether the gender of the interviewer has a role in their linguistic behavior. These demographic variables were correlated with three linguistic variables ([ɛ:], [ş], [u:]) and their variants. Based on his data analysis, Walters (1989, p. 298) concludes:

> No single sociodemographic group appears to be the innovators or the conservatives. Rather, these patterns of the behavior of these individuals are intimately tied to their life experiences, to possibilities offered them by history, by society, and through individual choice . . . no matter how we interpret these results, no matter what kind of "standard"-local, regional, national, supranational, learned/historical, covert, or overt-we have trouble characterizing the behavior of the individuals studied here.

Research indicates again and again that gender does not work alone in producing language variation. Haeri (1996) argues that approaching gender-based variation requires a consideration of such aspects as modernization and women's participation in public life. Vicente (2009) suggests that women's access to different varieties, particularly their access to SA may be implicated in defining their gender roles and their ability to participate in language change. A number of studies have shown that gender differences may be more visible when education is also a factor; it is educated women who tend to lead language change (Al-Wer, 2002). Age and social class also collaborate with gender in determining women's participation in language change. Jabeur (1987) observes that older women take pride in their use of the diphthongal variants, which mark social-class prestige. Al-Wer suggests that achieving an understanding of the relationship between linguistic variation and social factors in general necessitates consideration of identity dynamics. It should be noted that women's dissociation with SA forms may have to do with factors other than prestige. For example, the SA [q] variant is associated with masculinity in a number of Arabic settings, and therefore prestige alone may not explain women's preference to alternative forms. Miller (2007) contends that historical events and context play a critical role in language differentiation. For example, although women may be more prestige-conscious than men, it is important to consider the meaning of prestige from a local rather than a universal perspective.

To assume that gender by itself is responsible for language variation, or to argue that the patterns of gender-based variation are universal, automatically raises the question of whether the differences between men and women are biological or cultural. Chambers (2003) suggests, for example, that women have innately superior linguistic abilities compared to men. If this is the case, then the concept of gender as a spectrum of identities needs to be redefined to accommodate for the biological imbalance in natural ability. Biology-based language variation, however, does not explain the discordant patterns of variation across Arabic-speaking communities, nor those occurring cross-culturally. Labov (2001) suggests that the impact of gender on language variation is largely defined by the roles assigned to men and women in their social context, though his argument also does not explain the notable cross-cultural similarities in certain aspects of women's language behavior even when contextual factors are constant. Comparative studies on gender effects are needed to make any generalizations, especially as each culture defines gender roles differently.

6.3.2 Variation in relation to social class and education

Social class refers to culturally and discursively constructed categories that mark people's unequal access to power, valued resources, and career opportunities within a specific social setting. Distinct societies and groups use different criteria to mark hierarchies in the social system. While in some communities, social class may be *inherited* based on historical factors such as family ties or tribal affiliation, other societies allow individuals to move up and down the social ladder as an effect of their education, financial resources, profession, position, or affiliations. In yet other communities, social class is determined by the interaction of a number of historical, financial, and occupational factors, which is the case in most Arabic societies (Nydell, 2012). In this light, diverse social groups in the Arab region mark social status in varying ways. Though a community may be socially stratified according to specific criteria, language may not always play a part in indexing the social strata.

The correlation between social class and language variation has not been studied extensively because social class is not easily definable in most Arabic-speaking communities. In most cases, class interacts with a number of other demographic and social variables. When social class is operationalized, the existing data present conflicting evidence about its role in language variation (e.g., Habib, 2010; Haeri, 1991; Ibrahim, 1986; Schmidt, 1974). Several studies have established a relationship between social class and language variation and change. Haeri (1991) uses four indicators of social class in her study of language variation in Egypt, including parents' occupation, type of school attended, neighborhood of residence, and profession. Social class is correlated with both the palatalization of the sounds /t, d, ṭ, ḍ, tt, dd/ as well as the use of /q/. The four social-class indicators were given different weights ranging from 0.5 to 0.1. The researcher gathered data from interviews, recorded television and radio programs, and production, comprehension, and elicited-response experiments. In addition, Haeri used a picture-description task to identify the use of /q/ by children. She found that upper-middle-class and – to a lesser extent – upper-class women had a significantly higher percentage of palatalization than women in the medium and lower middle classes. Weak palatalization occurs when dental stops are produced with frication. Haeri concluded that palatalization was an innovation of upper-middle-class women; they use weak palatalization more frequently than the other social classes, and this use increases in formal style. Jabeur (1987) examined the alternation between the old urban diphthongs /ai/ and /aw/ and their monophthong variants /ii/ and /uu/ in Rades, a suburb of Tunis, Tunisia. He determined that social class is the main motivation for the maintenance of the diphthongs by older urban women. Walters (1989) confirms the same pattern in Korba and attributes this phenomenon to social class associated with high-class families. In the Qatari context, Al-Amadidhi (1985) describes a relationship between the affrication of the variant /q/ and social-group membership, age, and educational level, among other factors.

However, a number of studies have found no relationship between language variation and social class. Habib (2010) examined the alternation between the uvular stop [q] and the glottal stop [ʔ] in the natural speech of rural migrants in Hims, Syria. The [q] variant is a feature of their colloquial dialect, but some have adopted the urban [ʔ] variant in their speech. Habib collected naturally occurring speech from fifty-two speakers. Age, gender, residential area, and social class were factored into the study design. Social class − represented by people of lower-middle and upper-middle classes − was operationalized by four indices: income, residential area, occupation, and education. The data analysis showed a significant relationship between the variable use of these two sounds and the factors of age, gender, and residential area. The research revealed age to be the most highly significant predictor of language variation; the shift from [q] to [ʔ] was most noticeable among the younger generation. Social class did not play a role in this variation. Belnap (1991) found a considerable amount of variation in agreement forms among Egyptian speakers in tape-recorded naturalistic speech, but identified no relationship between this type of variation and demographic variables, including social class.

The discrepancy in these findings may be attributed to the fluid nature of social class in the Arab context and the difficulty that arises from any attempt to capture this complex social construct. Studies examining this variable have often adopted "universal" indicators of social class, such as occupation or parents' profession, which may not always index social class in Arab societies. For example, tribal affiliation and family history are two indices of social class that are more highly emphasized in the Arab region than they may be among other societies. Affiliation with an influential tribe is, to a certain extent, part of one's social class in Jordanian society, for example. In some Syrian cities as well, family history is an important mark of one's social class. In the city of Hims, for instance, families that formed the aristocracy during Syria's feudal system are generally considered − or more accurately consider themselves − a social class apart from other urban populations. The presence of these tribal/ancestry-related factors necessitates defining social class locally, within the specific context in which social actors interact and establish their relationships.

In some cases, social class may be partly marked by education. Education is often associated with formal learning and therefore scholastic or academic degree is often used as a measure of one's educational level, whereas informal or experience-based education is often not taken into account as it is not always easy to measure. Most existing variationist studies in the Arab context involve education as a speaker variable (e.g., Abdel-Jawad, 1981; Al-Jehani, 1985; Khtani, 1993; Al-Muhannadi, 1991; Al-Shehri, 1993; Al-Wer, 2002; Haeri, 1991; Holes, 1983; Schmidt, 1974). Some of these studies demonstrate education's role in language variation. For example, Holes (1983) examined several phonological and lexical variants in Bahrain and their correlation with education (literate vs. illiterate), ethnicity (urban vs. rural), and religion (Sunni vs. Shi'a). He found that all three social variables contribute to this type of variation. Al-Wer (2002) examined the variation between /θ/ and /t/ in Sult, Jordan, in relation to education, which she indexed by three levels: uneducated, grade school education, and college education. She observed that college-educated speakers produce the innovative form /t/ more frequently than less formally educated speakers. El Salman (2003) reports that new Palestinians who moved from Tirat Haifa in Palestine to Irbid, Jordan abandoned their /q/ variant in favor of the local Jordanian /g/ or non-local /ʔ/ sounds. Most of those who abandoned their original /q/ sound were educated speakers. According to El Salman, the few educated speakers who maintained the use of /q/ did so in "an attempt to standardize their speech to conform with Standard Arabic" (p. 423).

El Salman's findings concerning educated speakers' adoption of linguistic variables less associated with SA and more linked to QA are mirrored in a number of previous studies. Jabeur (1987) found a correlation between the extent to which rural immigrants in Rades deploy urban features in their speech and their educational level. Walters (1989) found that many young educated women in Korba (Tunisia) shift away from raising the vowel [ɛ:], which is associated with SA and marks traditional urban speech. Jassem (1987) examined language variation and alternation in the speech of immigrants from the Golan Heights in Damascus. These immigrants were exposed to three language varieties: Standard Arabic, their own dialects, and the local Damascene dialect. Jassem examined seven phonological variables and one morphological variable in relation to the social variables of gender, education, age, and area of residence. He found that educated speakers led the shift to the local Damascene variety. He also found that young women were more inclined to use the Damascene dialect in lieu of SA and their own dialects. In their study of language variation in Irbid, Jordan, Al-Ali and Arafa (2010) examined the relationship between the linguistic variables /θ/, /ð/, and /dʒ/ and the social variables of gender and education. The local variants (/θ/, /ð/, and /dʒ/) are identical to those found in SA, whereas their non-local variants diverge from their SA counterparts. The findings indicate that men and high school graduates tend to adopt the local variants, whereas women and college graduates prefer the non-local prestigious variants.

Based on previously reported patterns, Al-Wer (2008, p. 633) maintains that "what 'education' does not do is to promote the language associated with education." This is not surprising, as the process of "modernizing" classical Arabic was initiated by educated speakers (Abdulaziz, 1986). Educated speakers are also partly responsible for the introduction of many foreign words and neologisms into SA. Explaining the role of education in language variation based on her own data, as well as other relevant works, Al-Wer (2002) suggests that education is not necessarily an influential factor in language variation, but it functions as "a proxy variable," which stands in for a number of less obvious variables. The main underlying variable, according to Al-Wer, is the number and nature of contacts that educated individuals have with speakers of the target features (p. 633). In other words, educated speakers are exposed to multiple varieties, which impacts their language use. As noted above, speakers' access to diverse dialects may sometimes be key in understanding language variation.

6.3.3 Variation in relation to ethnicity and religion

As noted in the previous chapter, the several religious and ethnic groups in the Arab region share historical and social experiences that have become integral to their identity and social stability. Language and language use are two among the many social traditions and practices religious and ethnic groups share. In multiethnic and multireligious settings in particular, language may become a boundary-drawing factor between various ethnic and religious groups. This section will focus on language contact between religious and ethnic communities associated with particular language varieties. Two or more ethnic or religious groups who speak the same or different language varieties may converge or diverge linguistically for different reasons, such as identity factors, power relations, and sociopolitical circumstances. Power relations and shifts in power – not religion or ethnicity – seem to motivate much of the variation and change observed in these religious or ethnic dialects (Miller, 2004).

One of the pioneering studies on changes affecting communal dialects is Blanc's (1964) study on language change in Baghdad. Blanc examined the differences between three language varieties spoken by Muslim, Christian, and Jewish communities in Baghdad. Whereas Muslims spoke the *geltu* variety, which is similar to the Bedouin dialects of southern and western Iraq, Christians and Jews spoke the *qeltu* variety, which displays features that are similar to those found in the sedentary dialects of northern Iraq. Blanc suggests that the distinction between the dialects of the three communities did not exist in the fifteenth century but was a later development resulting from the migration of Bedouins from the Arabian Peninsula. The fact that these Bedouins were in positions of power and shared religious identity with the Muslim residents prompted the latter group to adopt features of the Bedouin dialects in an attempt to differentiate themselves from the other two groups, who maintained the features of their sedentary dialects. In this case, Bedouinization was motivated by religious and, possibly, power-related factors. One interesting finding in Blanc's study is that the Christian and Jewish communities were able to maintain the unique features of their dialects despite their coexistence with the Muslim community in the same city and for a long period of time, which is not a common scenario in majority-minority situations.

Using Blanc's study as a main point of reference, Abu-Haidar (1991) reports of a recent case of language change affecting the Christian dialect in Baghdad. The data came from interview-based recordings from Christians in Baghdad and in the diaspora. Nine of the participants lived in Baghdad at the time of the experiment, whereas eleven resided in Britain, and a single woman lived in Italy. The participants spoke the Christian variety, as well as the Muslim variety and SA. As noted by Blanc (1964), the Christian variety is a sedentary dialect spoken in Baghdad before the evolution of Baghdad's koineized Muslim dialect. The latter, according to Blanc, is a Bedouin-type variety that developed under the influence of Bedouin immigrants. Abu-Haidar describes a language change in progress resulting from Christians' adoption of linguistic features originating in the Muslim dialect. She reports numerous instances of lexical, phonological, morphological, and syntactic variation in the Christian dialect, which she attributes to interactions between Christian and Muslim speakers. She compared her findings to those of Blanc (1964) to display the extent of change in the Christian dialect. Phonologically, words like *neis* "people" came to be used along with *naas*, and a word like *kəslaan* "lazy" also shifted pronunciation to *kaslaan*. She also observed morphological changes in plural formation. Thus, instead of the broken-plural forms *xabeibiiz* "bakers" and *xayeiyiiṭ* "tailors," the participants also came to adopt the sound masculine plural forms *xabbaaziin* and *xayyaṭiin*. Syntactically, Abu-Haidar describes the use of independent pronouns instead of postpositional copula, as in:

(1)   taʕbaani yaani → taʕbaani ana "I (f.s.) am tired." (p. 147)

Abu-Haidar concludes that several marked features in the Christian dialect are undergoing "levelling," which she attributes to the influence of the Muslim dialect. This linguistic influence, according to Abu-Haidar, is the outcome of a power imbalance between Muslims and Christians in Baghdad.

In his study of the dialects of Bahrain, Holes (1983, 1987) makes a number of observations about the distribution and development of the Shi'a *Baharna* and Sunni *'Arab* dialects. The Baharna inhabited Bahrain before the 'Arab, and they spoke a sedentary dialect. The Sunnis immigrated to Bahrain in the eighteenth century, bringing with them a Bedouin dialect. Holes remarks that in neighborhoods where Shi'a groups were surrounded by Sunnis, the Shi'a would usually assimilate linguistically to the Sunni dialectal norms. However, where Sunnis were the minority group, they would maintain their Bedouin dialect. For example, Holes points to a high level of maintenance in Sunni-specific variants, such as /y/, /g/, /θ/, and /ð/, whereas he found a low level of maintenance in Shi'i-specific variants, such as /j/, /f/, /d/, and /ɣ/. In the town of

Muharraq, where the population is predominantly Sunni, the Shi'a minority dialect has become indistinguishable from the speech of the surrounding Sunnis. Holes attributes the Bedouinization of the sedentary dialect of the Baharna to the fact that speakers of the Bedouin dialect represent the "social group in which political and commercial power is concentrated, and whose dialect as a consequence has acquired a locally prestigious status" (Holes, 1983, p. 38). Holes also observes the development of a mixed urban dialect that favors the features of the Bedouin dialect associated with the Sunnis. This is true even in cases where features of the Shi'a sedentary dialect converge with those of SA.

Several other studies have documented variation in communal dialects in the Arab region (Amara, 2005; Amara, Spolsky, & Tushyeh, 1999; Behnstedt, 1989; Cohen, 1981; Levy, 1998). Amara (2005) and Amara, Spolsky, and Tushyeh (1999) examined the deployment of the phonemes /q/ and /θ/ and their variants /ʔ/ and /t/ among speakers of the Arabic dialect in Bethlehem. The participants were grouped in terms of religion and gender. Whereas Muslims and males tended to use /q/ and /θ/ variants, the authors found that Christians and women were more prone to use the /ʔ/ and /t/ sounds found in the *prestigious* urban dialect of Jerusalem. The same applies to the distinction between the Muslim and Jewish varieties of Arabic in the Meghreb, particularly in old cities, such as Fes in Morocco. According to Palva (2006) and Miller (2004), the Jewish varieties have maintained their distinctive features as old sedentary-based dialects, remaining largely unaffected by the neighboring koineized Muslim varieties. Miller attributes this type of language maintenance to spatial and social segregation in the city, and also to the fact that Muslim dialects were not associated with political power or with urban prestige until the twentieth century. The Jewish dialects were mostly affected by Spanish Andalusian speakers, Italian speakers in Tunis, and then by French settlers. However, the spread of the koineized Muslim varieties in the twentieth century has led to a number of changes in the Jewish dialects. Among these changes, for example, is the shift from /ʔ/ to /q/, the move from /θ/ and /ð/ to /s/ and /d/, and the severe reduction of short vowels (Palva, 2006).

Language contact may induce changes in language varieties associated with ethnic groups. As was the case for religious dialects, the change is usually influenced by the power relations governing the interaction among the ethnic groups involved. Studies focusing on the relationship between language change and ethnicity may be grouped into three categories. One group of studies focuses on variation emanating from contact between two or more Arabic-speaking communities with diverse ethnicities (Taqi, 2010). A second group of studies deals with variation in two or more Arabic dialects resulting from their simultaneous contact with non-Arabic speakers, usually in a context where Arabic is a minority language (Owens, 1995, 2000, 2001). And a third line of research handles changes in a single Arabic dialect as a result of its contact with a typologically distinct language, which cause that dialect to drift away from other Arabic dialects. This third category is by far the most researched type of variation and change in relation to ethnicity (Behnstedt, 2006; Caubet, 1998; Cohen, 1981; Levy, 1998; Miller, 2007; Taine-Cheikh, 2012).

As a representative of the first research trend, Taqi's (2010) study investigated phonological variation in the speech of three generations from two Kuwaiti ethnic groups: Najdis and Ajamis. The three generations are represented by three age groups: 50–60, 30–40, and 18–22 years. As the name suggests, the Najdis come from the region of Najd in current Saudi Arabia, whereas the Ajamis originate from Iran. According to Taqi, the Najdis have a higher social status than the Ajamis resulting from several sociohistorical and political reasons. Taqi's target phonological variables were [dʒ], [s], and [ɣ]. These phonemes are respectively realized by the Najdis as [y], [s], and [q], whereas Ajamis pronounce them as [dʒ], [ṣ], and [ɣ]. The three linguistic variables were correlated with the social variables of ethnicity, age, and gender. Taqi's findings indicate that the features of the Najdi dialect are generally more stable across generations compared to the Ajami features. The author also found a notable presence of the Najdi features in the Ajami dialect, which is a sign of a language shift toward the Najdi dialect, and this shift appeared most often among young, female participants.

Owen's study of Arab-non-Arab language contact in Maiduguri in northern Nigeria exemplifies the second research trend. Owens (1995, 2001) points to an interesting type of variation, where the Arabic dialects involved vary together. Arabs who originated from southern Egypt and resided in different parts of Africa began to migrate to Maiduguri from rural areas in Nigeria and from Chad (and to a lesser extent from Cameroon). Owens suggests these immigrants are at least three generations deep. The rural Nigerian and the Chadian immigrants possess distinct dialects. Due to a continuous influx of immigrants, the two varieties coexisted in the same setting. In the source rural Nigerian dialect, verbal agreement in first-person plural is realized as n- (n-uktub "we write"), as indicated by a survey of fifty speakers of this dialect. In Chadian Arabic, however, first-person agreement is realized as n- . . . -u (n-uktub-u). The language contact situation generated changes in both variants. Owen's survey of thirty speakers of Nigerian origin revealed that only 82% maintained their original n- agreement form. Similarly, only 83% of the Chadian-origin speakers maintained their original Chadian n- . . . -u form. This is a case of two-directional change, wherein both varieties are mutually influenced by language contact. Owens attributes this type of change to the minority status of Nigerian Arabic, and thus to its lack of an institutionalized norm, which can normalize different varieties. This in turn may be explained by the fact that Arab Nigerians possess no sociopolitical power.

The third case of change is wrought upon a given Arabic dialect in contact with a typologically distinct language, which results is variation between this dialect and other Arabic dialects. This phenomenon is clearly exemplified in the Maghrebi dialects. Although we do not have enough data delineating the exact features of the dialects spoken by the early Arab immigrants, we do know that the present Maghrebi dialects differ from other Arabic dialects in considerable ways. Many contextual and spatial factors may play a part in this deviation, but language contact with non-Arabic speaking ethnic groups, particularly Berber speakers, is likely to be implicated. Most of the varieties of the Maghreb may be described as mixed varieties that developed out of language contact between Arabs and other ethnic and religious groups, particularly the Berber and Jewish communities (Behnstedt, 2006; Cohen, 1981; Levy, 1998; Miller, 2006; Taine-Cheikh, 2012). Chtatou (1997) argues that a large proportion of the words that Moroccans use in their daily interactions come from Berber, and many of the unique phonetic and morphological features of Moroccan Arabic may be attributed to this type of mixing as well. Chtatou (1997, pp. 106–110) provides a list of salient features in Tarifit Berber that have found their way into some Maghrebi Arabic dialects. Most of these features are phonological, as the following cases show:

- Dropping of *hamza* word-initially, -medially and -finally, as in *xda* "took," *swwl* "asked," *luḍu* "ablution" (SA versions are *ʔaxaða, saʔala,* and *wuḍuʔ*[14]).
- The replacement of the deleted *hamza* by /y/ (and less so by /w/) to break the hiatus created by the deletion, as in *ryuus* "heads" (SA version is *ruʔuus*).
- Palatalization after the geminate voiced bilabial stop /bb/, geminate bilabial nasal /mm/, and geminate velar plosives /kk/ and /gg/, as in *qbbʷa* "dome" (SA version is *qubbah*).
- Adoption of Berber syllable structure, as in *k.tb*/C.CC "wrote."

In general, language contact between different religious or ethnic groups seems to generate dissimilar outcomes. In one scenario, the dialects retain their distinctive features due to social or spatial segregation, as is the case with the Christian dialect in Iraq and Jewish varieties in the Maghreb before the twentieth century. In a second scenario, a dialect belonging to a minority religious or ethnic group converges with another belonging to a majority religious or ethnic group. This applies to the Shi'i and Sunni dialects in Bahrain, as well as the 'Arabi and Ajami dialects in Kuwait. A third scenario involves mutual influence, as with the Nigerian and Chadian Arabic dialects in northern Nigeria. The direction and nature of change is often predicted by the social and political relationship between the various social groups involved, as well as the sociopolitical status of the dialects and their speakers.

6.3.4 Variation in relation to time and locality

Languages naturally evolve over time. Change becomes almost inevitable in language contact situations, particularly among minority languages and dialects. All of the present Arabic varieties are believed to be the outcome of changes that occurred over centuries, although we do not have enough data to expound upon how this process occurred. Because it requires a diachronic explanation of language variation, the study of language change is not feasible when data tracking the evolution of a language over longer periods of time are lacking. Researchers follow two approaches in bridging this gap of knowledge. One approach is to compare recent data about a given language variety with data collected previously on the same variety. Abu-Haidar (1991) for example, relies heavily on Blanc's (1964) study of the Christian, Jewish, and Muslim dialects in Baghdad to argue for an undergoing change in the Christian dialect. One challenge in this approach is that not all of the dialects have been documented in the previous literature. Even when data documenting the general features of a given dialect exists, some aspects of the dialect could be overlooked, and these may be the most critical aspects in language change. In other words, the fact that no comprehensive description of Arabic dialects exists prior to the twentieth century complicates the process of documenting change in these dialects over time. Therefore, researchers often follow a synchronic approach to language change, in which data is collected concurrently from people who lived during different times. Thus, the effects of time on language features and use are studied mostly through the social variable of *age*.

Researchers study the impact of age on language variation by simultaneously comparing speakers of different ages, family roles, or generational times. These speakers are compared and contrasted in terms of specific linguistic features or language use. With respect to age phases, a number of categories have been used in the literature, such as *infancy, childhood, adolescence, youth, middle age,* and *old age*, each of which is associated with predetermined age ranges, and is generally understood within their specific settings. As for family roles, typical categories include *children, parents,* and *grandparents*. In terms of generations, the temporal division between *first, second, third,* and *fourth* generations appears in various variationist studies. Generations consist of people born within a twenty- to thirty-year period, typically the time between offspring and parents. Regardless of the unit of measurement, the existing studies point to a consistent relationship between language change and age (e.g., Abdel-Jawad, 1981; Al-Essa, 2009; Al-Wer, 1991, 1999; Daher, 1999; Dendane, 2007; Ismail, 2007; Jabeur, 1987; Taqi, 2010; Walters, 1989).

Probably one of the most consistent findings in Arabic variationist research is that young people lead language change; they often adopt novel and innovative forms that deviate from the established linguistic norms of their speech communities (al-Rojaie, 2013; Al-Wer, 1991; Dendane, 2007; Ismail, 2007; Jabeur, 1987; Miller, 2004; Walters, 1989). Older people, by contrast, are more inclined to retain the conventional forms of their speech communities. Age works in tandem with a number of other social factors in marking the difference between old and young people. For example, compared to young people, older generations may have had fewer opportunities for contact with speakers of other language varieties due to limitations in transportation and communication technologies in their youth. These limitations in mobility and communication impinge upon their opportunities to gain sufficient linguistic exposure to varieties other than their own. The literacy rates are also generally lower in older generations than in younger generations because the former group may have had less access to schools and universities. Therefore, SA is usually not part of the linguistic package of many old people and may not play a role in language change for this group (Abdel-Jawad, 1986). It is also possible that old people are more resistant to change because of their nostalgia for and idealization of past experiences, including their attitudes toward their childhood language.

Age interacts with gender. Several studies have shown that, in cities where a koineized urban variety and an old sedentary variety coexist, old women are linguistically more conservative than men; they are more inclined than men to maintain the linguistic features associated with older sedentary varieties. This pattern has been reported among Tunisian women in Rades (Jabeur, 1987), in the Algerian city of Tlemcen (Belhadj-Tahar, 2013; Dendane, 2007), in Syria's capital Damascus (Daher, 1999), and in the Saudi city of Jeddah (Al-Essa, 2009). Again, this conservative behavior may have to do with older women's lack of access to different linguistic forms (Al-Wer, 2014; Haeri, 1991; Miller, 2004). Old women who do not work outside their homes, or who lack high literacy skills, may not have sufficient opportunities to be exposed to other dialectal forms, and therefore their use of the old sedentary-type dialects may occur simply as a matter of lack of access. In his study on the distribution of the variants /ʔ/, /q/, and /g/ in the speech of Tlemcenian women and men, Dendane (2007) suggests that old women opt for the sedentary /ʔ/ not only because of its relation to conventional values and identity, but also because it is a mark of femininity. On the other hand, men, especially young men, avoid the glottal stop variant because of its feminine associations. Dendane's study is one of several studies showing that age works together with a cohort of variables in affecting language change (Al-Essa, 2009; Daher, 1999; Ismail, 2007; Jabeur, 1987; Walters, 1991).

Age also interacts with locality, which explains the fact that some regional or local dialects change at a faster pace than others, or are more susceptible to language change than others. For example, Ismail (2007) examined the patterns of variation with respect to (1) the presence or absence of /h/ in the third-person feminine suffix /-ha/ and the plural suffix /-hon/ and (2) four variants of /r/ as an approximant, retroflex, alveolar fricative, and trill. Ismail compared the two linguistic variables through speech samples taken from fifty-six speakers in two localities in Damascus: Shagoor, an inner-city traditional neighborhood, and Dummar, a developing suburban district. In addition to their relation to locality, the linguistic variables were correlated with age and gender. The findings indicate that the variation in the /h/ variable is stable; thus, little intergenerational disparities are observed. As for the /r/ variable, however, age plays a significant role in an ongoing change toward the approximant variant. The change is initiated in the suburban district and is spreading to the inner-city neighborhood. The innovative variant is more visible in the speech of young women in Dummar, whereas in Shagoor, young men lead the change toward the approximant variant. Ismail suggests that in the traditional Shagoor neighborhood, most women are unemployed and therefore have little contact with speakers of other dialects. Young men, by contrast, have greater opportunities to interact with other speakers. Again, the findings indicate that age and locality may not by themselves explain the patterns of variation and change reported in this study.

The impact of locality on language variation has been studied extensively in relation to the relocation of Palestinians to Jordan and their contact with the Jordanian dialects. The Palestinian dialects are historically urban and rural in nature, whereas the Jordanian dialects are mostly rural and Bedouin (Abdel-Jawad, 1986). Abdel-Jawad (1986) investigated the distribution of the standard linguistic variable /q/ in the speech of urban Palestinians, rural Palestinians, and rural and Bedouin Jordanians. The phoneme /q/ is realized as /ʔ/ in the urban Palestinian dialect, /k/ in the rural Palestinian dialect, and /g/ in the Jordanian dialects. Abdel-Jawad found that the Bedouin and rural variants are gradually being replaced by more prestigious urban forms. This trend appears more in the speech of the younger generation than the older one. According to Abdel-Jawad, the aura of prestige and modernity is more appealing to the younger groups than the older ones. Interestingly, certain stigmatized linguistic forms, such as the variant /g/, are more maintained than others because they are "symbols of local identity, solidarity, pride in origin, and nationalism" (p. 61). As the author suggests, the results highlight the importance of considering attitudinal factors in understanding language variation and change. In a similar study, Al-Wer (1999) investigated the distribution of four phonological variables – /q/, /θ/, /ẓ/, and /dʒ/ – in the speech of 116 speakers from three Jordanian towns: Sult, Ajloun, and Karak. These variables have local variants, /g/, /θ/, /ẓ/, and /dʒ/, and innovative urban Palestinian variants, including /ʔ/, /t/, /ḍ/, and /j/. The author found that /g/ is the local variant most immune to change because of its symbolic function as an identity marker. Language maintenance here is motivated by community pressure to conform to a linguistically and geographically localized identity that is different from the "non-local and Palestinian identity" (p. 46). Less salient variables are mixed in the speech of the participants because they carry less symbolic weight for the speakers.

In general, age and locality are critical in accounting for language variation and change. However, when considering their role, it is important to consider the different sociocultural and demographic associations attached to each of these variables. Age differences may also mark differences in literacy skills, access to different varieties, attachments to traditional norms and practices, and overall positive attitudes either toward old or modern norms and ideals. Similarly, locality may provoke cultural, linguistic, and geographical attachments to a certain place. The affective dimension of locality is therefore indispensable for studying the relationship between locality and language variation.

6.4 VARIATION, POWER, LANGUAGE ATTITUDES, AND SOCIAL IDENTITIES

Language variation and change in the Arab region cannot be fully explained without understanding its diglossic context and the interdependence of its linguistic, political, historical, social, and ideological dimensions. With this in mind, in this section, I briefly outline three factors critical to understanding language variation and change in the Arab region: (1) power relations between social groups, (2) language attitudes toward language varieties, and (3) the role of certain linguistic variables in indexing identity. These factors intertwine with the above social and regional factors in explaining language variation.

One vital factor to understanding language convergence or divergence is the power dynamics between different social groups. Power is defined as "the capacity to influence the condition and terms of the everyday life of a community or society" (Bhavnani, 1988, p. 145). Fairclough (1989) argues that power is implicated in defining social categories. Social class, for example, involves the stratification of community members based on either their access to different social resources (e.g. education), or their ability to make decisions that influence other social groups (Bourdieu, 1977; Fairclough, 1989). Language itself may become a marker of power or a means of extending influence (Bourdieu, 1977), while at the same time, power may define how language is perceived, received, and used. A comparison between the status and usage of Arabic in the Middle Ages and the modern age demonstrates the role of power in defining the ways in which language is perceived and utilized. While Arabic was the language of prestige and science in the middle ages, it lacks this status in the modern age. Power always shifts according to changes in social, historical, and political processes and structures, and so does the status of languages and language varieties. However, power and social categories may manifest themselves distinctly in different cultures.

Power seems to be partly responsible for some of the patterns of language variation and change reported above. In most of the aforementioned studies, a dialect accommodates another when the latter is associated with politically and/or socioeconomically powerful groups. Blanc's explanation of the emergence of the Muslim's variety in Baghdad after the arrival of the influential Bedouin groups falls under this pattern, and so does Abu-Haidar's report of the convergence of the Christian dialect in that city with the Muslim dialect. Holes (1983) explains the changes in the Shi'a dialect in Bahrain in terms of attempts by Shi'a groups to converge with the more socioeconomically and politically powerful Sunni group. The widely reported process of linguistic urbanization among rural and Bedouin immigrants may be ascribed to the socioeconomic power of the city (Messaoudi, 2001). Likewise, gender-based language variation has been partly explained by power disparities between men and women (Sadiqi, 2003). Gender is a "social practice" that is affected by power relationships between male and female speakers (Eckert, 2000; Ehrlich, 1997; Sadiqi, 2003, 2006a). In this light, the notion of women deploying prestigious varieties may be seen as a strategy for attaining a status that they have historically been denied in the Arab region and elsewhere across the globe. At the same time, it is a means of re-addressing the uneven power relationships between men and women.

Language attitudes are another essential element for understanding language variation and they are interconnected with power relations. Labov (1972) suggests that language attitudes are at the heart of the study of language

variation and change. Different language varieties spark diverse images, stereotypes, and attitudes, both related to the dialects and to their speakers. The
idea of prestige and stigma has often been invoked in language variation and
change. Prestige and stigma are not fixed but change according to historical and
political circumstances. In sociolinguistic research, the terms "language prestige"
and "language power" reflect the power that a language variety accrues due
to its association with an influential social group. Dendane (2007) reports that
young male speakers in Tlemcen abandon some features of their local Tlemcenian dialect because of its association with femininity. Abdel-Jawad (1986)
indicates that many Jordanians are giving up the stigmatized forms in their dialect
and adopting more prestigious urban forms. Similarly, language attitudes prompt
many non-Cairene immigrants to adopt the Cairene dialect (Versteegh, 2001).
What is clear from these studies is that speakers often shift toward languages
that are viewed favorably in the society in which they operate (Al-Wer, 2014). This
may sometimes entail shifting away from one's local dialect toward another, more
prestigious variety.

The workings of identity transpire in a subtle way, but they can sometimes
play a role either in facilitating or impeding language change. Language variation
and change may be initiated by people who seek to project a modern or urban
identity (Abdel-Jawad, 1986; Al-Wer, 1991). Some speakers adopt a variety to
uphold a local or national identity (Abdel-Jawad, 1986; Suleiman, 1993). In fact,
even when a language variety is stigmatized, such as the Bedouin dialect in Jordan or Syria, speakers may converge with this variety when it indexes a particular form of identity. Abdel-Jawad (1986) and Al-Wer (1999) found that identity
factors are behind the retention of the linguistically and culturally salient /g/
sound among Jordanian speakers. On the other hand, speakers who seek to
project a modern identity converge toward the urban /ʔ/ sound (Daher, 1999;
Messaoudi, 2001). Fear of identity loss has been responsible for the preservation
of a number of minority dialects, such as the Jewish and Christian dialects in Iraq
(Blanc, 1964). Although identity dynamics are more subtle and less conscious
than many other social factors, the reported patterns provide ample evidence
for identity's role in language variation and change in different Arabic-speaking
communities.

It is important to indicate that none of these social factors work single-handedly
or in isolation from others. As noted above, each of these variables works within a
wider social, historical, and political reality, which reinforces the main claim of this
book concerning the interrelatedness of diglossia, language attitudes, identity
dynamics, and language use and behavior.

6.5 SUMMARY AND CONCLUSION

This chapter examined language variation and its different manifestations and
phenomena in the Arab region. The discussion in this chapter has focused on

two broad topics. The first examines the evolution of regional dialectology in the Arab region and its expansion to involve other areas of research. The earliest line of research on language variation in the Arab World has generated important descriptive studies on various Arabic dialects. The second half of the past century witnessed more research into phenomena related to language contact, particularly koineization and pidginization. The chapter examined the potential role of koineization – which is realized through a number of interrelated processes, such as leveling, mixing, and accommodation – in the evolution and formation of several Arabic dialects. Koineization is also examined within the framework of a number of hypotheses concerning the development of CA and the modern regional dialects in the Arab region (Anis, 1959; Cohen 1962; Corriente, 1976; Ferguson, 1959b). Recent examples of koineization have been highlighted, particularly those leading to the emergence of mixed dialects in cities like Amman and Cairo (Al-Wer, 2007; Woidich, 1994). As for pidginization, the chapter examined Versteegh's (1984) hypothesis about the progression of the modern Arabic dialects through a process of creolization, pidginization, and decreolization. More recent cases of Arabic-based pidiginization and creolization in Africa and the Gulf States were reviewed.

Social dialectology has gained a prominent place at the locus of variationist research since the 1960s, particularly with the emergence of the Labovian paradigm and its concentration on the role of social factors in language variation and change. Thus, the second part of this chapter focused on social dialectology, with particular attention paid to the social antecedents of language variation in the Arab World. Among the various social factors that are critical to accounting for language variation and change, gender stands out. The relationship between gender and language variation has been extended in this chapter, beyond the foci of mainstream variationist research, to incorporate three perspectives: (1) variations in marking grammatical gender, (2) variations in the language practices of men and women, and (3) variations in men's and women's roles in language change. The chapter also examined the role of social class, education, ethnicity, religion, time, and locality in language variation and change. It has been argued that these factors work conjointly rather than independently, and therefore a deeper understanding of language variation and change requires a consideration of as many social variables as possible. It has also been argued that power relationships, language attitudes, and identity factors may be involved in language variation and change. In short, taking into account the complexity of social reality helps provide a more comprehensive picture of the mechanisms underlying language variation and change, which is particularly needed in situations where change is studied synchronically and may therefore be in progress.

I conclude this chapter by noting that Arabic variationist research has been heavily influenced by research developments in Europe and North America and has derived most of its themes and assumptions from studies based in those regions. As has already been mentioned by various scholars, it is important to consider the unique facets of the Arabic diglossic situation (e.g., Haeri, 1991), and to view social factors from an emic point of view because social factors do not have a fixed meaning but rather change cross-culturally.

NOTES

1 Most of the variationist studies have focused on language production, but a growing trend has been focusing on language perception as well.

2 Language variation and change has also been explained within the framework of optimality theory. Optimality theory supposes that a set of universal yet conflicting constraints exists in the grammars of human languages. Variation arises from constraint interactions within the grammar, though researchers disagree on the nature of the mechanisms governing such interactions (see, for example, Anttila, 1997; Boersma & Hayes, 2001; Coetzee, 2006). A number of less common approaches have been followed, such as Implications Scales (DeCamp, 1971; see also Gibson, 2006), but these are rarely used in approaching variation in the Arab context.

3 Language contact involves several areas, such as bilingualism, language maintenance, language shift, language death, language socialization, and language use. In keeping with the theme of this chapter, I focus only on issues related to language variation and change, namely koineization and pidgins and creoles.

4 Researchers disagree on the definition of a koine and the exact processes involved in its formation (see Siegel, 1985).

5 The literature abounds with other terms that overlap to a great extent (see Trudgill, 1986). Researchers also disagree with respect to the meanings of these terms.

6 See Ferguson 1959b for a complete list of these features.

7 The picture of the linguistic situation in the pre-Islamic era is far from clear, although different hypotheses have been proposed to explain the situation then (see Abboud-Haggar, 2006; Versteegh, 2004 for an overview of the different hypotheses).

8 This has been dramatically changing after the independence of the Arab countries.

9 This argument has been recently challenged by Herin (2010), who argues that the Sult dialect originates from the Horani dialects in northern Jordan.

10 Al-Sharkawi (2010) proposes that the dialects were the result of different linguistic and non-linguistic factors. However, the primary factor, according to Al-Sharkawi, was modified input by Arabic speakers, which underlines the role of the learners in determining the outcome of "second language learning."

11 The Gulf States include Bahrain, Kuwdfait, Oman, Qatar, Saudi Arabia, and United Arab Emirates.

12 See McElhinny (2003) for a detailed discussion of the polemics surrounding the concepts of gender, sex, and sexuality.

13 The study of women-related genres is not part of variationist research, and much of it falls out of the scope of sociolinguistics; it may fall under literary criticism, political science, communication, history, etc. As Vicente (2009) correctly suggests, only a few studies on women and gender in the Arab societies approached this topic from a sociolinguistic perspective.

14 These forms also diverge from those found in most other Arabic dialects.

CHAPTER 7

Codeswitching

In sociolinguistic terms, codeswitching (CS) describes the speech of bilinguals/ multilinguals or bidialectals/multidiaectals who juxtapose elements from two or more language varieties in a single utterance or piece of discourse. Although CS is as old as language contact and has been documented as early as the fourteenth century (Argenter, 2001), formal studies of this phenomenon have not found their way into bilingual literature until the past century. Early studies on bilingual communities have presented CS as a language deficiency resulting from certain gaps in speakers' lexicon or morphosyntax (Bloomfield, 1927; Weinreich, 1968). The systematic study of CS in the past few decades, however, has brought to scholarly attention the regularized nature of CS in terms not only of its structure, but also its sociolinguistic functions and the meanings it holds within discourse.

The study of CS has been approached from three main perspectives: syntactic/grammatical, psycholinguistic, and sociolinguistic. A grammatical approach examines the structural aspects of CS, its goal being to determine the syntactic and morphosyntactic constraints on language alternation, and to discover whether CS conforms to certain universal principles of grammar.[1] A psycholinguistic approach deals with the cognitive aspect of CS for the purpose of pinpointing the mechanism through which language codes are organized in the brains of bilinguals and how this organization affects their language acquisition and production. Studies in second language acquisition often adopt the psycholinguistic framework in order to describe the learners' language abilities and practices. A sociolinguistic approach is concerned with the role of social and pragmatic factors in CS, the aim being to determine the social meaning and function of CS within discourse. As the first two lie outside the scope of the current work, the following review will focus only on the social and pragmatic aspects of CS.

Mainstream research in bilingualism posits that CS is a creative act of communication employed for various pragmatic and sociolinguistic purposes (Appel & Muysken, 1987; Bentahila, 1983b; Clyne, 2003; Eid, 2002; Gumperz, 1982; Heller, 1988; Holes, 2004; Myers-Scotton, 1993b; Valdés, 1981). For example, CS is viewed as a mechanism for identity negotiation, situational marking, social-group membership, upward mobility, social solidarity, face management, discursive salience, and linguistic economy (Auer, 1998; Bentahila, 1983b;

Bhatt & Bolonyai, 2011; Kachru, 1977; Myers-Scotton, 1993b; Wei, 1994). It has been claimed that some of these sociolinguistic and pragmatic functions are "universal" in the sense that they apply invariably to CS between diverse language pairs and in different speech communities, though sometimes with certain meanings given extra salience in different contexts.

This chapter explores the social and pragmatic functions of CS in the Arab context. Before examining these functions, I will start with a short discussion of the terminology used to describe CS and related phenomenon. The short discussion is followed by a section outlining the main theoretical approaches to CS in sociolinguistic research, starting with a brief historical overview of this social phenomenon. Such an overview is essential for gaining proper perspective on the relationship between the global study of CS and its study in the Arabic sociolinguistic context. Indeed, many Arabic sociolinguistic studies have used these frameworks in their approaches to bilingual CS between QA and typologically distinct languages, and to bidialectal CS between SA and QA or between different colloquial varieties.

7.1 TYPOLOGY: CODESWITCHING, CODE-MIXING, STYLE SHIFTING, AND BORROWING

The existing literature abounds with terms pertaining to language-contact phenomena, including codeswitching, borrowing, code-mixing, and style shifting. The loose, overlapping, and inconsistent use of these terms necessitates drawing clear distinctions between them. Such distinctions can be based on structure, context, use, and frequency.

Codeswitching is not borrowing. While in CS "two grammars and vocabularies are used in producing a sentence or a text," borrowing simply involves the adoption of lexical elements from one language into the lexicon of another language (Muysken, 2000, p. 70). Callahan (2004, p. 5) makes a further distinction by suggesting that borrowed "word forms" become part of the grammar of the receiving language, whereas in CS "the forms from each language, though contiguous, remain discrete in at least some respects." Callahan identifies three criteria for distinguishing between CS and borrowing: structure, frequency, and discourse function. Thus, borrowing often involves cases where a *single* word or expression is *phonologically adapted* by the borrowing language with no salient discourse *function*. On the other hand, CS goes beyond individual words, which retain some of their phonological features, and achieves a pragmatic or social function in the discourse. While a number of other CS researchers have identified different criteria for demarcating the lines between CS and borrowing (e.g., Lipski, 2005; Myers-Scotton, 1992), this basic distinction between the two concepts is generally accepted (Pfaff, 1979; Poplack, 1980).

Unlike the CS/borrowing dichotomy, the fine line between CS and code-mixing is often neglected, blurred, or contested. Several authors have indeed used the term code-mixing in reference to what has been identified by mainstream studies as CS (e.g., Ho, 2007). A number of researchers have distinguished the two terms on a functional rather than structural basis. For example, Auer (1998, p. 16) suggests CS and code-mixing are structurally indistinguishable – both involve frequent alternations between two languages. However, while in CS alternation between codes serves a conversational function, the individual cases of alternation in code-mixing "receive neither discourse- nor participant-related interpretations." Still other authors have established specific criteria for differentiating the two terms. For example, Kachru (1983) uses the term CS to refer to switches within the sentence and code-mixing to shifts across sentences. McCormick (1995) argues that code-mixing is often restricted to single words or shorter elements, whereas CS involves the alternation of longer elements of speech. To complicate matters further, many authors disregard this distinction altogether (Bokamba, 1988; Eastman, 1992; Milory & Muysken, 1995; Myers-Scotton, 1993a). For example, Eastman (1992, p. 1) contends that any effort to distinguish CS and code-mixing is "doomed," stressing that "When people use a *mixed language* regularly, *codeswitching* represents the norm" [italics added]. Eastman's assertion substantiates the mainstream view of the relationship between the two terms.

A similar controversy has brewed over the distinction between CS and style shifting. According to Myers-Scotton (1993a), CS refers to the alternation between two or more language varieties within the same conversation, where language varieties can refer to "different languages, or dialects or styles of the same language" (p. 2). Likewise, Romaine (1995) asserts that from a sociolinguistic and pragmatic perspective, the distinction between CS and style shifting is irrelevant, as they each perform specific functions in the discourse. Other researchers have placed CS and style shifting in entirely different domains, assuming the former to be a characteristic of bilingual or bidialectal speakers, whereas the latter pertains only to monolinguals (e.g., Ervin-Tripp, 2001; Labov, 1966). Labov uses the term "style shifting" to refer to consistent changes in the linguistic forms used by a speaker in accordance to changes in topics, participants, or the social variables.

Although distinctions between the constructs of CS code-mixing, borrowing, and style shifting are still being debated, I will follow Myers-Scotton (1993 1993a), Muysken (2000), among others, in adopting the term CS as a cover term that refers to the use of different elements from two languages, dialects, or styles within the same sentence or piece of discourse.

7.2 THEORETICAL APPROACHES TO CODESWITCHING

The early descriptive studies of bilingual communities gave rise to three basic sociolinguistic questions: why does language alternation occur? What is its meaning? And, how is it socially relevant? For example, in his study on Mexican Americans in Tucson, Arizona, Barker (1947) was perplexed to find that bilinguals alternated between English and Spanish on different occasions "without apparent cause" (1947, p. 186). Barker, however, did observe these bilinguals often allocating Spanish to intimate interactions with family members and English to formal conversation involving Anglo-Americans. However, their language choice fluctuated in other situations, allowing a more fluid mixing of the two languages. In terms of interpreting the meaning and function of CS, early accounts presented CS as a means of filling in a language deficiency. For example, Weinreich (1968, p. 73) maintained that "the ideal bilingual switches from one language to another according to appropriate changes in the speech situation (interlocutors, topics, etc.), but not in an unchanged speech situation and certainly not within a single sentence." According to Weinreich's description, bilinguals who switch in an "unchanged speech situation" or "within a single sentence" are non-ideal; their improper switching bears out language deficiency.

Although he was not particularly concerned with CS per se, Ferguson, in his seminal work on diglossia, paved the way for what researchers would later describe as situational CS. Ferguson suggested that in diglossic communities, speakers alternate between the two varieties based on the context of their discourse. In particular, speakers shift to the High variety in formal situations and to the Low variety in informal settings. Fishman (1971) extended Ferguson's model by proposing his domain model of multilingualism, which states that multilingual speakers use one variety/language based on their perception of the *domain* in which they find themselves. According to Fishman, a "domain" refers to the particular context in which the use of one language is more appropriate than another, and it involves three main parameters: interlocutors, occasion, and topics. Hence, as Fishman puts it, "'Proper' usage dictates that only one of the theoretically coavailable languages or varieties will be chosen by particular classes of *interlocutors* on particular kinds of *occasion* to discuss particular kinds of *topics*." (p. 437). Fishman's model therefore predicts a straightforward association between linguistic choices and the social domains in which those choices are made.

Deeper analyses of CS were yet to come. Gumperz (1964) presented CS in a new light in a series of studies on the dialects of Hindi. He not only linked CS to immediate context, but also to relationships of social class/caste. Gumperz notes that many speakers in Khalapur (a village in northern India) alternate between village dialects, regional dialects, and standard Hindi in their discourse. For example, village inhabitants use the village dialects with local residents, regional dialects when speaking to people from outside their villages and in small market centers, and standard Hindi in formal settings and larger cities. In the socioeconomically stratified community of India, elite groups also change features of their vernacular based on how formal their relationships with their interlocutors are. They use one form of a particular vernacular (moti boli) with family members, children, relatives, and servants, and another (Saf boli) outside these informal relationships and when addressing elders. Even in a single setting, switching is sometimes motivated by social relationships between speakers. For example, speakers change their forms of address depending on the socioeconomic or religious status of their interlocutors, and this is not exclusive to CS.

Blom and Gumperz's 1972 study in Hemnesberget (Norway) represents one of the earliest studies on the social functions of CS in its current use. The researchers differentiate between situational CS and metaphorical CS, and they identify the particular functions of each. Situational CS is the result of changes in situational variables, including interlocutors, setting, and the type of activity in which speakers are engaged. Like Ferguson (1959a) and Fishman (1971), Blom and Gumperz suggest language choice in terms of CS is restricted and predictable. Blom and Gumperz noticed that speakers in Hemnesberget (Norway) typically use Ranamal, the local dialect, to identify with the local values of their local community or in "heart-to-heart" talk, whereas they use Bokmal, the standard variety, for official and formal purposes. Metaphorical CS is carried out to achieve particular communicative effects even when the situational factors remain unchanged. Gumperz (1982, pp. 75–82) grouped these communicative effects into six social functions: (1) quotation; (2) addressee specification; (3) interjection; (4) reiteration; (5) message qualification; and (6) personification vs. objectification. Moreover, he recast the social dimension of CS on the basis of the distinction between the "we code" and the "they code" (p. 66) – a distinction that underlines one of the main social functions of bilingual CS as a tool for highlighting variances in social distance or solidarity.

The nature and function of CS is further explored by Goffman (1981), who linked the functions of CS to the notions of *framing*, *footing*, and *keying*. Framing denotes the way in which an individual interprets and organizes interactions and experiences in a meaningful way, often based on his/her cultural orientation and conditioning. Footing refers to the "participant's alignment, or set, or stance, or posture, or projected self" (p. 128) within the interaction. This self-projection is a common feature of daily interactions and can occur within a single sentence or across sentences. A speaker can assume different roles based on his/her projected alignment in relation to listeners, type of activity, and content of speech. Although footing is not solely related to language alternation, it often involves CS. *Keying* is a means by which an utterance or an action is understood in relation to another and in the context of a particular framework. Thus, according to Goffman, a consideration of the functions of CS for the speaker should involve not merely the context in which shifting occurs but also the frame and mode of the conversation, the assumptions of the interlocutors, and the dynamics of the interaction.

Based on conversation-analysis techniques and Goffman's notion of "interaction order," Auer (1998) proposed a sequential approach to CS. According to Auer (1998, pp. 1–2), proper analysis of CS "first and foremost requires close attention to be paid to the details of its production in the emerging conversational context which it both shapes and responds to." In this bottom-up approach to CS analysis, code choice emerges in the course of interaction as a result of a negotiation process between participants. Auer further claims the sequential structure of language negotiation is "sufficiently autonomous both from grammar (syntax) and from the larger societal and ideological structures to which the languages in question and their choice for a given interactional episode are related" (p. 4). Such an approach pays little attention to social, macro-contextual elements – participants, topic, setting, etc. – and focuses more on conversational structure. Auer's sequential approach implies that understanding every instance of CS would require considering the preceding and following utterances, only with secondary attention to more external sociolinguistic factors.

Another framework within which CS has been analyzed is Bourdieu's (1977) social capital theory. According to Bourdieu (1977, 1999), social actors are positioned within macro- and micro-systems of power relations. The relationships highlighting differences in social standing are regulated through valued resources (capitals), in specific spheres of struggle (fields), and by legitimation (symbolic violence). Bourdieu conceptualizes valued resources as capital that can be acquired, used, and recreated. Capital can take different forms, including economic (material wealth), cultural (knowledge of cultural norms and practices that give access to power), and social (access to individuals or organizations associated with power) capital. Capital exists in various social *fields*, which link individuals and institutions in a network of social relations. The relative position of social agents in structural power relationships in any given field is determined by their available forms of capital. This stratification of capital explains why social actors "try to maximise their gains and accumulate resources under different forms of capital (economic, social, cultural, and symbolic)" (Navarro, 2006). Bourdieu draws attention to *language* as a form of cultural capital that may be used to present oneself and to define relationships among interlocutors. Like other forms of cultural capital, language has a symbolic value that varies from one linguistic market to another. This value may be assessed by individuals or communities within linguistic markets, whether in complex communications, or even an interaction as small as a passing conversation between two people. Individuals tend to acquire and use linguistic capital helpful in each social field or that which gives them access to other forms of economic and social capital. Because of its value as a cultural capital and its link to social and economic capital, language is both an instrument and an index of power and power relationships. This explains why individuals adapt their language output to conform to the valued linguistic capital in different linguistic markets.

Giles and his associates (Coupland & Giles, 1988; Giles, Coupland, & Coupland, 1991; Giles & Smith, 1979) propose that much of the adjustments and shifts in people's interactions may be explained by their attempts to accommodate others. Giles et al. (1991, p. 2) see accommodation as "a multiply organized and contextually complex set of alternatives, ubiquitously available to communicators in face-to-face talk." Accommodation may take different forms, including convergence, divergence, and cooperativeness, as well as interactional synchrony, listener adaptedness, person-centered/other-directed speech, and role/perspective taking (see Giles et al., 1991 for details). In addition, accommodation subsumes the notion of positive politeness, which is an important facet of politeness theory also used to explain CS behavior (Brown & Levinson, 1987). The two main dynamics of accommodation are convergence and divergence, the former signaling the speakers' attempt to reduce verbal and non-verbal differences with others and the latter denoting the individuals' endeavor to accentuate these differences. In the case of convergence, speakers may sometimes be perceived as condescending if they overaccommodate their listeners. Giles and his associates link accommodation to a number of social factors, such as (1) social consequences in aspects of communication like attitudes and behaviors, (2) macro-societal factors such as prestige, power, and identity, (3) intergroup variances (age, gender, ethnicity, etc.), (4) discursive practices in naturalistic settings, and (5) language shifts that accommodate factors like language dominance (Giles et al., 1991, p. 4).

Taking insight from Grice's cooperative principle, Myers-Scotton (1993b, 2005) presents her "Markedness Model" to explain the social motivations driving CS. The Markedness Model rests on the negotiation principle, which posits that speakers choose a particular code based on the rights and obligations (RO) that they seek to establish with other speakers in the conversation and its setting. According to Myers-Scotton, for any communicative situation there exists an expected RO set, determined by the social norms of the community. Three *maxims* develop out of from this principle. The unmarked choice maxim directs "Make your choice the unmarked index of the unmarked RO set in talk exchanges when you wish to establish or affirm that RO set" (p. 114). The marked choice maxim states "Make a marked code choice which is not the unmarked index of the unmarked RO set in the interaction when you wish to establish a new RO set as unmarked for the current exchange" (p. 131). The exploratory choice maxim stipulates, "When an unmarked choice is not clear, use CS to make alternate exploratory choices as candidates for an unmarked choice and thereby as an index of an RO set which you favor" (142). In this model, language choice is governed by the rights and obligations of the interlocutors (assuming the speakers all agree upon the applicable RO set). Thus, identification with the expected RO set would lead to unmarked CS, whereas dis-identification with the expected RO set would produce marked CS. In choosing a particular code, speakers decide whether to follow the normative RO set or to seek a new one. Speakers opt for marked CS "to negotiate a change in the expected social distance holding between participants, either increasing or decreasing it" (p. 132). Marked choices are often accompanied by prosodic features such as distinct pauses or extended commentary on the switch. Myers-Scotton argues that "unmarked CS should not occur at all in narrow diglossic communities (the Arabic-speaking nations of the Middle East, at least, if not the other exemplars included in Ferguson 1959)" (p. 128). Myers-Scotton bases her argument on the assumption that speakers of Arabic who alternate between the standard and colloquial varieties of the language do not identify with the normative RO set.

More recently, Myers-Scotton and Bolonyai (2001, p. 1) reformulated the Markedness Model into their more explicit Rational Choice model. They criticize previous accounts of CS, which ascribe language choices to larger societal conventions, constraints, actors, or discourse structure. Instead, they invoke Rational Choice Theory to propose that "choices lie ultimately with the individual and are rationally based." As rational beings, speakers assess the possible choices available to them in terms of cost–benefit analysis and choose the one that is most productive in their current context. In this process, speakers consider the internal consistency of their choice and the best available evidence for the soundness of their rationale. For example, Myers-Scotton and Bolonyai notice that, in an interaction between a Hungarian–English bilingual boy and his mother, the boy often shifts to English, even though Hungarian is the preferred language for family interactions. In such a case, the boy circumvents the societal and discursive constraints on CS in order to attain his own subjective goals. The two researchers do not negate the role of societal factors or conversational structure, but consider them only one component among many that inform the Rational Choice model.

Highlighting the value of context in determining the functions of CS, Heller (1992) argues that CS can only be understood within both an interpretive and interactional framework. Within this theoretical model, verbal behavior should be interpreted with regard to the specific social and historical dimensions of a particular setting. In other words, the functions of CS vary from one setting to another, and this variance is driven by social and historical factors. Based on her ethnographic study in Ontario and Quebec between 1978 and 1990, Heller suggests that English–French CS is a political strategy, "especially as a strategy of ethnic mobilisation" (p. 123). CS becomes part of other symbolic resources used to control and regulate access to other forms of power. In elaborating her argument, Heller draws on Bourdieu's notions of symbolic capital and symbolic marketplace as well as Gumperz's concepts of speech economies and verbal repertoires (Bourdieu, 1977; Gumperz, 1982). A distinction is made between *conventional* CS, which affirms the existing power relations, and *anti-conventional* CS, which becomes a form of resistance. Heller shows how after the 1960s, CS was used as a means of French national mobilization. In this case, speakers employ CS with the goal of restructuring asymmetric relations of power. Thus speakers reevaluate the respective worth of French and English, both as symbolic resources in and of themselves, and as tools for regulating access to other material and symbolic resources. While the corporate demand for French-English bilinguals is perceived by Francophones as a way to preserve French language and identity, it provides Anglophones with a means to penetrate the Francophone-controlled corporate culture, while still laying claim to an Anglophone identity and its associated value in the international market.

In an attempt to explain the variation in CS patterns across different communities, Bhatt and Bolonyai (2011) propose a theoretic framework of optimality. They identify five principles that underlie some of the main functions of CS in different communities. These principles include Faith, Power, Solidarity, Face, and Perspective. In any community, the optimal output of the process of ranking these principles determines the sociocognitive functions of CS. This ordering is influenced by "speaker motivation and macro-social factors such as group membership, identity affiliations, and the politics of bilingual contact" (p. 2). This suggests that variance in the functions of CS in different communities is established by the way in which these principles are ordered in relation to one another. To illustrate their model, Bhatt and Bolonyai compared CS in Hindi–Kashmiri–English to Hungarian–English CS. They found that in Hindi–Kashmiri–English CS, Face outweighs Power, which in turn outweighs Solidarity, whereas in the Hungarian–English CS, Solidarity outranks Face and Power, both of which share a similar ranking.

Overall, discord characterizes the literature on the social aspect of CS. Different researchers disagree not only in regards to the social function and meaning of CS within discourse, but also on the appropriate approach for analysis. While some sociolinguists attribute code alternation to situational factors, others link it to social conventions, identity negotiation, self-assertion, speech accommodation, and politico-economic inclinations (Appel & Muysken, 1987; Auer, 1998; Bentahila, 1983b; Bhatt & Bolonyai, 2011; Blom & Gumperz, 1972; Clyne, 2003; Gal, 1998; Giles & Powesland, 1997; Gumperz, 1982; Heller, 1988; Kachru, 1977; Milroy & Wei, 1995; Myers-Scotton, 1993b; Valdés, 1981; Wei, 1994). Still others suggest that the meaning of code choice resides mainly in the conversation structure with respect to the negotiation process. Some of these differences are motivated by theoretical considerations, such as the specific approach to CS, but others are simply due to contextual factors.

7.3 CODESWITCHING IN THE ARAB CONTEXT

Given the number of language varieties available to Arabic speakers in diverse contexts, the use of CS as a form of social interaction becomes expected. While the initial reaction to Ferguson's model of diglossia has inspired numerous studies on middle and in-between varieties, the last two decades or so have witnessed a growing tendency to approach the juxtaposition of SA and QA as a form of CS (Albirini, 2011, 2014a; Bassiouney, 2006, 2013; Holes, 1993, 2004; Mazraani, 1997; Mejdell, 1999, 2006; Rabie, 1991; Saeed, 1997, among many others). For the sake of simplicity of analysis, I will distinguish between three types of CS, although their social and pragmatic functions often overlap: (1) *bilingual* CS between QA and typologically distinct languages, mainly French and English, (2) *bidialectal* CS between SA and QA, and (3) CS in written discourse. I will further distinguish between bidialectal CS in monitored and unmonitored speech. This distinction is motivated not only by organizational reasons, but also by the need to clarify some differences in the mechanisms governing each of these forms of CS.

7.3.1 Bilingual codeswitching between Arabic and French/English

A number of studies have focused on the alternation between QA and typologically distinct languages (e.g., Abbasi, 1977; Al-Dashti, 1998; Al-Enazi, 2002; Belazi, 1991; Bentahila, 1983b; Bentahila & Davies, 2002; Caubet, 2002; Davies & Bentahila, 2006b, 2008; Ennaji, 2005; Sadiqi, 2003; Safi, 1992). Some of these studies focused on QA–French CS in the Maghreb region simply because French and QA are used in everyday interactions at home, at schools and universities, and in the media, business, and other social spheres. However, most of the studies on QA–English CS are contextualized in English-speaking countries, particularly the United States, where Arabic–English bilinguals use English more "naturally" in their daily communications. I will outline two representative studies of QA–French CS and two studies focusing on QA–English CS in informal face-to-face interactions. In addition, I will examine other domains in which bilingual CS appears. These selected studies use methodologies commonly employed in CS research that may be relevant for future studies on bilingual CS. I will conclude this section by pointing to some common sociolinguistic patterns in bilingual CS as reflected in these studies.

Bentahila (1983b) examined the social motivations of CS between French and the Moroccan dialect of Arabic. The data came from recorded natural conversations among balanced Moroccan bilinguals. The conversations occurred in a home setting and lasted seven and a half hours. A variety of topics were discussed in these conversations, including food, world, politics, and education. Bentahila identifies three broad functions of CS in his data. First, speakers use French for topics related to medicine, education, and administration, and to indicate numbers, date, and time. On the other hand, Moroccan Arabic is used for religious topics and for insults and swearing. Sometimes language choice allows speakers to select words with particular connotations, or to avoid words that may be embarrassing in a particular context. In (1), for example, the speaker uses the French word *la toilette* "the toilet" to avoid embarrassment. Second, CS is used as a rhetorical device through which speakers may emphasize a point, intensify a contrast, gain the floor, change the topic of discourse, or introduce a quotation. In (2), for example, the speaker uses one expression in French and then reiterates it in the Moroccan dialect. Last, speakers may shift to one language in order to express themselves better, especially in situations where they forget words in the other language.

(1) *w kayn lli mšaw I la toilette*

  "and there are those who went to the lavatory." (Bentahila, 1983b, p. 237)

(2) *je ne lui plais pas, quoi, maʕjbtuš*

  "he doesn't like me, what, he doesn't like me." (Bentahila, 1983b, p. 236)

In a similar context, Belazi (1991) examined CS between Tunisian Arabic and French in informal conversations among educated Tunisian speakers in relaxed social gatherings. Belazi assumed the role of full participant in these gatherings as he recorded the data (twenty recordings, approximately one hour each). Most of the CS patterns that featured in Bentahila's study were also present in Belazi's data. For example, the subjects use Arabic when discussing non-technical or intimate topics, whereas they switch to French when the topic is technical or when the speakers aim to encode their social status. This form of CS may be seen as motivated by topic or speaker factors. Belazi also reports of a rhetorical function of CS, which appears in the use of French to highlight an important discursive segment, to underlie the seriousness of a point, or to discuss factual or objective information. Arabic is used to substantiate the speaker's message in the form of examples, illustrations, and stories derived from the speech of everyday life. Belazi suggests that the distribution and uses of the two language varieties in this form of bilingual CS are related to the dominant attitudes toward the roles and uses of French and Arabic in the Tunisian sociolinguistic landscape where French is associated with education, modernity, and economic success, and Arabic is linked to religiousness, conservatism, and nationalism.

Turning to QA–English CS, Safi (1992) examined the structure and functions of CS between English and the Saudi dialect. Safi used a single recording of a two-hour meeting among eight Saudi undergraduate and graduate students in the United States. Regarding the social functions of CS, Safi found that the distinction between the "we code" and the "they code" is blurred in the speakers' interactions. For example, discourse markers, such as fillers (e.g., yaʕni, zein, and ok) are expressed in both Arabic and English. Similarly, both languages contribute to interjections. However, whereas Saudi Arabic is used to mark politeness and emphasis (e.g., law samaħt "if you please"), English is used for cursing. Likewise, Arabic appears in phrases that convey religious and national feelings, whereas English is used to convey more serious, business-like attitudes to the topic under discussion. These distinct functions are illustrated in examples (3) and (4). The first example is spoken by a male student and the second by a female student who was reporting on an interaction with "a high-ranking male officer" in her university.

(3)   *They had a beautiful* mubxara

       "*They had a beautiful* incense burner." (Safi, 1992, p. 75)

(4)   Talabni waħda minil-*posters* illi ʕindi

       "He asked for one of the *posters* that I have." (Safi, 1992, p. 76)

According to Safi, the selection of the Saudi/Arabic term *mubxara* "incense burner" is more compatible with feelings of national belonging, whereas shifting to the English term *posters* underscores the business format of the officer's request and allows the speaker to avoid the potential negative connotations associated with the corresponding Arabic term if used in this context (namely, *ṣuwar* "photographs/pictures").

Like Safi (1992), Al-Enazi (2002) examined the syntactic constraints and social functions of CS between English and the Saudi dialect among Saudi bilinguals, though he included both children and adults in his research. Fifteen children and ten male adults formed the study sample. Thirty hours of audio-recorded data were gathered in informal meetings involving Saudi children and male graduate and undergraduate students in the United States. Al-Enazi found that English dominated among children, whereas Saudi Arabic was more common among adults. As to the social functions of CS, Al-Enazi found English to be allocated to academic terms (e.g., "dissertation," "presentation," and "comprehensive exam"), dates and numbers, specification and clarification, and interruptions and disagreements. Speakers also used English to claim prestige or authority, often by using *weighty terms*, such as *legitimate* and *protocol*. By contrast, Arabic is assigned to religious expressions (*ṣalah* "prayer," *ḥaraam* "forbidden," and *al-Qibla* "direction of Mecca"), discourse markers (e.g. *yaʕni* "I mean"), and culture-specific terms (e.g., *gahwa* "coffee"). Speakers also use Arabic to give oaths or make confirmations (*wa-Allah* "by God"). Like Safi and Bentahila, Al-Enazi found that English and Saudi Arabic may sometimes be used to perform similar functions, such as reiteration.

Apart from its use in everyday interactions, bilingual CS has been reported to occur pervasively in rap and rai song lyrics – two forms of music that are popular in the Maghreb and the West. In a series of studies on this topic, Davies and Bentahila (2006b, 2008; Bentahila & Davies, 2002) illustrate the ways in which CS is used as a resource to enhance the structure of songs, appeal to multiple audiences, and add to the aesthetic quality of the music. For example, CS is used to strike a balance between the goals of localizing musical genres and globalizing them, i.e., making them accessible to both Moroccan and Western audiences. According to Davies and Bentahila, localization effects are realized by the use of the Moroccan dialect, whereas the globalization impact is attained by deploying different lexical items and expressions from French (also some Spanish and English). Sometimes, CS is used to reflect shifts in viewpoints, to maintain the rhyme and line divisions of song lyrics, to enhance messages conveyed in the lyrics (often through words that carry nuanced connotations in one language and not the other), and to draw attention to specific meanings in the text. For example, most of the words pertaining to "love" and "love affairs" (e.g., *amour* "love," *souffrance* "suffering," etc.) are rendered in French.

Although they involve different languages and occur in different contexts and formats, studies focusing on bilingual CS between QA and English/French bring to light a number of convergent patterns. First, all of these studies suggest that at least some of the functions allocated to QA and English/French do not overlap. For example, English and French are often associated with technical and academic terms or themes, whereas QA is reserved for religious and culture-specific topics. However, QA and French/English may share the same function, as in reiteration. Second, language prestige does not always impact the social and pragmatic functions of one or either of the codes, possibly because language prestige is not always convertible to pragmatic gains in everyday interactions. SA does not seem to have a notable presence in bilingual CS. This is not surprising if we consider the fact that most of these studies focused on informal everyday life conversations where SA is rarely used. Future research may want to investigate whether CS between SA and typologically distinct languages exists in certain situations and, if so, to determine the reasons behind its use. Last, a number of studies have recently explored CS between QA and other local languages, such as Berber (Hoffman, 2006; Kossmann, 2012; Sadiqi, 2003, 2006b). These studies show that, in the very rare cases in which it is used by Berber–Arabic bilinguals, this form of switching is often restricted to lexical borrowings (Sadiqi, 2003) or to mark a change in topic (Kossmann, 2012).

7.3.2 Bidialectal codeswitching between SA and QA

One of the main criticisms leveled at Ferguson's model of diglossia concerns the allocation of SA and QA to non-overlapping domains of use. Critics maintain that SA and QA interact in a variety of contexts. This form of interaction is governed by different social, pragmatic, contextual, demographic, and affective factors, and often generates a wide range of sociolinguistic patterns and functions. A basic question in the relevant CS literature is whether speakers of Arabic – particularly educated speakers – have the facility to utilize SA and QA in their discursive practices (Hudson, 2002). This question highlights one of the fundamental assumptions in bidialectal CS research, namely, that educated Arabic speakers have at least a functional oral command of SA that enables them to use it strategically to attain different sociolinguistic and pragmatic goals. Another important consideration in bidialectal CS is whether the speech is monitored or unmonitored. I will focus on these two important questions before I discuss the modes of CS between SA and QA.

Speaking abilities in SA among educated Arabic speakers

The study of the social and pragmatic functions of CS presupposes that bilingual and bidialectal speakers have the oral linguistic skills to manipulate the two codes for different purposes. This assumption has been explicitly or implicitly questioned by a number of researchers (Hudson, 2002; Parkinson, 1993, 1996) but, to date, only a very few studies have investigated this important postulation empirically. For example, Parkinson (1993) sought to determine Egyptian speakers' *knowledge* of MSA. Education, age, and sex were factored into the analysis. Parkinson used a battery of tests to examine the participants' skills in grammar, reading, writing, listening, and speaking. He observed a notable variability in the participants' command of MSA. For example, he describes Egyptians with a high school education as "abominably fluent" in the sense that their discourse can be understood but it is rife with mistakes and colloquialisms (p. 69). Egyptians with college educations are described as "competent" users of MSA; they can be clearly understood, but their production has mistakes as well. Those with specialized Arabic education are described as having "professional competence" in the language in the sense that they use it skillfully and effectively in their discourse.

In this section, I report on a study that examines whether educated Arabic speakers are able to carry on and sustain *conversations* in SA without resorting to QA or other languages they may speak. It is not the purpose of this study to examine Arabic speakers' knowledge of SA as this is a multifaceted topic that requires testing various skills and employing multiple tasks. Additionally, the study investigates whether the use of SA is influenced by the discourse topic. The study was conducted during my fieldwork in Egypt, Jordan, Morocco, and Saudi Arabia. As noted in Chapter 3, much of my research activities were performed on university campuses in the host countries. The target population of the current study was educated speakers of Arabic in Egypt, Jordan, Morocco, and Saudi Arabia. A conveniently selected sample of forty professors and forty college students participated in the study.[2] The participants were distributed equally among the four countries, that is, each country was represented by ten professors and ten college students. The focus on both professors and students aimed to trace any patterns of change between a relatively older generation and a younger generation.[3] All of the participants were born and raised to Arab parents in their respective countries, and all finished their schooling in an Arab country. All of the participants had spent the past five years or more in the Arab region at the time of the experiment. None of the participating professors or students specialized in Arabic literature or related fields. The relevant demographics are illustrated in Table 7.1. The analysis reported here does not investigate the role of gender, discipline, or school simply because the sample is relatively small to allow comparisons of various subgroups.

The participants were simply asked to talk exclusively in SA about three topics: life after death, the political and cultural relationship between the East and the West, and their pastime, which together represent the domains of religious discourse, political and cultural discussions, and everyday life speech. The inclusion of these three topics in the study was necessary to investigate the role of topic in determining the consistency of SA use. The participants were informed about the purpose of this experiment, namely, to better our understanding of educated Arab speakers' ability to carry on and sustain conversation in SA. The participants were asked to talk for five minutes about each of the three topics. I timed the start of the narratives and asked the participants to stop at the end of the five minutes allocated to each. When speakers stopped before they finished the five minutes, I asked one or more questions (based on the content of their narratives) to prompt them to complete the five-minute narratives. My interjections were excluded from the analysis. The subjects were recorded as they completed the tasks. The recordings were transcribed verbatim into Word documents. In coding the switches to QA, speakers of all four language varieties were consulted when

Table 7.1 Summary of the demographics of the participants in the SA-narrative tasks

		Egyptian		Jordanian		Moroccan		Saudi	
		Professor	Student	Professor	Student	Professor	Student	Professor	Student
Gender	Male	7	5	3	6	7	4	10	10
	Female	3	5	7	4	3	6	0	0
Field	P. science*	8	3	2	3	2	3	1	4
	S. science	2	7	8	7	8	7	9	6
School	Public	9	9	3	4	4	8	10	10
	Private	1	1	7	6	6	2	0	0

*P. science = physical science; S. science = social science

ambiguous cases arose. The verification process was conducted mainly with the help of Arab students at Utah State University.

The criteria for whether an element belonged to SA or QA were partly informed by Eid's (1988) guidelines in determining switches between SA and QA. Eid suggests that the identification of switches should be based on cases where clear SA or QA forms are used. This principle excludes *ambiguous cases*, where language forms are shared by the two varieties (p. 56). For example, the word ʕaamil "factor" cannot start a switch to SA or QA because it belongs to both. However, phonological and morphological cues are sometimes used to make a distinction between the forms of the two varieties (e.g., *kursi* [chair] in SA vs. *kərse* in Jordanian Arabic). *Modified forms*, those belonging to one variety but that are morphologically or phonologically transformed according to the rules of the other, are categorized in their respective varieties based on the presence or absence of similar alternative forms available to the speaker (pp. 55–56). For example, a word like *raaħa* "went.3SM" is considered a QA form, even though it ends with SA indicative-mood marker, namely *-a*. This is because the alternative SA form *ðahaba* was conceivably available to the speaker (just as it would expectedly be available to educated speakers of Arabic in general). It is for this same reason that a word like *ðahab* "went.3SM" is counted as SA even when it ends with no indicative-mood marking (which is characteristic of SA verbs). Finally, words that exist exclusively in SA but whose phonological forms have been influenced (but not completely changed) by the dialects are considered SA words (e.g., *yistaṭiiʕ* "be able to" instead of *yastaṭiiʕ*; *limaaza* "why" instead of *limaaða*). When produced by Egyptian participants, SA words pronounced with the Egyptian /g/ were classified as SA elements if their other properties and context marks them as SA.[4]

As for English words, Callahan's (2004) guidelines were followed in distinguishing *borrowed* English words that have become parts of the Arabic language from those that are not. According to Callahan, "borrowed" words and expressions are characterized by their use in everyday speech, their phonological adaptation to the rules of the borrowing language, and their lack of clear discourse function. Most of the terms related to computer and internet technologies, such as *internet*, *computer*, and *Facebook*, fall under this category, and for this reason such terms were not counted as switches. However, when alternative Arabic terms are more common, then the English words were considered as switches. For example, the data contained the word "cell phone," which is rarely used in comparison to the Arabic word *jawwaal/khilyawi* "mobile." Tables 7.2 and 7.3 summarize the number of words produced by the professor and student groups in the four countries.

Considering the word count per minute assigned to each topic, a number of patterns emerge with respect to the overall comparative *fluency* of the professor and student groups. Among professors, Moroccans have greater fluency in SA than their Egyptian, Jordanian, and Saudi counterparts, while fluency rates were similar among the latter three groups. With students, Moroccan speakers again displayed higher fluency than the other student groups. A comparison across

Table 7.2 Word count per narrative

	Religion		Politics & culture		Pastime	
	Professors	Students	Professors	Students	Professors	Students
Egyptian	4,283	4,405	4,142	4,123	3,862	3,967
Jordanian	4,231	3,978	4,537	3,947	4,006	4,312
Moroccan	4,403	4,362	4,785	4,595	4,471	4,585
Saudi	4,496	4,204	4,066	3,714	3,924	4,011

Table 7.3 Overall word count in the three narratives

	Professors	Students
Egyptian	12,287	12,495
Jordanian	12,774	12,237
Moroccan	13,659	13,542
Saudi	12,486	11,929

the professor and student groups indicates that the Jordanian and Saudi professors have a comparatively higher fluency in SA than the Jordanian and Saudi students, whereas the Egyptian professors lag slightly behind Egyptian students in terms of fluency in SA. The Moroccan professors and students display a comparable fluency in SA. Apart from word count, I counted the frequency and types of switches in each of the narratives.[5] The switches were classified into eight main types, including:

- Whole clause,
- Phrase or clause fragment (i.e., a clause that is missing at least one component but has at least two adjacent and related words),
- Content words (nouns, adjectives, adverbs, and verbs: verbs and their affixes were considered one unit, based on Maratsos's [1991] notion of the morphological unity of verbs; multiword numbers, rates, and percentages also fell under this category),
- Function words (pronouns, demonstratives, relativizers, prepositions, conjunctions, expletives, negative particles, possessive particle),
- Bound morphemes (e.g., when the verb is in SA and the aspectual marker is in QA),
- Fillers and parentheticals,
- Idioms and fixed expressions, and
- English words.

The selection of these categories was informed by Bentahila and Davies's (1995) study on bilingual CS in the Moroccan context. The data lacked any switches to French. All of the switches to English were single words (e.g., drink) or compound nouns (e.g., movie show), and therefore no further subgrouping was done to English switches. The following examples illustrate these switches in context (also see Appendices for sample narratives):

(5) laa yuugad fii l-Ɂislaam tawaakul. *Mafeeš ħaaga Ɂismaha . . . Ɂinsaan yatruk kul šeiɁ wiyɁuul laa . . . rabinaa hayurzuɁni*

"There is no dependence on others in Islam. *There is not a thing named . . . a person leaves everything and says yah. . . . God will provide for me*." (Egyptian)

(6) jaaɁuu lana ṭabaʕan biħaḍaarah gamiilah *Ɂilli hiyya* alħammaamaat alruumaaniyyah

"They brough to us, of course, a beautiful civilization, *which is* the Roman baths." (Egyptian)

(7) fa-haðaa fiʕlan *Ɂaaʕid* fii faraaɣ kabiir

"Therefore this is really *living* in a big emptiness." (Egyptian)

(8) alħamdu lilah Ɂanni maħẓuuẓah fi xtiyaar aṣḍiqaaɁi *miš* fii haðihi al-fatrah faqaṭ

"Thanks to God. I am lucky in choosing my friends . . . *not* in this period only." (Jordanian)

(9) fa-haðihi l-biiɁah *bituʕ*tabar magaal xiṣb li-Ɂay dawlah Ɂuxraa

"Therefore this environment *is* considered a fertile field for any other country." (Egyptian)

(10) wa-yasaɁaluuna-hum bi-šaklin xaaṣ ʕan raɁyi-hum . . . -him bi-dawr ħukuumati-him fi . . . *šu ismuh* . . . fi . . . fi al fi. . . . qaraaraati-him

"And they ask them particularly about their opinion about the role of their government in . . . *what is the name?* . . . in . . . in the . . . in their decisions." (Jordanian)

(11) laa aṭfaalii *min ɣeir šar* aṭfaalii alɁaan kibaar fii aljaamiʕah laa yuujad ladyhim waqt.

"No my children . . . *no evil* . . . my children are now grown up in the university . . . they do not have time." (Jordanian)

(12) Ɂatanaawal ʕašaaɁi . . . rubbama maʕa drink basiiṭa

"I have my dinner . . . perhabs with a small drink." (Jordanian)

In (5), the speaker starts a sentence in SA, but then introduces another sentence in QA. In (6), however, the speaker switches to QA only in a sentence fragment, namely *Ɂilli hiyya* "which is." Similarly, in (7), (8), and (9), the speakers shift to QA to render the content word *Ɂaaʕid* "living/sitting in," the function word *miš* "not," and the bound morpheme *bi-*, which is the marker of the progressive case. Examples (10) and (11) mark the interjection of the colloquial parenthetical phrase *šu ismuh* "what is the name," which is used when one cannot recall the right word or name, and the colloquial expression *min ɣeir šar* "no evil" in pieces of SA discourse. The last example involves the use of the English word "drink" in the SA sentence.

The following four tables summarize the frequency and types of CS in the three narratives of the professors. As the tables show, the four groups of speakers share a number of common patterns. First, participants in each of the four groups shift to QA to varying extents. Second, based on the range of shifts, it is clear that a number of speakers in each group are able to sustain conversations in SA without the need to shift to QA or English, whereas others resort to QA quite frequently. This makes it difficult to make any generalizations about the extent to which this group of speakers may sustain the use of SA in their oral

Table 7.4 Frequency and type of switches in religion-focused narratives by professors

	Egyptian	*Jordanian*	*Moroccan*	*Saudi*
Whole clause	4	1	0	2
Phrase or part of a clause	20	3	6	9
Content word	44	9	24	21
Function word	30	7	5	8
Bound morpheme	9	3	2	0
Fillers and parentheticals	2	1	4	4
Idioms and fixed expressions	2	1	0	0
English	1	5	0	0

Table 7.5 Frequency and type of switches in politics-focused narratives by professors

	Egyptian	*Jordanian*	*Moroccan*	*Saudi*
Whole clause	2	1	0	1
Phrase or part of a clause	21	5	4	10
Content word	43	21	21	27
Function word	32	9	5	9
Bound morpheme	8	1	1	0
Fillers and parentheticals	0	5	2	4
Idioms and fixed expressions	0	0	0	0
English	3	11	0	1

Table 7.6 Frequency and type of switches in pastime-focused narratives by professors

	Egyptian	Jordanian	Moroccan	Saudi
Whole clause	7	2	0	1
Phrase or part of a clause	30	9	7	13
Content word	103	20	26	39
Function word	32	8	7	11
Bound morpheme	11	2	1	0
Fillers and parentheticals	3	1	3	3
Idioms and fixed expressions	0	1	0	0
English	5	17	2	5

Table 7.7 Overall number and range of switches in professors' narratives on religion, politics, and pastime

	Religion		Politics & culture		Pastime	
	No.	Range	No.	Range	No.	Range
Egyptian	112	0–57	109	1–28	191	2–61
Jordanian	30	0–14	53	1–19	60	0–24
Moroccan	41	0–10	33	0–7	46	0–9
Saudi	44	0–9	52	0–12	72	0–13

production. A third and last commonality is that, generally speaking, the four groups shifted to QA more often in addressing the topic of pastime activities than when discussing religious or political themes. This may be attributed to the nature of these topics in context, as some everyday activities are typically expressed in specific QA and English words (e.g., *min ɣeir šarr* "no evil"). The four groups, however, diverged in a number of respects. For example, the Egyptian group surpassed their counterparts in terms of the overall number of switches to QA. On the other hand, the Moroccan speakers exhibited the least amount of QA elements in their production. Moreover, the Moroccan speakers showed less of a tendency than the others to mix SA with English.

Relatively similar patterns emerged in the narratives of college students across the four groups. Like the professors, the college students resorted to QA to varying degrees in their narratives. Like their seniors, too, the students displayed notable variability in the number and type of switches, with some generating unmixed SA narratives and others incorporating a relatively high volume of QA and English elements into their productions. For all four groups, the non-SA forms were more sizable in the pastime narrative than in politics or religion. A final similarity is that all of the participants switched more at the word and phrase levels and less so at the level of clause.

In terms of differences, the data shows that the Moroccan college students were clearly ahead of their Egyptian, Jordanian, and Saudi counterparts in terms of their ability to sustain the use of SA in their discourse. Like the Moroccan professors, Moroccan students were also less inclined to mix SA with English. Contrastingly, the Jordanian group showed a comparably high presence of English words in their output. However, when we compare the professors and students, it becomes clear that the Jordanian college students were the group that showed the most notable divergence from their senior counterparts in terms of the number of switches to QA and English, followed by the Saudi and Egyptian groups.

When we compare the numbers and types of switches produced by professors versus students, a number of patterns emerge. The students in each of the four groups use more English elements in their narratives than professors,

Table 7.8 Frequency and type of switches in religion-focused narratives by students

	Egyptian	Jordanian	Moroccan	Saudi
Whole clause	1	2	0	1
Phrase or part of a clause	4	5	4	1
Content word	45	37	34	29
Function word	12	8	11	5
Bound morpheme	7	5	0	0
Fillers and parentheticals	1	2	3	3
Idioms and fixed expressions	2	1	0	0
English	0	1	0	0

Table 7.9 Frequency and type of switches in politics-focused narratives by students

	Egyptian	Jordanian	Moroccan	Saudi
Whole clause	2	3	1	1
Phrase or part of a clause	7	4	5	8
Content word	29	40	27	49
Function word	13	9	6	10
Bound morpheme	3	4	1	0
Fillers and parentheticals	0	3	1	4
Idioms and fixed expressions	0	1	0	0
English	7	14	3	11

Table 7.10 Frequency and type of switches in pastime-focused narratives by students

	Egyptian	Jordanian	Moroccan	Saudi
Whole clause	1	2	0	3
Phrase or part of a clause	9	5	6	9
Content word	47	38	25	53
Function word	14	11	5	9
Bound morpheme	5	8	1	0
Fillers and parentheticals	2	4	2	5
Idioms and fixed expressions	0	2	0	1
English	8	19	6	13

Table 7.11 Overall number and range of switches in students' narratives on religion, politics, and pastime

	Religion		Politics & culture		Pastime	
	No.	Range	No.	Range	No.	Range
Egyptian	72	0–20	61	0–16	86	0–19
Jordanian	61	0–13	78	0–15	89	0–22
Moroccan	52	0–11	44	0–9	45	0–13
Saudi	39	0–8	83	0–18	93	1–17

particularly in the pastime narrative. This may be due the spread of information and communication technologies, which provide younger generations with new contact opportunities with the outside world. This may also have to do with the global influence of English and its mounting presence in the economic, social, and educational spheres. The gap in the frequency of English words between professors and students appears particularly in the case of Jordanian and Saudi speakers. English has a stronger presence in Jordan and Saudi Arabia, possibly because of the political, economic, and social influence of the United States in these two countries.

As for QA switches, the Egyptian college students made fewer shifts to QA in comparison to the Egyptian professors. Four main reasons may account for this pattern. First, historically, most of the professors in the study lived their youths in a time when the link between Egyptian identity and the Egyptian dialect was at its height, which may have positively impacted their attitudes toward their dialect. However, this link may not be as strong in the case of the Egyptian students given the relatively receding political and cultural role of Egypt in the region. Second, the emergence of satellite television has granted the younger Arab generation greater exposure to SA, which was not always available to the older generation. Third, although Egyptian dialect is still widely used in television programs, other dialects such as those of the Gulf and the Levant are becoming profuse on different media, and therefore the Egyptians' attitudes toward their dialect as the dialectal lingua franca in the Arab region is not warranted. Last, the growing sense of religious identity in Egypt, mostly at the individual level (Nydell, 2012), draws more attention to the need for mastering SA.

The results present a complex picture of the participants' abilities to use SA and sustain it in conversations. One of the most visible patterns in the data is the notable variability in the extent to which different speakers resort to QA to develop their narratives. While some narratives were rendered in unmixed SA, others were replete with QA and English elements. This variability precludes the possibility of making any solid, data-driven generalizations concerning the ability of educated Arabic speakers to sustain the use of SA in their discourse. Generally speaking, however, the majority of speakers may be described as *functional* speakers of SA in the sense that they could carry on conversations in SA, only with unsystematic introductions of QA. This is evidenced by the fact the speakers in all of the student and professor groups rarely shift to QA or English at the clause level, the exception being the Egyptian professors. While they may resort frequently to their respective dialects, they do it mainly at the level of content words and other small constituents of speech, and not with full sentences. This type of *functional* proficiency may allow the speakers to mobilize SA for certain purposes and functions.

The disparity in the performance of the Moroccan and Mashriqi groups (i.e., Egyptians, Jordanians, and Saudis) may be explained by four main interrelated reasons. These reasons are not exhaustive, nor do they apply to every speaker of the dialects under study, but they may reflect general trends in the four speech communities. Considering the difference between the Moroccan and Egyptian participants, the performance of the Egyptian participants may be explained first by the status and value of the Egyptian dialect compared to the Moroccan dialect in their respective speech communities and in the Arab region in general. The Egyptian dialect has been used extensively along with SA as a medium of oral and written discourse, such as in poetry, drama, novels, short stories, and entertainment media, unlike Moroccan Arabic, which is largely restricted to the Moroccan context. Second, many Egyptian speakers generally assume that the Egyptian dialect is understood by the majority of Arabic-speaking people because of the popularity of Egyptian entertainment media – an assumption that places less pressure on them to use SA in communicating with Arabic speakers of other nationalities. By contrast, their Moroccan counterparts lack this advantage and may therefore need SA to be able to communicate effectively with speakers of other Arabic dialects.

The third reason driving Moroccans' superior use of SA is that Egyptian speakers generally have relatively more positive views of their dialects than Moroccan speakers, as has been confirmed in the two previous chapters. The Moroccan speakers have less favorable views of their dialect and tend to favor

SA. The sharp value distinction between SA and QA makes the shift from SA to QA less likely and less positive for the Moroccan speakers than it may be for their Egyptian counterparts. A fourth factor concerns the widely invoked relationship between the Egyptian national identity and the country's dialect. Although this relationship was propagated largely during the colonial period, there are still some Egyptian speakers who embrace it (Rosenbaum, 2011). This relationship may have had a negative influence on how some Egyptian speakers relate to SA or use it in their daily lives. The situation in Morocco is different because the link between the Moroccan dialect and national Moroccan identity may not be clearly established for various historical and cultural reasons. Among these are the existence of a large Berber community who would readily adopt SA as part of their Muslim identity but may not embrace the Moroccan dialect as part of their religious or ethnic identity. Moreover, Morocco is characterized by the presence of competing languages, including French, which serves as a reminder of the exclusion policies against SA.

The difference between the Moroccan and the Jordanian speakers may be explained by similar factors. First, like their Egyptian counterparts, many Jordanian speakers assume that the Jordanian dialect is understood by the majority of Arabic speakers, making them less concerned about the need to use SA for intelligibility purposes. Second, as has been noted in the two previous chapters, many Jordanian speakers are more keen on acquiring and practicing English than SA for practical reasons, which may have influenced their pursuit of using SA. Third, the Jordanians also have a heightened sense of national identity which developed as a result of the influx of refugees from Iraq, Libya, Lebanon, and Syria during armed conflicts in the region. QA acquires its significance from the fact that it is a major marker of the Jordanian versus non-Jordanian identity. The Saudis also have a heighted sense of national identity due to the relatively comfortable economic conditions of many Saudis, compared to other Arab nationals, and the putative religious position of Saudi Arabia in the Muslim world. The sense of national pride is furthered by the assumption that the Saudi dialect is close to SA and may have originated in some old Arabic dialect(s). These positive attitudes may explain the fact that Saudis and Jordanians rarely shift to SA to accommodate other Arab nationals in day-to-day communication. One cannot discount other educational, social, and individual factors, but the role of attitudes and identity is a crucial factor in the disparity between the Mashriqi speakers and the Moroccan speakers.

Last, the data reveals a notable presence of English terms in the speech of the Jordanian and Saudi college students. It is intriguing that the presence of English is more transparent in the narratives of the Jordanian and Saudi students than those of the Egyptian and Moroccan students in the study. As has been noted in Chapter 4, the Jordanian and Saudi student groups have more positive attitudes toward English than the other two groups. This suggests that speakers' language attitudes reflect directly on their language use and abilities (Albirini, 2014b). While the Jordanian and Saudi speakers shift to their second language (i.e., English), the Moroccan data does not show a single instance of French. Bentahila and Davies (1995) compared the linguistic output of old-generation Moroccans and Moroccan youth. They found a notable presence of French in the speech of the older generation, whereas younger Moroccan speakers used French parsimoniously, mainly in small constituents, such as noun phrases. Again, the receding role of French in the international arena, the Moroccan speakers' views of French in comparison to English, and the fact that French is generally seen as a variety imposed on Moroccan society may explain the absence of French in the speech of the Moroccan participants. These observations are tentative because of the small sample of participants, and therefore they may not warrant generalization. I am planning to expand the data collection to verify the generalizability of the claims.

The concepts of monitored speech versus unmonitored speech

A distinction between *monitored* and *unmonitored* speech is necessary for grasping the different forms of CS and the asymmetrical distribution of SA and QA in various forms of interaction. Monitored speech occurs in scenarios where speakers address a large actual or anticipated audience,[6] as in religious sermons, political speeches, and televised non-entertainment-related interviews, debates, and reports. In such cases, forms of speech are expected to be more formal and the linguistic functions to be performed are more serious, important, or intellectual than those used in everyday interactions. A number of scholars have alluded to this notion, but often with references to the relationship between the mode of speech and the formality of setting (e.g., Holes, 1995, 2004; Mejdell, 1999). The concept of monitored speech, as used in this work, goes beyond the issue of setting to include the function (intellectual, important, and serious topics[7]), audience (relatively large), and *expected* variety (typically, but not always, SA). In the variationist tradition, monitored speech has been deemed less natural and authentic than spontaneous speech in relaxed conversations (Bucholtz, 2003; Coupland, 2007; Labov et al., 1968). However, this postulation originates in and often relates to the American and similar contexts. The application of this criterion to the Arabic diglossic context would leave the majority of news reports, religious sermons, political speeches, university lecturers, and several other forms of SA-rendered speech out of the scope of the *authenticity* metric. For many Arabic speakers, however, SA is the more *natural* way of rendering a political speech, news report, or religious sermon. The unmarkedness of SA in such domains has been verified empirically (Rabie, 1991).

Monitored speech is an integral part of public speech in the Arabic sociolinguistic scene because, when monitored, speakers often try to construct their public image partly through linguistic moves. Thus, they would usually pay closer attention to their language use and base their choices not only on their communicative goals and attitudinal positions, but also the needs, attitudes, and reactions

of a wider audience of Arabic interlocutors and listeners. Monitored speech sometimes demands the speaker's awareness of the sociolinguistic patterns, roles,
and practices that meet the expectations of immediate and potential audiences,
as is the case of most interviews. Thus, it may illustrate what is sociolinguistically (un)acceptable by members of a given speech community, when, where,
and by whom. In this sense, monitored speech becomes part of "social awareness," which, in Labovian terms, leads to specific linguistic patterns following the
general sociolinguistic norms of the society – though the latter term applies to
all types of speech and communication. Albirini's (2011) function-based representation of diglossia (discussed in Chapter 2) is based on monitored speech.
In other words, it reflects the speakers' understanding of how language should
be used by different members of society, and it suggests that these perspectives often inform their language usage and choices. The same may be said of
Ferguson's (1959a) model, which has been described as an abstract/ideational
model of the distribution of SA and QA (Caton, 1991). Both may become ide-
ational if applied to informal, everyday conversations.

Unmonitored speech, on the other hand, occurs in everyday conversations
and other casual forms of communication. It conforms to Labov's description of
everyday speech as "the most systematic and regular form of language" (Labov
et al., 1968, p. 167). Unlike monitored speech, which often adheres to the speech
community's discursive and communicative norms, everyday interactions often
depend on demographic, interpersonal/group, contextual, and pragmatic factors.
Moreover, because it is typically based on one-on-one interactions in everyday
life, unmonitored speech often involves negotiation of roles, meanings, and identities. Therefore, one would expect more variance in the patterns and functions of
CS in unmonitored speech than in speech under observation. However, as it will
be shown below, even in this form of speech, there are some patterns of CS that
are more regular than others. What follows will be a more detailed elaboration on
the use of SA and QA in monitored vs. unmonitored speech.

Bidialectal codeswitching between SA and QA in monitored speech

The majority of studies on CS between SA and QA in monitored speech situations have been contextualized in religious and political speeches, though some
have focused on less formal domains, such as soccer commentaries (Abu-Haidar
1991; Albirini, 2011; Bassiouney, 2006, 2013; Harrell, 1964; Holes, 1987, 1993;
Mazraani, 1997; Mejdell, 1999, 2006; Rabie, 1991; Saeed, 1997; Soliman, 2008;
Taine-Cheikh, 2002). It is widely accepted and empirically verified that SA is used
substantially in religious and political discourse in Arabic (Holes, 2004; Saeed,
1997), and this assumption drives the focus on these domains, as well as interest
in exploring the changing roles of QA and SA (Soliman, 2008).

One consistent finding with respect to bidialectal CS is that some of the main
functions of SA and QA, as the High and Low varieties, are preserved in mixed

SA–QA discourse. Thus, SA is often designated for important or serious issues, whereas QA is adopted for less significant topics. For example, Saeed (1997) focused on the pragmatic functions of switching from SA to each of three Arabic regional dialects (Egyptian, Kuwaiti, and Yemeni) in the formal context of religious discourse. In particular, the study investigated whether CS serves any communicative purposes and sought to identify the nature of these purposes should they come to light in the research. In addition, Saeed examined the frequency of shifting to QA in this formal context. He used audio and video tapes for three religious scholars from Egypt, Kuwait, and Yemen to investigate these questions. The findings indicate that the three scholars switch codes in their speech with considerable frequency. The pragmatic motivations for CS fall into three categories: (1) iconic/rhetorical (e.g. to quote or to simplify); (2) structural (triggered by linguistic structure); and (3) other (e.g., due to linguistic incompetence). Saeed argues that the iconic/rhetorical function of CS seems to underlie most of the shifts between dialects. Using SA largely depends on whether the speaker seeks to introduce a point to which he attaches importance or value or to quote "true examples," whereas QA is used to achieve a variety of goals including indexing unimportant topics, simplifying explanations, inducing "hypothetical examples," deploying "fillers," and creating a sense of humor.

In political speeches, CS seems to have a similarly rhetorical function with a particular focus on persuasion (Holes, 1993; Jarraya, 2013; Mazraani, 1997). Holes (1993), for example, focused on code choice (*style shifting* in Holes's terms) in the political speeches of the former president of Egypt, Jamal Abdulnasser. Holes uses six extracts from political speeches delivered by Abdulnasser between 1956 and 1965. He notices that Abdulnasser is keenly aware of the rhetorical effects of his code choice. Indeed, the politician sometimes uses SA and QA completely unmixed and sometimes mixes them into a third linguistic variety. SA is used to mark the politician's authority over his audience, to express abstract idealized values, and to arouse pan-Arab sentiment. On the other hand, QA is used to show solidarity with the audience, to explain the "nitty-gritty" or personal side of politics, and to kindle Egyptian nationalism and values. Moreover, whereas SA is used to lay out broad but central messages, QA is dedicated to follow-up explanation and commentary. Similar results were reported by Mazraani (1997), who extended the analysis of political speeches to include − in addition to Jamal Abdulnasser − the late presidents of Iraq and Libya, Saddam Hussein and Mu'ammar Al-Qadhdhafi. Mazraani found that the three politicians employ CS to enhance the emotive and oratorical effectiveness of their speeches and to appeal to their audiences' emotions. Based on her study of the former Tunisian president Ben Ali's final speech, Jarraya (2013) similarly found that Ben Ali infused his language with QA elements to convey emotions more persuasively.

CS is sometimes attributed to personal choice rather than societal mandates. For example, Bassiouney (2006) examined the social functions and syntactic constraints of CS between Modern Standard Arabic (MSA) and Egyptian Colloquial Arabic (ECA). Her data included four oral sermons, four political speeches, and one university lecture. In terms of the social functions of CS, Bassiouney found the speaker to be the most important factor in deciding when CS occurs. Moreover, language choice in her data was not always related to a particular discourse function. That being said, she found that speakers often state abstract facts in MSA, or employ MSA to lend a tone of seriousness to the topic, and then elaborate through more concrete examples in ECA. In a more recent work, Bassiouney (2013) used three religious sermons "to show how Islamic preachers can manipulate the linguistic situation to convey a religious message" (p. 49). Her findings again indicate that "Using SA, ECA or alternating between both, is a matter of choice" (p. 64). Speakers may use the two varieties to negotiate relationships or establish solidarity with their audience, for example, or to clarify the preacher's attitude toward the topic. At the same time, however, she contends that "each stretch of discourse is still unique," (p. 65) suggesting that whether there is a conscious motivation behind the switch depends on structural factors.

Albirini (2011) argues that CS is a social mechanism that simply materializes the statuses and functions of SA and QA as the High and Low codes, respectively, of the Arabic sociolinguistic landscape. Albirini (2011) investigated the sociolinguistic functions of CS between SA and three varieties of colloquial Arabic, namely Egyptian, Gulf, and Levantine. Three sets of naturally produced data were employed, representing the domains of religious lectures and discussions, political debates and interviews, and play-by-play soccer commentaries. The naturalistic data came from thirty-five audio and video recordings of educated speakers of Arabic. The research revealed that switches between SA and QA occur in all three forms of discourse – political, religious, and sports-announcing – which differ considerably in their level of formality. CS between SA and QA regulates and preserves the statuses and functions of the two varieties as the High and Low codes in the discourse. Thus, switching to SA is linked to important, serious, and intellectual functions as well as functions requiring eloquent or complex style (e.g., rhyming poetry, abstract theorization, etc.). These patterns materialize the very status, role, and functions SA assumes as the High variety in the Arab diglossic situation. Likewise, QA is brought to the scene for simple everyday functions often less grave or important, such as joking and simplification of previously stated ideas. These functions characteristically reflect the status and functions of QA as the Low variety in the Arabic sociolinguistic arena. Thus, the construct of diglossia is proven relevant to the current situation of Arabic by the demonstrated allocation of SA and QA to distinct communicative functions.

Apart from its functional partitioning role, CS also marks the speaker's attitude toward certain details in the discourse, often indexing his/her positive attitudes toward SA-related functions and negative attitudes toward those delivered in QA (Albirini, 2011; Saeed, 1997). Saeed (1997) argues that speakers switch to QA to indicate their negative attitudes to the topic or point under discussion. Furthering the idea, Albirini (2011) suggests that the very act of switching, based on High/Low functions, pinpoints a change in the speaker's attitude. Speakers' positive or negative attitudes are materialized through their choice of the

High and Low varieties. For example, jokes and insults are often rendered in QA, whereas pedantic speech is typically conveyed in SA, and this attitudinal shift is also often accompanied by changes in the tone, pitch, and focus. In other words, the attitudinal asymmetry between SA and QA may materialize behaviorally in language use. This suggests that the relationship between language use and language attitudes may be empirically grounded in formal monitored speech.

A third important function of SA–QA CS in monitored speech is indexing speakers' pan-Arab and Muslim identities. However, this function seems to be restricted to the speaker's shift to SA. Albirini (2011) observed that speakers switch to SA to emphasize their pan-Arab or Muslim affiliation, mobilizing such concepts as *Umma* "nation," which are often invoked in pan-Arab and pan-Muslim contexts (*Al-Umma Al-Arabiyya* "The Arab nation" and *Ummatu l-Islam* "Muslim nation"). Speakers mobilize their membership in pan-Arab and Muslim communities by using a variety they share with their listeners while simultaneously setting aside their national or local dialects, as examples (13) and (14) show:

(13) *ʔna bistaɣrib ... hal ʔintiqaadat.* Naħnu, ka-juzʔ min haðihi l-ʔumma, natawaqqaʕ al-ʕawn min ʔašiqqaʔina fi lduwal al-ʕarabiyya.

"*I am surprised by these criticisms.* We [Palestinians], as part of this nation, expect help from our brothers in the Arab states." (Albirini, 2010, p. 123)

(14) *haadi l-ħamli š-šaʕwaaʔ leiš?* Naħnu muslimuun wa naʕtaz bi-ðaalek

"*Why is this severe campaign?* We are Muslims and we are proud about that." (Albirini, 2010, p. 123)

In (13), the speaker expresses his astonishment at the criticism raised against the Palestinian people by some Arab regimes, who, according to him, are expected help rather than criticize Palestinians. The speaker here appeals to Arab national identity to imply the obligation of Arab regimes to support the Palestinians. In (14), the preacher speaks about what he sees as a disparagement of Islamic symbols. Then, he shifts to SA to highlight the pride involved in Muslim affiliation. Albirini's data shows that SA is the only code employed for activating pan-Arab or Muslim identity – not surprising, as SA has historically been one of the few cultural assets shared among Arabs and Muslims.

It should be noted that recent studies point to a growing presence of QA in monitored speech, even in religious discourse, which is often considered the most formal form of discourse. Soliman (2008) conducted a case study on CS between SA and Egyptian Arabic in the religious speeches of an Egyptian preacher who is renowned for his remarkable reliance on the Egyptian dialect. Since this particular preacher is known for his extensive use of Egyptian Arabic, the researcher set to investigate the phonological, syntactical, and morphological features of his speech as well as the attitudes of educated Egyptians toward his use of Egyptian Arabic. The findings of the study show that Egyptian Arabic occurred with notable frequency in the religious discourse of this particular subject. SA was used for reciting Qur'anic verses, mentioning Prophetic narrations, giving quotations, and supplicating at the beginning and the end of the sermon. The other parts of the preaching were mainly in Egyptian Arabic. The surveyed educated Egyptians seemed to have an overall positive attitude toward the use of the Egyptian variety in the religious domain. Although this case study may not represent the typical patterns of language use in religious discourse, as the author himself acknowledges, it is still an important indicator of "the changing role of SA in religious discourse," as the title of the work in fact denotes.

To summarize, CS in monitored speech is characterized by the allocation of SA and QA to a number of distinct functions that reflect their respective statuses as High and Low varieties. It is also one of the mechanisms through which speakers verbalize their positive or negative attitudes to different parts of their discourse. In addition, switching to SA may index the speaker's pan-Arab or Muslim identity. This suggests that the link between SA and identity is the result of not only sociohistorical factors (e.g., the relationship between SA and Arab nationalism) and formal and informal institutions (schools, media, policy), but also the communicative practices of speakers of Arabic. Lastly, the sociolinguistic expectations concerning language use and CS in monitored speech may be violated by individual speakers, as Soliman's study shows, but these individual cases often do not represent the overarching patterns in this type of discourse.

Bidialectal codeswitching between SA and QA in unmonitored speech

In Chapter 2, I explained that Arabic varieties may be classified according to diverse approaches. When CS in dialect-contact situations is concerned, however, it is useful to differentiate between two dialectal groupings: national/state-based (Egyptian, Moroccan, Qatari, etc.) and local (urban, rural, and Bedouin). The majority of CS studies have been embedded within these two topological frameworks, and therefore examining CS research through these typological lenses may provide useful insights into the mechanisms of CS in their respective settings.

The Arabic state-based dialects diverge from each other in a number of ways, and therefore individuals coming from different Arab countries may find themselves obliged to switch codes to be able to communicate effectively. This type of CS is different from the one discussed above in three interrelated respects. First, the context of CS between SA and QA in monitored speech is characteristically formal, whereas CS between SA and the national QA varieties typically occurs in less formal or informal contexts. Second, in monitored speech situations, the linguistic common ground (Clark, 1996) for conversation is SA, whereas in the latter case the linguistic common ground is ambiguous or absent, and therefore speakers have to build or negotiate this important aspect of their interaction based on linguistic and non-linguistic factors. Last, the use of the national varieties inevitably invokes a number of political, attitudinal/ideological, and identity-related factors, which enter into the communication equation and affect the patterns of CS.

Among the earliest studies to examine the functions of CS between Arabs from different nationalities were those conducted by Abu-Melhim (1991, 1992), both of which generally report similar methodologies, theoretical frameworks, and findings. Abu-Melhim's 1992 study focused on the accommodation strategies implemented by educated bilingual Arabic-English speakers in their interactions. Informal conversations were arranged between ten speakers of the urban varieties in Egypt, Jordan, Iraq, Morocco, and Saudi Arabia (a pair of opposite-sex participants from each country). A questionnaire and follow-up phone interviews were conducted to elucidate the participants' language choices and attitudes. Abu-Melhim based his analysis on the assumption that speakers have the choice of using Classical Arabic (CA), Modern Standard Arabic (MSA), Educated Spoken Arabic (ESA), their respective colloquial dialects, and English. The findings indicate that the speakers often use their respective colloquial dialects, ESA, and English in their communication. They rarely shift to CA, MSA, or the colloquial varieties of their interlocutors. Contrary to common expectations, the Egyptian (particularly the Cairene) dialect was not preferred as the lingua franca in this context nor was it used consistently by the participants. Rather, the lingua franca in this context was "a combination of ESA and English" (p. 230). Moreover, when the participants switched away from their respective dialects, female participants tended to adopt different colloquial varieties, unlike the male participants who used both SA and their own colloquial dialects in their language switches. Finally, the Christian participants used more SA than their Muslim counterparts. Abu-Melhim attributes most of the CS patterns found in his studies, particularly the participants' abstention from switching to colloquial varieties other than their own, to attitudinal factors and national feelings toward the dialects involved.

Shiri (2002) reported similar findings in her study of interactions between Tunisian broadcasters and journalists living in London and their Middle Eastern coworkers (most of whom came from Egypt and the Levant). The study took place in two broadcasting companies. The author assumed the role of the observer–reporter. Five informants participated in the study (two males and three females). Unlike Abu-Melhim's four-dimensional classification of Arabic varieties (CA, MSA, ESA, and state-based colloquials), Shiri's typological approach acknowledges three varieties of Arabic: Sharqi dialects, Maghrebi dialects, and Fusha. She notes that the division is based on the informants' common perceptions of the distinction between Tunisian Arabic and the varieties spoken in the Middle East. Shiri found that all her Tunisian informants engaged in various forms of communicative accommodation. Thus, they sometimes deployed "Sharqi" features and words in their dialect, used a "third variety," shifted to Fusha, or resorted to English words to converge with their Middle Eastern interlocutors. In the follow-up interviews, the informants extended the explanation of language use beyond accommodation to include psychological concerns (e.g., fear of rejection, reduction of differences, and show of friendliness) and long-held attitudes toward the Sharqi and Maghrebi dialects (Maghrebi dialects are often viewed unfavorably, whereas the Sharqi dialects are considered closer to *Fuṣħa*). In addition, the participants' language usage reflected their attempts to "show off" their linguistic skills as multilingual speakers (which is viewed positively in Tunisia) and their bid to mark common membership in the Arabic-speaking community.

Taking insights from previous work on accommodation and making use of Content Analysis and Critical Discourse Analysis techniques, Albirini (in progress) examines the dynamics of interdialectal and bilingual CS in informal and semi-formal conversations and interviews involving educated speakers of Arabic. Starting with the assumption that some Arabic speakers accommodate their listeners linguistically, the study examined when, where, how, and why speech accommodation takes places, what governs the dynamics of this phenomenon, and what other factors are involved in language use in interdialectal and bilingual CS between Arabs from different Arab countries. Four types of data were used: arranged home-based conversations between speakers of the Egyptian, Jordanian, and Moroccan dialects, naturally occurring discussions in the mosque between speakers of the Egyptian, Moroccan, Saudi, and Syrian dialects, focus-group interactions between the author and Egyptian, Jordanian, Moroccan, and Saudi speakers, and interviews conducted by the author with Egyptian, Jordanian, Moroccan, and Saudi speakers. Whereas the focus-group interactions and the interviews were recorded during my fieldwork in Egypt, Jordan, Morocco, and Saudi Arabia, the other two data sets were recorded independently in two different sites in the United States. Follow-up interviews were used with a number of informants in each case. The preliminary findings show that the respondents rely predominantly on their respective dialects. Less prevalent are instances of shifting to SA, infusing QA with elements from SA, shifting to alternative QA varieties, and assuming the variety of the addressee. The degree of shifting away from one's colloquial variety depends on six main considerations:

- the native dialect of the speaker (Moroccans being the most profuse in their CS away from their dialect),
- the context of the discourse (house, university campus, café, or mosque),
- sociocognitive motivations (reducing differences),
- dynamics of the interaction (topics, argumentation, politeness, and turn taking),
- pragmatic moves (intelligibility), and
- sociopolitical aspects (power, ideology, and language insecurity).

Considering these factors together may explain why speakers shift, or shift more extensively in some contexts and turns than in others. However, the most important determinant of CS is the attitudinal and ideological stand that speakers have both prior to and during the interactions. In general, the dynamics of the interaction play a critical role in language choice.

A number of patterns emerge from the three studies reviewed above. First, language prestige is not a main determinant of CS patterns. Unlike the common assumption that Arabic speakers resort to SA or the Egyptian variety as a default form of interdialectal communication, these studies show that speakers rely more on their dialectal forms or mixed forms in their communication (Abu-Melhim, 1992; Shiri, 2002). SA is still used but on a limited scale. Accommodation seems to underlie the major part of CS in intercommunication between speakers of different national Arab dialects. Various other motives stand behind the speakers' accommodation of their interlocutors, including ideological/attitudinal, psychological, social, contextual, and discursive factors.

Within unmonitored speech, CS also occurs between SA and the local dialects or among the local dialects themselves. The dynamics of this form of CS are different from those underlying other forms of CS simply because the relationships that govern the local dialects and bind their speakers in this context are unique. First, the governmental policies and rhetoric that feed Arab nationalism at the regional and state levels – and its linguistic, cultural, social, political, economic, literary symbols – is not projected to operate at the local level. Thus, the strong national sentiments that may influence language choice when Arabs from different countries meet is not active in the case of local sociolinguistic encounters. This does not mean that identity dynamics are not at play in this type of CS, but that they are not amenable to nationalist rhetoric and symbolism (including language). Second, the relationship that holds speakers from the same Arab country is usually more durable than that between Arab nationals because of their geographical proximity and shared spheres of social activity. Thus, the subtleties of the interactions among Arab locals versus Arab nationals are dissimilar because the relationship that binds speakers in each case is unique. It is well known that interpersonal and intergroup relationships influence language use and choice (Auer, 1998; Gumperz, 1962). Last, speakers of the local Arabic dialects do usually understand each other, and therefore (un)intelligibility may not explain code choice in this context. This means that accommodation may not be motivated by mere intelligibility factors.

CS between SA and the local dialects has been explicated by a wide range of linguistic, affective, demographic, social, and economic factors. Albirini (2014a) indicates that speakers in his study use CS in everyday speech mainly for pragmatic gains. He examined the role of sociopragmatic factors in CS in the community of Al-'Keidaat Bedouins in Syria. Audio-recorded data was collected from two Bedouin wedding parties (both involving Al-'Keidaat Bedouins) and thirty-seven interactions involving five Bedouins in the workplace. The author undertook the role of uninvolved observer as he recorded the material. The data analysis betokens that Bedouin speakers use their multidialectal package to build ingroup relationships and enhance their ability to access different forms of social capital. For example, the Bedouins use the Bedouin dialect in Bedouin-dominated social fields (e.g., wedding party), because this variety helps them to index their Bedouin identities, which in turn guarantee their positions in tribe-based networks.

These intra-tribal social connections are, for Bedouins, a form of social capital and socioeconomic power. In the workplace, however, they resort to the urban dialect to build social relationships and networks with the urban and rural people, which lie at the heart of the practices of inclusion in and exclusion from institutionalized power relations in the workplace. Based on the finding, Albirini argues that, in everyday interactions, speakers' use of the Bedouin and urban dialects is more sociopragmatically driven than based on the often-invoked *prestige* of specific language varieties.

CS practices may materialize in the form of replacement of *features, words,* or *expressions* from one dialect by those from another. This type of CS is often motivated by factors related to prestige, accommodation, identity negotiation, and demographics (Abdel-Jawad, 1987; Amara, 2005; Al-Wer, 2007; Miller, 2005; Sawaie 1994; Suleiman, 1993). For example, a number of studies have found that Bedouin and rural speakers adopt some urban linguistic features in their interactions with speakers of these dialects, which has often been attributed to the "prestige," "beauty," "sophistication," and "femininity" of the urban dialects (e.g., Abdel-Jawad, 1981, 1986; Habib, 2010; Sawaie, 1994). Suleiman (1993) argues that Bedouin speakers switch to the rural and urban dialects in the multiethnic Jordan to express common nationality with speakers of these dialects. Parkinson (1996, p. 92) underscores the fact that some Arabic speakers infuse their SA speech with QA numbers to make themselves "accessible" to their listeners. In this context, shifting to the interlocutor's code becomes a form of communicative accommodation strategy, in which the speaker approximates his speech to that of his interlocutor to reduce dissimilarities between them and therefore gain social approval (Giles & Powesland, 1997, p. 233). This interpretation may also suggest that some aspects of SA are not "accessible" or understood by the listeners – a claim that may be questionable, especially in contexts where educated speakers of Arabic are involved. Al-Wer (2007) shows that many urban Palestinian speakers in Jordan adopt variables from the Bedouin dialects because of the national acclaim of Bedouin traditions and customs. These studies indicate that social considerations may inspire CS even when it operates below the word level, and it may result in enduring changes in the features of a given dialect.

The CS literature suggests that the functions allotted to SA and QA in monitored speech may also appear in unmonitored speech situations. Holes (1993) indicates speakers may use SA when they are in a "teaching" mode. He illustrates this through two anecdotes, one involving an agricultural extension officer advising illiterate village farmers in Bahrain and another involving a Syrian schoolteacher addressing a group of Jordanian visitors (who are still part of the Levant). In both cases, the speakers use SA in the process of formally addressing their audiences, often concluding their SA-delivered teaching with QA commentary. A similar pattern is reported by Albirini (2014a), who observed that speakers in informal or semi-formal situations (work environment) resort to SA when assuming a didactic role. Likewise, Versteegh (2001) notes that Arab informants often infuse their elicited QA speech tokens with different SA elements or may switch to SA, although these types of interaction may not be considered as part of monitored speech. Versteegh, however, attributes this form of switching to the informant's perception of the prestige associated with the standard language. Holes (2004) indicates that when educated Bahrainis discuss "serious" topics, especially topics of pan-Arab concern, they rely mainly on SA. However, when they tackle non-serious topics, especially topics pertaining to local affairs, they resort to QA. Irrespective of the motive or explanation, these patterns of CS are important because they show that the distribution of SA and QA in monitored speech may in some cases be replicated in unmonitored speech. In other words, there is always a chance of overlap between these two forms of CS. However, this again seems to depend on the functions or topics performed.

Last, in situations where the monitored–unmonitored speech dichotomy becomes fuzzy, speakers tend to mix SA and QA more frequently. For example, Holes (2004) recounts an interview situation where the interviewer uses a mixture of "levels" between SA and QA because the interviewee, who is an educated and cultured man, responds to his questions in a relaxed and casual way, using the colloquial Bahraini dialect. According to Holes, the interviewer fluctuates among these levels because the serious nature of his questions and yet the relaxed reaction of the interviewee obliges him not to use pure SA so that he does not sound pompous nor to use pure QA so that he does not sound as if he was demoting his guest's ability to understand the questions in SA. Mejdell (1999) focuses on broadcast interviews in which Najiib Maḥfouẓ, an Egyptian Noble Prize winner for literature, talks about his life. Like Holes (1993), Mejdell approaches her subject's use of SA and QA as a form of style shifting. Her findings point to a notable fluctuation in the style of Maḥfouẓ, with some stretches of discourse approximating SA or QA and some incorporating features from both. Mejdell attributes mixed style to the ambiguity of the "media situation," which combines the informality of face-to-face interactions and the formality of "public performance" (p. 323). Topic was not an important determinant of language choice. In another study, Mejdell (2006) analyzes a panel presentation at a seminar that confirms her previous findings and points additionally to the role of the structural proximity of SA and QA in the mixed style of the speakers.

In summary, the diverse patterns and motives of CS in everyday speech, both between SA and the local dialects or among the local dialects themselves, make any generalizations about the functions of CS in everyday interactions difficult. This is because many variables intervenes in the dynamics of this type of CS – most of which are *external* to the language varieties involved, such as gender, nationality, and education.

7.3.3 Codeswitching in written discourse

Written discourse is dissimilar to oral communication because of its nature as a self-conscious, planned, and editable textual interaction between the author and the readers. The written form has its own unique style, rhetoric, and structure that are not always compatible with the oral form. The writer's ability to edit and polish their work should therefore reflect finer awareness of the "conventions" of written discourse and the general expectations of the readership in a given context. This is significant in the Arab context because of the common assumption that SA is largely a written language or that writing is a functional domain of SA[8] (Mejdell, 2006; Rosenbaum, 2011). Traditionally, written discourse was assigned to SA not only because of the status of SA as a formal and prestigious variety, but also because the topics that writers dealt with in the pre-renaissance period were "traditional topics," focusing on religion, literatures, law, politics, etc. In fact, these topics are still largely transmitted textually in SA. However, the introduction of new literary genres (novel, short story, prose verse, etc.) and new concepts, terms, and styles has allowed for the introduction of QA into written, mainly literary, discourse. It has been argued that the use of QA is sparked by the stylistic demands of the new literary genres (Somekh, 1991).

Both the bilingual and the bidialectal types of CS transpire in literary work. Available research suggests that bilingual CS occurs in works written predominantly in languages other than Arabic. For example, Albakry and Hancock (2008) examined the juxtaposition of English and Egyptian Arabic in Ahdaf Soueif's *The Map of Love*, a novel shortlisted for the 1999 British Booker Prize award. The author was born in Egypt, but spent significant parts of her life in England. Since she was fluent in both English and Egyptian Arabic, this novel was written in English and imbued with elements from the Egyptian dialect. Albakry and Hancock notice that the writer intersperses her text with many Arabic words to preserve the original connotations and "sociocultural implications" of these expression (p. 226). For example, Soueif draws on such words as *ʕam* "paternal uncle" and *khal* "maternal uncle," which are titles of respect in the Egyptian culture. The novelist also brings into play a number of words and expressions that refer to Arab customs, traditions, history, and social life such as *mawwal* "a form of traditional music," *suħuur* "meal eaten in preparation for fasting," *kattar kheirak* "may God increase your bounty; thanks," and *mashaʔa Allah* "what God willed; an expression of admiration." Interestingly, the novelist also sprinkles her text with a few SA words, such as *amrad* "a man with no facial hair," to mark a character's high educational level or to signal a change in contextual formality. This pattern of CS is particularly informative because it reflects the author's awareness of the diglossic distribution of SA and QA even in written discourse. The juxtaposition of SA and typologically distinct languages has not figured predominantly in the CS literature, and therefore this type of CS presents a promising venue for future research.

Bidialectal CS appears particularly in literary works written by Egyptian writers (Mejdell, 2008b; Rosenbaum, 2011). Most of the existing studies have examined CS patterns as they relate to a single literary text or the literary work of a single author. Abdel-Malek (1972) examined the implications of diglossia on the novels of Yuusif Al-Sibaaʻi. Abdel-Malek traces the Egyptian novelist's "linguistic struggle" to reconcile his literary style with the realities of the diglossic situation in which he and his characters live. Although he started his novel-writing career with a conscious effort to "prevent colloquial expressions from sneaking in," Al-Sibaaʻi eventually found "the characters of the novel conversing – in spite of [him] – in colloquial" (cited in Abdel-Malek, 1972, p. 134). The novelist eventually settled on a compromised SA–QA style that is relatively acceptable by language "purists" in Egypt and at the same time leaves the impression that "characters converse in the normal speech of everyday life" (p. 134). Abdel-Malek lists a number of mechanisms that the novelist used to bridge the gap between SA and the Egyptian dialect, including borrowed expressions and grammatical constructions (e.g., *la muʔaxza* "excuse me," *miš baṭṭaal* "not too bad"), "Low-Standard" vocabulary (e.g., *naayim* instead of *naaʔim* "sleeping"), modified Egyptian expressions (e.g., *saliim miʔa fi-lmiʔa* "wholly sound/healthy"), and case-less nouns (Abdel-Malek, 1972). Abdel-Malek suggests that the style that Al-Sibaaʻi has adopted may be common among other novelists in similar situations.

Several subsequent studies have confirmed Abdel-Malek's perspicacious remark and extended its validity to other literary genres, such as poetry, zajal, short stories, and drama (e.g., Eid, 2002; Holes, 1995, 2004; Mejdell, 1999, 2006; Radwan, 2004; Rosenbaum, 2000, 2011; Semah, 1995). Some of these studies have focused on the evolution and spread of new branches of colloquial literary genres, such as "colloquial poetry" and "colloquial zajal" (Radwan, 2004; Semah, 1995). These studies have uncovered principal distinctions between literary genres written in SA and QA: whereas the SA-based forms of literature are still largely conceived as "high" compositions, the QA-based literary forms are often considered as "low" productions that may be best described as "a means of entertainment for the uneducated masses" (Semah, 1995, p. 81). Two further characteristics of the new genres are also underscored: (1) their appeal to the general population because of their accessible style, vocabulary, and themes, and, (2), the relationship between QA and the notion of building a relationship between the author and his audience (Radwan, 2004). Again, the reasoning behind the use of QA in these contexts points to the implicit functional polarity between SA and QA in literary genres. This polarity may be embedded in a single text or may transpire cross-textually (i.e., when comparing texts written in SA versus those composed in QA).

CS in the sense of coexistence of SA and QA side by side in the same text is observed in literary genres involving dialogues, such as novels, short stories, and drama. Dialogues are supposed to reflect everyday conversation, and therefore the use of SA for this purpose may place the authenticity of the text at risk. Holes (2004) provides a rich description of the different strategies that playwrights, novelists, and short-story writers use to ease the tension between the mode of their characters' speech and their code choice. For example, Tawfiq Al-Hakim, a renowned Egyptian playwright, uses a "third language," which follows the conventions of SA, but with minor modifications in vowels and grammatical inflections. On the other hand, Yuusif Idris, a staunch advocate of QA, uses SA only to reflect disparities in educational levels or social classes or to deride pedants and authority figures. In some of his works, Idris uses SA to reflect formality and non-local values or to draw attention to "marked" language uses (Holes, 2004, p. 377).

Eid (2002) examined language choice in written discourse by eight Egyptian short-story writers. Her data come from the writers' works between 1986 and 1997. Eid's analysis of the short stories shows that certain features of the collo- quial Egyptian dialect appear to varying extents in the stories. However, most of the colloquial forms in the narrative part of the short stories were mainly lexical, phonological, and minor grammatical issues. In the dialogue part, however, more salient features of the colloquial Egyptian variety, including syntactic features, transpire. Eid attributes this pattern to the fact that dialogues reflect everyday interactions where the colloquial variety is used. However, she remarks that the work of one of her subjects seems to be free of the "overt" properties of the col- loquial and that this is the case both in the narratives and the dialogues. Likewise, in a series of studies on the use of the Egyptian dialect in different literary genres, Rosenbaum (2000, 2004, 2011) documents not only the increasing presence of QA in a number of literary genres, but also the frequent alternation between SA and QA in the same genre and literary work. Such alternation, which Rosenbaum identifies as a form of *Fuṣhaammiyya*, may be found even in texts written by literary figures who oppose the use of QA in literature, such as Najiib Maḥfouẓ. Rosenbaum (2011, p. 331) comes to the conclusion that "Today the use of CEA [Colloquial Egyptian Arabic] side by side with MSA is not only tolerated by Egyp- tian writers, but in many cases is sought for and desired." Similarly, in a survey of a collection of Egyptian literary works in the period 2003–2005, Mejdell (2006) found that dialogues written in *Al-Fuṣha* represented only about 50% of dialogic text, whereas the rest is marked by a notable presence of QA or sometimes the mixing of the two varieties in "creative" ways.

A number of studies have investigated CS practices in newspapers (Abuhakema, 2013; Gully, 1997; Ibrahim, 2010; Sayahi, 2014). Ibrahim (2010) examined CS between SA and the Egyptian dialect in three newspapers: *Al-Ahram, Ad-Dastuur,* and *Al-Masri Al-Yawm.* The first newspaper is run by the government and the other two are run by the opposition. The data consisted of thirty-five issues from each newspaper. Ibrahim found that the state-run news- paper did not contain any switches to the Egyptian dialect, except in caricatures. By contrast, the opposition newspapers incorporated instances of intersentential and intra-sentential CS in different sections, including the headlines. She also found that switching to the colloquial variety was most visible in sections in which language "bore a resemblance to actual speech than it did to the language of a written article" (p. 31). Abuhakema (2013) examined 270 commercial advertise- ments in two Jordanian and two Palestinian newspapers: *Al-Ghad, Ad-Dostour, Al-Quds,* and *Al-Ayyam.* The researcher reported a notable presence of the col- loquial dialects in the advertisements, which affects lexical choice and the mor- phosyntactic structure of the advertisements. Abuhakema argues that switching to the colloquial varieities has become characteristic of a new literary genre that serves to enhance the communicative and persuasive force of advertisements and their appeal to wider audiences.

The existing studies provide a complex picture of the distribution and mixing of SA and QA in written discourse. While in some cases the "traditional" functions and statuses of SA and QA seem to be preserved (Albakry & Hancock, 2008; Eid, 2002), in others QA seems to assume functions customarily assigned to SA (Mejdell, 2006; Rosenbaum, 2000, 2011). QA transpires particularly in dialogues resembling *everyday interactions*, which shows the authors' sensitivity to the diglossic distribution of SA and QA. However, as Rosenbaum (2011) observes, the notable presence of QA in literary works seems to be unique to the Egyptian context. The tradition of writing in the Egyptian dialect is well-established and well-documented (Rosenbaum, 2011). The use of the Egyptian dialect in literary genres is made possible by the Egyptians' positive attitudes toward their dialect; the Egyptian dialect is seen as a medium appropriate for fulfilling certain functions in written discourse.

7.4 CODESWITCHING IN RELATION TO DIGLOSSIA, ATTITUDES, AND IDENTITY

The patterns of CS presented above demonstrate the complex relationship between CS and the social variables of diglossia, language attitudes, and identities. First, CS is intricately related to diglossia because the very existence of two varieties in the same context warrants switching between them to attain different communicative and affective goals. The patterns of CS reported above allow us to reconsider the notion of middle or in-between varieties. Generally speaking, Arabic speakers are able to separate or mix SA and QA to attain different social and pragmatic function (Holes, 2004). However, when the two varieties mix, they do not mold into a fixed and definite form that may be pinpointed in terms of specific lexical patterns, grammatical structures, and morphological features. Moreover, the product of bidialectal CS is not exclusive to the Arab context, but emulates the patterns found in CS literature worldwide, where two languages or language varieties contribute lexical and morphological elements to a single word, sentence, or larger piece of discourse (Bouman, 1998; Myers-Scotton, 1993a; Romaine, 1995). Since the relevant literature regards this type of code juxtaposition as CS, and not as middle language, there is no reason not to apply the same logic in similar cases between SA and QA. Speakers mingle elements from SA and QA in their oral and written discourses. However, even in this case, it is normally possible to identify the mixture, separate the mixed elements, and attribute them to their respective dialects (sometimes with the help of contextual factors; see Eid, 2002).

CS practices are intricately related to language attitudes. The case study reported above shows that Egyptian speakers shift to their dialects more frequently than the three other groups, particularly the Moroccan group. Considering the fact that the Egyptian participants have comparatively the most positive attitudes toward their colloquial dialect and the Moroccans have the least positive attitudes toward their colloquial dialect (Chapter 4), the patterns of CS point to a likely relationship between language attitudes and the degree to which speakers draw on their colloquial dialects. Speakers who view their dialects positively may adapt to using their dialects even in contexts where SA is expected, especially when the speech community endorses this use *attitudinally* in oral and written discourses. On the other hand, speakers who accord disproportionate values to the colloquial dialects and SA are more likely to maintain the functional distinction between the two varieties. For educated Arabic speakers, this in turn may necessitate commanding SA to be able to carry out the functions associated with the High code. Undoubtedly, several educational, social, and political factors may also be involved, but language attitudes seem to be implicated in the extent to which the participants resort to their colloquial dialects in SA-based narratives.

Educated Arabic speakers are generally aware of the implications of choosing one variety or another in their speech. When they have proper command of SA, they may use unmixed SA for certain functions, and they may mix SA and QA even when performing such serious tasks as political speeches (Holes, 1993; Mazraani, 1997). This often depends on the language attitudes of the speaker and the audience. In the case of the former president of Egypt Abdulnasser, for example, the speaker influences and is influenced by the attitudes of his audience. In his political speeches, Abdulnasser draws on SA to exercise authority over the audience, but he sometimes shifts *gradually* to QA to avoid "insulting" his audience (Holes, 1993; Versteegh, 2001). Even in written narratives a writer is influenced by the attitudes of the audience toward the concurrence of SA and QA in the same text. Al-Sibaa'i exemplifies a writer's negotiation of CS practice with his audience through his progress from using pure SA literature, to heavily QA-saturated texts, to balanced SA–QA writing that could please Arab purists but is compatible with everyday conversations. However, such a move is only possible because the general societal attitudes toward QA permit it. Such a practice is probably less feasible in Arabic-speaking communities where the prevalent language attitudes do not condone QA use in written discourse, as in Saudi Arabia. Language attitudes do not only impact when and where CS may occur, but may also signal the affective dimension of CS. Saeed (1997) and Albirini (2011) suggest that the very act of CS often reflects a change in the attitude of the speaker toward the functions performed (e.g., shifting from comic to serious discourse).

Identity factors also impact CS behavior. Not only are diverse identity forms shaped by social discourses and realities, but they are also indexed by the daily linguistic practices of Arabic speakers. Studies point to a link between SA use and the expression of Muslim and pan-Arab identities (Albirini, 2011). Likewise, the indexation of one's membership within the Arab community is carried out by using linguistic forms that approximate SA (Shiri, 2002). When speakers try to pinpoint their distinct national identities, they retain their national dialects and resist acts of linguistic accommodation (Abu-Melhim, 1992). Even at a more local level, speakers may use CS to construct, instate, or recreate their preferred identities (Albirini, 2014a; Al-Wer, 2007; Gibson, 2002; Holes, 1995; Suleiman, 1993). The most striking examples of identity–language relationship appear in cases when one's identity is challenged (Albirini, in progress). In such a case, speakers would mobilize their linguistic resources to construct their preferred identities, even when this may lead to the violation of common linguistic norms.

7.5 SUMMARY AND CONCLUSION

This chapter examined the use of CS for different social and pragmatic purposes. Three general types of CS were examined: bilingual CS, bidialectal CS, and CS in written discourse. It has been indicated that, although their functions may overlap, these types of CS often have distinct functions. In bilingual CS, QA is often allocated to religious and culturally specific topics, whereas English/ French are used for technical, academic, and business-related topics. SA seems to be absent within the realm of bilingual CS, except in literary writing. In bidialectal CS, SA, the "High" variety, is normally reserved for serious, important, and intellectual functions, whereas QA, as the "Low" variety, is used in for functions that carry less significance to the main themes of the discourse, such as simplification, explanation, joking, and insulting. In written discourse, QA has found a secure niche in dialogues along with SA, but its presence seems to be on the rise in different literary genres, principally in the Egyptian context (Mejdell, 2006; Rosenbaum, 2011).

A relevant distinction in bidialectal CS, as the dominant mode of CS in the Arabic sociolinguistic situation, is made between monitored and unmonitored speech. The former often calls for the use of SA, whereas the latter often involves the use of QA. CS in monitored speech situations reflects the general social and linguistic expectations of the speech community, upon which representations of diglossia are based, including Ferguson's model. In unmonitored speech, the functions of CS are influenced by interpersonal and intergroup factors and involve negotiation of roles, meanings, and identities. When Arab nationals and locals interact, they engage in the latter type of CS and therefore have to use their linguistic packages to negotiate their roles and identities. Moreover, when used by Arab locals, CS is often governed mainly by pragmatic reasons. Thus, the disproportionate prestige of SA and QA carries little weight on language choice in everyday speech.

The chapter highlights the intricate relationship between CS, diglossia, attitudes, and identity. For example, the proliferation of CS in written discourse in Egypt may be seen as reflective of the generally positive attitudes of many Egyptians toward their dialect and their strong sense of national identity. It should be noted that some patterns of bidialectal CS can be partially explained by the existing models of CS, even though these were mostly based on the experiences of bilingual communities. For example, switching to QA, the simpler code, in religious discourse may occasionally be motivated by the need to accommodate the listeners (Giles & Powesland, 1997), who may find difficulty grasping certain SA terms and expressions. Likewise, CS may be seen as a politeness strategy (Brown & Levinson, 1987) employed by speakers who are compelled to threaten an addressee's positive or negative face (e.g., in cursing). This suggests that, although bidialectal CS is motivated by reasons that may be historically, linguistically, and ideologically different from those found in bilingual contexts, they display similarities in certain details. It is reasonable, however, to say that the broad sociolinguistic functions of CS between SA and QA seem to be largely shaped by contextually specific factors, particularly the roles and statuses of the two codes in the Arabic-speaking communities.

NOTES

1 A large number of studies have focused on the structural aspects of CS between QA and Dutch/English/French (Aabi, 2004; Al-Enazi, 2002; Al-Mansour, 1998; Atawneh, 1992; Belazi, Rubin, & Toribio, 1994; Bentahila & Davies, 1983, 1997; Boumans, 1998; Eid, 1992; Nortier, 1990; Owens, 2005; among many others) and between SA and QA (Albirini, 2010; Bassiouney, 2006; Boussofara-Omar, 1999, 2003; Eid, 1988; Moshref, 2012).
2 Since the participants *volunteered* to take part in this study, it is possible that their competency in SA is higher than the average professor and college student.
3 *Education* may not be considered a point of difference between professors and college students because, beyond college, developing one's skills in SA depends on individual efforts rather than on specific SA coursework.
4 This case study does not focus on grammatical or stylistic errors.
5 I plan to expand the focus and scope of this study and to involve more participants in a future project.
6 How "large" an audience is relative and depends on context. For example, most religious sermons are attended by hundreds of worshippers, whereas the audience of a political speech may be in the thousands or even millions.
7 The constructs of *importance* or *seriousness* may be relative (sometimes subjective), but here I am using these two words in very general sense. For example, a discussion about entertainment media is often not considered a serious topic, whereas a debate about the Arab Spring is.
8 This argument has been challenged in the relevant literature (e.g., Eid, 2002).

CHAPTER 8

Digital media and language use

The past two decades have witnessed an unprecedented worldwide diffusion of various digital communication technologies and media.[1] The internet, which is increasingly recognized as one of the main centers of human activity, is becoming a staple of communication and information access across the Arab region. According to the *Arab Social Media Report*, which is produced and updated annually by Dubai School of Government, the number of internet users in the Arab region as of May 2013 was around 125 million with a growth rate of 60% since May 2011. The same report indicates that the total number of active Facebook users in the Arab region as of May 2013 was 54,552,875. The average Facebook penetration rate in the Arab countries was over 19%, up from 12% in June 2012. The percentage of users below the age of thirty was 68% of the total number of Facebook users. The total number of active Twitter users in the Arab region reached 3,766,160 as of March 2013. In 2013, the estimated number of tweets produced by Twitter users in the Arab World was 10,832,000 tweets per day. The Dubai School of Government carried out a survey including 3,373 participants from the twenty-two Arab countries. The survey indicated that 85% of the total number of respondents reported that online communication has enhanced their social communications, and 71% agreed that social media is replacing traditional face-to-face communications. These figures suggest that electronically mediated communication has become an integral part of everyday life experiences for many Arabic-speaking individuals, and especially among the youth.

There are a number of features for online communications in the so-called virtual world that set them apart from face-to-face communications in real-life situations. For example, face-to-face communications are largely oral, whereas online communications, especially messaging, emails, forums, and other social media, are mostly written. Despite their written form, however, electronically mediated communications are not as formal as traditional forms of writings, as has been confirmed in a number of studies (Androutsopoulos, 2013b; Crystal, 2001; Mimouna, 2012; Perez-Sabater, 2012; Van Gass, 2008; Whitty & Carr, 2006). Electronically mediated interactions are often based on a register that involves spoken and written linguistic features (Perez-Sabater, 2012). Moreover, online communication is decentralized in the sense that it is not controlled by a single entity, which problematizes the concepts of authorship, readership, text authority, and linguistic norms. In cyber-activism, for example, any individual with access to the internet can author *political texts* to a given audience without the need to consider the accuracy of the information or the linguistic norms in the target genre. Often, internet users write to a *cognitively constructed* audience, and therefore the concept of *audience awareness*, which is critical in traditional forms of writing, is reduced severely (Boyd, 2006). The virtual, imagined audience can be created through the users' discursive practices, language choices, and articulations of certain identity forms. This in turn influences their language use in terms of vocabulary selection, structure, and content. Another important aspect of cyberspace is that virtual communities are not necessarily defined by geography or history, and therefore the discursive practices of the interlocutors play a critical role in defining membership in a given online community, which is often based on shared interests. Lastly, online interactions are characterized by reduced contextual and non-verbal cues, such as gestures, voices, and facial expressions. Because of the absence of non-verbal cues, the interactions are often less personal and less involved (Ramirez et al., 2002). This explains why in many cases internet users may easily ignore interactants online, while they would not do so in similar offline situations. The absence of non-verbal cues also means that speakers have to rely mainly on their linguistic resources to express themselves, anchor themselves in the virtual community, and define themselves in relation to others.

The changes that the digital media have introduced in the modes and spaces of communication as well as in the relationship that binds interlocutors challenge some of key concepts and formulations in sociolinguistic research. These challenges have lately resonated in sociolinguistic research, particularly in connection with the global spread of English and the concurrent attempts to reconfigure the relationship between language, speech communities, and social context in the digital age (Blommaert, 2010; Coupland, 2003; Fairclough, 2006). As Blommaert (2010, p. 1) suggests, "globalization forces sociolinguistics to unthink its classic distinctions and biases and to rethink itself as a sociolinguistics of mobile resources, framed in terms of trans-contextual networks, flows and movements." However, because language, speech communities, and context are intricately related to other key sociolinguistic concepts, such as language attitudes, social identities, and language use, the implications of digital media can indeed be dramatic and far-reaching. Sociolinguistic studies on digital communication have focused on five main areas, including

- Language and globalization
- Multilingualism and language choice
- Language and online forms of identities
- Language variation and change
- Language use and interpersonal relationships (Androutsopoulos, 2013a; Thurlow & Mroczek, 2011)

These areas have not received equal scholarly attention in different social contexts due to the dissimilar circumstances surrounding the introduction and use of digital media in diverse social environments.

Much of the discussion on the use of the internet and its related technologies in the Arab region has focused mainly on the technologies themselves rather than on the linguistic, sociocultural, ideological, and human dimensions. However, a new wave of studies has lately been investigating the sociolinguistic changes that the new technologies have introduced into the Arabic sociolinguistic landscape. In particular, recent studies have focused on issues of representation, multilingualism, language use and CS patterns, language change, language attitudes, and identity. These topics are the main focus of this chapter. In particular, the chapter examines four main interrelated topics: (1) the sociolinguistic landscape of digital media, (2) the sociolinguistic changes induced by the new technologies in terms of new linguistic forms, mixed forms, and language varieties, (3) the effects of the new media on Arabic speakers' language attitudes and identities, and (4) the functional distribution of SA, QA, and English on social media in particular. The study of the sociolinguistic aspects of online communications is important as it may inform us about the current sociolinguistic situation in the Arab societies, the influence of new technologies on Arabic speakers' language use and identities, and the relationship between online and offline language use. Before examining these topics the chapter starts with a brief historical sketch concerning the evolution of information and communication technologies and the circumstances surrounding their introduction into the Arab region.

8.1 THE EVOLUTION OF DIGITAL MEDIA: A HISTORICAL SKETCH

The evolution of the internet was driven by development ideologies that evolved in the West after World War II. These ideologies have focused on technology and science to enhance "large scale industrialization, militarization, and national political power" (Shahidullah, 1991, p. 55). These ideologies were directly correlated to two interrelated issues, the first being the Western powers' fear of losing their political and economic edge in the aftermath of World War II, and the second being the national liberation movements throughout the "third world." The internet itself was developed in the late 1960s to provide "a secure and survivable communication network for organizations engaged in defense-related research" (Internet Society, 2006). However, it was not until the early 1990s that the internet was commercialized under corporate economic pressures. Western corporations aimed at harnessing the internet to create "an infinitely expanding cybermarket" (Scolve, 1998, p. 9). The commercialization of the internet has allowed the corporate to shift emphasis from producing and controlling material goods to controlling information (Agre, 2003).

The shift to an information-based economy has necessitated new information-based domains and new markets. This explains the intense competition among major technology industries to extend their reach to universities, schools, and other public spheres (Noble, 1998). The ensuing information revolution has generated a dynamic economic sector, incorporating web-based companies, virtual universities, cyber-stores, and so on. Commercial undertakings have become a characteristic feature of the World Wide Web in particular, shaping its design, tone, content, language, and usage. These developments have prompted the technology industries to internationalize the new medium, extending its reach to more than 2.41 billion international users in almost two decades (Internet World Stats, 2012). This technological explosion did not happen by chance, especially if we consider the huge profits that the electronic corporate giants (Google, Facebook, Yahoo, Ebay, Amazon, etc.) have reaped from online business. For example, in 2013, the standalone revenue of Google was $15.7 billion, Ebay 10.7 billion, Facebook 2.6 billion, and Yahoo 1.4 billion. The internationalization of the internet not only helped international corporations extend their marketplace worldwide but also facilitated the world's shift to a more open and global society. The same countries and forces that control international business and economy also nurtured the culture and subsequent adoption of the internet. By extension, the English language became not only an option, but a must dictated by international standards in business, communication, and global labor.

The internet made its way into most Arab countries in the 1990s, starting with Tunisia in 1991. The dissemination of the internet in the Arab region was associated with promises of economic development opportunities, positive social change, and political participation opportunities for disenfranchised groups (Wheeler, 2006). It was argued that the internet and related network technologies support economic growth, contribute to human resource advancement, and make possible leapfrogging over certain development constraints. Moreover, they empower individuals in the exercise of their right to receive, produce, and circulate information and ideas beyond national borders. Further, they facilitate intercultural communication where differences of race, ethnicity, and class disappear. Interestingly, while network technologies have often been conceptualized in terms of "exchange" of ideas and tools between different individuals and groups on equal basis, the existing literature suggests that the Arab region serves mainly as a consumer within this technology-based "exchange" (Albirini, 2007). The Arab World's consumption is not limited to technology products, but also to the linguistically and culturally diverse content that comes with these products. Thus, rather than being as an information-exchange medium, the internet is a channel of one-way flow of new multilingual and multicultural patterns into the Arab region as well as the rest of the non-Western world.

During the early stages of its introduction into the Arab region, the internet played a marginal role in the social, economic, and political realms of the Arab societies. In addition to issues of censorship and control, language was one of the main factors that hindered the integration of the internet in the Arab region because only those who were skilled in English and other world languages could utilize the new media (Abdulla, 2007). Another reason was the high cost of internet access. Moreover, the totalitarian regimes of the Middle East were hesitant to embrace the new media for fear of political dissent, often under the pretext of preserving national or religious identity. However, with the creation of systems, platforms, and interfaces that support Arabic, the internet gained much popularity, especially among the Arab youth. Internet use was first restricted to public places (e.g., internet cafés, universities, libraries, etc.), but home-based access soon became the norm. According to the *Arab Social Media Report* (2013), 88% of the overall internet users in the Arab region have home access to the internet, whereas 54% access it at work, and less so through mobile data (31%), internet cafés (22%), public places (21%), and school/college (12%). The majority of Arab countries made computer education one of the subjects taught in their schools and universities. Computer education courses used translated books that relied heavily on English terminology (Gunter & Dickinson, 2013). Moreover, computer science majors became widespread across the Arab region. While in some countries, this discipline is taught either in English or French (e.g., Oman, UAE, Morocco, Algeria, and Tunisia), others have used Arabicizied textbooks that still contained many English words (e.g., internet, hard drive, floppy, CD, computer, message, etc.).

The early uses of the internet in the Arab region were restricted mainly to entertainment (e.g., gaming, chatting, etc.) (Rohozinski, 2004; Teitelbaum, 2002). However, there is a growing tendency to use it for a wide array of purposes, including but not limited to, communication, socialization, information retrieval, sociolinguistic activism, sociopolitical activism, and education. The sociopolitical aspect of the new technologies transpired particularly in the Arab Spring in such countries as Tunisia, Libya, Egypt, Yemen, Syria, and Bahrain (e.g., Dabashi, 2012; Holtschke, 2013; Howard & Hussain, 2013; Pollack et al., 2011). Sociolinguistic activism appears, for example, in the number of websites dedicated to the promotion of minority languages, such as Kurdish and Berber (Merolla, 2002; Sheyholislami, 2008). Regardless of the end to which the internet applications are put, there is a common feeling in the Arab region that the internet is bringing forth significant changes to the Arabic sociolinguistic landscape, which will be the topic of the remaining sections.

8.2 THE SOCIOLINGUISTIC LANDSCAPE OF DIGITAL MEDIA: MULTILINGUALISM VS. DIGLOSSIA

In his influential work *The Bias of Communication*, Harold Innis (1951) argues that the development of new means of communication always leads to the dominance of some languages or language varieties at the expense of others. For example, the oral tradition and the vernaculars associated with this tradition were dominant in ancient Greece, but they were eclipsed by the introduction of parchment codex and the concomitant emergence of Latin as the lingua franca in the Christian world. The spread of Islam westward, its reliance on paper, and its revitalization of the Greek classics led to the reemergence of the vernaculars and the weakening of Latin, which eventually led to the development of the many European dialects. The development of the press helped create standardized national languages that were promoted within the boundaries of the European nation-states. Although Innis did not live long to witness the new digital media, research on information and communication technologies point to the emergence of new linguistic forms in the sociolinguistic landscape of digital media itself, which is also reflected in real-life communications.

One of the main features of digital communication technologies is multilingualism, which has been recently been cast in several interrelated terms, such as polylingualism, metrolingualism, and translanguagism,[2] describing the fact that a plethora of languages are embedded, disseminated, and used in information and communication technologies to the extent that it is difficult for minority groups, particularly non-English speakers, to be able to use information and communication technologies effectively if they are not multilingual. In November 2003, the *Journal of Computer-Mediated Communication* published a special issue focusing on this particular topic: "The Multilingual Internet: Language, Culture and Communication in Instant Messaging, Email and Chat." Multilingualism has many faces in cyberspace. One important facet of multilingualism is reflected in the designs, frames, advertisements, webpage content, discussion forums, chatrooms, and emails, which are often encoded in different languages, but particularly English. Multilingual content appears on most Arabic commercial websites, where Arabic and English texts appear side by side on a single webpage. This scene has become common on many Arab websites and social-media pages. Some popular applications and websites that target Arab internet users do not have full Arabic interface, as in the case of Amazon.com and Souq.com. Internet shoppers in the Arab region therefore have to possess functional knowledge of English to be able to navigate through such websites. The need becomes more urgent for researchers, businessmen, or professionals who may seek to access a wide range of data from different sources. In this case, being multilingual, especially with respect to the English language, becomes required rather than optional.

In the multilingual cyberspace, however, Arabic is notably underrepresented. For example, a 2014 study by World Wide Web Technology Surveys shows that websites with Arabic language content accounts for only 0.8% of the overall World Wide Web, thus trailing behind twelve other world languages. English-based websites occupy 56.1% of the overall content of the World Wide Web. Arabic contributes very little to the growing number of web applications and online businesses simply because most of these applications and businesses are developed in the United States and other technologically developed countries and have adopted English as their primary language for international purposes. For example, it was not until recently that Arabic interfaces have been added to Facebook (2009) and Twitter (2012). The same applies to educational websites and applications, which are rare in the Arab region.[3] In fact, the Arabic language is underrepresented on the internet even when compared to less dominant languages like Italian, Polish, Portuguese, Russian, and Turkish. More pressure is subsequently placed on Arab governments to promote and adopt English in international business and technological pursuits because English dominates the internet and its related technologies and businesses. This in turn forces internet users in Arab countries to rely more and more on English, which is seen as the lingua franca of the internet.

In a 2007 symposium on Arabic in the Age of Globalization held in Egypt, the Chair of the Egyptian Arab Academy Mahmoud Haafez pointed to the existence of more than 250 Egyptian private schools that use English as the medium of instruction and teach Arabic only as one of the curricular subjects. As Haafez indicated, parents see the acquisition of English as an indispensable skill for the "digital age," which may explain the mounting demand for English schools. The number may be even greater in the Gulf countries, where international businesses are flourishing and a high proportion of the workforce are international workers. Scholars, teachers, businessmen, students, and other social actors are increasingly relying on English to access various educational, news, shopping, and entertainment websites. The underrepresentation of Arabic on the internet in general and in the configuration of many internet applications inspired most of the early studies' work on issues of language incompatibility and support for Arabic on the internet and its related applications (Samy, 2006). It is possibly for the same reason that many internet users in the Arab region seem to be more comfortable writing in English rather than in Arabic (Taki, 2010; Riegert & Ramsay, 2012; Warschauer et al., 2002). Moreover, with the absence of coordinated efforts by the Arab academies to find Arabic equivalents to English media terminology, Arabic has borrowed a large number of English words, which appear widely in online content and communications. In his book *The Youth and the Language of the Modern Age: A Sociolinguistic Study*, Siraaj (2013) argues that the considerable number of English borrowings, especially with respect to internet-related terms, makes multilingualism one of the most visible facets of the Arabic-based internet content and online communications in general. The coexistence of English with Arabic has been reportedly found in websites, blogs, Tweets, Facebook comments, text messages, and emails (e.g., Alfaifi, 2013; Al-Khatib and Sabbah, 2008; Bianchi, 2013; Bruns, Highfield, & Burgess, 2013; Etling et al., 2010; Mimouna, 2012; Palfreyman & al Khalil, 2003; Riegert & Ramsay, 2012; Sakr, 2013; Strong & Hareb, 2012; Warschauer et al., 2002). The ubiquity of English online means that, even when they opt to use Arabic in their interactions, speakers may eventually have to resort to English to be able to interact with interlocutors who rely predominantly on English.

A second feature of electronic communication has to do with the very nature of this type of communication. Because of its rather informal nature, online communications have been said to have a negative effect on formal written languages

(Crystal, 2001). The existing literature suggests that internet users distinguish between "casual" online writing and other forms of writing (e.g., academic writing), and they are usually less attentive to language rules, structures, and spelling in online interactions (Baron, 2009; Lenhart et al., 2008). This means that Arabic speakers who use SA online may have to modify or change some of its rules to fit within the "casual" nature of online written texts. Moreover, the QA varieties, which have been used predominantly in oral communication, are nowadays used regularly in online writing (Al-Khalil, 2008; Mimouna, 2012; Palfreyman & al Khalil, 2003; Warschauer et al., 2002). Thus, writing is no longer confined to or associated exclusively with SA, and the normative boundaries between SA and QA may be blurred on digital communication media. In their study of email messages by 257 Jordanian undergraduate students, Al-Tamimi and Gorgis (2007) found that the majority of the students use casual writing styles in their messages similar to their spoken speech. Moreover, the senders use English and Romanized Jordanian Arabic extensively in their writings. The authors point to an emerging variety which they describe as a "pidgin" because it is simplified, contains much mixing between English and Arabic, and uses Roman letters extensively. Similarly, Mimouna (2012) found that email communications by Algerian college students were more based on the spoken colloquial Algerian variety than on the conventions of the standard written variety. As will be explained in the case study below, the language used in most social media pages is replete with colloquialisms, foreign words, inconsistent spelling, and stylistic innovations. The new forms may in the long run change some of the writing "conventions" or the structure of SA in online communications.

A critical question in this respect is whether online multilingualism could translate into multilingualism in real-life settings, given the common argument that online and offline communication patterns influence each other (Androutsopoulos, 2013b). To test this assumption, a simple experiment was conducted during my fieldwork in Jordan. In the streets of Amman, I assumed the role of a foreigner asking for an internet café close to my hotel. My opening comment in English was, "Hello. I arrived in Jordan a few days ago, and I am not familiar with the area here. Do you know of any nearby internet café?" The question was posed to fifty-three ordinary young walkers.[4] The responses fell under three categories.[5] Forty-five respondents replied to me in English and gave instructions in English, often with grammatical mistakes. For example, one of the respondents replied, "There an internet café . . . in the street Mecca . . . You know the mall . . . big mall . . . I forgot the name . . . in the mall." Another remarked, "I think you find internet in Marj Al-Ħamaam . . . close to here . . . close to l-bank l-ʕarabi l-Kuwaiti . . ." Six of the informants responded in English, indicating, ironically, that they do not speak English. Typical responses for this group were "No English. Speak Arabic?" or "No speak English." The remaining two respondents replied back in Arabic, indicating that they do not know English. To check whether respondents in the first group were aware of English internet-related terminology, I further asked the respondents in the first group, "What internet services do internet cafés offer? . . . what internet services are available in Jordan?" Almost all of the respondents[6] could list in English at least three common applications. The most commonly recalled applications were in order: Facebook, email, and WhatsApp. This indicates that English-related terminology is common and is possibly accessible in recall to informants.

In the formal interviews, I asked the college-student informants whether they use any internet applications. All of the 76 interviewees indicated that they use different applications, such as Facebook, WhatsApp, Skype, Email, Twitter, LinkedIn, chatrooms, and the World Wide Web. When I inquired about the language they use, most of the Egyptian, Jordanian, and Saudi informants indicated that they alternate between Arabic and English. Only nine respondents indicated that they use English exclusively in their online communications (two Egyptians, four Jordanians, and three Saudis), and eight others reported their reliance mostly on Arabic (three Egyptians, two Jordanian, and three Saudis). All of the Moroccans, on the other hand, indicated that they employ Arabic in addition to English and/or French. When I asked why they use English (and French in the case of the Moroccans), some participants indicated that they learned most of the technical words in English/French, and that is why it is "easier" or "quicker" for them to come up with the English/French words than to think of their Arabic equivalents. This is consistent with previous findings about the use of English in digital communication media (Reigert & Ramsay, 2012). Another group viewed their use of English online as a way to practice their English language skills. A third group attributed their use of English to difficulties with the Arabic keyboards (e.g., small Arabic letters). I also asked them about whether they use Arabic or Roman letters in their writings. The majority reported that they alternate between the Arabic and the Latin scripts. The claim about the multilingual nature of online communications in the Arab region is manifest in the informants' mastery level and reported use of English in their online interactions.

Last, an important aspect of digital communications is the evidence that minority languages, particularly Berber and Kurdish, have become widely used in online writing (Hoffman, 2006; Loukili, 2007; Merolla, 2002; Sheyholislami, 2008). These languages used to have limited venues of expression in the written form. However, they are gaining more space in the virtual world. Cyberspace allows minority communities to formulate and circulate discourses that help establish their own views of their languages and identities and undermine the corresponding mainstream narratives. There are several websites that are dedicated for promoting minority languages, and some focus on creating specific standards of written and oral forms among speakers of different Berber and Kurdish languages/dialects. As one prime example, the Kurdish Academy of Language, which is largely an online entity, is supported by several Kurdish activists, academicians, and organizations that coordinate efforts to serve the Kurdish languages. On the Berber side, the Amazigh World Organization publishes articles that raise awareness of the Berber language and culture in four languages, which are ordered from top to bottom as follows: Tamazight, English, French, and Arabic.

Such websites have been used by Berber and Kurdish speakers to maintain their languages and to promote awareness of the importance of their use in daily speech. These online activities seek to strengthen the presence of Berber and Kurdish online and increase their speakers' dedication to their languages not only online but also in real-world language use (Merolla, 2002; Sheyholislami, 2008).

8.3 CODESWITCHING AND THE EMERGENCE OF NEW LINGUISTIC FORMS

Apart from multilingualism as a feature of the media themselves or of their content, there is a growing scholarly interest in multilingual *practices* in electronically mediated communications. One of the most remarkable multilingual activities online is the use of more than one linguistic variety in the course of a single sentence or a piece of discourse, in a way similar to CS in real-life situations (Androutsopoulos, 2013b; Dorleijn & Nortier, 2009; Hinrichs, 2006). It is not surprising therefore that this type of CS has been approached from the same perspectives and has employed the same methods as conversational CS in real-life situations. Just like its counterpart in offline communication, online CS has been found to be often contextually and/or functionally motivated, rather than random (Alfaifi, 2013; Al-Khatib & Sabbah, 2008; Bianchi, 2013; Mimouna, 2012; Palfreyman & al Khalil, 2003; Salia, 2011; Warschauer et al., 2002). In other words, online written CS follows stylistic and social conventions that are similar to those found in spoken communications offline.

The existing studies have focused mainly on *bilingual* CS between Arabic and English/French. For example, Al-Khatib and Sabbah (2008) investigated the frequency and functions of CS in text messages used by Jordanian university students. The researchers analyzed a total of 181 messages produced by forty-six students, in addition to data collected from self-reported questionnaires and interviews. The findings indicate that, rather than using English or Arabic independently, the participants often switched between the two languages in their text messages. Arabic was reserved for discussing religion and culture, whereas English was used for prestige, academic or technical terms, and euphemisms. Warschauer and his associates (2002) investigated CS strategies in sample email messages and online chats written by four young Egyptian professionals working in information technology. The results largely replicate the patterns reported by Al-Khatib and Sabbah. The researchers also reported that the extent of shifting from Arabic to English correlated positively with the length of the participants' experience in the field. Thus, those who have worked longer in the field switched more often to English than those with less work experience. Alfaifi (2013) examined the use of intra-sentential CS on Facebook, focusing on comments made by ten Saudi Arabic-English bilinguals. Alfaifi found that the comments dealt with ten main topics, including gossip, humor, technology, compliments, achievement, film and music, family, makeup, travel, and religion. While the participants switched codes when discussing all of these themes, the highest percent of intra-sentential CS occurred in the topics of gossip and humor. Arabic was used in religious topics, whereas English was mainly used for technical and academic terms. These findings suggest that the topic of discussion affects the amount and type of switches.

Bianchi (2013) examined a 323-message thread on Mahjoob.com to identify functions of CS between Arabic, English, and Arabizi. The researcher found that Arabic is used to discuss the topics of poetry, humor, and culture, whereas English is used to address work- and study-related topics. Arabizi was implemented for "general discussion" (p. 90). Mimouna (2012) uncovered similar patterns of CS in his study of Algerian college students' use of email; the participants shifted customarily away from Algerian Arabic to English or French to fulfil certain communicative needs, such as the need to use technical terms or to economize in the email. In a study of instant messaging among female students in the United Arab Emirates, Palfreyman and al Khalil (2003) observed that Arabic is used for formulaic phrases, unlike English, which is reserved for university-related topics. Salia (2011) explored the comments made by a group of Moroccan friends and classmates on shared Facebook posts. It is reported that all speakers use the colloquial Moroccan dialect most of the time, but occasionally shift to English or French. The extent to which they adhere to Moroccan Arabic is based on whether they had education in English and/or French. Salia describes the alternation between English/French and Moroccan Arabic as a form of "code-weaving," which leads to the emergence of an "international code" containing terms that "are no longer markers of specific languages" (pp. 23–24). Salia cites words like "thanks, merci, hi, lol, peace, oui, yo (or yow) and bye" as specimen of this international code. Based on the reported findings, it seems that the functions of CS between Arabic and English emulate but are not identical to those found in real-life communications (see Chapter 7); Arabic is used for cultural and religious subjects, whereas English is used for technical, academic, and business topics. Moreover, the functions of CS seem to be consistent regardless of whether online interactions are synchronic (as in chatting or instant messages) or asynchronic (as in emails or Facebook comments). This suggests that text planning and editing do not play a critical factor in the patterns of written CS online.

Bilingual CS is also evident in how internet users write. Thus, even when Arabic speakers choose to use Arabic in their online interactions, CS may still take place between the Arabic script and other scripts and writing systems. Arabic speakers may encode their Arabic text using Arabic script, Romanized Arabic script, phonetic alphabet, new abbreviations (*JAK* for *Jazakumu Allahu khairan* "thank you"), syllabograms (e.g., *LOL* for "laughing out loud"), logograms (e.g., a smiley for anger), numbers (e.g., 5 for the letter ﺥ), and punctuation marks (e.g., *?* "What do you mean?") (Mimouna, 2012; Palfreyman, 2001; Palfreyman & al Khalil, 2003; Warschauer et al., 2002; Yaghan, 2008). The high frequency of mixing between Arabic and English at all levels has led to the coinage of terms such as Arabic-English, Romanized Arabic, Arabish, and Arabizi – all basically referring to colloquial Arabic speech rendered in a mixture of English letters and Arabic numbers and infused with borrowed English words and abbreviations. According to Yaghan (2008, pp. 42–44), Arabizi is characterized by a number of features, including the use of

- English consonants for their Arabic counterparts (ب → b),
- the English vowels a, o, and e (or a combination thereof) for the Arabic short vowels or the elimination of vowels altogether,
- borrowed English words (e.g., ok),
- common English abbreviations (e.g., plz for "please" or thnx for "thanks"),
- capital letters to indicate emotions, and
- special symbols to represent affixes (e.g., @ for the plural suffix – aat in Arabic).

Yaghan notes that there are other conventions that are specific to individual Arab countries, such as the representation of different letters (e.g., q, k, a, g for the standard /q/ sound). Siraaj (2013) argues that the main feature of Arabizi is the use of many Arabicized English words, such as dallet "delete (imperative),"
šawden "shut down (imperative), and sayyef "save" (imperative). What is interesting about these words is that they are adapted to the allomorphy of Arabic verbs, that is, the consonants of the English words are treated as Arabic roots that are then mapped onto Arabic verbal templates. This may be considered as a case of code-integration because the line between Arabic and English is blurred even within single words. Siraaj (2013) notes that internet-related terms have been used to change sayings of wisdom and poetry, citing such common sayings as ɣalṭat ɣuɣul b-ʔalf "a mistake by Google is like one thousand mistake [done by others]," which is a pun upon the common Arab saying ɣalṭat š-šaaṭir b-ʔalf "a mistake by a smart person is like a thousand by others."

One of the central questions that have motivated sociolinguistic studies of language behavior in the virtual world is why Arabic speakers employ Arabizi rather than Arabic script in their online communications. Most of the studies cited above have partly set out to answer this question (Al-Khatib & Sabbah, 2008; Allmann, 2009; Mimouna, 2012; Palfreyman & al Khalil, 2003; Siraaj, 2013; Yaghan, 2008). Yaghan summarizes these reasons in four main points based on his interviews with Egyptian undergraduate college students. First, Arab youth use Arabizi because most internet applications and media, including Facebook, Twitter, email, and instant messages did not support Arabic upon their first introduction into the Arab region, and therefore English took precedence over Arabic and it has continued to do so. Reigert and Ramsay (2012), similarly, found that their participants feel more comfortable with English script because they became accustomed to it. Second, because many internet-related terms and expressions are in English, speakers find it more convenient to write the whole text in English rather than switch constantly between Arabic and English scripts. Third, some Arabic speakers feel that the Arabic letters are designed for Classical Arabic and are not appropriate for *slang* where a single sound may have different representations in different Arabic dialects (e.g., the standard q sound can be expressed as q, g, k, a, etc. in different dialects). One may argue that Arabizi has different versions, each representing a unique Arabic dialect, and these diverse versions vary mainly with respect to the phonology and lexicon just as the colloquial Arabic varieties differ mainly in terms of these two areas. Moreover, since English has lower case and upper case letters, emotions can be expressed more easily in English letters. Last, according to Yaghan (2008), most applications allow greater word limit in English than in Arabic, which makes English more economical. In general, the existing literature suggests that Arabizi is used largely for technical, pragmatic, or stylistic purposes (e.g., circumventing orthographic incompatibilities), which explains its commonality among the Arab youth. However, based on personal interactions with a number of college students in Egypt, Jordan, Morocco, and Saudi Arabia, it seems that this type of CS is also related to the prestige associated with English; sprinkling the Arabic text with a few English words or with electronically conventionalized English abbreviations (e.g., w8 "wait") often gives a sense of technical sophistication, modernity, and multilingual skills, all of which are highly desired attributes among the Arab youth.

The literature lacks virtually any empirical studies on the functions of CS between SA and QA, despite their widely observed coexistence in digital communications. An important question in this regard is whether electronically mediated communications may be considered a form of monitored or unmonitored discourse and how this distinction may affect the distribution of SA and QA. To answer this question, it is important to remember that when the internet user is *anonymous*, the distinction becomes irrelevant because the relationship between the internet user and the audience cannot be established. However, when the identity of the internet user is known, whether online communication is viewed as monitored or unmonitored depends largely on who the *imagined* audience is and how the internet user presents himself/herself in relation to this audience. In visiting the Facebook pages of a number of Arab politicians and religious figures, I found that both the posts and the comments on their pages are largely in SA – although the commentary contained some stylistic colloquialisms. However, the posts and comments made on the Facebook pages of several singers were largely in the colloquial dialects. The imagined audience could be educated and religious people in the first case and song lovers in the second. If these groups of speakers seek to assume their traditional roles and address their imagined target audiences, it would not be surprising that SA is used by the former group and QA by the latter. However, as will be discussed below, the distinction between monitored and unmonitored speech is only one of several other factors that determine the selection of SA and QA in digitally mediated communications.

In general, despite the freshness of research on the sociolinguistic aspects of electronically mediated communication, the few existing studies point to important multilingual practices by Arab internet users, which manifest themselves in the widespread use of English terminology, Arabicized English borrowings,

English–Arabic CS, and Anglicized varieties of written Colloquial Arabic. Another facet of this multilingual behavior is the widespread use of QA in digitally processed writing, such as text messages, Facebook comments, tweets, emails, chatting, discussion forums, and blogs. Although they originate in the virtual world, these practices may foreshadow changes in the patterns of communication in the physical world. As Castells (2009) argues, although information and communication technologies are not used by everyone, their global impact has overtaken the daily activities of most people around the world. This is discussed in more detail in the next section.

8.4 DIGITAL MEDIA, LANGUAGE CHANGE, LANGUAGE ATTITUDES, AND SOCIAL IDENTITIES

The linguistic changes that the internet and its related media and applications have introduced into the Arabic sociolinguistic scene are interesting for theories of language change. It is well known that language change does not operate in isolation; it is always embedded within larger societal communities, environments, processes, and structures. At the same time, language change may function as an agent of social change. The emergence of new linguistic forms in a given speech community may lead to the construction of new concepts, practices, and social realities. According to Labov (1972, 2001), language change is often motivated by *the nonconformity principle*, according to which younger generations shift away from or even defy a linguistic norm set by an older generation by using new linguistic forms. The new linguistic forms can be generalized to the whole community when they are associated with positive social traits (e.g., upward social mobility), thus eventually becoming the new linguistic norm. Milroy (1987) suggests that language change is mainly driven by the structure of the social networks that bind different social actors. According to Milroy's social network theory, strongly connected social networks tend to be resistant to linguistic innovations and change, whereas weakly connected networks are more open to linguistic change. Social network theory has been used to explain the linguistic changes introduced by digital media, where the assumption is that the relationship that binds speakers is usually not as strong as that among people in the physical world (Androutsopoulos, 2007). However, the internet has redefined the concept of social network because it is now based more on the users' online discursive practices and identity performances than on other social bonds (nation, ethnicity, religion, etc.). That is why the interrelationship between language use and identity dynamics is an important facet of digital communication.

More recent approaches view language change as an evolutionary process that often implicates new speakers' ability to replicate an existing model of linguistic competency possessed by previous generations (e.g., Keller, 1994; Ritt, 2004). The new speakers' ability to replicate the competencies of an existing model depends on the opportunities that they have to be exposed to language use in context. When multiple linguistic models or options are available, these speakers would usually choose among linguistic forms depending on their inter-actional objectives. Linguistic choices may lead to large-scale linguistic changes when certain linguistic forms are adopted by many individuals. Thus, social, atti-tudinal, and identity-related factors are only secondary to language use and indi-vidual choice. These theoretical frameworks are important for understanding the linguistic changes that are occurring as a result of the use of electronically medi-ated communication by many Arabic speakers. The changes often implicate the use of English in various social spheres not only because English is associated with upward social mobility (e.g., better jobs) or it ensures connectivity to a global community and wider information databases, but also because some of the main interests of the Arab youth (e.g., social websites, entertainment, blogs, etc.) are better served in English than in Arabic. Siraaj (2013, p. 284) reflects on these changes as follows:

> English as a live language passes more and more from the public to the private in their [the Arab youth's] lives. It does not only enter into the behavior of a group of our youth – in its capacity as the language of study, reading, global culture, and social mobility– but it is also the desired language that they adopt in their text messages and daily activities, for composing poetry, and for forging their individual emotions . . . that is, it became the linguistic medium that is closer to them and more truthful to their feelings, their life details, and their present preoccupations [my translation].

It should be noted that language change is just one manifestation of other social changes in the Arab social reality, where the Western, particularly Amer-ican, modes of behavior are becoming the standard that the Arab youth follow (Siraaj, 2013).

The linguistic changes induced by the digital media present challenges to the concept of *identity* in its broad sense. Digital technologies open up new rela-tionships that are not necessarily built on specific ethnic, national, religious, or territorial affiliations. As a result, members of the virtual communities are not bound by the same structures, ideals, and traditions that hold the physical com-munities together. For example, the denominator of territory, which is critical for certain forms of identity, is not at play online. In a virtual community, speakers may assume personal and social identities that may not necessarily conform to their identities in real-life situations. In fact, the new forms of identity may chal-lenge or resist the socialization processes, historical discourses, and social and linguistic authorities that have traditionally reproduced the history-based forms of identity. The structures of networked communities are defined largely by lan-guage choice and language use, and therefore internet users may define and redefine themselves through discursive practices. In most cases, the formation of identity follows the rules of the specific virtual communities in which internet users choose to participate and is mediated by languages that may not be their daily use languages in the physical world. Wilson and Dunn (2011) examined the identity, language, and location of Facebook users and Tweeters in the Egyptian revolution. They found that the community of Facebook users and Tweeters came from diverse locations (Egypt, Middle East and North Africa, North America, and Europe), and they use more than one language (English, French, German, Japanese, Arabic, Italian, and "other" languages). What is remarkable in Wilson and Dunn's data is that this community of anti-Egyptian-regime individuals is tied by a common language, namely English, which, according to the authors, encodes 95% of the Facebook comments and tweets. English represents the lingua franca for this potentially multinational, multiethnic, and multicultural community and for many similarly diverse communities online. This is an example of a virtual community where the link between the language and the identity of the Arab internet users is fluid and unsettled.

One of the most important aspects of digital technologies is that they allow speakers to transcend physical time and space and to encounter multiple global and local perspectives. The dynamics of globalism and localness, which are propelled by the new media, may require speakers to create a third space where the representation of identity comes in two languages (Bhatt, 2008). As Bhatt (2008) observes, language "hybridity" may stem from broader socio-ideological tensions of self-representation and identity in the simultaneously globally and locally oriented media. These tensions have recently been reported in the case of Arabic speakers. For example, a study conducted by Wannas-Jones (2003) on Canadian Arab youth revealed that the participants' identities are not as settled in the traditional sense as for older generations. Unlike their parents, Arab Canadian youth adapt to different local and global perspectives derived from their daily lives in the Canadian society and their exposure to global media channels, such as Aljazeera and CNN. Reigert and Ramsay (2012) observed that Lebanese bloggers use a mixture of Arabic, English, and French, which reflects the hybridity of the Lebanese culture and identity.

When a group of speakers embraces a hegemonic non-native language, identity tensions may give way to identity assimilation. From this perspective, the Arabic language may indeed lose its function as the symbol of Arab identity as a result of English spreading via information and communication technologies (Khalil, 2005). In fact, Bishr (2007) claims that Arabic is no longer the language of Arab identity because the Arab youth no longer feel attached to their language and are no more keen on mastering it or using it in their lives. He expects that the Arab youth will dissolve culturally by adopting a global identity and linguistically by embracing both English and the colloquial varieties of their nation-states. Bishr cites the deteriorating status of SA in education, news, and other formal domains along with the Arabic speakers' weak command of SA as indicators of the dissociation between SA and the Arab identity. In general, online multilingual activities are intricately related to the fluidity of identity in the physical space. The use of multiple languages online may drive users to self-identify with speakers of different languages in diverse virtual communities just as their identity performances may be influenced by the languages that shape their communication patterns. However, although the youth are influenced by their online language use, they are still anchored in the sociolinguistic, sociopolitical, and socioeconomic realities of their offline communities, which exert influences on their identities. Thus, despite their importance, digital media remain only one of several players in identity construction offline.

Apart from English, Arabic is also being challenged by minority languages, such as Berber and Kurdish. Eriksen (2007) argues that, contrary to the common belief that the internet has weakened people's sense of national identity, the internet has maintained nations and strengthened people's feelings of national belonging. For this claim, Eriksen singles out "Nations which have lost their territory (such as Afrikaner-led South Africa), nations which are dispersed for political reasons (such as Tamil Sri Lanka or Kurdistan), nations with large temporary overseas diasporas (such as Scandinavian countries, with their large communities in Spain during winter), or nations where many citizens work abroad temporarily or permanently (such as India or Caribbean island-states)" (p. 1). Eriksen cites the fact that members of these nations maintain a strong presence on the internet. Eriksen's assertion resonates with the thesis that minority groups often seek and create venues to deconstruct the dominant discourses and circulate counter discourses that fit within their versions of identity (Fraser, 1990). The internet and its related technologies have equipped minority groups with the tools needed to disseminate their own discourses and languages.

Berber and Kurdish are thriving on the internet in terms of use in oral and written communications. This representation on the internet is raising awareness of the language and identity of Berber and Kurdish speakers by providing a forum for linking together Berber and Kurdish communities from different geographical spaces (Merolla, 2002; Sheyholislami, 2008). Thus, the digital media does not merely play a role in the maintenance of these languages by providing expanded venues for their continued use, but also provide a platform for linking Berber and Kurdish speakers to their language, which is a main marker of their distinct identities. Moreover, digital media provide opportunities for bottom-up language development that may undermine the top-down language policies – such as Arabicization policies – in countries where significant Berber and Kurdish populations exist (e.g., Morocco, Algeria, and Iraq). More importantly, they challenge the link between Berber and Kurdish speakers and the Arabic language, particularly SA, which used to be a shared denominator between Arabs, Berbers, and Kurds. Due to the open and decentralized nature of digital media, however, online communications may also lead to linguistic and identity fragmentation within the minority Kurdish and Berber communities. For example, Sheyholislami (2008) examined the online discursive practices of Kurdish speakers in Kurdistan Iraq and in the diaspora. He found that these practices did not lead to a unified Kurdish identity, but to multiple ones. As noted previously, this is because Kurdish, like Berber, is not one language/dialect but a multitude of languages/dialects. Identity fragmentation and reconfiguration therefore occur across the Arab region, even among minority groups.

The language-identity axis is problematized on a third frontier in the Arab context, namely the relationship between SA and QA online (Al-Saleem, 2011; Khalil, 2011; Kouloughli, 2010; Warschauer et al., 2002). There is growing evidence that SA is not the preferred medium of encoding online messages and texts. This trend has become particularly visible after the Arab Spring; QA has been used on a large scale in cyber-activism to approach wider audiences. Khalil (2011, p. 1) argues that activists used QA "for a freer, more direct approach to their readers, which has been more effective in communicating their message than the use of CA or MSA would have been." Warschauer et al. (2002) found that Classical Arabic was the least preferred code in online interactions by Egyptians, whereas English was the preferred language, together with a Romanized version of colloquial Egyptian Arabic. Similarly, Al-Saleem (2011) found that SA was almost absent in Facebook comments made by her Jordanian undergraduate student participants. Observing the same pattern, Gully (2012, p. 4) calls attention to "The proliferation of YouTube video clips available in a range of Arabic dialects." The increasing presence of QA online and its growing use in writing has been a main concern in Arab intellectual circles, particularly with regard to the changing role of SA and QA online. In an interview on Aljazeera Channel, Ahmad Ṭawqan, a Jordanian high school teacher of Arabic and a presenter at a 2009 conference titled *The Arabic Language in Jordanian Institutions: Its Realities and Ways to Elevate It* argued that he and his colleagues do not use SA in interacting with their students because "they [the students] see that we speak a language [SA] from a different planet, which is not understood by the new generation, who is controlled by the internet and satellite television" (Aljazeera.net, 24 October 2009). Ṭawqan's argument invokes one of the main objectives of the conference, which is how to bridge the widening gap between the Arab youth and SA. In the opening speech of this particular conference, the president of the Jordanian Arab Academy Abdulkariim Khalifah emphasized the importance of relinking the Arab youth to their language because the "Arab nation may not be able to innovate and to contribute to science except through its national language" (published on Aljazeera.net, 24 October 2009). It should be noted that, despite the growing use of QA in online writing, SA is still widely used, particularly in online newspapers, official government websites, personal web pages, or even personal social-media pages, as it will be shown below.

The proliferation of websites, Facebook pages, and blogs that are dedicated for promoting QA represents another linguistic and ideological challenge to the status and role of SA. Since the use of paper in the middle ages, SA has been the privileged variety in documents written in the Arab region. Print media maintained the dominance of SA in the writing domain, despite the unsystematic appearance of QA in some modern writings (e.g., novels, poetry, etc.) (Mejdell, 2006, 2008b). While traditional print media sought language unification insofar as, to a large extent, only standard language varieties appeared in print, digital media have facilitated language diversification in the sense that they allow almost *everyone* with access to the internet to use their preferred codes. In addition, digital media allow internet users to express their language attitudes and index their preferred social identities online through language. In a study tracing the development of blogosphere activities in Lebanon, Haugbolle (2007) found that Lebanese bloggers use the Lebanese colloquial dialect purposefully and playfully to challenge the authority and status of SA as well as the authoritative cultural voices in Lebanon in general. Wikipedia Masry, which was launched in November 2008 and written in colloquial Egyptian Arabic, is an example of websites that challenge the authority of SA and present an alternative linguistic representative of the Egyptian identity. Panovic (2010) suggests that the language ideologies of the founders of Wikipedia Masry materialize clearly in the style they choose, which exaggerates and overemphasizes the differences between the Egyptian dialect and SA. The message that the reader gets is that Egyptian dialect is distinct from SA, which in turn connotes that SA does not represent the Egyptians. Another example illustrating the promotion of QA is the spread of online QA dictionaries, grammar lessons, and colloquial courses. For example, the *Al-Mu'jam.com* and *Kalmasoft.com* offer online dictionaries for, respectively, eighteen and nineteen different Arabic colloquial dialects. Although they are still in the process of development, these dictionaries, ideologically speaking, embody a necessary step toward the potential recognition and codification of the various QA varieties.

The Arabic speakers' online linguistic practices, which seem to favor English and QA over SA as a means of expression and interaction, stand in contrast to the dominant ideologies of representation and identity in the Arab region. The existing studies suggest that, although Arabic speakers may use multiple languages in their online activities, they do not necessarily view these languages as representative of themselves or their culture. For example, Al-Saleem (2011) examined language use on Facebook by forty-four Jordanian undergraduate students. The findings revealed that English was the main medium of communication used by the participants. Nonetheless, the participants did not view English as an emblem of their identity or culture. Riegert and Ramsay (2012) and Jurkiewicz (2011) found that the bloggers that they interviewed made a conscious decision to use SA because it is "the prestigious Arabic script language used in literature and traditional media throughout the Arab region, the use of which says something about class and social standing" (Riegert & Ramsay, 2012, p. 290). Similarly, Arab internet users seem to have negative attitudes toward mixed bilingual forms, such as Arabizi. For example, Yaghan (2008) found that his Egyptian participants had unfavorable views of Arabizi, which they saw as a distortion of the Arabic language. Mimouna (2012) discovered that, although most of his Algerian participants used Arabizi in their online interactions, they still had negative attitudes toward this practice. Bani-Ismail (2012) found that the majority of his 503 Jordanian college-student participants did not approve Arabizi and were opposed to its use outside social media.

In my fieldwork interviews, I asked the participants about their opinions of Arabizi. The vast majority of the participants criticized this form of writing, describing it as "childish," "ugly," "careless," and "deformed way of expression." Only three participants described it as "fun," "personal choice," and "not a problem." When I asked for their opinions concerning people who use Arabizi, the majority of the participants again described them as "childish," "irresponsible," "disrespectful," "lacking in character," and "destructive people." When asked for explanations, the answers almost always had to do with their "carelessness" about their *native* language and identity. A few participants, however, viewed Arabizi users neutrally, explaining that it is a matter of "preference," "easiness," and "habit." In the course of my interaction with a number of the interviewees, I found that some of those who had negative attitudes toward Arabizi reported using it regularly in their online interactions. In general, however, the socially negative attitudes toward Arabizi may in fact have played a role in its receding presence, as it will be explained below. It should be noted that multilingual skills and practices are generally welcomed in the Arab region, but Arabizi is not so, possibly because it considered as a form of CS, which is generally viewed negatively in different speech communities (Bentahila, 1983a; Caubet, 2002; Hussein, 1999; Saidat, 2010). However, when identity concerns are raised, even multilingual practices may be viewed negatively. These attitudes may be credited for the survival of SA online because the continued communicative role and value of SA in the Arab societies rests largely on attitudinal and identity-related factors.

Recent concerns over the shrinking presence of SA online and its diminishing use among the Arab youth have instigated calls to revitalize the link between the Arab youth and their Arab identity in which the Arabic language plays a critical role. One aspect of this effort is the creation of Arabic platforms for computer-mediated applications through the coordinated efforts of technology experts and institutions across the Arab region (see Abdulla, 2007; Laroussi, 2003 for a review).[7] Another aspect of resistance to the dissociation between SA and the youth's local identity is manifest in the number of conferences, meetings, and publications dedicated for this purpose. For example, Jordan, an Arab country well known for its high rates of internet users and English language use (Al-Saleem, 2011), has hosted a series of conferences in the past few years to handle the growing sense of identity crisis in the light of the spread of English and the deterioration of SA in online and offline communication. In November 2011, a conference held in Alzarqa University and titled *The Arabic Language: A Praised Past and a Desired Future* had one of its main objectives discussing the status of Arabic on digital media and ways to improve its presence and power online. In November 2012, another conference titled *Developing Arabic Digital Content* focused on developing quality Arabic content that may create a link between Arab internet users, their culture, and their identity. Such intellectual gatherings may reflect a wider concern in the Arab societies about the need to retain or reinstate the link between SA and the identity of the Arab youth. Thus, while language *use* on digital media platforms seems to instigate the formation of a global identity that is related to English, local efforts motivated by language ideologies represent a competing force that seeks to reiterate the link between SA and Arab identity.

Language ideologies stand behind the sporadic and individual online and offline attempts across the Arab region to counteract the impact of digital media on the language–identity nexus. Among such sociolinguistic initiatives is the creation of websites for promoting SA, such as *Al-Fasiiħ Network for the Sciences of the Arabic Language*, *Forum for Fusħa Arabic and its Literatures*, and *The Arabic Tongue*. Online sociolinguistic activism is also found in online "campaigns," such as "Together to changing colloquial songs to standard," whose goal is to increase the accessibility of SA to Arab song lovers. A third form of initiatives focuses on using SA in everyday speech, such as the "Day without 'Aamiyya" campaign in the University of Ajman (UAE), which has been commended as a way "for breaking the anxiety barrier between our children and their language [SA]" (by Khaled Al-Khajeh, *Al-Bayaan* newspaper, 26 November 2013). However, because of the embryonic nature of these initiatives and their limited tangible impact on actual language use, there have recently been calls for political decisions to revitalize the role of SA in key formal domains, such as education and media, with the hope that this step will reorient the Arab youth toward using SA. This was one of the main recommendations of a 2012 conference in Saudi Arabia titled *The Arabic Language and Keeping up with the Modern Age*. Between 10–12 February 2014, I attended a conference titled *New Directions for Teaching Arabic as a Second Language* in Saudi Arabia. As the title suggests, the conference focused on the teaching/learning of Arabic as second language. Nonetheless, a number of papers engaged in discussions on the lack of political will in the Arab region to support SA and to activate its role in formal education. Online sociolinguistic activism remains largely ineffective in reversing the QA tide on the digital media, which may support the current approaches to language change, as being driven by language use and language choice rather than by language ideologies.

Before concluding this section, it is important to indicate that the digital media has been critical in aiding Arabic speakers in the diaspora to maintain their link to the Arabic language, culture, and identity (Blakely, 2005; Marley, 2013; Nagel & Staeheli, 2004). In her study of the acculturation patterns of thirty Arab immigrant women in Detroit, Blakely (2005) found that the majority of the participants use Arabic websites, Arabic-supported applications and communication media, and satellite television to stay connected to the Arabic language and culture and to help maintain their sense of belonging to the Arab culture. Similarly, Marley (2013) examined language use offline and online by children of British-Moroccan parents. She discovered that the children enjoyed using the Moroccan dialect online, which contributed to the development of a more positive attitude toward this dialect and helped them create bilingual identities. In their study of the politics of identity and citizenship among Arab-American immigrants, Nagel and Staeheli (2004) examined fifty-two websites of Arab-American organizations. The findings revealed that these websites capitalized on the Arabic language, culture, and history to promote the link between Arab Americans and their Arab culture, identity, and roots. It should be noted, however, that the new media by themselves are not enough to realize language maintenance or revitalization or to reestablish the link between language and identity (Fishman, 2001). They are just a means through which ideas and experiences are exchanged and virtual communities are created, which may not necessarily translate into changes in sociolinguistic realities.

8.5 CASE STUDY

One focus of this chapter is the distribution of SA and QA on digital media. Investigating this area is important because it may furnish us with a better understanding of the uses of SA and QA online and whether they diverge from or converge with those found offline. This may also help in identifying some of the sociolinguistic changes in the functions of these two varieties and language use in general. The literature virtually lacks any substantial empirical study designed specifically for researching this subject. The present study examined the distribution and functions of SA, QA, and English on social media because it is by far the most popular media used by the Arab youth, which encompasses several types of media at once. For example, social media, and Facebook in particular, is used for communication (e.g., status update), information sharing, entertainment (e.g., shared pictures and videos), sociopolitical activism, sociolinguistic activism, interpersonal relations, and socialization. The multipurpose uses of Facebook make it an ideal site for examining multiple voices, communication patterns, personalities, language attitudes, and identity performances. From this perspective, it is somewhat similar to real-life situations where such diversity of purposes, functions, speakers, and contexts is common. Two research questions were pursued in this case study: (1) what are the social functions of SA, QA, and English in comments posted on Facebook? And, (2) how do these functions compare to those found in offline interactions? The second question may shed light on the patterns of convergence and divergence between online and offline language use.

In this study, comments made by Facebookers on the Syrian Revolution page were examined. This page has over nine hundred thousand subscribers, keeping in mind that the number fluctuates based on the level of involvement of the members; some subscribers may drop out sometimes just due to "inactivity," whereas others may join in. The subscribers to this Facebook page have different social, linguistic, ethnic, political, and religious backgrounds, which is evident in their comments and personal Facebook pages. The page users' diverse composition makes it a good candidate for examining the functional distribution of the three language varieties (SA, QA, and English) in social media, particularly Facebook. Instead of gathering data selectively, a random day was chosen for data collection, which was Friday, 31 January 2014. Friday is usually the most eventful day of the week because many Facebook wall posts are provided on the Syrian

Revolution page, corresponding to the comparatively more dramatic events on the ground, and therefore more comments from members are expected, especially that Friday starts a weekend in the Arab region.

The total number of comments on 31 January 2014 was 2,993, ranging in length from a single word to 875 words. All of these comments were copied and pasted to a Word document. Out of these 2,993 comments, 885 were excluded because they were repetitive (i.e., posted several times), were posted by the administrators of the page, or were simply links to external videos, websites, or other Facebook pages. When a comment combined text and external link, the external link was removed and excluded from the word count. There was only a single comment with Arabic text followed by English translation, which was counted as two comments for frequency purposes. Other than this comment, the corpus lacked any comment containing Arabic and English scripts simultaneously, i.e., in the body of the comment. The overall number of comments examined in this study was 2,108. After removing the profile names, the dates and times of the comments, and Facebook-inserted data (e.g., "reply"), and all other non-comment data, the total word count was 33,816. As Table 8.1 shows, the bulk of the comments were in Arabic, followed by those in English, then Arabizi, and Other languages.

In addition to the comments on the Facebook page of the Syrian Revolution, I examined the personal Facebook pages of fifty subscribers to the Syrian Revolution Facebook page. The selection involved the authors of the chronologically first fifty comments posted on 31 January 2014. Facebook pages with clearly identifying information, especially those combining real names and photos were excluded for anonymity purposes. Also excluded were pages with no or very little activity since the beginning of 2014. In what follows, I outline the main functions of SA, QA, and English, as they appear in the Facebook comments. Some of the comments were delivered in a single language variety, whereas others involved using two codes (particularly SA and QA). The goal of this study is to examine the functions of the three language varieties regardless of whether they occur in one-code textual stretches or in mixed-code pieces of discourse. I restrict my account to systematic patterns of language use that seem to underlie particular pragmatic and sociolinguistic functions. Hence, unsystematic and individual cases are not reported. Undeniably, some cases may not have special social functions.

Table 8.1 Number of comments and words in Arabic, English, and Other languages

	Arabic	English	Arabizi	English-Arabizi	Other
No. of comments	2,032	40	24	3	9
No. of words	32,432	947	173	33	231

Moreover, the examples provided here are representative, rather than exhaustive, of the patterns observed in the data. Comments rendered in Arabic are shown in Arabic script as they appeared on the Facebook pages to distinguish them from English-scripted Arabic comments (i.e., in Arabizi). Last, I point to differences between monologues, one-to-one type of comments, and one-to-many type of comments. The mode of communication sometimes, but not always, affects code choice, and it is therefore relevant to the patterns observed.

The different linguistic forms were categorized as belonging to SA and DA based on the researcher's own intuition and the judgment of another native speaker of the Syrian dialect. In cases of mixed SA–QA sentences, the beginning of a switch was based on clear cases, where a language form is not shared by the two varieties (Eid, 1988). The word *xaaf* "be afraid," for example, cannot start a switch either to SA or DA because it belongs to both. Since the data analyzed is written, morphological cues were sometimes used to make a distinction between the forms of the two varieties (e.g., *yaktubuun* "write.3p" in SA vs. *yaktubuu* in QA). The sounds /q/, /ð/, /θ/, and /ẓ/, which are found mainly in SA, were the default forms used in online texts, and therefore they were not a determining factor in identifying SA or QA words. Words containing such letters were assigned to SA or QA based on contextual information. The transcribed data was coded following the procedure recommended by Glesne (2010) for data cataloging using analytic codes, categorization, and theme-searching. The first step was to systematically read the transcribed data and then code those segments that are relevant to the research questions. In formulating the codes, both the immediate event in which the speech took place as well as the broader Arabic sociolinguistic context were taken into account. As Heller (1988) suggests, the employment of an approach that is both top-down and bottom-up allows for explaining the text in its relevant setting as well as its sociolinguistic function. After this basic grouping of data, recurring codes within each group were identified and then labeled into coding patterns. Last, the relationships between coded patterns were sought and then assembled into themes and subthemes. These broad themes were compared to those found in the relevant literature for cross-referencing purposes. Linguistic analysis followed the coding process and resulted in the findings below.

8.5.1 Functions of SA

The data analysis shows that speakers use SA to: (1) highlight the importance of a segment of discourse, (2) introduce direct speech, (3) produce rhyming stretches of discourse, (4) theorize or preach, and (5) index their personal identities. These will be explained with reference to the status, function, and usage of SA in the Arabic sociolinguistic arena.

Probably the most visible motivation for Facebookers' use of SA is to give an air of importance to a particular piece of information. This explains why comments tagged as "important" or "urgent" are typically followed by SA text. The use of SA here is meant to present the comments or the events that they describe as significant and worthy of attention. In (1), for example, the Facebooker introduces a potentially important piece of news concerning the initiation of the second round of Geneva negotiations between the Syrian regime and the Opposition. The same applies to (2), where the Facebook user seems to present a seemingly important suggestion to deal with the assassinations and the car bombs that have taken the lives of several Opposition leaders. The comment posters' names are removed for anonymity purposes.

(1)   عــــــــــاجل

الابراهيمي يبلغ النظام والائتلاف بجولة مفاوضات ثانية في 10 من فبراير

"Urgent
Al-Ibrahimi informs the regime and the coalition of a second negotiation round in 10 February."

(2)   هااااااااام جدا للنشر

يجب على جميع الفصائل الاسلامية و كتائب الجيش الحر تشكيل سرايا وفصائل استخبارتية خارجية من أجل تفادي المفخخات والاغتيالات...

"Very important for publication
All Islamic factions and Free Syrian battalions have to form external intelligence companies and sections to avoid car bombs and assassinations."

A second function for SA use is direct quoting. Direct quotations often involve statements made by well-known political or historical figures, which sometimes become the subject of further analysis by the Facebooker. Such quotes may also be introduced for rhetorical effectiveness (i.e., accuracy and conciseness purposes). This may correspond to what Bhatt and Bolonyai (2008) call the "Economy Principle." In other words, the user seeks to communicate the idea with the minimum number of words, while at the same time avoiding to put the message awkwardly in his or her own words. This seems to be the rationale for the quote in (3), which cites a statement by Al-Jarba, the former head of the Syrian Opposition Coalition. Another form of direct quotation is the citation of Qur'anic verses or Prophetic sayings to lend authority and credibility to the Facebooker's argument. In (4), the Facebook user invites other users to pray to God for relief and supports the invitation by a quote from the Qur'an.

(3)   أحدث تصريحات الجربا:

الجربا: أؤكد التزام المعارضة السورية ببحث تشكيل هيئة حكم انتقالي كاملة الصلاحيات

"A-Jerba's latest statements:
Al-Jerba: I emphasize the Syrian Opposition's commitment to discuss the formation of a full-power transitional government."

(4)   ان الله يستجيب دعاء المظلومين.. "امن يجيب المضطر اذا دعاه ويكشف السوء.."

"God answers the call of the oppressed: 'Is not He Who answers the wronged one when he cries unto Him and removes the evil'".

Third, SA is employed when Facebookers produce rhyming stretches of discourse, which transpire frequently in lines of poetry and religious supplications, as in examples (5) and (6), respectively. The lines of poetry in (5) are posted on the owner's personal Facebook page, but it is attributed to a "martyred" friend. (6), on the other hand, introduces a rhyming supplication with a longer stretch of SA-based supplication. In Arabic, speakers often produce rhyming stretches of discourse in order to generate greater affective impact on their audience. This is also a sign of eloquence and mastery of the language. The personal pages examined in this study were replete with lines of poetry, almost all of which were in SA. This form of language use can only be understood if we consider the common perception of SA as the "eloquent language," which, to many Arabs, is the only medium suited for delivering eloquent, high-style, and linguistically complex structures.

(5) أخشى أن أموت و لا أراها

فإذا متتُ ادفنوني في ثراها

وأخبروها كم أحبها و أهواها

كم اشتقتُ يوماً أن أرى ضحاها

قولوا لها لم يفارقني أبداً شذاها

لم يبرح طيفها عيني لم أنساها

"I fear that I die without seeing her [Syria]
But if I die bury me in her soil
And tell her how much I love her and adore her
How I longed to see her sunrise
Tell her that her fragrance never abandoned me
Her image never left my eye and I never forgot her"

(6) اللهم رب الأرباب مجري السحاب منزل الكتاب هازم الأحزاب . . .

"O God, The Lord of the lords, the mover of the clouds, the sender of the Book, and defeater of the Confederates . . ."

Fourth, Facebookers deploy SA to theorize or preach. Here a Facebook user addresses other users assuming the role of a theorist, a wise person, or a preacher. In most cases, the Facebooker would digress from the flow of an interaction thread to provide a reflective monologue about certain events. Although speakers sometimes theorize in QA, the data shows that SA is the common code for this purpose. In (7), SA is utilized to present a thoughtful and ostensibly

"objective" comment on how to deal with groups with different political and ideological orientations, and in (8) it is used in a preaching comment on the meanings
of death and grief in the current events. The reliance on SA in this context may
be explained by the fact that using SA in the Arab sociolinguistic context often
correlates with education, knowledge, and sophistication.

(7)   لا جرم أن تختلف مع جماعة معينة من الناس لهم توجه معين فليس بالضرورة أن
توافقهم وألا تخالفهم، ولكن الجريمة أن تختلف مع إنسانيتك بتأييد الامتهان وسلب
كرامة الإنسان ضد هذه الجماعة

> "It is not a crime to differ with a certain group of people who have a
> certain orientation, and it is not required that you agree with them or
> that you never disagree with them. But the crime is to disagree with your
> human nature by supporting the humiliation and mortification of this
> group."

(8)   لا يكون التمكين حتى يتم الابتلاء . . . ولن تموت نفس حتى تستوفي رزقها وأجلها . . .
وانا لنحزن على اخوة وأبناء وآباء وأمهات ووورود نرجوا ان تكون اطيارا في جنان
الخلد. . . . غير ان الحزن الحقيقي على ايام تمر ونتخاذل فيها عن نصرة أهلنا ديارنا
ودماءنا . . .

> "There is no empowerment without test, and a soul will not die until it
> consumes its provision and lifespan . . . We grieve over brothers, sons,
> fathers, mothers, and roses that we hope to be birds in everlasting
> paradise. But the true grieve is over days that pass with us falling behind
> in supporting our people, lands, and bloods . . ."

Last, SA is the code used for self-representation. This function appears particularly on the Facebookers' personal pages, where the wall posts are predominantly in SA, with only a few posts rendered in English and even fewer in QA.
Marwick and Boyd (2011, p. 97) suggest that "Personal homepages, arguably
the first multi-media online identity presentations, are highly managed and limited
in collaborative scope; people tend to present themselves in fixed, singular, and
self-conscious ways." Similarly, Walker (2000) argues that "All home pages reveal
identity, whether or not that is the intention of their authors." Because they present
the identity of their constructors and owners to a public, yet largely undefined,
audience, personal Facebook pages aim to exhibit the Facebook page owner in
the best possible manner. The use of SA here may help page owners to index one
of the most desired social attributes in the Arab region, namely education. The use
of SA in this context may also have to do with the Arabs' generally positive attitude
toward SA or their approach to it as the common medium of written discourse.

Overall, it seems that the motivational patterns of SA use are linked with
importance, eloquence, and linguistic sophistication. These patterns materialize
the status and functions that SA assumes as the High variety in the Arab diglossic situation. These patterns transpired in both the public page of the Syrian

Revolution and in the personal pages of the Facebookers. SA is also associated with self-representation, which characterizes the majority of the personal Facebook pages examined in this study. It should be noted that SA appeared mostly in monologues and in one-to-many modes of communication, which is clearly the case in wall posts and in the preaching and theorizing comments.

8.5.2 Functions of QA

The functions of SA, as they appear in the Facebook comments, are qualitatively different from those underlying QA use. The data indicates that speakers shift to QA to (1) make sarcastic, often underhandedly offensive, remarks, (2) introduce daily-life sayings, and (3) scold or insult. These types of uses occurred both in the public and personal Facebook pages.

One of the most visible patterns of employing QA is for sarcasm. Sarcasm enables users to discuss offensive issues in an indirect way – a pattern that has been reported in previous literature (Riegert & Ramsay, 2012). In (9), for example, the Facebooker uses the word *friends* sarcastically to criticize the symbolic aid that Syria's Friends are offering to the Opposition, which has not improved their situation. In (10), the Facebook user invokes the inactivity of the Free Syrian Army in the face of current escalations by the regime and Hezbollah militia. The Facebooker criticizes this inactivity by wondering if it will be justified by statements similar to those made by the regime itself whenever its forces are attacked by a foreign power, citing the regime's common phrase "we reserve the right to retaliate," which has never materialized. The regime's ironic claim to be *resistant*, while unable to react against external attacks on its own soil is invoked to criticize the Free Syrian Army overtly and the regime itself covertly for inaction.

(9) بالنسبة للنظام لاحاجة لفضحه ولم يبقى لي كلام، أما لأصدقاء سوريا، كفانا نمصمص لهاياتكم البلاستيك، التي لاتغنينا، لأسكاتنا عن أوجاعنا والبكاء والجوع، كالأطفال لثلاث سنوات، ونحن بحاجة لحليب وغذاء وسقف فوق رؤوسنا، ... العمى إذا أصدقاء وهيك صار فينا، لو كنتم أعداء، ياالطبييييف شو كان صار، الحمد لله .. الله سترنا ولو، ... وووه

> "As for the regime, there is no need to expose it and I have nothing left to say. As for Syria's Friends, we are tired of your plastic soothers ... which are of no avail to silence our pains, and weeping, and hunger – like three-year old children when we are in need for milk and food and a roof above our heads ... *Slur You are Friends, and this is what has happened to us ... If you were to be enemies, O my God, what would have happened. Thanks to God. God has protected us maaaaaaaaaaaaan.*"

(10) وين [...] وين الجيش الحر شو صايرين ممانعين وبيحتفظوا بحق الرد .. حسبنا الله ونعم الوكيل

"Where is [name]? Where is the Free Syrian Army? Have you become resistant and you reserve the right to retaliate. Allah is sufficient for us and He is the best Disposer of affairs."

Second, Facebook users employ QA to induce daily-life sayings. The purpose of introducing these sayings is to allow the audience to grasp the commenter's point, concretize a certain idea or concept, or dramatize the point under discussion by adding an affective dimension to it. In (11), the Facebooker questions the meager support of the Gulf States for the Syrian people, concluding the remark with the common folk saying *smell and do not taste*. The daily-life saying in (12) is interesting because it appears on a Facebook page that is almost exclusively encoded in SA. This saying, however, was delivered in QA, which sets it strikingly apart from the other SA-based text. The consistent employment of QA to deliver folk sayings underscores the Facebookers' awareness of the functional allocation of QA to this type of sayings.

(11)   أين تأثير وقوة دول الخليج لدعم الشعب السوري وأين صداقاتهم مع الغرب
وامريكا لا بل واين امكانياتهم المالية والتي لم نرى منها الا اليسير على مبدأ شم
ولا تدوق ومثل الشحادة [. . .]

"Where is the influence and power of the Gulf states in supporting
the Syrian people and where are their friendships with the West and
America? Also where are their financial capabilities of which we saw
only little, following the principle *smell and do not taste like begging* [. . .]"

(12)   شو بينفع السيف للي ما عندو مراجل !!!

"What use is the sword for someone who does not have courage!!!"

Finally, QA is employed for scolding or insulting, unless these verbal acts are embedded in a prayer or supplication, which then can be either in SA or QA. It is illuminating that these verbal acts are associated with QA, sometimes even when contextualized in SA-based pieces of discourse. In (13), for example, the Facebooker disparages a member of the Opposition Coalition for what he/she sees as irrational statement, namely, "progressing backward." Although the user starts his criticism by what seems to be an objective statement, which is rendered in SA, he/she shifts to QA to deride this member for attaining no real gains for the Opposition in preparation for Geneva 2 negotiations. In (14), the Facebook user responds in QA to news about the death of a British physician named Abbas Khan under torture in the prisons of the Syrian regime, using a common slur *May they be inflicted by the breaking of their necks*, which is here directed against those who stand with the regime.

(13)   عضو بائتلاف العرصات يقول تقدمنا في جنيف2 بالرجوع الى جنيف1 !! في عاقل
بيتقدم لورا ؟؟؟؟؟ اعربولنا ياها

"A member of the Coalition of *Slur*[8] says that we have progressed in Geneva 2 by going back to Geneva 1!! *Is there a rational being who progresses backward????? Explain it to us grammatically.*"

(14)   يبلاهم بكسر رقبتهم كل من والاهم وشد على ايديهم

"*May they be inflicted by the breaking of their necks,* everyone who aligns with them and supports them!"

In general, QA is brought into use for low-prestige, accessible, everyday functions, which are associated with the status and role of QA in the Arabic sociolinguistic arena. It should be noted that, generally speaking, QA is used more often than SA in one-to-one communications, which appears occasionally in Facebookers' dialogues on wall posts by the Syrian Revolution page administrators, and appear more clearly in users' reactions to wall posts on personal pages. For example, the interaction in (15) starts with a statement made mostly in SA. The statement criticizes the people of Hama city for their minimal contribution to the Revolution. A Facebooker responds in QA, contending the comment and listing a number of activities illustrating the involvement of Hama-city people in the Revolution. The poster of the first comment responds back in QA to reiterate his/her claim, in a fashion similar to daily-life interactions.

(15)   الحق يقال ريف حماة مع الثورة وابطال ويحققون انتصارات - اما اهل المدينة جبناء وخايفين وكأنه لاعلاقة لهم بالثورة وكأنهم ليسوا سوريين - ياحيف , ضاعت الرجولة.
جبناء وخايفين ؟ واكبر مظاهرات الثورة طلعت من عندن واول مجازر الثورة صارت فيهن نسيت ال 100 شهيد اللي استشهدو بأول رمضان بالثورة وصارت ريحة الهوا دم من كتر الشهداء.. اتقي الله يارجل. . .
وبعد ال100 شهيد شو صار - طارت الرجال وصارت مثل الحمام متخابية بالاعشاش . . .

User 1: "The people of Hama countryside are with the Revolution and heroes and achieve victories. As for the people of the city, they are cowards and *afraid*...as though they have no relationship with the Revolution...as though they are not Syrians. *How shameful!* Manhood is lost."

User 2: "*Cowards and afraid? And the biggest demonstrations of the revolution started by them and the first massacres were inflicted on them. Have you forgotten the 100 martyrs that died in the first day of Ramadan in the revolution and the smell of the air was blood because of the big number of martyrs.* Be conscious of God man."

User 1: "*And after the 100 martyrs what happened. The men flew and became like pigeons hiding in the nest...*"

In general, QA seems to be the preferred code in online dialogues that emulate daily-life interactions, even when these interactions are written. The one-to-one type of Facebook-based dialogues are similar to online chatting, which often relies heavily on the colloquial dialects (Mimouna, 2012). One-to-many comments, however, are possibly closer to online blogs, which have been found to be associated with SA (Riegert & Ramsay, 2012). This suggests that the mode of interaction plays a role in language choice and language use online.

8.5.3 Functions of English

The use of English on the Facebook pages being examined seems to be motivated by three main factors. First, some Facebookers seem to lack functional knowledge of the Arabic language. This is apparent, for example, in a number of repetitive comments that appeared on different wall posts calling for dissimilar reactions. The comment below, for example, was made repeatedly in reaction to wall posts discussing dissimilar events, such as the death of children, weeping women and men, military operations, interviews, news updates, refugee issues, and general discussions of the Syrian situation.

(16)   the Lord God bless good family and keep them, Amen!

A second group of Facebookers use English because it seems easier or more convenient to them, as has been suggested by previous studies (e.g., Riegert & Ramsay, 2012; Yaghan, 2008). This is evidenced by the fact that some of the Facebookers use both English and English-scripted Arabic in several comments, as the two comments in (17a, b) show. The second sentence is interesting because the Facebook user employs the QA word *Tfou* "spit on," which clearly indicates that he/she is aware of the extreme offensiveness of the act of "spitting on someone" as a sign of contempt.

(17)   a. Glory to the real heroes

b. TFOU [name]

"Spit on [name]"

The third and the most important function of using English in Facebook commentary was to convey a global message to an international audience. In (18), the Facebooker uses English to make his humanitarian appeal reach as many Facebook users as possible. If the humanitarian organization that the comment poster represents is based in Spain, as the comment suggests, the comment becomes more compelling in showing the global appeal of English for addressing a wide audience. The same applies to example (19), where the author of the comment uses both English and Arabic to make the message reach as many people as possible. Although the English comment is not written in perfect English, the message is still clear to readers who are familiar with the Syrian situation. The perception of English as the lingua franca in online communication appears in comments made to a wall post showing the mother of the British physician Abbas Khan weeping and condemning the regime for torturing her son to death. Several of the comments made to this posting were in English, as in (20) and (21). The use of English here may also be a form of solidarity with the mother, assuming that the Pakistani-born mother who is living in Britain could speak English.

(18)   To help our Syrian refugees who are suffering from cold and hunger you can help us in our campain from Spain by clicking on this photo: [. . .] Thank youu

(19)   Before 2 years we asked . . . Anti air. . . . No one answer

We need only Anti Air.. to protect our children

فقط نحتاج مضاد طيران.. لنحمي أطفالنا

(20)   Sorry mother for what happened to your son. We all are your sons.

(21)   u r my mother

Before concluding this section, it is important to note two distinct patterns with respect to the use of English in the data. The first pattern concerns the insertion of borrowed Arabic-scripted or Arabicized English words in some of the wall posts and comments found on personal Facebook pages. As examples (22) and (23) illustrate, words like virus, Facebook, YouTube, and Skype are fully integrated in the text. Some terms, such as بروفايل "profile," نت 'net,' and شات "chat" occurred less profusely in the data.

(22)   سألنى الفيس بوك كيف حالى اجيب ان حالى من حال السوريين المقصوفين عند الفرن الالى فى حلفايا حالى مثل حال السوريين المقصوفين فى كل سوريا صحيح انا شخصيا لم اقصف لكن قصفت احلامى وافكارى انا لا اريد خبزا بعد اليوم فخبز سوريا ممزوج بالدم وعنب سوريتنا ممزوج بالدم لازال الفيس يسألنى عن حالى ترى اهو اعمى لم يرى نشرات الاخبار واليوتيوب وكل وسائل الاعلام رأت حالى والاهم ان الله يعلم بحالى ا سألك ربى فرجا قريبا

"**Facebook** asked about my situation. I answer that my situation is like the situation of the bombarded Syrians at the bakery in Hilfaaya . . . like the situation of the Syrians who are bombarded everywhere in Syria. It is true that I personally was not bombarded, but my dreams and thoughts were bombarded. I no longer need bread, because Syria's bread is mixed with blood and Syria's grape is mixed with blood. Face[book] still asks me about my condition. Is it blind? Did not it see news broadcasts and **YouTube**, while all the media saw my condition and, more importantly, God knows my condition? I ask you my Lord a quick exit."

(23)   هام . . .

فايروس جديد على السكايب تحت اسم: تغيير لون فيس بوك (:
يرجى من جميع النشطاء الحذر

"Important. . .
A new **virus** on **Skype** under the name: changing the color of
Facebook.
All activists are requested to exercise caution."

The second pattern concerns the use of mixed English-Arabizi comments, which is the only case of bilingual CS found in the data. This pattern appeared only in a few instances, and were characterized by the incorporation of religion phrases in the English text (using Arabizi) or the dramatization of the comment by incorporating culturally or contextually loaded terms. The religious-connotation function is captured in examples (24) and (25), where the Facebookers employ English throughout the comment, but then write religious phrases such as ALLAHim "O God," *MasaALLAH* [maša'a Allah] "what God willed," and *ya rab* "O Lord" in English-scripted Arabic. The second example employs the Arabic term *barmil* "barrel," referring to the exploding barrels thrown by the regime's planes on Opposition-held areas, possibly because the term *barmil* is charged with more dramatic meanings in the Syrian context; it is associated with death and destruction, which is not the case with its English equivalent, *barrel*. The consistent use of English script even in Arabic words and phrases maybe related to ease of use, as previous studies have suggested (Riegert & Ramsay, 2012; Yaghan, 2008).

(24) ALLAHim bless you ANGEL KIDS MasaALLAH

(25) I hope they drop on [name] barmil soon ya rab.

8.5.4 Discussion

The findings indicate that SA and QA still have some distinctive functions when used in social media. Thus, SA is used to (1) highlight the importance of a segment of discourse, (2) introduce direct quotations, (3) produce rhyming stretches of discourse, (4) theorize or take a pedantic stand, and (5) index Facebookers' self-representations. The patterns of SA use can be classified under the constructs of *importance*, *linguistic sophistication*, and *self-representation*, which reflect the status of SA as the High variety in the Arabic sociolinguistic scene and the variety with which most Arabic speakers associate (see Chapters 2 and 5). QA is employed to (1) to make sarcasm, (2) introduce daily-life sayings, and (3) scold or insult. The patterns of QA use can be classified under the constructs of *low-prestige* and *accessibility*, which again reflect the status of QA as the Low variety in the Arab sociolinguistic arena. This suggests that the functions of SA and QA online overlap with some of their functions offline (e.g., Albirini, 2011; Bassiouney, 2006; Haeri, 2000; Holes, 1993, 2004; Saeed, 1997).

However, the picture becomes more complicated when we consider some of the overlapping functions of SA and QA in online interactions especially when we compare the patterns of language use in this chapter and those reported in the previous chapter. Functions that are traditionally allocated exclusively to SA (e.g., formulaic expressions) or exclusively to QA (e.g., joking) are expressed in either SA or QA in online interactions. This is probably the main functional change that can be detected in the data, although such a conclusion necessitates a larger corpus with data derived from various digital media applications (e.g., email, instant messages, chatting, blogs, etc.). SA encodes the vast majority of wall posts by the administrators of the Syrian Revolution page or the administrators of local Syrian Revolution pages representing the different Syrian cities, towns, and villages (tansiiqiyyaat). Most of the wall posts on the personal Facebook pages are in SA as well. By contrast, QA text is frequent in the subscribers' comments, particularly in one-to-one interactions between two individual Facebookers, which somehow emulate everyday life interactions. The use of Arabizi seems to be a matter of convenience and easiness, as previous studies suggest (Yaghan, 2008). English manifests its status as a global language in online communication by encoding messages that seem to address an international audience. Thus, English maintains its status as a global language in both the virtual and the physical worlds.

The data points to the infrequent occurrence of Arabizi on both the public and the personal Facebook pages being evaluated. The decline in using Arabizi online could be due to the integration of Arabic platforms in social media, which makes it easier for Arabic speakers to utilize Arabic script. This decline could also have been influenced by the negative attitudes toward Arabizi in the Arab societies. Arabizi may have been "tolerated" when writing in the Arabic script was difficult, but now that this is no longer the case, many Arabic speakers see the use of Arabizi as an "eccentric" language behavior. Similarly, although English still enjoys a relatively high presence in the data, this presence is not as strong as previous studies have suggested (Alfaifi, 2013; Al-Khatib and Sabbah, 2008; Bianchi, 2013; Bruns, Highfield, & Burgess, 2013; Etling et al., 2010; Mimouna, 2012; Palfreyman & Al-Khalil, 2003; Riegert & Ramsay, 2012; Sakr, 2013; Strong & Hareb, 2012; Warschauer et al., 2002). Technical support for Arabic is partly involved as a factor, but it is not the main factor if we consider the findings of recent research reporting the widespread use of English and Arabizi on social media. Admittedly, the data presented here may not represent the different trends of language use on social media. For example, Facebook pages owned by actors and singers may contain more QA, Arabizi, and possibly English than does the Syrian Revolution page. By the same token, Facebook pages owned by well-known politicians or religious figures may contain more SA and less QA, Arabizi, and English than the Syrian Revolution page.

Syrians, who constitute the majority of the subscribers to this sociopolitically oriented page, are renowned to have a good grasp of SA and highly positive attitudes toward its use, which is another potential variable in the infrequent use of English and Arabizi. The predominance of Arabic, in its SA and QA versions, may further be explained by Syrians' sense of attachment to their homeland, which, to many Syrians, has been missed or is likely to be missed for an indefinite period of time. Syrians index their sense of attachment to the homeland behaviorally by using more Arabic than English and Arabizi. Geopolitical conditions therefore play a critical role in language use (Albirini et al., 2011). The extendibility of the conclusions of the present study to online language use in other Arab contexts may require independent empirical studies. It is worth noting that the English version of the Arabic Facebook page of the Syrian Revolution is, based on observation rather than systematic study, mostly encoded in English because it is directed toward an international audience.

Another important finding in this case study is that most of the Facebook page owners self-present themselves through SA. The use of SA in most homepages under examination may be explained from three interrelated perspectives. First, using SA may be seen as a statement of identity, which reflects the link between SA and Arab identity in general. This interpretation goes along with previous studies that point to the Arab internet users' language choice and their conscious selection of SA as a form of alignment with Arab identity – a case that has been reported by Jurkiewicz (2011) and Riegert and Ramsay (2012) in their studies of Lebanese bloggers' language behavior. A second interpretation has to do with the relative prestige of SA as an index of education and possibly sociopolitical sophistication, especially considering the nature of the Facebook page being studied and the possible character of those subscribing to it. In their interviews with the Lebanese bloggers, Riegert and Ramsay report that some of their participants showed a preference for blogging in SA because its link to "class and social standing" (p. 290). The last potential explanation concerns the readership of the personal Facebook pages. Facebook page owners who seek a wide readership and possibly social relationships from different Arab countries may choose SA to encode their text because it is widely understood across the Arab region.

Finally, just as offline language use may lean more toward SA or QA, depending on functional usage and speaker variables, online language use is also marked by similar variability. As the examples above illustrate, some comments are rendered entirely in SA or entirely in QA, whereas others mix the two varieties both intra-sententially and intersentementially. However, as has been noted in Chapter 2, it is difficult to assign such differences to discrete, in-between language varieties mainly because the rules of mixing SA and QA are not fixed.

8.6 Summary and conclusion

This chapter examined the impact of the spread of digital media on Arabic speakers' language practices online and their extended effects on their language behavior offline. One of the main implications for electronically mediated communication is the use of English in young Arabic speakers' online interactions, which presents English as a major competitor for SA and QA on digital media. Another feature of online interactions is the widespread use of QA as a written variety and the formation of new writing conventions, which are resembled by Arabizi. The spread of English, English-scripted Arabic, and QA has been perceived as a threat to the link between SA and Arab identity, which has prompted a number of sporadic initiatives across the Arab region to face the identity risks involved in the weakening status and use of SA among the Arab youth. Just as offline communications in the Arab region are characterized by switching among different languages or language varieties, online communication in the Arab region are also marked by the deployment of more than one language variety, particularly SA, QA, and English. Whereas SA is mostly used for important functions (e.g., theorizing), QA is used for less important functions (e.g., scolding) and English is used for conveying messages that target a global audience.

The increasing availability of digital media and the widespread reliance on digital communications raise a number of questions that are central for envisaging the future direction of the existent global and local languages in the Arab region. Chapter 5 indicates that the spread of English has sparked debates in Arab intellectual circles concerning the instrumentalist view and the cultural view of language. Most Arabic speakers view the learning and use of English from an instrumentalist perspective. The question is whether the direction of this debate will change in the light of the increasing spread of English not only on digital media but also in real-life communication. Will the colloquial Arabic dialects be recognized, codified, and standardized as a result of their mounting use in online writing and the impressive amount of support that they receive from online sociolinguistic activism? Will the language ideologies that have sustained the status of SA in the Arab societies give way to social realities where SA is hardly used by young Arabic speakers? If SA were to lose its currency as a *used* language, what bonds may hold the linguistically, culturally, economically, and politically diverse Arab communities and what is the future of Arab identity? These questions are central for the Arabic sociolinguistic scene in the coming years because, as noted above, digital technologies have recently become the center of communicative activities by Arabic speakers, and they may contribute largely to the future shape of the Arabic sociolinguistic scene.

NOTES

1 The term "digital media" is used here to refer in particular to the internet and its related technologies (computer, social media, email, messaging, etc.). Traditional media that has been relocated to the World Wide Web, such as online newspapers and online television broadcasting are also included in this definition.
2 See Androutsopoulos (2013b) for a review of these terms.

3 Kelly-Holmes's (2006) study on commercial language practices on the internet shows a growing presence of Arabic. However, this growth is confined to the region of the Middle East and North Africa and does reflect the worldwide presence of Arabic online.

4 Female participants were not included in this experiment because of cultural issues (i.e., it is generally inappropriate to approach an unfamiliar young woman in a public space).

5 A number of informants inquired, in Arabic, whether I am an Arab or not. My response was to re-pose the question in English.

6 Some of the respondents did not respond directly, saying for example, "everything," in which case I asked them for examples or illustrations.

7 In 2009, the International Corporation for Assigned Names and Numbers (ICANN) recognized a new platform, which allows web addresses to be written in a number of non-Latin alphabets, including Arabic.

8 The exact meaning of this word is controversial, though it is generally understood to refer to an immoral person.

CHAPTER 9

Heritage Arabic speakers
A different paradigm

The previous chapters have focused mostly on speakers of Arabic who are born and raised in the Arab region. The diglossic situation in which they live, as well as the prevalent language attitudes and identity dynamics at play in their speech communities, all generally influence the language behavior of these speakers. Moreover, the speakers' deployment of their linguistic repertoires in different contexts and situations usually reflects the general trends of language use in their communities. This chapter explores just what patterns we expect to see in terms of language usage and the construction of attitudes and identity in speakers of Arabic who are removed from the "diglossic" context, especially when they do not operate in well-defined Arabic speech communities. To this end, the chapter focuses on heritage Arabic speakers in the United States, i.e., those who are raised by Arab parents in a context where diglossia and the concept of an Arab speech community are nonexistent.

Heritage speakers are children of immigrants who grew up speaking their parents' language at home and then shifted to a dominant language (English, in the US case) as they grew older because of increased contact with speakers of the dominant language. The typical linguistic trajectory of these speakers involves stable exposure to the heritage language in early childhood, extensive use of English at school and with peers, and gradual attrition of their heritage languages as they progress in age. In the case of heritage speakers of Arabic, many of them are exposed to their parents' variety of colloquial Arabic in the home. Some may get exposed to the Standard variety of Arabic at some point in their education (e.g., Sunday schools) or through other communication channels. Since the colloquial dialects of their parents are generally neither written nor used in major media channels, heritage speakers have limited input in the varieties of Arabic with which they are familiar and have little chance to use them outside their homes. This is coupled with the fact that their strong command of English places no pressure on them to use their heritage dialects in the public sphere (Shiri, 2010). As a result of their limited proficiency in their heritage language, these speakers often encounter interpersonal, sociocultural, and psychological challenges in terms of relationships with their families, relatives, and heritage communities.

From an acquisition point of view, heritage speakers are different from monolingual Arabic speakers in that they acquire their heritage language, i.e., Arabic, under reduced input conditions (Albirini, 2014b). Their heritage language development is typically interrupted after they shift to the second, and dominant, language (i.e., English), and some aspects of their acquired knowledge may undergo attrition as they progress in age and come to rely more on English. Because they have another *competing* linguistic system used for everyday communication, there is often a chance for interference from this dominant system (Albirini & Benmamoun, 2014a; Rouchdy, 2013). As speakers of Arabic, however, heritage speakers may not be merely defined in terms of language knowledge or proficiency. Many heritage speakers may still have attachments to the Arabic language in its colloquial and standard versions as well as to aspects of the Arab culture and heritage. With such a complex array of influences – both in character and identity construction and also coming from the environment – it is fascinating to examine language use by speakers who live in contexts where some of the basic conditions for developing sociolinguistic competencies in Arabic are lacking, and yet still consider themselves somewhat related to the Arabic-speaking community (based on attitude and identity factors) (Albirini, 2014b).

In this chapter, I provide a brief overview of the historical and sociolinguistic state of affairs in Arab communities in the USA, although most of the patterns observed among Americans can be found in heritage communities in other parts of the world. I have selected heritage speakers in the United States because much of the existing literature focuses on this speech community, whereas not much *sociolinguistic research* has been done on heritage Arabic speakers, say, in Africa, South America, or South Asia. Wherever relevant, however, I explain supporting evidence from other heritage speech communities, particularly in Europe (see Boumans & de Ruiter, 2002; Caubet, 2001). The experiences of heritage speakers in the context under study may likely resemble those found in other contexts mainly because of their similarity in the majority–minority contact situation, the type of heritage-language exposure, and the motives for learning and using the heritage language. Differences undoubtedly exist, and these will be pointed out as well.

9.1 HERITAGE SPEAKERS IN THE USA: A HISTORICAL SKETCH

The earliest records of Arabic in the United States date back to the eighteenth century, when millions of Africans were enslaved and transported from Africa to the "New World." These slaves formed the main workforce on plantations and other emerging industries (e.g., tobacco), especially in the eighteenth and nineteenth centuries (Osman & Forbes, 2004). The new settlers not only brought with them their physical labor, but also their values, beliefs, cultural traditions, and customs. In addition, they brought their languages, including Arabic. Omar Ibn Said, a Muslim scholar from Senegal who was transported to North America and forced into slavery in the eighteenth century, wrote the earliest available document of Arabic writing on American soil.[1] In his manuscript, Omar Ibn Said records in Arabic his own autobiography as a slave (Osman & Forbes, 2004). Although only a few other documents survived from this historical period, the use of the Arabic language by Omar Ibn Said is an indication that Arabic may have been used by other African slaves at least for religious purposes. The extent to which Arabic was used as a written or oral language, however, remains largely unclear. Unfortunately, historical records provide little evidence on whether the Arabic language used by some African slaves was passed on to later generations of African-American Muslims.

The presence of Arabic in more visible form in the US dates back to the nineteenth century, when a large number of immigrants moved mainly from Greater Syria and settled in major cities such as New York, Boston, and Detroit (Suleiman, 1999). This immigrant wave was mainly instigated by socioeconomic struggles (poverty, population increase, and unemployment), political unrest, and the quest for new opportunities in the "New World" (Suleiman, 1999). According to US immigration records, about 130,000 Arab immigrants were living in the US by the 1930s. Despite their small number, these early immigrants built a strong communal solidarity and tried to preserve their heritage language and culture. For example, a number of literary figures formed the "Pen League" (*al-Rabita al-Qalamiyya*), and later founded an important school of modern Arabic literature, with its aims directly linked to Arab audiences both in the US and back home (Kayyali, 2006). However, most of these early Arab immigrants eventually assimilated into the American culture due to social pressures to adopt American language, values, and customs, as well as the immigrants' lack of contact with their home countries or with their Arab compatriots in the new land, particularly given the fact that most of them were trying to survive socially and economically in the new milieu (Abdelhady, 2014; Orfalea, 2006; Suleiman, 1999). Thus, the majority of them found little opportunities to use their Arabic language or used it minimally in their attempt to develop their skills in English as a prerequisite for economic success in the competitive American society.

The second major wave of Arab immigration began after World War II and continued till the late 1960s (Abdelhady, 2014; Suleiman, 1999). This wave brought to America a diverse array of people coming from different Arab countries, including Lebanese, Syrians, Egyptians, Palestinians, Iraqis, Jordanians, and Yemenis and smaller numbers of people from the Maghreb and the Gulf regions. Post-1948 Palestinian refugees constituted a substantial part of this wave of Arab immigrants (Abdelhady, 2014; Orfalea, 2006; Suleiman, 1999). Most of these immigrants were educated professionals: professors, doctors, lawyers, engineers, and teachers. They differed from the first wave in that most of them were keener on maintaining the use of Arabic among their children so that the new generation could continue to relate to the Arab culture. The number of Arabic and Islamic schools, dedicated in part to creating an environment in which second- and third-generation Arab Americans can use the language of their parents, especially in the face of the limited opportunities to practice Arabic outside the home, provides clear indication of this passion for instilling a knowledge of Arabic in their children. This phase in Arab-American history is also marked by growing unity among many Arab Americans and a growing awareness of their common Arab identity, community, and ethnic origins (Abdelhady, 2014).

The third wave of immigration occurred between 1967 and 2000, spurred by changes in American immigration policy and by the various political tensions in the region, including the Lebanese and Yemeni civil wars, the Israeli-Palestinian conflict, and the Iran-Iraq war (Abdelhady, 2014; Suleiman, 1999). Members of this third wave of immigrants, like their predecessors in the second wave, came from diverse places in the Arab region and many were highly educated (Orfalea, 2006). This is reflected in the fact that Arab Americans average higher than the median American in terms of post-secondary education and household income. These new immigrants were involved in the political life of the United States, which is evident in the formation of several civil and political entities, such as the Council on American–Islamic Relations (CAIR). This political involvement also helped increase the visibility of the Arab community in American social life. Unlike previous immigrations, members of the third wave shared a strong awareness of their ethnic roots and were keen on displaying these roots through social and intellectual activities (Salaita, 2005). According to the US Census Bureau, the number of Arab Americans reached 1.2 million people in the year 2000 – a 100% jump in just two decades (the number was 610,000 in 1980). The US Census Bureau indicates that 68% of individuals who are above fifteen and who descend from Arabic origin reported that they speak a language other than English at home (most likely Arabic).

The fourth wave of immigration took place after 2001. The most notable source of migration was Iraq (Rouchdy, 2013). These immigrants are generally less educated and less versed with English than their predecessors. However, the flow of Arab immigrants from other Arab countries, such as Egypt, Morocco, and Jordan, never stopped. Many of these immigrants were students who finished their graduate degrees and settled in the United States after finding work opportunities. The continuous immigration from the Arab region has helped with the "intergenerational transmission" and vitality of Arabic among heritage speakers (Campbell & Christian, 2003). The diversity in the background, education, and language experiences of Arab immigrants makes the Arab population in the United States very heterogeneous, reflecting the diversity of the Arab region itself, but adding to it the dimension of being a member of a minority group and speaking a minority language. Some of these immigrants speak English fluently and some have limited abilities in English and rely more on Arabic in everyday speech or on a "pidginized" form of English (Rouchdy, 2013). It should be noted that this last phase is marked by a heightened sense of identity, ethnic belonging, and heritage among Arab immigrants and American-born Arabs in response to the pervading anti-Arab sentiments and racial discriminations against Arab Americans (Abdelhady, 2014).

In the past two decades or so, much scholarly and public attention has been given to heritage speakers. One of the main reasons behind the interest in heritage languages in general is the need to exploit the valuable resources that bilinguals have, especially in light of the scarcity of college graduates with high proficiency in languages other than English (ACTFL, 2002; Allen, 2007). Bilingual language policies that recognize and support heritage languages as a resource for national development are responsible for establishing a number of bilingual and immersion schools in a number of major cities, such as New York, Columbus (OH), Los Angeles, and Detroit. Moreover, in the past four years or so, a number of initiatives have been started to promote the maintenance of heritage languages. For example, the goal of the National Heritage-Language Resource Center (NHLRC) at UCLA, which is funded by the US Department of Education, is to "develop effective pedagogical approaches to teaching heritage language learners, first by creating a research base and then by pursuing curriculum design, materials development, and teacher education" (NHLRC mission statement, 2010). The Center identifies over 55 million people in the US as speakers of languages other English, including Arabic.

While the literature on heritage communities seems to be growing rapidly, especially with regard to their language proficiencies and language use (Albirini, Benmamoun, & Saadah, 2011; Benmamoun, Albirini, Montrul, & Saadah, 2014; Bos, 1997; Boumans, 2006; El Aissati, 1996), more and more studies are focusing on the sociolinguistic experiences of these speakers, including their language attitudes, identities, and CS as well as the relationship between their language use and other social factors (e.g., Abu-Haidar, 2002; Albirini, 2014b; Almubayei, 2007; Boumans & de Ruiter, 2002; Kenny, 2002; Martin, 2009; Othman, 2006; Rieschild & Tent, 2008; Seymour-Jorn, 2004). These areas are the focus of the remaining sections. Before delving into these topics, I briefly look at two important concepts that are relevant to understanding the languages and the language behavior of heritage speakers: speech community and diglossic context. From a sociolinguistic perspective, an understanding of these two parameters is critical for explaining the differences between heritage speakers and native speakers of Arabic in the Arab region.

9.2 HERITAGE SPEAKERS AND THE DIGLOSSIC CONTEXT

As humans, we are born with some ability to acquire language, and we are also situated in contexts that provide the framework for our language use and interaction with others. Context is defined by such immediate situational elements as time, place, event, occasion, and speakers, as well as by larger social norms, power relationships, cultural traditions, ideological concepts, and discursive practices (Eckert, 2000; Fairclough, 1989; Fowler, 1985; Goodwin, 2003; Hall, 1996; Rampton, 1995). Schegloff (1992, p. 195) distinguishes between external or distal context, on one hand, and discourse or proximal context, on the other. The former type of context reflects the different social orders in a speech community as well as "the ecological, regional, national, and cultural settings" (p. 195). The latter type situates utterances in their immediate context in discourse. According to Schegloff, both forms of context are needed to understand language use and language behavior in general. Since the dimensions of context are not uniform cross-culturally, the uses to which language is put may be realized differently in different sociocultural contexts.

Edwards (1992, p. 50) argues that, for minority languages and speakers, context in is defined by several factors, which include

- demographics (e.g., number and concentration of speakers),
- sociology (e.g., nature of migration),
- linguistics (speakers' language capabilities),
- psychology (attitudes toward the language by the speakers and by the majority groups and the relation between the language and identity politics),
- history (e.g., history of the language and its speakers),
- politics (e.g., official recognition of the language),
- geography (where the language is spoken),
- education (educational support for the language),
- religion (relationship between the language and religion),
- economics (economic strength of the group), and
- media (language and group representation in the media).

These factors are relevant for understanding the general situation of Arabic as a heritage language in the United States, because a comparison between English and Arabic in this context definitely puts Arabic at a notable advantage due to issues related to status, use, written tradition, standardization, attitudes, available varieties, and bilingual competencies of heritage Arabic speakers.

One significant dimension of context that has received little attention in the literature, particularly with respect to heritage speakers of Arabic, is the diglossic situation of the Arabic language (in its standard and colloquial varieties). The diglossic situation of the Arab speech communities is a critical part of the sociolinguistic experience of members of the Arabic-speaking community. For example, Arabic speakers may hear QA in their everyday interactions in the market and on the streets and may attend a lecture and listen to religious speeches in SA. This constant exposure to SA and QA in context allows speakers of Arabic not only to internalize the distribution, functions, and statuses of SA and QA in different forms of discourse, but also to use them in their own speech to attain different communicative goals (Holes, 1993, 2004; Saeed, 1997; Van Mol, 2003; Versteegh, 2001). Members of such speech communities develop a range of diglossic competencies based on their understanding of the interplay of SA and QA in different social domains. These multiple competencies enable speakers of Arabic to perform various language activities and fulfill different roles in response to situational and functional factors. Although some speakers of Arabic may not be able to use SA in their everyday speech, the majority can understand SA when it is used in political discourse, in print, in news reports, in academic lectures, and in religious speeches. Moreover, they are often able to judge whether SA is used appropriately with respect to both context and function.

Unlike monolingual speakers of Arabic, who have firsthand experience with the diglossic situation and its main variables and intricacies, heritage speakers live in a context in which neither SA nor QA are used in the public sphere, and where Arabic holds virtually no status within the American sociolinguistic landscape. In America, English is the majority language that is used in daily interactions, on television, and in most other communication channels. Moreover, English is the language of education, media, and government. In terms of prestige, English is unchallenged in the American context due to its socioeconomic power, its global status, and its attachment to particular types of identities (see the discussion below about identity).[2] Also, many Americans hold negative attitudes toward speakers of languages other than English (Canagarajah, 2008; Mucherah, 2008; Ovando, Collier, & Combs, 2006). The English-Only movement, whose aim is to preserve the monolingual character of the United States, is one representation of this general attitude against bilingualism. The discriminatory views toward Arabs and Muslims in the United States − which are widely documented in the literature − affect their social identities (Abdelhady, 2014; Wingfield, 2006). The general attitude of prejudice constitutes part of the context in which heritage speakers live and within which they have to compromise their language behavior, attitudes, and social identities.

The fact that the sociolinguistic milieu affords no place for the heritage language in the public sphere may explain why many heritage speakers of Arabic, and their parents, prioritize English over Arabic in terms of acquisition and use (Martin, 2009). Pursuit of economic and educational success may be a factor, but, according to the United States Census Bureau (2003), most second- or third-generation Arab Americans tend to speak English even at home. Suleiman (1999) found that 75% of all Arab Americans speak English "very well," and the majority of them use it extensively both inside and outside their homes. This tendency to rely heavily on English allows it to replace Arabic in everyday communications, and even at home, and this may be one of the reasons behind the widely observed phenomenon of Arabic language loss among second-, third-, and fourth-generation Arab Americans.

Many heritage Arabic speakers are exposed to the Standard variety of Arabic at some point in their education (e.g., Sunday schools) or through informal communication channels (e.g., television), but they seldom use it in their everyday interactions, except possibly for reading printed texts (e.g., the Qur'an). This explains why many heritage speakers take college-level SA classes to get literacy skills in SA (Husseinali, 2006). Heritage speakers may be aware of SA and QA and may recognize some of the linguistic differences between the two varieties (Albirini & Benmamoun, 2014a; Shiri, 2010). However, because they are removed from the diglossic context of SA and QA and the functionality of these varieties in context, they are often not fully aware of their contextually proper uses and roles, and they are often unable to use them effectively and strategically in their discourse. Diglossia is thus an abstract notion that is never realized in the daily social lives of Arab-American heritage speakers, and is not, as in the Arab region, a sociolinguistic reality that is materialized by the speakers themselves. Thus, heritage speakers diverge from native speakers of Arabic, who *acquire* SA and QA and enact their functions and distributions in discourse because they are situated in the Arab context. This shows that the speech of social actors is governed by the sociolinguistic context in which they live and function.

9.3 SPEECH COMMUNITY VERSUS HERITAGE COMMUNITY

Speech communities are the framework within which language use, language attitudes, and language-related identities develop over time based on shared practices and beliefs among the community members.[3] Speech communities serve as both a framework for language use and a source of language input for speakers. It has been suggested that a speech community supports the stability of language and language use by providing confirming evidence and opportunities to practice linguistic and pragmatic norms (Köpke, 2007; Sharwood Smith & van Buren, 1991). According to Gumperz (1972, p. 219), a speech community is "a group of people who through regular interaction develop a shared language usage." Ferguson (1996, pp. 54–55) defines a speech community as "a social group held together by frequency of social interaction patterns and set off from the surrounding areas by weaknesses in the lines of communications." For Morgan (2014, p. 1), speech communities refer to "groups that share values and attitudes about language use, varieties and practices." These definitions indicate that members of a speech community are connected by common patterns of verbal communication that are based on predictable and consistent guidelines in their social milieu. Language represents not only an important facet of communication patterns, cultural traits, and identity, but also a major means through which members of a given speech community display and enact their participation in the community. Individual irregularities exist, but as Gumperz (1982, p. 24) indicates, even individual patterns "show systematic regularities at the level of social facts."

Speech communities, with their historical roots, norms, and structures, set the boundaries within which individuals can use their languages, construct their language attitudes, and define themselves in relation to others. An important function of a speech community is thus to regulate what is linguistically acceptable and unacceptable in different social settings. Language users therefore must select their utterances based on the recognized norms and expectations of the speech community (Gumperz, 1972). In fact, Milroy and Milroy (2002) suggest that the boundaries between different speech communities are largely based on the adherence of their members to different social norms and speech patterns. Morgan (2014, p. 1) argues that a speech community may be ill-defined in cases of "constant relocations, mass migration, transmigration, ever-evolving technology and globalization." This is because the conventional face-to-face interactions that set the norms and conventions of language use among community members become disrupted.

The concept of speech community is important for understanding the language behavior of heritage Arabic speakers for three interrelated reasons. These three main issues underlie the fact that Arab-American communities do not form ideal speech communities because some of the main dimensions of speech communities, such as rich language exposure, sense of social identity, and shared language attitudes, are limited due to the majority–minority language situation in which these speakers live. These issues also show the integral relationship between a speech community and social context. First, heritage speakers of Arabic are situated in speech communities that are governed by norms and expectations different from those found in the Arab region. Because English is the dominant language in almost all societal domains, it is difficult for most heritage speakers to learn the norms of Arabic language use based on firsthand experiences with native speakers of the language. In other words, they lack the social model that their monolingual counterparts in the Arab region have. Second, the population of Arab Americans is dispersed across the fifty American states, but with higher concentrations in the northeast, California, and Florida (Arab American Institute, 2009). Even when several Arab-American families may live nearby in the same town or city, they rarely form coherent speech communities. Most heritage Arabic speakers and their families have little connection with other speakers of Arabic in their communities simply because the relatively small number of Arab Americans are separated not only by distance, but by diverse backgrounds and lifestyles, and by their degree of assimilation into the broader American society (Sarroub, 2005). This means that most heritage speakers of Arabic are linguistically connected mostly with their immediate or extended families rather than with wider Arab speech communities. They are less likely to have consistent interactions with the other Arab Americans, and are therefore less likely to develop sensitivity to the use of Arabic in different societal contexts. Even inside the home, heritage speakers are not much exposed to the sociocultural patterns of Arabic language use because QA competes with English (Shiri, 2010), whereas SA is probably out of the question in this domain. Edwards (1992, p. 39) considers the "internal spatial cohesion" among members of a social group as an important consideration in the development of a speech community.

The third and last reason for the relevance of the concept of speech community to understanding heritage Arabic speakers in the US is the powerful impact that the prevailing negative feelings toward Arabs have on heritage speakers' attitudes toward their heritage language. Heritage speakers react differently to these negative feelings, with some interested in linguistic and cultural assimilation and others seeking to link themselves to their heritage language and culture.

Likewise, heritage speakers have multiple identities based on their different associations and connections in the Arab World and the United States (Albirini, 2014b; Bale, 2010; Martin, 2009). These divergent attitudes and identities play a critical role in how heritage speakers approach Arabic and how they use it in their daily lives. According to Labov (1972, p.120) socioaffective factors, including language attitudes and identities and "overt types of evaluative behavior" are what distinguish different speech communities. Similarly, Morgan (2014) argues that language combines members of a speech community not only symbolically but ideologically as well. This means that these attitudinal and ideological orientations have an impact on the formation and exact delineation of a speech community. When these attitudes and identities are ambivalent, speech communities are more fluid and less distinct.

The main meeting places for many Arab Americans are religious centers (mosques and churches) and university campuses where several student associations are created. However, again due to the diversity of the attendees, English remains the main medium of interaction in these community institutions, although Standard Arabic may be used often as the subject of learning in some Islamic centers. The colloquial varieties are sometimes used in rare cases when speakers of the same dialect interact. Many Arab-American parents send their children to Sunday school for different reasons. First, some parents are keen to have their children learn the Arabic language, especially SA, for religious purposes (e.g., to read the Qur'an). Arab parents share this interest with many Muslim parents who also want their children to acquire Arabic because of their affiliation with the Muslim faith. A second group of parents seeks for their children to learn the Arabic language and culture, so as to facilitate their connection with the cultures and traditions of the parents' home countries. Third, some parents view their children's attendance of Sunday school as means of building bridges among Arab children and youth with the hope that together they can form miniature Arab speech communities in their local settings. The reality, however, is that most of these children interact among one another using English, rather than Arabic, which precludes the development of a speech community in this context.

The fact that heritage speakers of Arabic are removed from the Arabic sociolinguistic contexts and are not immersed in "real" Arab speech communities may largely explain the commonly observed phenomenon of language loss among this group, which is the subject of the next section.

9.4 LANGUAGE LOSS AND MAINTENANCE AMONG HERITAGE SPEAKERS

Language loss and maintenance are generally discussed in relation to a number of related sociolinguistic phenomena, such as language shift, language death, language dominance, and language obsolescence (Fase, Jaspaert, & Kroon, 1992). Sociolinguistic studies have used specific terms depending on the population, language, and context in which these phenomena occur. In minority–majority language contact situations, such as the Arabic–English situation in the United States, language loss and maintenance are widely used in describing the situation of the minority language in relation to the majority language. According to Fase and his colleagues (1992, p. 4), language loss refers to "changes in language proficiency," whereas "language maintenance refers both [to] retention of use and proficiency." These two aspects are pertinent to individual members of minority communities rather than to whole groups. However, as Fase and his associates suggest, the aggregate effects of this sociolinguistic phenomenon on speakers of minority languages eventually alter the communication patterns and coherence of the whole community. For the sociolinguist, language loss becomes a worthy area of study when it develops into a social phenomenon rather than a case of individual occurrences. Researchers generally distinguish between partial and total loss, only the latter is named "loss," whereas the former is often labeled "attrition" (Clyne, 1992). These terms, however, will be used interchangeably in this work.

According to Clyne (1992), changes in the grammar of the minority language are the major indicator of language loss. A number of studies have documented different areas of language loss among heritage speakers of Arabic. In terms of syntax and syntax interfaces with other domains, heritage speakers diverge from their monolingual counterparts in a number of respects. For example, using data from elicited narratives in the colloquial Egyptian and Palestinian dialects, Albirini, Benmamoun, and Saadah (2011) found that heritage speakers of Arabic use overt pronominals in sentences that pragmatically prefer the pro-drop strategies, whereas this phenomenon almost disappeared in the output of their monolingual counterparts. Likewise, Albirini and Benmamoun (2014a) found that heritage speakers are not always successful in establishing long-distance dependencies between a pronoun and its antecedent in restrictive relative clauses, as in (1) below, or maintaining word order in construct state phrases, as in (2). Albirini and Benmamoun (2015) found that heritage Egyptian speakers have incomplete knowledge of the syntax of negation, as in (3).

(1) miš mətzakkra   šu   hummi l-ətlaati lli saʔal
     NEG remembering.f what they   the-three that asked.3SM

   "I do not remember what the three things that he asked are" (Albirini & Benmamoun, 2014a, p. 266)

(2) ʔiħna bi-l-ʕuluum   l-faḍaaʔ fii haaði nəṣṣ s-sini
     we   in-the-sciences the-space in this.f half the-year

   "We are in the space science [class] this semester" (Albirini & Benmamoun, 2014a, p. 262)

(3) huwwa   miš raaħ l-kaftiria
     He   Neg went the-cafeteria

   "He did not go to the cafeteria." (Albirini & Benmamoun, 2015, p. 482)

In terms of morphology, heritage speakers are reported to have major problems with subject-verb agreement and noun-adjective agreement morphology (Albirini, Benmamoun, & Chakrani, 2013; Albirini et al., 2011). The gaps in agreement morphology appear particularly when the modified noun is not masculine singular, which is considered the simplest, earliest to acquire, and default form of agreement, as has been confirmed in child acquisition studies (Omar, 1973). Root and pattern morphology, particularly in terms of plural formation, is another fragile area in the language proficiencies of heritage speakers of Arabic (Albirini & Benmamoun, 2014b; Benmamoun et al., 2014; El Aissati, 1996). For example, studies have shown that heritage speakers have an incomplete knowledge of the notion of the root. Moreover, they are not always accurate in deploying the correct templates of broken plural nouns (e.g., *ħawaamir* "donkey" [correct form is *ħamiir*]).

With respect to the lexicon it has been reported that heritage speakers have notable lexical gaps, as well as difficulties in lexical selection and subcategorization requirements (Albirini, 2014b; Albirini et al., 2011). For example, Albirini and Benmamoun (2014b) found that when provided with a list of common words, heritage speakers were able to identify only 62% of the stimuli compared to 99.78% for monolingual Arabic speakers. Likewise, heritage speakers show different gaps in their use of numbers, prepositions, and possessives (Albirini, 2014b; Albirini et al., 2011), as examples (4), (5), and (6) demonstrate. In example (4), the speaker uses the number *ʔitnein* before the dual noun, which is not needed in Arabic in the pre-nominal position and leaves the noun *ʔax* "brother" in the singular form. In (5), the speaker uses the preposition *li* "to" after transitive verb *yitgawwiz* "marry." This could also be a case of transfer from English, which allows the use of a preposition after the verb in this context (i.e., "be married to"). Example (6) marks the incorrect usage of *maʕ* "with" to indicate general possession, rather than the more specific meaning of possession of things carried on at the time of speech.

(4) *ʔana ʕindi ʔitnein ʔax
     I   at-me two   brother

     "I have two brothers" (Albirini et al., 2011, p. 289)

(5) yitgawwiz li-yasamin
     marry.3SM to-Jasmine

     "He (Aladdin) marries Jasmine." (Albirini et al., 2011, p. 292)

(6) *huwwa maʕu   matʕam hoon
     he   with-him restaurant here

     "He has a restaurant here." (Albirini et al., 2011, p. 294)

In terms of phonetics and phonology, contrary to the common assumption that heritage speakers sound like native speakers of the colloquial Arabic dialects, a number of recent studies have shown that most of them diverge from native speakers of Arabic in subtle ways. For example, Khattab (2002) showed that children of Lebanese descent have acquired the voice onset time (VOT) patterns of their heritage Arabic varieties, but their VOT patterns are mixed with the Yorkshire variety of English, which they use more frequently in their daily speech. Similarly, Saadah (2011) found that not all heritage speakers are accurate in vowel production in monosyllabic words of the pattern CVC, which could be extended to both heritage children and adults.

Another manifestation of language loss is the use of simplification or generalization of unmarked forms – strategies that have also been reported in the pidginization and creolization literature (Clyne, 1992). This subtle form of loss has been verified in the language of heritage speakers of Arabic. For example, Albirini et al. (2011) report that Egyptian heritage speakers overuse the SVO word order even in contexts where VSO is preferred, possibly because the former is common in English and/or is syntactically simpler than the latter. In verbal sentences, heritage speakers tend to overuse participial forms instead of inflected verbal forms, which may reflect a tendency to use lexical items that are morphologically simpler. In a study on agreement morphology, Albirini, Benmamoun, and Chakrani (2013) found that heritage speakers extended the default and morphologically simple agreement paradigms of the sound masculine to other agreement paradigms. Likewise, Benmamoun, Albirini, Montrul, and Saadah (2014) found that heritage speakers of Arabic deploy the unmarked feminine suffixal plural as the default pattern, a finding that a number of researchers have reported in language by monolingual Arab children (e.g., Albirini, 2015; Omar, 1973; Ravid & Farah, 1999).

While the existing studies focus mainly on *areas* of language loss among heritage speakers of Arabic,[4] more studies are needed to document the *process* of language loss and the different social and affective factors that contribute to this process. However, as Fase and his colleagues (1992) note, this area is difficult to document because language loss is a slow process. What is important, however, is to detect the predictors of language loss and maintenance in heritage communities and, whenever possible, to take the necessary steps to counteract this process. Language loss has been ascribed mainly to lack of enough exposure to the Arabic language and to the limited opportunities to use the language on regular basis. However, social factors have also been found to be a major contributor to these language gaps (Almubayei, 2007; Bale, 2010; El Aissati, 1996; Ibrahim & Allam, 2006; Martin, 2009; Reischild & Tent, 2008; Rouchdy, 1992, 2013; Sehlaoui, 2011; Shiri, 2010; among others). In other words, language loss is a social phenomenon as well as a linguistic phenomenon. Among the social variables that play a role in language loss are social networking, community relations, language attitudes, identity sentiments, family involvement, and demographics such as gender and age of onset of bilingualism (Albirini, 2014b; Almubayei, 2007; Martin, 2009; Oriyama, 2010; Rieschild & Tent, 2008; Rouchdy, 2013).

Almubayei (2007) examined the ethnic, cultural, and religious identities of Arab Americans in relation to the preservation of Arabic as a heritage language.

She reported that the two focus groups comprising her sample (first-generation and second-generation Arab Americans) emphasized the role of ethnic identity in their keenness to preserve Arabic. Reischild and Tent (2008) found that religion and gender are related to Arab Australians' attitudes to heritage Arabic and their desire to preserve it. Martin (2009) found that parents' attitudes toward heritage Arabic are associated with language preservation. Based on a survey of Arab Americans learning Arabic at Wayne State University, Rouchdy (2013) identified five main motives behind their learning of Arabic, which include (1) ethnic identity, (2) religious affiliation, (3) fulfilling a language requirement, (4) importance of Arabic from a global perspective, and (5) influence of parental advice. Rouchdy anticipated that Arabic would persist in the sociolinguistic lives of Arab Americans because of its strong ties to their ethnic identities, religious affiliations, and cultural backgrounds. Using data from a USA-wide survey of learners of different heritage languages (including Arab learners), Carreira and Kagan (2011) reported that heritage learners had positive attitudes to their heritage languages and that their primary interest in studying them was to relate to communities of speakers in the United States and to know more about their roots.

Overall, the conditions surrounding the acquisition and use of Arabic in the diaspora, particularly with respect to the absence of a speech community and removal from the diglossic context, become manifest in the language abilities of heritage speakers of Arabic. Two other areas externalize language loss among heritage speakers of Arabic: language interference and CS to English. According to Clyne (1992), these two phenomena are the most observable manifestations of language loss in minority languages.

9.5 LANGUAGE DOMINANCE AND INTERFERENCE

Language dominance transpires distinctly in different sociolinguistic contexts. Ferguson (1996) identifies three main indicators of language dominance in countries where two or more languages are well-established in the speech community. First, dominant languages are spoken by "more than half of the population of the country" (p. 270). A second benchmark is the extent to which a certain language is learned by speakers of other languages in a given country. A last benchmark is the extent to which a given language is used in official domains or for national purposes, such as laws, government schools, and official texts. In the literature on heritage speakers, language dominance refers to cases in which a bilingual speaker has greater proficiency and fluency in, as well as accessibility to, one language in comparison to others. Lanza (2004) observes that in language contact situations, the typical pattern of bilingualism is that of unbalanced bilingualism, where the bilingual speaker is often more competent or is simply more inclined to use one language at the expense of another. Thus, as Lanza (2004) argues, the notion of balanced bilingualism is a theoretical construct that does not mirror the reality of actual language use and proficiency among the vast majority of bilinguals. Unbalanced bilingualism[5] becomes more transparent in the case of majority–minority language situations, where heritage speakers are typically more competent in the majority language than in their heritage minority language. Previous studies note that, once they shift to English, typically at school age, heritage children start using the majority language in everyday communication, even with their siblings and parents in the home (Anderson, 1999, 2001; Silva-Corvalán, 1994, 2003).

One consequence of the dominance of the majority language is language interference (or negative transfer), which involves the overextension of forms, concepts, and structures from one language into similar but not identical ones in another language. The influence of the dominant language becomes progressively more visible with age, especially in light of diminishing input/use of the minority language and the extensive reliance on the dominant language (Domínguez, 2009; Pavlenko & Jarvis, 2002). The effects of interference may take different forms, including simplification, overregularization, borrowing, avoidance, omission, restructuring, convergence, and misinterpretation (Altenberg, 1991; Cornips & Hulk, 2006; Klee, 1996; Montrul, 2004; Montrul & Bowles, 2009; Montrul & Ionin, 2010; Pavlenko, 2004; Polinsky, 1997, 2008; Rothman, 2007; Rouchdy, 1992, 2013; Schmid, 2002; Seliger & Vago, 1991).

Language interference has been widely documented in the literature on heritage speakers of Arabic. For example, Albirini and Benmamoun (2014a) examined four linguistic areas in three oral narratives collected from Egyptian and Palestinian heritage speakers in the United States: plural and dual morphology, possessive constructions, and restrictive relative clauses. The focus was mainly on how the dominant language (English) influences the structure and use of these areas in connected discourse. The findings suggest that interference effects appear in forms that are marked (e.g. broken plurals), infrequent (duals), or characterized by processing difficulty (e.g., dependencies in relative clauses). In example (7), the speaker places the number *tintein* "two" before the plural noun *banaat* "girls," thus producing a structure equivalent to the English phrase *two sisters*. In (8), however, the speaker replaces the default relative complementizer *lli* with the *wh*-phrase *wein* "where?" after the relativized noun *l-ʕamaara* "the building." This sequence results in an ungrammatical sentence, equivalent to the English sentence *Many of my friends live in the building where I live now*. The construction of both sentences is based on or is influenced by comparable structures found in English.

(7) ʕind-ha tintein banaat
     at-her two.F girls

     "She has two girls." (Albirini & Benmamoun, 2014a, p. 258)

(8) ktiir min ʔaṣħaab-i ʕaayšiin bi-l-ʕamaara *wein ʔana ʕaayeš halla?
     many of friends-my living   in-the-building where I   live   now

     "Many of my friends live in the building in which I live now." (Albirini & Benmamoun, 2014a, p. 264)

Similar findings were reported in a number of other studies. For example, El Aissati (1996) examined the knowledge that Moroccans living in the Netherlands possess regarding different linguistic areas. One of these areas was plural formation. The participants were provided with a list of singular nouns and were asked to give their plural forms. The results indicated that, unlike Moroccan monolinguals, the heritage participants used the suffixation strategy for regular and irregular plurals. Bos (1997) tested Moroccan heritage children's comprehension of complex clauses involving three agents (e.g. "The lion which the monkey kisses is hitting the bear"). The findings indicate that the heritage speakers were less accurate than their monolingual peers in terms of VSO sentences, but not SVO sentences. Moreover, they performed best with sentences where the head noun is the Subject of the main clause and the relative clause, whereas their monolingual counterparts performed best with sentences in which the main noun is the Object of the main clause and the Subject of the relative clause. Using an oral narrative procedure, Boumans (2006) compared Moroccan immigrants and monolinguals in terms of the use of synthetic and analytic constructions for expressing possession. The immigrant speakers showed a notable preference for the analytic construction compared to those residing in Morocco. As Boumans suggests, this trend in the Moroccan heritage Arabic may be attributed to the influence of Dutch as the dominant language.

Overall, the patterns of language interference suggest that the majority language not only diminishes the role of the minority language in the speech of heritage speakers of Arabic, but also contributes directly or indirectly to the loss of different features and their replacement with similar forms derived from the dominant language.

9.6 CODESWITCHING BY HERITAGE SPEAKERS

One of the most visible and intriguing aspects of heritage speakers' language usage regards the frequency with which they switch to English and to a lesser degree, to SA (Albirini, 2014b; Albirini et al., 2011; Nortier, 1990; Othman, 2006; Rouchdy, 2013). In this respect, they may look like native speakers, who often alternate between SA and QA, and they may incorporate English words and phrases in naturally produced speech or in elicited narrative tasks. The similarities become more apparent when one examines the accuracy with which heritage speakers combine components from these languages and language varieties, which demonstrates their command of the general morphosyntactic rules of their dialects. In other words, their CS illustrates that they have internalized the rules for, and constraints on, the integration of linguistic elements from multiple languages (Benmamoun, Montrul, & Polinsky, 2010). This is important if we consider accounts suggesting that CS is governed by a unitary morphosyntactic system (e.g., Myers-Scotton, 1993a).

CS may take different forms. Muysken (2000) identifies three patterns of CS that are common in the speech of bilinguals: insertion, alternation, and congruent lexicalization. In the insertion pattern, mixed sentences are built on the grammatical structure of one language into which are integrated elements from the other language, usually single words or constituents. In the alternation pattern, both languages contribute to mixed sentences, each preserving its own structure. In the congruent lexicalization pattern, "the grammatical structure is shared by languages A and B, and words from both languages are inserted more or less randomly" (Muysken, 2000, p. 8). These patterns do not usually have similar presence or proportion in bilinguals' output. The existing studies show that insertion and, to a lesser extent, alternation are the dominant patterns of CS in the speech of Arabic heritage speakers (Albirini, 2014b; Albirini et al., 2011; Othman, 2006). Strikingly, when they converse in QA, heritage speakers are able to use QA as the matrix language and embed elements from English or SA into their QA-based discourse. Most of the inserted constituents are content words, particularly nouns, verbs, and adjectives (Albirini, 2014b; Othman, 2006). Likewise, when the language of discourse is English, they are able to insert constituents from QA or SA accurately. Examples (9) through (12) illustrate cases of CS between QA and English in QA-based narratives and English-based interviews with heritage Arabic speakers.

(9)   bazuur ʔusrit-i   f-*Cleveland*, bas miš *frequently*
      visit.1s family-my in-*Cleveland*, but not *frequently*

      "I visit my family in Cleveland, but not frequently." (Albirini, 2014b, p. 744)

(10) humme ʕaayšiin fi-s-*suburbs*   fi *Chicago*
      they   living   in-the-*suburbs* in *Chicago*

      "They live in the suburbs of Chicago." (Albirini, 2014b, p. 744)

(11) ʔahamm   ʔiši fi haada l-*major* ʔin-i baħǝbb-u
      The most important thing in this the-*major* that-I like-it

      "The most important thing in this major is that I like it." (Albirini, 2014b, p. 744)

(12) *I meet them on campus and sometimes in the* masjid

      "I meet them on campus and sometimes in the mosque." (unpublished excerpt from an interview with an Egyptian heritage speaker; see Albirini, 2014b)

In example (9), the speaker uses the negation marker *miš* before the adverb *frequently*, which is the common particle deployed before adverbs in Egyptian Arabic. In (10), the speaker not only positions the definite article before the English noun *suburbs*, which is expected in this context, but also applies the Arabic rules of allomorphy to match the definite article to the noun. Thus, the assimilated form of the definite article, namely s- "the," is used before *suburbs* because the latter starts with coronal consonant /s/. Moreover, the whole determiner phrase *s-suburbs* "the suburbs" is accurately embedded under the preposition *fi* "in." In (11), the English noun *major* is felicitously introduced by the non-assimilated form of the definite article *l-* "the." In addition, the speaker places the demonstrative *haada* "this" before the determiner phrase *l-major*, whose Arabic equivalent (namely, *t-taxaṣṣuṣ*) takes this particular demonstrative, which modifies singular masculine nouns. Further, when an object pronoun is used to refer to the word *major* after the verb *ħabb*, it is used in its singular masculine form, namely − *u*. Overall, heritage speakers are successful in integrating various English words into their Arabic sentences, which may reflect their knowledge of the underlying structure of their heritage language system. The same applies to the last example, where the word *masjid* "mosque" is embedded felicitously into the determiner phrase headed by *the*.

This notable accuracy appears in cases of CS between QA and SA, where the integration of the SA elements does not violate the structural form or soundness of the QA-based sentences. In example (13), the speaker inserts the Standard Arabic *ʔaxawaat* "sisters," instead of the corresponding dialectal forms *ʔixwaat/xawaat*. Likewise, the speaker in (14) resorts to a dual morpheme used almost exclusively in SA, namely, *Seifaan* "two summers." The shift to SA (as well as English) is largely triggered by the need to find substitutes for the appropriate forms which may not be retrieved easily from the lexicons of some of these speakers.

(13) ʔana ʕind-i talaata *ʔaxawaat.*
     I   at-me three *sisters*

   "I have three sisters." (Albirini & Benmamoun, 2014a, p. 256)

(14) nsaafir   ʔila misr   kul   ṣeif   or ṣeifaan
     Travel.1pl *to* Egypt every summer or summers.D

   "We travel to Egypt every summer or every two summers [every other summer]." (Albirini & Benmamoun, 2014a, p. 259)

Unlike insertion, *alternation* involves the embedding of a sequence of elements into the matrix language, specifically when this sequence is not part of a larger constituent (Muysken, 2000). Alternation appears clearly in examples (15) and (16), where the sequences *here around my place* and *they send leaflets* can stand alone as constituents that are separate from the preceding or following elements. The speakers' able juxtaposition of different constituents from distinct languages reflects knowledge of the underlying structure of both languages, which according to Muysken (2000) is a mark of language maintenance that characterizes the speech of both new immigrants and proficient bilinguals.

Thus, despite their loss of certain features of Arabic, heritage speakers generally maintain a working knowledge of the language.[6]

(15) ma-fi-š   maħillat kitira *here around my place*
     NEG-there-NEG   shops many *here around my place*

    "There are not many shops here around my place." (Othman, 2006, p. 50)

(16) saʕat   yaʕni *they send leaflets* wi ʔašyaaʔ tanya
     Sometimes means *they send leaflets* and things other

    "Sometimes they send leaflets and other things." (Othman, 2006, p. 51)

    Although heritage speakers, like their monolingual counterparts, are generally accurate in their use of CS at the morphosyntactic level, they differ from native speakers in three important respects. First, heritage speakers often switch from QA to SA and back to fill in gaps in their lexical knowledge or for retrieval purposes, as has been shown above (Albirini, 2014b; Albirini et al., 2011; Othman, 2006). Second, heritage speakers' alternations between SA and QA are not always situationally or contextually appropriate. For example, Albirini (2014b) and Albirini, Benmamoun, and Saadah (2011) asked heritage and native speakers of Arabic to produce narratives in QA that focus on themselves (hobbies, study, friends, etc.) and their families. While native speakers used QA for the most part, and shifted to English only for technical and university-related words, heritage speakers infused their QA narratives with SA and English components lacking a consistent pattern. The use of SA in particular is situationally and thematically inappropriate in this context. As noted above, this phenomenon may occur because while heritage speakers are familiar with the existence of two varieties, they still approach both as "Arabic language," without being fully aware of their social functions and distributions. Moreover, previous studies on CS in Arab contexts show that native speakers of Arabic do not usually mix elements from SA and a typologically distinct language. Thus, the mixing of QA, SA, and English is relatively unique to heritage speakers.

    The third way in which heritage speakers diverge from native speakers is that their use of CS does not always serve social or pragmatic purposes. For example, Othman (2006, p. 63) found that "the informants' reliance on switching is restricted to a limited group of conversational functions, and that they rely on Arabic for fulfilling most of these functions." Likewise, Elsaadany (2003) found that, although CS occurs along with changes in the topic, it does not often have clear "communicative functions." This stands in contrast to native speakers of Arabic, who deploy these varieties (typically at the sentence or discourse level) strategically to attain various goals (Holes, 2004; Saeed, 1997). Thus, switching from one variety to another serves sociopragmatic functions in the case of native speakers, while its use by heritage speakers seems to be largely related to cross-dialectal influence and possibly processing difficulty. Heritage and bilingual speakers have been reported to resort to their primary language, either to counter processing delays resulting from complex structures, or simply because certain forms are more accessible to them in one language/variety than in another (Jiménez Jiménez, 2004). Even when CS seems to reflect a change in domain or topic (e.g., religion), the direction of the switching is not always predictable. For example, Othman (2006) cites the following example, in which he contends that words related to religion are often rendered in English. However, previous studies on heritage children suggest that words related to religion are often delivered in QA (Al-Enazi, 2002). To reconcile these two accounts, one has to assume that heritage speakers may use SA, QA, or English to mark their shift to specific domains or topics, but this does not entail a fixed association between a particular code and a corresponding domain or topic.

(17) Mumkin in-nas taʕtaqid in il-biʔa hina mumkin tinassi-na
      Possible *the-people think that the-environment here possible make-forget-us*

      i-*religion* lakin il-*opposite* tamaman.
      the-*religion* but the-*opposite* totally

      "People may think that the environment here can make us forget the *religion*, but the *opposite* is absolutely true." (Othman, 2006, p. 57–58)

However, the sociopragmatic functions of CS seem to transpire clearly in written discourse. For example, Albakry and Siler (2012) examined the CS strategies used in *A Map of Home* by Randa Jarrar (2009), a Palestinian novelist who was born in the United States, raised in Kuwait, and moved back to the United States when she was still a child. The novelist associates many religious terms (*sura* "chapter in the Qur'an," and *hajj* "pilgrimage") and family expressions (e.g., *geddo* "grandpa," and *baba* "father") with QA, whereas she reserves English for most of the narrative. Likewise, she uses many hybrid sentences to reflect her own cultural hybridity as an Arab American, and to reflect the "presence of her Middle Eastern culture" (Albakry & Siler, 2012, p. 114). Albakry and Siler also notice how the author uses the two codes (Arabic and English) to express *shifts of view* in terms of voice and the cultural lenses through which the text should be understood. For them, the use of code-mixing in the novel allows Jarrar to depict herself as an example of a heritage speaker who dwells on the borderline between two communities, cultures, and languages.

Before concluding this section, two issues need to be highlighted. First, heritage speakers deploy CS frequently and competently like their native speakers, though they seem to be less competent in using CS for social purposes. Lanza (2004) argues that bilingual children need to acquire grammatical competence as well as communicative competence, which involves contextual and social appropriateness, to be able to use their language properly. The heritage speakers' unique use of CS may be due to the absence of the diglossic context and the lack of a well-defined Arab speech community through which they can obtain opportunities for learning proper language use in different contexts. Second, although manifestations of language loss are widely documented among heritage speakers of Arabic, they are not likely to lose their heritage language (i.e., Arabic) for two reasons. First, many Arab immigrants – and some of their children – still use Arabic in religious and social gatherings, even though on a limited scale, which prevents the complete disappearance of Arabic from their social lives. Second, many heritage speakers of Arabic and their parents associate Arabic with their Muslim and Arab identities and generally have favorable attitudes toward Arabic, as the language of heritage – another hindrance to complete language loss. The following two sections will focus on language attitudes and the social identities of heritage speakers of Arabic.

9.7 LANGUAGE ATTITUDES OF HERITAGE SPEAKERS

One of the important factors that accounts for the loss or maintenance of a particular language in a given speech community is the attitude of its speakers (Baker, 1992; Fishman, 1991; Wilson, 2013). Valdés (1992, p. 50) maintains that "the attitudes of circumstantial bilinguals toward their own group and their ethnic identity will determine their willingness to maintain or abandon their heritage language." Positive attitudes toward one's heritage language often translate into increased efforts to acquire it, use it, and keep it alive in the social life of the family or community. On the other hand, negative attitudes lead to apathy about the destiny of the language in the community and reluctance to maintain it. Lukmani (1972) argues that an individual's motivation to acquire and use a language is influenced by such factors as attitudes toward the language itself and its value in one's life, attitudes toward the community and people who speak the language, and the purpose behind learning a language. Understanding attitudes toward the acquisition and maintenance of minority languages also requires an examination of the dominant social beliefs about minority languages, and about linguistic and cultural diversity in a given community.

Language attitudes are intricately related to language use and maintenance. Crawford (2000) indicates that negative attitudes circulating in the dominant culture may dissuade members of minority groups from acquiring or using minority languages. Moreover, the prevailing attitudes in public life may deter parents' transfer of minority languages to their children. Ruiz (1984) maintains that language attitudes are influenced by one of three common societal approaches to minority languages: (1) language as a problem, (2) language as a right, and (3) language as a resource. The first approach views minority languages as an obstacle to integration and success in society, or as a threat to national unity and identity (Ricento, 2005), and therefore speakers of minority languages may feel that they have to abandon their home languages as they learn the dominant language. This attitude dominated in the United States during the first and second waves of Arab immigration. The second approach considers the acquisition of minority languages as a right that non-dominant groups hold as a way to retain their cultural heritage and bilingualism. This attitude was debated during the third wave of Arab immigration. The third approach sees minority languages as a resource for speakers, their families, communities, and society at large. This attitude is a late development in US history, and it often accompanies calls for linguistic and cultural pluralism in American society, although this approach has also been problematized for its underlying instrumentalist perspective of heritage languages (Ricento, 2005). The instrumental view of language is particularly relevant for so-called "critical-need languages," which include Arabic, whose learning has been promoted for national security interests, particularly after 2001.

Given the reportedly negative attitudes toward minority languages in general, and toward Arabic in particular, one may expect Arab parents to adopt the language-as-a-problem approach to the acquisition and use of Arabic by their children, as has been shown in studies of parental attitudes toward other heritage languages (Canagarajah, 2008; Mucherah, 2008). One would also expect that that the societal pressure to learn English, as part of the cultural assimilation and economic success, would adversely influence Arab parents' desire for their children to learn and use Arabic. However, the existing literature suggests that this is not the case: the majority of Arab parents view Arabic as an asset that connects heritage speakers to their parents' culture, tradition, and history. For example, Martin (2009) explored the language practices and attitudes of ninety-four Arab-American parents toward Arabic and examined these practices and attitudes in relation to perceived societal racism. The findings indicate that parents hold positive attitudes toward Arabic and engage in various practices to retain Arabic in their families. Results also indicate that racism is not significantly associated with the parents' language attitudes or language maintenance efforts. Similar results were reported by Rouchdy (2013), who indicated that her participants viewed their parents' positive attitudes and support as a main motive for learning and speaking Arabic. Likewise, Seymour-Jorn (2004) found that the majority of heritage students were studying Arabic under the pressure of their parents and family members.

While the parents' role is critical, it is not the only factor involved in shaping the attitudes of Arabic heritage speakers toward the language. Wilson (2013) argues that heritage speakers' attitudes toward the maintenance of their heritage languages depend upon whether they view its value from an extrinsic or intrinsic perspective. An extrinsic orientation is grounded in the instrumental view of language as a means of communication, education, and economic success, whereas the intrinsic position links language to sentiments, values, and ideals. Although both dimensions are important, the intrinsic value of the language often creates a stronger bond between the language and its speakers. Existing studies on Arabic show that heritage speakers have favorable attitudes toward Arabic more for its symbolic value than for its communicative value. This means that for them school-based practices that promote the acquisition of English for educational attainment and economic opportunity do not thwart the development of positive attitudes toward "home-learned" languages. Kenny (1992) explored the attitudes of twenty-eight high school students in Dearborn toward Arabic. The students were taking classes in SA at the time of the study. The students' responses to a questionnaire revealed favorable attitudes toward learning Arabic to read religious texts, learn more about their culture and literature, and communicate with family and community members. Qawasmeh (2011) used a questionnaire to investigate the attitudes of seventy Muslim Arabs in Vancouver toward Arabic. She also examined the participants' use of the language. The researcher reported that the participants used Arabic (along with English) in various domains, thus reflecting the notable vitality of Arabic in the social life of the community. The researcher attributes this language vitality to the participants' sense of pride in their Arab identity, positive attitudes toward Arabic, and regular use of the language in social and religious realms built on community support.

Albirini (2014b) examined the attitudes of forty heritage speakers (twenty Egyptians and twenty Palestinians) toward Arabic, particularly in terms of their perceptions of the beauty, usefulness, and importance of Arabic as well as their desire to use it and pass it on to their children. Elicited narratives were used for measuring their proficiency, and a questionnaire and interview methods were used to correlate language proficiency with language attitudes and other social factors. The findings indicate that the participants had a robust knowledge of their heritage languages, despite the existence of knowledge gaps in specific areas of their speech. Moreover, most of the participants expressed notable affection for Arabic, mainly because of its perceived beauty, its link to their heritage and cultural identity, and its importance for their personal and professional lives and for future generations. Strikingly, although most of them were neutral with regard to the usefulness of Arabic in their daily lives, the informants confirmed their positive attitudes toward it for religious and cultural purposes and for communication. Similar results are reported by Rouchdy (2013) in her survey of seventy-nine heritage-speaker students at Wayne State University. Out of the seventy-nine participants, seventy-four indicated that "Arabic is very important to them," asserting its relationship to their ethnic identity and religious affiliation (p. 145).

With respect to the two varieties of Arabic, heritage speakers' attitudes toward SA and QA resemble those held by their parents. SA is perceived as the prestige variety, which is associated with literacy, education, Arab literary tradition, media, and religion (for those with Muslim background). By contrast, QA is perceived as a less prestigious variety that is associated with everyday speech. In his investigation of the language attitudes of twenty-five heritage students at the University of Buffalo, New York, Dweik (1997) found that students regarded SA as the language of knowledge and prestige while they saw QA as proper only for informal oral interactions. Still, the participants viewed both as valuable and they considered their coexistence unproblematic. Albirini (2014b) reported similar findings with respect to the perceived statuses and values of both varieties, although some held a more favorable opinion of SA because of its association with education, literacy, religion, and Arab media. While some of the interviewees related SA to the ability to read Arabic, particularly media and religious books, others simply replicated the common arguments used in the Arab World about the value of SA, as the following interview excerpt indicates:

> To me, Fuṣħa is more important because it's the language of education and media.... It's taught at schools and universities.... It's the language of religion ... like it's the language of the Qur'an ... So I feel like ... Fuṣħa is used in important social spheres. I'm not sure if 'Aaamiyya can be used ... or is appropriate in any of these spheres.

Since many heritage speakers may have had limited opportunities for SA exposure and use in context, their attitudes toward SA and QA may simply reflect those of their families and immigrant communities. Their views of the importance and prestige of SA may explain why most of them attend SA classes. When attempts are made to teach QA classes (even in their dialects), most of them would not take these classes, notwithstanding their limited proficiency in these dialects. Another explanation for these positive attitudes concerns the relationship between SA and Qur'anic literacy, which has been found to be the main motive for studying SA among various Muslim groups in the USA and Europe (Jaspal & Colyle, 2010; Rosowsky, 2007). Overall, heritage Arabic speakers' favorable attitudes may be critical for the retention of their heritage languages (Fishman, 1991). Another socioaffective factor intertwined with language attitudes, and which plays an important role in Arabic language maintenance in the diaspora, is the strong sense of Arab identity that characterizes many Arab immigrants and Arab-born Americans.

9.8 IDENTITY CONFLICT

Throughout the history of the United States, language ideologies and language policies were influenced by endeavors to construct the American national identity. Because of the United States' unique ethnic diversity, language has often been perceived as a major symbol of Americans' unity and identity. At the same time, linguistic and cultural diversity has sometimes been perceived as a menace to the unified national identity of America.[7] As Ricento (2005) argues, "the claims for public space for non-English languages have in the past been, and continue to be, viewed as threats to national unity." That is why the use of languages other than English in the public domain has sometimes been considered "un-American." A number of federal and state initiatives, such as the English Language Unity Act, the English for the Children act in California, and similar initiatives in other states, have aimed to exclude minority language instruction from public schools. Lobby groups, such as English First and US English, have been actively involved in promoting English-only legislations at the federal and state levels (Crawford, 2000). The English-Only movement has been successful in curtailing the use of minority languages and somehow stigmatizing multilingualism and multicultural-ism in several social domains. The major thrust behind the English-Only move-ment is the preservation of national unity and identity of the United States.

In the early waves of Arab immigration, Arab Americans and their children were an invisible group, partly because of their small numbers and their assimi-lation into American culture, but also because not much *negative* attention was given to them in the media, especially when the US was battling communism and its main representative, the Soviet Union. This explains why most of the early studies on Arab Americans and their children show a tendency to forsake their Arab identities in favor of symbols of American identity. For example, based on his study of language shift among Christian Lebanese in Buffalo, New York, Dweik (1997, p. 117) documents a notable shift away from the use of Arabic in the social life of this group because "it had no religious or nationalistic value for these Lebanese." Similarly, in his study of Maronite Lebanese Arabs, Ahdab-Yehia (1983) found that many Christian Maronites in the Detroit area have changed their Arabic-sounding names to Anglicized ones (e.g., Butrus to Peter) as part of their identity transformation. Aruri (1969) reported that many Muslim and Christian Arabs in Springfield, Massachusetts, replaced their Arabic names with English names. Sawaie (1992) predicted that Arabic will have a marginal future role in the Arab-American community because many second-generation heritage speakers are abandoning their loyalties to their Arabic heritage and language in the face of daily societal pressures.

The main link between many heritage speakers and the Arabic language is constructed through their religious affiliation as Muslims mainly because SA is associated with Islamic texts and liturgy. For example, in her study of Shi'a Leba-nese families in Dearborn, Michigan, Ajrouch (1999) found that her participants viewed the use of Arabic for reading religious texts and prayers as the main factor contributing to their efforts to maintain it. Ajrouch argues that religion is the strongest basis of group identity among this Shi'a community and the main motive for their efforts to ensure its continuity. Similarly, Almubayei (2007) used focus-group interviews with first- and second-generation Arab Americans in Ari-zona. The researcher found that both groups considered Arabic an important element of their identities as Muslims, and they highlighted its importance for reading religious texts and acts of worship. Similar results were reported in a num-ber of other studies (Albirini, 2014b; Rouchdy, 2013). Rouchdy (2013, p. 144) suggests, "It [SA] is a language from which members of the different speech communities draw support and upon which they build their Arab American ethos in the Diaspora. Hence, it creates a bond of solidarity and an ethnic identity that raises a feeling of 'us versus them.'" When the Muslim identity is evoked, most heritage speakers of Arabic associate it with SA because it is the lan-guage of Qur'an and other religious texts. SA also brings Arabs and non-Arab Muslims together through religious affiliation. For Christian Arabs, SA does not have the same religious significance (Ahdab-Yehia, 1983; Dweik, 1997; Stiffler, 2010). This suggests that religious identity plays a role in language perception and maintenance.

Since the tragic events of September 2001, the common rhetoric characterizing Arabs as the "other," or sometimes even as "the enemy," has influenced Arab Americans' sense of identity in remarkable ways (Abdelhady, 2014; Eid, 2007; Haddad, 2004). Although post-9/11 language policies have drawn attention to heritage languages as a national resource, there is an apprehension, especially in security programs, of the double loyalty of Arab-born Americans between their heritage countries and their home/residence country. The discourse of "otherness" of Arabs and Arab Americans has fostered their sense of identity as "not-fully" American and has obliged many Arab Americans, even those who have assimilated into American culture, to fall back on their Arab roots and identity. As Juteau (1997) suggests, minority communities' self-perceptions are often influenced by the majority group's projection of themselves and others. This interest in Arab identity and heritage has helped many Arab Americans recognize and reestablish the link between the Arabic language and their cultural and historical roots, which is materialized in the sharp increase in the number of heritage Arabic speakers taking college-level Arabic courses since 2001 (Allen, 2007; Carreira & Kagan, 2011). As the existing studies indicate, the majority of these students take Arabic for reasons related to their Arab identity and heritage (Kenny, 1992; Rouchdy, 1992, 2013; Seymour-Jorn, 2004). Community-based studies also show that both parents and children view Arabic as an essential component of their home culture and historical roots, and of their Arab identity (Albirini, 2014b; Almubayei, 2007; Bitar, 2009; Gogonas, 2011; Gomaa, 2011). Moreover, the maintenance of Arab-ethnic and cultural identity and the preservation of Arabic as a community resource for communication are increasingly seen as interdependent. These changes confirm the common view of group language as a potent representation of ethnic identity, especially in minority language situations (Kroon, 1990).

Heritage speakers are defined more by ethnic and "religious" identities and less by regional identities. This is because their depiction as "the other" has often been based on their "Arabness" and "Islamness," rather than on their affiliation to a particular Arab nationality. Moreover, many heritage speakers are not aware of the politically driven rhetoric that has been nurturing the rising sense of state-based nationalism in various Arab countries. The Arabic language has been identified as one of the major symbols of Arab identity among Arab Americans (Bale, 2010). However, it seems that the strength of this link is not uniform across different Arabic-speaking groups – especially among groups that have undergone dissimilar sociopolitical experience in recent history. Albirini (2014b) found that Palestinian heritage speakers show greater commitment to the Arabic language than their Egyptian counterparts because it ties in strongly with their identity, heritage, and history, which explains their keenness to acquire it and to pass it on to their children. This may have to do with the continuous influx of

Palestinians to the United States through family connections. It may also relate to their attempt to foster a sense of community in the face of the identity risks they encounter as a displaced group in a dominant culture. Bitar (2009) found that his Palestinian participants emphasized the connection between the Palestinian dialect and their history and identity. The Palestinian participants were keen to preserve and use the Palestinian dialect because of its link to Palestine and its closeness to SA.

Although many heritage speakers display pride in their Arab ethnicity and Muslim affiliation, the majority of them still see themselves as Americans. For example, Almubayei (2007) found that the majority of her participants maintained that "it [English] is the language with which Arab Americans identify themselves as Americans" and they view it as part of their "ethnic and cultural identity alongside with Arabic" (p. 112). The participants, however, were concerned that total immersion in English would lead to indifference or disinterest in "the Arabic side of their identity." Albirini (2014b) asked his Egyptian and Palestinian participants whether they identify themselves as primarily Arab, primarily American, or both. The vast majority of the participants identified themselves as both Arab and American. Albirini also used an ethnic identity scale that assessed the extent to which the participants (1) felt positively about their ethnicity, (2) felt attached to members, groups, or organizations of the same ethnic group, and (3) engaged in exploring their ethnicity and its sociocultural expressions. Although the scores of both groups showed similarly positive tendencies toward their ethnic Arab identities, the Palestinian speakers expressed greater interest than their Egyptian counterparts in exploring their ethnicity and its cultural expressions. The difference may be due to the fact that some Palestinian parents are vesting the Arabic language with a greater sense of identity than their Egyptian counterparts, possibly because of the geopolitical context from which Palestinian parents come. Language may be one of the strongest links to their Palestinian and Arab roots in a world in which many Palestinians feel a strong need to maintain those ties (Albirini et al., 2011). However, both groups still considered English an important part of their identity as Arab Americans living in the United States.

How does the heritage Arabic speakers' sense of identity reflect on their language proficiencies, language use, and language maintenance? The literature suggests that heritage speakers' sense of their ethnic identity has a direct impact on their language skills as well as their language-maintenance efforts (Almubayei, 2007; Bale, 2010; Gogonas, 2011; Gomaa, 2011; Rouchdy, 2013; Seymour-Jorn, 2004). For example, Albirini (2014b) reported that heritage speakers' language attitudes and sense of ethnic identity are positively related to language input, which was relevant to both language use and overall language proficiency. The Palestinian speakers showed a greater sense of ethnic identity than the Egyptian participants (because of their apprehension of identity loss), which had prompted them to explore Palestinian cultural artifacts and traditions. This may translate into greater chances exposure to the target language.

In his study of Egyptian heritage speakers in Greece, Gogonas (2011) found that second-generation Egyptian Muslims have better command of Arabic than Coptic Egyptians, who in turn have a better mastery of Greek than their Muslim counterparts. Gogonas argues that the Egyptian Muslims have better command of Arabic because it is a core facet of their Muslim and Arab identities, which is not the case for the Coptic Egyptians who seek to assimilate into Greek society. Similarly, Caubet (2004) argues that Arabic has a more symbolic value, which explains its regular use by many Arab immigrants and their children. The relationship between socio-affective factors and language maintenance, however, is still an understudied area that needs further in-depth investigation through empirical studies dedicated particularly to this purpose.

Overall, the literature points to a symbiotic relationship between language and ethnic identity. The vitality of the Arabic language is critical for the liveliness of ethnic and religious identities and their relevant conventions, values, and practices. While the dominant expectations with respect to the use of English, cultural assimilation, and display of Americanism may limit heritage speakers' desire to acquire and use their heritage language, their positive attitudes toward Arabic and their strong sense of ethnic and religious affiliations are likely to ensure the endurance of Arabic in their social lives (Bale, 2010; Rouchdy, 2013).

9.9 SUMMARY AND CONCLUSION

This chapter examined language use, language attitudes, and identity dynamics in a population that speaks Arabic, but is removed from the Arabic diglossic context and the Arab speech community and is situated in a context where the distribution and functions of SA and QA are not materialized in everyday communication. This situation results in language loss and attrition among heritage speakers of Arabic, which is reflected in gaps in grammar, language interference, and CS between English and Arabic. One of the most striking consequences of this situation is that heritage speakers lack the ability to deploy SA and QA in a functionally and contextually proper way in their speech. This appears particularly in their CS practices where the mixing of SA and QA does not necessarily have clear social or pragmatic functions.

However, as Bale (2010) suggests, Arabic is expected to survive even outside its "home" because of the international presence of Arabic as a mother tongue for more than 300 million people in the Arab region and as a language of worship for nearly two billion Muslims. More importantly, Arabic is expected to persist in the social lives of heritage speakers because of the generally favorable attitudes toward it in Arab diaspora communities and its link to their Arab and Islamic identities. This socioaffective factor is responsible for the increasing number of media and community programs in Arabic, which provide a source of continued input for heritage speakers, especially those who are interested in maintaining their language. The continued use of Arabic by heritage speakers shows that language attitudes and identity feelings are critical for the maintenance of Arabic in the diaspora, just as they are crucial for the continued survival of SA in the Arab region.

NOTES

1 The well-known Abdulrahman Ibrahim Ibn Sori also wrote in Arabic. The earliest documented work for Abdulrahman Ibrahim Ibn Sori was a personal letter written in 1826 (Alford, 2007).
2 Here, the focus is on English as a typologically distinct language rather than the different varieties of American English (e.g., Standard American English versus African-American English).
3 A number of researchers (e.g., Coupland, 2007; Eckert, 2000) have used the term *community of practice* instead of *speech community*.
4 Very few studies have examined heritage speakers' knowledge of SA. For example, Albirini (2014c) examined the knowledge that heritage speakers of Arabic in elementary SA classrooms possess with respect to sentential negation in SA. The subjects were asked to negate forty verbal sentences (in the present, past, future, and imperative) and forty verbless sentences (with nominal, adjectival, and prepositional predicates as well as existential constructions). The study showed that these speakers were able to negate these different constructions in only 23.55% of the cases.
5 The term "unbalanced bilingualism" applies to the majority of heritage speakers, who have at least basic knowledge of Arabic as well as English. Heritage speakers who do not acquire or who lose Arabic completely are often called "early bilinguals." However, the existing studies suggest that "early bilingualism" is rare among heritage speakers of Arabic.
6 Undoubtedly, there are some exceptions, but the focus here is on general trends.
7 Although these viewpoints may be widespread – as is reported in the literature – to generalize this opinion as one that has swept America misrepresents the divided nature of American political and linguistic ideologies. These conservative viewpoints have historically coexisted with another, possibly more common, thrust toward tolerance and respect for cultural diversity.

CHAPTER 10

General conclusion

The book has focused on the subjects of diglossia, language attitudes, social identities, variation, and codeswitching and their individual and combined impact on the language behavior of Arabic speakers. Since these five variables do not operate in a social vacuum, the book has also examined their relationships to key aspects of the Arabic sociolinguistic situation, such as language prestige, language policies, language standardization, and so on. The discussions on these various topics highlight a number of sociolinguistic patterns, some of which are deep-rooted in the Arabic sociolinguistic scene, while others are emerging and taking shape as a result of larger social, political, and economic changes in Arab societies. This chapter summarizes these longstanding and recent sociolinguistic patterns and, whenever applicable, points to potential areas of research to address the current gaps in these areas.

10.1 PATTERNS OF SOCIOLINGUISTIC STASIS

The most distinctive feature of the Arabic sociolinguistic situation is diglossia, which has continued to influence language use in the Arab context for centuries. Diglossia is represented by the coexistence of two codes – Standard Arabic and Colloquial Arabic – each conferred a different status and assigned different roles. While the contextual representation of diglossia negates the possibility of contextual overlap between the two codes (Ferguson, 1959a), there is a growing body of literature documenting the coexistence of SA and QA in the same context. However, this coexistence is regularized by assigning different functions to SA and QA in the same piece of discourse. In other words, it helps speakers perform functions that may differ in importance and seriousness, even in a single speech event. For example, even though he/she may rely primarily on SA in the course of a political debate, a politician may resort to QA when joking. Despite the frequent mixing of SA and QA, the postulation of middle varieties between SA and QA is not warranted; the CS literature both in face-to-face interaction and in online communication points out the lack of systematic rules of mixing SA and QA in such a way that a discernible variety may be identified.

From a theoretical perspective, diglossia is still conceptualized as a problem in the relevant literature, particularly in the field of education. However, empirical data shows that it is not perceived as such by the majority of Arabic speakers, except for those who have negative attitudes toward QA and view it as a threat to the status of SA or to the link between SA and their Arab and Muslim identities. The problematization of diglossia in educational settings is underlined by the perspective that SA is a barrier to children's educational achievement; SA delays learning the subject matter because of the time that students take to acquire it. Empirical studies, however, show that the "problems" surrounding the teaching of SA are not language-specific but are related to several external variables, such as parents' involvement, exposure to SA inside and outside school, and teaching methods (Abu-Rabia, 2000; Aram, Korat, & Hassunah-Arafat, 2013; Hassunah-Arafat, 2010). The argument against the use of SA in education raises three interrelated questions:

(1) What is the relationship between SA skills (e.g., reading and writing abilities) and scholastic achievement and how is this relationship different from its counterparts worldwide?

(2) What is the impact of QA on the formal acquisition of SA at school?

(3) How do inside and outside school practices and variables influence the acquisition of SA and how do they impact scholastic attainment?

Addressing these questions empirically may provide a more realistic picture of the role of SA in the reportedly declining scholastic achievement among Arab children.

As has been historically the case, diglossia is still sustained by a number of sociocontextual and socioaffective factors. Among the factors that are indispensable to understanding the dissimilar values and functional distribution of SA and QA are language attitudes. Language attitudes are implicated in the elevated status of SA, its continued role in language policies, and the very survival of the underused SA as a living language in the Arab context. Similarly, language attitudes are involved in defining the status of QA as the Low code, its exclusion from language planning, and the resistance to its codification and standardization even though it is the means of everyday interactions. In addition to language attitudes, the Arabic diglossic situation is sustained by identity dynamics that pull in two opposite directions; one is the direction of pan-Arab identity, which is represented by SA, while another is moving in the direction of state-based identities, which is represented by the colloquial varieties in each of the Arab countries. SA is linked to the Arab past history and heritage, and is an important vestige of a tradition marked by achievement, stability, and prosperity. It is also linked to Islamic texts and liturgy and therefore is considered indispensable to Arab Muslims in their rituals and as an indicator of their religious identities. Unlike SA, QA is associated with the political, linguistic, and cultural fragmentation of the Arab societies, and it marks divergent local and state-based identities. The identity–language bond becomes critical in defining the status and role of SA and QA as the High variety and Low variety, respectively.

A last persistent pattern to be discussed concerns the Arabic speakers' frequent alternation between SA and QA in contexts of varying levels of formality. The dynamics of CS differ based on whether it occurs in monitored or unmonitored speech. In monitored speech, CS typically follows the general societal norms with respect to the uses and distribution of SA and QA. It is within this type of CS that the representations of diglossia should be understood. In unmonitored speech, however, CS is motivated mostly by demographic, pragmatic, contextual, and interpersonal factors. Moreover, it involves negotiation of roles, meanings, and identities. It should be noted that educated Arabic speakers have varying skills in SA; some have a notable ability to carry out and sustain conversations in SA, while others are less able to do so. This suggests that, when educated Arabic speakers engage in extended discourse in SA, certain switches, particularly word-level switches, to QA may be triggered by limitations in SA skills rather than by social factors. One interesting pattern in the CS literature is the lack of alternation between SA and typological distinct languages, such as English and French. The absence of this type of CS may be due to the fact that most of the existing studies on bilingual CS are contextualized in daily interactions where QA is mostly used. However, this phenomenon is sociolinguistically interesting and ought to be studied systematically.

10.2 PATTERNS OF SOCIOLINGUISTIC CHANGE

While the above patterns exhibit the durability of a number of sociolinguistic trends for decades now, there emerge new patterns that reflect recent changes in theories, approaches, or social realities in the Arab region. Methodologically, the book draws attention to the changing meaning of *context, community, communication,* and *language variety*. Arabizi presents an interesting case because it encodes Arabic texts in Latin letters, numbers, English abbreviations, phonetic alphabet, syllabograms, logograms, and punctuation marks. Moreover, it does not always have a fixed orthography. This "variety" is not spoken and is often limited to certain online contexts. Another example concerns the concept of community, which has become fluid in the virtual world of digital media; it is often constructed through the discursive practices and identity performances of the internet users. This means that speakers may create and recreate their personal identities online without the need to anchor these identities in the social realities of the physical world. Overall, digital communication presents new modes and venues of expression, which have transformed key concepts and practices in the Arabic sociolinguistic situation, including the features of written discourse.

One of the conceptual developments in the field of Arabic sociolinguistics is the reassessment of the common approach to SA as a second language for Arabic speakers. This postulation takes insights from language acquisition research, where order of acquisition becomes critical in defining the mother tongue, and it is rationalized by considering the fact that the *formal* learning of SA takes place at school. This line of reasoning has recently been challenged by empirical data, which attest Arab children's ability to understand and speak SA at an early stage of their language development (Aram, Korat, & Hassunah-Arafat, 2013; Haeri, 2000; Sabir & Safi, 2008; Saiegh-Haddad et al., 2011). The children's ability to comprehend and use SA ensues from their *informal* exposure to SA through different communication channels, such as children's cartoons, children's stories, religious speeches, Qur'anic recitations, news reports, and other oral and written forms of discourse. The book also highlights the need to implement sociolinguistic criteria for defining the concept of mother tongue, which ought to be based on such issues as representation, identity, and localness. The application of sociolinguistic criteria presents SA as a mother tongue for many Arabic speakers who see SA as a main marker of their Arab identities or explicitly claim SA as their mother tongue.

A second emergent pattern concerns the changing attitudes toward English, which had traditionally been perceived as an "intruding" language in the post-independence Arab countries. More recent studies show that the Arab youth have favorable attitudes toward English and embrace it in their offline and online communications (Bishr, 2007; Khalil, 2005; Shaaban & Ghaith, 2002, 2003; Siraaj, 2013). English–Arabic codeswitching is gaining popularity in everyday face-to-face speech as well as on online interactions. The attitudinal and behavioral "adoption" of English stems from its indexicality of modernity, education, and technical sophistication and also from pragmatic necessities, given its status as the international language of science, technology, and business. In Bourdieuan terms (Bourdieu, 1977), the adoption of English by the Arab youth is a process of accruing social capital given the power assigned to English locally and internationally. Although the majority of Arab youth still see SA as a marker of their identity as Arabs or Muslims, their adoption of English may be seen as part of their emulation of a broader sociocultural model. This attitude is translated culturally by adopting Western lifestyles and linguistically through acquiring English. Like English, French is still associated with modernity and technology in the Maghreb countries. However, French is generally conceived as a colonially imposed language and therefore it receives less favorable attitudes. This partly explains the slowly receding role of French in the Maghreb countries in comparison to English (Battenburg, 2006; Bentahila & Davies, 1995; Chakrani, 2010).

The favorable attitudes toward English coincide with less favorable attitudes to SA among the Arab youth, which also reflects the diminishing role of SA as a spoken language across the Arab region. This may explain why intellectual discussions in the Arab region have been colored by alarmist tones concerning the rise of English as a major competitor to SA. The competition between SA and English is seen as multidimensional; it cuts across social space, structure, identity, politics, and ideology. SA is also increasingly challenged by the realities of QA use in domains that were traditionally reserved for the Standard variety. For example, QA coexists with SA in online communication, in some media channels, and even in print media (Eid, 2002; Ibrahim, 2010; Mejdell, 2006; Rosenbaum, 2011). SA and QA may exist independently in written discourse, as is the case in online blogging and chatting, respectively, or they mix together intra-sententially or intersententially, as in novels and short stories. Thus, the ideologically protective attitudes toward SA do not necessarily mirror actual language use where QA and English are gradually gaining ground in Arabic speakers' everyday communications. The current intellectual endeavors to "save" SA are noteworthy in the sense that the status of SA, which was taken for granted after the Arab states' independence, is nowadays highly contested. The Arab intellectuals have to elaborately justify the importance of SA for the Arab and Muslim identity.

A third development is the official recognition of Berber and Kurdish on the political map of the Arab World, their growing use in formal domains, and the shift in some of the narratives of Kurdish and Berber speakers from a focus on ethnolinguistic identity to national recognition. While the historical narratives underlying the shared ethnic identities and languages of Berber- and Kurdish-speaking peoples have been successful in bringing recognition to Berber and Kurdish languages, new historical narratives are needed to deconstruct the current state-based identities and construct new national identities based on territorial and political grounds. The Berber, Kurdish, and state-based forms of identity are part of a larger process of the identity fragmentation in the Arab region that threaten the traditional forms of national, ethnic, and religious identities. The political front has witnessed the practical disappearance of pan-Arab rhetoric and the emergence of state-based nationalisms that are fed by loyalties to ruling families or personages. On the religious front, pan-Islamic rhetoric is substituted by loyalties to sects or individual religious figures. Possibly the only form of identity that persists is ethnic identities, which is what holds Arabs' sense of shared identity. The Arabic language is crucial for this form of identity because the Arab ethnicity is based less on racial, religious, or territorial commonalties, and more on a shared tongue. However, even this form of shared identity is unsettled, given the possibility of redrawing the ethnicity lines for political ends – a prospect supported by state-based nationalisms, religious secticisms, and the politics of ethnolinguistic identity in minority communities.

A fourth pattern of change concerns heritage Arabic speakers, children of Arab immigrants who are born and raised in contexts where diglossia is nonexistent. Previous research on this population in the United States suggests that most second-generation Arab Americans assimilate culturally and linguistically in the American context in their effort to acquire the dominant language and function in the larger society in which they live. However, recent studies, particularly after September 11th, show an increased keenness among this group to acquire their heritage language and to use it in communication within their families, communities, and their parents' home countries. Language maintenance is stimulated by the discourse of "otherness" that American media has been propagating with respect to Arab and Muslim Americans, which has raised their awareness of their roots and enhanced their attitudes toward Arabic. This shows that language use is intricately related to language attitudes and identity feelings. The relationship between language maintenance and the socioaffective factors of language attitudes and identity may also explain Arabic speakers' divergent abilities to use SA (Chapter 7). The Moroccan participants surpassed their Egyptian, Jordanian, and Saudi counterparts in terms of ability to sustain conversations in SA, which is possibly due to their positive attitudes toward SA. On the other hand, the Egyptian, Jordanian, and Saudi participants have more positive attitudes to their colloquial varieties and English, which impinges on their discursive skills in SA.

The study reported in Chapter 7 also reveals that the Egyptian college students have better skills in SA compared to Egyptian professors. This advantage may have to do with intergenerational changes in identity dynamics and language attitudes between a generation that experienced the elevation of the Egyptian dialect – as the dialectal lingua franca in the Arab region – and a heightened sense of Egyptian identity and a newer generation whose language attitudes and sense of Egyptian identity are potentially less strong. Similarly, the Jordanian students' less favorable attitudes to SA, compared to English, could be responsible for the decline in their mastery of SA, compared to the Jordanian professors. It is again doubtful that this trend has to do with differences in the level of education; otherwise, this should apply to the Egyptian and Moroccan participants as well, which is not the case. These changes are gradually becoming part of the current intellectual discourse in the Arab region, thus replacing the rhetoric about SA admiration, pan-Arabism, and Arabicization with more practical issues about the lack of SA mastery by the Arab youth and its educational, ideological, and political implications for the continued use of SA.

10.3 POTENTIAL TRAJECTORIES IN THE ARABIC SOCIOLINGUISTIC SITUATION

It is difficult to predict the progression of the Arabic sociolinguistic situation due to the sociopolitical volatility of the Arab region. However, if we project the future sociolinguistic trajectory as an extension of existing trends in the Arab region, two main routes may ensue.

One possible development concerns the move of the Arab region from diglossia to multilingualism as a result of the growing reliance on English in business, technology, and science, the widespread use of English in digital communication, and the incorporation of many English words in everyday interactions. Just as French became part of the Maghreb sociolinguistic scene largely by military force, English may as well become part of the broader Arabic sociolinguistic landscape by economic force, an implied "force of conviction" that English is *needed* for international communications, world trade, and economic competitiveness. Dubai resembles an example of this type of multilingualism, but other parts of the Arab region may follow suit (Siraaj, 2013). Apart from the spread of English, the prospect of multilingualism is bolstered by the precarious status of SA and its deteriorating use across the Arab region.

Alternatively, diglossia may persist as the sociolinguistic norm if the current sporadic *intellectual* efforts to maintain SA summon further social or sociopolitical measures to regulate the spread of English and counteract its influence on everyday language use. They may entail revitalizing the Arabicization policies in its two dimensions: promoting Arabic in key official domains, such as education and media, and implementing a unified Arab policy for incorporating borrowed English terms. This scenario necessitates mobilizing the attitudinal and identity-based associations of SA as the language of Arab heritage and history. This scheme, however, entails working against the currently prevalent trends of language use across the Arab region. If we accept the more recent conception of language change as mainly based on language use (Keller, 1994; Ritt, 2004), then this scenario is more challenging and less expected to succeed in reversing the current patterns of language use, especially among the Arab youth.

Another potential development concerns the possible contraction of domains in which SA in its spoken form appears. This extrapolation is based on three interrelated trends. First, many young Arabs do not have as highly positive views of SA as previous studies show (e.g., Dash & Tucker, 1975; Haeri, 2000) mainly because of its presumed difficulty and its distance from their daily language use. Second, members of the younger generation do not have a strong command of SA possibly because they see little need to use it in their personal and professional lives. Last, the Arab youth underestimate the link between SA and their Arab identity mainly because political pan-Arabism is no longer a reality. The Arab youth are fostered in social environments where state-based nationalism and loyalty to the state or ruling family/figure is overemphasized, which may make the link between SA and Arab identity absurd to them. The emergence of digital communications and the practical need to master English in digitally mediated communication further alienates the Arab youth from SA. Eventually, the ideologies that have upheld the status, role, and use of SA may capitulate to realities of language usage.

A last possible development concerns the growth of bilingual CS between Arabic and English. While bilingual CS between Arabic and typologically distinct languages has traditionally been situated in the Maghreb region or in the Western world, there is a growing evidence that Arabic–English CS is on the rise across the Arab region (Alfaifi, 2013; Al-Khatib & Sabbah, 2008; Bianchi, 2013; Mimouna, 2012; Palfreyman & al Khalil, 2003; Salia, 2011; Warschauer et al., 2002). This trend is expected to grow along with the growing role of English in the international arena and in the Arab region in particular. However, as indicated above, how likely these developments are to occur hinges on other sociopolitical developments in the volatile Arab region. The recent efforts on the part of many Arab intellectuals to maintain and promote SA may curtail the current trends of mixing Arabic and English in a number of contexts. Again, this requires working against the current tide of actual language use, which may eventually determine the trajectory of the sociolinguistic changes in the Arab region.

Bibliography

Aabi, M. (2004). On parameterization and the syntax of code switching. *Al-Lughāt wa al-lisāniyāt* [Languages and Linguistics], *13*, 67–83.

Abbasi, A. (1977). *A sociolinguistic analysis of multilingualism in Morocco.* (Unpublished doctoral dissertation). University of Texas, Austin.

Abboud-Haggar, S. (2005). Teaching Arabic dialectology in European Universities: why, what, and how. In A. Elgibali (Ed.), *Investigating Arabic: Current parameters in analysis and learning* (pp. 117–132). Leiden: Brill.

Abboud-Haggar, S. (2006). Dialect genesis. In K. Versteegh, M. Eid, A. Elgibali, M. Woidich, & A. Zaborski (Eds.), *Encyclopedia of Arabic language and linguistics* (pp. 613–622). Leiden: Brill.

Abdelhady, A., Makoni, B., Makoni, S., & Mugaddam, A. (2011). The sociolinguistics of nationalism in the Sudan: The politicisation of Arabic and the Arabicisation of politics. *Current Issues in Language Planning, 12*(4), 457–501.

Abdelhady, D. (2014). The sociopolitical history of Arabs in the United States: Assimilation, ethnicity, and global citizenship. In S.C. Nassar-McMillan, K.J. Ajrouch, & J. Hakim-Larson (Eds.), *Biopsychosocial perspectives on Arab Americans* (pp. 17–43). New York, NY: Springer.

Abdel-Jawad, H.R. (1981). Lexical and phonological variation in spoken Arabic of Amman. (Unpublished doctoral dissertation). University of Pennsylvania, Philadelphia.

Abdel-Jawad, H.R. (1986). The emergence of an urban dialect in the Jordanian urban centres. *International Journal of the Sociology of Language, 61*, 53–63.

Abdel-Jawad, H.R. (1987). Cross-dialectal variation in Arabic: Competing prestigious forms. *Language in Society, 16*, 359–368.

Abdel-Jawad, H. R. (1989). Language and women's place with special reference to Arabic. *Language Sciences, 11*(3), 305–324.

Abdel-Malek, Z. (1972). The influence of diglossia on the novels of Yuusif al-Sibaa'i. *Journal of Arabic Literature, 3*, 132–141.

Abdulaliim, M. (2012). *Al-lugha al-'arabiyya w-ṣiraa' al-hawiyya* [The Arabic language and the identity struggle]. Paper presented at the First International Conference on the Arabic Language, Beirut, 19–23 March. Retrieved from www.alarabiah.org/index.php?op=view_all_studies&id=15

Abdulaziz, M.H. (1986). Factors in the development of modern Arabic usage. *International Journal of the Sociology of Language, 62*, 11–24.

Abdul-Hassan, R.S. (1988). Variation in the Educated Spoken Arabic of Iraq: A sociolinguistic study. (Unpublished doctoral dissertation). University of Leeds, UK.

Abduljabbar, A. (1996). *Muhadhdhab iqtiḍaa' al-ṣiraat al-mustaqiim: Mukhalafat ahl al-jaḥiim* [edited version of *Necessity of straight path: Disagreeing with the people of hellfire*]. Amman, Jordan: Daar Al-Rissalah.

Abdulla, R. (2007). *The Internet in the Arab World: Egypt and beyond*. New York: Peter Lang, International Academic Publishers.

Abdul-Raof, H. (2004). The Qur'an: Limits of translatability. In S. Faiq (Ed.), *Cultural encounters in translation from Arabic* (pp. 91–107). Clevedon: Multilingual Matters.

Abou, S., Kaspartan, C. & Haddad, K. (1996). *Anatomie de la Francophonie Libanaise*. Beirut: Universite Saint-Joseph.

Aboud, F., & Doyle, A. (1993). The early development of ethnic identity and attitudes. In M.E. Bernal & G.P. Knight (Eds.), *Ethnic identity: Formation and transmission among Hispanics and other minorities* (pp. 47–59). New York: State University of New York Press.

Abou-Seida, A. (1971). Diglossia in Egyptian Arabic: Prolegomena to a pan-Arabic sociolinguistic study. (Unpublished doctoral dissertation). University of Texas, Austin.

Abu-Haidar, F. (1989). Are Iraqi women more prestige conscious than men? Sex differentiation in Baghdadi Arabic. *Language in Society, 18*, 471–481.

Abu-Haidar, F. (1991). *Christian Arabic of Baghdad*. Wiesbaden: Otto Harrassowitz.

Abu-Haidar, F. (1996). Turkish as a marker of ethnic identity and religious affiliation. In Y. Suleiman (Ed.), *Language and identity in the Middle East and North Africa* (pp. 117–133). Richmond: Curzon.

Abu-Haidar, F. (2002). Arabic and English in conflict: Iraqis in the UK. In A. Rouchdy (Ed.), *Language contact and language conflict in Arabic: Variations on a sociolinguistic theme* (pp. 286–296). London: RoutledgeCurzon.

Abuhakema, G. (2013). Code switching and code mixing in Arabic written advertisements: Patterns, aspects, and the question of prestige and standardization. *The International Journal of Language, Culture and Society, 38*, 173–186.

Abu-Lughod, L. (1986). *Veiled sentiments: Honor and poetry in a Bedouin society*. Berkeley and Los Angeles: University of California Press.

Abu-Lughod, L. (1990). The romance of resistance: Tracing transformations of power through Bedouin women. *American Ethnologist, 17*(1), 41–55.

Abu-Melhim, A.H. (1991). Code-switching and linguistic accommodation in Arabic. In B. Comrie & M. Eid (Eds.), *Perspectives on Arabic Linguistics III: Papers from the Third Annual Symposium on Arabic Linguistics*. Amsterdam: John Benjamins.

Abu-Melhim, A.H. (1992). Communication across Arabic dialects: Code-switching and linguistic accommodation in informal conversational interactions. (Unpublished doctoral dissertation). Texas A&M University, College Station.

Abu Nasser, M., & Benmamoun, E. (In press). Quantifying lexical and pronunciation variation between three Arabic varieties. *Perspectives on Arabic Linguistics*.

Abu Nasser, M., Benmamoun, E., & Hasegawa-Johnson, M. (2013). Pronunciation Variation Metric for four dialects of Arabic, presentation at AIDA 10 (Association Internationale de Dialectologie Arabe), Qatar University.

Abu-Rabia, S. (2000). Effects of exposure to literary Arabic on reading comprehension in a diglossic situation. *Reading and Writing, 13*(1–2), 147–157.

Ager, D.E. (2001). *Motivation in language planning and language policy*. Clevedon: Multilingual Matters.

Agheyisi, R., & Fishman, J. (1970). Language attitude studies: A brief survey of method-ological approaches. *Anthropological Linguistics, 12*(5), 137–157.

Agre, P. (2003). Surveillance and capture: Two models of privacy. In Wardrip-Fruin & Mont-fort (Eds.), *The new media reader* (pp. 741–760). Cambridge, MA: The MIT Press.

Ahdab-Yehia, M. (1983). The Lebanese Maronites: Patterns of continuity and change. In S. Y. Abraham & N. Abraham (Eds.), *Arabs in the new world: Studies on Arab-American communities* (pp. 148–162). Detroit: Wayne State University.

Ajrouch, K. (1999). Family and ethnic identity in an Arab-American community. In M. Sulei-man (Ed.), *Arabs in America* (pp. 129–139). Philadelphia: Temple University Press.

Ajzen, I., & Fishbein, M. (1980). *Understanding attitudes and predicting social behavior.* Englewood Cliffs, NJ: Prentice-Hall.

Akbacak, M., Vergyri, D., Stolcke, A., Scheffer, N., & Mandal, A. (2011). Effective Arabic Dialect Classification Using Diverse Phonotactic Models. In the Proceedings of Inter-speech, 737–740.

Akman, V. (2000). Rethinking context as a social construct. *Journal of Pragmatics, 32,* 743–759.

Al-Abed Al-Haq, F. (1994). *Toward a theoretical framework for the study of Arabicization planning.* Paper presented at *The first International conference on Literature, Lin-guistics, and Translation*, Yarmouk University, Irbid, Jordan.

Al-Abed Al-Haq, F. (1998). Language attitude and the promotion of standard Arabic and Arabicization. *Al-'Arabiyya, 31,* 21–37.

Al-Abed Al-Haq, F., & Al-Masaeid, A. L. (2009). Islam and language planning in the Arab world: A case study in Jordan. *Iranian Journal of Language Studies, 3*(3), 267–302.

Al-Ahdal, H. (1989). A Sociolinguistic description of speech in Makkah. (Unpublished doctoral thesis). University of Reading, UK.

Al-Ali, M., & Arafa, H. (2010). An experimental sociolinguistic study of language variation in Jordanian Arabic. *Buckingham Journal of Language and Linguistics, 3,* 207–230.

Al-Amadidhi, D. (1985). Lexical and sociolinguistic variation in Qatari Arabic. (Unpub-lished doctoral thesis). University of Edinbrugh, UK.

Al-Asal, M., & Smadi, O. (2012). Arabicization and Arabic expanding techniques used in science lectures in two Arab universities. *Asian Perspectives in the Arts and Human-ities, 2*(1), 15–38.

Albakry, M., & Hancock, P. (2008). Code switching in Ahdaf Soueif's "The Map of Love." *Language and Literature, 17*(3), 221–234.

Albakry, M. & Siler, J. (2012). Into the Arab-American borderland: Bilingual creativity in Randa Jarrar's "Map of Home." *Arab Studies Quarterly, 34*(2), 109–121.

Al-Batal, M. (2002). Identity and language tension in Lebanon: The Arabic of local news at LBCT. In A. Rouchdy (Ed.), *Language contact and language conflict in Arabic: Vari-ations on a sociolinguistic theme* (pp. 91–115). London: RoutledgeCurzon.

Al-Batal, M., & Belnap, R. K. (2006). The teaching and learning of Arabic in the United States: Realities, needs, and future directions. In K. M. Wahba, Z. A. Taha, & L. England (Eds.), *Handbook for Arabic language teaching professionals* (pp. 389–399). Mah-wah, NJ: Lawrence Erlbaum.

Albirini, A. (2007). The Internet in developing countries: A medium of economic, cultural and political domination. *International Journal of Education and Development using ICT, 4*(1), 49–65.

Albirini, A. (2010). The structure and functions of codeswitching between Standard Arabic and dialectal Arabic. (Unpublished doctoral thesis). University of Illinois Urbana-Champaign.

Albirini, A. (2011). The sociolinguistic functions of codeswitching between standard Arabic and dialectal Arabic. *Language in Society, 40,* 537–562.

Albirini, A. (2015). Factors affecting the acquisition of plural morphology in Jordanian Arabic. *Journal of Child Language, 42*(4), 734–762.

Albirini, A. (2014a). The socio-pragmatics of dialectal codeswitching by the Al-'Keidaat Bedouin speakers. *Intercultural Pragmatics, 11*(1), 121–147.

Albirini, A. (2014b). Toward understanding the variability in the language proficiencies of Arabic heritage speakers. *International Journal of Bilingualism, 18*(6), 730–765.

Albirini, A. (2014c). The role of the colloquial varieties in the acquisition of the standard variety: the case of Arabic heritage speakers. *Foreign Language Annals, 47*(3), 371–389.

Albirini, A. (in progress). The ideologies of language accommodation.

Albirini, A., & Benmamoun, E. (2014a). Aspects of second language transfer in the oral production of Egyptian and Palestinian heritage speakers. *International Journal of Bilingualism, 18*(3), 244–273.

Albirini, A. & Benmamoun, E. (2015). Factors affecting the retention of sentential negation in heritage Egyptian Arabic. *Bilingualism: Language and Cognition, 18*(3), 470–489.

Albirini, A. & Benmamoun, E. (2014b). Concatenative and non-concatenative plural formation in L1, L2, and heritage speakers. *Modern Language Journal, 98*(3), 854–871.

Albirini, A., Benmamoun, A., & Saadah, E. (2011). Grammatical features of Egyptian and Palestinian Arabic heritage speakers' oral production. *Studies in Second Language Acquisition, 33,* 273–303.

Albirini, A., Benmamoun, E., & Chakrani, B. (2013). Gender and number agreement in the oral production of Arabic heritage speakers. *Bilingualism: Language and Cognition, 16*(1), 1–18.

Al-Ḍabiib, A (2001). *Al-lugha al-'arabiyyah fii 'aṣr al-'awlamah* [The Arabic language in the age of globalization]. Riyadh, Saudi Arabia: Dar Al-'Beikaan.

Al-Dashti, A. (1998). Language choice in the state of Kuwait: A sociolinguistic investigation. (Unpublished doctoral dissertation). University of Essex, UK.

Aldawri, A. (1984). *Al-takween at-taariikhi li-l-'umma l-'Arabiyya: Diraasa fi l-hawiyya wa-l-wa'y* [The historical establishment of the Arab nation: A study in identity and awareness]. Beirut: Markaz Diraasaat al-Wahda al-'Arabiyya.

Al-Dibs, Š. (1934). *Thikra Anis Salloum* [Memoir of Anis Salloum]. Damascus: Ibn Raidoum.

Al-Enazi, M.H. (2002). The syntactic form and social functions of Saudi Arabic-English code switching among bilingual Saudis in the United States. (Unpublished doctoral dissertation). Indiana University of Pennsylvania, Indiana.

Al-Essa, A. (2009). When Najd meets Hijaz: Dialect contact in Jeddah. In E. Al-Wer & R. de Jong, *Arabic dialectology* (pp. 203–222). Amsterdam: Brill.

Alfaifi, S. (2013). Code-switching among bilingual Saudis on Facebook. (Unpublished doctoral dissertation). Southern Illinois University, Carbondale.

Al-Fasiiħ Network for the Sciences of the Arabic Language. Retrieved from www.alfaseeh.com/vb/forum.php

Alford, T. (2007). *Prince among slaves*. Oxford: Oxford University Press.

Alghamdi, F. (2014). The usage of newly borrowed color terms in Arabic: Gender and regional variations. (Unpublished doctoral dissertation). Southern Illinois University, Carbondale.

Al-Husari, S. (1985). *Fi Al-Adab wa-l-Lugha wa-'alaqatuhuma bi-l-qawmiyyah* [About literature and language and their relationship to nationalism]. Beirut: Markaz Diraasaat Al-Wahda Al-'arabiyya.

Al-Jaabiri, M.A. (1989). *Takwiin al-'aql al-'Arabiyy* [Formation of the Arab mind]. Beirut: Markaz Diraasaat Al-Waħda al-'Arabiyya.

Al-Jaabiri, M.A. (1995). *Mas'alat al-huwiyyah: Al-'uruubah wa-l-islaam was l-gharb* [The identity question: Arabism, Islam, and the West]. Beirut: Markaz Diraasaat Al-Waħda Al-'Arabiyya.

Al-Jaahiẓ, A. (1983). *Rassa'il al-Jaahiẓ* [Al-Jaahiẓ's Letters]. Beirut: Dar Al-Nahḍa Al-'Arabiyya.

Al-Jallad, A. (2009). The polygenesis of the Neo-Arabic dialects. *Journal of Semitic Studies, 54*(2), 515–536.

Al-Jehani, N.M. (1985). Sociostylistic stratification of Arabic in Makkah. (Unpublished doctoral dissertation). University of Michigan, Ann Arbor.

Al-Kahtany, A.H. (1997). The "Problem" of diglossia in the Arab world: An attitudinal study of modern standard Arabic and the Arabic dialects. *Al-'Arabiyya, 30*, 30–31.

Al-Khatib, M. (1988). Sociolinguistic change in an expanding urban context. (Unpublished doctoral dissertation). University of Durham, UK.

Al-Khatib, M. (2007). Innovative foreign and second language education in the Middle East and North Africa. In N.V. Deusen-Scholl & N.H. Hornberger (Eds.), *Encyclopedia of language and education (2nd Ed.): Second and foreign language education* (pp. 227–237). New York: Springer.

Al-Khatib, M. (2008). E-mails as a mode of communication among Jordanian university students: A sociolinguistic perspective. *International Journal of Language, Society and Culture, 25*, 1–17.

Al-Khatib, M., & Farghal, M. (1999). English borrowing in Jordanian Arabic: Distribution, functions, and attitudes. *Grazer Linguistische Studien, 52*, 1–18.

Al-Khatib, M., & Sabbah, E. (2008). Language choice in mobile text messages among Jordanian university students. *SKY Journal of Linguistics, 21*, 37–65.

Allen, R. (2007). Arabic – "flavor of the moment": Whence, why, and how? *Modern Language Journal, 91*(2), 258–261.

Allmann, K. (2009). Arabic language use online: Social, political, and technological dimensions of multilingual internet communication. *Monitor*, 61–76.

Al-Maghrebi, A. (1908). *Al-Ishtiqaaq wa-Ta'riib*. Fajjalah, Egypt: Al-Hilal Publications.

Al-Mansour, N. (1998). Linguistic constraints on code-switching: A case study of Saudi-spoken Arabic-English code-switcing. (Unpublished doctoral dissertation). University of Florida, Gainesville.

Almubayei, D. (2007). Language and the shaping of the Arab-American identity. *UTA Working Papers in Linguistics, 2*, 91–119.

Al-Muhammadi, Š. (2013). *Al-'amaala al-ajnabiyya bi-duwal al-khaliij al-'arabi wa ishkaaliyyat al-hawiyya al-thaqaafiyya al-wattaniyya* [Foreign workers in the Gulf states and problem for the cultural nation-state identity]. Paper presented at the Second

International Conference on the Arabic Language. Retrieved from www.alarabiah. org/index.php?op=view_all_studies&id=19

Al-Muhannadi, M. (1991). A sociolinguistic study of women's speech in Qatar. (Unpublished doctoral dissertation). University of Essex, UK.

Al-Muusa, N. (2003). *Al-thunaa'iyyaat fii qaḍaaya al-lugha al-'arabiyya min 'aṣr al-nahḍah ila 'aṣr l-'awlamah* [Dualisms in questions about the Arabic language from the renaissance to globalization]. Beirut: Daar Al-Shurooq.

Al-Nafisi, A. (1999). Iran wa al-khaliij [Iran and the Gulf]. Kuwait: Daar Qirtaas.

Al-Nassar, Ṣ. (2012). *ḍa'f al-ṭalabah fi l-lugha al-'arabiyya: qiraa'a fi asbaab al-ḍa'f wa-aathaarih fi ḍaw' al-buħuuth wa-l-diraasaat al-'ilmiyya.* [Students' weakness in the Arabic language: Reading into the causes of the weakness and its effects in the light of findings from scholarly research and studies]. Paper presented at the First International Conference on the Arabic Language, Beirut, 19–23 March. Retrieved from www.alarabiah.org/index.php?op=view_all_studies&id=15

Al Natour, M. (2012). Forms and rhetoric of resistance to oppressive authority in the contemporary Arabic novel. (Unpublished doctoral thesis). University of Arkansas, Fayetteville.

Al-Oliemat, A. (1998). Attitudes of Jordanian members of Parliament towards Arabization from a language planning perspective. (Master's thesis). Yarmouk University, Irbid, Jordan.

Alosh, M. (1997). *Learner, text, and context in foreign language acquisition.* Columbus, OH: Ohio State University Press.

Alosh, M. (2009). The Arabic language continuum: At which point to start? *NECTFL Review, 64,* 53–58.

Al-Rafi'i, M. S. (2002). *Tahta raayet Al-Qur'an* [Under the banner of Qur'an]. Saida, Lebanon: Al-Maktaba Al-'Aṣriyya.

Al-Rojaie, Y. (2013). Regional dialect leveling in Najdi Arabic: The case of the deaffrication of [k] in the Qaṣīmī dialect. *Language Variation and Change, 25*(1), 43–63.

Al-Sa'di, A. (2012). *Ad-da'wa ila 'aamiyyat al-lughah al-'arabiyyah manhaj li-ba'd al-madaaris al-lughawiyyah al-hadiithah* [The call for colloquialization of the Arabic language, a methodology for some modern language schools]. Paper presented at the First International Conference on the Arabic Language, Beirut, 19–23 March. Retrieved from www.alarabiah.org/index.php?op=view_all_studies&id=15

Al-Saħmaraani, A. (2002). *Waylaat al-'awlamah 'ala d-diin wa-l-lugha wa-l-thaqaafah* [Scourges of globalization on religion, language, and culture]. Beirut: Daar Al-Nafaa'is.

Al-Saleem, S. (2011). Language and identity in social networking sites. *International Journal of Humanities and Social Science, 1*(19), 197–202.

Al-Salem, A. (2012). Juhuud al-mamlaka al-'arabiyya al-sa'uudiyya fii ja'l al-'arabiyya lugha 'aalamiyya [Efforts of the Kingdom of Saudi Arabia in making Arabic a global language]. Paper presented at the First International Conference on the Arabic Language, Beirut, 19–23 March. Retrieved from http://www.arabiclanguageic.org/view_page.php?id=2091

Al-Sharkawi, M. (2010). *The ecology of Arabic: A study of Arabicization.* Leiden: Brill.

Al-Shehri, A. (1993). Urbanisation and linguistic variation and change: A sociolinguistic study of the impact of urbanization on the linguistic behaviour of urbanised rural immigrants in Hijaz, Saudi Arabia. (Unpublished doctoral dissertation). University of Essex, UK.

Al-Tamimi, Y., & Gorgis, D. (2007). Romanised Jordanian Arabic e-messages. *International Journal of Language, Society and Culture, 21,* 1–12.

Al-Tawhiidi, A. (2002). *Al-Imtaaʿ wa-l-muʾaanasa* [Entertainment and sociability]. Almesh-kat.com Books. Available at: www.almeshkat.net.

Altenberg, E. (1991). Assessing first language vulnerability to attrition. In H. Seliger & R. Vago (Eds.), *First language attrition* (pp. 189–206). Cambridge, UK: Cambridge University Press.

Al-Toma, S. (1961). The Arabic writing system and proposals for its reform. *Middle East Journal, 15*(4), 403–415.

Al-Toma, S. (1969). *The problem of diglossia in Arabic: A comparative study of classical and Iraqi Arabic.* Cambridge, MA: Harvard University Press.

Al-Wer, E. (1991). Phonological variation in the speech of women from three urban areas in Jordan. (Unpublished doctoral thesis). University of Essex, UK.

Al-Wer, E. (1999). Why do different variables behave differently? Data from Arabic. In Y. Suleiman (Ed.), *Language and society in the Middle East and North Africa: Studies in identity and variation* (pp. 38–58). Richmond: Curzon.

Al-Wer, E. (2002). Education as a speaker variable. In A. Rouchdy (Ed.), *Language contact and language conflict in Arabic: Variations on a sociolinguistic theme* (pp. 41–53). London: RoutledgeCurzon.

Al-Wer, E. (2008). Variation. In K. Versteegh, M. Eid, A. Elgibali, M. Woidich, & A. Zaborski, (Eds.), *Encyclopedia of Arabic language and linguistics* (pp. 627–37). Leiden: Brill.

Al-Wer, E. (2007). The formation of the dialect of Amman: From chaos to order. In C. Miller, E. Al-Wer, D. Caubet, & J. Watson (Eds.), *Arabic in the city: Issues in dialect contact and language variation* (pp. 55–76). London: Routledge.

Al-Wer, E. (2014). Language and gender in the Middle East and North Africa. In S. Ehrlich, M. Meyerhoff, & J. Holmes (Eds.), *The handbook of language, gender, and sexuality (2nd Ed.)* (pp. 396–411). Oxford: Wiley-Blackwell.

Al-Wer, E., & De Jong, R. (2009). *Arabic dialectology.* Leiden: Brill.

Amara, M. (2005). Language, migration and urbanization: The case of Bethlehem. *Linguistics, 43*, 883–902.

Amara, M., Spolsky, B., Tushyeh, H. (1999). Sociolinguistic reflexes of socio-political patterns in Bethlehem: Preliminary studies. In Y. Suleiman (Ed.), *Language and Society in the Middle East and North Africa: Studies in variation and identity* (pp. 58–80). London: Curzon Press.

Anderson, C. (2013). I talk it and I feel it: Language attitudes of Moroccan University Students. (Unpublished doctoral dissertation). Swarthmore College, Swarthmore, PA.

Anderson, G.L. (1989). Critical ethnography in education: Origins, current status, and new directions. *Review of Educational Research, 59*(3), 249–270.

Anderson, R. (1999). Loss of gender agreement in L1 attrition: Preliminary results. *Bilingual Research Journal, 23*, 319–338.

Anderson, R. (2001). Lexical morphology and verb use in child first language loss. A preliminary case study investigation. *International Journal of Bilingualism, 5*, 377–401.

Androutsopoulos, J. (2007). Language choice and code-switching in German-based diasporic web forums. In B. Danet, & S. Herring (Eds.), *The multilingual internet: Language, culture and communication online* (pp. 340–361). Oxford: Oxford University Press.

Androutsopoulos, J. (2013a). Computer-mediated communications and linguistic landscapes. In J. Holmes & K. Hazen (Eds.), *Research methods in sociolinguistics: A practical guide.* (pp. 47–90). Oxford: Wiley-Blackwell.

Androutsopoulos, J. (2013b). Networked multilingualism: Some language practices on Facebook and their implications. *International Journal of Bilingualism*, Epub DOI: 10.1177/1367006913489198.

Anis, I. (1959). *Muḥaḍaraat 'an mustaqbal al-lugha al-muštaraka.* Cairo: The Arab League.

Antaki, C., & Widdicombe, S. (1998). Identity as an achievement and as a tool. In C. Antaki & S. Widdicombe (Eds.), *Identities in talk* (pp. 1–14). Thousand Oaks, CA: Sage.

Antonius, G. (1938). *The Arab Awakening: The story of the Arab national movement.* London: Hamish Hamilton.

Anttila, A. (1997). Deriving variation from grammar. In F. Hinskens, R. van Hout, & W. L. Wetzels (Eds.), *Variation, change and phonological theory* (pp. 35–68). Amsterdam: John Benjamins.

Aoun, J., Benmamoun, E., & Choueiri, L. (2010). *The Syntax of Arabic.* Cambridge, UK: Cambridge University Press.

Appadurai, A. (1986). Theory in anthropology: Center and periphery. *Comparative Studies in Society and History, 28*(2), 356–361.

Appel, R., & Muysken, P. (1987). *Language contact and bilingualism.* New York: Edward Arnold.

Aram, D., Korat, O., & Hassunah-Arafat, S. (2013). *The contribution of early home literacy activities to first grade reading and writing achievements in Arabic.* Springer. Epub ahead of print. DOI 10.1007/s11145-013-9430-y.

Argenter, J. A. (2001). Code switching and dialogism: Verbal practices among Catalan Jews in the middle Ages. *Language in Society, 30,* 377–402.

Aruri, N. H. (1969). The Arab-American community of Springfield, Massachusetts. In E. C. Hagopian & A. Paden (Eds.), *The Arab American: Studies in assimilation* (pp. 50–66). Wilmette, IL: Medina University International Press.

Asker, A., & Martin-Jones, M. (2013). A classroom is not a classroom if students are talking to me in Berber: Language ideologies and multilingual resources in secondary school English classes in Libya. *Language and Education, 27*(4), 343–355.

Atawneh, A. (1992). Codemixing in Arabic-English bilinguals. In E. Broselow, M. Eid, & J. MacCarthy (Eds.), *Perspectives on Arabic Linguistics IV* (pp. 219–241). Amsterdam: John Benjamins.

Auer, P. (1998). *Codeswitching in conversation: Language, interaction and identity.* London: Routledge.

Aune, K. (2003). Prior pidginization and creolization in Moroccan Arabic. (Unpublished master's thesis). The University of Montana, Missoula.

Avram, A. (2010). An outline of Romanian pidgin Arabic. *Journal of Language Contact, 3,* 20–36.

Ayari, S. (1996). Diglossia and illiteracy in the Arab world. *Language, Culture and Curriculum, 9*(3) 243–253.

Badawi, S. A. (1973). *Mustawayat al-lugha al-'arabiyya al-mu'asira fi misr* [Levels of Contemporary Arabic in Egypt]. Cairo: Dar al-Ma'arif.

Baker, C. (1992). *Attitudes and language.* Clevedon: Multilingual Matters.

Bakhtin, M. (1986). The problem of speech genres. In C. Emerson & M. Holquist (Eds.), *Speech genres and other late essays* (V. W. McGee, trans.) (pp. 60–102). Austin, TX: University of Texas Press.

Bakir, M. (2010). Notes on the verbal system of Gulf Pidgin Arabic. *Journal of Pidgin and Creole Languages, 25*(2), 201–228.

Bale, J. (2010). Arabic as a heritage language in the United States. *International Multilingual Research Journal, 4*(2), 125–151.

Bani-Ismail, I. (2012). "Arabizi" as used by undergraduate students in some Jordanian universities: A sociolinguistic study. (Master's thesis). Yarmouk University, Irbid, Jordan.

Barakat, H. (1993). *The Arab World.* Berkeley, CA: University of California Press.

Barkat, M., Ohala, J., & Pellegrino, F. (1999). Prosody as a distinctive feature for the discrimination of Arabic dialects. In Proceedings of *Eurospeech 99.* Budapest, Hungary, September 5–9.

Barker, G. (1947). Social functions of language in a Mexican-American community. *Acta-Americana, 5,* 185–202.

Barnett, M. (1995). Sovereignty, nationalism, and regional order in the Arab States System. *International Organization, 49*(3), 479–510.

Baron, N. S. (2009). Are digital media changing language? *Educational Leadership, 66*(6), 42–46.

Barontini, A., & Ziamari, K. (2009). Comment des (jeunes) femmes marocaines parlent "masculine": tentative de définition sociolinguistique [How (young) Moroccan women speak "masculine": Attempted sociolinguistic definition]. *Estudios de Dialectología Norteafricana y Andalusí (EDNA), 13,* 153–172.

Bassiouney, R. (2006). *Functions of code switching in Egypt: Evidence from monologues.* Leiden: Brill.

Bassiouney, R. (2009a). The variety of housewives and cockroaches: Examining code-choice in advertisements in Egypt. In E. Al-Wer & R. de Jong (Eds.), *Arabic Dialectology* (pp. 273–285). Amsterdam: Brill.

Bassiouney, R. (2009b). *Arabic sociolinguistics.* Edinburgh: Edinburgh University Press.

Bassiouney, R. (2010). Identity and code-choice in the speech of educated women and men in Egypt: Evidence from talk shows. In R. Bassiouney (Ed.), *Arabic and the media* (pp. 97–123). Leiden: Brill.

Bassiouney, R. (2013). The social motivation of code-switching in mosque sermons in Egypt. *International Journal of the Sociology of Language, 220,* 49–66.

Bateson, M.C. (1967). *Arabic language handbook.* Washington, DC: Center for Applied Linguistics.

Battenburg, J. (2006). English language teaching in Tunisia, 5–12. Retrieved from http://cla.calpoly.edu/$jbattenb/world/tunisia.html.

Bayyoumi, S. (2005). *Umm al-lughaat: diraasah fii khaṣaa'iṣ al-lughah al-'arabiyyah wa-l-nuhooḍ bi-ha* [The mother of languages: A study in the attributes of the Arabic language and uplifting it]. Egypt: Kotobarabia.com.

Behnstedt, P. (1989). Christlisch-Aleppinische Texte. *Zeischrift für Arabische Linguistik, 20,* 43–96.

Behnstedt, P. (1997). *Sprachatlas von Syrien.* Wiesbaden: Harrassowitz Verlag.

Behnstedt, P. (2006). Dialect geography. In K. Versteegh, M. Eid, A. Elgibali, M. Woidich, & A. Zaborski, (Eds.), Encyclopedia of Arabic language and linguistics (pp. 583–593). Leiden: Brill.

Behnstedt, P., & Woidich, M. (2013). Dialectology. In J. Owens (Ed.), *The Oxford handbook of Arabic linguistics* (pp. 300–325). Oxford: Oxford University Press.

Belazi, H.M. (1991). Multilingualism in Tunisia and code-switching among educated Tunisian bilinguals. (Unpublished doctoral dissertation). Cornell University, Ithaca, NY.

Belazi, H.M., Rubin, E.J., & Toribio, A.J. (1994). Code-switching and X-Bar Theory: The functional head constraint. *Linguistic Inquiry, 25*, 221–237.

Belhadj-Tahar, K. (2013). Aspects of women's bilingual behaviour in Tlemcen speech community. (Unpublished master's thesis). Abou Bakr Belkaid University, Tlemcen.

Belnap, K. (1991). Grammatical agreement variation in Cairene Arabic. (Unpublished doctoral thesis). University of Pennsylvania, Philadelphia.

Benmamoun, E. (2000). *The feature structure of functional categories.* New York: Oxford University Press.

Benmamoun, E. (2001). Language identities in Morocco: A historical overview. *Studies in the Linguistic Sciences, 31*(1), 95–106.

Benmamoun, E., Abunasser, M., Al-Sabbagh, R., Bidaoui, A., & Shalash, D. (2014). The location of sentential negation in Arabic varieties. *Brill's Annual of Afroasiatic Languages and Linguistics.*

Benmamoun, E., Albirini, A., Montrul, S., & Saadah, E. (2014). Arabic plurals and root and pattern morphology in Palestinian and Egyptian heritage speakers. *Linguistic Approaches to Bilingualism, 4*(1), 89–123.

Benmamoun, E., Montrul, S., & Polinsky, M. (2010). White paper: Prolegomena to heritage linguistics. Retrieved from http://nhlrc.ucla.edu/pdf/HL-whitepaper.pdf.

Benrabah, M. (2007). Language-in-education planning in Algeria: Historical development and current issues. *Language Policy, 6*, 225–252.

Benrabah, M. (2013). *Language conflict in Algeria: From colonialism to post-independence.* Bristol: Multilingual Matters.

Bentahila, A. (1983a). *Language attitudes among Arabic-French bilinguals in Morocco.* Bristol: Multilingual Matters.

Bentahila, A. (1983b). Motivations for code-switching among Arabic-French bilinguals in Morocco. *Language and Communication, 3*(3), 233–243.

Bentahila, A., & Davies, E. (1983). The syntax of Arabic-French code-switching. *Lingua, 59*, 301–330.

Bentahila, A., & Davies, E. (1995). Patterns of code-switching and patterns of language contact. *Lingua, 96*, 75–93.

Bentahila, A., & Davies, E. (1998). Codeswitching: An unequal partnership. In R. Jacobson (Ed.), *Codeswitching worldwide* (pp. 25–49). Berlin: Mouton De Gruyter.

Bentahila, A., & Davies, E. (2002). Language mixing in rai music: Localisation or globalisation? *Language and Communication, 22*, 187–207.

Bhatt, M.R. (2008). In other words: Language mixing, identity representations, and third space. *Journal of Sociolinguistics, 12*(2), 177–200.

Bhatt, R. & Bolonyai, A. (2008). Code-switching and optimal grammars. Proceedings of the Annual Meeting of the Chicago Linguistic Society, *44*(2), 109–122.

Bhatt, R., & Bolonyai, A. (2011). Code-switching and the optimal grammar of bilingual language use. *Bilingualism: Language and Cognition, 14*(4), 522–546.

Bhavnani, K.-K. (1988). What's power got to do with it? Empowerment and social research. In I. Parke & J. Shotter (Eds.), *Deconstructing social psychology* (pp. 141–152). London: Routledge.

Bianchi, R. (2013). Arab English: The Case of 3arabizi/Arabish on Mahjoob.com. *Voices in Asia Journal, 1*(1), 82–96.

Bishr, K. (2007). *Al-Lugha Al-'arabiyya bayna l-wahm wa suu'i l-fahm* [Arabic language between illusion and misunderstanding]. Cairo: Daar Al-Ghariib.

Bitar, S. (2009). Palestinian-Levantine Dialect Diaspora: Exploring its role in maintaining Palestinian cultural heritage & identity. (Master's thesis). The University of Montana, Missoula.

Bitar, S. (2011). Language, identity, and Arab nationalism: Case study of Palestine. *Journal of Middle Eastern and Islamic Studies (in Asia)*, 5(4), 48–64.

Bizri, F. (2010). *Pidgin Madame: Une grammaire de la servitude*. Paris: Geuthner.

Blakely, J. (2005). Acculturation and the use of media among Arab women immigrants living in metropolitan Detroit. (Unpublished doctoral dissertation). Regent University, Virginia Beach, VA.

Blanc, H. (1960). Style variations in Arabic: A sample of interdialectal conversation. In C.A. Ferguson (Ed.), *Contributions to Arabic linguistics* (pp. 81–156). Cambridge, MA: Harvard University Press.

Blanc, H. (1964). *Communal dialects of Baghdad*. Cambridge, MA: Harvard University Press.

Blau, J. (1981). *The renaissance of modern Hebrew and modern standard Arabic: Parallels and differences in the revival of two Semitic languages*. Berkeley, CA: University of California Press.

Blau, J., & Suleiman, Y. (1996). Language and ethnic identity in Kurdistan: A historical overview. In Y. Suleiman (Ed.), *Language and identity in the Middle East and North Africa* (pp. 153–164). Richmond: Curzon.

Blom, J. P., & Gumperz, J. J. (1972). Social meaning in linguistic structure: Code-switching in Norway. In J. J. Gumperz & D. Hymes (Eds.), *Directions in sociolinguistics: The ethnography of communication* (pp. 407–434). New York: Holt, Reinehart and Winston.

Blommaert, J. (2010). *The sociolinguistics of Globalization*. Cambridge, UK: Cambridge University Press.

Bloomfield, L. (1927). Literate and illiterate speech. *American Speech, 2*, 432–439.

Boersma, P., & Hayes, B. (2001). Empirical tests of the gradual learning algorithm. *Linguistic Inquiry 32*, 45–86.

Bokamba, E. (1988). Code-mixing, language variation and linguistic theory: Evidence from Bantu languages. *Lingua, 76*, 21–62.

Bos, P. (1997). *Development of bilingualism: A study of school-age Moroccan children in the Netherlands*. Tilburg, the Netherlands: Tilburg University Press.

Bouamrane, A. (1986). Aspects of the sociolinguistic situation in Algeria. (Unpublished doctoral dissertation). University of Aberdeen, UK.

Boumans, L. (1998). *The syntax of codeswitching: Analyzing Moroccan Arabic/Dutch conversation*. Tilburg: Tilburg University Press.

Boumans, L. (2006). The attributive possessive in Moroccan Arabic spoken by young bilinguals in the Netherlands and their peers in Morocco. *Bilingualism: Language and Cognition, 9*, 213–231.

Boumans, L., & de Ruiter, J.J. (2002). Moroccan Arabic in the European diaspora. In A. Rouchdy (Ed.), *Language contact and language conflict phenomena in Arabic* (pp. 259–285). London: Routledge-Curzon.

Bourdieu, P. (1977). *Outline of a theory of practice*. Cambridge, UK: Cambridge University Press.

Bourdieu, P. (1999). *Language and symbolic power*. Cambridge, MA: Harvard University Press.

Boussofara-Omar, N. (1999). Arabic diglossic switching: An application of Myers-Scotton's MLF model. (Unpublished doctoral dissertation). University of Texas, Austin.

Boussofara-Omar, N. (2003). Revisiting Arabic diglossic switching in light of the MLF model and its sub-models: The 4-M model and the Abstract Level model. *Bilingualism: Language and Cognition, 6*(1), 33–46.

Boyd, D. (2006). Friends, friendsters, and top 8: Writing community into being on social network sites. *First Monday, 11*(12). Retrieved from http://firstmonday.org/htbin/cgiwrap/bin/ojs/index.php/fm/article/view/1418/1336

Britain, D. (2009). "Big bright lights" versus "green and pleasant land"? The unhelpful dichotomy of "urban" v "rural" in dialectology. In E. Al-Wer & R. de Jong (Eds.), *Arabic dialectology* (pp. 223–248). Leiden: Brill.

Brosh, H., & Olshtain, E. (1995). Language skills and the curriculum of a diglossic language. *Foreign Language Annals, 28*(2), 247–260.

Brown, P., & Levinson, S. C. (1987). *Politeness: Some universals in language usage*. Cambridge, UK: Cambridge University Press.

Bruns, A., Highfield, T., & Burgess, J. (2013). The Arab Spring and social media audiences: English and Arabic Twitter users and their networks. *American Behavioral Scientist, 57*(7), 871–898.

Brustad, K. (2000). *The syntax of spoken Arabic: A comparative study of Moroccan, Egyptian, Syrian, and Kuwaiti dialects*. Washington, DC: Georgetown University Press.

Bucholtz, M. (2003). Sociolinguistic nostalgia and the authentication of identity. *Journal of Sociolinguistics, 7*(3), 398–416.

Bucholtz, M., & Hall, K. (2004). Language and identity. In A. Duranti (Ed.), *A companion to linguistic anthropology* (pp. 369–394). Malden, MA: Blackwell.

Bucholtz, M., Liang, A. C., & Sutton, L. (1999). *Reinventing identities*. Oxford: Oxford University Press.

Burrows, M. (1986). "Mission civilisatrice": French cultural policy in the Middle East, 1860–1914. *The Historical Journal, 29*(1), 109–135.

Cadora, F. (1992). *Bedouin, village, and urban Arabic: An ecolinguistic study*. Leiden: Brill.

Callahan, L. (2004). *Spanish/English codeswitching in a written corpus*. Amsterdam: John Benjamins.

Cameron, D. (2006). Gender and the English language. In B. Aarts & A. McMahon (Eds.), *The handbook of English linguistics* (pp. 724–741). Oxford: Blackwell.

Campbell, R., & Christian, D. (2003). Directions in research: Intergenerational transmission of heritage languages. *Heritage Language Journal, 1*(1), 1–44.

Canagarajah, A. S. (2008). Language shift and the family: Questions from the Sri Lankan Tamil diaspora. *Journal of Sociolinguistics, 12*(2), 143–176.

Cantineau, J. (1937). Etudes sur quelques parlers de nomades arabes d'Orient. *Annales de l'Institut d'Etudes Orientales, 2*, 1–118.

Carreira, M., & Kagan, O. (2011). The results of the heritage language survey: Implications for teaching, curriculum design, and professional development. *Foreign Language Annals, 44*(1), 40–64.

Castells, M. (2009). *The rise of the network society* (2nd ed.). Oxford: Wiley-Blackwell.

Caton, S. (1991). Diglossia in North Yemen: A case of competing linguistic communities. *Southwest Journal of Linguistics, 10*(1), 143–159.

Caubet, D. (1998). Étude sociolinguistique des traits préhilaliens dans un dialecte en voie d'urbanisation à Fès. In J. Aguadé, P. Cressier & Á. Vincente (Eds.), *Peuplement et *arabisationau Maghreb occidental. Dialectologie et histoire* (pp. 165–175). Madrid and Zaragoza: Casa de Velazquez.

Caubet, D. (2001). Maghrebine Arabic in France. In G. Extra & D. Gorter (Eds.), *The other languages of Europe: Demographic, sociolinguistic, and educational perspectives* (pp. 261–277). Clevedon: Multilingual Matters.

Caubet, D. (2002). Jeux de langues: humor and codeswitching in the Maghreb. In A. Rouchdy (Ed.), *Language contact and language conflict phenomena in Arabic* (pp. 233–258). London: RoutledgeCurzon.

Caubet, D. (2004). *Les mots du bled.* Paris: L'Harmattan.

Chakrani, B. (2010). A sociolinguistic investigation of language attitudes among youth in Morocco. (Unpublished doctoral dissertation). University of Illinois, Urbana-Champaign.

Chakrani, B. (2012). Arabic standardization. History of and motivation for Arabic standardization. *The Encyclopedia of Applied Linguistics.* DOI: 10.1002/9781405198431. wbeal0036.

Chambers, J.K. (2003). *Sociolinguistic theory: Linguistic variation and its social significance.* Oxford: Blackwell.

Chambers, J.K. (2013). Studying language variation: An informal epistemology (2nd ed.). In J.K. Chambers & N. Schilling-Estes (Eds.), *The handbook of language variation and change* (pp. 1–15). Oxford: Blackwell.

Chambers, J.K., & Schilling-Estes, N. (Eds.) (2013). *The handbook of language variation and change.* Oxford: Blackwell.

Chatty, D. (2010). The Bedouin in contemporary Syria: The persistence of tribal authority and control. *The Middle East Journal, 64*(1), 29–49.

Chejne, A. (1969). *The Arabic language: Its role in history.* Minneapolis: University of Minnesota Press.

Cheshire, J. (2002). Sex and gender in variation research. In J.K. Chambers, P.J. Trudgill, & N. Schilling-Estes (Eds.), *The handbook of language variation and change* (pp. 423–443). Oxford: Blackwell.

Chomsky, N. (1965). *Aspects of the theory of syntax.* Cambridge, MA: MIT.

Chtato, M. (1997). The influence of the Berber language on Moroccan Arabic. *International Journal of the Sociology of Language, 123*(1), 101–118.

Clark, H. (1996). *Using language.* Cambridge, UK: Cambridge University Press.

Clyne, M. (Ed.) (1992). *Pluricentric languages: Differing norms in different nations.* Berlin: De Gruyter Mouton.

Clyne, M. (2003). *Dynamics of language contact: English and immigrant languages.* Cambridge, UK: Cambridge University Press.

Coetzee, A.W. (2006). Variation as accessing "non-optimal" candidates. *Phonology, 23,* 337–385.

Cohen, D. (1962). Koinè, langues communes ou dialectes arabes. *Arabica, 9,* 119–144.

Cohen, D. (1973). Variantes, variétés dialectales et contacts linguistiques en domaine arabe. *Bulletin de la Société de Linguistique de Paris, 68,* 215–248.

Cohen, D. (1981). Remarques historiques et sociolinguistiques sur les parlers des juifs maghrébins. *International Journal of the Sociology of Language, 30,* 91–106.

Cohen, D., & Caubet, D. (2000). Un questionnaire différentiel pour la dialectologie arabe. *Oriente Moderno* XIX (LXXX), n. s. 1. *Studi di Dialettologia Araba,* 1–23.

Cole, J. (2007). *Napoleon's Egypt: Invading the Middle East.* New York: Palgrave McMillan.

Conversi, D. (1995). Reassessing current theories of nationalism: Nationalism as boundary maintenance and creation. *Nationalism and Ethnic Politics, 1*(1), 73–85.

Cooper, R. (1989). *Language planning and social change.* Cambridge, UK: Cambridge University Press.

Cooper, R. L., & Fishman, J. A. (1974). The study of language attitudes. *International Journal of the Sociology of Language, 3*, 5–19.

Cornips, L., & Hulk, A. (2006). External and internal factors in bilingual and bidialectal language development: Grammatical gender of the Dutch definite article. In C. Lefebvre, L. White, & C. Jourdan (Eds.), *L2 acquisition and Creole genesis: Dialogues* (pp. 355–378). Amsterdam: John Benjamins.

Corriente, F. (1976). From Old Arabic to Classical Arabic through the pre-Islamic koine: Some notes on the native grammarians' sources, attitudes and goals. *Journal of Semitic Studies, 21*, 64–98.

Coulmas, F. (Ed.) (1997). *The handbook of sociolinguistics.* Oxford: Blackwell.

Coupland, N. (2001). Dialect stylization in radio talk. *Language in society, 30*(3), 345–375.

Coupland, N. (2003). Introduction: Sociolinguistics and globalization. *Journal of Sociolinguistics, 7*(4), 465–472.

Coupland, N. (2007). *Style: Language variation and identity.* Cambridge, UK: Cambridge University Press.

Coupland, N., & Giles, H. (1988). Introduction: The communicative contexts of accommodation. *Language & Communication, 8*, 175–182.

Cowan, W. (1968). Notes toward a definition of modern standard Arabic. *Language Learning, 18*, 29–34.

Crawford, J. (2000). *At war with diversity: US language policy in an age of anxiety.* Clevedon: Multilingual Matters.

Creswell, J. (2003). *Research design: Qualitative, quantitative, and mixed methods.* Thousand Oaks, CA: Sage.

Critchfield, A. (2010). The other. In R. Jackson & M. Logg (Eds.), *Encyclopedia of identity* (vol. 1) (pp. 519–526). Thousand Oaks, CA: Sage.

Croft, W. (2000). *Explaining language change: An evolutionary approach.* London: Longman.

Croft, W. (2006). The relevance of an evolutionary model to historical linguistics. In O.N. Thomsen (Ed.), *Competing models of linguistic change: Evolution and beyond* (pp. 91–132). Amsterdam: John Benjamins.

Crotty, M. (1998). *The Foundations of social research: Meaning and perspective in the research process.* London: Sage.

Crystal, D. (2000). *Language death.* Cambridge, UK: Cambridge University Press.

Crystal, D. (2001). *Language and the internet.* Cambridge, UK: Cambridge University Press.

Cummins, J. (2000). Forward. In R. González & I. Melis (Eds.), *Language ideologies: Education and the social implications of official language* (pp. ix–xxi). Mahwah, NJ: Lawrence Erlbaum.

Dabashi, H. (2012). *The Arab Spring: The end of postcolonialism.* New York: Zed Books.

Daher, J. (1998). Gender in linguistic variation: The variable (q) in Damascus Arabic. In *Perspectives on Arabic linguistics,* (vol. XI, pp. 183–205). Amsterdam: John Benjamins.

Daher, J. (1999). (θ) and (ð) as ternary and binary variables in Damascene Arabic. In *Perspectives on Arabic linguistics*, xii (pp. 163–202). Amsterdam: John Benjamins.

Daoud, M. (2012). Political identity formation in postwar Lebanon. (Unpublished doctoral dissertation). Lebanese American University, Lebanon.

Davies, E., & Bentahila, A. (2006a). Ethnicity and language. In K. Versteegh, M. Eid, A. Elgibali, M. Woidich, & A. Zaborski, (Eds.), *Encyclopedia of Arabic language and linguistics* (pp. ii: 58-D5). Leiden: Brill.

Davies, E., & Bentahila, A. (2006b). Code switching and the globalisation of popular music: the case of North African rap and rai. *Multilingua, 25*, 367–392.

Davies, E., & Bentahila, A. (2008). Code switching as a poetic device: Examples from rai lyrics. *Language & Communication, 28*, 1–20.

Dawisha, A. (2002). *Arab nationalism in the twentieth century: From triumph to despair.* Princeton, NJ: Princeton University Press.

Dawood, M. (2012). *'alaaqat al-lugha al-'arabiyya bi-l-siyaada al-waṭaniyyah wa-l-hawiyyah* [The relationship of the Arabic language to national sovereignty and identity]. Paper presented at the First International Conference on the Arabic Language, Beirut, 19–23 March. Retrieved from www.alarabiah.org/index.php?op=view_all_studies&id=15

DeCamp, D. (1971). Implicational scales and sociolinguistic linearity. *Linguistics, 9*(73), 30–43.

De Fina, A. (2007). Code-switching and the construction of ethnic identity in a community of practice. *Language in Society, 36*(3), 371–392.

Debrix, F. (Ed.) (2003). *Language, agency, and politics in a constructed world.* New York: M.E. Sharpe.

De Jong (2009). *Arabic dialectology* (pp. 77–98). Leiden: Brill.

Dendane, Z. (2007). Sociolinguistic variation and attitudes towards language behaviours in an Algerian context: The case of Tlemcen Arabic. (Unpublished doctorate thesis). University of Oran.

Domínguez, L. (2009). Charting the route of bilingual development: Contributions from heritage speakers' early acquisition. *International Journal of Bilingualism, 13*(2), 271–287.

Dorian, N. (1994). Varieties of variation in a very small place: Social homogeneity, prestige norms and linguistic variation. *Language, 70*, 631–696.

Dorleijn, M., & Nortier, J. (2009). Code-switching and the internet. In B.E. Bullock & A.J. Toribio (Eds.), *The Cambridge handbook of linguistic code-switching* (pp. 127–141). Cambridge, UK: Cambridge University Press.

Dubai School of Government. Arab Social Media Report. Retrieved from www.arabsocial-mediareport.com/home/index.aspx?&PriMenuID=1&mnu=Pri

Dweik, B.S. (1997). Attitudes of Arab students towards al-Fusha wal-Ammiyya. *Al-'Arabiyya, 30*, 48–31.

Eades, D. (2009). The Arabic dialect of a Šawāwī community of Northern Oman. In E. Al-Wer & R. De Jong (Eds.), *Arabic dialectology* (pp. 77–98). Leiden: Brill.

Eastman, C.M. (1983). *Language planning: An introduction.* Novato, CA: Chandler & Sharp Publishers.

Eastman, C.M. (1992). Codeswitching as an urban language contact phenomenon. *Journal of Multilingual and Multicultural Development, 13*, 1–17.

Eckert, P. (2000). *Language variation as a social practice: The linguistic construction of identity in Belten High.* Oxford: Blackwell.

Eckert, P. (2012). Three waves of variation study: The emergence of meaning in the study of variation. *Annual Review of Anthropology, 41*, 87–100.

Eckert, P., & McConnell-Ginet, S. (2003). *Language and gender.* Cambridge, UK: Cambridge University Press.

Edwards, J. (1992). Sociopolitical aspects of language maintenance and loss: Towards a typology of minority language situations. In W. Fase, K. Jaspaert, & S. Kroon (Eds.), *Maintenance and loss of minority languages* (pp. 37–54). Amsterdam: John Benjamins.

Ehrlich, S. (1997). Gender as social practice: Implications for second language acquisition. *Studies in Second Language Acquisition, 19*, 421–446.

Eid, M. (1988). Principles of code switching between standard and Egyptian Arabic. *Al-'Arabiyya, 21*, 51–79.

Eid, M. (1990). Arabic linguistics: The current scene. In M. Eid (Ed.), *Perspectives on Arabic Linguistics I* (pp. 3–37). Amsterdam: John Benjamins.

Eid, M. (1992). Directionality in Arabic-English code-switching. In A. Rouchdy (Ed.), *The Arabic language in America* (pp. 50–71). Detroit: Wayne State University Press.

Eid, M. (1994). "What's in a name?" Women in Egyptian obituaries. In Y. Suleiman (Ed.), *Arabic Sociolinguistics: issues and perspectives* (pp. 80–101). Richmond: Curzon.

Eid, M. (2002). Language is a choice: Variation in Egyptian women's written discourse. In Rouchdy, A. (Ed.), *Language contact and language conflict in Arabic: Variations on a sociolinguistic theme* (pp. 203–232). London: RoutledgeCurzon.

Eid, M. (2007). Arabic on the media: Hybridity and styles. In E. Ditters & H. Motzki (Eds.), *Approaches to Arabic linguistics: Presented to Kees Versteegh on the occasion of his sixtieth birthday* (pp. 403–434). Leiden: Brill.

Eid, P. (2003). The Interplay between ethnicity, religion, and gender among second-generation Christian and Muslim Arabs in Montreal. *Canadian Ethnic Studies, 35*(2), 30–60.

Eisele, J. C. (2002). Approaching diglossia: Authorities, values, and representations. In Rouchdy, A. (Ed.), *Language contact and language conflict in Arabic: Variations on a sociolinguistic theme* (pp. 3–23). London: RoutledgeCurzon.

El Aissati, A. (1996). Language loss among native speakers of Moroccan Arabic in the Netherlands. (Unpublished doctoral dissertation). University of Nijmegen, Netherlands.

El-Anani, M. (1971). Forms of address in Jordanian Arabic with some additional reference to speech fellowships. (Unpublished doctoral dissertation). University of Leeds, UK.

El-Dash, L., & Tucker, R. (1975). Subjective reactions to various speech styles in Egypt. *Linguistics, 166*, 33–54.

El-Hassan, S. (1977). Educated spoken Arabic in Egypt and the Levant: A critical review of diglossia and related concepts. *Archivum Linguisticum, 8*(2), 112–132.

Elsaadany, K. (2003). Code-alternation among Arab speakers in America. *Umm Al-Qura University Journal of Educational, Social Sciences and Humanities, 15*(2), 67–92.

El Saadawi, N. (1980). *The hidden face of Eve: Women in the Arab world.* London: Zed Press.

El Salman, M. (2003). The use of the /q/ variants in the Arabic dialect of Tirat Haifa. *Anthropological Linguistics, 45*(4), 413–426.

Elster, J. (1979). *Ulysses and the sirens.* Cambridge, UK: Cambridge University Press.

Elverskog, L. (1999). Verb morphology in Educated spoken Arabic. (Unpublished doctoral dissertation). Indiana University, Bloomington.

El-Yasin, M. (1985). Basic word order In Classical Arabic and Jordanian Arabic. *Lingua, 65*, 107–122.

Embarki, M., Yeou, M., Guilleminot, C., & Al Maqtari, S. (2007). An acoustic study of coarticulation in Modern Standard Arabic and dialectal Arabic: Pharyngealized vs non-pharyngealized articulation. Proceedings of the 16th ICPhS, Saarbrücken, 141–146.

Ennaji, M. (1988). Language planning in Morocco and changes in Arabic. International Journal of the Sociology of Language, 74, 9–39.

Ennaji, M. (1997). The sociology of Berber: Change and continuity. International Journal of the Sociology of Language, 123(1), 23–40.

Ennaji, M. (2005). Multilingualism, cultural identity, and education in Morocco. New York: Springer.

Ennaji, M. (2007). Arabic sociolinguistics and cultural diversity in Morocco. In E. Benmamoun (Ed.), Perspectives of Arabic linguistics XIX: Papers from the Nineteenth Annual Symposium on Arabic Linguistics (pp. 267–277). Amsterdam: John Benjamins.

Eriksen, T. (2007). Nationalism and the Internet. Nations and Nationalism, 13(1), 1–17.

Errihani, M. (2006). Language policy in Morocco: Problems and prospects of teaching Tamazight. Journal of North African Studies, 11(2), 143–154.

Ervin-Tripp, S. (2001). Variety, style-shifting, and ideology. In P. Eckert & J. Rickford (Eds.), Style and sociolinguistic variation (pp. 44–56). Cambridge, UK: Cambridge University Press.

Etling, B., Kelly, J., Faris, R., & Palfrey, J. (2010). Mapping the Arabic blogosphere: Politics and dissent online. New Media & Society, 12(8), 1225–1243.

Eviatar, Z., & Ibrahim, R. (2000). Bilingual is as bilingual does: Metalinguistic abilities of Arabic-speaking children. Applied Psycholinguistics, 21(4), 451–471.

Fahmy, Z. (2010). Media-capitalism: Colloquial mass culture and nationalism in Egypt, 1908–18. International Journal of Middle East Studies, 42, 83–103.

Fairclough, N. (1989). Language and power. London: Longman.

Fairclough, N (2006). Language and globalization. London: Routledge.

Fairclough, N., & Wodak, R. (1997). Critical discourse analysis. In T.A. van Dijk (Ed.), Discourse as social interaction (pp. 258–284). London: Sage.

Faiza, D. (2013). Arabization planning: Algeria as an instance. IOSR Journal of Humanities and Social Science, 18(4), 25–28.

Fase, W., Jaspaert, K., & Kroon, S. (1992). Introductory remarks. In W. Fase, K. Jaspaert, & S. Kroon (Eds.), Maintenance and loss of minority languages. Amsterdam: John Benjamins.

Fasold, R. (1991). The sociolinguistics of society. Oxford: Blackwell.

Ferguson, C. (1959a). Diglossia. Word, 15, 325–340.

Ferguson, C. (1959b). The Arabic koine. In R.K. Belnap & N. Haerixe (Eds.), Structuralist studies in Arabic linguistics: Charles A. Ferguson's papers, 1954–1994 (pp. 50–69). Leiden: Brill.

Ferguson, C. (1968). Myths about Arabic. In J. A. Fishman (ed.), Readings in the Sociology of Language (pp. 375–381). The Hague: De Gruyter Mouton.

Ferguson, C. (1991). Diglossia revisited. South West Journal of Linguistics, 10, 214–234.

Ferguson, C. (1996). Sociolinguistic perspectives: Papers on language in society, 1959–1994. Oxford: Oxford University Press.

Fetterman, D.M. (1989). Ethnography: Step by step. Newbury Park, CA: Sage.

Finlay, L. (2002). Negotiating the swamp: The opportunity and challenge of reflexivity in research practice. Qualitative Research, 2(2), 209–230.

Fishman, J.A. (1971). *Sociolinguistics.* Rowley, MA: Newbury House.

Fishman, J.A. (1967). Bilingualism with and without diglossia, diglossia with and without bilingualism. *Journal of Social Issues, 23,* 29–38.

Fishman, J.A. (1974). Language modernization and planning in comparison with other types of language modernization and planning. In J. Fishman (Ed.), *Advances in language planning* (pp. 79–102). The Hague, the Netherlands: De Gruyter Mouton.

Fishman, J.A. (1991). *Reversing language shift.* Clevedon: Multilingual Matters.

Fishman, J.A. (2001). *Can threatened languages be saved?* Clevedon: Multilingual.

Forum for Fusħa Arabic and its Literatures. Retrieved at www.ahlalhdeeth.com/vb/forum display.php?f=33

Fowler, R. (1985). Power. In T. Van Dijk (Ed.), *Handbook of discourse analysis: Discourse analysis in society* (vol. 4) (pp. 61–82). New York: Academic Press.

Fox, J. (2013). An introduction to religion and politics: Theory and practice. London: Routledge.

Fraser, N. (1990). Rethinking the public sphere: A contribution to the critique of actually existing democracy. *Social Text, 25/26,* 56–80.

Fück, J. (1950). *Arabiya: Untersuchungen zur arabischen Sprach- und Stilgeschichte.* Berlin: Akademie Verlag.

Gal, S. (1998). Multiplicity and contention among language ideologies. In B. Schieffelin, K. Woolard, P. Kroskrity (Eds.), *Language ideologies: Practice and theory* (pp. 317–331). Oxford: Oxford University Press.

Garafanga, J. (2007). Code-switching as a conversational strategy. In R. Auer & L. Wei (Eds.), *Handbook of multilingualism and multilingual communication* (pp. 271–314). Berlin: De Gruyter Mouton.

García-Sánchez, I. (2010). The politics of Arabic language education: Moroccan immigrant children's language socialization into ethnic and religious identities. *Linguistics and Education: An International Research Journal, 21*(3), 171–196.

Garrett, P. (2010). *Attitudes to language.* Cambridge, UK: Cambridge University Press.

Garrett, P., Coupland, N., & Williams, A. (2003). *Investigating language attitudes: Social meanings of dialect, ethnicity and performance.* Cardiff: University of Wales Press.

Garvin, P. (1993). A conceptual framework for the study of language standardization. *International Journal of the Sociology of Language, 100/101,* 37–54.

Gay, L.R., & Airasian, P. (2000). *Educational research: Competencies for analysis and application* (6th ed.). Upper Saddle River, NJ: Prentice-Hall.

Genoni, M. (2010). History of otherness. In R. Jackson & M. Hogg (Eds.), *Encyclopedia of identity* (vol. 1) (pp. 526–530). Thousand Oaks, CA: Sage.

Ghazali, S., Hamdi, R., & Barkat, M. (2002). *Speech rhythm variation in Arabic dialects.* Paper presented at *Speech Prosody* conference, Aix-en-Provence, France 11–13 April.

Ghazi, H. (2009). *Language standardisation and the question of the Kurdish varieties: The language debate in Iraqi Kurdistan.* Paper presented at the International Conference: The Kurds and Kurdistan: Identity, Politics History. 2–3 April, University of Exeter.

Gibson, M. (2002). Dialect levelling in Tunisian Arabic: Towards a new spoken standard. In A. Rouchdy (Ed.), *Language contact and language conflict in Arabic: Variations on a sociolinguistic theme* (pp. 24–40). London: RoutledgeCurzon.

Gibson, M. (2006). Implicational Scale. In K. Versteegh, M. Eid, A. Elgibali, M. Woidich, & A. Zaborski (Eds.), *Encyclopedia of Arabic language and linguistics* (pp. 318–325). Leiden: Brill.

Giles, H., & Billings, A. (2004). Assessing language attitudes: Speaker evaluation studies. In A. Davies & C. Elder (Eds.), *The handbook of applied linguistics* (pp. 187–209). Malden, MA: Blackwell.

Giles, H., Coupland, J., & Coupland, N. (1991). Accommodation theory: Communication, context, and consequence. In H. Giles, J. Coupland, & N. Coupland (Eds.), *Contexts of accommodation* (pp. 1–68). Cambridge, UK: Cambridge University Press.

Giles, H., & Powesland, P. (1997). Accommodation theory. In N. Coupland & A. Jaworski (Eds.), *Sociolinguistics: A reader* (pp. 232–239). Basingstoke: Palgrave Macmillan. (Reprinted from H. Giles & P. Powesland, P. (1975). *Speech style and social evaluation* (pp. 154–170). London: Academic Press.

Giles, H., & Smith, P. (1979). Accommodation theory: Optimal levels of convergence. In H. Giles & R. St. Clair (Eds.), *Language and social psychology* (pp. 45–65). Oxford: Blackwell.

Gill, H. (1999). Language choice, language policy and the tradition-modernity debate in culturally mixed postcolonial communities: France and the francophone Maghreb as a case study. In Y. Suleiman (Ed.), *Language and society in the Middle East and North Africa* (pp. 122–136). Richmond: Curzon.

Glesne, C. (2010). *Becoming qualitative researchers: An introduction* (4th ed.). Boston: Pearson.

Goffman, E. (1981). *Forms of talk*. Philadelphia: University of Pennsylvania Press.

Gogonas, N. (2011). Religion as a core value in language maintenance: Arabic speakers in Greece. *International Migration, 50*(2), 113–126.

Gomaa, Y. A. (2011). Language maintenance and transmission: The case of Egyptian Arabic in Durham, UK. *International Journal of English Linguistics, 1*(1), 46–53.

Goodwin, M.H. (2003). The relevance of ethnicity, class, and gender in children's peer negotiations. In J. Holmes & M. Meyerhoff (Eds.), *The handbook of language and gender* (pp. 229–251) Oxford: Blackwell.

Gordon, M. (2013). *Labov: A guide for the perplexed*. New York: Bloomsbury Academic.

Gralewski, M. (2011). The philosophical underpinnings of social constructionist discourse analysis. *Lodz Papers in Pragmatics, 7*(1), 155–171.

Grandguillaume, G. (1990). Language and legitimacy in the Maghreb. In B. Weinstein (Ed.), *Language policy and political development* (pp. 150–166). Norwood, NJ: Ablex Publishing.

Gully, A. (1997). The discourse of Arabic advertising: Preliminary investigations. *Journal of Arabic and Islamic Studies, 1*, 1–49.

Gully, A. (2012). It's only a flaming game: A case study of Arabic computer-mediated communication. *British Journal of Middle Eastern Studies, 39*(1), 1–18.

Gumperz, J. (1962). Types of linguistic communities. *Anthropological Linguistics, 4*(1), 28–40. Reprinted in J. Fishman (Ed.), *Readings in the sociology of language* (pp. 460–472). Berlin: De Gruyter Mouton.

Gumperz, J. (1964). Linguistic and social interaction in two communities. *American Anthropologist, 66*(6), 137–153.

Gumperz, J. (1972). The speech community. In P. P. Giglioli (Ed.), *Language and social context: Selected readings, 9* (pp. 219–231). Baltimore: Penguin Books.

Gumperz, J. (1976). The sociolinguistic significance of conversational code-switching. In *Papers on language and context, working paper no. 46.* (pp. 1–26). Berkeley: University of California Language Behaviour Research Laboratory.

Gumperz, J. (1982). *Discourse strategies*. Cambridge, UK: Cambridge University Press.

Gumperz, J. (1992). Contextualization and understanding. In A. Duranti & C. Goodwin (Eds.), *Rethinking context: Language as an interactive phenomenon* (pp. 229–252). Cambridge, UK: Cambridge University Press.

Gumperz, J. (1993). Transcribing conversational exchanges. In J. A. Edwards & M.D. Lampert (Eds.), *Talking data. Transcription and coding in discourse research* (pp. 91–121). Hillsdale, NJ: Lawrence Erlbaum.

Gumperz J.J. (1982). *Language and social identity*. Cambridge, UK: Cambridge University Press.

Gunter, B., & Dickinson, R. (2013). *News media in the Arab world: A study of 10 Arab and Muslim countries*. New York: Bloomsbury.

Haak, M., DeJong, R., & Versteegh, K. (Eds.) (2004). *Approaches to Arabic dialects: A collection of articles presented to Manfred Woidich on the occasion of his sixtieth birthday*. Leiden: Brill.

Habib, R. (2010). Rural migration and language variation in Hims, Syria. *SKY Journal of Linguistics, 23*, 61–99.

Hachimi, A. (2001). Shifting sands: Language and gender in Moroccan Arabic. In M. Hellinger & H. Bußmann (Eds.), *Gender across languages: The linguistic representation of women and men* (pp. 27–51). Amsterdam: John Benjamins.

Hachimi, A. (2007). Becoming Casablancan: Fessis in Casablanca as a case study. In C. Miller, E. Al-Wer, D. Caubet, & J. Watson (Eds.), *Arabic in the city: Issues in language variation and change* (pp. 97–122). London: Routledge.

Hachimi, A. (2011). Réinterprétation sociale d'un vieux parler citadin maghrébin à Casablanca. *Langage et Société, 138*(4), 21–42.

Hachimi, A. (2012). The urban and the urbane: Identities, language ideologies, and Arabic dialects in Morocco. *Language in Society, 41*, 321–341.

Hachimi, A. (2013). The Maghreb-Mashreq language ideology and the politics of identity in a globalized Arab world. *Journal of Sociolinguistics, 17*(3), 269–296.

Haddad, Y.Y. (2004). *Not quite American? The shaping of Arab and Muslim identity in the US*. Waco, TX: Baylor University Press.

Haeri, N. (1991). Sociolinguistic variation in Cairene Arabic: Palatalization and the Qaf in the speech of men and women. (Unpublished doctoral thesis). University of Pennsylvania, Philadelphia.

Haeri, N. (1996). *The sociolinguistic market of Cairo: Gender, class, and education*. London: Kegan Paul International.

Haeri, N (1997). The reproduction of symbolic capital: Language, state, and class in Egypt. *World Journal of Human Sciences, 38*(5), 795–816.

Haeri, N. (2000). Form and ideology: Arabic sociolinguistics and beyond. *Annual Review of Anthropology, 29*, 61–87.

Haeri, N. (2003). *Sacred language, ordinary people: dilemmas of culture and politics in Egypt*. New York: Palgrave Macmillan.

Hall, S. (1996). Who needs "identity"? In S. Hall & P. du Gay (Eds.), *Questions of cultural identity* (pp. 1–17). London: Sage.

Halliday, M. (1978). *Language as social semiotic: The social interpretation of language and meaning*. London: Edward Arnold.

Hamad, O. (1913). Kayfa nu'azziz al-jinsiyya al-'arabiyya [How to reinforce the Arabic nationality]. *Al-Mufiid*, 3 November.

Hamaada, S. (2012). *Al-lugha wa-l-huwiyya al-'arabiyya fi muwaajahat 'aṣr al-ma'luumaat wa-l-'awlamah – diraasa taħliiliyyah* [The Arabic language and identity in the face of the age of information and globalization – An analytic study]. Paper presented at the First International Conference on the Arabic Language, Beirut, 19–23 March. Retrieved from www.alarabiah.org/index.php?op=view_all_studies&id=15

Hammond, M. (2007). *Popular culture in the Arab World.* Cairo: American University in Cairo Press.

Hannaoui, A. (1987). Diglossia, media Arabic, and language policy in Morocco. (Unpublished doctoral dissertation). State University of New York, New York.

Harrell, R. (1964). A Linguistic Analysis of Egyptian Radio Arabic. In C. Ferguson (Ed.), *Contributions to Arabic Linguistics* (pp. 1–77). Cambridge, MA: Harvard University Press.

Harris, W. (1988). *Interpretive acts: In search of meaning.* Oxford: Clarendon.

Hashimi, A. (2012). *Al-lugha al-'arabiyya bayna l-fuṣħa wa-l-'aamiyyah* [The Arabic language between the standard and the colloquial]. Paper presented at the First International Conference on the Arabic Language, Beirut, 19–23 March. Retrieved from www.alarabiah.org/index.php?op=view_all_studies&id=19

Hassanpour, A. (2012). The indivisibility of the nation and its linguistic divisions. *International Journal of the Sociology of Language, 217,* 49–73.

Hassunah-Arafat, S. (2010). Maternal mediation during a shared book-reading activity and its contribution to children' literacy in kindergarten and first grade: Evidence from the Arab family. (Unpublished doctoral dissertation). Bar-Ilan University, Israel.

Haugbolle, S. (2007). From A-list to Webtifada: Developments in the Lebanese blogosphere 2005–2006. *Arab Media & Society, 1.* Retrieved from http://www.arabmediasociety.com/?article=40

Haugen, E. (1966). *Language conflict and language planning: The case of modern Norwegian.* Cambridge, MA: Harvard University Press.

Haugen E. (1994). Standardization. In R. Asher & J. Simpson (Ed.), *The encyclopedia of language and linguistics* (pp. 4340–4342). New York: Pergamon Press.

Hawkins, P. (1983). Diglossia revisited. *Language Sciences, 5*(1), 1–20.

Hawkins, S. (2010). National symbols and national identity: Currency and constructing cosmopolitans in Tunisia. *Culture and Power, 17*(2–3), 228–254.

Hazen, K. (2007). The study of variation in historical perspective. In R. Bayley & C. Lucas (Eds.), Sociolinguistic variation: Theories, methods, and applications (pp. 70–89). Cambridge, UK: Cambridge University Press.

Hecht, M. L. (1993). 2002- a research odyssey: toward the development of a communication theory of identity. *Communication Monographs, 60,* 76–82.

Heine, B. (1982). *The Nubi Language of Kibera – an Arabic Creole.* Berlin: Dietrich Reimer.

Heller, M. (1988). Strategic ambiguity: Codeswitching in the management of conflict. In M. Heller (Ed.), *Code switching: Anthropological and sociological perspectives* (pp. 77–96). Berlin: De Gruyter Mouton.

Heller, M. (1992). The politics of codeswitching and language choice. In C. Eastman (Ed.), *Codeswitching* (pp. 123–142). Clevedon: Multilingual Matters.

Herin, B. (2010). Le parler arabe de Salt (Jordanie): Phonologie, morphologie et éléments de syntaxe. (Unpublished doctoral dissertation). Université Libre du Bruxelles, Belgium.

Heugh, K. (2002). Recovering multilingualism: Language policy developments in South Africa. In R. Mesthrie (Ed.), *Language in South Africa* (pp. 449–75). Cambridge, UK: Cambridge University Press.

Hinrichs, L. (2006). *Code-switching on the web: English and Jamaican Creole in e-mail communication.* Amsterdam: John Benjamins.

Hitti, P. (1996). *The Arabs: A short history* (2nd ed). Washington, DC: Regnery Publishing.

Ho, J. (2007). Code-mixing: Linguistic form and socio-cultural meaning. *International Jouranl of Language, Society and Culture, 21,* 1–8.

Hoffman, K. (2006). Berber language ideologies, maintenance, and contraction: Gendered variation in the indigenous margins of Morocco. *Language and Communication, 26,* 144–167.

Holes, C. (1983). Patterns of communal language in Bahrain. *Language in Society, 12*(4), 433–457.

Holes, C. (1987). *Language variation and change in a modernising Arab State: The case of Bahrain.* London: Kegan Paul International.

Holes, C. (1993). The use of variation: A study of the political speeches of Gamal Abd al-Nasir. *Perspectives on Arabic Linguistics: Papers from the Annual Symposium on Arabic Linguistics, V* (pp. 13–45). Amsterdam: John Benjamins.

Holes, C. (1995). Community, dialect, and urbanization in the Arabic-speaking Middle East. *Bulletin of the School of Oriental and African Studies, 58*(2), 270–287.

Holes, C. (1996). The Arabic dialects of south eastern Arabia in a socio-historical perspective. *Zeischrift für Arabische Linguistik,* 36–50.

Holes, C. (2004). *Modern Arabic: structures, functions, and varieties.* Washington, DC: Georgetown University Press.

Holes, C. (2006). Gulf States. In K. Versteegh, M. Eid, A. Elgibali, M. Woidich, & A. Zaborski (Eds.), *Encyclopedia of Arabic language and linguistics* (pp. 210–216). Leiden: Brill.

Holmes, J. (2006). Workplace narratives, professional identity, and relational practice. In A. de Fina, D. Schiffrin, & M. Bamberg (Eds.), *Discourse and identity* (pp. 166–187). Cambridge, UK: Cambridge University Press.

Holmes, J., & Meyerhoff, M. (Eds.) (2003). *The handbook of language and gender.* Oxford: Blackwell.

Holt, M. (1994). Algeria: Language, nation and state. In Y. Suleiman (Ed.), *Arabic sociolinguistics* (pp. 25–41). Richmond: Curzon.

Holtschke, E. (2013). *The role of media during the Arab spring with particular focus on Libya.* Germany: GRIN Verlag.

Hourani, A. H. (1991). *A history of the Arab peoples.* London, UK: Faber and Faber.

Howard, P., & Hussain, M. (2013). *Democracy's fourth wave? Digital media and the Arab Spring.* Oxford: Oxford University Press.

Hudson, A. (2002). Outline of a theory of diglossia. *International Journal of the Sociology of Language, 157,* 1–48.

Hudson, R. A. (1996). *Sociolinguistics.* Cambridge, UK: Cambridge University Press.

Huntington, S. P. (1996). *The clash of civilizations and the remaking of world order.* New York: Simon & Schuster.

Hussein, R. (1980). The case of triglossia in Arabic (with special emphasis on Jordan). (Unpublished doctoral dissertation). State University of New, York-Buffalo.

Hussein, R. (1999). Code-alteration among Arab college students. *World Englishes, 18*(2), 281–289.

Hussein, R., & El-Ali, N. (1989). Subjective reactions of rural university students toward different varieties of Arabic. *Al-'Arabiyya, 22*(1–2), 37–54.

Husseinali, G. (2006). Who is studying Arabic and why? A survey of Arabic students' orientations at a major university. *Foreign Language Annals, 39*(3), 395–412.

Hymes, D. (1972). On communicative competence. In J. Pride & J. Holmes (Eds.), *Socio-linguistics* (pp. 269–293). Harmondsworth: Penguin.

Ibn Katheer, I. (1999). *Tafseer Al-qur'aan Al-'adheem, 4* [Interpretation of the Great Qur'an]. Riyadh: Daar Teibah.

Ibn Khaldun, A. (1995 [1406]). *Muqaddimat Ibn Khaldun (with Commentary by D. Al-Huwaidi)*. Saida, Lebanon: Al-Maktaba Al-'Aṣriyya.

Ibn Qutayba, D. (1996). *'uyuun Al-Akhbaar*. Cairo: Daar Al-Kutub Al-Masriyya.

Ibrahim, M. (1986). Standard and prestige language: A problem in Arabic sociolinguistics. *Anthropological Linguistics, 28*, 115–126.

Ibrahim, M. (1989). Communicating in Arabic: Problems and prospects. In F. Coulmas (Ed.), *Language adaptation*. Cambridge, UK: Cambridge University Press.

Ibrahim, R., & Aharon-Peretz, J. (2005). Is literary Arabic a second language for native Arab speakers? Evidence from a semantic priming study. *Journal of Psycholinguist Research, 34*(1), 51–70.

Ibrahim, Z. (2000). Myths about Arabic revisited. *Al-'Arabiyya, 33*, 13–27.

Ibrahim, Z. (2007). Lexical variation in Modern Standard Arabic. In K. Versteegh, M. Eid, A. Elgibali, M. Woidich, & A. Zaborski (Eds.), *Encyclopedia of Arabic language and Linguistics* (pp. 13–21). Leiden: Brill.

Ibrahim, Z. (2010). Cases of written code-switching in Egyptian opposition newspapers. In R. Bassiouney (Ed.), *Arabic and the media: Linguistic analyses and applications* (pp. 23–46). Leiden: Brill.

Ibrahim, Z., & Allam, J. (2006). Arabic learners and heritage students redefined: Present and future. In K.M. Wahba, Z.A. Taha, & L. England (Eds.), *Handbook for Arabic language teaching professionals in the 21st century* (pp. 437–446). Mahwah, NJ: Lawrence Erlbaum.

Ingham, B. (2009). The Dialect of the Euphrates Bedouin, a fringe Mesopotamian dialect. In E. Al-Wer & R. De Jong (Eds.), *Arabic dialectology* (pp. 99–108). Leiden: Brill.

Innis, H. (1951). *The bias of communication*. Toronto: University of Toronto Press.

Internet Society. (2006). A brief history of the Internet and related networks. Retrieved from www.isoc.org/Internet/history/cerf.shtml

Internet World Stats. (2012). The internet usage and population statistics. Retrieved from www.internetworldstats.com/stats.htm

Irvine, A. (2011). Duration, dominance and depth in telephone and face-to-face interviews: A comparative exploration. *International Journal of Qualitative Methods, 20*(3), 202–220.

Irvine, J., & Gal, S. (2000). Language ideology and linguistic differentiation. In P. Kroskrity (Ed.), *Regimes of language* (pp. 35–84). Sante Fe, NM: School of American Research Press.

Ismail, H. (2007). The urban and suburban modes: Patterns of linguistic variation and change in Damascus. In C. Miller, E. Al-Wer, D. Caubet, & J. Watson (Eds.), *Arabic in the city: Issues in dialect contact and language variation* (pp. 188–212). London: Routledge.

Jaber, R. (2013). Gender and age effects on lexical choice in the baghdadi speech community: A cognitive sociolinguistic analysis. (Unpublished doctoral dissertation). Universiti Utara Malaysia, Malaysia.

Jabeur, M. (1987). A sociolinguistic study in Tunisia: Rades. (Unpublished doctoral dissertation). University of Reading, UK.

Jarrar, R. (2009). *A map of home.* New York: Penguin Books.

Jarraya, S. (2013). Persuasion in political discourse: Tunisian President Ben Ali's last speech as a case study. (Master's thesis). Syracuse University, Syracuse.

Jaspal, R., & Coyle, A. (2010). Arabic is the language of the Muslims–that's how it was supposed to be: Exploring language and religious identity through reflective accounts from young British-born South Asians. *Mental Health, Religion & Culture, 13*(1), 17–36.

Jassem, Z. (1987). Phonological variation and change in immigrant speech: A sociolinguistic study of a 1967 Arab-Israeli war immigrant speech community in Damascus, Syria. (Unpublished doctoral dissertation). Durham University, UK.

Jiménez Jiménez, A. F. (2004). A sociocultural approach to language attrition. In M. S. Schmid, B. Köpke, M. Keijzer & L. Weilemar (Eds.), *First language attrition: Interdisciplinary perspective on methodological issues,* (pp. 61–80). Amsterdam: John Benjamins.

Johnstone, B. (2000). *Qualitative methods in sociolinguistics.* Oxford: Oxford University Press.

Jones, R.J. (2000). Egyptian Copts in Detroit: Ethnic community and long-distance nationalism. In N. Abraham & A. Shryock (Eds.), *Arab Detroit: From margin to mainstream* (pp. 219–240). Detroit: Wayne State University Press.

Jones, S., Torres, V., & Arminio, J. (2014). *Negotiating the complexities of qualitative research in higher education.* London: Routledge.

Joseph, J.E. (2004). *Language and identity: National, ethnic, religious.* New York: Palgrave Macmillan.

Juffermans, K., & Van der Aa, J. (2013). Introduction to the special issue: Analyzing voice in educational discourse. *Anthropology & Education Quarterly, 44*(2), 112–123.

Jurkiewicz, S. (2011). *Of islands and windows–publicness in the Lebanese blogosphere.* Oriente Moderno, *XCL*(1), 139–155.

Juteau, D. (1997). Multicultural citizenship: The challenge of pluralism in Canada. In V.M. Bader, (Ed.), *Citizenship and exclusion* (pp. 96–112). London: Macmillan.

Kachru, B. (1977). Code-switching as a communicative strategy in India. In M. Saville-Troike (Ed.), *Linguistics and anthropology: Georgetown University round table on languages and linguistics.* Washington DC: Georgetown University Press.

Kachru, B. (Ed.) (1982). *The other tongue: English across cultures.* Urbana, IL: University of Illinois Press.

Kachru, B. (1983). On mixing. In B. Kachru (Ed.), *The Indianization of English: The English language in India* (pp. 193–207). Oxford: Oxford University Press.

Kahane, H. (1986). A Typology of the prestige language. *Language, 62*(3), 495–508.

Kallas, E. (2007). Nationalism and language. In K. Versteegh, M. Eid, A. Elgibali, M. Woidich, & A. Zaborski, (Eds.), *Encyclopedia of Arabic language and linguistics* (pp. 343–353). Leiden: Brill.

Kaplan, R.B., & Baldauf, R.B. (1997). *Language planning: From practice to theory.* Clevedon: Multilingual Matters.

Katz, D. (1960). The functional approach to the study of attitude. *The Public Opinion Quarterly, 24*(2), 163–204.

Kaye, A. (1972). Remarks on diglossia in Arabic: Well-defined vs. Ill-defined. *Linguistics, 81*, 32–48.

Kaye, A. (1975). More on diglossia in Arabic (Review of the book *The Problems of Diglossia in Arabic: A Comparative Study of Classical and Iraqi Arabic* by S.J. Altoma). *International Journal of Middle East Studies, 6*(3), 325–340.

Kaye, A. (1994). Formal vs informal Arabic: Diglossia, triglossia, tetraglossia etc., multiglossia viewed as a continuum. *Zeitschrift für Arabische Linguistik, 27*, 47–66.

Kayyali, R. (2006). *The Arab Americans.* Westport, CT: Greenwood Publishing.

Keating, E., & Mirus, G. (2003). American Sign Language in virtual space: Interactions between deaf users of computer-mediated video communication and the impact of technology on language practices, *Language in Society, 32*, 693–714.

Kedourie, E. (1993). *Nationalism* (4th ed.). London: Wiley-Blackwell.

Keita, S.O.Y. (2010). Biocultural emergence of the Amazigh (Berbers) in Africa: Comment on Frigi et al. *Human Biology, 82*(4), 385–393.

Keller, R. (1994). *On language change: The invisible hand in language.* London: Routledge.

Kelly-Holmes, H. (2006). Multilingualism and commercial language practices on the Internet. *Journal of Sociolinguistics, 10*(4), 507–519.

Kenny, K.D. (1992). Arab-Americans learning Arabic: Motivations and attitudes. In A. Rouchdy (Ed.), *The Arabic language in America* (pp. 119–161). Detroit: Wayne State University Press.

Kenny, K.D. (2002). Code-switch fluency and language attrition in an Arab immigrant community. In A. Rouchdy (Ed.), *Language contact and language conflict in Arabic: Variations on a sociolinguistic theme* (pp. 331–352). London: RoutledgeCurzon.

Kerswill, F. (2013). Koineization. In J.K. Chambers & N. Schilling-Estes (Eds.), *The handbook of language variation and change* (pp. 519–536). Oxford: Blackwell.

Khalil, J. (2005). Blending in: Arab television and the search for programming ideas. *Transnational Broadcasting Journal, 13*. Retrieved from www.tbsjournal.com/archives/Wint 2004.htm

Khalil, S. (2011). *The evolution of the Arabic language through online writing: The explosion of 2011.* Proceedings of British Society for Middle Eastern Studies (BRISMES) 2012 Graduate Conference Papers. Durham, UK. Retrieved from www.isn.ethz.ch/Digital-Library/Publications/Detail/?ots591=0c54e3b3-1e9c-be1e-2c24-a6a8c7060233&lng=en&id=151357

Khamis-Dakwar, R., & Froud, K. (2007). Lexical processing in two language varieties: An event related brain potential study of Arabic native speakers. In M. Mughazy (Ed.), *Perspectives on Arabic linguistics XX* (pp. 153–168). Amsterdam: John Benjamins.

Khamis-Dakwar, R., Froud, K., & Gordon, P. (2012), Acquiring diglossia: Mutual influences of formal and colloquial Arabic on children's grammaticality judgments. *Journal of Child Language, 39*, 1–29.

Khan, M. (1958). Arab nationalism. *Pakistan Horizon, 11*(4), 295–300.

Kharraki, A. (2001). Moroccan sex-based linguistic difference in bargaining. *Discourse and Society, 12*, 615–632.

Khattab, G. (2002). VOT production in English and Arabic bilingual and monolingual children. In D. Parkinson & E. Benmamoun (Eds.), *Perspectives on Arabic linguistics* (pp. 1–38). Amsterdam: John Benjamins.

Khtani, A.S. (1992). The impact of social change on linguistic behaviour: Phonological variation in spoken Arabic, Asir, Saudi Arabia. (Unpublished doctoral dissertation). University of Essex, UK.

Klee, C. (1996). The Spanish of the Peruvian Andes: The influence of Quechua on Spanish language structure. In A. Roca & J.B. Jensen (Eds.), *Spanish in contact: Issues in bilingualism* (pp. 73–92). Somerville, MA: Cascadilla Press.

Kossmann, M. (2012). Berber-Arabic code-switching in Imouzzar du Kandar (Morocco). *STUF – Language Typology and Universals Sprachtypologie und Universalienforschung, 65*(4), 369–382.

Kouloughli, D.E. (2010). L'Arabe est-il réfractaire au changement? *Actes du Colloque International La Langue* (pp. 207–229). Casablanca: Fondation Zakoura Education.

Köpke, B. (2007). Language attrition at the crossroads of brain, mind, and society. In B. Köpke, M. Schmid, M. Keijzer, & S. Dostert (Eds.), *Language attrition: Theoretical perspectives* (pp. 9–38). Amsterdam: John Benjamins.

Kroon, S. (1990). Some remarks on ethnic identity, language and education. *Innovation: The European Journal of Social Science Research, 3*(3), 421–435.

Kroskrity, P. (1993). *Language, history and identity: Ethnolinguistic studies of the Arizona Tewa.* Tucson: University of Arizona Press.

Kroskrity, P. (2000). Regimenting languages: Language ideology perspectives. In P. Kroskrity (Ed.), *Regimes of language* (pp. 1–34). Santa Fe, NM: School of American Research Press.

Krumbacher, K. (1902). *Das Problem der neugriechischen Schriftsprache.* München: königliche Bayerische Akademie.

Kurath, H. (1972). *Studies in area linguistics.* Bloomington, IN: Indiana University Press.

Kurdali, M. (2010 [1948]). *Al-Muthakkaraat* [The memoirs]. Riyadh: Dar s-Salaf.

Labov, W. (1963). The social motivation of a sound change. *Word, 19,* 273–303.

Labov, W. (1966). *The social stratification of English in New York City.* Washington: Center for Applied Linguistics.

Labov, W. (1972). *Sociolinguistic patterns.* Philadelphia: University of Pennsylvania Press.

Labov, W. (1981). Field methods used by the project on linguistic change and variation. Sociolinguistic Working Paper 81. Austin: South Western Educational Development Laboratory.

Labov, W. (2001). *Principles of Linguistic Change* (vol. 2: Social factors). Oxford: Blackwell.

Labov, W., Ash, S., & Boberg, C. (2005). *Atlas of North American English.* Berlin: De Gruyter Mouton.

Labov, W., Cohen, P., Robins, C., & Lewis, J. (1968). A study of the Nonstandard English of Negro and Puerto Rican speakers in New York City. Final Report, Cooperative Research Project No. 3288, United States Office of Education.

Lanza, E. (2004). *Language mixing in infant bilingualism: A sociolinguistic perspective.* Oxford: Oxford University Press.

Laroussi, F. (2003). Arabic and the new technologies. In J. Maurais & M. Morris (Eds.), *Languages in a globalising world* (pp. 250–259). Cambridge, UK: Cambridge University Press.

Lather, P., (2003 [1986]). Issues of validity in openly ideological research: Between a rock and a soft place. In Y. Lincoln & N. Denzin (Eds.), *Turning points in qualitative research* (pp. 185–215). Lanham, MD: Rowman and Littlefield.

Lawson-Sako, S., & Sachdev, I. (1996). Ethnolinguistic communication in Tunisian streets. In Y. Suleiman (Ed.), *Language and ethnic identity in the Middle East and North Africa* (pp. 61–79). Richmond: Curzon.

Lawson, S., & Sachdev, I. (2000). Codeswitching in Tunisia: Attitudinal and behavioral dimensions. *Journal of Pragmatics, 32*(9), 1343–1361.

Le Page, R.B., & Tabouret-Keller, A. (1985). *Acts of identity: Creole-based approaches to language and ethnicity.* Cambridge, UK: Cambridge University Press.

Leikin, M., Ibrahim, R., & Eghbaria, H. (2013). The influence of diglossia in Arabic on narrative ability: Evidence from analysis of the linguistic and narrative structure of discourse among preschool children. Springer, Epub ahead of print. DOI: 10.1007/s11145–013–9462–3.

Lenhart, A., Arafeh, S., Smith, A., & Macgill, A.R. (2008). Writing, technology and teens. Washington, DC: Pew Internet & American Life Project and the College Board's National Commission on Writing.

Levy, S. (1998). Parlers arabes pré-hilaliens: traits et tendances'. *Langues et Littératures. Contact et Evolution historique des langues au Maroc*, vol. XVI (pp. 185–198). Rabat: Publication de la Faculté des Lettres et des Sciences Humaines.

Lincoln, Y.S., & Guba, E.G. (2000). Paradigmatic controversies, contradictions, and emerging confluences. In N.K. Denzin & Y.S. Lincoln (Eds.), *Handbook of qualitative research (2nd Ed.).* Thousand Oaks: Sage.

Lipski, J.M. (2005). Code-switching or borrowing? No sé *so* no puedo decir, *you know.* In L. Sayahi & M. Westmoreland (Eds.), *Selected proceedings of the Second Workshop on Spanish Sociolinguistics* (pp. 1–15). Somerville, MA: Cascadilla Proceedings Project.

Lo, M. (2009). *Understanding Muslim discourse: Language, tradition, and the message of Bin Laden.* Lanham, MA: University Press of America.

Lori, A. (1990). Self-concept, tolerance of ambiguity, English achievement, Arabic achievement and overall school achievement as factors contributing to Bahraini high school seniors' attitudes toward learning English as a foreign language. (Unpublished doctoral dissertation). Indiana University, Bloomington, IN.

Loseke, D. (2007). The study of identity as cultural, institutional, organization and personal narratives: Theoretical and empirical integrations. *Sociological Quarterly, 48,* 661–688.

Loukili, A. (2007). *Moroccan diaspora, Internet and national imagination: Building a community online through the Internet portal Yabiladi.* Paper presented at the Nordic Africa Days, Uppsala, Sweden.

Lucas, C. (2007). Jespersen's cycle in Arabic and Berber. *Transactions of the Philological Society, 105*(3), 398–431.

Luffin, X. (2007). Pidgin Arabic: Bongor Arabic. In K. Versteegh, M. Eid, A. Elgibali, M. Woidich, & A. Zaborski (Eds.), *Encyclopedia of Arabic language and linguistics* (pp. 634–639). Leiden: Brill.

Lukmani, Y. (1972). Motivation to learn and language proficiency. *Language Learning, 22,* 261–273.

Maamouri, M. (1998). *Language education and human development: Arabic diglossia and its impact on the quality of education in the Arab Region*. The Mediterranean development forum, Washington, DC: The World.

Maddy-Weitzman, B. (2001). Contested identities: Berbers, "Berberism" and the state in North Africa. *Journal of North African Studies, 6*(3), 23–47.

Maddy-Weitzman, B., & Zisenwine, D. (Eds.) (2013). *Contemporary Morocco: State, politics and society under Mohammed VI*. London: Routledge.

Magidow, A. (2013). Towards a sociohistorical reconstruction of pre-Islamic Arabic dialect diversity. (Unpublished doctoral dissertation). University of Texas, Austin.

Mahmoud, A. (2000). Modem standard Arabic vs. non-standard Arabic: Where do Arab students of EFL transfer from? *Language, Culture and Curriculum, 13*(2), 126–136.

Mahmoud, Y. (1986). Arabic after diglossia. In J. Fishman (Ed.), *The Fergusonian impact* (pp. 239–251). Berlin: De Gruyter Mouton.

Mahmud, U.A. (1979). Linguistic change and variation in the aspectual system of Juba Arabic. (Unpublished doctoral thesis). Georgetown University, Washington, DC.

Makdisi, U. (1996). Reconstructing the nation-state: The modernity of sectarianism in Lebanon. *Middle East Report, No. 200, Minorities in the Middle East: Power and the Politics of Difference*, 23–26.

Makdisi, U. (2002). After 1860: Debating religion, reform, and nationalism in the Ottoman Empire. *International Journal of Middle East Studies, 34*(4), 601–617.

Makoni, S., & Pennycook, A. (2007). Disinventing and reconstituting languages. In S. Makoni & A. Pennycook (Eds.), *Disinventing and reconstituting languages* (pp. 1–41). Clevedon: Multilingual Matters.

Mansour, G. (1993). *Multilingualism and nation building*. Clevedon: Multilingual Matters.

Maratsos, M. (1991). How the acquisition of nouns may be different from that of verbs. In N.A. Krasnegor & D.M. Rumbaugh (Eds.), *Biological and behavioral determinants of language development* (pp. 67–88). Hillsdale, NJ: Lawrence Erlbaum.

Marçais, W. (1930). La diglossie arabe. L'Enseignement public. *Revue pédagogique, 104*(12), 401–409.

Marley, D. (2002). Diversity and uniformity. Linguistic fact and fiction in Morocco. In K. Salhi (Ed.), *French in and out of France: Language policies, intercultural antagonisms and dialogue* (pp. 335–376). Bern: Peter Lang.

Marley, D. (2004). Language attitudes in Morocco following recent changes in language policy. *Language Policy, 3*(1), 25–46.

Marley, D. (2013). The role of online communication in raising awareness of bilingual identity. *Multilingua, 32*(4), 485–505.

Martin, N. (2009). Arab American parents' attitudes toward their children's heritage language maintenance and language practices. (Master's thesis). University of North Carolina, Chapel Hill.

Marwick, A., & Boyd, D. (2011). I tweet honestly, I tweet passionately: Twitter users, context collapse, and the imagined audience. *New Media and Society, 13*, 96–113.

May, S.A. (1997). Critical ethnography. In N.H. Hornberger & D. Corson (Eds.), *Research methods in language and education* (pp. 197–206). *Encyclopedia of language and education* (vol. 8). Dordrecht: Kluwer.

Mazraani, N. (1997). *Aspects of language variation in Arabic political speech-making*. Richmond: Curzon.

McArthur, T. (2002). *Oxford Guide to World English*. Oxford: Oxford University Press.

McCormick, K. (1995). Code-switching, code-mixing and convergence in Cape Town. In R. Mesthrie (Ed.), *Language and social history* (pp. 193–208). Cape Town: David Philip Publishers.

McDowall, D. (2004). *A modern history of the Kurds* (3rd ed.). London: I.B. Tauris.

McElhinny, B. (2003). Theorizing gender in sociolinguistics and linguistic anthropology. In J. Holmes & M. Meyerhoff (Eds.), *The handbook of language and gender* (pp. 21–42). Oxford: Blackwell.

McLoughlin, L. (2009). The teaching of Arabic as a foreign language (TAFL) at tertiary level in the twenty-first century: now where do we go? *NECTFL Review, 64*, 68–70.

Meho, L. I., & Maglaughlin, K. (2001). *Kurdish culture and society: An annotated bibliography*. Westport, CT: Greenwood Press.

Meiseles, G. (1980). Educated spoken Arabic and the Arabic language continuum. *Archivum Linguisticum, 11*, 118–143.

Mejdell, G. (1999). Switching, mixing-code interaction in spoken Arabic. In B. Brendemoen, E. Lanza & E. Ryen (Eds.), *Language encounters across time and space* (pp. 225–241). Oslo: Novus.

Mejdell, G. (2006). *Mixed styles in spoken Arabic in Egypt*. Leiden: Brill.

Mejdell, G. (2008a). Is modern Fusha a "Standard" language? In Z. Ibrahim & S. Makhlouf (Eds.), *Linguistics in the age of globalization* (pp. 41–52). Cairo: American University in Cairo Press.

Mejdell, G. (2008b). What is happening to lughatunā l-gamīla? Recent media representations and social practice in Egypt. *Journal of Arabic and Islamic Studies, 8*, 108–124.

Merolla, D. (2002). Digital imagination and the "landscapes of group identities": The flourishing of theatre, video and "Amazigh Net" in the Maghrib and Berber diaspora. *Journal of North African Studies, 7*(4), 122–131.

Mertens, D.A. (2010). *Research and evaluation in education and psychology* (3rd ed.). Thousand Oaks, CA: Sage.

Messaoudi, L. (2001). Urbanisation linguistique et dynamique langagières dans la ville de Rabat. In T. Bulot, C. Bauvois, & P. Blanchet (Eds.), *Sociolinguistique urbaine. Variations linguistiques, images urbaines et sociales*. Rennes: Presses de l'Université de Rennes.

Mesthrie, R., & Swann, J. (2009). From variation to hybridity. In J. Maybin & J. Swann (Eds.), *The Routledge companion to English language studies* (pp. 76–107). London: Routledge.

Miller C. (1997). Pour une étude du contact dialectal en zone urbaine: Le Caire. Proceedings of the 16th International Congress of linguistics, Paris.

Miller, C. (2002). The Relevance of Arabic-based Pidgin/Creoles for Arabic linguistics. In G. Mansour & M. Doss (Eds.), *Al-Lugha* (pp. 7–45). Cairo: Arab Development Center.

Miller, C. (2003). Linguistic policies and the issue of ethno-linguistic minorities in the Middle East. In A. Usuki and H. Kato (Eds.), *Islam in the Middle Eastern studies: Muslims and minorities* (pp. 149–174). Osaka: Japan Center for Area Studies.

Miller, C. (2004). Variation and change in Arabic urban vernaculars. In M. Haak, R. DeJong & K. Versteegh (Eds.), *Approaches to Arabic dialects: A collection of articles presented to Manfred Woidich on the occasion of his sixtieth birthday* (pp. 177–206). Leiden: Brill.

Miller, C. (2005). Between accommodation and resistance: Upper Egyptian migrants in Cairo. *Linguistics, 43,* 903–956.

Miller, C. (2006). Juba Arabic. In K. Versteegh, M. Eid, A. Elgibali, M. Woidich, & A. Zaborski (Eds.), *Encyclopedia of Arabic language and linguistics* (pp. 517–525). Leiden: Brill.

Miller, C. (2007). Arabic urban vernaculars: Development and change. In C. Miller, E. Al-Wer, D. Caubet, &. J. Watson (Eds.), *Arabic in the city: Issues in dialect contact and language variation* (pp. 1–31). London: Routledge.

Milroy, J. (2001). Language ideologies and the consequences of standardization. *Journal of Sociolinguistics, 5*(4), 530–555.

Milroy, J., & Milroy, L. (2002). *Authority in language: Investigating standard English* (3rd ed.). London: Routledge.

Milroy, L. (1987). *Language and social networks.* Oxford: Blackwell.

Milroy, L., & Gordon, M. (2003). *Sociolinguistics: Method and interpretation.* Oxford: Blackwell.

Milroy, L., & Milroy, J. (1992). Social network and social class: Toward an integrated socio-linguistic model. *Language in society, 21*(01), 1–26.

Milroy, L., & Muysken, P. (1995). *One speaker, two languages: Cross-disciplinary perspectives on code-switching.* Cambridge, UK: Cambridge University Press.

Milroy, L., & Wei, L. (1995). A social network approach to code-switching: The example of a bilingual community in Britain. In L. Milroy & P. Muysken (Eds.), *One speaker, two languages: Cross-disciplinary perspectives on code-switching* (pp. 136–157). New York: Press Syndicate of the University of Cambridge.

Mimouna, B. (2012). Is English there? Investigating language use among young Algerian users of internet. (Unpublished doctoral dissertation). University of Oran, Algeria.

Mitchell, T. (1982). More than a matter of "writing with the learning, pronouncing with the vulgar": Some preliminary observations on the Arabic Koine. In E. Hass (Ed.), *Standard languages: Spoken and written* (pp. 123–156). Manchester, UK: Manchester University Press.

Mitchell, T. (1986). What is educated spoken Arabic? *International Journal of the Sociology of Language, 61,* 7–32.

Mitchell, T., & El-Hassan, S. (1994). *Modality, mood, and aspect in spoken Arabic, with special reference to Egypt and the Levant.* New York: Kegan Paul International.

Mizher, R., & Al-Abed Al-Haq, F. (2014). Attitudes towards using Standard Arabic among academic staff at Balqa Applied University/Center in Jordan: A sociolinguistic study. *International Journal of English Linguistics, 4*(1), 53–59.

Montgomery, M. (2008). *An introduction to language and society* (3rd ed.). London: Routledge.

Montrul, S. (2004). Subject and object expression in Spanish heritage speakers: A case of morpho-syntactic convergence. *Bilingualism: Language and Cognition, 7*(2), 125–142.

Montrul, S., & Bowles, M. (2009). Back to basics: Differential Object Marking under incomplete acquisition in Spanish heritage speakers. *Bilingualism: Language and Cognition, 12*(3), 363–383.

Montrul, S., & Ionin, T. (2010). Transfer effects in the interpretation of definite articles by Spanish heritage speakers. *Bilingualism: Language and Cognition, 13*(4), 449–473.

Moore, M. (1997). On national self-determination. *Political Studies, XLV*(5), 900–913.

Morgan, M. (2014). *Speech communities.* Cambridge, UK: Cambridge University Press.

Moshref, O. (2012). Corpus study of tense, aspect, and modality in diglossic speech in Cairene Arabic. (Unpublished doctoral dissertation). University of Illinois, Urbana-Champaign.

Mostari, H. (2004). A sociolinguistic perspective on Arabisation and language use in Algeria. *Language Problems and Language Planning, 28*(1), 25–44.

Mouhssine, O. (1995). Ambivalence du discourse sur l'arabisation. *International Journal of the Sociology of Language, 112*, 45–62.

Mubaarak, M. (1985). *Nahwa Wa'yin Lughawiyy* [Toward a language awareness]. Beirut: Mu'assasat Al-Risaalah.

Mucherah, W. (2008). Immigrants' perceptions of their native language: Challenges to actual use and maintenance. *Journal of Language, Identity, and Education, 7*(3/4), 188–205.

Muñoz-Cobo, B. (2008). Terms of address in Moroccan Arabic: Language and identity. *Estudios de dialectología norteafricana y andalusí, 12*, 93–103.

Murad, M. K. (2007). Language attitudes of Iraqi native speakers of Arabic: A sociolinguistic investigation. (Unpublished master's thesis). University of Kansas, Lawrence, KS.

Musa, F. (2013). Al-lugha Al-'Arabiyyah: Huwiyyatuha wa taħaddiyaat al-muħaafatha 'alayha [The Arabic language: Its identity and the challenges facing its maintenance]. Paper presented at the Second International Conference on the Arabic Language, Dubai, 7–10 May. Retrieved from www.alarabiah.org/index.php?op=view_all_studies&id=19

Musa, S. (1958). *Tarbiyat Salaama Musa* (2nd ed.). [Education of Salaama Musa]. Beirut: Daar Al-Ma'aaref.

Muysken, P. (2000). *Bilingual speech: A typology of code-mixing.* Cambridge, UK: Cambridge University Press.

Myers-Scotton, C. (1992). Comparing codeswitching and borrowing. In C. Eastman (Ed.), *Codeswitching* (pp. 19–39). Clevedon: Multilingual Matters.

Myers-Scotton, C. (1993a). *Dueling Languages: Grammatical structure in codeswitching.* Oxford: Clarendon.

Myers-Scotton, C. (1993b). *Social motivations for code switching: Evidence from Africa.* Oxford: Oxford University Press.

Myers-Scotton, C. (2005). *Multiple voices: An introduction to bilingualism.* Malden, MA: Blackwell.

Myers-Scotton, C., & Bolonyai, A. (2001). Calculating speakers: Codeswitching in a rational choice model. *Language in Society, 30*, 1–28.

Nader, L. (1962). A note on attitudes and the use of language. *Anthropological Linguistics, 4* (6), 24–29.

Næss, U. G. (2008). Gulf Pidgin Arabic: Individual strategies or a structured variety? (Master's thesis). University of Oslo, Oslo, Norway.

Nagel, C. R., & Staeheli, L. A. (2004). *Citizenship, identity, and transnationalism migration: Arab immigrants to the United States. Space and Polity, 8*(1), 3–24. Retrieved from http://scholarcommons.sc.edu/geog_facpub.

Nasr, A. (2010). The advertising construction of identity in Lebanese television. (Unpublished doctoral dissertation). University of Texas, Austin.

Nassar, H. (1956). *Al-Mu'jam Al-'Arabyy: Nash'atuhu wa-Tatawuruhu* [The Arabic dictionary: Its creation and development]. Cairo: Maktabat Misr.

Navarro, Z. (2006). In search of a cultural interpretation of power: The contribution of Pierre Bourdieu. *Institute of Development Studies Bulletin, 37*(6), 1–22.

Newman, D. (2002). The phonetic status of Arabic within the world's languages: The uniqueness of the lughat al-daad. *Antwerp Papers in Linguistics, 100*, 65–75.

Nielsen, H.L. (1996). How to teach Arabic communicatively: Toward a theoretical framework for TAFL. In A. Elgibali (Ed.), *Understanding Arabic* (pp. 211–239). Cairo: American University of Cairo Press.

Noble, D. (1998). Selling academe to the technology industry. *Thought & Action Journal, 14*(1), 29–40.

Nortier, J. (1990). *Dutch-Moroccan Arabic code switching among young Moroccans in the Netherlands.* Dordrecht: Kluwer.

Nourddiin, K. (2012). *Istikhdaam al-kalimaat al-ajnabiyya fi l-lugha al-'arabiyya wa-mawqif al-majaami' al-'arabiyya min thaalik* [The use of foreign words in the Arabic language and the attitudes of the Arab academies toward it]. Paper presented at the First International Conference on the Arabic Language, Beirut, 19–23 March. Retrieved from www.alarabiah.org/index.php?op=view_all_studies&id=15

Nydell, M.K. (2012). *Understanding Arabs: A contemporary guide to Arab society.* Boston, MA: Nicholas Brealey.

O'Shea, M. (2004). *Trapped between the map and reality: Geography and perceptions of Kurdistan.* London: Routledge.

Omar, M. (1973). *The acquisition of Egyptian Arabic as a native language.* The Hague: Mouton.

Orfalea, G. (2006). *The Arab Americans: A history.* New York: Olive Branch Press.

Oriyama, K. (2010) Heritage language maintenance and Japanese identity formation: What role can schooling and ethnic community contact play? *Heritage Language Journal, 7*(2), 76–111.

Osman, G., & Forbes, C. (2004). Representing the West in the Arabic language: The slave narrative of Omar Ibn Said. *Journal of Islamic Studies, 15*(3), 331–343.

Othman, M. (2006). Language choice among Arabic-English bilinguals in Manchester, Britain. (Master's thesis). University of Manchester, UK.

Ouassini, A. (2013). Between Islamophobia and the ummah: How Spanish Moroccans are negotiating their identities in post 3–11 Madrid. (Unpublished doctoral dissertation). University of Nevada, Las Vegas.

Ovando, C.J., Combs, M.C., & Collier, V.P. (2006). *Bilingual and ESL classrooms: Teaching in multicultural contexts* (4th ed.). New York: McGraw Hill.

Owens, J. (1985). The origins of East African Arabic Nubi. *Anthropological Linguistics, 27*, 229–271.

Owens, J. (1991). Nubi, genetic linguistics and language classification. *Anthropological Linguistics, 33*, 1–30.

Owens, J. (1995). Minority languages and urban norms: A case study. *Linguistics, 33*, 305–358.

Owens, J. (1998). *Variation in the Spoken Arabic of Maiduguri, Nigeria.* Amsterdam: John Benjamins.

Owens, J. (2000). *Arabic as a minority language.* Berlin: Mouton De Gruyter.

Owens, J. (2001). Arabic sociolinguistics. *Arabica, XLVIII*, 419–469.

Owens, J. (2005). Bare forms and lexical insertions in codeswitching: A processing-based account. *Bilingualism: Language and Cognition, 8*, 23–38.

Palfreyman, D. (2001). Informal Latinized orthographies. *Linguist List, 12*(12–2760). Retrieved from http://linguistlist.org/issues/12/12-2760.html

Palfreyman, D., & al Khalil, M. (2003). A funky language for teenzz to use: Representing Gulf Arabic in instant messaging. *Journal of Computer-Mediated Communication, 9*(1). Retrieved from http://jcmc.indiana.edu/vol9/issue1/index.html

Palmer, J. (2008). Arabic diglossia: Student perceptions of spoken Arabic after living in the Arabic-speaking world. *Arizona Working Papers in Second Language Acquisition and Teaching, 15*, 81–95.

Palva, H. (1982). Patterns of koineization in modern colloquial Arabic. *Acta Orientalia, 43*, 13–32.

Palva, H. (1994). Bedouin and sedentary elements in the dialect of Es Salt: Diachronic notes on the sociolinguistic development. In D. Caubet & M. Vanhove (Eds.), *Actes des premières journées internationales de dialectologie arabe de Paris* (pp. 459–469). Paris: INALCO.

Palva, H. (2006). Dialects: Classification. In K. Versteegh, M. Eid, A. Elgibali, M. Woidich, & A. Zaborski (Eds.), *Encyclopedia of Arabic language and linguistics* (pp. 604–613). Leiden: Brill.

Palva, H. (2013). G. A. Wallin's contributions to the study of Arabic dialects. *Studia Orientalia, 114*, 511–530.

Panovic, I (2010). The beginnings of Wikipedia Masry. *Al-Logha, 8*, 93–127.

Parkinson, D. (1991). Searching for modem fusha: Real life formal Arabic. *Al-'Arabiyya, 24*, 31–64.

Parkinson, D. (1993). Knowing standard Arabic: Testing Egyptians' MSA abilities. In M. Eid & C. Holes (Eds.), *Perspectives on Arabic linguistics: Papers from the Annual Symposium on Arabic Linguistics, V* (pp. 47–73). Amsterdam: John Benjamins.

Parkinson, D. (1996). Variability in Standard Arabic grammar skills. In A. Elgibali (Ed.), *Understanding Arabic: Essays in contemporary Arabic linguistics in honor of El-Said Badawi* (pp. 91–102). Cairo: American University in Cairo Press.

Parkinson, D. (2003). Verbal features in oral Fuṣḥa performances in Cairo. *International Journal of the Sociology of Language, 163*, 27–41.

Parkinson, D.B. (1985). *Constructing the social context of communication: Terms of address in Egyptian Arabic*. Berlin: Mouton De Gruyter.

Patel, A. (2013). *The Arab Nahdah: The making of the intellectual and humanist movement*. Edinburgh: Edinburgh University Press.

Patton, M. (1990). *Qualitative evaluation and research methods* (2nd ed.). Thousand Oaks, CA: Sage.

Pauwels, A. (1986). Diglossia, immigrant dialects and language maintenance in Australia: The case of Limburgs and Swabian. *Journal of Multilingual and Multicultural Development, 7*, 13–30.

Pavlenko, A. (2004). L2 influence and L1 attrition in adult bilingualism. In M. Schmid, B. Köpke, M. Keijzer, & L. Weilemar (Eds.), *First language attrition: Interdisciplinary perspectives on methodological issues* (pp. 47–59). Amsterdam: John Benjamins.

Pavlenko, A., & Jarvis, S. (2002). Bidirectional transfer. *Applied Linguistics, 23*(2), 190–214.

Pavlou, P., & Papapavlou, A. (2004). Issues of dialect use in education from the Greek Cypriot perspective. *International Journal of Applied Linguistics, 14*(2), 243–258.

Peacock, J. (2001). *The anthropological lens: Harsh light, soft focus*. Cambridge, UK: Cambridge University Press.

Pennycook, A. (2004). Performativity and language studies. *Critical Inquiry in Language Studies: An International Journal, 1*(1), 1–19.

Pereira, C. (2007). Urbanization and dialect change: The Arabic dialect of Tripoli (Libya). In C. Miller, E. Al-Wer, D. Caubet, & J. Watson (Eds.), *Arabic in the city: Issues in dialect contact and language variation* (pp. 77–96). London: Routledge.

Pérez-Sabater, C. (2012). The linguistics of social networking: A study of writing conventions on Facebook. *Linguistik Online, 56*(6), 111–130.

Pfaff, C. (1979). Constraints on language mixing: Intrasentential codeswitching and borrowing in Spanish/English. *Language, 55,* 291–318.

Phillips, D. C. (1990). Subjectivity and objectivity: An objective inquiry. In E. Eisner & A. Peshkin (Eds.), *Qualitative inquiry in education: The continuing debate.* New York: Teachers College Press.

Phoenix, A. (2010). Ethnicities. In M. Wetherell & C.T. Mohanty (Eds.), *The SAGE handbook of identities.* (pp. 297–320). Thousand Oaks, CA: Sage.

Piscatori, J. (1986). *Islam in a world of nation-states.* Cambridge, UK: Cambridge University Press.

Polinsky, M. (1997). American Russian: Language loss meets language acquisition. In W. Brown, E. Dornisch, N. Kondrashova, & D. Zec (Eds.), *Formal approaches to Slavic linguistics* (pp. 370–407). Ann Arbor, MI: Michigan Slavic Publications.

Polinsky, M. (2008). Gender under incomplete acquisition: Heritage speaker's knowledge of noun categorization. *Heritage Language Journal, 6*(1), 40–71.

Pollack, K., Byman, D., Al-Turk, A., Baev, P., Doran, M., Elgindy, K., Grand, S. Hamid, S., Jones, B., Maloney, S. Pollack, J., Riedel, B., Santini, R., Shaikh, S., Sharqieh, I., Taspinar, Ö, Telham, S., & Yerkes, S. (2011). *Arab awakening: America and the transformation of the Middle East.* Washington, DC: Brookings Institution Press.

Poplack, S. (1980). Sometimes I'll start a sentence in English y termino en español: Toward a typology of code-switching. *Linguistics, 18,* 581–618.

Procházka, S. (2003). The Bedouin Arabic dialects of Urfa. In I. Ferrando & J. Sandoval (Eds.), *AIDA 5th Conference Proceedings* (pp. 75–88). Cadiz: Universidad de Cadiz.

Qawasmeh, R. (2011). Language use and language attitudes among the Muslim Arabs of Vancouver/Canada: A sociolinguistic study. (Master's thesis). Middle East University, Beirut, Lebanon.

Qaymasoon, J. (2013). *Al-lugha al-'arabiyya wa-tashkiil al-hawiyya fi ẓill al-'awlamah* [The Arabic language and identity formation in globalization]. Paper presented at the First International Conference on the Arabic Language, Beirut, 19–23 March. Retrieved from www.alarabiah.org/index.php?op=view_all_studies&id=15

Rabie, M. (1991). A sociolinguistic study of diglossia of Egyptian radio Arabic: An ethnographic approach. (Unpublished doctoral dissertation). University of Texas, Austin.

Radwan, N. (2004). Two masters of Egyptian 'Āmmiyya poetry. *Journal of Arabic Literature, 35*(2), 221–243.

Ramirez, A., Jr., Walther, J. B., Burgoon, J. K., & Sunnafrank, M. (2002). Information seeking strategies, uncertainty, and computer-mediated communication: Toward a conceptual model. *Human Communication Research, 28*(2), 213–228.

Rampton, B. (1995). *Crossings: Language and ethnicity among adolescents.* London: Routledge.

Randall, M., & Samimi, M. (2010). The status of English in Dubai. *English Today, 26,* 43–50.

Ravid, D., & Farah, R. (1999). Learning about noun plurals in early Palestinian Arabic. *First Language, 19*, 187–206.

Rayhaan, F. (2012). *Al-lugha al-ʻarabiyya wa-huwiyya l-qawmiyya al-ʻarabiyya ṣinwaan* [The Arabic language and the Arab national identity are twins]. Paper presented at the First International Conference on the Arabic Language, Beirut, 19–23 March. Retrieved from www.alarabiah.org/index.php?op=view_all_studies&id=15

Reagan, T. (2009). *Language matters: Reflections on educational linguistics*. Charlotte, NC: Information Age Publishing.

Reagan, T. G. (2002). Language planning and language policy: Past, present and future. In R. Mesthrie (Ed.), *Language in South Africa* (pp. 419–433). Cambridge, UK: Cambridge University Press.

Redouane, R. (1998). Arabisation in the Moroccan educational system: Problems and prospects. *Language, Culture and Curriculum, 11*(2), 195–203.

Ricento, A. (2005). Problems with the 'language-as-resource' discourse in the promotion of heritage languages in the U.S.A. *Journal of Sociolinguistics, 9*(3), 348–368.

Riegert, K., & Ramsay, G. (2012). Activists, individualists, and comics: The counter-publicness of Lebanese blogs. *Television & New Media, 14*(4), 286–303.

Rieschild, R., & Tent, J. (2008). *Bilinguality, gender, and religion as influences on Arabic-Heritage Australian youths' attitudes to their ambient languages and cultures*. Paper presented at the 17th *Sociolinguistics Symposium* at Free University of Amsterdam, 3–5 April.

Ritt, N. (2004). *Selfish sounds and linguistic evolution*. Cambridge, UK: Cambridge University Press.

Rohozinski, R. (2004). *"Secret Agents" and "Undercover Brothers": The hidden information revolution in the Arab World*. A paper presented at the Fifth Mediterranean Social and Political Research Meeting (Florence & Montecatini Terme) 24–28 March.

Romaine, S. (1994). *Language in society. An introduction to sociolinguistics*. Oxford: Oxford University Press.

Romaine, S. (1995). *Bilingualism*. Oxford: Blackwell.

Rosenbaum, G. (2000). "Fushammiyya": Alternating style in Egyptian prose. *Zeitschrift for arabische Linguistik, 38*, 68–87.

Rosenbaum, G. (2004). Egyptian Arabic as a written language. *Jerusalem Studies in Arabic and Islam, 29*, 281–340.

Rosenbaum, G. (2011). The rise and expansion of Colloquial Egyptian Arabic as a literary language. In R. Sela-Sheffy & G. Toury (Eds.), *Culture contacts and the making of cultures* (pp. 323–344). Tel Aviv: Tel Aviv University, Unit of Culture Research.

Rosenhouse, J., & Dbayyat, N. (2006). Gender switch in female speech of an urbanized Arabic dialect in Israel. *Anthropological Linguistics, 48*(2), 169–186.

Rosowsky, A. (2007). Qurʼanic literacy: Its central role in the life of UK Muslim communities. *NALDIC Quarterly, 5*(2), 44.

Rothman, J. (2007). Heritage speaker competence differences, language change and input type: Inflected infinitives in heritage Brazilian Portuguese. *International Journal of Bilingualism, 11*(4), 359–389.

Rouchdy, A. (1992). Borrowing in Arab-American speech. In A. Rouchdy (Ed.), *The Arab language in America* (pp. 36–49). Detroit: Wayne State University Press.

Rouchdy, A. (2013). Language conflict and identity: Arabic in the American diaspora. In A. Rouchdy (Ed.), *Language contact and language conflict in Arabic: Variations on a sociolinguistic theme* (pp. 133–148). London: Routledge.

Royal, A. M. (1985). Male/female pharyngalization patterns in Cairo Arabic: A sociolinguistic study of two neighborhoods. (Unpublished doctoral thesis). University of Texas, Austin.

Rubin, H., & Rubin. I. (2005). *Qualitative interviewing: The art of hearing data.* (2nd ed.). Thousand Oaks, CA: Sage.

Ruiz, R. (1984). Orientations in language planning. *NABE Journal, 8,* 15–34.

Ryan, E., Giles, H., & Sebastian, R. (1982). An integrative perspective for the study of attitudes toward language variation. In E. Ryan & H. Giles (Eds.), *Attitudes towards language variation* (pp. 1–19). London: Edward Arnold.

Ryding, K. (1991). Proficiency despite diglossia: A new approach for Arabic. *Modern Language Journal, 75*(2), 212–218.

Ryding, K. (2005). *A reference grammar of modern standard Arabic.* Cambridge, UK: Cambridge University Press.

Ryding, K. (2009). Educated Spoken Arabic: A flexible spoken standard. *NECTFL Review, 64,* 49–52.

Sa'aada, A. (2014 [1938]). *Nushuu' Al-umam* [The creation of nations]. Beirut: Sa'aada Cultural Foundation.

Saadah, E. (2011). The production of Arabic vowels by English L2 learners and heritage speakers of Arabic. (Unpublished doctoral dissertation). University of Illinois, Urbana-Champaign.

Sa'ar, A. (2007). Masculine talk: On the subconscious use of masculine linguistic forms among Hebrew- and Arabic-speaking women in Israel. *Signs: Journal of Women in Culture and Society, 32*(2), 405–429.

Sabir, M., & Safi, S. (2008). Developmental diglossia: Diglossic switching and the Equivalence Constraint. *JKAU Arts and Humanities, 16*(2), 91–110.

Sadiqi, F. (1995). The language of women in the city of Fés, Morocco. *International Journal of the Sociology of Language, 112,* 63–79.

Sadiqi, F. (1997). The place of Berber in Morocco. *International Journal of the Sociology of Language, 123,* 7–21.

Sadiqi, F. (2003). *Women, gender and language in Morocco.* Leiden: Brill.

Sadiqi, F. (2006a). Language and gender. In K. Versteegh, M. Eid, A. Elgibali, M. Woidich, & A. Zaborski, (Eds.), *Encyclopedia of Arabic language and linguistics* (pp. 642–650). Leiden: Brill.

Sadiqi, F. (2006b). The gendered use of Arabic and other languages in Morocco. In D. Parkinson & E. Benmamoun (Eds.), *Perspectives on Arabic linguistics* (pp. 1–41). Amsterdam: John Benjamins.

Saeed, A. (1997). The pragmatics of codeswitching Fusha Arabic to Aammiyyah Arabic in religious oriented discourse. (Unpublished doctoral dissertation). Ball State University, Muncie, IN.

Safi, S. (1992). Functions of codeswitching: Saudi Arabic in the United States. In A. Rouchdy (Ed.), *The Arabic language in America* (pp. 72–80). Detroit: Wayne State University.

Said, E. (1978). *Orientalism.* New York: Pantheon.

Saidat, A. (2006). The syntax of Quranic Classical Arabic: A principles and parameters approach. (Unpublished doctoral dissertation). University of Texas, Arlington.

Saidat, A. (2010). Language attitude: The case of Jordan. *International Journal of Academic Research, 2*(2), 235–243.

Saiegh-Haddad, E. (2005). Correlates of reading fluency in Arabic: Diglossic and orthographic factors. *Reading and Writing, 18*(6), 559–582.

Saiegh-Haddad, E., Levin, I., Hende, N., & Ziv, M. (2011). The linguistic affiliation constraint and phoneme recognition in diglossic Arabic. *Journal of Child Language, 38,* 297–315.

Sakr, L. (2013). A digital humanities approach: Text, the Internet, and the Egyptian Uprising. *Middle East Critique, 22*(3), 247–263.

Salaita, S. (2005). Ethnic identity and imperative patriotism: Arab Americans before and after 9/11. *College Literature, 32*(2), 146–168.

Salam, A. (1980). Phonological variation in educated spoken Arabic: A study of the uvular and related plosive types. *Bulletin of the School of Oriental and African Studies, 43,* 77–100.

Salia, R. (2011). Between Arabic and French lies the dialect: Moroccan code-weaving on Facebook. (Undergraduate thesis). Columbia University, New York.

Samy, W. (2006). Internet. In K. Versteegh, Eid, M., A. Elgibali, M. Woldich & A. Zaborski (eds.), *Encyclopedia of Arabic language and linguistics* (pp. 380–387). Leiden: Brill.

Sarroub, L. (2005). Discontinuities and differences among Muslim Arab-Americans: Making it at home and school. In M.L. Dantas & P.C. Manyak (Eds.), *Home-school connections in a multicultural society: Learning from and with culturally and linguistically diverse families* (pp. 76–93). London: Routledge.

Sarrouf, Y. (1929). Al-lughah Al-'arabiyyah wa l-ta'riib wa-l-tazammut fiih [The Arabic Language, Arabization, and strictness in it]. *Al-Muqtataf, 74*(5), 250–265.

Saville-Troike, M. (1989). The ethnographic analysis of communicative events. In M. Saville-Troike (Ed.), *The ethnography of communication: An introduction* (pp. 107–139). Oxford: Blackwell.

Sawaie, M. (1992). Arabic in the melting pot: Will it survive? In A. Rouchdy (Ed.), *The Arabic language in America* (pp. 83–99). Detroit: Wayne State University Press.

Sawaie, M. (1994). *Linguistic variation and speakers' attitudes.* Damascus: Al Jaffar & Al Jabi Publisher.

Sawaie, M. (2006). Language academies. In K. Versteegh, M. Eid, A. Elgibali, M. Woidich, & A. Zaborski (Eds.), *Encyclopedia of Arabic language and linguistics* (pp. 634–42). Leiden: Brill.

Sayadi, M. (1982). Al-ta'riib wa dawruhu fi tad'iim Al-wujuud al-'arabiyy was l-waħdah al-'arabiyyah [Arabization and its role in supporting the Arab existence and unity]. Beirut: Markaz Diraasaat Al-Waħda Al-'Arabiyya.

Sayahi, L. (2014). *Diglossia and language contact: Language variation and change in North Africa.* Cambridge, UK: Cambridge University Press.

Schegloff, E. (1992). In another context. In A. Duranti & C. Goodwin (Eds.), *Rethinking context: Language as an interactive phenomenon* (pp. 191–227). Cambridge, UK: Cambridge University Press.

Schiffman, H.F. (1996). *Linguistic culture and language policy.* London: Routledge.

Schiffman, H.F. (1997). Diglossia as a sociolinguistic situation. In F. Coulmas (Ed.), *The handbook of sociolinguistics* (pp. 205–216). London: Basil Blackwell.

Schilling-Estes, N. (2013). Investigating stylistic variation. In J.K. Chambers & N. Schilling-Estes (Eds.), *The handbook of language variation and change* (pp. 327–349). Oxford: Blackwell.

Schmid, M. (2002). *First language attrition, use and maintenance: The case of German Jews in Anglophone countries.* Amsterdam: John Benjamins.

Schmidt, R. W. (1974). Sociolinguistic variation in Spoken Egyptian Arabic: A re-examination of the concept of diglossia. (Unpublished doctoral dissertation). Georgetown University, Washington, DC.

Schmidt, R. W. (1986). Applied sociolinguistics: The case of Arabic as a second language. *Anthropological linguistics, 28*(1), 55–72.

Schulz, D. (1981). *Diglossia and variation in formal spoken Arabic in Egypt.* (Unpublished doctoral dissertation). University of Wisconsin, Madison.

Schwandt, T. (2000). Three epistemological stances from qualitative inquiry: interpretivism, hermeneutics, and social constructivism. In N. K. Denzin & Y. S. Lincoln (Eds.), *Handbook of qualitative research* (2nd ed.) (pp. 189–214). Thousand Oaks: Sage.

Scolve, R. (1998). The democratic use of technology. *Thought & Action Journal, 14*(1), 9–18.

Sehlaoui, A. (2011). Language learning, heritage, and literacy in the USA: The case of Arabic. *Language, Culture, and Curriculum, 21*(3), 280–291.

Seliger, H. W., & Vago, R. M. (1991). The study of first language attrition: An overview. In H. W. Seliger & R. M. Vago (Eds.), *First language attrition* (pp. 3–15). Cambridge, UK: Cambridge University Press.

Semah, D. (1995). Modern Arabic Zajal and the quest for freedom. *Journal of Arabic Literature, 26*(1/2), 80–92.

Seymour-Jorn, C. (2004). Arabic language learning among Arab immigrants in Milwaukee, Wisconsin: A study of attitudes and motivations. *Journal of Muslim Minority Affairs, 24*(1), 109–122.

Shaaban, K. (2006). Language policies and planning. In K. Versteegh, M. Eid, A. Elgibali, M. Woidich, & A. Zaborski (Eds.), *Encyclopedia of Arabic language and linguistics* (pp. 694–707). Leiden: Brill.

Shaaban, K., & Ghaith, G. (2002). University students' perceptions of the ethnolinguistic vitality of Arabic, French and English in Lebanon. *Journal of Sociolinguistics, 6*(4), 557–574.

Shaaban, K., & Ghaith, G. (2003). Effect of religion, first foreign language, and gender on the perception of the utility of language. *Journal of Language Identity & Education, 2*(1), 53–77.

Shaalan, K. (2014). A survey of Arabic named entity recognition and classification. *Computational Linguistics, 40*(2), 469–510.

Shahidullah, S. (1991). *Capacity-building in science and technology in the third world.* Boulder, CO: Westview Press.

Shahiid, A. (2002). Tajribat Sourya fi ta'riib al-'uluum fi al-ta'liim al-'aali [Syria's experience in Arabizing education in higher education]. A paper presented at The Arabic Language, Where To? Symposium, Umm Al-Qura University, Mecca, Saudi Arabia, 1–3 November. Retrieved from http://uqu.edu.sa/page/ar/148364.

Sharwood Smith, M. A., & van Buren, P. (1991). First language attrition and the parameter-setting model. In H. Seliger & R. Vago (Eds.), *Language attrition: Structural and theoretical perspectives.* Cambridge, UK: Cambridge University Press.

Sherazade, B. (1993). Gender and ethnicity: Language attitudes and use in an Algerian context. (Unpublished doctoral dissertation). University of Columbia, New York.

Sheyholislami, J. (2008). Identity, discourse, and the media: The case of the Kurds. (Unpublished doctoral dissertation). Carleton University, Canada.

Shiri, S. (2002). Speak Arabic please! Tunisian Arabic speakers' linguistic accommodation to Middle Easterners. In A. Rouchdy (Ed.), *Language contact and language conflict in Arabic* (pp. 149–174). London: Routledge Curzon.

Shiri, S. (2010). Arabic in the United States. In K. Potowski (Ed.), *Linguistic diversity in the United States* (pp. 206–222). Cambridge, UK: Cambridge University Press.

Shohamy, E. (2006). *Language policy: Hidden agendas and new approaches.* London: Routledge.

Shryock, A., & Lin, A. (2009). Arab American identities in question. In the Detroit Arab American Study Team (Eds.), *Citizenship and crisis: Arab Detroit after 9/11* (pp. 35–68). New York: Russell Sage Foundation.

Siegel, J. (1985). Koines and koineization. *Language in Society, 14,* 357–378.

Silva-Corvalán, C. (1994). *Language contact and change: Spanish in Los Angeles.* Oxford. Oxford University Press.

Silva-Corvalán, C. (2003). Linguistic consequences of reduced input in bilingual first language acquisition. In S. Montrul & F. Ordóñez (Eds.), *Linguistic theory and language development in Hispanic languages* (pp. 375–397). Somerville, MA: Cascadilla Press.

Silverstein, M. (1992). The indeterminacy of contextualization: When is enough enough? In P. Auer & A. Di Luzio (Eds.), *The contextualization of language* (pp. 55–76). Amsterdam: John Benjamins.

Silverstein, M. (2003). Indexical order and the dialectics of sociolinguistic life. *Language & Communication, 23,* 193–229.

Silverstein, P. (1996). Realizing myth: The Berber movement in Algeria and France. *Middle East Report, 200/26*(3), 11–15.

Simon, B. (2004). *Identity in modern society: A social psychological perspective.* Malden, MA: Blackwell.

Siraaj, N. (2013). *Al-shabaab wa lughatu al-'asr* [The youth and the language of the contemporary age]. Beirut: Mu'assatu Al-Fikr Al-'Arabiyy.

Sirles, C. (1999). Politics and Arabization: The evolution of postindependence North Africa. *International Journal of the Sociology of Language, 137*(1), 115–130.

Smart, J. R. (1990). Pidginization in Gulf Arabic: A first report. *Anthropological Linguistics, 32,* 83–118.

Smith, A. (1981). States and homelands: The social and geopolitical implications of national territory. *Millennium: Journal of International Studies, 10*(3), 187–202.

Smith, A. (1986). *The ethnic origins of nations.* Oxford: Blackwell.

Soliman, A. (2008). The changing role of Arabic in religious discourse: A sociolinguistic study of Egyptian Arabic. (Unpublished Doctoral dissertation). Indiana University of Pennsylvania, Indiana, PA.

Soltan, U. (2007). On formal feature licensing in minimalism: Aspects of standard Arabic morphosyntax. (Unpublished doctoral dissertation). University of Maryland, College Park.

Somekh, S. (1991). *Genre and language in modern Arabic literature.* Wiesbaden: Otto Harrassowitz.

Somers, M. (1994). The narrative constitution of identity: A relational and network approach. *Theory and Society, 23*(4), 5–49.

Spencer, J. (2001). Ethnography after post-modernism. In P. Atkinson, A. Coffey, S. Delamont, J. Lofland, & L. Lofland (Eds.), *Handbook of ethnography.* Thousand Oaks, CA: Sage.

Spolsky, B. (2004). *Language policy.* Cambridge, UK: Cambridge University Press.

Stanley, L., & Wise, S. (1993). *Breaking out again: Feminist ontology and epistemology.* London: Routledge.

Stavans, I. (2000). Spanglish: Tickling the tongue. *World Literature Today.* Retrieved from http://isites.harvard.edu/fs/docs/icb.topic653576.files/Spanglish%20Tickling%20 the%20Tong ue.pdf

Stiffler, M. (2010). Authentic Arabs, authentic Christians: Antiochian Orthodox and the mobilization of cultural identity. (Unpublished doctoral dissertation). University of Michigan, Ann Arbor, MI.

Strong, C., & Hareb, H. (2012). Social media fashion among digitally fluent young Arabic women in the UAE. *Journal of Middle East Media, 8*(1), 1–21.

Suleiman, M. (1999). Introduction: The Arab immigrant experience. In M. Suleiman (Ed.), *Arabs in America: Building a new future* (pp. 1–24). Philadelphia: Temple University Press.

Suleiman, Y. (1993). The language situation in Jordan and codeswitching: A new interpretation, *New Arabian Studies*, 1–20.

Suleiman, Y. (1994). *Arabic sociolinguistics: Issues and perspectives.* Richmond: Curzon.

Suleiman, Y. (1996). *Language and identity in the Middle East and North Africa.* Richmond: Curzon.

Suleiman, Y. (2003). *The Arabic language and national identity.* Edinburgh: Edinburgh University Press.

Suleiman, Y. (2004). *A war of words: Language and conflict in the Middle East.* Cambridge, UK: Cambridge University Press.

Suleiman, Y. (2011). *Arabic, self and identity: A study in conflict and displacement.* Oxford: Oxford University Press.

Suleiman, Y. (2012). Ideology and the standardization of Arabic. In R. Bassiouney & Katz (Eds.), *Arabic language and linguistics* (pp. 201–213). Washington, DC: Georgetown University Press.

Suleiman, Y. (2013). *Arabic in the fray: Language ideology and cultural politics.* Edinburgh: Edinburgh University Press

Tabarani, G. G. (2008). *How Iran plans to fight America and dominate the Middle East.* Bloomington, IN: Author House.

Tagliamonte, S. (2011). *Variationist sociolinguistics: Change, observation, interpretation.* Oxford: Wiley-Blackwell.

Taha, Z. (2006). Toward pragmatic competency in Arabic. In K. Wahba, Z. Taha, & L. England (Eds.), *Handbook for Arabic language teaching professionals in the 21st century* (pp. 353–362). Mahwah, NJ: Lawrence Erlbaum.

Taine-Cheikh, C. (2002). De la variation linguistique dans le prêche populaire Mauritianien. In A. Rouchdy (ed.), *Language contact and language conflict in Arabic variations on a sociolinguistic theme* (pp. 177–202). New York: Curzon.

Taine-Cheikh, C. (2012). On the usefulness and limits of a geographic perspective in dialectology: Arabic and Berber examples. *Language Typology and Universals, 65*(1), 26–46.

Taki, M. (2010). Bloggers and the blogosphere in Lebanon & Syria: Meanings and activities. (Unpublished doctoral dissertation). University of Westminster, UK.

Taqi, H. (2010). Two ethnicities, three generations: Phonological variation and change in Kuwait. (Unpublished doctoral thesis). University of Newcastle, UK.

Tashakkori, A., & Teddlie, C. (2010). *Sage handbook of mixed methods in social & behavioral research.* Thousand Oaks, CA: Sage.

Teitelbaum, J. (2002). Dueling for da'wa: State vs. society on the Saudi internet. *Middle East Journal, 56*(2), 222–239.

Temples, A. (2013). Constructing Arabic as heritage: Investment in language, literacy, and identity among young U.S. learners. (Unpublished doctoral dissertation). Georgia State University, Atlanta, GA.

The Arabic Tongue. Retrieved from www.lisanarabi.com/vb/showthread.php?t=25

Thurlow, C., & Mroczek, K. (2011). *Digital discourse: Language in the new media.* Oxford: Oxford University Press.

Todd, J. (2011). *The politics of language policy in Morocco: The 2003 Berber language initiative.* (Unpublished doctoral dissertation). University of Wisconsin, Madison.

Tollefson, J.W. (2000). Policy and ideology in the spread of English. In J. K. Hall & W. G. Eggington (Eds.), *The sociopolitics of English language* (pp. 7–22). Clevedon: Multilingual Matters.

Tollin, S. (2012). Y aunque no lo creas, that works: A study of Spanish-English language mixing. (Master's thesis). University of Oslo, Oslo.

Tosco, M. (1995). A pidgin verbal system: The case of Juba Arabic. *Anthropological Linguistics, 37*, 423–459.

Tosco, M., & Manfredi, S. (2013). Pidgins and creoles. In J. Owens (Ed.), *The Oxford handbook of Arabic linguistics* (pp. 495–519). Oxford: Oxford University Press.

Trabelsi, C. (1991). De quelques aspects du langage des femmes de Tunis. *International Journal of the Sociology of Language, 87*, 87–98.

Trentman, E. (2011). L2 Arabic dialect comprehension: Empirical evidence for the transfer of familiar dialect knowledge to unfamiliar dialects. *L2 Journal, 3*, 22–49.

Trudgill, P. (1974). *The social differentiation of English in Norwich.* Cambridge, UK: Cambridge University Press.

Trudgill, P. (1986). *Dialects in contact.* Oxford: Basil Blackwell.

Trudgill, P. (2004). *New-dialect formation: The inevitability of colonial Englishes.* Edinburgh: Edinburgh University Press.

Trudgill, P. (2009). Contact, isolation, and complexity in Arabic. In E. Al-Wer & R. de Jong, *Arabic dialectology* (pp. 173–186). Leiden: Brill.

United States Census Bureau. (2003). American community survey. Retrieved from http://www.census.gov/acs/www/library/by_year/2003/

Valdés, G. (1981). Codeswitching as deliberate verbal strategy: A microanalysis of direct and indirect requests among bilingual Chicano speakers. In R. Duran (Ed.), *Latino language and communicative behavior* (pp. 95–107). Norwood, NJ: Ablex.

Valdés, G. (1992). The role of the foreign language teaching profession in maintaining non-English languages in the United States. In H. Byrnes (Ed.), *Languages for a multicultural world in transition: 1993 Northeast Conference reports* (pp. 29–71). Skokie, IL: National Textbook Company.

Vali, A. (2003). *Genealogies of the Kurds: Constructions of nation and national identity in Kurdish historical writing. Essays on the origins of Kurdish nationalism.* Costa Mesa: Mazda Publishing.

Valppu, J. (2013). Finnish students' uses of and attitudes towards English on Facebook. (Master's thesis). University of Jyväskylä, Finland.

Van Dijk, T.A. (2008). *Discourse and context: A sociocognitive approach.* Cambridge, UK: Cambridge University Press.

Van Gass, K. (2008). Language contact in computer-mediated communication: Afrikaans-English code switching on internet relay chat (IRC). *South African Linguistics and Applied Language Studies, 26*(4), 429–444.

Van Mol, M. (2003). *Variation in Modern Standard Arabic in radio news broadcasts: A synchronic descriptive investigation into the use of complementary particles.* Leuven, Belgium: Peeters Publishers.

Versteegh, K. (1984). *Pidginization and creolization: The case of Arabic.* Amsterdam: John Benjamins.

Versteegh, K. (1993). Levelling in the Sudan: From Arabic creole to Arabic dialect. *International Journal of the Sociology of Language, 99*, 65–79.

Versteegh, K. (1996). Linguistic attitudes and the origin of speech in the Arab world. In A. Elgibali (Ed.), *Understanding Arabic* (pp. 15–31). Cairo: American University in Cairo Press.

Versteegh, K. (1997). *Landmarks in linguistic thought* III. London: Routledge.

Versteegh, K. (2001). *The Arabic language.* Edinburgh: Edinburgh University Press.

Versteegh, K. (2004). Pidginization and creolization revisited: The case of Arabic. In M. Haak, R. de Jong & K. Versteegh (Eds.), *Approaches to Arabic dialects* (pp. 359–372). Leiden: Brill.

Vicente, A. (2009). Gender and language boundaries in the Arab world: Current issues and perspectives. *Estudios de dialectología norteafricana y andalusí, 13*, 7–30.

Wahba, K. (1996). Linguistic variation in Alexandrian Arabic: The feature of stress. In A. Elgibali (Ed.), *Understanding Arabic: Essays in contemporary Arabic linguistics in honor of El-Said Badawi* (pp. 103–128). Cairo: American University in Cairo Press.

Walker, K. (2000). It's difficult to hide it: The presentation of self on internet home pages. *Qualitative Sociology, 23*, 99–120.

Wallin, G. (1851). Notes taken during a journey through part of Northern Arabia, in 1848. *Journal of the Royal Geographical Society, 20*, 293–344.

Walters, K. (1989). Social change, and linguistic variation in Korba, a small Tunisian town. (Unpublished doctoral dissertation). University of Texas, Austin.

Walters, K. (1991). Women, men, and linguistic variation in the Arab world. In B. Comrie and M. Eid (Eds.), *Perspectives on Arabic Linguistics III* (pp. 199–229). Amsterdam: John Benjamins.

Walters, K. (1996). Diglossia, linguistic variation, and language change in Arabic. In M. Eid (Ed.), *Perspectives on Arabic linguistics VIII* (pp. 157–197). Amsterdam: John Benjamins.

Walters, K. (2003). Fergies prescience: The changing nature of diglossia in Tunisia. *International Journal of the Sociology of Language, 163*, 77–109.

Walters, K. (2006). Language attitudes. In K. Versteegh, M. Eid, A. Elgibali, M. Woidich, & A. Zaborski (Eds.), *Encyclopedia of Arabic language and linguistics* (pp. 650–664), Leiden: Brill.

Walters, K. (2011). Gendering French in Tunisia: Language ideologies and nationalism. *International Journal of the Sociology of Language, 211*, 83–111.

Wannas-Jones, J. (2003). Globalization and the reconciliation of dissonant hybrid identities: A case study of Canadian-Arab youths. (Unpublished doctoral dissertation). University of Alberta, Canada.

Ward, K. (2000). *Religion and community.* Oxford: Clarendon Press.

Warschauer, M., El Said, G., & Zohry, A. (2002). Language.com: Language choice online: Globalization and identity in Egypt. *Journal of Computer-Mediated Communication, 7*(4), 1–18.

Webber, J. (1997). Jews and Judaism in contemporary Europe: Religious or ethnic group? *Ethnic and Racial Studies, 20*, 225–252.

Wei, L. (1994). *Three generations, two languages, one family language: Language choice and language shift in a Chinese community in Britain*. Clevedon: Multilingual Matters.

Weinreich, U. (1968). *Languages in contact*. The Hague: Mouton.

Weinreich, U., Labov, W., & Herzog, M. (1968). Empirical foundations for a theory of language change. In W. Lehmann & Y. Malkiel (Eds.), *Directions for historical linguistics* (pp. 95–195), Austin: University of Texas Press.

Wellens, I. (2005). *The Nubi language of Uganda*. Leiden: Brill

Wetzstein, J. G. (1868). Sprachliches aus den Zeltlagern der syrischen Wüste. *Zeitschrift der Deutschen Morgenländischen Gesellschaft*, 22, 69–194.

Wheeler, D. (2006). *The Internet in the Middle East: Global expectations and local imaginations in Kuwait*. Albany, NY: State University of New York Press.

Whitty, M. T., & Carr, A. N. (2006). *Cyberspace romance: The psychology of online relationships*. Basingstoke: Palgrave Macmillan.

Wild, S. (2006). Arabic language. In O. Leaman (Ed.), *The Qur'an: An encyclopedia* (pp. 49–54). London: Routledge.

Williams, C. H. (1991). Language planning and social change: Ecological speculations. In D. Marshall (Ed.), *Focus on language planning: Essays in honour of Joshua A. Fishman* (pp. 53–74). Amsterdam: John Benjamins.

Wilmsen, D. (2006). What is communicative Arabic? In K. Wahba, Z. Taha, & L. England (Eds.), *Handbook for Arabic language teaching professionals in the 21st century* (pp. 125–138). Mahwah, NJ: Lawrence Erlbaum.

Wilson, C., & Dunn, A. (2011). Digital media in the Egyptian Revolution: Descriptive analysis from the Tahrir data sets. *International Journal of Communication, 5*, 1248–1272.

Wilson, D. (2013). The intersection of identity, gender, and attitudes toward maintenance among beginning Spanish as a heritage language students. *Southwest Journal of Linguistics, 31*(1), 177–198.

Wingfield, M. (2006). Arab Americans: Into the multicultural mainstream. *Equity & Excellence in Education, 39*, 253–266.

Wodak, R., & Meyer, M. (Eds.) (2009). *Methods of critical discourse analysis* (2nd ed.). Thousand Oaks, CA: Sage.

Woidich, M. (1994). Cairo Arabic and the Egyptian dialects. In D. Caubet & M. Vanhove (Eds.), *Actes des premières journées internationales de dialectologie arabe de Paris* (pp. 493–507). Paris: INALCO.

Woidich, M. (1996). Rural dialect of Egyptian Arabic: An overview. *Égypte-monde arabe* [Les langues en Égypte], *27–28*, 325–354.

Wolfram, W. (1991). The linguistic variable: Fact and fantasy. *American Speech, 66*(1), 22–32.

Wolfram, W. (2006). Variation and language, an overview. In K. Brown (Ed.), *Encyclopedia of Language and Linguistics* (pp. 333–341). Oxford: Elsevier.

Wolfram, W., & Fasold, R. (1974). *The study of social dialects in American English*. New York: Prentice-Hall.

Wolfson, N. (1986). Research methodology and the question of validity. *TESOL Quarterly, 20*(4), 82–92.

World Bank (2014). *World development indicators: Urban development*. Retrieved from http://data.worldbank.org/topic/urban-development

Wright, S. (2004). *Language policy and language planning: From nationalism to globalization*. New York: Palgrave Macmillan.

Yaghan, M. (2008). "Arabizi": A contemporary style of Arabic slang. *Massachusetts Institute of Technology Design Issues, 24*(2), 39–52.

Yassin, M.A.F. (1975). A linguistic study of forms of address in Kuwaiti colloquial Arabic. (Unpublished doctoral dissertation). University of Leeds, UK.

Younes, M. (2006). Integrating the Colloquial with *Fushā* in the Arabic-as-a-foreign-language classroom. In K.M. Wahba, Z.A. Taha, & L. England (Ed.), *Handbook for Arabic language teaching professionals in the 21st century* (pp. 157–166). Mahwah, NJ: Lawrence Erlbaum.

Younes, M. (2009). The case for integration in the Arabic-as-a-foreign language classroom. *NECTFL Review, 64*, 59–67.

Youssi, A. (1995). The Moroccan triglossia: Facts and implications. *International Journal of the Sociology of Language, 112*, 29–44.

Zaidan, J. (1988). *Al-lugha Al-Arabiyya Kaa?inun Hayy* [The Arabic language: A living Being]. Beirut, Lebanon: Daar Al-Jeel.

Zakaria, A. (1983). *'Ashaa'ir Al-Sham* [Clans of Greater Syria]. Damascus: Daar Al-Fikr.

Zakharia, Z. (2008). Languages, schooling, and the (re-)construction of identity in contemporary Lebanon. (Unpublished doctoral dissertation). Columbia University, New York.

Zeine, Z. (1977). The Arab lands. In P. M. Holt, A. Lambton, & B. Lewis (Eds.), *The Cambridge history of Islam* (pp. 566–594). Cambridge, UK: Cambridge University Press.

Zimbardo, P., Ebbesen, E., & Maslach, C. (1977). *Influencing attitudes and changing behavior*. Addison-Wesley Publishing Company.

Zimmerman, D.H. (1992). Achieving context: Openings in emergency calls. In G. Watson & R. M. Seiler (Eds.), *Text in context: Contributions to ethnomethodology* (pp. 35–51). Thousand Oaks, CA: Sage.

Zisser, E. (2006). Who's afraid of Syrian nationalism? National and state identity in Syria. *Middle Eastern Studies, 42*(2), 179–198.

Zughoul, M. (1980). Diglossia in Arabic: Investigating solutions, *Anthropological Linguistics, 22*(5), 201–217.

Zuwaini, S. (2012). *Al-ḥiraak al-'jtimaa'i li-l-lugha al- 'arabiyya wa ṭ-ṭakhṭiiṭ al-lughawi wa-l-hawiyyah al-waṭaniyyah* [Social mobilization for the Arabic language and language planning and national identity]. Paper presented at the First International Conference on the Arabic Language, Beirut, 19–23 March. Retrieved from www.alarabiah.org/index.php?op=view_all_studies&id=15

Zwettler, M. (1978). *The oral tradition of Classical Arabic poetry*. Columbus, OH: Ohio State University Press.

APPENDICES

APPENDIX 1

Questionnaire: Arabic and English versions

جامعة ولاية يوتا

استبيان الآراء اللغوية

الدكتور عبد الكافي البيريني

هذا الاستبيان جزء من دراسة تهدف إلى فهم آراء الناطقين باللغة العربية بمختلف اللغات و اللهجات المحكية في حياتهم. يتألف الاستبيان من سبعة أقسام. يبتدأ كل قسم ببعض التعليمات التي تخص ذلك القسم فقط. قبل أن تبدأ بالإجابة على كل قسم الرجاء قراءة التعليمات بدقة ثمَّ الإجابة بصراحة حسب الشكل المطلوب. إن نجاح هذا البحث متوقف على جدية ونزاهة أجوبتكم. لا تحتوي هذه الاستمارة على أية معلومات تعرّف بالمشارك. الرجاء الإجابة على جميع الأسئلة.

	معلومات عامة		
1.	الرمز : لا تكتب هنا	2. التاريخ:	3. البلد الاصلي:
4.	الجنس:	5. العمر:	6. الدين:
7.	معدل دخل أسرتك الشهري بعملة بلدك:		
8.	الاصل العرقي: □ عربي □ غير عربي (حدد):		
9.	اللغات التي تتكلمها: □ العربية الفصحى □ العربية العامية □ الانكليزية □ الفرنسية □ لغة أخرى (حدد):		
10.	أعلى شهادة حصلت عليها: □ مدرسة ابتدائية أو اعدادية □ مدرسة ثانوية □ إجازة/بكالوريوس □ ماجستير □ دكتوراة		
11.	في أي مجال من المجالات التالية تعمل أو تدرس الآن: □ التربية □ الكمبيوتر □ الطب □ الهندسة □ عامل حرّ □ السياحة □ التجارة □ الحقوق □ السياسة □ عمل آخر (حدد):		
12.	في أي مجال من المجالات التالية تود الدراسة أو العمل مستقبلا : □ التربية □ الكمبيوتر □ الطب □ الهندسة □ عامل حرّ □ السياحة □ التجارة □ الحقوق □ السياسة □ عمل آخر (حدد):		

					13. ماهي الاماكن التي زرتها وكم كانت مدة الزيارة: □ بلاد عربية (حدد البلد و المدة): .... □ بلاد تسود فيها الانكليزية (حدد البلد و المدة): .... □ بلاد تسود فيها الفرنسية (حدد البلد و المدة) .... □ لغات أخرى (حدد البلد و المدة): ....

رتّب اللغات بملأ الفراغات بالنقاط التالية: 4 = الخيار الأول/المفضل، 3= الخيار الثاني، 2= الخيار الثالث، 1= الخيار الرابع، 0= الخيار الخامس/الأخير

لغات أخرى	اللغة الفرنسية	اللغة الانكليزية	العربية العاميّة	العربية الفصحى	
					1. اللغة الرسمية في العالم العربي يجب أن تكون
					2. وددت لو أنّ بإمكان العرب التحدث بـ
					3. اللغة التي يجب المحافظة عليها هي
					4. يجب مناقشة الدين بـ
					5. لغة التجارة و الأعمال يجب أن تكون
					6. لغتي المفضلة هي
					7. لو كان لدي فرصة تعلم لغة واحدة في حياتي لاخترت
					8. أفضّلُ قراءة الكتب و الجرائد و المجلات بـ
					9. لغة الإعلام يجب أن تكون
					10. لغة التعليم من المرحلة الابتدائية إلى المرحلة الجامعية يجب أن تكون
					11. أثناء القيام بأعمالهم على موظفي الحكومة استعمال
					12. اللغة التي أحب أن أتحدّث بها في الغالب هي
					13. الأشخاص الذين يحبّون أن يظهروا كمتدينين يستعملون
					14. اللغة الأوثق ارتباطاً بثقافتي هي
					15. الأشخاص الذين يحبّون أن يظهروا كعصريين يستعملون
					16. أفضل لغة لدراسة العلوم والتكنولوجيا هي
					17. لكي أحصل على وظيفة جيدة يجب أن أتقن

	لغات أخرى	اللغة الفرنسية	اللغة الانكليزية	العربية العامّية	العربية الفصحى
18. اللغة الأكثر غنىً من حيث التعبير هي					
19. الأشخاص الذين يحبّون أن يظهروا كمتفتّحين يستعملون					
20. اللغة الأكثر الفائدة الأكثر لي في حياتي اليومية هي					
21. اللغة الأكثر تأثيراً على المستمع هي					
22. اللغة ذات الفائدة الأكبر لي في حياتي المهنية هي					
23. المثقفون العرب يتكلمون بـ					
24. لكي تكون عربياً من المهم التحدّث بـ					
25. معظم الموسيقى التي أستمع إليها بـ					
26. معظم المواقع الالكترونية التي أزورها بـ					
27. غالباً ما أكتب الرسائل الالكترونية (الإيميل) بـ					
28. الكتب التي أقرأها بـ					
29. معظم القنوات والبرامج التلفزيونية التي أشاهدها بـ					
30. عندما أبعث رسائل نَصيّة هاتفيّة غالباً أستعمل					
31. معظم برامج الراديو التي أستمع إليها بـ					
32. عندما أكون مع عائلتي أو أصدقائي أو معارفي أتحدث بـ					
33. معظم الأفلام التي أشاهدها بـ					
34. أستمع إلى التعليقات الرياضية بـ					
35. عندما أتحدّث مع أشخاص لا أعرفهم، أستعمل					
36. لو أنّ هناك لغة أحاول إتقانها ، لكانت					

حدد اللغات التي ستستخدمها في كلٍ من الحالات التالية بملأ الفراغات بالنقاط التالية: 4 = دائماً، 3= غالباً، 2= أحياناً، 1= نادراً، 0= لا أبداً

لغات أخرى	اللغة الفرنسية	اللغة الانكليزية	العربية العاميّة	العربية الفصحى		
					مع أفراد العائلة في البيت	1.
					مع الأصدقاء و المعارف	2.
					مع نادل في مطعم	3.
					لتكتب أو تروي قصة شعبية	4.
					مع الزملاء في العمل أو في المدرسة/الجامعة	5.
					في مسلسل في الراديو	6.
					لتكتب رسالة شخصية	7.
					لتقدّم تقرير أخباري	8.
					لتلقي خطاب سياسي	9.
					لتلقي خطبة دينية	10.
					لتلقي محاضرة في الجامعة	11.
					لتلقي قصيدة	12.
					لتسبّ	13.
					لتمزح أو تهرّج	14.
					لتوبّخ أو تهين	15.
					لتقول أمثال أو أقوال شعبية تستخدم في الحياة اليومية	16.
					لتتحدث عن موضوع غير مهم أو غير ذي شأن	17.
					لتبسّط فكرة أو تضرب مثال من الحياة اليومية	18.
					لتناقش موضوع هام في اجتماع عمل	19.
					لتتحدّث بكلام فصيح أو مقفى (منظوم)	20.
					لتظهر كشخص متعلم متحذلق	21.
					لتُعبّر عن هويتك العربية أو انتمائك العربي	22.
					لتؤكّد على أهمية الموضوع الذي تتحدث عنه	23.
					لتقتبس شخص حرفياً	24.

رتب اللغات من حيث ارتباطها بالسمات التالية وذلك باستخدام النقاط التالية: 4 = الخيار الأول/المفضل،   3= الخيار الثاني،   2= الخيار الثالث،   1= الخيار الرابع،   0= الخيار الخامس/الأخير

لغات أخرى	اللغة الفرنسية	اللغة الانكليزيّة	العربية العاميّة	العربية الفصحى	
					1. الصفة الرسمية
					2. الدولية
					3. الارتباط بمعرفة القراءة والكتابة
					4. تعددية الإستخدام
					5. القوة أو السلطة
					6. العملية
					7. الفصاحة
					8. الجمال
					9. الأصالة
					10. المرموقية (البرستيج)
					11. النقاء
					12. الغنى

من فضلك ضع دائرة حول الرقم الذي يحدد مدى موافقتك أو عدم موافقتك مع كل من العبارات التالية.

أعارض بقوة	أعارض	حيادي	أوافق	أوافق بقوة	
0	1	2	3	4	1. لا أرغب في أن يعرف الناس هويتي العربية
0	1	2	3	4	2. أنا سعيد أنني من أصول عربية
0	1	2	3	4	3. أفتخر كثيراً بالتراث العربي
0	1	2	3	4	4. أحب العادات والتقاليد العربية، مثل اللباس و التحيّة
0	1	2	3	4	5. أحب أن أزيد معرفتي بأصولي وثقافتي العربية
0	1	2	3	4	6. أحب أن أكون عضواً في هيئات و مجموعات يتكون معظمها من العرب
0	1	2	3	4	7. أستمتع بالاختلاط مع أناس ذوي أصول غير عربية.
0	1	2	3	4	8. أحب الاشتراك في نشاطات ثقافية عربية، مثل الأكل و الموسيقى.
0	1	2	3	4	9. لا أشعر بارتباط قوي بالأرض العربية.

	أوافق بقوة	أوافق	حيادي	أعارض	أعارض بقوة
10. أفضّل مصادقة أشخاص من أصول غير عربية	4	3	2	1	0
11. ديني هو جزء منّي.	4	3	2	1	0
12. ليس للثقافة العربية صلة بحياتي الشخصية	4	3	2	1	0

حدد مدى مقدرتك على التحدث باللغات التالية بوضع دائرة حول الرقم المناسب

	أتكلمها بطلاقة	أتكلمها جيد جداً	أتكلمها جيداً	أتكلمها بشكل مقبول	أتكلمها بشكل ضعيف	لا أتكلمها إطلاقاً
1. العربية الفصحى	5	4	3	2	1	0
2. العربية العاميّة	5	4	3	2	1	0
3. اللغة الانكليزية	5	4	3	2	1	0
4. اللغة الفرنسية	5	4	3	2	1	0
5. لغات أخرى (حدد):	5	4	3	2	1	0

حدد مدى مقدرتك على فهم اللغات التالية بوضع دائرة حول الرقم المناسب

	أفهمها تماماً	أفهمها جيد جداً	أفهمها جيداً	أفهمها بشكل مقبول	أفهمها بشكل ضعيف	لا أفهمها إطلاقاً
1. العربية الفصحى	5	4	3	2	1	0
2. العربية العاميّة	5	4	3	2	1	0
3. اللغة الانكليزية	5	4	3	2	1	0
4. اللغة الفرنسية	5	4	3	2	1	0
5. لغات أخرى (حدد):	5	4	3	2	1	0

شكرا على منحي بعضا من وقتكم للإجابة على هذه الأسئلة

Utah State University
Language Attitudes Questionnaire

By Abdulkafi Albirini

The following questionnaire is a part of a study that aims to understand the Arab people's attitudes toward the different languages and spoken varieties in their lives. The questionnaire consists of seven sections. Each section begins with some directions pertaining to that part only. As you begin each section, please read the directions carefully and provide your responses candidly in the format requested. The success of this research depends on your serious and honest answers. No information identifying you will appear anywhere on this question-naire. Please make sure to respond to all the questions.

General Information		
1. Code: Don't write here	2. Date:	3. Country of origin:
4. Gender: ☐ Male ☐ Female	5. Age:	6. Religion:
7. Monthly average household income in your country's currency:		
8. What is your ethnic origin: ☐ Arab ☐ Non-Arab (specify)		
9. What languages do you speak? ☐ Standard Arabic ☐ Colloquial Arabic ☐ English ☐ French ☐ Other (specify)...............		
10. What is your highest completed academic degree? ☐ Elementary/middle school ☐ High school ☐ Bachelors ☐ Master's ☐ Doctorate		
11. In which of these areas do you work/study? ☐ education ☐ computers ☐ medicine ☐ engineering ☐ freelance worker ☐ tourism ☐ commerce ☐ law ☐ politics ☐ Other (specify)...............		
12. In which of these areas do you want to work in the future? ☐ education ☐ computers ☐ medicine ☐ engineering ☐ freelance worker ☐ tourism ☐ commerce ☐ law ☐ politics ☐ Other (specify)...............		
13. Which of these places have you visited and for how long? ☐ Arab countries (specify country and duration): ☐ English-speaking countries (specify country and duration): ☐ French-speaking countries (specify country and duration): ☐ Other (specify country and duration):		

(*continued*)

	Standard Arabic	Colloquial Arabic	English	French	Other
Rank the languages by filling in the blanks using these numbers: 4=first favorite, 3=second favorite, 2=third favorite, 1=fourth favorite, 0=fifth favorite					
1. The official language in the Arab world should be					
2. I wish Arabs can converse in					
3. The language that we need to maintain is					
4. Religion should be discussed in					
5. The language of business should be					
6. The language(s) that I prefer is/are					
7. If I had been given the chance to learn one language in my life, I would have chosen					
8. I prefer reading books, newspapers, magazines in					
9. The language of media should be					
10. The language of education from elementary school to university should be					
11. When at work, government employees should use					
12. The language that I like to speak most is					
13. People who want to appear religious use					
14. The language that relates best to my culture is					
15. People who want to appear modern use					
16. The best language for studying science and technology is					
17. To obtain a good job, I need to master					

	Standard Arabic	Colloquial Arabic	English	French	Other
18. The language(s) rich in expression is/are					
19. People who want to appear open-minded speak					
20. The language that is most useful for my daily life is					
21. The language(s) that impacts the listener most is/are					
22. The language that is most useful for my professional life is					
23. Educated Arab people speak in					
24. To be an Arab, it is important to speak					
25. The majority of the music that I listen to is in					
26. Most of the websites that I visit are in					
27. I write my emails mostly in					
28. The books that I read are in					
29. Most of the TV channels and programs that I watch are in					
30. When I text someone, I text them in					
31. Most of the radio programs I listen to are in					
32. When I am with family, friends, and acquaintances, I speak					
33. The majority of the movies that I watch are in					
34. I listen to sports commentary in					
35. When I interact with people that I do not know, I speak					
36. If there is a language that I would try to master, it would be					

(continued)

		Standard Arabic	Colloquial Arabic	English	French	Other
1.	With family members at home					
2.	With friends and acquaintances					
3.	With a waiter in a restaurant					
4.	To write or narrate a folk story					
5.	With colleagues at work or in school/college					
6.	In a radio soap opera					
7.	To write a personal letter					
8.	To do a news report					
9.	If you were to give a political speech					
10.	If you were to give a religious sermon					
11.	If you were to give a university lecture					
12.	To deliver a poem					
13.	To swear					
14.	To joke					
15.	To scold or insult					
16.	To introduce daily-life sayings					
17.	To chat about unimportant issue					
18.	To simplify an idea or exemplify it through real-life example					
19.	To discuss an important issue in a business meeting					
20.	To produce eloquent or rhyming stretches of discourse					
21.	To take a pedantic stand					

Indicate the language(s) that you will use in each of the following cases by filling in the blanks using these numbers: 4=always, 3=mostly, 2= sometimes, 1= rarely, 0=never

		Standard Arabic	Colloquial Arabic	English	French	Other
22.	To indicate your pan-Arab identity					
23.	To emphasize the seriousness of the topic					
24.	To cite someone literally					

Rank the language(s) in terms of their association with the following attributes by using these numbers: 4=first favorite, 3=second favorite, 2=third favorite, 1=fourth favorite, 0=fifth favorite.

		Standard Arabic	Colloquial Arabic	English	French	Other
1.	Formality or official status					
2.	Internationality					
3.	Literacy					
4.	Versatility					
5.	Power or authority					
6.	Practicality					
7.	Eloquence					
8.	Beauty					
9.	Originality					
10.	Prestige					
11.	Purity					
12.	Richness					

Please indicate your reaction to each of the following statements by circling the number that represents your level of agreement or disagreement with it.

		Strongly agree	Agree	Neutral	Disagree	Strongly disagree
1.	I do not like to be identified as an Arab.	4	3	2	1	0
2.	I am happy that I am a member of an Arab ethnic group.	4	3	2	1	0
3.	I have a lot of pride in the Arab heritage.	4	3	2	1	0
4.	I like the Arab traditions and customs, such as dress and greetings.	4	3	2	1	0

(continued)

	Strongly agree	Agree	Neutral	Disagree	Strongly disagree
5. I like to learn more about my Arab cultural and ethnic background.	4	3	2	1	0
6. I like to be a member of organizations or social groups that are mostly composed of Arabs.	4	3	2	1	0
7. I enjoy being around people from ethnic groups other than Arabs.	4	3	2	1	0
8. I like to participate in Arab cultural practices, such as food and music.	4	3	2	1	0
9. I do not feel a strong attachment to the Arab land.	4	3	2	1	0
10. I prefer to befriend people from other ethnic groups.	4	3	2	1	0
11. My religion is part of who I am.	4	3	2	1	0
12. The Arabic culture is not relevant to my personal life.	4	3	2	1	0

Indicate your ability to **speak** each of the following languages by circling the appropriate numbers.

	Fluent	Very good	Good	Fair	Poor	None
1. Standard Arabic	5	4	3	2	1	0
2. Colloquial Arabic	5	4	3	2	1	0
3. English	5	4	3	2	1	0
4. French	5	4	3	2	1	0
5. Other (specify):	5	4	3	2	1	0

Indicate your ability to **comprehend** each of the following languages by circling the appropriate numbers.

	Fluent	Very good	Good	Fair	Poor	None
1. Standard Arabic	5	4	3	2	1	0
2. Colloquial Arabic	5	4	3	2	1	0
3. English	5	4	3	2	1	0
4. French	5	4	3	2	1	0
5. Other (specify):	5	4	3	2	1	0

Thank you for taking the time to answer these questions.

APPENDIX 2

Semi-structured interview: Arabic and English versions

1. هل تتكلم العربية؟
2. أي نوع من العربية تتكلم؟
3. ما هي لغتك الأم؟ لماذا؟
4. بشكل عام، أيهما تفضل أو تحب أكثر: الفصحى أم العامية؟ (لماذا؟)*
5. ما هي اللهجة العربية المفضلة بالنسبة لك؟ (لماذا؟)
6. ما هي أصعب لهجة عربية بالنسبة لك؟
7. ما هي أسهل لهجة عربية بالنسبة لك ؟
8. ما هي أقرب لهجة للفصحى برأيك؟ (كيف؟)
9. هل ترى أي مشكلة في وجود لغة فصحى ولهجات عامية في المجتمعات العربية؟ (لماذا؟)
10. لو أردنا استبدال الفصحى بإحدى اللهجات العامية، فأي لهجة ستختار أنت شخصياً؟
11. ما رأيك بانتشار اللغة الإنكليزية في المجتمع المصري/الأردني/المغربي/السعودي؟
12. ما رأيك بالناس الذين يمزجون الفصحى بالعامية في الخطب الدينية؟
13. ما رأيك بالناس الذين يمزجون الفصحى بالعامية في الخطابات السياسية؟
14. ما رأيك بالناس الذين يمزجون الفصحى بالعامية في حديثهم اليومي؟
15. ما رأيك باستخدام اللغة الإنكليزية من قبل بعض العرب؟
16. ما رأيك باستخدام اللغة الفرنسية من قبل بعض العرب؟
17. ماذا تمثل الفصحى بالنسبة لك؟
18. ماذا تمثل العامية/الدارجة بالنسبة لك؟
19. ماذا تمثل اللغة الإنكليزية بالنسبة لك؟
20. ما هي اللغة أو اللهجة اللي تمثل هويتك كعربي؟
21. ما هي اللغة أو اللهجة اللي تمثل هويتك كمصري/أردني/مغربي/سعودي؟
22. ما هي اللغة أو اللهجة اللي تمثل هويتك بشكل عام؟
23. ما مدى استخدامك للفصحى والعامية واللغة الإنكليزية؟ (أين ومتى تستخدم كلاً من هذه اللغات؟)
24. ما رأيك بسياسات التعريب في مصر/الأردن/المغرب/السعودية (أقصد بالتعريب هنا استخدام الفصحى في التعليم والدوائر الرسمية)؟
25. ما رأيك بالدعوة لتبني العامية في التعليم؟
26. ما رأيك بالدعوة لاستخدام العامية بدلاً من الفصحى في الكتابة ... طبعاً بعد تطوير ضوابط تهجئة وقواعد للهجات العامية؟

27. هل تستخدم الانترنت أو أياً من تطبيقاته؟
28. ما هي اللغات أو اللهجات التي تستخدمها عند استعمالك لهذه التطبيقات؟
29. هل تستخدم العربيزي؟
30. ما رأيك بالعربيزي وبالناس الذين يستخدمونه في التواصل على الانترنت؟
31. هل لديك أي أسئلة أو تعليقات لي؟

1 Do you speak Arabic?
2 What form of Arabic do you speak?
3 What is your mother tongue? (Why?)*
4 In general, which do you prefer or like more: Al-Fuṣħa or Al-ʻAamiyya? (Why?)
5 What is your favorite Arabic colloquial dialect? (Why?)
6 What is the most difficult Arabic dialect to you?
7 What is the easiest Arabic dialect to you?
8 What is the dialect closest to Al-Fuṣħa? How?
9 Do you see any problem in the existence of Al-Fuṣħa or Al-ʻAamiyya dialects in the Arab societies? (Why?)
10 If we were to replace Al-Fuṣħa with one of the colloquial dialects, which one would you personally choose?
11 What is your opinion of the spread of English in the Egyptian/Jordanian/Moroccan/Saudi society?
12 What do you think of people who mix Al-Fuṣħa and Al-ʻAamiyya in religious speeches?
13 What do you think of people who mix Al-Fuṣħa and Al-ʻAamiyya in political speeches?
14 What do you think of people who mix Al-Fuṣħa and Al-ʻAamiyya in everyday life?
15 What do you think of the use of English by some Arabic speakers?
16 What do you think of the use of French by some Arabic speakers?
17 What does Al-Fuṣħa represent for you?
18 What does Al-ʻAamiyya represent for you?
19 What does English represent to you?
20 Which language or dialect represents your identity as an Arab?
21 Which language or dialect represents your identity as an Egyptian/Jordanian/Moroccan/Saudi?
22 Which language or dialect represents your identity in general?
23 To what extent do you use Al-Fuṣħa, Al-ʻAamiyya, and English? (When and where do you use these varieties?)
24 What do you think of the Arabicization policy in Egypt/Jordan/Morocco/Saudi Arabia…I mean by Arabicization using Al-Fuṣħa in education and official circles?
25 What do you think of the call for adopting Al-ʻAamiyya in education?

26 What do you think of the call for using Al-'Aamiyya instead of Al-Fuṣḥa in writing…of course after developing orthographic and grammatical rules for Al-'Aamiyya?
27 Do you use the internet or any of its application?
28 What language or languages do you use in communicating with others on these applications?
29 Do you use Arabizi?
30 What do you think of Arabizi and of the people who use it online?
31 Do you have any questions or comments for me?

NOTE

* Parenthetical text refers to follow-up questions used when explanation was needed.

APPENDIX 3

Interview and narrative transcription conventions

INTERVIEW TRANSCRIPTION

. . . = incomplete thoughts, hesitations, self-interruptions, filled pauses, unde-ciphered text, and word fragments that do not change the meaning of the text

(. . .) = speakers' words edited out (used when a quoted text is an incomplete sentence or multiple ideas expressed in sentences that are separated by unrelated text)

[] explanation added for clarification of meaning

Prolonged sounds and syllables and silent pauses are not represented in the transcriptions.

SA NARRATIVE TRANSCRIPTION

. . . = incomplete thoughts, hesitations, self-interruptions, filled pauses, unde-ciphered text, and word fragments that do not change the meaning of the text

(. . .) = speakers' words edited out (used when a quoted text is an incomplete sentence or multiple ideas expressed in sentences that are separated by unrelated text)

[] explanation added for clarification of meaning

<< >>question posed by the interviewer

Prolonged sounds and syllables and silent pauses are not represented in the transcriptions.

APPENDIX 4

Sample narratives in SA

NARRATIVE 1: LIFE AFTER DEATH: EGYPTIAN PROFESSOR #9

أتصور أن الحياة بعد الموت هي صورة.. . الوجه الآخر للحياة التي نحياها اليوم مع الاختلاف في وجود مفهوم العدالة، حيث أن العدالة . . . والقصاص هما المعيار الأساسي الذي تتساوى فيه جميع البشر في الحياة بعد الموت . . . وأنّ الحياة بعد الموت هي بداية وليست نهاية كما يعتقد الكثير من الناس . . . من وجهة نظري على أقل تقدير . . . بل يذهب بتفكيري وفلسفتي وقناعتي إلى ما هو أبعد من ذلك . . . من حيث أنني أحيانا أتصور أن الحياة بعد الموت هي بداية . . . من مفهوم أن سوف نعيش كل واحد منا سوف يعيش حياة أخرى في شكل . . . في أشكال أخرى في ذوات أخرى . . . سنقوم بأدوار ثانية . . . هذا مرتبط في وجهة نظري على . . . أخرى . . . على كوكب الأرض . . . ربما أكون كائن في المريخ في فترة من فترات حياتي ربما أكون كائن في كوكب آخر وأنّ دائما هناك أشباه لي عبر العصور.. ومن هنا أحيانا أتصور وأفكر ماذا كنت . . . أو أرى نفسي . . . لو في العصر المملوكي على أي شاكلة أو العصر العثماني أو العصر الفاطمي أو العصر الأندلسي . . . في أي فترة . . . بحكم تكويني النفسي . . . من . . . سأجد نفسي على أي صورة وعلى أي هوية من الهويات . . . من هذا المنطلق . . . من هذا المفهوم أتصور أن الحياة بعد الموت هي ليست غيبيّة بقدر ما بنكوّن تصوراتنا عنها وماذا نكون. . .

>> <<. . . تؤثر هذه النظرة على حياتي اليومية بأنني أحيا حياتي بشكل مفهوم صوفي طوال الوقت أبحث عن الوجه الآخر من الأحداث اليومية وطوال الوقت أنا مشغولة بما يسمى بعلم الدلالة.. وأنّ كل شيء ليس عبثا وأنّ كل حدث يحدث في حياتي اليومية له دلالة ما . . . سواء على شكل تنبيه ينبهني أو على شكل . . . تهيئة حواسي لاستقبال حدث جلل. . . طوال الوقت أشعر أن الحياة اليومية .. فيها نوع من أنواع الرد الفعل بيني أنا كشخص وبين الحدث الذي يحدث لي. . . . >> << هو أنا أحيانا بحكم تكوين تفكيري. . . أنا أرفض في كثير من الأوقات التفكير في الحياة في القبر من المفهوم الذي يصوره لنا الذين يتكلمون نيابة عن الدين. . . بمعنى أحيانا أهرب بتفكيري أو أرفض. . . تفكيري يرفض أن هناك ما يسمى بالثعبان الأقرع . . . في الحياة . . . في القبر . . . أحيانا يشطح بتفكيري . . . بطريئة مختلفة أنني أرى الله، كيفية إن أنا. . . كيف أرى الله .. أتصور دائما. . . دائما أقول. . . حتى لابنتي أن الله سبحانه وتعالى ليس هتلر لأن يمثل بنا لكن هو رحيما بنا . . . هناك شكل ما من أشكال العدالة لكن يعجز تفكيري على كيف ستكون هذه العدالة.

NARRATIVE 2: THE RELATIONSHIP BETWEEN THE EAST AND THE WEST: MOROCCAN PROFESSOR #10

علاقة الشرق بالغرب . . . . . . أنا أؤمن بما يقول إدوارد سعيد أن الغرب خلق الشرق بمعنى أننا لا يمكن أن نقول أن الشرق خُلق من. . . كَردِّ فعل للغرب. هذا تقسيم جغرافي جيواستراتيجي خلقه الغرب لكي يربطوا جميع مشاكلهم بالشرق وليحلوا مشاكلهم عن طريق. . . عن طريق الشرق وبواسطة الشرق. بمعنى أن خيرات الشرق. . . أن الغرب دائما كان يفكر في الديموقراطية ولكن لما استعمر لم يفكر في الديموقراطية، أخرج الديموقراطية لما انتهى من الاستعمار. . . لما أصبح الغرب . . . غنيا. إذن طوّر مفاهيمه وعلى حساب الشرق في كثير من الأشياء ولكن لم يحاسب نفسه عن الشرق إلا بعد أن أنهى من مهامه وخلق نظرية جديدة بعد الانتهاء من مهامه. نفس الشيء بالنسبة للأمم المتحدة، خلقت الأمم المتحدة للدفاع عن مصالح الغرب عوض الدفاع عن مصالح الشرق لماذا لأن الذي يسير الأمم المتحدة هو الغرب. فمهوم الغرب إذاً في هذه الحالة هو القوة في حين أنّ الشرق قوته لا توازي قوة الغرب وفي هذه الحالة يصعب علي أن أجيب عن هذا التوازن الحقيقة بين الشرق والغرب.

الإشكال المطروح الآن هو هل للشرق مكانة في. . . دوليا إذن مفهوم الغرب والشرق هي مفاهيم خلقت لحل مشاكل جيواستراتيجية بقدر ما .. لا .. بقدر ما نعتمد عليها فقط لتحديد أنّ هذه دولة متقدمة أو غير متقدمة وللدول المتقدمة الصلاحية في أن تقوم الدولة غير المتقدمة. وهذه مفاهيم في الحقيقة برجماتية [. . .] ليس فيها ولا حقوق الإنسان ولا أي شيء وأكثر مثال على ذلك وهو أن تنطبق على الدول الغربية أمور حقوق الإنسان مثلا التي يحاسبون عليها الشرق في حين أن الغرب أول من لا يحترمها مثلا.

إذن هذا يعني أن. . . مفهوم .. هناك المقولة المشهورة أن لا أحد يمكن أن يقول للأسد . . .أن يسب الأسد وينتقد الأسد لأن هذا الأسد، لا أتحدث عن الأسد السوري ولكن أتحدث عن الأسد ملك الحيوانات. . . بمعنى أن هذا هو.. ضمن مفهوم. . . بمعنى أن الآن التصور للشرق. . .الشرق له ثقافة وعادات، هذه العادات لها أصول باعتبار. . . باعتبار سنوات أو باعتبار تاريخها بصفة عامة، لها أصول ولها عادات إن قارنتها بعادات بعض الثقافات اللي هي الغربية سأقول إنها ثقافات محافظة لها إيجابيتها كما لها سلبياتها ولكن لا يمكن أن يحاسب مثلا الشرق عن ضعف ثقافته وحضارته باعتبار أن الغرب الذي هو نموذج التطور هو النموذج الثقافي في حين ان استمرارية الحياة غير مرتبط بالمحافظة على بعض العادات والتقاليد والتي تجعل بعض الدول هي أكثر. . . لها مورود قوي في حين أن الدول الأخرى مورودها شبه سطحي لدرجة أنه، ربما مع مرور الوقت ستتغير الأشياء وتختلف. . . إذا عاداتنا الشرقية من ثقافتنا الشرقية و ثقافتنا الشرقية لا تعني أننا فقط. . .أن ثقافتنا مختلفة عن ثقافة الغرب ولكن تصورنا للأشياء مختلف، لأن هناك عوامل تاريخية وهناك عوامل دينية وهناك عوامل حضارية كلها تتحكم فينا. . .الغرب .. له .. طبعا فَهمَ الحياة بزاوية أخرى كيف يصل إلى الحياة . . .وإلى الرفاه في الحياة وكيف يصل إلى هذا. إذا أصبحت الآن. . . التوازن بين مصلحة البلد، رفاه الشعب كيف يصلون إلى رفاه الشعب وكيف يدافعون عن هذا الرفاه، إذا كنت من الدول المتقدمة تحاول أن تستعمر الدول الشرقية لأنها أضعف لماذا لانك [. . .] أنت تبحث عن رفاه بلدك إذاً على حساب رفاه دولة أخرى. إذا

حين تحاسب الناس عن رفاه بلدك ورفاه دول أخرى دائما تقول إنّ بلدي أقوى وإنّ بلدي له .. أكثر ديموقراطية ولكن هذه الديموقراطية لن يحصل عليها الإنسان البسيط في الدول المتقدمة إلا إذا كانت على حساب الدول الأخرى. إذاً بمعنى أنّ مفهوم الشر والخير مفهوم الديموقراطية وعدم الديموقراطية مفهوم. . . مثلا مفهوم الطاقة التي مثلا في بعض الدول اللي هي غير موجودة كيف يمكن أن تحصل على هذه الطاقة إذا لم يكن على حساب أشياء كثيرة التي تحتاج إليها الدول الغربية لكي تحصل بها على الطاقة بالمجان . . .

NARRATIVE 3: PASTIME: JORDANIAN STUDENT #2

في الحقيقة أنا شخصيا لا أحب الـ . . . الأشياء التافهة . . . أحب أن أملي وقتي بشيء يهمني ويفيدني بغض النظر إن كان ماليا أو فكريا . . . أنا أتاجر في الأجهزة الإلكترونية خصوصا اللابتوبات فأبي يملك شركة كبيرة . . . تعتبر من أكبر الشركات في الأردن . . . في هذا الوقت أتاجر في هذه اللابتوبات . . . أذهب إلى العقبة كثيراً ممكن خلال يوم أذهب مرتان في العقبة . . . إلى العقبة ذهابا وإيابا . . . إضافة إلى ذلك أحب السباحة . . . أحب القراءة . . . نوعية خاصة من الكتب . . . أحب أن أدخن السيجار . . . يعني فلنقل هذا روتين لا أستطيع التخلي عنه . . . تدخين السيجار ضروريّ جدا . . . وأنا معجب كثيرا في هوليود وفي أفلامها وفي طريقة تصويرها وفي القضايا التي تطرحها بغض النظر إن كانت بعضها تخلو من المصداقية التاريخية ولكن أحب مشاهدتها وبما أني أدرس الترجمة أحب مشاهدة هذه الأفلام بترجمة عربية . . . كي أشاهد كيف أترجم . . . وما هي الأخطاء التي يرتكبونها. بالإضافة إلى أني أحب الأكل كثيرا فممكن أن أأكل في اليوم ستة أو سبعة وجبات ومن بينهم اثنتان مع أُرُز . . . بالإضافة إلى ذلك . . . أقضي كثير من الوقت في القيادة . . . فَ ملتزم بأخي وأختي في إيصالهم إلى الجامعة والمدرسة .. آم . . . فقط . . .

>> << >> نعم أنا قررت أني أتعلم الطبخ منذ ثلاث سنوات فأنا أطبخ الأكل الإيطالي خصوصا الـ spaghetti و [. . .]. و من ثم سأتجه إلى الطبخ العربي بإذن الله

>> << >> لا بالإيطالي لأنه أسهل بكثير

>> << >> أستطيع أن أقول أني مدمن على السباحة . . . أنا لدي ثلاث شهادات مبتدئين وشباب ومحترفين من مدرسة فيلادافيا. تعلمت السباحة منذ الصغر لموقف حدث معي . . . بعد هذا الموقف قررت أن أتعلم السباحة أنا وأختي وأخي نحن ثلاثتنا كنا نجيد السباحة جيدا ونتمتع بها وأصبحت إدمان وضرورة لدينا.

>> << >> في المدرسة النموذجية في العقبة لأني أذهب كثيرا في مسبح مدرسة فيلادافيا

>> << >> لا إنه اشتراك يومي قد كنت مشترك شهريا ولكن نظرا لضيق وقتي مع توسع الدراسة والـ . . . الاقتراب من التخرج فأصبحت اشتراك بشكل يومي أذهب يوميا عفوا بشكل يومي ليس شهريا . . . لأن . . . شهري أصبح ملتزما ويجب علي أن أذهب في أيام محددة ولكني أذهب حاليا باشتراك يومي عندما يُتاح . . . يتيح لي الوقت.

>> << >> بدايةً . . . أولويتي الأولى هي الطعام وتقبيل أمي . . . من ثم مشاهدة برشلونة . . . من ثم العمل . . . من ثم الدراسة . . . من ثم السباحة . . . والقراءة وغيره ولكن الدراسة تأتي في مرتبة متأخرة.

APPENDIX 5

Sample interview transcript

1. هل تتكلمين العربية؟
بالطبع أتكلم العربية.

2. أي نوع من العربية تتكلمين؟
أتكلم اللهجة الأردنية أو الشامية . . .لأن أبي أردني وأمي فلسطينية. . . وأتكلم الفصحى قليلًا فقط.

3. ما هي لغتك الأم؟
لغتي الأم. . . تقصد التي تعلمتها من الصغر. . .هي اللهجة الأردنية . . .ولكن الفصحى . . . الفصحى. . . لغة أم بالنسبة لي من حيث أنها أساس اللهجات العربية جميعها. . .أو أمّ اللهجات.. فالفصحى هي الأصل والعاميات هي الفروع.

4. بشكل عام، أيهما تفضلين أو تحبين أكثر: الفصحى أم العامية؟
أفضل الفصحى بالطبع لأنها أقوى وأجمل وأعرق. و كما قلت هي أصل العاميات.

5. ما هي اللهجة العربية المفضلة بالنسبة لك؟ ولماذا؟
اللهجة الأردنية. . لماذا! لأنني أردنية . . لكن اللهجة الأردنية أيضاً قريبة من الفصحى. يعني هي مفهومة حتى لغير الأردنيين. . . فهناك. . .مثلاً عندي صديقات غير أردنيات يفهمون اللهجة الأردنية. . ليس هناك مشاكل . . .

6. ما هي أصعب لهجة عربية بالنسبة لك؟
لهجة أهل المغرب بشكل عام. يعني لهجة المغرب وتونس والجزائر.

7. ما هي أسهل لهجة عربية بالنسبة لك ؟
اللهجة الارنية
طيب غير الأردنية
اللهجة الفلسطينية والسورية والمصرية

8. ما هي أقرب لهجة للفصحى برأيك؟
اللهجة الأرنية أيضاً
لماذا؟
يعني الأردنيون ينطقون الحروف بوضوح وخاصة الحروف الصعبة مثل الـ ”ذ“ و الـ ”ظ“ و الـ ”ث“... يعني أنا لا أستخدم هذه الحروف لكن معظم الأردنيين خاصةً في الشمال والجنوب يستخدمونهم. وأيضاً القواعد... المفردات معروفة...معظمها مأخوذة من الفصحى.

9. هل ترين أي مشكلة في وجود لغة فصحى ولهجات عامية في المجتمعات العربية ؟
لا. بالنسبة لي ليست هناك مشكلة. يعني هذا لا يُشكّل مشكلة فهم أو تواصل بالنسبة لي مع الناس الآخرين. إذا تكلم معي شخص بالعامية أفهمه وإذا تكلم بالفصحى أفهمه. يعني... أيضاً ...هذا شيء تعودنا عليه...صار جزء من حياتنا اليومية.

لو أردنا استبدال الفصحى بإحدى اللهجات العامية، فأي لهجة ستختارينها أنت شخصياً؟

10. أنا لا أحبذ هذا الخيار. . . يعني أنا لا أظن أن أي لهجة من اللهجات العربية يمكن أن تقوم في مقام الفصحى.

طيباً لو افترضنا جداً أن هناك لهجة بديلة للفصحى فما هي برأيك.

طبعاً كأردنية أفضل اللهجة الأردنية.

11. ما رأيك بانتشار اللغة الإنكليزية في المجتمع الأردني؟

هذا موضوع معقّد. فأنا أظن أن اللغة الإنكليزية مهمة . . .يعني في التجارة والسفر

هذا موضوع معقّد. فأنا أظن أن اللغة الإنكليزية مهمة ...يعني في التجارة والسفر والإنترنت وغيرها. فمن هذه الناحية... يجب أن يتعلمها الناس. لكن في... هناك ...تصبح هناك مشكلة عندما تؤثر على ثقافة المجتمع... وهذا موجود يعني بشكل واضح في الأردن. يعني بعض الناس يفتخرون أنهم يتكلمون بالإنكليزية. و يمكن أنك رأيت آرمات المحلات بالانكليزية وفي الشوارع وغيره. في رأيي هذه مشكلة.

12. ما رأيك بالناس الذين يمزجون الفصحى بالعامية في الخطب الدينية؟

أنا شخصياً . . .أنا لا أحب أن أسمع الخطب بالعامية. يعني بعض الشيوخ لا أسمع لهم لأنهم يتكلمون بالعامية كثيراً.

لماذا؟

يعني العادة أن نسمع الخطبة بالفصحى. . .هي كذلك. . .الناس تعودت. . .تعودنا على هذا الشيء. وأظن . . .ذلك يجعل الخطبة أقوى.

13. ما رأيك بالناس الذين يمزجون الفصحى بالعامية في الخطابات السياسية؟

أيضاً يجب أن تكون بالفصحى.

لماذا؟

يعني من غير . . . من غير المعقول أن شخص مهم . . .أو له منصب في الدولة لا يعرف التحدث بالفصحى.

14. ما رأيك بالناس الذين يمزجون الفصحى بالعامية في حديثهم اليومي؟

هذا قليل و سيكون غريباً لو سمعته. ولكن يعني . . .لو حصل ذلك سأحترم الشخص الذي يقوم بذلك.

15. ما رأيك باستخدام اللغة الإنكليزية من قبل بعض العرب؟

كما قلت... أنا لا أحبّ ذلك...يعني إلا للضرورة...مثلًا في العمل أوغير ذلك.

لماذا؟

أولاً هذا سيكون غريب. . . وثانياً يعني طالما إن الشخص يتكلم مع العرب فيجب أن يتحدث بالعربية.

16. ما رأيك باستخدام اللغة الفرنسية من قبل بعض العرب؟

نفس الشيء. لا أحبّ ذلك. وأظن أن هذا نادر جداً أو غير موجود في الأردن على كل حال.

17. ماذا تمثل الفصحى بالنسبة لك؟

الفصحى هي لغة العرب جميعاً...يعني هي اللغة التي يمكن لكل العرب أن يتكلمو بها مع بعضهم...وهي لغة القرآن.

18. ماذا تمثل العامية بالنسبة لك؟

هي اللغة التي أتحدث بها مع أهلي وأصدقائي كل يوم.

19. ماذا تمثل اللغة الإنكليزية بالنسبة لك؟

لغة التجارة والكومبيوتر والسفر. . .وربما بعض الوظائف.

20. ما هي اللغة أو اللهجة اللي تمثل هويتك كإنسانة عربية؟

الفصحى

لماذا؟

لأنها لغة كل الشعوب العربية. وهي لغة العرب من زمن طويل. وهي اللغة التي نزل بها القرآن. فأنا كمسلمة و كمسلمة محافظة أعتبر اللغة العربية أهم لغة بالنسبة لي .

21. ما هي اللغة أو اللهجة التي تمثل هويتك كأردنية؟

اللهجة الأرنية.

22. ما هي اللغة أو اللهجة التي تمثل هويتك بشكل عام؟

الفصحى

23. ما مدى استخدامك للفصحى والعامية واللغة الإنكليزية؟

طبعاً أستخدم العامية كل يوم. . .مع الأهل والأصدقاء و. . .وفي الجامعة والسوق و. . .لأستخدم الفصحى إلا قليلاً. . . يعني مثلاً في دروس اللغة العربية أحياناً. . . الإنكليزية أيضاً لا أستخدمها إلا قليلاً. لكن أحياناً أشاهد القنوات الإنكليزية وأزور بعض المواقع الالكترونية الإنجليزية.

24. ما رأيك بسياسات التعريب في الأردن (أقصد بالتعريب هنا استخدام الفصحى في التعليم والدوائر الرسمية)؟

أظنّ أن التعريب شيء مهمّ لكي يتعلم الأولاد . . . الأطفال. . . لكي يتعلمو اللغة العربية بشكل جيد. لكن من خلال تجربتي أظنّ أن معظم المدرسين يستخدمون العامية وليس الفصحى أو يستخدموا فصحى مكسرة.. .فيجب أن يكون هناك اعتناء أكثر بتعليم اللغة العربية . . . يعني الفصحى للأطفال.

ماذا عن تعريب الكلمات الأجنبية؟

واللهِ لا أعرف كثيراً عن هذا الموضوع. ولكن أظنّ أن ذلك مهمّ أيضاً. يعني هناك كلمات أجنبية كثيرة نستخدمها . . .فهذه يجب أن تكون لها ترجمة في العربية.

25. ما رأيك بالدعوة لتبني العامية في التعليم؟

لاأوافق على هذا لأن ذلك يعني إضعاف الفصحى ونسيانها. وبالتالي لن تستطيع الأجيال القادمة معرفة القراءة والكتابة بالفصحى. . . و ذلك ما يعني فقدان الصلة مع ارثهم الثقافي.

26. ما رأيك بالدعوة لاستخدام العامية بدلاً من الفصحى في الكتابة . . . طبعاً بعد تطوير ضوابط تهجئة وقواعد للهجات العامية؟

أيضاً أنا ليس مع هذه الفكرة لأني. . . العامية ليست قوية مثل الفصحى وليست. . .لا. . .ليست لها قواعد واضحة أو معروفة.. ثمّ أيضاً هناك لهجات كثيرة في الأردن، فأي لهجة. . .يعني. . .أيها يمكن أن نستخدمها.

27. هل تستخدمين الانترنت أو أياً من تطبيقاته؟
نعم أستخدم الانترنت . . . أستخدم الايميل والفيسبوك والواتسب. يعني هذه أكثر شيء.

28. ما هي اللغات أو اللهجات التي تستخدمينها عند استعمالك لهذه التطبيقات؟
أستخدم العامية وأحياناً الإنكليزية.
متى تستخدمين الإنكليزية؟
فقط عندما أكلّم ناس غير عرب. أحيانا أعتبر ذلك تدرّب . . . أتدرّب لأحسنّ لغتي الإنكليزية.

29. هل تستخدمين العربيزي؟
نعم وليس دائماً؟ أستخدم العربيزي مع أصدقائي فقط يعني خاصة . . . خاصة بعض الأصدقاء الذين يستخدمون العربيزي.
لماذا تستخدمين العربيزي؟
والله لأعرف . . . لأظن أن هناك سبب مقنع . . . ولكن تعودت على ذلك في الحديث مع بعض الأصدقاء.

30. ما رأيك بالعربيزي وبالناس الذين يستخدمونه في التواصل على الانترنت؟
في الحقيقة أنا لا أحب ذلك، ولكن يعني أصبح شيء مألوف بالنسبة لي. يعني تعودت عليه.

31. هل لديك أي أسئلة أو تعليقات لي؟
لا. ليس عندي أسئلة.

شكراً جزيلًا لك.

APPENDIX 6

Summary of by-item scores on the Attitudes Scale

EGYPTIAN GROUP

		Standard Arabic	Colloquial Arabic	English	French	Other
1.	The official language in the Arab world should be	3.64	2.75	2.11	1.02	0.35
2.	I wish Arabs can converse in	3.47	2.49	2.33	1.20	0.41
3.	The language that we need to maintain is	3.84	2.36	2.19	1.14	0.31
4.	Religion should be discussed in	3.63	2.77	1.95	1.02	0.32
5.	The language of business should be	2.83	2.64	2.72	1.33	0.41
6.	The language(s) that I prefer is/are	2.90	2.56	2.65	1.15	0.45
7.	If I had been given the chance to learn one language in my life, I would have chosen	2.77	1.55	2.55	1.68	1.17
8.	I prefer reading books, newspapers, magazines in	3.27	2.82	2.31	0.99	0.43
9.	The language of media should be	3.39	2.59	2.13	1.11	0.39
10.	The language of education from elementary school to university should be	3.61	1.88	2.55	1.39	0.51
11.	When at work, government employees should use	3.06	2.82	2.31	1.09	0.34
12.	The language that I like to speak most is	2.70	2.85	2.60	1.27	0.50

	Standard Arabic	Colloquial Arabic	English	French	Other
13. People who want to appear religious use	3.70	2.58	1.95	1.10	0.20
14. The language that relates best to my culture is	3.42	2.88	2.22	1.03	0.22
15. People who want to appear modern use	1.43	1.95	3.50	2.14	0.64
16. The best language for studying science and technology is	2.50	1.63	3.33	1.81	0.48
17. To obtain a good job, I need to master	2.16	1.20	3.53	2.11	0.81
18. The language(s) rich in expression is/are	3.50	2.07	2.50	1.43	0.26
19. People who want to appear open-minded speak	1.72	1.73	3.49	2.27	0.65
20. The language that is most useful for my daily life is	2.68	2.83	2.68	1.28	0.43
21. The language(s) that impacts the listener most is/are	2.70	3.06	2.63	1.24	0.27
22. The language that is most useful for my professional life is	2.41	1.99	3.18	1.51	0.74
23. Educated Arab people speak in	3.48	2.02	2.63	1.35	0.39
24. To be an Arab, it is important to speak	3.72	2.75	2.19	1.13	0.24
25. The majority of the music that I listen to is in	2.17	3.05	2.64	1.22	0.60
26. Most of the websites that I visit are in	2.67	2.56	3.03	1.18	0.44
27. I write my emails mostly in	2.49	2.89	2.97	1.17	0.52
28. The books that I read are in	3.39	2.53	2.47	1.08	0.44
29. Most of the TV channels and programs that I watch are in	2.64	3.23	2.57	1.00	0.48

(continued)

		Standard Arabic	Colloquial Arabic	English	French	Other
30.	When I text someone, I text them in	2.42	3.03	2.80	1.10	0.52
31.	Most of the radio programs I listen to are in	2.64	3.20	2.39	0.95	0.38
32.	When I am with family, friends, and acquaintances, I speak	2.28	3.68	2.33	1.03	0.40
33.	The majority of the movies that I watch are in	1.97	3.12	3.08	1.07	0.56
34.	I listen to sports commentary in	2.65	3.30	2.20	0.92	0.34
35.	When I interact with people that I do not know, I speak	2.36	3.55	2.48	0.95	0.43
36.	If there is a language that I would try to master, it would be	2.49	1.45	2.68	1.91	1.04

JORDANIAN GROUP

		Standard Arabic	Colloquial Arabic	English	French	Other
1.	The official language in the Arab world should be	3.62	3.13	2.45	1.21	0.46
2.	I wish Arabs can converse in	3.63	2.67	2.90	1.44	0.60
3.	The language that we need to maintain is	4.00	2.44	2.18	0.63	0.10
4.	Religion should be discussed in	3.58	2.78	1.87	1.48	1.12
5.	The language of business should be	3.44	2.35	3.35	1.69	0.96
6.	The language(s) that I prefer is/are	2.81	2.98	3.38	1.56	0.46
7.	If I had been given the chance to learn one language in my life, I would have chosen	2.98	1.45	2.96	2.06	1.33

	Standard Arabic	Colloquial Arabic	English	French	Other
8. I prefer reading books, newspapers, magazines in	3.57	2.30	3.48	0.94	0.40
9. The language of media should be	3.75	1.86	3.38	1.43	0.63
10. The language of education from elementary school to university should be	3.62	1.88	3.19	1.67	0.75
11. When at work, government employees should use	3.40	2.31	2.64	1.25	0.67
12. The language that I like to speak most is	2.54	3.04	3.38	1.19	0.52
13. People who want to appear religious use	3.60	2.13	1.42	1.00	0.26
14. The language that relates best to my culture is	3.48	2.85	2.02	0.57	0.42
15. People who want to appear modern use	1.02	2.37	3.83	2.90	1.10
16. The best language for studying science and technology is	2.56	1.60	3.77	1.19	0.85
17. To obtain a good job, I need to master	2.02	1.50	3.83	2.28	1.13
18. The language(s) rich in expression is/are	3.29	2.62	2.60	1.33	0.33
19. People who want to appear open-minded speak	1.96	2.31	3.71	2.76	1.33
20. The language that is most useful for my daily life is	2.15	3.29	3.20	1.22	0.46
21. The language(s) that impacts the listener most is/are	2.94	2.54	2.99	1.22	0.67
22. The language that is most useful for my professional life is	2.73	2.75	3.69	1.17	0.54
23. Educated Arab people speak in	3.96	2.58	2.96	1.52	0.83

(*continued*)

	Standard Arabic	Colloquial Arabic	English	French	Other
24. To be an Arab, it is important to speak	3.71	3.04	2.10	0.96	0.50
25. The majority of the music that I listen to is in	1.43	2.71	2.77	0.74	0.77
26. Most of the websites that I visit are in	2.12	1.63	2.78	0.54	0.42
27. I write my emails mostly in	1.77	2.21	3.75	0.33	0.12
28. The books that I read are in	3.29	1.04	2.56	0.18	0.00
29. Most of the TV channels and programs that I watch are in	2.12	3.48	2.84	0.33	0.50
30. When I text someone, I text them in	1.56	3.31	3.29	0.10	0.12
31. Most of the radio programs I listen to are in	1.77	3.38	2.84	0.13	0.13
32. When I am with family, friends, and acquaintances, I speak	0.87	3.83	2.64	0.23	0.33
33. The majority of the movies that I watch are in	1.19	2.40	3.37	0.34	0.71
34. I listen to sports commentary in	1.92	2.88	1.88	0.10	0.00
35. When I interact with people that I do not know, I speak	1.19	3.75	2.60	0.22	0.19
36. If there is a language that I would try to master, it would be	2.24	1.92	2.42	2.38	1.71

MOROCCAN GROUP

	Standard Arabic	Colloquial Arabic	English	French	Other
1. The official language in the Arab world should be	3.69	1.98	2.24	1.58	0.23
2. I wish Arabs can converse in	3.46	1.69	2.68	1.77	0.43

	Standard Arabic	Colloquial Arabic	English	French	Other
3. The language that we need to maintain is	3.76	2.12	2.33	1.57	0.68
4. Religion should be discussed in	3.82	2.33	2.26	1.57	0.44
5. The language of business should be	2.82	1.90	3.13	2.23	0.52
6. The language(s) that I prefer is/are	2.95	1.99	3.16	1.90	0.93
7. If I had been given the chance to learn one language in my life, I would have chosen	2.95	1.53	2.97	2.06	1.02
8. I prefer reading books, newspapers, magazines in	2.94	1.55	3.19	2.15	0.62
9. The language of media should be	3.18	1.77	2.78	2.01	0.57
10. The language of education from elementary school to university should be	3.23	1.33	2.84	2.18	0.69
11. When at work, government employees should use	3.47	2.11	2.23	1.90	0.39
12. The language that I like to speak most is	2.63	2.35	3.09	2.03	0.67
13. People who want to appear religious use	3.77	2.59	1.85	1.42	0.41
14. The language that relates best to my culture is	3.39	2.75	1.79	2.00	0.84
15. People who want to appear modern use	2.07	1.42	3.25	3.05	0.80
16. The best language for studying science and technology is	2.39	1.36	3.34	2.60	0.41
17. To obtain a good job, I need to master	2.42	1.38	3.30	2.95	0.72
18. The language(s) rich in expression is/are	3.55	1.68	2.86	2.39	0.51
19. People who want to appear open-minded speak	2.30	1.44	3.20	2.95	0.89

(*continued*)

	Standard Arabic	Colloquial Arabic	English	French	Other
20. The language that is most useful for my daily life is	2.62	2.29	2.98	2.24	0.82
21. The language(s) that impacts the listener most is/are	2.94	2.26	2.78	2.33	0.74
22. The language that is most useful for my professional life is	2.38	1.62	3.32	2.83	0.61
23. Educated Arab people speak in	3.51	1.73	2.74	2.12	0.44
24. To be an Arab, it is important to speak	3.77	2.45	1.96	1.69	0.36
25. The majority of the music that I listen to is in	2.48	1.66	2.05	2.44	1.02
26. Most of the websites that I visit are in	2.29	1.42	3.05	2.84	0.77
27. I write my emails mostly in	2.29	1.70	2.99	2.70	0.42
28. The books that I read are in	2.87	1.47	1.93	2.48	0.40
29. Most of the TV channels and programs that I watch are in	2.64	1.84	2.02	2.41	0.53
30. When I text someone, I text them in	2.02	2.47	2.70	2.54	0.59
31. Most of the radio programs I listen to are in	2.59	2.62	2.18	2.47	0.58
32. When I am with family, friends, and acquaintances, I speak	1.98	3.25	2.04	2.27	0.68
33. The majority of the movies that I watch are in	2.04	2.22	3.07	2.46	0.59
34. I listen to sports commentary in	3.14	2.50	2.02	1.97	0.53
35. When I interact with people that I do not know, I speak	2.39	2.90	2.24	2.31	0.36
36. If there is a language that I would try to master, it would be	2.71	1.71	2.61	2.50	1.62

SAUDI GROUP

		Standard Arabic	Colloquial Arabic	English	French	Other
1.	The official language in the Arab world should be	3.77	2.98	2.33	1.04	0.35
2.	I wish Arabs can converse in	3.75	2.80	2.54	1.23	0.51
3.	The language that we need to maintain is	4.00	2.50	2.21	0.70	0.09
4.	Religion should be discussed in	3.82	2.75	1.96	1.44	0.58
5.	The language of business should be	3.61	2.32	3.27	1.57	0.72
6.	The language(s) that I prefer is/are	3.01	2.82	3.15	1.52	0.42
7.	If I had been given the chance to learn one language in my life, I would have chosen	3.18	1.53	2.75	1.89	0.96
8.	I prefer reading books, newspapers, magazines in	3.85	2.32	3.07	0.90	0.30
9.	The language of media should be	3.96	2.02	3.07	1.36	0.56
10.	The language of education from elementary school to university should be	3.73	1.93	2.77	1.70	0.65
11.	When at work, government employees should use	3.61	2.40	2.17	1.20	0.53
12.	The language that I like to speak most is	2.65	3.30	2.99	1.13	0.33
13.	People who want to appear religious use	3.67	2.30	1.79	1.01	0.21
14.	The language that relates best to my culture is	3.55	2.97	2.04	0.59	0.23
15.	People who want to appear modern use	1.21	2.82	3.73	2.77	0.80
16.	The best language for studying science and technology is	2.73	1.66	3.70	1.17	0.42

(*continued*)

		Standard Arabic	Colloquial Arabic	English	French	Other
17.	To obtain a good job, I need to master	2.39	1.74	3.73	2.21	0.69
18.	The language(s) rich in expression is/are	3.54	2.65	2.65	1.39	0.20
19.	People who want to appear open-minded speak	2.15	1.81	3.68	2.68	0.88
20.	The language that is most useful for my daily life is	2.57	3.31	2.82	1.13	0.30
21.	The language(s) that impacts the listener most is/are	3.23	2.30	3.00	1.21	0.36
22.	The language that is most useful for my professional life is	2.96	2.64	3.65	1.17	0.46
23.	Educated Arab people speak in	3.96	2.51	2.74	1.46	0.63
24.	To be an Arab, it is important to speak	3.86	3.06	2.04	0.94	0.32
25.	The majority of the music that I listen to is in	1.72	2.99	2.89	0.84	0.58
26.	Most of the websites that I visit are in	2.47	1.74	3.68	0.53	0.23
27.	I write my emails mostly in	2.16	2.25	3.20	0.44	0.10
28.	The books that I read are in	3.62	0.87	2.32	0.28	0.00
29.	Most of the TV channels and programs that I watch are in	2.34	3.25	3.01	0.38	0.25
30.	When I text someone, I text them in	1.85	3.45	2.81	0.20	0.04
31.	Most of the radio programs I listen to are in	2.11	3.09	2.73	0.20	0.13
32.	When I am with family, friends, and acquaintances, I speak	1.41	3.95	2.42	0.31	0.27
33.	The majority of the movies that I watch are in	1.58	2.44	3.66	0.38	0.29

	Standard Arabic	Colloquial Arabic	English	French	Other
34. I listen to sports commentary in	2.37	2.94	2.15	0.20	0.00
35. When I interact with people that I do not know, I speak	1.63	3.77	2.67	0.29	0.08
36. If there is a language that I would try to master, it would be	2.32	1.52	2.64	2.28	0.68

APPENDIX 7

Summary of by-item scores on the Identity Scale

		Egyptians	Jordanians	Moroccans	Saudis
1.	I do not like to be identified as an Arab.	0.57	0.37	1.05	0.19
2.	I am happy that I am a member of an Arab ethnic group.	3.70	3.49	3.67	3.70
3.	I have a lot of pride in the Arab heritage.	3.73	3.71	3.71	3.84
4.	I like the Arab traditions and customs, such as dress, greetings, etc.	3.31	3.38	3.34	3.56
5.	I like to learn more about my Arab cultural and ethnic background.	3.62	3.49	3.37	3.69
6.	I like to be a member of organizations or social groups that are mostly composed of Arabs.	3.00	2.92	2.66	3.04
7.	I enjoy being around people from ethnic groups other than Arabs.	3.10	3.15	3.26	3.28
8.	I like to participate in Arab cultural practices, such as special food or music.	3.25	3.24	3.04	3.05
9.	I do not feel a strong attachment to the Arab land.	1.14	1.35	1.54	1.27
10.	I prefer to befriend people from other ethnic groups.	2.51	2.04	2.61	2.01
11.	My religion is part of who I am.	3.91	3.67	3.59	3.86
12.	The Arabic culture is not relevant to my personal life.	0.95	1.35	1.01	1.06

APPENDIX 8

Transcripts of children's videos and rubric for answering comprehension questions

NARRATIVE ONE

Sinbad, Episode 50, Part 2: excerpt (8:02–9:07).
www.youtube.com/watch?v=IXfXFXGHddE

- كم انا مسرورة يا سندباد لرؤيتكم جميعاً سالمين
- شكراً يا حورية البحر. هذه الجرة التي أهداني إياها صديقٌ من بغداد ساعدتنا كثيراً
- ولكن أما زلت تنوي الذهاب إلى قصر الزعيم الأزرق
- نعم ولا شيء في الدنيا يجعلني أغير رأيي أبداً
- ولكن من المستحيل أن تتغلبوا وحدكم على هذا الشرير وأعوانه
- أنت على حق فهو لن يقع في حيلة الجرة. يجب أن نجد وسيلة أخرى للإيقاع به
- وجدتها. لماذا لاتطلبون العون من صخر وأهله جميعاً. هه.
- صحيح فعلاً. صخر وأهله يستطيعون التغلب على الزعيم. فعلاً. هاي سندباد. هيا بنا نبحث عنهم.
- و لكن...
- لا تخف أيضاً يمكن أن نساعدك. عندنا أصدقاءٌ كثيرون من النورس وغيرهم من الطيور. سأطلب من أصدقائي أن يبحثو معكم. والآن الوداع. لن أوصيكم مرةً أخرى بالحذر. الوداع
- الوداع يا حورية.

NARRATIVE TWO

Sasuki, Episode 10: 6:29–7:31
http://youtube.com/watch?v=EB0nV2v63z8

- ألا ترى معي أن القائد سانادا قاسي القلب؟ أنا أفهم وضعه لكنّ هذا لا يعني أن تموت الآنسة يوكي. ألست موافقاً معي. ألست موافقاً. تكلّم. ألست مقتنعاً؟

- الآنسة يوكي جعلتك تفقد عقلك. يجب علينا أن نتفهم وضع القائد سانادا. فهمت؟
- وضع القائد سانادا. تبدو واثقاً مما تقول يا جامبو. لماذا؟
- أجل. أنا أكبر منك.
- كلا كلا كلا كلا. لن أسمع كلام القائد هذه المرّة. أنا ذاهب لأنقذ الآنسة يوكي. سأذهب الآن. هه.
- سازوكي
- أنت يا سايزو
- سازوكي. يجب أن تطيع أوامر القائد. أنا أفهم شعورك ولكن.
- تفهم شعوري؟ حياة الآنسة يوكي في خطر. هل حقاً تفهم شعوري يا سايزو.
- أهه
- ماذا تقول يا سايزو
- لم أعد أحتمل.

NARRATIVE THREE

Sinaan, Episode 29, Part II 4:05–5:08
www.youtube.com/watch?v=WFixbJmJn6k

- يا إلهي. كل هذه الأشياء لفيفي؟
- أهلاً بكم جميعاً
- أهلاً بك. هل رأيتم ذلك بأنفسكم. إنّ فيفي تلميذةٌ مجتهدة.
- إنّها حقاً تلميذةٌ مجتهدة.
- بالمناسبة. فإنّ صغار هذه الغابة لا يدرسون إطلاقاً
- الصحّة أهم من أي شيء
- كلا كلا فالصغار يجب أن يدرسوا منذ البداية. والآن سأختبركم. اذكروا لي اسم هذا الحيوان.
- هاه. إنّه سمكٌ كبير
- لايوجد مثل هذا في النهر.
- إنّه ليس من أنواع السمك المعروفة.
- ههههههه
- فيفي لاينبغي الضحك
- ماسم هذا السمك؟
- إنّه من نوع الحوت وحجمه يكون أكبر من هذا البيت.
- هاه... صحيح؟ لا أصدّق هذا
- هناك حيوانات عديدة في عالمنا الكبير
- أوه هذا صحيح.

NARRATIVE FOUR

Abtaal Al-Malaa'ib, Episode 48: 0:55–2:04
www.youtube.com/watch?v=SXJ-UwZtsJA

- حسنٌ. حتى الآن لم أستطع أن أصدّق أننا واجهنا مثل هذه الهزيمة النكراء.
- وأنا أيضاً. ضربات كِن كانت عظيمة.
- كيف نستطيع أن نتجنّب ضرباته الرائعة؟ هذا ما يجب أن نفكر فيه جدياً.
- لكنّ حميدو صدّ ضربته وأحرز هدفاً. وهذا يكفينا. أليس كذلك؟
- لا تكن سخيفاً
- حميدو ما بك؟ ما الذي أثار غضبك هكذا؟
- ماذا تعني بقولك كفايةً لنا؟ هل تعني أنهم سعداء بالهدف الوحيد الذي أحرزته. هل تمزحون.
- اسمع يا حميدو
- بل أنت اسمعني. لا تنسى أننا خسرنا المباراة. يجب أن تهتموا بحقيقة أننا خسرنا المباراة فعلاً. ولو كان كِن هنا كان سيقول أنا أشعر بالخجل لأنني لعبت معكم مباراةً أيها الأولاد. إنكم لا تعرفون لعبة كرة القدم ولن ألعب معكم مباراةً بعد الآن.

NARRATIVE FIVE

Hikaayaat 'Aalamiyya: Ba'i'u t-tuffah: 2:30–3:30
www.youtube.com/watch?v=Fplbuvr5e9c

- ماذا حدث أيها العجوز ماذا تريد الآن
- أرجوك. أتوسل إليك أن تعطيَني واحدةً فقط
- وأنا أيضاً أرجوك
- إذا أردت تفاحة ادفع الثمن. هيّا.
- أقبل بأسوء تفاحة
- لا يوجد لديّ ثمرة سيئة. اسمع. هل أنت صديق لهذا الرجل؟ هيّا خذه وابتعد من هنا. خذه.
- لا أنا لستُ صديقاً له. أتفهم؟
- لا بأس لكن يجب أن يبتعد من هنا. هيّا. خذه وابتعد.
- اسمعني لديك عدد كبير من التفاح. لماذا لا تعطي هذا العجوز واحدةً منها فقط؟
- قلت لك لا وأنا أعني ذلك. هذه تجارة. نعم. حسناً لمَ لا تقوم أنت بشراء واحدة؟
- هاه

RUBRIC FOR ANSWERING COMPREHENSION QUESTIONS

Category	Points	Criteria
Full answer	2	Answer is complete
		Answer is accurate
Partial answer	1	Answer lacks some detail
		Answer is partially accurate
		Answer is partially understandable
		Answer is provided together with other possible answers
Wrong answer	0	No answer is provided
		Answer is inaccurate
		Answer is not understandable

Index